Fodor's 99

Scotland

P9-CAM-035

The complete guide, thoroughly up-to-date

Packed with details that will make your trip

The must-see sights, off and on the beaten path

What to see, what to skip

Mix-and-match vacation itineraries

City strolls, countryside adventures

Smart lodging and dining options

Essential local do's and taboos

Transportation tips, distances and directions

Key contacts, savvy travel tips

When to go, what to pack

Clear, accurate, easy-to-use maps

Fodor's Travel Publications, Inc.
New York • Toronto • London • Sydney • Auckland
www.fodors.com

Fodor's Scotland

EDITOR: Caragh Rockwood

Area Editor: Beth Ingpen, with Gilbert Summers
Editorial Contributors: Robert Blake, David Brown, Kay Hammond, John Hutchinson, Christina Knight, Stacey Kulig, Helayne Schiff, Gilbert Summers
Editorial Production: Linda K. Schmidt
Maps: David Lindroth, *cartographer*; Steven K. Amsterdam, *map editor*
Design: Fabrizio La Rocca, *creative director*; Guido Caroti, *associate art director*; Jolie Novak, *photo editor*
Production/Manufacturing: Mike Costa
Cover Photograph: Catherine Karnow/Woodfin Camp

Copyright

Special Sales

Fodor's Travel Publications are available at special discounts for bulk purchases for sales promotions or premiums. Special editions, including personalized covers, excerpts of existing guides, and corporate imprints, can be created in large quantities for special needs. For more information, contact your local bookseller or write to Special Markets, Fodor's Travel Publications, 201 East 50th Street, New York, NY 10022. Inquiries from Canada should be directed to your local Canadian bookseller or sent to Random House of Canada, Ltd., Marketing Department, 2775 Matheson Boulevard East, Mississauga, Ontario L4W 4P7. Inquiries from the United Kingdom should be sent to Fodor's Travel Publications, 20 Vauxhall Bridge Road, London SW1V 2SA, England.

PRINTED IN THE UNITED STATES OF AMERICA

10 9 8 7 6 5 4 3 2 1

CONTENTS

Maps

ON THE ROAD WITH FODOR'S

WHEN I PLAN A VACATION, the first thing I do is cast around among my friends and colleagues to find someone who's just been where I'm going. That's because there's no substitute for a recommendation from a good friend who knows your tastes, your budget, and your circumstances, someone who's just been there. Unfortunately, such friends are few and far between. So it's nice to know that there's *Fodor's Scotland*.

In the first place, this book won't stay home when you hit the road. It will accompany you every step of the way, steering you away from wrong turns and wrong choices and never expecting a thing in return. It includes a wonderful, full-color map from Rand McNally, the world's largest commercial mapmaker. Most important of all, it's written and assiduously updated by the kind of people you *would* hit up for travel tips if you knew them. They're as choosy as your pickiest friend, except they've probably seen a lot more of Scotland. In these pages, they don't send you chasing down every town and sight in Scotland but have instead selected the best ones, the ones that are worthy of your time and money. To make it easy for you to put it all together in the time you have, they've created short, medium, and long itineraries and, in cities, neighborhood walks that you can mix and match in a snap. Just tear out the map at the perforation, and join us on the road in Scotland.

About Our Writers

Our success in helping to make your trip the best of all possible vacations is a credit to the hard work of our extraordinary writers. We'd also like to thank British Airways for its ever-exceptional service and generosity.

The information in these pages is largely the work of **Beth Ingpen.** A longtime editorial contributor to *Fodor's Scotland*, Beth works as a freelance editor and writer. She was previously publishing manager with the Royal Society of Edinburgh, Scotland's premier learned society, and spent lunchtimes soaking up that city's culture, particularly in its art galleries and concert halls. She has recently become an expert at holidays with small children, with their very different needs and interests. She is assisted by her husband, **Gilbert Summers,** a native Scot who has spent the last 14 years writing numerous guidebooks and articles about his home country. His aim is to make visitors realize that there is a much more diverse nation behind the "haggis and tartan" image (Gilbert has never worn a kilt in his life). They live out in the barley fields in the rural northeast, within sight of the sea.

New This Year

To *Fodor's Scotland,* we've added some "Close-Up" features to enrich your travels here—they highlight Charles Rennie Mackintosh (Chapter 4); Sir Walter Scott (Chapter 5); Hollywood's recent interest in Scotland (Chapter 7); and clans and tartans (Chapter 11). Check them out.

Connections

We're pleased that the American Society of Travel Agents continues to endorse Fodor's as its guidebook of choice. ASTA is the world's largest and most influential travel trade association, operating in more than 170 countries, with 27,000 members pledged to adhere to a strict code of ethics reflecting the Society's motto, "Integrity in Travel." ASTA shares Fodor's devotion to providing smart, honest travel information and advice to travelers, and we've long recommended that our readers—even those who have guidebooks and traveling friends—consult ASTA member agents for the experience and professionalism they bring to your vacation planning.

On Fodor's Web site (www.fodors.com), check out the new Resource Center, an online companion to the Gold Guide section of this book, complete with useful hot links to related sites. In our forums, you can also get lively advice from other travelers and more great tips from Fodor's experts worldwide.

How to Use This Book

Organization

Up front is the **Gold Guide,** an easy-to-use section arranged alphabetically by topic. Under each listing you'll find tips and information that will help you accomplish what you need to in Scotland. You'll also find addresses and telephone numbers of organizations and companies that offer destination-related services and detailed information and publications.

The first chapter in the guide, Destination: Scotland helps get you in the mood for your trip. New and Noteworthy cues you in on trends and happenings, What's Where gets you oriented, Pleasures and Pastimes describes the activities and sights that make Scotland unique, Great Itineraries lays out a selection of complete trips, Fodor's Choice showcases our top picks, and Festivals and Seasonal Events alerts you to special events you'll want to seek out.

Chapters in *Fodor's Scotland* are arranged by region. Each city chapter begins with Exploring information, which is divided into neighborhood sections; each recommends a walking or driving tour and lists sights in alphabetical order. Each regional chapter is divided by geographical area; within each area, towns are covered in logical geographical order, and attractive stretches of road and minor points of interest between them are indicated by the designation *En Route*. And within town sections, all restaurants and lodgings are grouped.

To help you decide what to visit in the time you have, all chapters begin with our recommended itineraries. The A to Z section that ends all chapters covers getting there and getting around. It also provides helpful contacts and resources. At the end of the book you'll find Portraits, with a chronology covering Scotland.

Icons and Symbols

★ Our special recommendations
✕ Restaurant
🏠 Lodging establishment
✕🏠 Lodging establishment whose restaurant warrants a special trip
☺ Good for kids (rubber duck)
☞ Sends you to another section of the guide for more information
✉ Address

☎ Telephone number
☺ Opening and closing times
💳 Admission prices (those we give apply to adults; substantially reduced fees are almost always available for children, students, and senior citizens)

Numbers in white and black circles ③ ❸ that appear on the maps, in the margins, and within the tours correspond to one another.

Dining and Lodging

The restaurants and lodgings we list are the cream of the crop in each price range. Price charts appear in the Pleasures and Pastimes section that follows each regional chapter introduction; in city chapters, price charts are in the dining and lodging sections, right before the reviews.

Hotel Facilities

We always list the facilities that are available—but we don't specify whether you'll be charged extra to use them: When pricing accommodations, always ask what's included. In addition, assume that all rooms have private baths unless noted otherwise. In addition, when you book a room, be sure to mention if you have a disability or are traveling with children, if you prefer a private bath or a certain type of bed, or if you have specific dietary needs or other concerns.

Restaurant Reservations and Dress Codes

Reservations are always a good idea; we mention them only when they're essential or are not accepted. Book as far ahead as you can, and reconfirm as soon as you arrive. Unless otherwise noted, the restaurants listed are open daily for lunch and dinner. We mention dress only when men are required to wear a jacket or a jacket and tie. Look for an overview of local dining-out habits in the Gold Guide.

Credit Cards

The following abbreviations are used: **AE,** American Express; **DC,** Diners Club; **MC,** MasterCard; and **V,** Visa.

Don't Forget to Write

You can use this book in the confidence that all prices and opening times are based on information supplied to us at press time; Fodor's cannot accept responsibility for any errors. Time inevitably brings changes, so always confirm information when it matters—especially if you're making a detour to visit a specific place.

Were the restaurants we recommended as described? Did our hotel picks exceed your expectations? Did you find a museum we recommended a waste of time? Keeping a travel guide fresh and up-to-date is a big job, and we welcome your feedback, positive *and* negative. If you have complaints, we'll look into them and revise our entries when the facts warrant it. If you've discovered a special place that we haven't included, we'll pass the infor- mation along to our correspondents and have them check it out. So send us your thoughts via e-mail at editors@fodors.com (specifying the name of the book on the subject line) or on paper in care of the Scotland editor at Fodor's, 201 East 50th Street, New York, New York 10022. In the meantime, have a wonderful trip!

Karen Cure
Editorial Director

Scotland

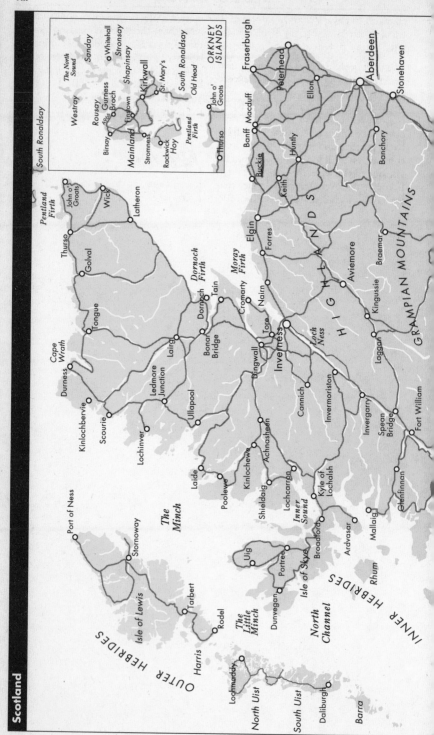

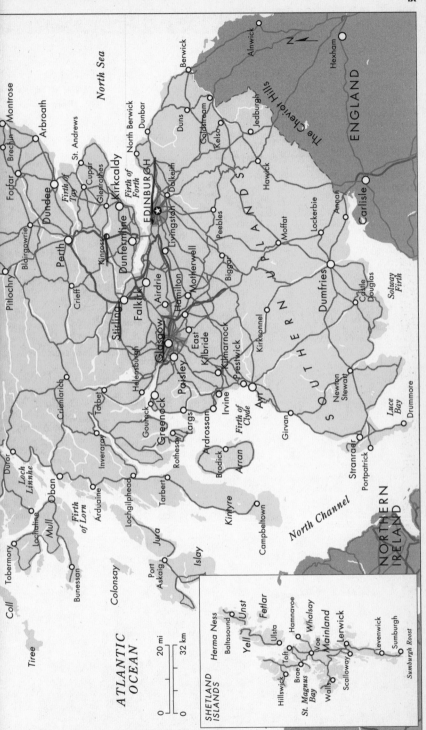

Europe

Reykjavík
ICELAND

NORTHERN
IRELAND

SCOTLAND

NORWAY
Bergen

North
Sea

Skagerra

Edinburgh

Belfast

DENMARK

IRELAND

Irish
Sea

UNITED

Dublin

KINGDOM

Hamburg

WALES

ENGLAND

NETHERLANDS

Amsterdam

Cardiff

The Hague

GERM

London

Rotterdam

ATLANTIC
OCEAN

English Channel

Brussels

Bonn

BELGIUM

Paris

LUXEMBOURG

Frankfurt

FRANCE

Zürich

Munich

Bern

SWITZERLAND

Lyon

LIECHTENSTEIN

Milan

Venic

Monte
Carlo

PORTUGAL

Madrid

ANDORRA

Marseille

Nice

MONACO

Florence

Lisbon

Barcelona

Corsica

SPAIN

Sardinia

Tyrrhenia

Seville

Granada

Balearic
Islands

Gibraltar

Mediterranean Sea

MOROCCO

ALGERIA

0   400 miles

TUNISIA

0   600 km

SMART TRAVEL TIPS A TO Z

Basic Information on Traveling in Scotland, Savvy Tips to Make Your Trip a Breeze, and Companies and Organizations to Contact

AIR TRAVEL

BOOKING YOUR FLIGHT

Price is just one factor to consider when booking a flight: frequency of service and even a carrier's safety record are often just as important. Major airlines offer the greatest number of departures. Smaller airlines—including regional and no-frills airlines—usually have a limited number of flights daily. On the other hand, so-called low-cost airlines usually are cheaper, and their fares impose fewer restrictions, such as advance-purchase requirements. Safety-wise, low-cost carriers as a group have a good history—about equal to that of major carriers.

When you book, **look for nonstop flights** and **remember that "direct" flights stop at least once.** Try to **avoid connecting flights,** which require a change of plane. Two airlines may jointly operate a connecting flight, so ask if your airline operates every segment—you may find that your preferred carrier flies you only part of the way. International flights on a country's flag carrier are almost always nonstop; U.S. airlines often fly direct.

CARRIERS

When flying internationally, you must usually choose between a domestic carrier, the national flag carrier of the country you are visiting, and a foreign carrier from a third country. You may, for example, choose to fly British Airways to Scotland. National flag carriers have the greatest number of nonstops. Domestic carriers may have better connections to your home town and serve a greater number of gateway cities. Third-party carriers may have a price advantage.

Although a small country, Scotland has a significant internal air network. Contact **British Airways Express** for details of flights from Glasgow, Edinburgh, Aberdeen, and Inverness to the farthest corners of the Scottish mainland and to the islands. Check out details of discounts and passes: For example, British Airways has in the past offered a Highland Rover Pass, which gave substantial savings on a total of 5 flights around Scotland in the winter season. **easyJet** also flies between Glasgow, Edinburgh, Aberdeen, and Inverness (plus to Belfast and London Luton).

Many carriers have prohibited smoking on all of their international flights; others allow smoking only on certain routes or certain departures, so **contact your carrier regarding its smoking policy.**

➤ MAJOR AIRLINES: Nonstop flights to Glasgow: **British Airways** (☎ 800/247–9297). Via other carriers in London and/or Manchester: **American Airlines** (☎ 800/433–7300). **Continental** (☎ 800/525–0280). **Delta** (☎ 800/221–1212). **Northwest Airlines** (☎ 800/447–4747). **TWA** (☎ 800/892–4141). **United** (☎ 800/241–6522). **Virgin Atlantic** (☎ 800/862–8621).

➤ FROM LONDON TO EDINBURGH AND GLASGOW: **British Airways** (☎ 0345/222–111) flies from Heathrow; **KLM UK** ☎ 0990/074074) flies from Stansted and London City; **Ryanair** (☎ 01292/678000) flies from Stansted (to Prestwick); **British Midland** (☎ 0345/554–554) flies from Heathrow; and **easyJet** (☎ 990/292929) flies from London Luton and Belfast.

➤ WITHIN SCOTLAND: **British Airways Express** (☎ 0345/222111). **easyJet** (☎ 990/292929).

CHARTERS

Charters usually have the lowest fares but are the least dependable. Departures are infrequent and seldom on time, flights can be delayed for up to

48 hours or can be canceled for any reason up to 10 days before you're scheduled to leave. Itineraries and prices can change after you've booked your flight.

In the U.S., the Department of Transportation's Aviation Consumer Protection Division has jurisdiction over charters and provides a certain degree of protection. The DOT requires that money paid to charter operators be held in escrow, so if you can't pay with a credit card, **always make your check payable to a charter carrier's escrow account.** The name of the bank should be in the charter contract. If you have any problems with a charter operator, contact the DOT (☞ Airline Complaints, *below*). If you buy a charter package that includes both air and land arrangements, remember that the escrow requirement applies only to the air component.

CHECK IN & BOARDING

Airlines routinely overbook planes, assuming that not everyone with a ticket will show up, but sometimes everyone does. When that happens, airlines ask for volunteers to give up their seats. In return these volunteers usually get a certificate for a free flight and are rebooked on the next flight out. If there are not enough volunteers, the airline must choose who will be denied boarding. The first to get bumped are passengers who checked in late and those flying on discounted tickets, so **get to the gate and check in as early as possible,** especially during peak periods.

Although the trend on international flights is to drop reconfirmation requirements, many airlines still ask you to reconfirm each leg of your international itinerary. Failure to do so may result in your reservation being canceled.

Always **bring a government-issued photo ID to the airport.** You may be asked to show it before you are allowed to check in.

CONSOLIDATORS

Consolidators buy tickets for scheduled international flights at reduced rates from the airlines, then sell them at prices that beat the best fare available directly from the airlines, usually without restrictions. Sometimes you can even get your money back if you need to return the ticket. Carefully read the fine print detailing penalties for changes and cancellations, and **confirm your consolidator reservation with the airline.**

➤ CONSOLIDATORS: **Cheap Tickets** (☎ 800/377–1000). **Up & Away Travel** (☎ 212/889–2345). **Discount Travel Network** (☎ 800/576–1600). **Unitravel** (☎ 800/325–2222). **World Travel Network** (☎ 800/409–6753).

COURIERS

When you fly as a courier, you trade your checked-luggage space for a ticket deeply subsidized by a courier service. It's all perfectly legitimate, but there are restrictions: You can usually book your flight only a week or two in advance, your length of stay may be set for a certain number of days, and you probably won't be able to book a companion on the same flight.

CUTTING COSTS

The least-expensive airfares to Scotland are priced for round-trip travel and usually must be purchased in advance. It's smart to **call a number of airlines, and when you are quoted a good price, book it on the spot**—the same fare may not be available the next day. Airlines generally allow you to change your return date for a fee. If you don't use your ticket, you can apply the cost toward the purchase of a new ticket, again for a small charge. However, most low-fare tickets are nonrefundable. To get the lowest airfare, **check different routings.** Compare prices of flights to and from different airports if your destination or home city has more than one gateway. Also price off-peak flights, which may be significantly less expensive.

Travel agents, especially those who specialize in finding the lowest fares (☞ Discounts & Deals, *below*), can be especially helpful when booking a plane ticket. When you're quoted a price, **ask your agent if the price is likely to get any lower.** Good agents know the seasonal fluctuations of airfares and can usually anticipate a sale or fare war. However, waiting can be risky: The fare could go *up* as seats become scarce, and you may wait so long that your preferred flight sells out. A wait-and-see strategy works best if your plans are flexible. If you must arrive and depart on certain dates, don't delay.

At certain (less popular) times of year, airlines may offer travel passes covering a certain number of flights within Scotland, which offer considerable savings over the cost of the flights booked individually. Inquire before your arrival in Scotland as to what is available.

If you intend to fly to Scotland from London, **take advantage of the current fare wars** on internal routes—notably between London's four airports and Glasgow/Edinburgh. Among the cheapest are Ryanair between London Stansted (with its excellent rail links from London's Liverpool Street Station) and Glasgow Prestwick, and easyJet, offering bargain fares from London Luton (with good rail links from central London) to Glasgow, Edinburgh, Aberdeen, and Inverness. Even British Airways now offers competitive fares on some flights.

FLYING TIMES

Flying time is 6½ hours from New York, 7½ hours from Chicago, and 10 hours from Los Angeles.

HOW TO COMPLAIN

If your baggage goes astray or your flight goes awry, complain right away. Most carriers require that you **file a claim immediately.**

➤ AIRLINE COMPLAINTS: U.S. Department of Transportation **Aviation Consumer Protection Division** (✉ C-75, Room 4107, Washington, DC 20590, ☎ 202/366–2220). **Federal Aviation Administration Consumer Hotline** (☎ 800/322–7873).

AIRPORTS & TRANSFERS

AIRPORTS

The major gateway to Scotland is Glasgow Airport, about 7 mi outside of Glasgow. Edinburgh Airport, 7 mi from the city, does not offer transatlantic flights, but does offer connec-

tions for dozens of European cities and hourly flights to London Gatwick and Heathrow.

➤ AIRPORT INFORMATION: **Glasgow Airport** (☎ 0141/887–1111). **Edinburgh Airport** (☎ 0131/333–1000).

TRANSFERS

Lothian Regional Transport runs buses between Edinburgh Airport's main terminal building and Waverley Bridge, in the city center and within easy reach of several hotels. The buses run every 15 minutes on weekdays (9–5) and less frequently (roughly every hour) during off-peak hours and on weekends. The trip takes about 30 minutes (about 45 minutes during rush hour). Single fare for Lothian Regional Transport is £3.20; for Guide Friday, £3.50.

Express buses run from Glasgow Airport to near the Glasgow Central railway station (☎ 0345/484950) and to the Glasgow Buchanan Street bus station (☎ 0141/332–7133). There is service every 15 minutes throughout the day (every 30 minutes in winter). The fare is about £2.50.

➤ TAXIS & SHUTTLES: **Lothian Regional Transport** (☎ 0131/555–6363) and **Guide Friday** (☎ 0131/556–2244).

BIKE TRAVEL

Because Scotland's main roads are continually being upgraded, it is easier than ever for bicyclists to access the network of quieter rural roads in such areas as Dumfries and Galloway, the Borders, and much of eastern Scotland, especially Grampian. Still, care must be taken in getting from some town centers to rural riding areas, so if in doubt, ask a local. In a few areas of the Highlands, notably in northwestern Scotland, the rugged nature of the terrain and limited population have resulted in the lack of side roads, making it more difficult—sometimes impossible—to plan a minor-road route in these areas.

The best months for cycling in Scotland are May, June, and September, when the roads are often quieter and the weather is usually better. Winds are predominantly from the southwest, so plan your route accordingly.

A variety of agencies are now promoting "safe routes" for recreational cyclists in Scotland. These routes are signposted, and the agencies have produced maps or leaflets showing where they run. Perhaps best known is the Glasgow–Loch Lomond–Killin Cycleway, which makes use of former railway track beds, forest trails, quiet rural side roads, and some main roads. The Glasgow to Irvine Cycle Route runs south and west of Glasgow and links with the Johnstone and Greenock Railway Path. In Edinburgh there is the Innocent Railway Path from Holyrood Path to St. Leonards. Contact the relevant tourist board for more information.

BIKES IN FLIGHT

Most airlines will accommodate bikes as luggage, provided they are dismantled and put into a box. Call to see if your airline sells bike boxes (about $5; bike bags are at least $100) although you can often pick them up free at bike shops. International travelers can sometimes substitute a bike for a piece of checked luggage for free; otherwise, it will cost about $100. Domestic and Canadian airlines charge a $25–$50 fee.

BIKES ON BUSES

Although some rural bus services will transport cycles if space is available, you usually can't count on getting your bike on a bus. Be sure to check well in advance with the appropriate bus company.

BIKES ON FERRIES

Bicycles can be taken without any restrictions on car and passenger ferries in Scotland, and it is not generally necessary to book in advance. The three main ferry service operators (☞ Boat & Ferry Travel, *below*) are Caledonian MacBrayne, which charges from £1–£4 per journey for accompanied bicycles on some routes (on many routes, bicycles are carried free); Western Ferries, which carries accompanied bicycles free; and P & O Ferries, which charges from £3–£5 single to £6–£10 return fare in addition to the cost of a passenger ticket. On car ferries, check cycles early so that they can be loaded through the boat's car entrance.

BIKES ON TRAINS

ScotRail strongly advises making a reservation for you and your bike at least a month in advance. On several trains, reservations are compulsory. A leaflet containing the latest information is available through ScotRail and can be picked up at most manned train stations within Scotland.

BIKING OFF-ROAD

People in Scotland were cycling off-road long before the mountain bike was invented. Sometimes they cycled over rights of way in the Highlands; sometimes they biked cross-country to shorten the time taken to climb less accessible high hills. The growing popularity of mountain biking, however, has forced the Scots to focus on the suitability and availability of routes.

Scotland's legal position on off-road cycling is complex. Cycling is covered by road traffic laws because a bike is classified as a vehicle. In a strict legal sense, cycling off-road is only possible on specifically designated cycle tracks, routes that have a common-law right of way for cycles, or routes that have the consent of the landowner. Legally, cyclists are not allowed on pedestrian rights of way, but many landowners don't mind if cyclists use them. Nevertheless, it is best for off-road cyclists to seek local advice when planning routes.

ORGANIZATIONS

Cyclists' Touring Club (✉ National Headquarters, Cotterell House, 69 Meadrow, Godalming, Surrey, GU7 3HS, England, ☎ 01483/417217, 𝕱𝕬𝕏 01483/426994) actively campaigns for better cyclist facilities throughout the United Kingdom. It publishes a members magazine, route maps, and guides. **Sustrans Ltd.** (✉ 53 Cochrane St., Glasgow, G1 1HL, ☎ 0141/572–0234, 𝕱𝕬𝕏 0141/552–3599) is a nonprofit organization dedicated to providing environmentally friendly routes for cyclists, notably in and around cities.

PUBLICATIONS

The Scottish Tourist Board's (☞ Visitor Information, *below*) free brochure, **"Cycling in Scotland"** has some suggested routes and practical advice. The Ordnance Survey Landranger series of maps, which shows gradient, is invaluable for cyclists.

TOURS

Bespoke Highland Tours (✉ The Bothy, Camusdarach, Arisaig, Inverness-shire, PH39 4NT, ☎ FAX 01687/450272) arranges treks throughout the Highlands and the islands for cyclists and walkers of all abilities. **Scottish Border Trails** (✉ Drummore, Venlaw High Rd., Peebles, EH45 8RL, ☎ 01721/720336, FAX 01721/723004) runs off-road mountain bike treks in the Borders and vehicle-supported road tours on which your luggage is ferried between stops. **Wildcat Mountain Bike Tours** (✉ 15A Henderson St., Bridge of Allan, Stirling, FK9 4HN, ☎ FAX 01786/832321) sells guided, vehicle-supported tours throughout Scotland for novices and experts.

BOAT & FERRY TRAVEL

With so many islands, plus the great Firth of Clyde waterway, ferry services in Scotland are of paramount importance. Most of these now transport vehicles as well as foot passengers, although a number of the smaller ones are passengers only.

The main operator is Caledonian MacBrayne Ltd., known generally as Calmac. Services extend from the Firth of Clyde, where there is an extremely extensive network, right up to the northwest of Scotland and all of the Hebrides. Calmac offers an Island Rover runabout ticket, which is ideal for touring holidays in the islands, as well as an island-hopping scheme called Island Hopscotch, and inclusive holidays under the name Hebridean Driveaways, which include ferries, accommodations, and some meals.

The Dunoon–Gourock route on the Clyde, as well as a run from Islay (Port Askaig) to Jura, is served by Western Ferries.

P & O Ferries operates a car ferry for Orkney between Scrabster (near Thurso) or Aberdeen and Stromness (on the main island of Orkney, called Mainland) and for Shetland between Aberdeen and Lerwick. The main

ferries, the *St. Clair* and the *St. Sunniva*, have cabin accommodations and sail five times a week in each direction.

➤ FERRY LINES: **Caledonian MacBrayne** (✉ The Ferry Terminal, Gourock, ☎ 01475/650100, FAX 01475/637607; for reservations, ☎ 0990/650000, FAX 01475/637607). **Western Ferries** (☎ 01369/704452, FAX 01369/706020). **P & O Ferries** (✉ Orkney and Shetland Services, Box 5, Jamieson's Quay, Aberdeen, AB11 5NP, ☎ 01224/572615, FAX 01224/574411).

BUS TRAVEL

The country's bus network is extensive. Bus service is comprehensive in cities, less so in country districts. **Express service links main cities and towns,** connecting, for example, Glasgow and Edinburgh to Inverness, Aberdeen, Perth, Skye, Ayr, Dumfries, and Carlisle; or Inverness with Aberdeen, Wick, Thurso, and Fort William. These express services are very fast, and fares are quite reasonable.

For town, suburban, or short-distance journeys, you normally buy your ticket on the bus, from a paybox or the driver. Sometimes you need exact change. For longer journeys—for example, Glasgow–Inverness—it is usual to reserve and pay at the bus station booking office.

➤ INFORMATION & SCHEDULES: Contact any bus station, the **Travel Center** (✉ Buchanan Street Bus Station, Glasgow G2 3NP, ☎ 0141/332–7133), or the **Edinburgh and Scotland Information Centre** (✉ 3 Princes St., Edinburgh, EH2 2QP, ☎ 0131/557–1700, FAX 0131/473–3881).

DISCOUNT PASSES

On bus routes, Tourist Trail Pass offers complete freedom of travel on any National Express or Scottish Citylink services throughout the mainland UK. Four different permutations give up to 15 days of travel in 30 consecutive days. It is available from Scottish Citylink offices, most bus stations, and any National Express appointed agent.

FROM ENGLAND

Coaches (as long-distance and touring buses are usually called) usually provide the cheapest way to travel between England and Scotland; fares may be as much as one-third of the rail fares for comparable trips (though rail companies are now offering more competitive fares on some routes). About 20 companies operate service between major cities, including National Express. Journey time between London and Glasgow or Edinburgh is 8 to 8¼ hours. The main London terminal is Victoria Coach Station, but some Scottish companies use Gloucester Road Coach Station in west London, near the Penta Hotel. Many people travel to Scotland by coach; in summer a reservation three or four days ahead is advisable. Fares are about £26 round-trip.

➤ BUS LINES: **National Express** (✉ Buchanan Street Bus Station, Killermont St., Glasgow, G2 3NP, ☎ 0990/808080, FAX 0141/332−8055). Travel centers and travel agents also have details, and some travel agents sell tickets.

BUSINESS HOURS

BANKS

Banks are open weekdays 9:30− 3:30, some days to 4:45. Some banks have extended hours on Thursday evenings, and a few are open on Saturday mornings. Some also close for an hour at lunchtime. The major airports operate 24-hour banking services seven days a week.

SHOPS

Usual business hours are Monday− Saturday 9−5:30. Outside the main centers, most shops observe an early closing day once a week, often Wednesday or Thursday—they close at 1 PM and do not reopen until the following morning. In small villages, many also close for lunch. Department stores in large cities stay open for late-night shopping (usually until 7:30 or 8) one day a week. Apart from some newsstands and small food stores, many shops are closed on Sunday except in larger towns and cities, where main shopping malls may be open.

CAMERAS & COMPUTERS

EQUIPMENT PRECAUTIONS

Always **keep your film, tape, or computer disks out of the sun.** Carry an extra supply of batteries, and **be prepared to turn on your camera, camcorder, or laptop** to prove to security personnel that the device is real. Always **ask for hand inspection of film,** which becomes clouded after successive exposure to airport X-ray machines, and **keep videotapes and computer disks away from metal detectors.**

TRAVEL PHOTOGRAPHY

➤ PHOTO HELP: **Kodak Information Center** (☎ 800/242−2424). *Kodak Guide to Shooting Great Travel Pictures,* available in bookstores or from Fodor's Travel Publications (☎ 800/533−6478; $16.50 plus $4 shipping).

CAR RENTAL

If you're traveling to more than one country, make sure your rental contract permits you to take the car across borders and that the insurance policy covers you in every country you visit. Remember that unlike cars in the United States or the rest of Europe, British cars have the steering wheel on the right. Therefore, you may want to leave your rented car in Britain and pick up a left-side drive when you cross the Channel.

Rates in Glasgow begin at £45 a day and £253 a week for an economy car with a manual transmission, and unlimited mileage. This does not include tax on car rentals, which is 17.5%.

➤ MAJOR AGENCIES: **Alamo** (☎ 800/522−9696, 0800/272−2000 in the U.K.). **Avis** (☎ 800/331−1084, 800/879−2847 in Canada, 008/225−533 in Australia). **Budget** (☎ 800/527−0700, 0800/181181 in the U.K.). **Dollar** (☎ 800/800−4000; 0990/565656 in the U.K., where it is known as Eurodollar). **Hertz** (☎ 800/654−3001, 800/263−0600 in Canada, 0345/555888 in the U.K., 03/9222−2523 in Australia, 03/358−6777 in New Zealand). **National InterRent** (☎ 800/227−3876; 0345/222525 in the U.K., where it is known as Europcar InterRent).

THE GOLD GUIDE / SMART TRAVEL TIPS

CUTTING COSTS

To get the best deal, **book through a travel agent who is willing to shop around.**

Also **ask your travel agent about a company's customer-service record.** How has the company responded to late plane arrivals and vehicle mishaps? Are there often lines at the rental counter? If you're traveling during a holiday period, does a confirmed reservation guarantee you a car?

Be sure to **look into wholesalers,** companies that do not own fleets but rent in bulk from those that do and often offer better rates than traditional car-rental operations. Prices are best during off-peak periods. Rentals booked through wholesalers must be paid for before you leave the United States.

➤ RENTAL WHOLESALERS: **Auto Europe** (☎ 207/842–2000 or 800/223–5555, ℻ 800–235–6321). **DER Travel Services** (✉ 9501 W. Devon Ave., Rosemont, IL 60018, ☎ 800/782–2424, ℻ 800/282–7474 for information or 800/860–9944 for brochures). **Kemwel Holiday Autos** (☎ 914/835–5555 or 800/678–0678, ℻ 914/835–5126).

INSURANCE

When driving a rented car you are generally responsible for any damage to or loss of the vehicle. Before you rent, **see what coverage you already have** under the terms of your personal auto-insurance policy and credit cards.

Collision policies that car-rental companies sell for European rentals typically do not cover stolen vehicles. Before you buy additional coverage for theft, check with your credit-card company and personal auto insurance—you may already be covered.

REQUIREMENTS

In Scotland your own driver's license is acceptable. An International Driver's Permit is a good idea; it's available from the American or Canadian automobile association, and, in the United Kingdom, from the Automobile Association or Royal Automobile Club. These international

permits are universally recognized, and having one in your wallet may save you a problem with the local authorities.

SURCHARGES

Before you pick up a car in one city and leave it in another, **ask about drop-off charges or one-way service fees,** which can be substantial. Note, too, that some rental agencies charge extra if you return the car before the time specified in your contract. To avoid a hefty refueling fee, **fill the tank just before you turn in the car,** but be aware that gas stations near the rental outlet may overcharge.

CAR TRAVEL

AUTO CLUBS

➤ INFORMATION: **Australian Automobile Association** (☎ 06/247–7311). **Canadian Automobile Association** (CAA, ☎ 613/247–0117). **New Zealand Automobile Association** (☎ 09/377–4660). In the U.K.: **Automobile Association** (AA, ☎ 0990/500–600), **Royal Automobile Club** (RAC, ☎ 0990/722–722 for membership, 0345/121–345 for insurance). **American Automobile Association** (☎ 800/564–6222).

GASOLINE

Though costs have been remarkably stable in recent years, **expect to pay a good deal more for gasoline than in the United States,** about £2.90 a gallon (64p a liter) for unleaded—up to 10p a gallon higher in remote rural locations. Remember, too, that the British Imperial gallon is about 20% more in volume than the U.S. gallon. What you may find confusing is that although service stations advertise prices by the gallon (mainly for the benefit of the conservative British who continue to resist metrication), pumps actually measure in liters. A British gallon is approximately 4.5 liters.

Most gas stations stock 4-star (97 octane), unleaded, and super unleaded, plus diesel. Service stations are located at regular intervals on motorways and are usually open 24 hours a day, though stations elsewhere usually close from 9 PM to 7 AM, and in country areas many close at 6 PM and all day on Sunday. Most gas stations accept major credit cards.

ROAD CONDITIONS

A good network of superhighways, known as motorways, and divided highways, known as dual carriageways, extends throughout Britain, though in the remoter areas of Scotland where the motorway has not penetrated, travel is noticeably slower. Motorways shown with the prefix "M" are mainly two or three lanes in each direction, without any right-hand turns. If you'll be covering longer distances, these are the roads to use, though inevitably you'll see less of the countryside. Service areas are at most about an hour apart. Dual carriageways, usually shown on a map as a thick red line (often with a black line in the center) and the prefix "A" followed by a number perhaps with a bracket "T" (for example, A304[T]), are similar to motorways, except that right turns are sometimes permitted and you'll find both traffic lights and traffic circles on them.

The vast network of other main roads, which typical maps show as either single red "A" roads, or narrower brown "B" roads, also numbered, are for the most part the old coach and turnpike roads built for horses and carriages in the last century or earlier. Travel along these roads is a bit slower because passing is more difficult, and your trip will take longer than it would take along a motorway. On the other hand, you'll see much more of Scotland.

Minor roads (shown as yellow or white on most maps, unlettered and unnumbered) are the ancient lanes and byways of Britain, roads that are not only living history but a superb way of discovering the real Scotland. You have to drive along them slowly and carefully. On single-track roads, found in the north and west of Scotland, there isn't room for two vehicles to pass, and you must use a passing place if you meet an oncoming car or tractor, or if a car behind wishes to overtake. Never hold up traffic on single-track roads; it is considered extremely bad manners.

ROAD MAPS

The best general purpose touring map is the Scottish Tourist Board's Touring Map of Scotland (5 miles to the inch), widely available in bookshops, tourist information centers, or direct from the Scottish Tourist Board (☞ Visitor Information, *below*). Any bookshop in the main cities will usually sell a good range of maps. For walking or getting to know a smaller area, the Ordnance Survey Landranger series (1:50,000) cannot be beaten and, again, is widely available.

RULES OF THE ROAD

The most noticeable difference for the visitor is that when **in Britain, you drive on the left and steer the car on the right. Give yourself time to adjust to driving on the left**—especially if you pick up your car at the airport and are still suffering from jet lag.

One of the most complicated questions facing visitors to Britain is that of speed limits. In urban areas, except for certain freeways, it is generally 30 miles per hour (mph), but it is 40 mph on some main roads, as indicated by circular red signs. In rural areas the official limit is 60 mph on ordinary roads and 70 mph on divided highways and motorways—and traffic police can be hard on speeders, especially in urban areas. In other respects procedures are similar to those in the United States.

THE CHANNEL TUNNEL

Short of flying, the "Chunnel" is the fastest way to cross the English Channel: 35 minutes from Folkestone to Calais, 60 minutes from motorway to motorway, or 3 hours from London's Waterloo Station to Paris's Gare du Nord.

➤ CAR TRANSPORT: **Le Shuttle** (☎ 0990/353535 in the U.K.).

➤ PASSENGER SERVICE: In the U.K., **Eurostar** (☎ 0345/881881) and **InterCity Europe** (✉ Victoria Station, London, ☎ 0171/834–2345, 0171/828–0892 for credit-card bookings). In the U.S., **BritRail Travel** (☎ 800/677–8585) and **Rail Europe** (☎ 800/942–4866).

THE GOLD GUIDE / SMART TRAVEL TIPS

CHILDREN & TRAVEL

FLYING

If your children are two or older, **ask about children's airfares.** As a general rule, infants under two not occupying a seat fly at greatly reduced fares or even for free.

In general the adult baggage allowance applies to children paying half or more of the adult fare. When booking, **ask about carry-on allowances for those traveling with infants.** In general, for babies charged 10% of the adult fare you are allowed one carry-on bag and a collapsible stroller, which may have to be checked; you may be limited to less if the flight is full.

Experts agree that it's a good idea to use safety seats aloft for children weighing less than 40 pounds. Airlines, however, can set their own policies: U.S. carriers allow FAA-approved models but usually require that you buy a ticket, even if your child would otherwise ride free, since the seats must be strapped into regular seats. Airline rules vary, so it's important to **check your airline's policy about using safety seats during takeoff and landing.** Safety seats cannot obstruct the movement of other passengers in the row, so get an appropriate seat assignment as early as possible.

GROUP TRAVEL

When planning to take your kids on a tour, look for companies that specialize in family travel.

➤ FAMILY-FRIENDLY TOUR OPERATORS: **Grandtravel** (✉ 6900 Wisconsin Ave., Suite 706, Chevy Chase, MD 20815, ☎ 301/986–0790 or 800/247–7651) for people traveling with grandchildren ages 7–17. **Families Welcome!** (✉ 92 N. Main St., Ashland, OR 97520, ☎ 541/482–6121 or 800/326–0724, FAX 541/482–0660).

LODGING

The Scottish Tourist Board's two *Where to Stay* accommodation guides, *Hotels & Guest Houses* and *Bed & Breakfast,* indicate establishments which welcome children and have facilities for them, such as cots and high chairs. It is wise to mention the age of your children when booking accommodation—some of the more upscale country house hotels, in particular, do not allow children under a certain age, e.g. 12, to stay. On the other hand, you may well find that as soon as you arrive at your hotel or guest house, the children are warmly welcomed and a box of toys appears. Many tourist information centers have leaflets on activities for children in the surrounding area.

Although there is no general policy regarding hotel rates for children in Scotland, many hotels allow children under 14 to stay for free in their parents' room: enquire at time of booking. Many also have adjoining family rooms.

CRUISE TRAVEL

Many of the crossings from North America to Europe are repositioning sailings for ships that cruise the Caribbean in winter and European waters in summer. Sometimes rates are reduced, and fly/cruise packages are usually available. Check the travel pages of your Sunday newspaper or contact a travel agent for lines and sailing dates. To get the best deal on a cruise, **consult a cruise-only travel agency.**

SPECIAL-INTEREST CRUISES

Hebridean Island Cruises Ltd. (✉ Acorn Park, Skipton, North Yorkshire, BD23 2UE, ☎ 01756/701338, FAX 01756/701455) offers 6-, 7-, 8-, 13-, or 15-night luxury cruises aboard the MV *Hebridean Princess* around the Scottish islands, including all the Western Isles. The **National Trust for Scotland** (✉ Cruise Manager, National Trust for Scotland, 5 Charlotte Square, Edinburgh, EH2 4DU, ☎ 0131/226–5922) runs a regular cruise program with lectures on natural history. The destination changes each year, but may well include the West Coast or Northern Isles the year you wish to visit. The **Scottish Tourist Board**'s free brochure, "Watersports," includes details of many charter firms operating among the islands.

CUSTOMS & DUTIES

When shopping, **keep receipts** for all of your purchases. Upon reentering the country, **be ready to show customs officials what you've bought.** If you feel a duty is incorrect, appeal the assessment. If you object to the way your clearance was handled, get the inspector's badge number. In either case, first ask to see a supervisor, then write to the appropriate authorities, beginning with the port director at your point of entry.

IN SCOTLAND

Entering the United Kingdom, a traveler 17 or over can take in (1) 200 cigarettes or 100 cigarillos or 50 cigars or 250 grams of tobacco; (2) one liter of alcohol over 22% volume or two liters of fortified wine, sparkling wine or other liqueurs; (3) two liters of still table wine; (4) 60 ml of perfume and 250 ml of toilet water; (5) other goods to a value of £145 (no pooling of exemptions is allowed).

IN AUSTRALIA

Australia residents who are 18 or older may bring back $A400 worth of souvenirs and gifts (including jewelry), 250 cigarettes or 250 grams of tobacco, and 1,125 ml of alcohol (including wine, beer, and spirits). Residents under 18 may bring back $A200 worth of goods.

➤ INFORMATION: **Australian Customs Service** (Regional Director, ✉ Box 8, Sydney, NSW 2001, ☎ 02/9213–2000, FAX 02/9213–4000).

IN CANADA

Canadian residents who have been out of Canada for at least 7 days may bring in C$500 worth of goods duty-free. If you've been away less than 7 days but more than 48 hours, the duty-free allowance drops to C$200; if your trip lasts 24–48 hours, the allowance is C$50. You may not pool allowances with family members. Goods claimed under the C$500 exemption may follow you by mail; those claimed under the lesser exemptions must accompany you. Alcohol and tobacco products may be included in the 7-day and 48-hour exemptions but not in the 24-hour exemption. If you meet the age requirements of the province or territory through which you reenter Canada, you may bring in, duty-free, 1.14 liters (40 imperial ounces) of wine or liquor or 24 12-ounce cans or bottles of beer or ale. If you are 16 or older you may bring in, duty-free, 200 cigarettes and 50 cigars.

You may send an unlimited number of gifts worth up to C$60 each duty-free to Canada. Label the package UNSOLICITED GIFT—VALUE UNDER $60. Alcohol and tobacco are excluded.

➤ INFORMATION: **Revenue Canada** (✉ 2265 St. Laurent Blvd. S, Ottawa, Ontario K1G 4K3, ☎ 613/993–0534, 800/461–9999 in Canada).

IN NEW ZEALAND

Although greeted with a "Haere Mai" ("Welcome to New Zealand"), homeward-bound residents with goods to declare must present themselves for inspection. If you're 17 or older, you may bring back $700 worth of souvenirs and gifts. Your duty-free allowance also includes 4.5 liters of wine or beer; one 1,125-ml bottle of spirits; and either 200 cigarettes, 250 grams of tobacco, 50 cigars, or a combo of all three up to 250 grams.

➤ INFORMATION: **New Zealand Customs** (✉ Custom House, ✉ 50 Anzac Ave., Box 29, Auckland, New Zealand, ☎ 09/359–6655, ☎ 09/309–2978).

IN THE U.S.

U.S. residents may bring home $400 worth of foreign goods duty-free if they've been out of the country for at least 48 hours (and if they haven't used the $400 allowance or any part of it in the past 30 days).

U.S. residents 21 and older may bring back 1 liter of alcohol duty-free. In addition, regardless of your age, you are allowed 200 cigarettes and 100 non-Cuban cigars. Antiques, which the U.S. Customs Service defines as objects more than 100 years old, enter duty-free, as do original works of art done entirely by hand, including paintings, drawings, and sculptures.

You may also send packages home duty-free: up to $200 worth of goods for personal use, with a limit of one parcel per addressee per day (and no alcohol or tobacco products or perfume worth more than $5); label the package PERSONAL USE, and attach a list of its contents and their retail value. Do not label the package UNSOLICITED GIFT, or your duty-free exemption will drop to $100. Mailed items do not affect your duty-free allowance on your return.

➤ INFORMATION: **U.S. Customs Service** (Inquiries, ✉ Box 7407, Washington, DC 20044, ☎ 202/927–6724; complaints, Office of Regulations and Rulings, ✉ 1301 Constitution Ave. NW, Washington, DC 20229; registration of equipment, Resource Management, ✉ 1301 Constitution Ave. NW, Washington DC 20229, ☎ 202/927–0540).

DINING

MEALTIMES

In a country so involved in the tourism industry, "all day" meal places are becoming widespread. The normal lunch period, however, is 12:30–2:30. A few places offer "high tea"—one hot dish and masses of cakes, bread and butter, and jam, served with tea only, around 5:30–6:30.

DISABILITIES & ACCESSIBILITY

ACCESS IN SCOTLAND

In Scotland, many hotels offer facilities for wheelchair users, and special carriages are beginning to appear on intercity and long-distance trains. However, since much of Scotland's beauty is found in hidden hills and corners "off the beaten track," renting a car is probably a better option.

MAKING RESERVATIONS

When discussing accessibility with an operator or reservations agent, **ask hard questions.** Are there any stairs, inside *or* out? Are there grab bars next to the toilet *and* in the shower/tub? How wide is the doorway to the room? To the bathroom? For the most extensive facilities meeting the latest legal specifications, **opt for newer accommodations,** which are more likely to have been designed with access in mind. Older buildings or ships may have more limited facilities. Be sure to **discuss your needs before booking.**

TRANSPORTATION

Hertz (☎ 800/654–3131) can provide hand controls for its cars at its rental offices in Glasgow and Edinburgh. With advance notice, ScotRail staff will assist passengers with disabilities; inquire at any ScotRail area office.

➤ COMPLAINTS: **Disability Rights Section** (✉ U.S. Department of Justice, Civil Rights Division, ✉ Box 66738, Washington, DC 20035–6738, ☎ 202/514–0301 or 800/514–0301, TTY 202/514–0383 or 800/514–0383, FAX 202/307–1198) for general complaints. **Aviation Consumer Protection Division** (☞ Air Travel, *above*) for airline-related problems. **Civil Rights Office** (✉ U.S. Department of Transportation, Departmental Office of Civil Rights, S-30, ✉ 400 7th St. SW, Room 10215, Washington, DC, 20590, ☎ 202/366–4648, FAX 202/366–9371) for problems with surface transportation.

TRAVEL AGENCIES & TOUR OPERATORS

As a whole, the travel industry has become more aware of the needs of travelers with disabilities. In the U.S., the Americans with Disabilities Act requires that travel firms serve the needs of all travelers. Note, though, that some agencies and operators specialize in making travel arrangements for individuals and groups with disabilities.

➤ TRAVELERS WITH MOBILITY PROBLEMS: **Access Adventures** (✉ 206 Chestnut Ridge Rd., Rochester, NY 14624, ☎ 716/889–9096), run by a former physical-rehabilitation counselor. **Accessible Journeys** (✉ 35 W. Sellers Ave., Ridley Park, PA 19078, ☎ 610/521–0339 or 800/846–4537, FAX 610/521–6959), for escorted tours exclusively for travelers with mobility impairments. **Flying Wheels Travel** (✉ 143 W. Bridge St., Box 382, Owatonna, MN 55060, ☎ 507/451–5005 or 800/535–6790, FAX 507/451–1685), a travel agency specializing in customized tours and itineraries worldwide. **Hinsdale Travel Service** (✉ 201 E. Ogden Ave., Suite 100, Hinsdale, IL 60521, ☎ 630/325–1335), a travel agency that benefits from the advice of wheelchair traveler Janice Perkins.

DISCOUNTS & DEALS

Be a smart shopper and **compare all your options** before making any choice. A plane ticket bought with a promotional coupon may not be cheaper than the least expensive fare from a discount ticket agency. For high-price travel purchases, such as packages or tours, keep in mind that what you get is just as important as what you save. Just because something is cheap doesn't mean it's a bargain.

CREDIT-CARD BENEFITS

When you use your credit card to make travel purchases you may get free travel-accident insurance, collision-damage insurance, and medical or legal assistance, depending on the card and the bank that issued it. American Express, MasterCard, and Visa provide one or more of these services, so **get a copy of your credit card's travel-benefits policy.** If you are a member of an auto club, always **ask hotel and car-rental reservations agents about auto-club discounts.** Some clubs offer additional discounts on tours, cruises, and admission to attractions.

PACKAGE DEALS

Packages and guided tours can save you money, but don't confuse the two. When you buy a package, your travel remains independent, just as though you had planned and booked the trip yourself. Fly/drive packages, which combine airfare and car rental, are often a good deal.

ELECTRICITY

To use your U.S.-purchased electric-powered equipment, **bring a converter and adapter.** The electrical current in Scotland is 220 volts, 50 cycles alternating current (AC); wall outlets take plugs with two round oversize prongs and plugs with three prongs.

If your appliances are dual-voltage, you'll need only an adapter. Don't use 110-volt outlets, marked FOR SHAVERS ONLY, for high-wattage appliances such as blow-dryers. Most laptops operate equally well on 110 and 220 volts and so require only an adapter.

EMERGENCIES

To contact the police, fire brigade, ambulance service, or coast guard, **dial 999** from any telephone. No coins are needed for emergency calls from public telephone boxes.

GAY & LESBIAN TRAVEL

Outside the main cities, at least a sector of Scottish society is a little Calvinistic and not given to much in the way of open expression of heterosexuality, let alone anything else. In short, Scotland isn't California. However, most Scots also have an attitude of "live and let live," so it is unlikely you will encounter problems or any real hostility.

➤ GAY- AND LESBIAN-FRIENDLY TRAVEL AGENCIES: **Corniche Travel** (✉ 8721 Sunset Blvd., Suite 200, West Hollywood, CA 90069, ☎ 310/854–6000 or 800/429–8747, ℻ 310/659–7441). **Islanders Kennedy Travel** (✉ 183 W. 10th St., New York, NY 10014, ☎ 212/242–3222 or 800/988–1181, ℻ 212/929–8530). **Now Voyager** (✉ 4406 18th St., San Francisco, CA 94114, ☎ 415/626–1169 or 800/255–6951, ℻ 415/626–8626). **Yellowbrick Road** (✉ 1500 W. Balmoral Ave., Chicago, IL 60640, ☎ 773/561–1800 or 800/642–2488, ℻ 773/561–4497). **Skylink Travel and Tour** (✉ 3577 Moorland Ave., Santa Rosa, CA 95407, ☎ 707/585–8355 or 800/225–5759, ℻ 707/584–5637), serving lesbian travelers.

HEALTH

No particular shots are necessary for visiting Scotland from the USA. If you are traveling in the Highlands and islands in summer, **pack some midge repellent and antihistamine cream** to reduce swelling: the Highland midge is a force to be reckoned with.

MEDICAL PLANS

No one plans to get sick while traveling, but it happens, so **consider signing up with a medical-assistance company.** Members get doctor referrals, emergency evacuation or repatriation, 24-hour telephone hot lines for medical consultation, cash for emergencies, and other personal and legal assistance. Coverage varies by plan, so **review the benefits of each carefully.**

➤ MEDICAL-ASSISTANCE COMPANIES: **International SOS Assistance** (✉ 8 Neshaminy Interplex, Suite 207, Trevose, PA 19053, ☎ 215/245–4707 or 800/523–6586, FAX 215/244–9617; ✉ 12 Chemin Riant-bosson, 1217 Meyrin 1, Geneva, Switzerland, ☎ 4122/785–6464, FAX 4122/785–6424; ✉ 10 Anson Rd., 14-07/08 International Plaza, Singapore, 079903, ☎ 65/226–3936, FAX 65/226–3937).

HOLIDAYS

January 1–2; April 10, May 4; May 25; August 3 (Summer Bank Holiday); December 25–26, 28 (in lieu of December 26).

INSURANCE

Travel insurance is the best way to **protect yourself against financial loss.** The most useful plan is a comprehensive policy that includes coverage for trip cancellation and interruption, default, trip delay, and medical expenses (with a waiver for preexisting conditions).

Without insurance, you will lose all or most of your money if you cancel your trip, regardless of the reason. Default insurance covers you if your tour operator, airline, or cruise line goes out of business. Trip-delay covers unforeseen expenses that you may incur due to bad weather or mechanical delays. It's important to compare the fine print regarding trip-delay coverage when comparing policies.

For overseas travel, one of the most important components of travel insurance is its medical coverage. Supplemental health insurance will pick up the cost of your medical bills should you get sick or injured while traveling. U.S. residents should note that Medicare generally does not cover health-care costs outside the United States, nor do many privately issued policies. Residents of the United Kingdom can buy an annual travel-insurance policy valid for most vacations taken during the year in which the coverage is purchased. If you are pregnant or have a pre-existing condition, make sure you're covered. Australian travelers should buy travel insurance, including extra

medical coverage, whenever they go abroad, according to the Insurance Council of Australia.

Always **buy travel insurance directly from the insurance company;** if you buy it from a cruise line, airline, or tour operator that goes out of business you probably will not be covered for the agency or operator's default, a major risk. Before you make any purchase, **review your existing health and home-owner's policies** to find out whether they cover expenses incurred while traveling.

➤ TRAVEL INSURERS: In the U.S., **Access America** (✉ 6600 W. Broad St., Richmond, VA 23230, ☎ 804/285–3300 or 800/284–8300). **Travel Guard International** (✉ 1145 Clark St., Stevens Point, WI 54481, ☎ 715/345–0505 or 800/826–1300). In Canada, **Mutual of Omaha** (✉ Travel Division, ✉ 500 University Ave., Toronto, Ontario M5G 1V8, ☎ 416/598–4083, 800/268–8825 in Canada).

➤ INSURANCE INFORMATION: In the U.K., **Association of British Insurers** (✉ 51 Gresham St., London EC2V 7HQ, ☎ 0171/600–3333). In Australia, the **Insurance Council of Australia** (☎ 613/9614–1077, FAX 613/9614–7924).

LANGUAGE

"Much," said Doctor Johnson, "may be made of a Scotchman if he be caught young." This quote sums up—even today—the attitude of some English people to the Scots language. They simply assume that their English is superior. Since they speak the language of Parliament and much of the media, their arrogance is understandable. The Scots have long been made to feel uncomfortable about their mother tongue and have only themselves to blame, being until recently actively encouraged—at school, for example—to ape the dialect of the Thames Valley ("Standard English") in order to "get on" in life.

The Scots language (that is, Lowland Scots, not Gaelic) was a northern form of Middle English and in its day was the language used in the court and in literature. It borrowed from Scandinavian, Dutch, French, and

Gaelic. After a series of historical body blows—such as the decamping of the Scottish Court to England after 1603 and the printing of the King James Bible in English but not in Scots—it declined as a literary or official language. It survives, in various forms, virtually as an underground language spoken at home, in shops, on the playground, the farm, or the quayside among ordinary folk, especially in its heartland, in northeast Scotland. (There they describe Scots who use the brayed diphthongs of the English Thames Valley as speaking with a *bool in the mou*—marble in the mouth!)

Plenty of Scots speak English with only an accent and virtually all will "modulate" either unconsciously or out of politeness into understandable English when conversing with a nondialect speaker. As for Gaelic, that belongs to a different Celtic culture and, though threatened, hangs on in spite of the Highlands depopulation.

LODGING

The Scottish Tourist Board publishes two *Where to Stay* guides updated annually, *Hotels & Guest Houses* (£7.99) and *Bed & Breakfast* (£5.50), which give detailed information of facilities provided, and classify and grade the accommodation (☞ Hotels, *below*). The various area tourist boards also publish separate accommodation listings for their areas, annually, which can be obtained either from the Scottish Tourist Board or from the individual area tourist authority.

APARTMENT & VILLA RENTALS

If you want a home base that's roomy enough for a family and comes with cooking facilities, **consider a furnished rental.** These can save you money, especially if you're traveling with a large group of people. Home-exchange directories list rentals (often second homes owned by prospective house swappers), and some services search for a house or apartment for you (even a castle if that's your fancy) and handle the paperwork. Some send an illustrated catalog; others send photographs only of specific properties, sometimes at a charge. Up-front registration fees may apply.

➤ RENTAL AGENTS: **Drawbridge to Europe** (✉ 5456 Adams Rd., Talent, OR 97540, ☎ 541/512–8927 or 888/268–1148, ℻ 541/512–0978). **Europa-Let/Tropical Inn-Let** (✉ 92 N. Main St., Ashland, OR 97520, ☎ 541/482–5806 or 800/462–4486, ℻ 541/482–0660). **Hometours International** (✉ Box 11503, Knoxville, TN 37939, ☎ 423/690–8484 or 800/367–4668). **Interhome** (✉ 124 Little Falls Rd., Fairfield, NJ 07004, ☎ 973/882–6864 or 800/882–6864, ℻ 973/808–1742). **Property Rentals International** (✉ 1008 Mansfield Crossing Rd., Richmond, VA 23236, ☎ 804/378–6054 or 800/220–3332, ℻ 804/379–2073). **Rent-a-Home International** (✉ 7200 34th Ave. NW, Seattle, WA 98117, ☎ 206/789–9377 or 800/488–7368, ℻ 206/789–9379). **Vacation Home Rentals Worldwide** (✉ 235 Kensington Ave., Norwood, NJ 07648, ☎ 201/767–9393 or 800/633–3284, ℻ 201/767–5510).**Villas International** (✉ 605 Market St., San Francisco, CA 94105, ☎ 415/281–0910 or 800/221–2260, ℻ 415/281–0919). **Hideaways International** (✉ 767 Islington St., Portsmouth, NH 03801, ☎ 603/430–4433 or 800/843–4433, ℻ 603/430–4444; membership $99) is a club for travelers who arrange rentals among themselves.

CAMPING

Camping is an economical option for budget travelers. Consult *Forestry Commission Camping and Caravan Sites* (free from the **Forestry Commission,** ✉ 231 Corstorphine Rd., Edinburgh, EH12 7AT, Scotland, ☎ 0131/334–0303), or the Scottish Tourist Board publication, *Caravan & Camping Parks* (£3.99 or £4.50 including postage and packing). For help planning a bicycle camping trip, contact the **Camping and Caravanning Club** (✉ Greenfields House, Westwood Way, Coventry CV4 8JH, ☎ 01203/694995, ℻ 01203/694886).

FARMHOUSE & CROFTING HOLIDAYS

A popular option for families with children is a farmhouse holiday, combining the freedom of bed-and-breakfast accommodations with the hospitality of Scottish family life. Information is available from the

SMART TRAVEL TIPS / THE GOLD GUIDE

British Tourist Authority or the Scottish Tourist Board (☞ Visitor Information, *below*), from **Scottish Farmhouse Holidays** (✉ 10 Drumtenant, Ladybank, Fife, KY15 7UG, Scotland, ☎ 01337/830451, FAX 01337/831301), and from the **Farm Holiday Bureau** (✉ National Agricultural Centre, Stoneleigh, Warwickshire, England CV8 2LZ, ☎ 01203/696909, FAX 01293/696630).

HOME EXCHANGES

If you would like to exchange your home for someone else's, **join a home-exchange organization,** which will send you its updated listings of available exchanges for a year and will include your own listing in at least one of them. It's up to you to make specific arrangements.

➤ EXCHANGE CLUBS: **HomeLink International** (✉ Box 650, Key West, FL 33041, ☎ 305/294–7766 or 800/638–3841, FAX 305/294–1148; $83 per year).

HOSTELS

No matter what your age, you can **save on lodging costs by staying at hostels.** In some 5,000 locations in more than 70 countries around the world, Hostelling International (HI), the umbrella group for a number of national youth hostel associations, offers single-sex, dorm-style beds and, at many hostels, "couples" rooms and family accommodations. Membership in any HI national hostel association, open to travelers of all ages, allows you to stay in HI-affiliated hostels at member rates (one-year membership is about $25 for adults; hostels run about $10–$25 per night). Members also have priority if the hostel is full; they're eligible for discounts around the world, even on rail and bus travel in some countries.

➤ HOSTEL ORGANIZATIONS: **Hostelling International—American Youth Hostels** (✉ 733 15th St. NW, Suite 840, Washington, DC 20005, ☎ 202/783–6161, FAX 202/783–6171). **Hostelling International—Canada** (✉ 400-205 Catherine St., Ottawa, Ontario K2P 1C3, ☎ 613/237–7884, FAX 613/237–7868). Youth Hostel Association of England and Wales (✉ Trevelyan House, 8 St. Stephen's Hill,

St. Albans, Hertfordshire AL1 2DY, ☎ 01727/855215 or 01727/845047, FAX 01727/844126); membership in the U.S. $25, in Canada C$26.75, in the U.K. £9.30).

In Scotland, information is available from **The Scottish Youth Hostels Association** (✉ 7 Glebe Crescent, Stirling, FK8 2JA, ☎ 01786/891400, FAX 01786/891333). A list of independent hostels and bunkhouses is available from **Independent Backpackers' Hostels Scotland** (✉ Croft Bunkhouse and Bothy, 7 Portnalong, Isle of Skye, IV47 8SL, ☎ FAX 01478/640254).

HOTELS

Hotels in the larger cities are generally of good quality. Glasgow and Edinburgh have a number of superior establishments, as well as an extensive range of good hotels in all other price categories.

If you are touring around, you are not likely to be stranded: In recent years, even in the height of the season—July and August—hotel occupancy has run at about 80%. On the other hand, if you arrive in Edinburgh at festival time or some place where a big Highland Gathering or golf tournament is in progress, your choice of accommodations will be extremely limited, and your best bet will be to try for a room in a nearby village. To secure your first choice, **it's always good to reserve in advance,** either through a travel agent at home, directly with the facility, or through local Information Centers (see the individual city or regional chapters), making use of their "Book-a-Bed-Ahead" services. Telephone bookings made from home should be confirmed by letter, and country hotels expect you to turn up by about 6 PM.

Scotland was the first part of the United Kingdom to run a national "Classification and Grading Scheme" to take some of the guesswork out of booking accommodations. Though Fodor's does not use this rating system, you will see it in Scottish publications, and when you are considering a hotel, guest house, or bed-and-breakfast, make sure that you pay close attention to its classification and its grading. The classification part is easy. The number of crowns from zero to five tells you the range of the establishment's facilities. Zero crowns (confusingly described as "Listed") is basic, five crowns luxury. The grading part is actually more important. It purports to assess the quality of the place objectively. Very roughly, the ordinary is "Approved," the good "Commended," the very good "Highly Commended," and the "De Luxe" the best of all. Thus a two-crown "Highly Commended" is probably better value all around than a four-crown "Approved." The awards are part of the accommodations listing in the *Where to Stay* guides distributed at most tourist information centers. Not all establishments participate, but the scheme is becoming popular.

➤ RECOMMENDED HOTELS: **Scotland's Hotels of Distinction** (✉ Central Reservations Office, Box 14610, KY8 6ZA, ☎ 01333/360888, ℻ 01333/360809).

MAIL

POSTAL RATES

Airmail letters to the United States and Canada cost 43p, postcards 37p, aerograms 36p. Letters and postcards to Europe under 20 grams cost 31p (26p to other European Union member countries). Within the U.K. first-class letters cost 26p, second-class letters and postcards 20p.

RECEIVING MAIL

If you're uncertain where you'll be staying, you can **arrange to have your mail sent to American Express.** The service is free to cardholders; all others pay a small fee. You can also collect letters at any post office by addressing them to Poste Restante at the post office you nominate. In Edinburgh, a convenient central office is St. James Centre Post Office, St. James Centre, Edinburgh, EH1 3SR, Scotland.

MONEY

COSTS

A man's haircut will cost £4 and up; a woman's anywhere from £10 to £20. It costs about £1.50 to have a shirt laundered, from £5 to dry-clean a dress, and from £8 to dry-clean a man's suit. A local newspaper will cost you about 35p and a national daily, 45p. A pint of beer is around £1.60, and a serving of whisky about the same. A cup of coffee will run from 50p to £1, depending on where you drink it; a ham sandwich, £2; lunch in a pub, £4 and up (plus your drink).

A theater seat will cost from £5 to £30 in Edinburgh and Glasgow, less elsewhere. Nightclubs will take all they can get from you. For dining and lodging costs, *see* each chapter under that heading.

CREDIT & DEBIT CARDS

Should you use a credit card or a debit card when traveling? Both have benefits. A credit card allows you to delay payment and gives you certain rights as a consumer (☞ Consumer Protection, *above*). A debit card, also known as a check card, deducts funds directly from your checking account and helps you stay within your budget. When you want to rent a car, though, you may still need an old-fashioned credit card. Although you can always *pay* for your car with a debit card, some agencies will not allow you to *reserve* a car with a debit card.

Otherwise, the two types of plastic are virtually the same. Both will get you cash advances at ATMs worldwide if your card is properly programmed with your personal identification number (PIN). (For use in Scotland, your PIN must be four digits long.) Both offer excellent, wholesale exchange rates. And both protect you against unauthorized use if the card is lost or stolen. Your liability is limited to $50, as long as you report the card missing.

➤ ATM LOCATIONS: **Cirrus** (☎ 800/424–7787). **Plus** (☎ 800/843–7587) for locations in the U.S. and Canada, or visit your local bank.

➤ REPORTING LOST CARDS: **American Express** (☎ 312/935–3600 or 910/668–5309 in U.S. collect). **Diners Club** (☎ 303/779–1504 in U.S. collect). **Mastercard** (☎ 800/964–767 toll-free or 314/542–7111 in U.S. collect). **Visa** (☎ 800/985082 toll-free or 410/581–3836 in U.S. collect).

SMART TRAVEL TIPS / THE GOLD GUIDE

CURRENCY

Britain's currency is the pound sterling, which is divided into 100 pence (100p). Notes are issued in the values of £50, £20, £10, and £5 (also £1 in Scotland). Coins are issued to the values of £1, 50p, 20p, 10p, 5p, 2p, and 1p. Scottish coins are the same as English ones, but Scottish notes are issued by three banks: the Bank of Scotland, the Royal Bank of Scotland, and the Clydesdale Bank. They have the same face values as English notes, and English notes are interchangeable with them in Scotland. Scottish £1 notes are no longer legal tender outside Scotland. English banks and post offices will exchange them for you, but fewer and fewer English shops are accepting them.

At press time (summer 1998), the exchange rate for the pound sterling was 61p to the U.S. dollar and 40p to the Canadian dollar.

EXCHANGING MONEY

For the most favorable rates, **change money through banks.** Although fees charged for ATM transactions may be higher abroad than at home, Cirrus and Plus exchange rates are excellent, because they are based on wholesale rates offered only by major banks. You won't do as well at exchange booths in airports or rail and bus stations, in hotels, in restaurants, or in stores, although you may find their hours more convenient. To avoid lines at airport exchange booths, **get a bit of local currency before you leave home.**

➤ EXCHANGE SERVICES: **Chase Currency To Go** (☎ 800/935–9935; 935–9935 in NY, NJ, and CT). **International Currency Express** (☎ 888/842–0880 on the East Coast, 888/278–6628 on the West Coast). **Thomas Cook Currency Services** (☎ 800/287–7362 for telephone orders and retail locations).

TRAVELER'S CHECKS

Do you need traveler's checks? It depends on where you're headed. If you're going to rural areas and small towns, go with cash; traveler's checks are best used in cities. Lost or stolen checks can usually be replaced within 24 hours. To ensure a speedy refund, buy your own traveler's checks—don't let someone else pay for them: irregularities like this can cause delays. The person who bought the checks should make the call to request a refund.

PACKING

LUGGAGE

How many carry-on bags you can bring with you is up to the airline. Most allow two, but the limit is often reduced to one on certain flights. Gate agents will take excess baggage—including bags they deem oversize—from you as you board and add it to checked luggage. To avoid this situation, make sure that everything you carry aboard will fit under your seat. Also, get to the gate early, and request a seat at the back of the plane; you'll probably board first, while the overhead bins are still empty. Since big, bulky baggage attracts the attention of gate agents and flight attendants on a busy flight, make sure your carry-on is really a carry-on. Finally, a carry-on that's long and narrow is more likely to remain unnoticed than one that's wide and squarish.

If you are flying internationally, note that baggage allowances may be determined not by piece but by weight—generally 88 pounds (40 kilograms) in first class, 66 pounds (30 kilograms) in business class, and 44 pounds (20 kilograms) in economy.

Airline liability for baggage is limited to $1,250 per person on flights within the United States. On international flights it amounts to $9.07 per pound or $20 per kilogram for checked baggage (roughly $640 per 70-pound bag) and $400 per passenger for unchecked baggage. You can buy additional coverage at check-in for about $10 per $1,000 of coverage, but it excludes a rather extensive list of items, shown on your airline ticket.

Before departure, **itemize your bags' contents** and their worth, and label the bags with your name, address, and phone number. (If you use your home address, cover it so that potential thieves can't see it readily.) Inside each bag, **pack a copy of your itinerary.** At check-in, **make sure that** each bag is correctly tagged with the destination airport's three-letter code. If your bags arrive damaged or fail to arrive at all, file a written report with the airline before leaving the airport.

PACKING LIST

Travel light. Porters are more or less wholly extinct these days (and very expensive where you can find them).

In Scotland **casual clothes are de rigueur,** and very few hotels or restaurants insist on jackets and ties for men in the evenings. If you plan to attend some gala occasion, you may need evening wear. For summer, lightweight clothing is usually adequate, except in the evenings, when you'll need a jacket, sweater, or cardigan. A waterproof coat or parka is essential. Drip-dry and crease-resistant fabrics are a good bet, since only the most prestigious hotels have speedy laundering or dry-cleaning service.

Many visitors to Scotland appear to think it necessary to adopt a Scottish costume. It is not. Scots themselves do not wear tartan ties or Balmoral "bunnets" (caps), and only an enthusiastic minority prefer the kilt for everyday wear.

In your carry-on luggage **bring an extra pair of eyeglasses or contact lenses** and **enough of any medication you take** to last the entire trip. You may also want your doctor to write a spare prescription using the drug's generic name, since brand names may vary from country to country. **Never put prescription drugs or valuables in luggage to be checked.** To avoid customs delays, carry medications in their original packaging. And don't forget to copy down and carry addresses of offices that handle refunds of lost traveler's checks.

PASSPORTS & VISAS

When traveling internationally, **carry a passport even if you don't need one** (it's always the best form of I.D.), and make **two photocopies of the data page** (one for someone at home and another for you, carried separately from your passport). If you lose your passport, promptly call the nearest embassy or consulate and the local police.

ENTERING SCOTLAND

U.S., Canadian, New Zealand, and Australian citizens, even infants, need only a valid passport to enter Great Britain for stays of up to 90 days.

PASSPORT OFFICES

The best time to apply for a passport or to renew is during the fall and winter. Before any trip, be sure to check your passport's expiration date and, if necessary, renew it as soon as possible. (Some countries won't allow you to enter on a passport that's due to expire in six months or less.)

➤ AUSTRALIAN CITIZENS: **Australian Passport Office** (☎ 131–232).

➤ CANADIAN CITIZENS: **Passport Office** (☎ 819/994–3500 or 800/567–6868).

➤ NEW ZEALAND CITIZENS: **New Zealand Passport Office** (☎ 04/494–0700 for information on how to apply, 0800/727–776 for information on applications already submitted).

➤ U.S. CITIZENS: **National Passport Information Center** (☎ 900/225–5674; calls are charged at 35¢ per minute for automated service, $1.05 per minute for operator service).

SENIOR-CITIZEN TRAVEL

Scotland offers a wide variety of discounts and travel bargains for anyone over 60. **Look into the Senior Citizen Railcard;** it's available in all major railway stations and offers one-third off all rail fares. Travelers over 50 are eligible for the Vantage 50 Card (£8), which provides up to 30 percent off all long-distance National Express or Scottish Citylink coach fares in Britain.

Many hotels advertise off-season discounts for senior citizens, and some offer year-round savings. Budget-minded seniors may also **consider overnight accommodations at a university or college residence hall** (☞ Students, *below*).

For discounted admission to hundreds of museums, historic buildings, and attractions throughout Britain, senior citizens need show only their passport as proof of age. Reduced-rate tickets to theater and ballet are also available.

To qualify for age-related discounts, **mention your senior-citizen status up front** when booking hotel reservations (not when checking out) and before you're seated in restaurants (not when paying the bill). Note that discounts may be limited to certain menus, days, or hours. When renting a car, **ask about promotional car-rental discounts,** which can be cheaper than senior-citizen rates.

➤ ADVENTURES: **Overseas Adventure Travel** (✉ Grand Circle Corporation, 625 Mt. Auburn St., Cambridge, MA 02138, ☎ 617/876–0533 or 800/221–0814, FAX 617/876–0455).

➤ EDUCATIONAL PROGRAMS: **Elderhostel** (✉ 75 Federal St., 3rd floor, Boston, MA 02110, ☎ 617/426–8056). **Interhostel** (✉ University of New Hampshire, 6 Garrison Ave., Durham, NH 03824, ☎ 603/862–1147 or 800/733–9753, FAX 603/862–1113).

SIGHTSEEING TOURS

The **Scottish Tourist Guides Association** has members throughout Scotland who are fully qualified professional tourist guides able to offer walking tours in the major cities, half- or full-day tours or extended tours throughout Scotland, driver-guiding, and special study tours. Many of the guides have at least one second language other than English. Fees are negotiable with individual guides, a list of whom can be obtained from the above address.

➤ TOURIST GUIDES ASSOCIATION: **Scottish Tourist Guides Association** (✉ Kate Anderson, STGA, 2/4 Drumbryden Gardens, Edinburgh EH14 2NG, ☎ FAX 0131/453–1297).

STUDENT TRAVEL

DISCOUNT PASSES

A Student Coach Card from National Express, available to full-time students aged 17 and older, provides one-third off all long-distance coach fares in Britain; contact any National Express agent in Britain with evidence of student status. Those 16–25 are eligible for the same reduction via the National Express Discount Coach Card.

TRAVEL AGENCIES

To save money, **look into deals available through student-oriented travel agencies.** To qualify you'll need a bona fide student I.D. card. Members of international student groups are also eligible.

➤ STUDENT I.D.s & SERVICES: **Council on International Educational Exchange** (✉ CIEE, 205 E. 42nd St., 14th floor, New York, NY 10017, ☎ 212/822–2600 or 888/268–6245, FAX 212/822–2699), for mail orders only, in the United States. **Travel Cuts** (✉ 187 College St., Toronto, Ontario M5T 1P7, ☎ 416/979–2406 or 800/667–2887) in Canada.

➤ STUDENT TOURS: **Contiki Holidays** (✉ 300 Plaza Alicante, Suite 900, Garden Grove, CA 92840, ☎ 714/740–0808 or 800/266–8454, FAX 714/740–2034). **AESU Travel** (✉ 2 Hamill Rd., Suite 248, Baltimore, MD 21210-1807, ☎ 410/323–4416 or 800/638–7640, FAX 410/323–4498).

UNIVERSITY HOUSING

Many universities and colleges throughout Britain open their halls of residence to visitors during vacation periods—that is, from mid-March to mid-April, from July to September, and during the Christmas holidays. Campus accommodations—usually single rooms with access to lounges, libraries, and sports facilities—include breakfast and generally cost about $30 per night. Locations vary from city centers to bucolic lakeside parks.

➤ INFORMATION: **Scottish Universities Accommodation Consortium Campus Hotels** (✉ Box 808, Riccarton, Edinburgh, EH14 4AS, ☎ 0131/449–4034, FAX 0131/451–3199). **British Universities Accommodation Consortium** (✉ Box 1591, University Park, Nottingham, NG7 2RD, England, ☎ 0115/950–4571, FAX 0115/942–2505).

TAXES

VALUE-ADDED TAX (V.A.T.)

The British sales tax, VAT (Value Added Tax), is 17.5%. The tax is almost always included in quoted prices in shops, hotels, and restaurants. Overseas visitors to Scotland can reclaim the VAT on goods by using the Foreign Exchange Tax-Free Shopping arrangements, available only in participating shops. To **get a VAT refund,** you must complete a Tax-Free Shopping form at the shop where the goods are purchased (take your passport with you) and then present the form and the goods to HM Customs and Excise as you leave Great Britain.

Details on how to get a VAT refund and a list of stores offering tax-free shopping are available from the British Tourist Authority (☞ Visitor Information, *below*).

TAXIS

In Edinburgh, Glasgow, and the larger cities, taxis with their "Taxi" sign illuminated can be hailed in the street, or booked by telephone (expect a charge). Elsewhere, most communities of any size at all have a taxi service; your hotel or landlady will be able to supply telephone numbers. Very often you will find an advertisement for the local taxi service in public phone booths.

TELEPHONES

COUNTRY CODES

The country code for Great Britain is 44. When dialing a Scottish or British number from abroad, drop the initial 0 from the local area code. Cellular phone numbers, the 0800 toll-free code and local-rate 0345 numbers do not have a 1 after the initial 0, nor do a range of premium-rate numbers, e.g. 0891, and special-rate numbers, e.g. 0990.

DIRECTORY & OPERATOR INFORMATION

To call the operator, dial 100; directory inquiries (information), 192; international directory inquiries, 153.

INTERNATIONAL CALLS

To make international calls *from* Scotland, you must use the international access code 00. To call North America, dial 00–1–area code–number.

AT&T, MCI, and Sprint international access codes make calling the United States relatively convenient, but you may find the local access number

blocked in many hotel rooms. First ask the hotel operator to connect you. If the hotel operator balks, ask for an international operator, or dial the international operator yourself. One way to improve your odds of getting connected to your long-distance carrier is to travel with more than one company's calling card (a hotel may block Sprint, for example, but not MCI). If all else fails, call from a pay phone in the hotel lobby.

➤ ACCESS CODES: **AT&T Direct** (☎ 0800/890011). **MCI WorldPhone** (☎ 0800/890222). **Sprint International Access** (☎ 0800/890877).

TIPPING

Some restaurants and most hotels add a service charge of 10%–15% to the bill. In this case you are not expected to tip. If no service charge is indicated, add 10% to your total bill, but always check first. Taxi drivers should also get 10%, hairdressers and barbers 10%–15%. You are not expected to tip theater or movie theater ushers, elevator operators, or bartenders in pubs.

TOUR OPERATORS

Buying a prepackaged tour or independent vacation can make your trip to Scotland less expensive and more hassle-free. Because everything is prearranged, you'll spend less time planning.

Operators that handle several hundred thousand travelers per year can use their purchasing power to give you a good price. Their high volume may also indicate financial stability. But some small companies provide more personalized service; because they tend to specialize, they may also be more knowledgeable about a given area.

BOOKING WITH AN AGENT

Travel agents are excellent resources. In fact, large operators accept bookings made only through travel agents. But it's a good idea to **collect brochures from several agencies,** because some agents' suggestions may be influenced by relationships with tour and package firms that reward them for volume sales. If you have a special interest, **find an agent with expertise**

THE GOLD GUIDE / SMART TRAVEL TIPS

THE GOLD GUIDE / SMART TRAVEL TIPS

in that area; ASTA (☞ Travel Agencies, *below*) has a database of specialists worldwide.

Make sure your travel agent knows the accommodations and other services. Ask about the hotel's location, room size, beds, and whether it has a pool, room service, or programs for children, if you care about these. Has your agent been there in person or sent others you can contact?

Do some homework on your own, too: Local tourism boards can provide information about lesser-known and small-niche operators, some of which may sell only direct.

BUYER BEWARE

Each year consumers are stranded or lose their money when tour operators—even very large ones with excellent reputations—go out of business. So **check out the operator.** Find out how long the company has been in business, and ask several travel agents about its reputation. If the package or tour you are considering is priced lower than in your wildest dreams, **be skeptical.** Try to **book with a company that has a consumer-protection program.** If the operator has such a program, you'll find information about it in the company's brochure. If the operator you are considering does not offer some kind of consumer protection, then ask for references from satisfied customers.

In the U.S., members of the National Tour Association and United States Tour Operators Association are required to set aside funds to cover your payments and travel arrangements in case the company defaults. It's also a good idea to choose a company that participates in the American Society of Travel Agent's Tour Operator Program (TOP). This gives you a forum if there are any disputes between you and your tour operator; ASTA will act as mediator.

➤ TOUR-OPERATOR RECOMMENDATIONS: **American Society of Travel Agents** (☞ Travel Agencies, *below*). **National Tour Association** (✉ NTA, 546 E. Main St., Lexington, KY 40508, ☎ 606/226–4444 or 800/755–8687). **United States Tour Operators Association** (✉ USTOA, 342 Madison Ave., Suite 1522, New York, NY 10173, ☎ 212/599–6599 or 800/468–7862, FAX 212/599–6744).

COSTS

The more your package or tour includes, the better you can predict the ultimate cost of your vacation. Make sure you know exactly what is covered, and **beware of hidden costs.** Are taxes, tips, and service charges included? Transfers and baggage handling? Entertainment and excursions? These can add up.

Prices for packages and tours are usually quoted per person, based on two sharing a room. If traveling solo, you may be required to pay the full double-occupancy rate. Some operators eliminate this surcharge if you agree to be matched with a roommate of the same sex, even if one is not found by departure time.

GROUP TOURS

Among companies that sell tours to Scotland, the following are nationally known, have a proven reputation, and offer plenty of options. The classifications used below represent different price categories, and you'll probably encounter these terms when talking to a travel agent or tour operator. The key difference is usually in accommodations, which run from budget to better, and better-yet to best.

➤ SUPER-DELUXE: **Abercrombie & Kent** (✉ 1520 Kensington Rd., Oak Brook, IL 60521-2141, ☎ 630/954–2944 or 800/323–7308, FAX 630/954–3324). **Travcoa** (✉ Box 2630, 2350 S.E. Bristol St., Newport Beach, CA 92660, ☎ 714/476–2800 or 800/992–2003, FAX 714/476–2538).

➤ DELUXE: **Classique Tours**(✉ 8 Underwood Rd., Paisley PA3 1TD U.K., ☎ 0141/889–4050, FAX 0141/848–7616). **Globus** (✉ 5301 S. Federal Circle, Littleton, CO 80123-2980, ☎ 303/797–2800 or 800/221–0090, FAX 303/347–2080). **Maupintour** (✉ 1515 St. Andrews Dr., Lawrence, KS 66047, ☎ 785/843–1211 or 800/255–4266, FAX 785/843–8351). **Prestige Tours** (✉ Seaforth House, Barrie Rd.,

Hillington, Glasgow G52 4PX, U.K., ☎ 0141/810–3200 in U.K., ᴲᴬˣ 0141/810–3223 in U.K.).Tauck Tours (✉ Box 5027, 276 Post Rd. W, Westport, CT 06881-5027, ☎ 203/226–6911 or 800/468–2825, ᴲᴬˣ 203/221–6866).

➤ FIRST-CLASS: **Brendan Tours** (✉ 15137 Califa St., Van Nuys, CA 91411, ☎ 818/785–9696 or 800/421–8446, ᴲᴬˣ 818/902–9876). **British Airways Holidays** (☎ 800/247–9297). **Caravan Tours** (✉ 401 N. Michigan Ave., Chicago, IL 60611, ☎ 312/321–9800 or 800/227–2826, ᴲᴬˣ 312/321–9845). **CIE Tours** (✉ Box 501, 100 Hanover Ave., Cedar Knolls, NJ 07927-0501, ☎ 973/292–3899 or 800/243–8687, ᴲᴬˣ 973/292–0463). **Collette Tours** (✉ 162 Middle St., Pawtucket, RI 02860, ☎ 401/728–3805 or 800/340–5158, ᴲᴬˣ 401/728–4745). **DER Travel Services** (✉ 9501 W. Devon Ave., Rosemont, IL 60018, ☎ 800/782–2424, ᴲᴬˣ 800/282–7474 for information or 800/860–9944 for brochures). **Insight International Tours** (✉ 745 Atlantic Ave., #720, Boston, MA 02111, ☎ 617/482–2000 or 800/582–8380, ᴲᴬˣ 617/482–2884 or 800/622–5015). **Trafalgar Tours** (✉ 11 E. 26th St., New York, NY 10010, ☎ 212/689–8977 or 800/854–0103, ᴲᴬˣ 800/457–6644). **United Vacations** (☎ 800/328–6877).

➤ BUDGET: **Cosmos** (☞ Globus, *above*). **Trafalgar** (☞ *above*).

PACKAGES

Like group tours, independent vacation packages are available from major tour operators and airlines. The companies listed below offer vacation packages in a broad price range.

➤ AIR/HOTEL: **British Airways Holidays** (☎ 800/247–9297). **Celtic International Tours** (✉ 1860 Western Ave., Albany, NY 12203, ☎ 518/862–0042 or 800/833–4373). **CIE Tours** (☞ Group Tours, *above*). **DER Travel Services** (☞ Group Tours, *above*).

➤ CUSTOMIZED PACKAGES: **Five Star Touring** (✉ 60 E. 42nd St., #612, New York, NY 10165, ☎ 212/818–9140 or 800/792–7827, ᴲᴬˣ 212/818–9142).

THEME TRIPS

Perthshire Activity Line (✉ Lower City Mills, West Mill St., Perth PH1 5QP, ☎ 01738/444144, ᴲᴬˣ 01738/630416) offers a range of activities, from white-water rafting to painting. **Travel Contacts** (✉ Box 173, Camberley, GU15 1YE, England, ☎ 01276/677217, ᴲᴬˣ 01276/63477) represents 150 tour operators in Europe.

➤ BARGE/RIVER CRUISES: **Alden Yacht Charters** (✉ 1909 Alden Landing, Portsmouth, RI 02871, ☎ 401/683–1782 or 800/662–2628, ᴲᴬˣ 401/683–3668). **Le Boat** (✉ 10 S. Franklin Turnpike, #204B, Ramsey, NJ 07446, ☎ 201/236–2333 or 800/922–0291).

➤ BEER: **MIR Corporation** (✉ 85 S. Washington St., #210, Seattle, WA 98104, ☎ 206/624–7289 or 800/424–7289, ᴲᴬˣ 206/624–7360).

➤ BICYCLING: **Backroads** (✉ 801 Cedar St., Berkeley, CA 94710-1800, ☎ 510/527–1555 or 800/462–2848, ᴲᴬˣ 510-527–1444). **Himalayan Travel** (✉ 110 Prospect St., Stamford, CT 06901, ☎ 203/359–3711 or 800/225–2380, ᴲᴬˣ 203/359–3669). **Uniquely Europe** (✉ 2819 1st Ave., Ste. 280, Seattle, WA 98121-1113, ☎ 206/441–8682 or 800/426–3615, ᴲᴬˣ 206/441–8862). **Vermont Bicycle Touring** (✉ Box 711, Bristol, VT, 05443-0711, ☎ 800/245–3868 or 802/453–4811, ᴲᴬˣ 802/453–4806).

➤ GOLF: **Francine Atkins' Scotland/Ireland** (✉ 2 Ross Ct., Trophy Club, TX 76262, ☎ 817/491–1105 or 800/742–0355, ᴲᴬˣ 817/491–2025). **Golf International** (✉ 275 Madison Ave., New York, NY 10016, ☎ 212/986–9176 or 800/833–1389, ᴲᴬˣ 212/986–3720). **Golfpac** (✉ Box 162366, Altamonte Springs, FL 32716-2366, ☎ 407/260–2288 or 800/327–0878, ᴲᴬˣ 407/260–8989). **ITC Golf Tours** (✉ 4134 Atlantic Ave., #205, Long Beach, CA 90807, ☎ 310/595–6905 or 800/257–4981). **Scottish Golf and Travel Service** (✉ 12 Rutland Sq., Edinburgh, EH1 2BB, Scotland, ☎ 800/847–8064; 0131/221–1500 in U.K., FAX 800/546–3510). **Stine's Golftrips** (✉ 193 Towne Center Dr., Kissimmee, FL 34759, ☎ 407/933–0032, FAX 407/933–8857).

➤ HORSEBACK RIDING: **Cross Country International Equestrian Vacations** (✉ Box 1170, Millbrook, NY 12545, ☎ 914/677–6000 or 800/828–8768, FAX 914/677–6077).

➤ HORTICULTURE: **Brightwater Holidays** (✉ Eden Park House, Cupar Fife KY15 4HS, U.K., ☎ 01334/657155, FAX 01334/657144).

➤ LEARNING: **Earthwatch** (✉ Box 9104, 680 Mount Auburn St., Watertown, MA 02272, ☎ 617/926–8200 or 800/776–0188, FAX 617/926–8532) for research expeditions. **Natural Habitat Adventures** (✉ 2945 Center Green Ct., Boulder, CO 80301, ☎ 303/449–3711 or 800/543–8917, FAX 303/449–3712). **Questers** (✉ 381 Park Ave. S, New York, NY 10016, ☎ 212/251–0444 or 800/468–8668, FAX 212/251–0890). **Smithsonian Study Tours and Seminars** (✉ 1100 Jefferson Dr. SW, Room 3045, MRC 702, Washington, DC 20560, ☎ 202/357–4700, FAX 202/633–9250). **Victor Emanuel Nature Tours** (✉ Box 33008, Austin, TX 78764, ☎ 512/328–5221 or 800/328–8368, FAX 512/328–2919).

➤ MOTORCYCLE: **Edelweiss Bike Travel** (✉ 129 Hillside Ave., Williston Park, NY 11596, ☎ 516/746–6761 or 800/877–2784, FAX 516/746–6690).

➤ WALKING/HIKING: **Above the Clouds Trekking** (✉ Box 398, Worcester, MA 01602-0398, ☎ 800/233–4499 or 508/799–4499, FAX 508/797–4779). **Backroads** (☞ Bicycling, *above*). **Country Walkers** (✉ Box 180, Waterbury, VT 05676-0180, ☎ 802/244–1387 or 800/464–9255, FAX 802/244–5661). **English Lakeland Ramblers** (✉ 18 Stuyvesant Oval, Suite 1A, New York, NY 10009, ☎ 212/505–1020 or 800/724–8801, FAX 212/979–5342). **Himalayan Travel** (☞ Bicycling, *above*). **Uniquely Europe** (☞ Bicycling, *above*). **Walking the World** (✉ Box 1186, Fort Collins, CO 80522, ☎ 970/498–0500 or 800/340–9255, FAX 970/498–9100) spe-

cializes in tours for ages 50 and older. **Wilderness Travel** (✉ 1102 Ninth St., Berkeley, CA 94710, ☎ 510/558–2488 or 800/368–2794).

TRAIN TRAVEL

Scotland has a rail network extending all the way to Thurso and Wick, the most northerly stations in the British Isles. Lowland services, most of which originate in Glasgow or Edinburgh, are generally fast and reliable. A shuttle makes the 50-minute trip between the cities every half hour. (For information about Edinburgh's and Glasgow's train stations, *see* Chapters 3 and 4, respectively.)

Some lines in Scotland—all suburban services and lines north and west of Inverness—operate on one class only (standard). Long-distance services carry buffet and refreshment cars. One word of caution: **There are very few trains in the Highlands on Sundays.**

DISCOUNT PASSES

If you plan to travel by train in Scotland, **consider purchasing a BritRail Pass,** which also allows travel in England and Wales. Prices begin at $375 for eight days of first-class travel and $259 for eight days of second-class travel. Passes good for longer periods of time are also available, as are a Flexipass, a BritRail Senior Pass, a BritRail Youthpass, and a Freedom of Scotland Travelpass. Remember that EurailPasses are not honored in Great Britain.

But be aware that if you don't plan to cover many miles, you may come out ahead by buying individual tickets. Standard passes (BritRail Classic Passes) are available for 8 days ($375 in first class and $259 in second class), for 15 days ($575 and $395), for 22 days ($740 and $510), and one month ($860 and $590). BritRail Flexipasses allow you to travel for any 4, 8, or 15 days in one month, and 15 days in two months; you pay $315, $459, and $699 for the Flexipass one-month passes in first class, $219, $315, and $480 for second class, and $385 for the two-month pass.

The Freedom of Scotland Travelpass allows transportation on all Caledonian MacBrayne and Strathclyde ferries and discounts on some P & O ferry routes to the islands. You can travel any 4 days in an 8-day period ($110); 8 days in a 15-day period ($160); and 12 days in a 15-day period ($210).

The BritRail Youthpass and BritRail Youth Flexipass are available for second-class travel for those under 26 on their first travel day; fares for the Youthpass are $205, $318, $410, and $475 for 8, 15, and 22 days, and one month. The Youth Flexipass is $175 for 4 days of travel in one month, $253 for 8 days in one month, and $385 for 15 days in a 2-month period.

Although some passes may be purchased in Scotland, **you must purchase many passes stateside;** they're sold by travel agents as well as BritRail or Rail Europe.

Many travelers assume that rail passes guarantee them seats on the trains they wish to ride. Not so. You need to **book seats ahead even if you are using a rail pass;** seat reservations are required on some European trains, particularly high-speed trains, and are a good idea on trains that may be crowded—particularly in summer on popular routes. You will also need a reservation if you purchase overnight sleeping accommodations.

➤ DISCOUNT PASSES: BritRail Passes are available from most travel agents or from **BritRail Travel** (✉ 226 Westchester Ave., White Plains, NY 10604, ☎ 888/BRITRAIL or 800/ 677–8585; ✉ 2087 Dundas St. E., Suite 105, Mississauga, Ontario l4X 1M2, ☎ 905/602–4195 or 800/361– 7245) recently merged with **Rail Europe** (✉ 226 Westchester Ave., White Plains, NY 10604, ☎ 800/ 848–7245). In London, contact the **National Rail Enquiry Line** (☎ 0345/ 484950).

FARES

Train fares vary according to class of ticket purchased and distance traveled. The fare system is complex. Before you buy your ticket, be sure to stop at the Information Office/Travel Centre first and request the lowest fare to your destination and information

about any special offers. [...] about InterCity Saver, Sup[...] Super-APEX and APEX ti[...] about the Family Railcard [...] are with you. Note that yo[...] does *not* guarantee you a seat. For that you need a seat reservation, which if made at the time of ticket purchase is usually included in the ticket price, or if booked separately, must be paid for at a cost of £1 *per train* on your itinerary (that is, £2 if you need to book seats on two trains). You can opt to sit facing toward or away from the engine, and in a smoking or no-smoking compartment.

FROM ENGLAND

There are two main rail routes to Scotland from the south of England. The first, the west coast main line, runs from London Euston to Glasgow Central; it takes five and a half hours to make the 400-mile trip to central Scotland, and service is frequent and reliable, with one train every two hours on average. Useful for daytime travel to the Scottish Highlands, and equipped with an excellent restaurant car, is the direct train to Stirling and Aviemore, terminating at Inverness. For a restful route to the Scottish Highlands, take the overnight sleeper service, with air-conditioned, sound-proof sleeping carriages. It runs from London Euston, departing in late evening, to Perth, Stirling, Aviemore, and Inverness, where it arrives the following morning.

The second route is the east coast main line from London King's Cross to Edinburgh; it provides the quickest trip to the Scottish capital, and between 8 AM and 6 PM there are 16 trains to Edinburgh, three of them through to Aberdeen. Limited-stop expresses like the *Flying Scotsman* make the 393-mile London to Edinburgh journey in around four hours. Connecting services to most parts of Scotland—particularly the Western Highlands—are often better from Edinburgh than from Glasgow.

Trains from elsewhere in England are good: There is regular service from Birmingham, Manchester, Liverpool, and Bristol to Glasgow and Edinburgh. From Harwich (the port of

SMART TRAVEL TIPS / GOLD GUIDE

XXXV

call for ships from Holland, Germany, and Denmark), you can travel to Glasgow via Manchester. But it is faster to change at Peterborough for the east coast main line to Edinburgh. **Reservations for all sleeper services are essential.**

SCENIC ROUTES

Although many routes in Scotland run through extremely attractive countryside, several stand out: from Glasgow to Oban via Loch Lomond; to Fort William and Mallaig via Rannoch (ferry connection to Skye); from Edinburgh to Inverness via the Forth Bridge and Perth; from Inverness to Kyle of Lochalsh and to Wick; and from Inverness to Aberdeen.

A luxury private train, the *Royal Scotsman,* does scenic tours, partly under steam power, with banquets en route. This is a luxury experience: Some evenings require formal wear (black tie for men, evening dresses for women). Only 36 people are carried per trip. For trips within Scotland, there is a choice of a four-night (£2,450) or five-night (£3,100) tour.

➤ TRAIN TOURS: Book Royal Scotsman tours through **Abercrombie & Kent** (⌧ Sloane Square House, Holbein Pl., London SW1W 8NS, ☎ 0171/730–9600, ℻ 0171/730–9376; or ⌧ 1420 Kensington Rd., Oak Brook, IL 60521, ☎ 312/954–2944 or 800/323–7308).

TRAVEL AGENCIES

A good travel agent puts your needs first. Look for an agency that has been in business at least five years, emphasizes customer service, and has someone on staff who specializes in your destination. In addition, **make sure the agency belongs to a professional trade organization,** such as ASTA in the United States. (If your travel agency is also acting as your tour operator, *see* Buyer Beware in Tour Operators, *above*).

➤ LOCAL AGENT REFERRALS: American Society of Travel Agents (ASTA, ☎ 800/965–2782 24-hr hot line, ℻ 703/684–8319). Association of Canadian Travel Agents (⌧ Suite 201, 1729 Bank St., Ottawa, Ontario K1V 7Z5, ☎ 613/521–0474, ℻ 613/521–0805). Association of British

Travel Agents (⌧ 55–57 Newman St., London W1P 4AH, ☎ 0171/637–2444, ℻ 0171/637–0713). **Australian Federation of Travel Agents** (☎ 02/9264–3299). **Travel Agents' Association of New Zealand** (☎ 04/499–0104).

TRAVEL GEAR

Travel catalogs specialize in useful items, such as compact alarm clocks and travel irons, that can **save space when packing.** They also offer dual-voltage appliances, currency converters, and foreign-language phrase books.

➤ CATALOGS: **Magellan's** (☎ 800/962–4943, ℻ 805/568–5406). **Orvis Travel** (☎ 800/541–3541, ℻ 540/343–7053). **TravelSmith** (☎ 800/950–1600, ℻ 800/950–1656).

VISITOR INFORMATION

For general information about Scotland, contact the British and Scottish tourism offices.

➤ BRITISH TOURIST AUTHORITY: **U.S. Nationwide:** (⌧ 551 5th Ave., Suite 701, New York, NY 10176, ☎ 212/986–2200 or 800/462–2748, ℻ 212/986–1188 or 818/441–8265 24-Hour Fax Information Line). **Chicago:** (⌧ 625 N. Michigan Ave., Suite 1510, Chicago, IL 60611; walk-in service only). **Canada:** (⌧ 111 Avenue Rd., Suite 450, Toronto, Ontario M5R 3J8, ☎ 416/961–8124, ℻ 416/961–2175). **U.K.:** British Travel Centre, (⌧ 12 Regent St., London SW1Y 4PQ; no information by phone). **U.K.:** (⌧ Thames Tower, Black's Rd., London W6 9EL; mail inquiries only).

➤ SCOTTISH TOURIST BOARD: **U.K.:** ⌧ 23 Ravelston Terr., Edinburgh EH4 3EU, ☎ 0131/332–2433, ℻ 0131/315–4545; ⌧ 19 Cockspur St., London SW1Y 5BL, ☎ 0171/930–8661, ℻ 0171/930–1817.

WEB SITES

Do **check out the World Wide Web** when you're planning. You'll find everything from up-to-date weather forecasts to virtual tours of famous cities. Fodor's Web site, www.fodors.com, is a great place to start your on-line travels. For more information specifically on Scotland, visit www.holiday.scotland.net, the Scottish Tourist Board's Web site.

WHEN TO GO

The Scottish climate has been much maligned (sometimes with justification). You can be unlucky: You may spend a summer week in Scotland and experience nothing but low clouds and drizzle. But on the other hand, you may enjoy calm Mediterranean-like weather even in early spring and late fall.

Generally speaking, Scotland is three or four degrees cooler than southern England. The east is drier and colder than the west; Edinburgh's rainfall is comparable to Rome's, while Glasgow's is more like that in Vancouver—yet the cities are only 44 miles apart.

Long summer evenings grow longer still as you travel north. Dawn in Orkney and Shetland in June is at around 1 AM, no more than an hour or so after sunset. Winter days are very short.

Scotland has few thunderstorms and little fog, except for local mists near coasts. But there are often variable winds that reach gale force even in summer. They blow away the hordes of gnats and midges, the curse of the western Highlands.

CLIMATE

What follows are average daily maximum and minimum temperatures for major cities in Scotland.

➤ FORECASTS: **Weather Channel Connection** (☎ 900/932–8437), 95¢ per minute from a Touch-Tone phone.

Climate in Scotland

ABERDEEN

Jan.	43F	6C	May	54F	12C	Sept.	59F	15C
	36	2		43	6		49	9
Feb.	43F	6C	June	61F	16C	Oct.	54F	12C
	36	2		49	9		43	6
Mar.	47F	8C	July	63F	17C	Nov.	47F	8C
	36	2		52	11		40	4
Apr.	49F	9C	Aug.	63F	17C	Dec.	45F	7C
	40	4		52	11		36	2

EDINBURGH

Jan.	43F	6C	May	58F	14C	Sept.	61F	16C
	34	1		43	6		49	9
Feb.	43F	6C	June	63F	17C	Oct.	54F	12C
	34	1		49	9		45	7
Mar.	47F	8C	July	65F	18C	Nov.	49F	9C
	36	2		52	11		40	4
Apr.	52F	11C	Aug.	65F	18C	Dec.	45F	7C
	40	4		52	11		36	2

GLASGOW

Jan.	41F	5C	May	59F	15C	Sept.	61F	16C
	34	1		43	6		49	9
Feb.	45F	7C	June	65F	18C	Oct.	56F	13C
	34	1		49	9		43	6
Mar.	49F	9C	July	67F	19C	Nov.	49F	9C
	36	2		52	11		38	3
Apr.	54F	12C	Aug.	67F	19C	Dec.	45F	7C
	40	4		52	11		36	2

HIGHLANDS

Jan.	43F	6C	May	58F	14C	Sept.	61F	16C
	32	0		43	6		49	9
Feb.	45F	7C	June	63F	17C	Oct.	56F	13C
	34	1		49	9		43	6
Mar.	49F	9C	July	65F	18C	Nov.	49F	9C
	36	2		52	11		38	3
Apr.	52F	11C	Aug.	65F	18C	Dec.	45F	7C
	40	4		52	11		34	1

ORKNEY ISLANDS

Jan.	43F	6C	May	54F	12C	Sept.	58F	14C
	36	2		43	6		49	9
Feb.	43F	6C	June	58F	14C	Oct.	52F	11C
	36	2		47	8		45	7
Mar.	45F	7C	July	61F	16C	Nov.	47F	8C
	38	3		50	10		41	5
Apr.	49F	9C	Aug.	61F	16C	Dec.	45F	7C
	40	4		50	10		38	3

1 Destination: Scotland

THE PRIDE OF SCOTLAND

ON SOME OLD RECORDINGS of Scottish songs still in circulation, you may run across *Roamin' in the Gloamin'* or *I Love a Lassie* or one of the other comic ditties of Harry Lauder, a star of the music halls of the 1920s. With his garish kilt, short crooked walking stick, rich rolling *R*s, and *pawky* (cheerfully impudent) humor, chiefly based on the alleged meanness of the Scots, he impressed a Scottish character on the world. But his was, needless to say, a false impression and one the Scots have been trying to stamp out ever since.

How, then, do you characterize the Scots? Temperamentally, they are a mass of contradictions. They have been likened, not to a Scotch egg, but to a soft-boiled egg: a dour hard shell, a mushy middle. The Scots laugh and weep with almost Latin facility, but to strangers they are reserved, noncommittal, and in no hurry to make an impression. Historically, fortitude and resilience have been their hallmarks, and there are streaks of both resignation and pitiless ferocity in their makeup, warring with sentimentality and love of family. Very Scottish was the instant reaction of an elderly woman of Edinburgh 200 years ago, when news arrived of the defeat in Mysore in India and of the Scottish soldiers being fettered in irons, two by two: "God help the puir chiel that's chained tae oor Davie."

The Scots are in general suspicious of the go-getter. "Whiz kid" is a term of contempt. But they are by no means plodders, though it is true to say that they are determined and thorough, respecting success only when it has been a few hundred years in the making. Praise of some bright ambitious youngster is quenched with the sneer: "Him? Ah kent (knew) his faither."

Yet this is the nation that built commerce throughout the British Empire, opened wild territories, and was responsible for much of humankind's scientific and technological advancement, a nation boastful about things it is not too good at and shamefacedly modest about genuine achievements. Consider the following extract from a handout about the Edinburgh School of Medicine: "If one excepts a few discoveries such as that of 'fixed air' by Black, of the diverse functions of the nerve-roots by Bell, of the anaesthetic properties of chloroform by Simpson, of the invention of certain powerful drugs by Christison, and of the importance of antiseptic procedures by Lister, the influence of Edinburgh medicine has been of a steady constructive rather than a revolutionary type."

Among things that strike most newcomers to Scotland are the generosity of the Scots; their obsession with respectability; their satisfaction with themselves and their desire to stay as they are; and, above all, their passionate love of Scotland. An obstinate refusal to go along with English ideas has led to accusations that the nation has a head-in-the-sand attitude toward progress. But the Scots have their own ideas of progress, and they jealously guard the institutions that remain unique to them.

When it comes to education, Scotland has a proud record. The nation boasted four universities—St. Andrews, Aberdeen, Glasgow, and Edinburgh—when England had only two: Oxford and Cambridge. The *lad o' pairts* (man of talents)—the poor child of a feckless father and a fiercely self-sacrificing mother, sternly tutored by the village *dominie* (schoolmaster) and turned loose at the age of 13 with so firm a base of learning that he rose to the top of his profession—this type of lad is a phenomenon of Scottish social history. The sacrifices that boys made as a matter of course to further their education are an old Scottish tradition. "Meal Monday," the midsemester holiday at a Scottish university, is a survivor of the long weekend that once enabled students to return to their distant homes—on foot—and replenish the sack of "meal" (oatmeal) that was their only subsistence.

It is a British cliché that an English education teaches you to think and a Scottish education stuffs your head with information. The average Scot does appear to be better informed than his English neighbor and to discuss facts rather than ideas. Scots pride themselves on their international outlook and on being better linguists than the English. The Scots get on well with foreigners, and they offer strangers a kindly welcome and a civility not often found in the modern world.

Just as the Scots have their own traditions in education, so is their legal system distinct from England's. In England the police both investigate crime and prosecute suspects. In Scotland there is a public prosecutor directly responsible to the Lord Advocate (equivalent to England's Attorney General), who is himself accountable to Parliament.

For the most part, however, you will notice few practical differences except in terminology. The barrister in England becomes an advocate in Scotland. Law-office nameplates designate their occupants "S. S. C." (Solicitor to the Supreme Court) or "W. S." (Writer to the Signet); cases for prosecution go before the "procurator fiscal" and are tried by the "sheriff" or "sheriff-substitute." The terms are different in England, and procedures are slightly different, too, for Scotland is one of the few countries that still bases its legal system on the old Roman law.

Crimes with picturesque names from ancient times remain on the statute book: *hamesucken,* for example, means assaulting a person in his home. In criminal cases Scotland adds to "Guilty" and "Not Guilty" a third verdict: "Not Proven." This, say the cynics, signifies "Don't do it again."

The Presbyterian Church of Scotland—the "Kirk"—is entirely independent of the Church of England. Until the 20th century it was a power in the land and did much to shape Scottish character. There are still those who can remember when the minister visited houses like an inquisitor and put members of the families through their catechism, punishing or reprimanding those who were not word-perfect. On Sunday morning the elders patrolled the streets, ordering people into church and rebuking those who sat at home in their gardens.

Religion in Scotland, as elsewhere, has lost much of its grip. But the Kirk remains influential in rural districts, where Kirk officials are pillars of local society. Ministers and their wives are seen in all their somber glory in Edinburgh in springtime, when the General Assembly of the Kirk takes place, and, for a week or more, Scottish newspapers devote several column-inches daily to the deliberations.

THE EPISCOPALIAN CHURCH of Scotland has bishops, as its name implies (unlike the Kirk, where the ministers are all equal), and a more colorful ritual. Considered genteel, Episcopalianism in Scotland has been described rather sourly by the Scottish novelist Lewis Grassie Gibbon as "more a matter of social status than theological conviction . . . a grateful bourgeois acknowledgment of anglicisation."

Of the various nonconformist offshoots of the established Kirk, the Free Kirk of Scotland is the largest. It remains faithful to the monolithic unity of its forefathers, promoting the grim discipline that John Knox promoted long ago. The Free Kirk is strong in parts of the Outer Hebrides—Lewis, Harris, and North Uist. On Sunday in these areas no buses run, all the shops are shut, and there is a general atmosphere of a people cowering under the wrath of God. Among the fishing communities, especially those of the Northeast from Buckie to Peterhead, evangelical movements, such as the Close Brethren and Jehovah's Witnesses, have made impressive inroads.

Other than religion, Scotland on the whole is mercifully free of the class consciousness and social elitism that so often amuse or disgust foreign residents in England. But its turbulent history has left Scotland a legacy of sectarian bigotry comparable to that of Northern Ireland. Scotland's large minority population of Roman Catholics is still to some extent underprivileged. Catholics tend to stick together, Protestants to mix only with Protestants. Even the two most famous soccer teams in Scotland—Rangers and Celtic—are notorious for their sectarian bias.

A word, finally, is needed on the vexed subject of nomenclature. A "scotchman" is a nautical device for "scotching," or clamping, a running rope. It is not a native of Scotland. Though you may find some rather more conservative people refer to themselves as Scotchmen and consider themselves Scotch, most prefer Scot or

Scotsman and call themselves Scottish or Scots.

There are exceptions to this rule. Certain internationally known Scottish products are Scotch. There is Scotch whisky, Scotch wool, Scotch tweed, Scotch mist (persistent drizzling rain). A Scotch snap is a short accented note followed by a longer one—a phrase that is characteristic of Scottish music, though certainly not unique to it. A snack food of a hard-boiled egg wrapped in sausage meat and rolled in crumb coating, then fried, is a Scotch egg.

You may include the Scots in the broader term British, but they dislike the word *Brits*, and nothing infuriates them more than being called English. Nonetheless, there are a lot of Anglo-Scots, that is, people of Scottish birth who live in England or are the offspring of marriages between Scottish and English people. The term Anglo-Scots is not to be confused with Sassenachs, the Gaelic word for Saxon, which is applied facetiously or disdainfully to all the English. But at the same time, English people who live in Scotland remain English to their dying day, and their children after them. Similarly, the designation of North Britain for Scotland, which crept in during Victorian times, has now crept out again. It survives only in the names of a few North British hotels. Scots feel that it denies their national identity, and there are some who, on receiving a letter with "N. B." or "North Britain" in the address, will cross it out and return the envelope to the sender.

WHAT'S WHERE

Edinburgh

Scotland's capital makes a strong first impression—Edinburgh Castle looming from the crags of an ancient volcano; the Royal Mile stretching from the castle to the Palace of Holyroodhouse; the neoclassical monuments perched on Calton Hill; Arthur's Seat, a small mountain with steep slopes, little crags, and spectacular vistas over the city and the Firth of Forth. Like Rome, Edinburgh is built on seven hills, and it has an Old Town district that retains striking evidence of a colorful history. The medieval Old Town, with its winding closes (narrow, stone-arched walkways) contrasts sharply with the Georgian New

Town and its planned squares and streets. But Edinburgh offers more than just a unique architectural landscape—it's a cosmopolitan capital, rich in museums, pubs, and culture. It's the site of the famous International Festival, when tourists and performers descend upon the city in late summer to celebrate the arts. Even more obvious to the casual stroller during this time is the refreshingly irreverent Edinburgh Festival Fringe, unruly child of the official festival, which spills out of halls and theaters all over town.

Glasgow

Glasgow, Scotland's largest city, suffered gravely from the industrial decline of the 1960s and '70s, but recent efforts at commercial and cultural renewal have restored much of the style and grandeur it had in the 19th century, at the height of its economic power. Now it is again a vibrant metropolitan center with a thriving artistic life—so much so that it is the UK City of Architecture and Design in 1999. Glasgow is a convenient touring center, too, in easy reach of the Clyde coast to the south and with excellent transportation links to the rest of Scotland.

The Borders and the Southwest

The Borders area comprises the great rolling hills, moors, wooded river valleys, and farmland that stretch south from Lothian, the region crowned by Edinburgh, to England. All the distinctive features of Scotland—paper currency, architecture, opening hours of pubs and stores, food and drink, and accent—start right at the border; you won't find the Borders a diluted version of England. The Dumfries and Galloway region south of Glasgow is a hilly and sparsely populated area, divided from England by the Solway Firth; it's a region of somber forests and radiant gardens, where the palm, in places, is as much at home as the pine. The county seat is Dumfries, associated with Robert Burns (he spent the last years of his life here) in much the same way as the Borders are with Sir Walter Scott.

Fife and Angus

Fife, northwest of Edinburgh, has the distinction of being the sunniest and driest part of Scotland. This area is one of sandy beaches, fishing villages, and windswept cliffs, hills, and glens. The industrial west may hold little interest, but the east coast is home to the ancient university and golf town of St. Andrews, with its romantic stone houses and seaside ruins. Angus, whose main city, Dundee, is an industrial port, stretches to the northeast into the North Sea. The Angus glens provide scenic hikes through secluded plateaus surrounded by hills and mountains.

Aberdeen and the Northeast

Aberdeen, Scotland's third-largest city, is a sophisticated city built largely of glittering granite, and is a main port of North Sea oil operations. The Grampian region spreads out to the west, the terrain changing from coastline—some of the United Kingdom's wildest shorelines of high cliffs and sandy beaches—to farmland to forests to hills. Here, the Grampian mountains and the Cairngorms, beautiful regions of heather and forest, granite peaks and deep glens, are ideal terrain for hill walking in warm weather and skiing in cold weather. The northeast is also known for its wealth of castles and whisky distilleries.

The Central Highlands

The main towns of Perth and Stirling are easily accessible gateways to the Central Highlands, the rugged and spectacular terrain stretching north from Glasgow. This may not be the famed Highlands of the north, but there's plenty of wild country to be experienced in the Central Highlands; here you'll find lush green woodlands and lochs. Especially in the Trossachs, deep lochs shimmer at the foot of gently sloping hills covered in birch, oak, and pine. Loch Lomond (loch is Scots for lake), Scotland's largest, is here; Sir Walter Scott's poems about the area have ensured its popularity as a tourist destination.

Argyll and the Isles

Argyll, a remote, sparsely populated group of islands in western Scotland that forms part of the Inner Hebridean archipelago, is a transitional area between the Highlands and Lowlands, an environment ranging from lush landscapes to treeless islands, sea lochs to wooded hills. Oban, the hub of transportation for Argyll, is the main sea gateway for Mull and the Southern Islands. The Island of Mull has a rolling green landscape and its capital, Tobermory, has brightly painted houses that give it a Mediterranean look. Iona, near Mull, is Scotland's most important Christian site, with an abbey and a royal

graveyard. The Isle of Islay is synonymous with whisky—it produces seven malts. Jura is covered with wild mountains. Sweeping southward, the long Kintyre peninsula is a wonderland of sea views, spectacular sunsets, and prehistoric monuments. Arran is more developed than most southern isles, with mist-shrouded mountains in the north and farmland in the south.

Around the Great Glen

The Great Glen cuts through the Southern Highlands from Inverness to Fort William and is ringed by Scotland's tallest mountains and greatest lochs; it is considered by many to be the most dramatic, captivating landscape in Scotland. Of its lochs, the most famous is Loch Ness. Inverness, on the Moray Firth, is a major shipping port and the last substantial outpost as you head north. East of Fort William, Glen Nevis is home to Ben Nevis, Britain's highest peak. Serious climbers come from far and wide to scale it.

The Northern Highlands

The Highlands, a remote and wild area of Scotland, are the source of the country's most breathtaking scenery. The great surprises to unprepared visitors are the changing terrain and the stunning effects of light and shade, cloud, sunshine, and rainbows. In a couple of hours you may pass from heather, bracken, and springy turf to granite rock and bog, to serrated peak and snow-water lake, to the red Torridon sandstone of Wester Ross, and the flowery banks of Loch Ewe and Loch Maree. Sea inlets are deep and fjordlike. The black shapes of the isles cluster like basking whales on the skyline. Cliffs where quartzite gleams above crescents of hard sand lead around a northern shore that looks from the air as though it had been trimmed by an axe. Gaelic-speaking natives on the Isle of Skye live in villages along the coast; the varied interior has forested glens, hills of heather, rocky waterfalls, and the Cuillin Mountains. The Outer Hebrides, also known as the Western Isles, arc outward to the Atlantic; this is possibly the most rugged part of Scotland, with frequent wind and rain, and an often inhospitable landscape where anything that grows seems a gift. In between are hidden coves with awe-striking white sand beaches and turquoise waters. Westward, the next stop is North America.

The Northern Isles

The nearly unceasing wind in the Northern Isles creates a challenging climate that contributes to the feeling that you've reached the end of the world. Orkney, a grouping of almost 70 islands, 20 of them inhabited, has the greatest concentration of prehistoric sites in Scotland. The treeless Mainland, Orkney's major island, strikes a peculiar mix between farmland and prominent stone-age relics, including phenomenally well-preserved standing circles, brochs (circular towers), and tombs. Shetland's islands, with their dramatic vertical cliffs on the coastline and barren moors in the interior, aren't as rugged as you might think; the harshest winter weather is kept in check by the Gulf Stream. Winter days are sometimes no more than five hours long, whereas beautiful summer days last almost 20 hours, with a persistent twilight known as the "summer dim." There are few trees to be found, and no spot is farther than 3 mi from the blue-black sea. North Sea oil has brought great wealth to the Shetlands: some of Scotland's best roads are here, the buses are modern, and most homes are recently built.

PLEASURES AND PASTIMES

Biking

Cycling is an ideal way to see the country. A mountain bike with street tires is as good a touring bike as the traditional, slouch-forward road bikes. The flat lands of Fife, with its quiet side roads, offer good biking. Dotted with bike rental shops, the islands of Arran and Islay are also popular cycling destinations. Don't forget that although some terrain may be flat, as in the Northern Isles, the conditions may be hazardous—strong winds or thick mist—so always bring rain gear. Roads are narrow, not to mention sparse in the more remote Northern Highlands, Hebrides, and Northern Isles, and you are often sharing the road with trucks and buses; always try to wear high-visibility clothing. For a touring route, *see* Great Itineraries, *below.*

Castles

Castle fanatics will have a ball in Scotland: there's everything here from atmospheric medieval ruins, complete with gory tales, such as Kildrummy, to magnificent Georgian piles like Culzean, full of antiques and paintings, and surrounded by parkland. The North East of Scotland in particular, inland from Aberdeen, has a huge range of castles to admire, helpfully strung together along a "Castle Trail." Whether still in private ownership and full of family atmosphere, like Cawdor, or under the care of the National Trust for Scotland or of Historic Scotland, or just a jumble of stones atop a hill, Scotland's castles and forts vividly demonstrate the country's unsettled past and historically uneasy relationship with its southern neighbor.

Cultural Festivals

The Edinburgh International Festival is the spectacular flagship of mainstream cultural events, from theater to comedy skits. In fact, the capital suffers from Festival overkill in late August, partly due to the size of the Fringe, the less formal and more unruly part of the official festival. This huge grab bag of performances spreads out of halls and theaters onto the streets of the capital. Also adding to the throng are the Edinburgh Military Tattoo and a range of smaller events such as the Book Festival and the Jazz Festival. Folk festivals are also held in many places at various times of the year, as are themed festivals. One of the most spectacular festivals is Up Helly Aa, held in Shetland at the end of January, when Viking ceremonies culminate in the burning of a replica Viking longship.

Dining

The best Scottish restaurants are noted for the freshest seafood, excellent red meats and game, and the use of traditional ingredients such as oatmeal and wild berries in new and imaginative ways. City Scots usually take their midday meals in a pub, wine bar, bistro, or department store restaurant (which might not serve alcohol and which might ban smoking). When traveling, the Scot generally eats inexpensively and quickly at a country pub or village tearoom. Places like Glasgow, Edinburgh, and Aberdeen, of course, offer restaurants of cosmopolitan character and various price levels; of these, the more notable tend to open only in the evening. You will come across restaurants that offer a "Taste of Scotland" menu. The Taste of Scotland scheme, initiated by the Scottish Tourist Board but now run independently, has helped—almost by accident—to preserve some of the Scots language, especially the names for a variety of traditional dishes. Most smaller towns and many villages have at least one restaurant where—certainly if a local is in charge—the service is a reminder of a Highland tradition that ensured that no stranger could travel through the country without receiving a welcome.

To start the day with a full stomach, try a "traditional Scottish breakfast," which consists of bacon and fried eggs, served with sausage, fried mushrooms and tomatoes, and, often, fried bread or potato scones. Most places also serve kippers (smoked herring). All this is in addition to juice, porridge, cereal, toast, and other bread products.

Distillery Tours

The process of producing whisky is closely monitored by the British government. It is strictly commercially licensed and takes place only in Scotland's distilleries (and, in Scotland, the product is most definitely spelled "whisky," without an "e"). Many distilleries place strong emphasis on visitor facilities and attempt to inject some drama and excitement into a process that is visually undramatic but nevertheless requires skill, method, and large-scale investment. A typical visit includes some kind of audiovisual presentation and a tour, and then a dram is usually offered. No tour of Speyside or Islay is complete without taking in at least one distillery.

Gardens

Somewhat surprisingly perhaps, Scotland's lowland climate is very favorable to a wide variety of plants, and a highlight of a Scottish visit for any gardening enthusiast will be discovering its gardens. In the Southwest: Castle Kennedy Gardens (with landscape features built by soldiers under the command of their aristocratic field marshal), Logan Botanic Gardens (where tree ferns and cabbage palms thrive), Threave Gardens (where National Trust for Scotland gardeners train). or Arbigland Gardens (birthplace of John Paul Jones of U.S. naval fame) are all here to enjoy. On the east coast, in addition to the impressive Royal Botanic Gardens in Edinburgh, many of the stately homes, whether in private ownership or under National Trust for Scotland care, are surrounded by beautifully tended gardens and parkland. Even in the far northwestern Highlands, Inverewe defies the elements behind its shelterbelts to display luxuriant rhododendrons and South American shrubs. And that is just a few of the major gardens; in addition, many private gardens open for one or two days each summer for charity under "Scotland's Gardens Scheme": look for the yellow posters as you drive along, to discover some normally hidden delights.

Golf

Scotland is often called the "home of golf" and, brushing aside any suggestion that the game probably originated in the Low Countries, claims it for her own. Certainly, Scotland has a number of old established courses, often lying close to town centers, where, had it not been for the early rights of golfers, the land would have been swallowed up by developments long ago. Now, with more than 400 golf courses—some world-famous—Scotland is a destination for golfers the world over. St. Andrews is such a popular spot for golfers that reservations need to be made up to a year in advance for summer play. Courses are also in the major urban centers: 20 courses are within or close to Edinburgh, and seven courses are within Glasgow. For more information, *see* Chapter 2 and individual chapters.

Hiking

Hiking is a superb pursuit for getting to know Scotland's varied landscape of low-lying glens and major mountains. From Edinburgh's Arthur's Seat to Ben Nevis, Britain's tallest peak, Scotland offers an unlimited number of walking and hiking possibilities. However, it is essential to know how to use a map and compass, and to be properly equipped at all times: weather conditions can change very rapidly in Scotland's hills, even at low level, and people have been known to die of exposure even in high summer.

Pubs

The Scots enjoy their pub culture. Whether you join in a lively political discussion in a bar in Glasgow, or enjoy folk music and dancing in a rural pub in the Highlands, you'll find that a public house is the perfect site to experience the Scottish spirit and, of course, enjoy a pint or a wee dram. Most bars sell two kinds of beer—

lager and ale. Lager (try Tennent's or McEwan's), most familiar to American drinkers, is light-colored, heavily carbonated, and served cold. Ale (try McEwan "80 Shilling" and Caledonian "80") is dark, semi-carbonated, and served just below room temperature. An increasing number of pubs, especially in the major cities, also offer a small selection of "real ales"—hand-drawn beers produced by smaller breweries, which in their range of flavors are a revelation compared to the usual pub beers. All pubs also carry any number of single-malt and blended whiskies.

Scenic Drives

One of the best ways to see Scotland is to rent a car and drive (on the left side of the road, of course). The following are some of our favorite scenic routes: the road west of Aberdeen into Royal Deeside, on either bank of the River Dee (Aberdeen); the east bank of Loch Ness, from Fort Augustus to Inverness via Dores (Around the Great Glen); the route between Brig o' Turk and Aberfoyle in the Trossachs (Central Highlands); and the Drumbeg road, north of Lochinver (Northern Highlands). For planned routes, *see* Great Itineraries, *below.*

Shopping

The best buys in Britain in general are antiques, craft items, woolen goods, china, men's shoes, books, confectionery, and toys. In Scotland, many visitors go for tweeds, designer knitwear, Shetland and Fair Isle woolens, tartan rugs and fabrics, Edinburgh crystal, Caithness glass, malt whisky, Celtic silver, and pebble jewelry. The Scottish Highlands bristle with old *bothies* (farm buildings) that have been turned into small crafts workshops where visitors are welcome—but not pressured—to buy attractive handmade items of bone, silver, wood, pottery, leather, and glass. Handmade chocolates, often with whisky or Drambuie fillings, and the traditional "petticoat tail" shortbread in tin boxes are popular; so, too, at a more mundane level, are boiled sweets in jars from particular localities—Berwick cockles, Jethart snails, Edinburgh rock, and similar crunchy items. Dundee cake, a rich fruit mixture with almonds on top, and Dundee marmalades and heather honeys are among the other eatables that visitors take home from Scotland.

NEW AND NOTEWORTHY

Glasgow: UK City of Architecture and Design 1999

Glasgow in 1999 is the showcase for exhibitions in a comprehensive range of design disciplines, from product and graphic design to architecture and interiors, with a Glasgow, national, and international focus and covering both contemporary and historical design themes. Venues will include Glasgow's galleries and museums, a new Centre for Architecture, Design and the City, called The Lighthouse (created in a Charles Rennie Mackintosh–designed building that once housed the *Herald* newspaper offices), and more unconventional exhibition spaces citywide. Local community involvement is not forgotten, with new people-friendly housing, public open spaces, and an access guide for people with disabilities among much else.

New Hotel Grading Scheme

In 1998, the Scottish Tourist Board introduced a new quality assurance scheme that uses stars to indicate the quality of accommodation. Star quality grades indicate the quality of the welcome, the standard of service, and the condition of the accommodation. All types and sizes of accommodation are included in the scheme, from grand hotels to simple bed-and-breakfasts. Each property is graded every year, to ensure that standards are maintained. This new single-tier grading scheme is taking over from the previous two-tier scheme that assessed separately the quality of accommodation, ranging from Approved (basic) to De Luxe (the very best), and the facilities offered (from basic to 5 crown).

Developments in the Outer Hebrides

Although these islands may seem far away from central Scotland, they are surprisingly easy to reach by air or ferry and are currently experiencing a major investment in new attractions. The Year of the Viking is being celebrated in 1999, with themed exhibitions and visitor events throughout the islands. On South Uist, the Kildonan Museum and Heritage Centre, focusing on archaeology, local history, and culture, with crafts on show, is also a good place to stop for a bite to eat. Lewis and Harris have three new attractions: the Northton Genealogy Trust will offer an expanded genealogy service for tracing your Hebridean forebears; the West Side Story throws light on the natural environment, archaeology, culture, and history of the west side of Lewis; and the Harris Tweed Visitor Centre will explain the story and manufacture of this indigenous island product. At Carloway, Lewis, in addition to a new interpretative facility at Carloway Broch, phase two of the regeneration of the black house village of Gearrannan (Garenin) is underway, and on the island of Great Bernera, just off the west coast of Lewis, Iron Age houses have recently been discovered at Bosta and may be reconstructed. The Western Isles Tourist Board's website (http://www.witb.co.uk) can show you more.

Highland Estates

It isn't easy being a landowner in Scotland and making a chunk of Highland landscape pay its way. A number of sporting estates try to diversify by broadening their appeal to everyday visitors. Leading the way is the Rothiemurchus Estate near Aviemore on the A9, the main road from Perth to Inverness. This estate contains some of the finest Highland landscapes, including ancient pine forest and the high, remote slopes of the Cairngorm mountains. A variety of programs is available: everything from low-key guided walks and pathfinding to special-interest tours revealing the life of the estate and its diverse forestry, sporting, and conservation interests. You can try your hand at clay-pigeon shooting or go on safari in a four-wheel-drive vehicle. Traditional pursuits such as angling are also offered, and there's a good chance you'll see fish-eating ospreys help themselves to a meal at the estate's fish farm. Call 01479/810858 for information.

Hogmanay

With roots going back to the pagan era, Hogmanay (☞ Festivals and Seasonal Events, *below*) not long ago was *the* winter celebration in Scotland. Up until the 1950s children in some parts of Scotland would hang up their stockings on the night of December 31, rather than at Christmas. Since then, the influence of the mostly English-controlled media and the commercial pressures to conform have led the Scots to as enthusiastic a celebration of Christmas as the English. But Hogmanay has not died out as a night of celebration and overindulgence north of the Border, and today it's undergoing something of a revival. If you are in Scotland at the end of December, unless you have an invitation to a private party with Scottish friends, then Edinburgh is the place to celebrate this most Scottish of all celebrations. A program of events starts on December 30, runs through Hogmanay itself (the 31st), and continues into New Year's Day—often a very quiet day north of the Border, as the natives nurse their sore heads.

FODOR'S CHOICE

Buildings and Monuments

★ **The facade of Marischal College, Aberdeen.** This ornate facade, built in 1891, is part of the second-largest granite building in the world.

★ **Gearrannan Black House Village, Carloway, Isle of Lewis, Outer Hebrides (Northern Highlands).** Built without mortar and thatched on a timber framework without eaves, black houses were the traditional Hebridean home. At Gearrannan, a black house village is being brought "back to life" in a phased program of rebuilding.

★ **The Georgian House, Edinburgh.** In New Town's Charlotte Square, this house is decorated in period style to demonstrate the lifestyle of an affluent family living in the late 18th century.

★ **Traquair House, near Walkerburn (Borders).** This is said to be the oldest continually occupied house in Scotland. Be sure to sample the ale that is brewed on site in an 18th-century brewhouse.

★ **The Standing Stones of Callanish, Lewis (Northern Highlands).** This series of monoliths is considered second only to Stonehenge in England, and is thought to have been used for astronomical observations.

★ **Torosay Castle, Isle of Mull (Argyll and the Isles).** One of Mull's best-known castles, Torosay has a friendly air and gives visitors the run of much of the house.

★ **Cawdor Castle, Nairn (Around the Great Glen).** Shakespeare's Macbeth was Thane of Cawdor, but this 14th-century castle exudes 600 years of real, not fictional, history.

Lodging

⭐ **Auchterarder House, Auchterarder (Central Highlands).** This secluded Victorian country mansion offers bedrooms with original furnishings and views of the Perthshire countryside. ££££

⭐ **Kildrummy Castle, Kildrummy (Aberdeen and the Northeast).** An old Victorian country house is the peaceful setting for attentive service and award-winning cuisine. ££££

⭐ **22 Murrayfield Gardens.** An exceptionally friendly and comfortable bed-and-breakfast in a well-heeled suburb of Edinburgh, with easy parking and a 10-minute bus ride to the city center, has as its hosts a couple who will be delighted to help you get the most out of your visit. ££

⭐ **Channings, Edinburgh.** This elegant hotel comprises five Edwardian terraced houses; those facing north provide wonderful views of Fife. £££

⭐ **Clifton House, Nairn (Great Glen).** Original works of art, antique furnishings, and famed cuisine make this hotel unique. £££

⭐ **Cringletie House, Peebles (Borders).** Turrets and crow-step gables lend a traditional Scottish baronial style to this hotel, whose accommodations are simple and comfortable; the food is its major achievement. £££

Museums and Visitor Centers

⭐ **Auchindrain Museum (Argyll).** An 18th-century communal tenancy farm has been restored to illustrate early farming life in the Highlands.

⭐ **Burrell Collection (Glasgow).** Pollock County Park is the setting for one of Scotland's finest art collections, with exhibits ranging from Egyptian, Greek, and Roman artifacts to stained glass and French Impressionist paintings.

⭐ **Paisley Museum and Art Gallery (Glasgow).** Paisley, part of the Greater Glasgow suburban area, is home to this museum that tells the story of the woolen Paisley shawl, and describes the famous Paisley pattern and weaving techniques.

⭐ **Scottish Fisheries Museum (Fife).** In Anstruther, this museum illustrates the life of Scottish fishermen through documents, artifacts, paintings, and quayside floating exhibits.

⭐ **Scotland's Lighthouse Museum (Aberdeenshire).** Scotland's first lighthouse was built at Fraserburgh in the 1780s on top of a 16th-century castle. A climb to its topmost gallery can now form part of an information-packed visit to this museum on the history, science, and role of lighthouses over the centuries.

⭐ **Carnegie Birthplace Museum (Edinburgh and the Lothians).** In Dunfermline, the birthplace of Andrew Carnegie tells his life story.

Dining

⭐ **Auchterarder House, Auchterarder (Central Highlands).** This dining room filled with sparkling glassware is attached to a fine hotel (☞ *above*) and serves excellent cuisine. ££££

⭐ **The Old Monastery, Buckie (Aberdeen).** The setting is a Victorian former religious establishment, and the theme is ever present, from the Cloisters Bar to the Chapel Restaurant. Local specialties include fresh river fish and Aberdeen Angus beef. £££–££££

⭐ **The Atrium, Edinburgh.** This restaurant is a good place to go for pre- or post-theater dinner (the Traverse Theatre is next door) to sample Scottish ingredients combined in unusual ways; the menu changes daily. £££

⭐ **The Cellar, Anstruther (Fife).** The fact that this place is popular with locals is a good sign. Come here for top-quality fish, beef, and lamb, cooked in a simple, straightforward fashion. ££

⭐ **Yes, Glasgow.** This stylish restaurant belies its basement location, with careful lighting and mirrors setting off the dramatic red, purple, and cream color scheme. Try the "Surprise Menu": an eclectic four-course selection reflecting the best fresh produce available that day. ££–£££

GREAT ITINERARIES

Scottish tourist authorities have developed numerous tourist trails that encompass everything from Scotland's brooding castles to its pungent whisky distilleries. However, you should probably avoid these thematic trails during the height of summer, when crowds and buses tend to swarm the best-known sights. The following itineraries, conceived independently of the Tourist Board, are offered as a guide in planning individual travel. For more travel suggestions, be sure to consult the itineraries recommended in each chapter.

The Seaways of the West

From Glasgow, you and your rental car can escape into the Western Highlands in less than two hours, using a short ferry crossing to save time. Then, if it isn't raining, you'll discover why the romantic landscapes of the west, with their vanished clans and tales of Bonnie Prince Charlie, continue to hold an intense fascination for visitors.

DURATION➤ 4 to 6 Days

THE MAIN ROUTE➤ **1–2 Nights:** Go west from Glasgow on the A8 along the south bank of the meandering River Clyde to reach Wemyss Bay on the A78. Catch the ferry for the old-fashioned holiday resort of Rothesay on the island of Bute. Tour the hinterland and leave the island via the five-minute Rhubodach–Colintraive ferry and enjoy the typical western scenery around Cowal.

1 Night: Go south to Lochgilphead, take a quick peek at the Caledonian Canal, then head for Tarbert and the peninsular Mull of Kintyre. If you crave island scenery, you can hop across to the tiny island of Gigha. Otherwise, continue south toward Campbeltown.

1–3 Nights: Return north through Lochgilphead and head for Oban, a busy ferryport where tartan kitsch and tour buses form the backdrop. Cross from Oban to the dramatic Isle of Mull, eventually arriving at the tiny Isle of Iona, the ancient burial place of Scottish kings. Leave Iona and Mull via the Fishnish–Lochaline ferry, then loop north toward Acharacle for magnificent views of the small isles of Rhum, Eigg, and Muck.

1–3 Nights: If time permits continue west to Mallaig, a ferryport with connections to the rugged and wild Isle of Skye. Otherwise, head east to Fort William, taking the A82 southward toward the famous Loch Lomond before returning to Glasgow.

Anything but the Main Route

If you're on a whirlwind tour of Scotland, this driving tour offers discriminating adventurers the chance to skirt the tourist horde while still experiencing some of the country's better-known sights. This nearly circular tour starts in Dunfermline and ends in either Perth or Edinburgh, but it could be done in either direction. (A good road map is indispensable.)

DURATION➤ 4 to 7 Days

THE MAIN ROUTE➤ **1–2 Nights:** From Dunfermline, the ancient capital of Scotland and the birthplace of Andrew Carnegie, take the A823 northwest. This soon cuts through the green and rounded Ochil Hills, giving good views of the nearby Highlands. You can browse for antiques in Auchterarder before continuing to the pleasant Highland-edge town of Crieff (another good spot for bargain hunters).

1–2 Nights: From Crieff follow the A822 north into the Highlands through the Sma'Glen, but keep your eyes open for a sign reading GLEN QUAICH and KENMORE. This route rises through moors before zigzagging steeply down to the east end of Loch Tay. Head to Fortigall to join, a little way east, the B846. Take this high road over the hills to Tummel Bridge, then go east to join the main and busy A9 (there is no other option here). At Dalwhinnie take the A86 (via Loch Laggan) to cosmopolitan Fort William.

1 Night: From Fort William take the A82 north past Loch Lochy to Fort Augustus. Leave the busy A82 and keep to the scenic east bank of Loch Ness—home to the fabled and feared Loch Ness monster (locals call her Nessie). Continue to Inverness.

1–3 Nights: From Inverness take the A96 and then the A939 to Cawdor Castle, the haunting ground of Shakespeare's Macbeth. Continue south on the A939 and cross the wilds of Dava Moor to reach handsome Grantown-on-Spey. Continue toward Tomintoul and the Royal Deeside region (also known as Castle Country), stopping off at one of the region's many dramatic keeps—perhaps the castles at Corgarff, Balmoral, or Braemar. You can detour along the A93 to Aberdeen, a pleasant but commercial port city. Otherwise, rejoin the A9 and head south to Pitlochry, home to the Edradour Distillery, which claims to be the smallest single-malt distillery in Scotland. Head south along the banks of the River Tummel, joining the B867 at Dunkeld. Continue south for Perth and Edinburgh.

The Highlands and Islands by Bike

Happiness is zooming down a steep coastal hill with horizon-wide views of the rugged Highlands. Biking the eastern side of Scotland, around Aberdeen, is saner since the landscape is mostly soft and gentle. But in the coastal Highlands, from Oban to the Isle of Skye to Inverness, the country turns raw and wild. Cycling in this environment requires more than a little stamina, though dining and lodging facilities are generally closely spaced. The following itinerary starts in Glasgow and ends in Inverness. Some sections take advantage of specially designated cycle routes; others follow main and secondary roads where you must be wary of vehicular traffic. No matter what time of year you visit, bring rain gear.

DURATION➤ 8 to 14 Days

THE MAIN ROUTE➤ **1 Night:** From Glasgow take the train to Paisley to link with the Glasgow–Irvine Pedestrian and Cycle Route (maps available from Tourist Information Centers). From Paisley via Lochwinnoch and Kilwinning, the next 30 mi lead through tame countryside to Androssan, where you can catch a summer ferry to Brodick, on Arran island.

1–2 Nights: From Brodick follow the A841 clockwise around the island; or, if you're short on time, turn north toward Lochranza, where there's a frequent summer-only ferry to Claonaig. Continue to the quiet town of Kennacraig or larger Tarbert.

1–2 Nights: If time permits, follow the B8024 clockwise around Knapdale for outstanding views of the Hebridean islands.

Otherwise, continue north from Tarbert along the western bank of Loch Gilp. Your final destination in either case is the small, very pleasant town of Lochgilphead.

1–2 Nights: Take the minor road (B840) northeast to Ford at the southern end of Loch Awe, Scotland's longest loch. You can make a quick detour to Carnasserie Castle, just off the A816, or continue along the loch's northwestern side to the B845 junction. Follow the B845 to Taynuilt, where there's an unlabeled back road to Oban via Glen Lonan.

1 Night: North of Oban there are summer ferries to Craignure, on the Isle of Mull. On Mull, follow the A849 south past Torosay and Duart castles, then circle northward on the B8035 to reach Fishnish Pier, connected by ferry during summer with Lochaline. On the mainland, follow the A884 north to Strontian or Salen.

1 Night: Continue north along the coast, past Loch Ailort, to the A830 junction. Head west, either to Arisaig or Mallaig.

1–3 Nights: Summer ferries connect Mallaig with the rugged Isle of Skye. Once on Skye, if you're pressed for time, head north on the A851, then east on the A850 for the bridge to Kyle of Lochalsh. Otherwise, the A850 leads about 45 mi northwest to the lovely town of Portree and to the wild, spectacular seascapes of northern Skye. When you're ready, backtrack to the Kyle of Lochalsh bridge.

1–2 Nights: Continue northeast via the villages of Plockton and Stromeferry. It's a demanding uphill ride around the banks of Loch Carron, but there's plenty of accommodation in Lochcarron, and the subsequent ride between Ardarroch and Shieldaig is spectacular. So, too, is the short ride between Shieldaig and Torridon. From Torridon, bike 20 mi to Achnasheen and continue by bike or train to Inverness.

FESTIVALS AND SEASONAL EVENTS

➤ DEC. 30–JAN. 1: **Hogmanay** (Edinburgh Tourist Information, ☎ 0131/557–1700), Edinburgh's ancient, still thriving alternative to Christmas.

➤ JAN. 25: **Burns Night** dinners and other entertainments are held in memory of Robert Burns in Glasgow, Ayr, Dumfries, Edinburgh, and many other towns and villages.

➤ MID-JAN.–EARLY FEB.: **Celtic Connections** (✉ Glasgow Royal Concert Hall, 2 Sauchiehall St., Glasgow G2 3NY, ☎ 0141/353–4137), an ever-expanding annual homage to Celtic music, with musicians from all over the world, hands-on workshops, and much more.

➤ LAST TUESDAY IN JAN.: **Up Helly Aa** (details from Shetland Tourist Board, ✉ Market Cross, Lerwick, Shetland ZE1 0LU, ☎ 01595/693434), Shetlanders celebrate their Viking heritage, culminating in the burning of a replica Viking longship.

➤ LATE MAR.–EARLY APR.: **Edinburgh International Science Festival** (✉ 149 Rose St., Edinburgh

EH2 4LS, ☎ 0131/220–3977) aims to make science accessible, interesting, and, above all, fun, especially but not exclusively for children, at venues throughout the city.

➤ APR.: **Shetland Folk Festival** (details from Shetland Tourist Board; ☞ *above*) is one of the biggest folk gatherings in Scotland, set in the home of fiddle playing.

➤ EASTER: **Shoots and Roots** (☎ FAX 0131/554–3092), the Edinburgh Folk Festival, with the emphasis on folk/jazz and folk/rock crossovers.

➤ MID-MAY: The **Perth Festival of the Arts** (☎ 01738/21031) offers orchestral and choral concerts, drama, opera, recitals, and ballet throughout Perth, Tayside.

➤ LATE MAY: **Orkney Folk Festival** (✉ Box 4, Stromness, Orkney, ☎ 01856/851331) brings the folkies back up to the far north in their hundreds.

➤ THIRD WEEK IN JUNE: **St. Magnus Festival** (✉ Strandal, Nicolson St., Kirkwall, Orkney, ☎ 01856/872669) is a feast of classical and modern music, often showcasing new vocal or orchestral compositions.

➤ MID-AUG.–EARLY SEPT.: The **Edinburgh International Festival** (✉ 21 Market St., Edinburgh, EH1 1BW, ☎ 0131/226–4001), which runs for three weeks, is the world's largest festival of the arts. The **Edinburgh International Film Festival** (✉ Filmhouse, 88 Lothian Rd., Edinburgh EH3 9BZ, ☎ 0131/228–4051) concentrates on the best new films from all over the world. After dark is the **Edinburgh Military Tattoo** (✉ 22 Market St., Edinburgh, EH1 1DF, ☎ 0131/225–1188), a display of military expertise.

➤ SEPT.: The **Braemar Royal Highland Gathering** (✉ Princess Royal and Duke of Fife Memorial Park, Braemar, Grampian, ☎ 01339/755377) hosts kilted clansmen from all over Scotland.

➤ OCT.: **Shetland Accordian and Fiddle Festival** (details from Shetland Tourist Board; ☞ *above*) concentrates on two of the most popular instruments of folk musicians in Scotland.

➤ THIRD WEEKEND IN NOV.: **Shoots and Roots** (☎ FAX 0131/554–3092), the second half of Edinburgh's annual folk jamboree, this time with the focus on traditional music.

2 Scotland: The Home of Golf

Golfing Throughout the Country

By John
Hutchinson

THERE ARE MORE THAN 400 GOLF COURSES in Scotland and only 5 million local residents, so the country has probably the highest ratio of courses to people anywhere in the world. Some of these courses are world famous as venues for major championships, and if you're a golfer coming to Scotland you'll probably want to play the "famous names" sometime in your career. Telling your friends in the clubhouse back home that you got a birdie at the Road Hole on the Old Course in St. Andrews, where Lyle, Faldo, and Jacklin have played, somehow carries more weight in terms of prestige than an excellent round at an obscure but delightful little course that no one has ever heard of.

So, by all means, play the championship courses and get your prestige, but remember they are championship courses and, therefore, they are difficult; you may enjoy the actual game itself much more at an easier, if less well-known, course. Remember, too, that everyone else wants to play them, so booking can be more of a problem, particularly on peak days during the summer. Do book early, or, if you are staying in a hotel attached to a course, get them to book for you.

There has always been considerable debate as to who invented golf, but there is no doubt that its development into one of the most popular games in the world stems from Scotland. Like many other games that involve hitting a ball with a stick, golf evolved in the countries that border the North Sea during the Middle Ages and gradually took on its present form in the last 200 years.

The first written reference to golf, variously spelled as "gowf" or "goff," was as long ago as 1457, when James II (1430–60) of Scotland declared that both golf and football should be "utterly cryit doune and nocht usit" (publicly criticized and prohibited) because they were distracting his subjects from their archery practice. Mary, Queen of Scots (1542–87), it seems, was fond of golf. When in Edinburgh in 1567, she played on Leith Links and on Bruntsfield Links, perhaps the oldest course in the world where the game is still played. When in Fife, she played at Falkland near the palace and at St. Andrews itself.

Golf must surely rank as one of Scotland's earliest cultural exports. In 1603, when James VI (1566–1625) of Scotland also became James I of England, he moved his court to London. With him went his golf-loving friends, and they set up a course on Blackheath Common, then on the outskirts of London.

Golf clubs as we know them today first began in the middle of the 18th century. The earliest written evidence of the existence of a club is of the Honourable Company of Edinburgh Golfers, now residing at Muirfield, in 1744, and of the Royal & Ancient at St. Andrews in 1754. From then on, clubs sprang up all over Scotland: Royal Aberdeen (1780), Crail Golfing Society (1786), Dunbar (1794), and the Royal Perth Golfing Society (1824).

By the early years of the 19th century, golf clubs had been set up in England, and the game had begun to be carried all over the world by enthusiastic Scots. With them, these Scottish golf missionaries took their knowledge not only of golf, but of golf courses. Scotland is fortunate in that large parts of its coastline are natural golf courses, and the origins of bunkers and the word *links* (courses) are to be found in the sand dunes of the Scottish shore. But other countries were not so fortunate. The natural terrain did not exist, and courses had to be designed and created. Willie Park of Musselburgh (who laid out Sunningdale), James Braid, and C. K. Hutchison (whose crowning glory is at Gleneagles Hotel) are some of the best known of Scotland's golf course architects.

Golf has always had a peculiar classlessness in Scotland. It is a game for everyone, and for centuries towns and cities in Scotland have had their own golf courses for the enjoyment of the citizens. The snobbishness and exclusivity of golf clubs in some parts of the world have few echoes here. Admittedly, there are at least a few clubs that have always been noted for their exclusive air, and there are newer golf courses emerging as part of exclusive leisure complexes. These are exceptions to the long tradition of recreation for all. Golf in Scotland is usually a democratic game, played by ordinary folk as well as the rich and carefree.

Many of the important changes in the design and construction of balls and clubs were pioneered by the professional players who lived and worked around these town courses and who made the balls and clubs themselves. The original balls, called *featheries,* were leather bags stuffed with boiled feathers. Often they only lasted one round. When, in 1848, the gutta percha ball, called a *guttie,* was introduced, there was considerable friction, particularly in St. Andrews, between the makers of the two rival types of ball. The gutta percha proved superior and was in general use until the invention of the rubber-core ball in 1901.

Clubs were traditionally made of wood: shafts of ash, later hickory, and heads of thorn or some other hardwood like apple or pear. Heads were spliced then bound to the shaft with twine. Players generally managed with far fewer clubs than today. About 1628 the marquis of Montrose, a golf enthusiast, had a set of clubs made for him in St. Andrews that illustrates the range of clubs used in Stuart times: "Bonker clubis, a irone club, and twa play clubs."

Caddies—the word comes from the French *cadet,* a young boy, and was used, particularly in Edinburgh, for anyone who ran messages—carried the players' clubs around, usually under the arm. Golf carts did not come into fashion in Britain until the 1950s. Golf carts are still considered by some to be potentially injurious to the national health and moral fiber.

The technology of golf may change, but its addictive qualities are timeless. Toward the end of the 18th century, an Edinburgh golfer called Alexander McKellar regularly played golf all day and refused to stop even when it grew dark. One night his wife carried his dinner and nightcap on Bruntsfield Links where he was playing in an attempt to shame him into changing his ways. She failed.

And the addiction continues.

Where to Play

Scotland's courses are well spread throughout the country in all areas but the far northern Highlands and some of the islands, so finding a holiday golf course is never a problem. Most courses welcome visitors with the minimum of formalities, and some at surprisingly low cost. (Off season, a few clubs still use the "honest box," in which you drop your fees!)

Just three short pieces of advice, particularly for North Americans: 1) In Scotland the game is usually played fairly quickly, so it's best not to hang about if others are waiting; 2) caddy carts are hand-pulled carts for your clubs, not the driven golf carts that are more familiar to U.S. golfers and rarely available in Scotland; and 3) when they say "rough" they really mean "rough."

Unless specified otherwise below, course playing hours are generally 9 AM to sundown, which in June can be as late as 10 PM. For a complete list of courses, contact local tourist offices, and for more regional information, *see* Outdoor Activities and Sports *in* Chapters 3–12.

The Stewartry

At the very southern border, the Stewartry is a delightful part of Scotland set in the rich farmlands around Dumfries, a golfing vacation area since Victorian times. Powfoot and Southerness are enjoyable links courses along the shores of the Solway Firth, and inland, Dumfries and Moffat have long-established courses that provide superb golf in a clean, invigorating environment. There are also several fine nine-hole courses in the area.

Southerness. The first to be designed in Scotland after World War II (Mackenzie Ross, 1947), Southerness is a long course, played over extensive links with fine views southward over the Solway Firth. The greens are hard and fast, and the frequent winds make for some testing golf. ☎ 01387/880677. 18 holes. Yardage 6,566. Par 70. ⌨ *Weekdays £28 daily; weekends £40 daily.* ☉ *Daily. Advance reservations essential. Caddy carts (£1), catering.*

Ayrshire and the Clyde Coast

Lying just an hour to the south of Glasgow either by car or by train, Ayrshire and the Clyde Coast have been a holiday area for Glaswegians for generations. Few golfers need an introduction to the famous names of Turnberry, Royal Troon, Prestwick, or Western Gailes, all challenging links courses along this coast. In addition, there are at least 20 courses in the area within an hour's drive. Remember, too, that at major areas, such as Turnberry, Troon, and Ayr, there are several different courses to play from the same base.

Girvan. This is an old, established course with play along a narrow coastal strip and a more lush inland section next to the Water of Girvan—the neighborhood river that constitutes a particular hazard at the 15th, unless you are a big hitter. This is quite a scenic course, with good views of Ailsa Craig and the Clyde estuary. ☎ *01465/714346. 18 holes. Yardage 4,590. Par 64.* ⌨ *Weekdays £12.50/round, £19.65 daily; weekends £13/round, £25 daily.* ☉ *Daily. Caddy carts (£2), catering.*

Glasgow

The busy and thriving center of Scotland's industry and commerce, Glasgow is well known for its shopping, nightlife, art galleries, theaters, and restaurants. Less well known are the parks and gardens, affectionately called the "dear green places," that breathe life into the city. Most of the old city center golf courses have now moved out to the suburbs, but you can tee off from at least 30 different courses less than one hour from the city center. And remember that, in addition to these, all the Ayrshire courses are just down the road.

Dougalston. North of the city near Milngavie (pronounced mul-*gai*), Dougalston is a long, attractive course set among birch and pine trees with massive rhododendrons blooming in early summer. The Campsie Fells form a pleasing backdrop. ☎ *0141/9565750. 18 holes. Yardage 5,959. Par 69.* ⌨ *£14/round, £24 day.* ☉ *Daily after 3 PM. Caddy carts (£1.30/round).*

Killermont and Gailes, The Glasgow Golf Club. Originally the club played on Glasgow Green in the heart of the ancient city center, but as the pressure for space grew, the club moved north to the leafy suburb of Bearsden, on the road to Loch Lomond. The Killermont course was laid out by Tom Morris (1904) in beautiful parkland with ancient trees, fine greens, and an elegant clubhouse. Visitors are offered the facilities of the club's other course at Gailes near Irvine on the Firth of Clyde. The Glasgow Club's Tennant Cup (June) is the oldest open amateur tournament in the world. *Gailes: ☎ 0141/9422011. 18 holes. Yardage 6,301. Par 70. ✉ £42/round, £52 day; weekends £47/round. ☉ Weekdays 9–sundown, weekends after 2:30. Advance reservations essential. Practice area, caddy carts, catering.*

East Lothian

The sand dunes that stretch eastward from Edinburgh along the southern shore of the Firth of Forth made an ideal location for some of the earliest golf courses in the world. Muirfield is perhaps the most famous course in the area, but around it are more than a dozen others, at Gullane, North Berwick, Dunbar, and Aberlady and, nearer Edinburgh, at Longniddry, Prestonpans, and Musselburgh. All are links courses, many with views to the islands of the Firth of Forth and northward to Fife, and if you weary of the East Lothian courses, just 20 miles or so to the west, there are nearly 30 more within the city of Edinburgh.

Dunbar. This ancient golfing site by the sea even has a lighthouse at the 9th hole. It's a good choice for a typical east coast links course in a seaside town, but within easy reach of Edinburgh. *☎ 01368/862086. 18 holes. Yardage 6,426. Par 71. ✉ Weekdays £35 daily, weekends £45 daily. ☉ Fri.–Wed. after 9:30. Advance reservations essential. Practice area, caddies (by reservation), golf carts (£25/round, £35 daily), catering.*

Edinburgh

Edinburgh today is best known as Scotland's capital and home to the Edinburgh International Festival, the largest of its kind in the world. The city is also host to nearly 30 golf courses within its boundaries. Most are parkland courses, though along the shores of the Firth of Forth they take on more the characteristics of traditional links. Some of the courses are used by private clubs with difficult access for visitors; others belong to the city with easier access and much lower fees. Historians of golf should also visit and play on Bruntsfield Links where golf has been enjoyed for more than 450 years.

Barnton, Royal Burgess Golfing Society. One of the oldest golf clubs in the world (1735), whose members originally played on Bruntsfield Links; now its members and guests play on elegantly manicured parkland in the northwestern suburbs of the city. It's a long course with particularly fine greens. *☎ 0131/3392075. 18 holes. Yardage 6,111. Par 68. ✉ Weekdays £37 round, £47 daily. ☉ Weekdays. Advance reservations essential. Caddy carts (£2/round), golf carts (£5/round), catering.*

Braids. Two courses built by the city as urban development nearly 90 years ago forced golfers out of the center, Braids number 1 and Braids number 2 (no connection with James Braid) are beautifully laid out over a curiously rugged range of small hills in the southern suburbs. The views to the south and the Pentland Hills and north toward the skyline of the city are worth a visit in themselves. *☎ 0131/4476666. 18 holes. No. 1: Yardage 5,692. Par 70; No. 2: Yardage 5,412. Par 65. ✉ £8.50 round. ☉ Daily. Advanced reservations essential. Caddy carts (£1.75).*

Fife

Few would dispute the claim of St. Andrews to be the Home of Golf, holding as it does the Royal & Ancient, the organization that governs the sport worldwide. Golf has been played in the area since the sport's inception, and to play in Fife is for most golfers a cherished ambition. St. Andrews itself has a wide range of full 18-hole courses in addition to the famous Old Course, and along the north shores of the Firth of

Forth is a string of ancient villages, each with its harbor, ancient red-roofed buildings, and golf course. In all, there are about 30 courses in the area.

Ladybank. Fife is known for its choice of coastal courses, but this one offers an interesting inland contrast: although Ladybank is laid out on fairly level ground (Tom Morris, 1876), the fir woods, birches, and heathery rough give it a Highland flavor among the gentle Lowland fields. Qualifying rounds of the British Open are played here when the main championship is played at St. Andrews. ☎ *01337/830814. 18 holes. Yardage 6,617. Par 71. 🖃 May–Oct., weekdays £28/round, £38 daily, weekends £35/round; Nov.–Apr., weekdays £19/round, £27 daily, weekends £25/round. ☉ Daily. Advance reservations essential. Practice area, caddy carts, golf carts (£18/round), catering.*

Leven. Another fine Fife course used as a British Open qualifier, this one, a links course, feels like the more famous St. Andrews, with hummocky terrain and a tang of salt in the air. The 1st and 18th share the same fairway, and the 18th green has a burn running by it. ☎ *01333/428859. 18 holes. Yardage 6,436. Par 71. 🖃 Weekdays £22/round, £32 daily; weekends £26/round, £38 daily. ☉ Sun.–Fri.. Advance reservations essential. Catering.*

Perthshire

Perthshire has a variety of attractive country courses developed specifically for visiting golfers, rather than for large numbers of local club members. Gleneagles Hotel is, of course, the most famous of these golf resort hotels. Its facilities are considered outstanding compared with those anywhere in the world. But other courses in the area, set on the edges of beautiful Highland scenery, will delight any golfer. Crieff, Taymouth, and other courses are in the mountains; Blairgowrie and Perth are set amid the rich farmlands nearer the sea.

Callander. Callander was designed by Tom Morris (1913), and has a scenic upland feel in a town well prepared for the visitor. Pine and birch woods and hilly fairways offer fine views, especially toward Ben Ledi, and the tricky moorland layout demands accurate hitting off the tee. ☎ *01877/330975. 18 holes. Yardage 5,204. Par 66. 🖃 Weekdays £20/round, £26 daily; weekends £31 daily. ☉ Daily. Practice area, caddy carts, catering.*

Killin. A splendidly scenic course, Killin is typically Highland, with a roaring river, woodland birdsong, and backdrop of high green hills. There are a few surprises, including two blind shots to reach the green at the 4th. The village of Killin is attractive, almost alpine in feel, especially in spring when the hilltops may still be white. ☎ *01567/820312. 9 holes. Yardage 2,508. Par 65. 🖃 £11/round, £14 daily. ☉ Daily. Caddy carts, club rental, catering.*

Rosemount, Blairgowrie Golf Club. Well known to native golfers looking for an exciting challenge, Rosemount's 18 (Tom Morris, 1889), are laid out on rolling land in the pine, birch, and fir woods, which bring a wild air to the scene. You may encounter a browsing roe deer if you stray too far. There are, however, wide fairways and at least some large greens. ☎ *01250/872622, FAX 01250/875451. 18 holes. Yardage 6,588. Par 72. 🖃 Weekdays £50/round, £60 daily; weekends £55/round. ☉ Daily. Practice area, caddies, golf carts (£17), trolleys (£2.50), catering.*

Angus

East of Perthshire, north of the city of Dundee, lies a string of demanding courses along the shores of the North Sea and inland into the foothills of the Grampian Mountains. The most famous course in Angus is probably Carnoustie, one of several British Open Championship venues in Scotland, but there are many more along the same stretch of coast from Dundee northward as far as Stonehaven. Golfers who excel in windy conditions will particularly enjoy the breezes blowing eastward from the sea. Inland Edzell, Forfar, Brechin, and Kirriemuir all have courses nestling in the farmlands of Strathmore.

Carnoustie. Venue for the British Open Championship in 1999, the extensive coastal links around Carnoustie have been played since at least 1527. Open winners here have included Armour, Hogan, Cotton, Player, and Watson. Carnoustie was also once a training ground for golf coaches, many of whom went to the United States. The choice municipal course here is therefore full of historical snippets and local color, as well as being tough and full of interest. ☎ 01241/853789. *18 holes. Yardage 6,941. Par 72. ☎ £52/round, £156 for 3 days. ⊙ Weekdays 9–sundown, Sat. after 2, Sun. after 11:30. Advance reservations essential. Caddies, caddy carts (May–Oct. £2.50), catering.*

Aberdeenshire

The city of Aberdeen, Scotland's third largest, is particularly known for its sparkling granite buildings and the amazing displays of roses each summer. It also offers a good range of courses for the golfer. Aberdeen itself has six courses, and to the north, as far as Fraserburgh and Peterhead, there are five others, including the popular Cruden Bay. Royal Deeside has three, and in the rich farmlands to the north are three more with at least six nine-hole courses.

Balgownie, Royal Aberdeen Golf Club. This old, established club (1780) is the archetypal Scottish links course: long and testing over uneven ground, with the frequently added hazard of a sea breeze. Prickly gorse is inclined to close in and form an additional hurdle. The two courses are tucked behind the rough, grassy sand dunes, and there are surprisingly few views of the sea. One historical note: in 1783, this club originated the five-minute-search rule for a lost ball. ☎ 01224/702571, FAX 01224/826591. *18 holes. Yardage 6,550. Par 70. ☎ Weekdays £45/round, £60 daily; weekends £50/round. ⊙ Daily after 3:30. Handicap limit 20; letter of introduction required from visitor's home club. Advance reservations essential. Practice area, caddies, caddy carts (£3), catering.*

Ballater. This club has a holiday atmosphere and a course laid out along the sandy river flats of the River Dee, surrounded by the mountains of Royal Deeside. Originally opened in 1906, the club makes maximum use of the fine setting between river and woods and is ideal for a relaxing round of golf. The variety of shops and pleasant walks in nearby Ballater make this a good place for nongolfing partners. ☎ 013397/55567. *18 holes. Yardage 6,112. Par 70. ☎ Weekdays £18/round, £27 daily; weekends £21/round, £31 daily. ⊙ Daily. Advance reservations essential. Practice area, caddy carts (£2), catering.*

Cruden Bay. Another east coast Lowland course sheltered behind the extensive sand hills, this one offers a typical Scottish golf experience. Runnels and valleys, among other hazards, on the challenging fairways ensure plenty of excitement, and some of the holes are rated among the finest anywhere in Scotland. Like Gleneagles and Turnberry, this course owes its origins to an association with the grand railway hotels that were built in the heyday of steam. Unlike the other two, however, Cruden Bay's railway hotel and the railway itself have gone, but the course remains in fine shape. ☎ 01779/812285. *18 holes. Yardage 6,395. Par 70. ☎ £35/round, £50 daily, £150 weekly, £250 for 2 weeks. ⊙ Weekdays. Advance reservations essential. Practice area, covered driving range, caddy carts (£2), catering.*

Speyside

Set on the main A9 road an hour south of Inverness amid the Cairngorm Mountains, the valley of the River Spey is one of Scotland's most attractive all-year sports centers, with winter skiing and, in summer, sailing and canoeing, pony-trekking, fishing, and some fine golf. The main courses in the area are Newtonmore, Grantown-on-Spey, and Boat of Garten, all fine inland courses with wonderful views of the surrounding mountains and challenging golf provided by the springy turf and the heather. For a change of pace, the links courses along the coastline of the Moray Firth, with their seaside attractions, are only an hour's drive away.

Boat of Garten. Possibly one of the greatest "undiscovered" courses in Scotland and celebrating its centennial in 1998, Boat of Garten was redesigned and extended by famous golf architect James Braid in 1932. Each of the 18 holes is individual: some cut through birch wood and heathery rough, most have long views to the Cairngorms and a strong Highland ambience. An unusual feature is the preserved steam railway that runs along part of the course. The occasional puffing locomotive can hardly be considered a hazard. ☎ 01479/831282. *18 holes. Yardage 5,637. Par 69.* 🍴 *Weekdays £20 daily, weekends £25 daily.* ☉ *Daily. Starting sheet used on weekends. Advance reservations essential. Caddies, caddy carts, catering.*

Moray Coast

No one can say that the Lowlands of Scotland have a monopoly of Scotland's fine seaside golf courses. The Moray Coast, stretching eastward from Inverness, has some spectacular sand dunes, and these have been adapted to create stimulating and exciting links courses. The two courses at Nairn have long been known to golfers famous and unknown. Charlie Chaplin regularly played here. But in addition there are a dozen courses looking out over the sea from Inverness as far along as Fraserburgh, Banff, and Macduff and several inland amid the fertile Moray farmland.

Banff, Duff House Royal Golf Club. Although within moments of the sea, this club is a puzzling blend of a coastal course with a parkland setting. The course, only minutes from Banff center, lies within the parkland grounds of Duff House, a country house art gallery in an Adam mansion. The club has inherited the ancient traditions of seaside play (golf records here go back to the 17th century). Mature trees and gentle slopes create a pleasant playing atmosphere. ☎ 01261/812075. *18 holes. Yardage 6,161. Par 69.* 🍴 *Weekdays £18/round, £24 daily; weekends £25/round, £30 daily.* ☉ *Daily. Advance reservations essential. Practice area, caddy carts (£1), catering.*

Fraserburgh. This northeast fishing town has extensive links and dunes that seem to have grown up around the course rather than the other way around. Be prepared for a hill climb and a tough finish. ☎ 01346/518287. *18 holes (9 additional for warm-up). Yardage 5,917. Par 70.* 🍴 *Weekdays £14/round, £17 daily; weekends £18/round, £22 daily.* ☉ *Daily. Practice area, catering.*

Lossiemouth, Moray Golf Club. Discover the mild airs of the "Moray Riviera," as Tom Morris did in 1889 when he was inspired by the lie of the natural links. There are two courses plus a six-hole minicourse. There is lots of atmosphere here, with golfing memorabilia in the clubhouse, as well as the tale of the pre-World War I British prime minister, Asquith, who took a vacation in this out-of-the-way spot, yet still managed to be attacked by a crowd of militant suffragettes at the 17th. All other hazards on these testing courses are entirely natural, with the

18th hole providing a memorable finish. ☎ *01343/813330. 18 holes each (plus 6-hole minicourse). Yardage 6,585. Par 71.* ▨ *Old Course: weekdays £30/round, £40 daily; weekends £40/round, £50 daily. New Course: weekdays £17/round, £22 daily; weekends £25/round, £30 daily. Joint ticket (one round on each course), £35 weekdays, £45 weekends.* ☉ *Daily. Practice area, caddy carts (£2), catering.*

Nairn. Widely regarded in golfing circles as a truly great course, Nairn dates from 1887 and is the regular home of Scotland's Northern Open. Huge greens, aggressive gorse, a beach hazard for five of the holes, a steady prevailing wind, and distracting views across the Moray Firth to the northern hills make play here an unforgettable experience. ☎ *01667/453208. 18 holes. Yardage 6,772. Par 72.* ▨ *Weekdays £40/round, weekends £40/round.* ☉ *Daily. Advance reservations essential. Practice area, caddies, caddy carts, catering.*

Dornoch Firth

North of Inverness, the east coast is deeply indented with firths (the word is linked to the Norwegian "fiord") that border some excellent, relatively unknown golf courses. Royal Dornoch has recently been "discovered" by international golf writers, but knowledgeable golfers have been making the northern pilgrimage for well over a hundred years. There are half a dozen enjoyable links courses around Dornoch, and inland, another Victorian golfing holiday center, Strathpeffer, preserves much of the atmosphere those gentlemen of a past age set out to achieve.

Royal Dornoch. This course, laid out by Tom Morris in 1886 on a sort of coastal shelf behind the shore, has matured to become one of the world's finest. Its location in the north of Scotland, though less than an hour's drive from Inverness Airport, means that it is far from over-run even in peak season. It may not have the fame of a Gleneagles or a St. Andrews, but if time permits, Dornoch is an unforgettable golfing experience. The little town of Dornoch, behind the course, is sleepy and timeless. ☎ *01862/810219. 18 holes. Yardage 6,514. Par 70.* ▨ *Weekdays £40/round, £100 for 3 days; weekends £50/round.* ☉ *Daily. Handicap limit: men 24, women 35. Advance reservations essential. Practice area, caddies, caddy carts, catering.*

Argyll

The lochs and glens of Argyll in the west of Scotland have provided the scenic backdrop for family outings for generations. Wherever Scots take their holidays, golf courses are soon developed, so the string of courses north from the Mull of Kintyre all offer golf in a relaxed atmosphere with sea, beach, and hills not far away.

Machrihanish, by Campbeltown. A course that many enthusiasts discuss in hushed tones—it's a kind of out-of-the-way golfers' Shangri-la. It was laid out in 1876 by Tom Morris on the links around the sandy Machrihanish Bay. The drive off the first tee is across the beach to reach the green—an intimidating start to a memorable series of individual holes. If you are short on time, consider flying from Glasgow to nearby Campbeltown, the last town on the long peninsula of Kintyre. ☎ *01586/810277. 18 holes. Yardage 6,228. Par 70.* ▨ *Sun.–Fri. £21/round, £30 daily; Sat. £36 daily; £120 weekly.* ☉ *Daily. Advance reservations essential. Practice area, caddy carts, catering.*

3 Edinburgh and the Lothians

Scotland's capital makes a strong first impression: Edinburgh Castle looming from the crags of an ancient volcano; neoclassical monuments perched on Calton Hill; Arthur's Seat, a small mountain with steep slopes, little crags, and spectacular vistas of the Firth of Forth. Edinburgh offers more than just a unique historical and architectural landscape—it's a cosmopolitan capital, rich in museums and culture.

By Gilbert
Summers

THE FIRST-TIME VISITOR TO SCOTLAND may be surprised that the country still has a capital city at all, thinking perhaps that the seat of government was drained of all its resources and power after the union with England in 1707. Far from it. The Union of Parliaments brought with it a set of political partnerships—such as separate legal, ecclesiastical, and educational systems—that Edinburgh (-*burgh* is always pronounced *burra* in Scots) assimilated and integrated with its own surviving institutions. Now, nearly 300 years later, Edinburgh is once again to be the seat of a Scottish Parliament, albeit one with restricted powers. In the trying decades after the union, many influential Scots, both in Edinburgh and beyond, went through an identity crisis, but out of the 18th-century difficulties grew the Scottish Enlightenment, during which great strides were made by educated Scots in medicine, economics, and science.

By the mid-18th century, it had become the custom for wealthy Scottish landowners to spend the winter in town houses in the Old Town of Edinburgh, huddled between the high castle rock and the Royal Palace below. In the tall, crowded buildings of old Edinburgh, the well-to-do tended to have their rooms on the middle floors, while the "lower orders" occupied dwellings on the top and ground floors. Such an overcrowded arrangement bred plenty of unsavory and odorous hazards (more on this later), but it also bred ideas. Uniquely cross-fertilized in the coffeehouses and taverns, intellectual notions flourished among a people determined to remain Scottish, yet deprived of their identity in a political sense. One result was a campaign to expand and beautify the city, to give it a look worthy of its subsequent nickname, Athens of the North. Thus was the New Town of Edinburgh built, with broad streets and gracious buildings creating a harmony that even today's throbbing traffic cannot obscure.

Edinburgh today is the second-most-important financial center in the United Kingdom. Its residents come from all over Britain—not least of all because the city regularly ranks near the top of surveys that measure "quality of life"—and New Town apartments on fashionable streets sell for considerable sums. In some senses the city is showy and materialistic, but Edinburgh still supports several learned societies, many of which have their roots in the Scottish Enlightenment: the Royal Society of Edinburgh, for example, established in 1783 "for the advancement of learning and useful knowledge," is still an important forum for interdisciplinary activities, both in Edinburgh and in Scotland as a whole, publishing scientific papers, holding academic symposia and meetings, and administering research fellowships at many Scottish universities. Hand in hand with the city's academic and scientific life is a rich cultural life, with the Edinburgh International Festival attracting lovers of all the arts. Running for three weeks from mid-August into September, this is simply one of the top cultural and artistic festivals in the world. It attracts talent from all parts of the globe: first-tier orchestras and conductors, international dance troupes and ballet companies, and leading opera and theater performers.

Thousands of years ago, an eastward-grinding glacier encountered the tough basalt plug or core of an ancient volcano. It swept around the core, scouring steep cliffs and leaving a trail of material like the tail of a comet. This material formed a ramp, gently leading down from the rocky summit. On this *crag* and *tail* would grow the city of Edinburgh. The lands that rolled down to the sea were for centuries open country, between Castle Rock and the tiny community clustered by the shore that grew into Leith, Edinburgh's seaport. By the 12th century Edinburgh had become a walled town, still perched on the hill. Its shape was becoming clearer: like a fish with its head at the castle, backbone running down the ridge, with "ribs" leading briefly off on either side. The backbone gradually became the continuous thoroughfare now known as the Royal Mile, and the ribs became the closes (alleyways), some still surviving, that were the scene of many historic incidents. By the early 15th century Edinburgh had become the undisputed capital of Scotland. The bitter defeat of Scotland at Flodden in 1513, when Scotland aligned itself with France against England, caused a new defensive city wall to be built. Though the castle escaped, the city was burned by the English earl of Hertford under the orders of King Henry VIII (1491–1547) of England. By 1561, when Mary, Queen of Scots (1542–87), returned from France already widowed, the guest house of the Abbey of Holyrood had grown to become the Palace of Holyroodhouse. Mary's legacy to the city included the destruction of most of the earliest buildings of Edinburgh Castle, held by her supporters after she was forced to flee her homeland.

At the end of the 18th century, the grand New Town was taking shape, though it never was taken as far as the sea at Leith, which had been the original intention. Victorian suburbs added to the gradual sprawl. Despite the expansion, the guardian castle remained the focal point. Princes Street—a master stroke in city planning—was built up only on one side, allowing magnificent views of the great rock on which the fortress stands. Today you can marvel in a skyline of sheer drama and an aura of grandeur. Edinburgh Castle watches over the city, frowning down on Princes Street, now the main downtown shopping area, as if disapproving of its modern razzle-dazzle. Its ramparts still echo with gunfire each day when the traditional one-o'clock gun booms out over the city, startling unwary shoppers. To the east, the top of the New Town's Calton Hill is cluttered with sturdy neoclassical structures, somewhat like an abandoned set for a Greek tragedy.

These theatrical elements give a unique identity to downtown, but turn a corner, say, off George Street, and you will see not an endless cityscape, but blue sea and a patchwork of fields. This is the county of Fife, beyond the inlet of the North Sea called the Firth of Forth—a reminder, like the Highlands to the northwest glimpsed from Edinburgh's highest points, that the rest of Scotland lies within easy reach.

Pleasures and Pastimes

Biking

Edinburgh is a fairly compact, if hilly, city, and biking is a good way to get around, though careful route planning may be needed to avoid traffic. The East Lothian countryside, with its miles of twisting roads and light traffic, is within cycling distance of the city.

Dining

Edinburgh's restaurants offer a sophisticated, diverse mix of traditional and foreign cuisines, from Scottish to Mexican, Thai, Chinese, Greek, and Russian. Many restaurants offer set-price business lunches, often a good value.

Golf

You won't have to go far afield for golf—there are about 20 courses within or close to the city (not including the easily accessible East Lothian courses), many of which welcome visitors (☞ Chapter 2).

Lodging

Edinburgh offers a variety of accommodations, many in traditional Georgian properties, some even in the New Town, only a few minutes from downtown. There are also a number of upscale hotels in the downtown area, each with an international flavor.

Nightlife and the Arts

Edinburgh's nightlife is quite varied and includes dinner dances, discos, Scottish musical evenings, and *ceilidhs* (a mix of country dancing, music, and song pronounced *kay*-lees). Jazz and folk music in general are wide ranging. There are no nightclubs of the cabaret-and-striptease variety. Edinburgh is world renowned for its flagship arts event, the Edinburgh International Festival, now in its 53rd year, and there is no escaping a theater buzz if you visit the city from August to early September. The annual festival has attracted all sorts of international performers since its inception in 1947. Even more obvious to the casual stroller during this time is the refreshingly irreverent Edinburgh Festival Fringe, unruly child of the official festival, which spills out of halls and theaters and onto the streets all over town. At other times throughout the year, professional and amateur groups alike offer a range of cultural performances appropriate to a capital city, even if Edinburgh's neighbor and rival city, Glasgow, has the reputation of being more lively.

Shopping

To make the most of shopping in Edinburgh you will need at least two days, in part because the city's most interesting shops are scattered among several districts. Edinburgh's downtown has the usual chain stores, lined up shoulder to shoulder and offering identical goods. But within a few yards, down some of the side streets, you'll find shops offering more exclusive wares, such as designer clothing, unique craft items, 18th-century silverware, and wild-caught, smoked Scottish salmon.

As the capital city and an important tourist center, Edinburgh features a cross section of Scottish specialties, such as tartans and tweeds, rather than products peculiar to the Edinburgh area. Once you venture into Edinburgh's "villages"—perhaps Stockbridge, Bruntsfield, Morningside, or even the Old Town itself—you will find many unusual stores specializing in single items, such as antique clocks or designer knitwear using the finest Scottish wool or cashmere. In many cases the goods sold in these stores are unavailable elsewhere in Scotland.

If you are interested in antiques, Edinburgh should be a fruitful hunting ground. Scotland has a strong tradition of distinctive furniture makers, silversmiths, and artists; top-quality examples of their work can still be found, at a price. Most reputable dealers are able to arrange transport abroad for your purchases if you buy something too bulky to fit into your luggage.

EXPLORING EDINBURGH AND THE LOTHIANS

The Old Town, which bears a great measure of symbolic weight as the "heart of Scotland's capital," is for lovers of atmosphere and history. The New Town, by contrast, is for you if you appreciate the unique architectural heritage of Edinburgh's Enlightenment. If you belong in both categories, don't worry—the Old and the New Towns are only yards apart. The Old and the New are the essence of Edinburgh, even if, away from this central core, Victorian expansion and urban sprawl have greatly increased the city's dimensions. But Edinburgh, as cities go, is still compact, and much of the city center can be covered on foot.

The hills, green fields, beaches, and historic houses and castles in the countryside outside Edinburgh—Midlothian, West Lothian, and East

Lothian, collectively called the Lothians—can be reached quickly by bus or car, a welcome escape during festival crush at the height of summer.

Numbers in the text correspond to numbers in the margin and on the Exploring Edinburgh, West Lothian and the Forth Valley, and Midlothian and East Lothian maps.

Great Itineraries

Edinburgh's spectacular setting usually means a good first impression. You can be there for a day and think you know the place, as even a cursory bus tour will enable you to grasp the layout of castle, Royal Mile, Old Town, New Town, and so on. However, if your taste is more for leisurely strolling through the nooks and crannies of the Old Town closes, then allow three or four days for exploring.

IF YOU HAVE 2 DAYS

To start you off, make your way to Edinburgh Castle—not just the battlements—and spend some time there, just for its sense of history. Certainly, take a city bus tour as well. Your list of must-sees should also have the National Gallery of Scotland and, unless it is winter, the Georgian House for an idea of life in the New Town.

IF YOU HAVE 5 DAYS

Five days allows plenty of time for Old Town exploration, including the important museums of Huntly House and the People's Story (in the Canongate Tolbooth), and for a walk around the New Town with its Scottish National Portrait Gallery and the Scottish National Gallery of Modern Art, both well worth an hour or two. You should also have plenty of time for shopping, not only in areas close to the city center such as Rose Street and Victoria Street, but also in some of the less "touristy" areas like Bruntsfield. Make a foray to Leith to check out its array of eating places. You could also get out of town: hop on a bus out to Midlothian to see the stunning stone carving in Rosslyn Chapel at Roslin, and visit the Edinburgh Crystal Visitor Centre at Penicuik for crystal bargains. Consider spending another half day traveling out to South Queensferry to admire the Forth road and rail bridges, then visit palatial Hopetoun House, with its wealth of portraits and fine furniture.

IF YOU HAVE 8 DAYS

In eight days, in addition to a thorough exploration of Edinburgh's Old and New Towns, museums and galleries, and a shopping trip or two, you will not only have time to explore Leith, Roslin, and South Queensferry, but also take a couple of side trips from the city. Allow at least a day for each trip, so you have time to enjoy stately homes such as Dalmeny House for its Rothschild collection of sumptuous French furniture; a historic ruin such as Linlithgow Palace, with its Mary, Queen of Scots connection; or the magnificently sited Castle Campbell. At Gullane, with its splendid East Lothian beach, you can walk in the footsteps of Robert Louis Stevenson. Andrew Carnegie's Birthplace Museum at Dunfermline; Dunbar, with its John Muir Country Park; or the delightful market town of Haddington, with the nearby Lennoxlove House (which also boasts Mary, Queen of Scots associations) are other gems beyond the city limits. If it is Festival time, however, you can probably take in shows, concerts, and exhibitions for eight solid days and hardly stray from the city center.

Old Town

Time and progress (of a sort) have swept away some of the narrow closes and tall tenements of the Old Town, but enough remain for you to imagine the original shape of Scotland's capital. Probably every visitor to the city tours the castle, which is more than can be said for many of the city's residents. Its popularity as an attraction is due not only to the castle's historic and symbolic value, but also to the stupendous views offered from its battlements. Immediately below the Castle Esplanade the Royal Mile starts, running roughly west to east, from the castle to the Palace of Holyroodhouse, the queen's official residence in Scotland, and to the foot of Canongate. The Royal Mile's name changes as it progresses, from Castlehill to Lawnmarket, High Street, and Canongate.

A Good Walk

Start your exploration of the Old Town at **Edinburgh Castle** ①. After exploring its extensive complex of buildings, and admiring the view from the battlements, set off down the first part of the Royal Mile, stopping en route at your choice of the museums and other interesting ports of call: on **Castlehill** ②, Cannonball House, the **Outlook Tower** ③ and Camera Obscura, **Scotch Whisky Heritage Centre** ④, Tolbooth Kirk (a *tolbooth* was a town hall or prison, and *kirk* means church), and Upper Bow; and on **Lawnmarket** ⑤, **Gladstone's Land** ⑥ and the **Writers' Museum** ⑦.

At the junction of Lawnmarket with **George IV Bridge** ⑧, turn right onto the bridge then right again into Victoria Street, which winds down to the historic **Grassmarket** ⑨, where parts of the old city walls still stand. Retrace your steps to George IV Bridge, then detour again southward to see the **National Library of Scotland** ⑩, the **Kirk of the Greyfriars** ⑪, and the little statue of the faithful Greyfriars Bobby. On Chambers Street, at the foot of George IV Bridge, the impressive galleries of the **Royal Museum of Scotland and Museum of Scotland** ⑫ interest visitors of all ages.

Returning to the junction of George IV Bridge with the Royal Mile, turn right (eastward) down **High Street** ⑬ for the **Parliament House** ⑭, the **High Kirk of St. Giles** ⑮, the Mercat Cross, and the elegant City Chambers, bringing a flavor of the New Town's neoclassicism to the Old Town's severity. Farther down on the right is the Tron Kirk, with the **Museum of Childhood** ⑯ and **Brass Rubbing Centre** ⑰ beyond. **John Knox House** ⑱ and the **Netherbow Arts Centre** ⑲ are on this section of the Royal Mile, which immediately afterward becomes **Canongate** ⑳.

A short distance down Canongate on the left is **Canongate Tolbooth** ㉑; **Huntly House** ㉒ is opposite, and the **Canongate Kirk** ㉓ and Acheson House are nearby. This walk ends, as it started, on a high point: the **Palace of Holyroodhouse** ㉔, full of historic and architectural interest and some fine paintings, tapestries, and furnishings to admire, in **Holyrood Park** ㉕. Being erected nearby is the new Scottish Parliament building, scheduled to be completed by 2002.

TIMING

The walk could be accomplished in a day, but to give the major sights—the castle, Palace of Holyroodhouse, and Royal Museum of Scotland—the time they deserve, and also see at least some of the other attractions properly, you should allow two days. We suggest that you end the first day with an afternoon in the Royal Museum of Scotland, and spend the second afternoon at Holyroodhouse.

Sights to See

🕊 ⑰ **Brass Rubbing Centre.** No experience is needed to create do-it-yourself replicas from original Pictish stones and markers, rare Scottish brasses, and medieval church brasses. All the materials are here, and children find the pastime quite absorbing. It's down a close opposite the Museum of Childhood. ⊠ *Trinity Apse, Chalmers Close,* ☎ *0131/556–4364.* 🖃 *Free; rubbings 90p–£17 each.* ⊘ *Mon.–Sat. 10–5, Sun. (during festival only) noon–5.*

⓴ Canongate. Named for the canons who once ran the abbey at Holyrood, Canongate is now the site of the Palace of Holyroodhouse. In Scots, "gate" means "street." Canongate itself was originally an independent "burgh," another Scottish term used to refer to a community with trading rights granted by the monarch. Canongate is home to the Canongate Kirk and graveyard, Canongate Tolbooth, Huntly House, and Acheson House (☞ *below*). ⊠ *Section of Royal Mile from end of High St. to the Abbey Strand at the entrance to the Palace of Holyroodhouse.*

㉓ Canongate Kirk. The graveyard of the Canongate Kirk, built in 1688, is the burial place of some notable Scots, including Adam Smith (1723–90), author of *The Wealth of Nations* (1776), and who once lived in 17th-century Panmure House nearby. You can also visit the grave of the undervalued Scots poet Robert Fergusson (1750–74). The fact that Fergusson's grave is even marked is due to the efforts of the much more famous Robert Burns (1759–96). On a visit to the city Burns was dismayed to find the grave had no headstone, so he commissioned an architect—by the name of Robert Burn—to design one. (Burn reportedly took two years to complete the commission, so Burns, in turn, took two years to pay.) Burn also designed the Nelson Monument, the tall column on Calton Hill (☞ *below*) to the north, which you can see from the graveyard.

Against the eastern wall of the graveyard is a bronze sculpture of the head of Mrs. Agnes McLehose, "Clarinda" of the copious correspondence Robert Burns engaged in while confined to his lodgings with an injured leg in 1788. Burns and Mrs. McLehose—an attractive and talented woman who had been abandoned by her husband—exchanged passionate letters for some six weeks that year, Burns signing his name "Sylvander"; Mrs. McLehose, "Clarinda." The missives were dispatched across town by a postal service that delivered them for a penny an hour. The curiously literary affair ended when Burns left Edinburgh to take up a farm tenancy and marry Jean Armour.

Opposite Canongate graveyard is **Acheson House** (circa 1633), once a fine town mansion, which, like so much of the property in the Canongate, fell on hard times. It has been restored, as has the 1628 **Moray House,** a little farther up the street. ⊠ *Canongate,* ☎ *0131/556–3515.* ⊘ *June–Sept., Mon.–Sat. 10:30–4:30, Sun. services 10 and 11:15.*

㉑ Canongate Tolbooth. Nearly every city and town in Scotland once had a tolbooth. Originally a customs house where tolls were gathered, a tolbooth came to mean "town hall" and later "prison" because detention cells were housed in the basement. The building where Canongate's town council once met now houses a museum, the **People's Story,** which focuses on the lives of "ordinary" people from the 18th century to today. The museum describes how this now in some ways rather sterile street, Canongate, once bustled with the activities of the various tradesmen needed to supply life's essentials in the days before superstores. Special displays include a reconstruction of a cooper's workshop and a 1940s kitchen. ⊠ *Canongate,* ☎ *0131/529–4057.* 🖃 *Free.* ⊘ *Mon.–Sat. 10–5, Sun. (during festival only) 2–5.*

NEED A BREAK?　　You can get a good cup of tea and a sticky cake, a quintessentially Scottish indulgence, from **Clarinda's** (⊠ 69 Canongate, ☎ 0131/557–1888) or the **Abbey Strand Tearoom** (⊠ The Sanctuary, Abbey Strand, ☎ no phone), near the palace gates.

Edinburgh

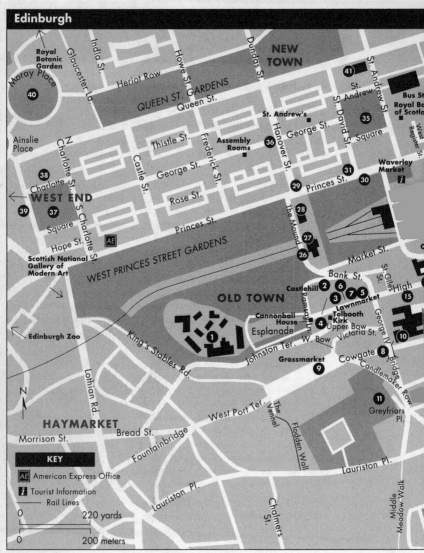

Brass Rubbing Centre, **17**
Calton Hill, **33**
Canongate, **20**
Canongate Kirk, **23**
Canongate Tolbooth, **21**
Castlehill, **2**
Charlotte Square, **37**

Edinburgh Castle, **1**
George IV Bridge, **8**
George Street, **36**
Georgian House, **38**
Gladstone's Land, **6**
Grassmarket, **9**
High Kirk of St. Giles, **15**
High Street, **13**

Holyrood Park, **25**
Huntly House, **22**
Jenners, **31**
John Knox House, **18**
Kirk of the Greyfriars, **11**
Lawnmarket, **5**
Moray Place, **40**
The Mound, **26**

Museum of Childhood, **16**
National Gallery of Scotland, **27**
National Library of Scotland, **10**
Netherbow Arts Centre, **19**
Outlook Tower, **3**

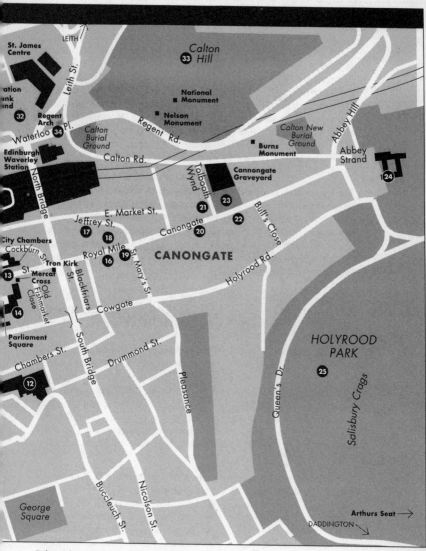

Palace of
Holyroodhouse, **24**
Parliament House, **14**
Princes Street, **29**
Register House, **32**
Royal Museum of
Scotland and
Museum of
Scotland, **12**

Royal Scottish
Academy, **28**
St. Andrew Square, **35**
Scotch Whisky
Heritage Centre, **4**
Scott Monument, **30**
Scottish National
Portrait Gallery, **41**

Writers'
Museum, **7**
Warterloo Palace, **34**
West Register
House, **39**

❷ **Castlehill.** In the late 16th century, witches were brought to what is now a street in the Royal Mile to be burnt at the stake, as a bronze plaque recalls. The cannonball embedded in the west gable of Castlehill's **Cannonball House** was, according to legend, fired from the castle during the Jacobite rebellion in 1745 led by Charles Edward Stuart (or Bonnie Prince Charlie, 1720–88), the most romantic of the Stuart pretenders to the British throne. Most authorities agree on a more prosaic explanation, however, saying it was a height marker for Edinburgh's first piped water-supply system, installed in 1681. Atop the Gothic **Tolbooth Kirk,** built in 1842–44 for the General Assembly of the Church of Scotland church, is, at 240 ft, the tallest spire in the city. It is the new home of the Edinburgh Festival offices, the **Festival Centre** (✉ Castlehill).

The **Upper Bow,** running from Lawnmarket to Victoria Street, was once the main route westward from the town and castle. Before Victoria Street (☞ *below*) was built in the late 19th century, the Upper Bow led down into a narrow dark thoroughfare coursing between a canyon of tenements. All traffic struggled up and down this steep slope from the Grassmarket, which joins the now-truncated West Bow at its lower end. ✉ *East of the Esplanade and west of Lawnmarket.*

NEED A BREAK?
A number of atmospheric pubs and restaurants bustle on this section of the Royal Mile. Try the friendly pub **Jolly Judge** (✉ James Ct., ☎ 0131/ 225-2669), where firelight brightens the dark-wood beams.

❶ **Edinburgh Castle.** Archaeological investigations have established that the rock on which the castle stands was inhabited as far back as 1000 BC, in the latter part of the Bronze Age. There have been fortifications here since the mysterious people called the Picts first used it as a stronghold in the 3rd and 4th centuries AD. The Picts were dislodged by Saxon invaders from northern England in AD 452, and for the next 1,300 years the site saw countless battles and skirmishes. The castle has been held by Scots and Englishmen, Catholics and Protestants, soldiers and royalty.

The oldest surviving building is the tiny 11th-century **St. Margaret's Chapel,** named in honor of Saxon Queen Margaret (1046–93), who had persuaded her husband, King Malcolm III (circa 1031–93), to move his court from Dunfermline to Edinburgh because the latter's environs— the Lothians—were occupied by Saxon settlers with whom she felt more at home, or so the story goes. (Dunfermline was surrounded by Celts.) The chapel was the only building spared when the castle was razed in 1313 by the Scots, having won it back from their English foes. The **Crown Room** contains the **Honours of Scotland**—the crown, scepter, and sword that once graced the Scottish monarch. Upon the **Stone of Scone,** in the Crown Room, Scottish monarchs once sat to be crowned. In **Queen Mary's apartments** Mary, Queen of Scots, gave birth to the future James VI of Scotland (1566–1625), who was also to rule England as James I. In 1573 the castle defended Mary as the rightful Catholic queen of Scotland; it was her last stronghold and was virtually destroyed by English artillery. The **Great Hall** displays arms and armor under an impressive vaulted, beamed ceiling. Scottish parliament meetings were held here until 1840. During the Napoleonic Wars (1803–15), the castle contained French prisoners of war, whose carvings can still be seen on the vaults under the Great Hall.

Several military features of interest include the **Scottish National War Memorial,** the **Scottish United Services Museum,** and the famous 15th-century Belgian-made cannon *Mons Meg.* This enormous piece of artillery has been silent since 1682, when it exploded while firing a salute for the duke of York; it now stands in an ancient hall behind the Half-Moon Battery, the curving ramparts that give Edinburgh Castle its distinctive appearance from miles away. Contrary to what you may hear from locals, it is not *Mons Meg* but the battery's time gun that goes off with a bang every weekday at 1 PM, frightening visitors and reminding Edinburghers to check their watches.

The **Esplanade,** the huge forecourt of the castle, was built in the 18th century as a parade ground, using earth from the foundation of the Royal Exchange (now the City Chambers) to widen and level the area. Although it now serves as the castle parking lot, it comes alive with color each year during the festival, when it is used for the Tattoo, a magnificent military display and pageant. ☎ *0131/668–8800.* ✉ *£6.* ◷ *Apr.–Sept., daily 9:30–5:15; Oct.–Mar., daily 9:30–4:15.*

NEED A BREAK?
At the castle, **Mills Mount Restaurant** (✉ Edinburgh Castle) serves coffee, light lunches, and afternoon tea in bright premises with panoramic views over the city.

❽ George IV Bridge. It is not immediately obvious that this is in fact a bridge, as buildings are closely packed most of the way along both sides. But these buildings descend several stories below street level, as can be seen by looking over the short lengths of parapet.

At the corner of George IV Bridge and Candlemaker Row, near the Greyfriars church, stands one of the most photographed sculptures in Scotland, *Greyfriars Bobby.* This famous Skye terrier kept vigil beside his master's grave in the churchyard for 14 years, leaving only for a short time each day to be fed at a nearby pub after the one-o'clock salute from the castle. ✉ *Between Bank St. and intersection with Candlemaker Row.*

❻ Gladstone's Land. The narrow, six-story tenement, next to the Assembly Hall on Lawnmarket, is a survivor from the 17th century, demonstrating typical 17th-century Scottish architectural features, including an arcaded ground floor and an entrance at second-floor level (livestock sometimes inhabited the ground floor). It is furnished in the style of a 17th-century merchant's house. ✉ *377B Lawnmarket,* ☎ *0131/226–5856.* ✉ *£3.* ◷ *Easter–Oct., Mon.–Sat. 10–5, Sun. 2–5 (last admission 4:30).*

❾ Grassmarket. An area that was for centuries an agricultural market now hosts numerous shops, bars, and restaurants, making it a hive of activity at night.

Sections of the Old Town wall can be approximately traced on the north (castle) side by a series of steps that runs steeply up from Grassmarket to Johnston Terrace above. By far the best-preserved section of the wall, however, is to be found by crossing to the South Side and climbing the steps of the lane called the Vennel. Here you can see a section of the 16th-century **Flodden Wall,** which comes in from the east and turns southward at Telfer's Wall, a 17th-century extension. From here there are outstanding views northward to the castle.

The **cobbled cross** marks the site of the town gallows. Among those hanged here were many 17th-century Covenanters. Judges were known to issue the death sentence for these religious reformers with the words, "Let them glorify God in the Grassmarket."

From the northeast corner of the Grassmarket, **Victoria Street,** a 19th-century addition to the Old Town, leads up to George IV Bridge. Shops sell antiques, new designer clothing, and high-quality gifts.

⑮ **High Kirk of St. Giles.** Originally the city's parish church, St. Giles's briefly became a cathedral in 1633 and is now often called St. Giles's Cathedral. There has been a church here since AD 854, although most of the present structure dates from 1829. The spire, however, was completed in 1495. The **Chapel of the Order of the Thistle,** bearing the belligerent national motto NEMO ME IMPUNE LACESSIT ("No one provokes me with impunity"), was added in 1911. ⊠ *High St.,* ☎ *0131/ 225–4363.* ⌨ *Kirk free, Thistle Chapel suggested donation £1.* ⊙ *Mon.–Sat. 9–5 (until 7 in summer), Sun. 1–5. Services: Sun. 8, 10, and 11:30 AM, 6 and 8 PM (music program only at 8); Mon.–Fri. 8 AM, noon; Sat. noon, 6 PM.*

⑬ **High Street.** One of the four streets making up the Royal Mile, High Street contains some of the Old Town's most impressive buildings and sights, which merit individual entries. However, there are also other, less obvious historic relics to be seen. Near Parliament Square, look on the west side for a **heart** set in cobbles. This marks the site of the vanished Tolbooth, the center of city life from the 15th century until the building's demolition in 1817. This ancient civic edifice, formerly housing the Scottish parliament and used as a prison from 1640 onward, inspired Sir Walter Scott's (1771–1832) novel *The Heart of Midlothian.*

Just outside Parliament House the **Mercat Cross** (*mercat* means market), a focus of public attention for centuries, is still the site of royal proclamations. The cross itself is modern, but part of its shaft is as old as the city. Across High Street from St. Giles's Cathedral are the **City Chambers,** now the seat of local government. Built by John Fergus, who adapted a design of John Adam in 1753, the chambers were originally known as the Royal Exchange and intended to be a place where merchants and lawyers could conduct business. Note that the building drops 11 stories to Cockburn Street on its north side.

A *tron* is a weigh beam used in public weigh houses, and the **Tron Kirk** was named after a salt tron that used to stand nearby. The kirk itself was built after 1633, when St. Giles's became an Episcopal cathedral for a brief time. In this church in 1693 a minister offered an often-quoted prayer for the local government: "Lord, hae mercy on aa [every] fool and idiot, and particularly on the Magistrates of Edinburgh."

You would once have passed out of the safety of the town walls through a gate called the **Netherbow Port.** Look for the brass studs in the street cobbles that mark its location. A plaque outside the Netherbow Arts Centre (☞ *below*) depicts the gate. ⊠ *Between Lawnmarket and Canongate.*

㉕ **Holyrood Park.** Behind the palace lie the open grounds and looming crags of Holyrood Park, the hunting ground of early Scottish kings. At the Edinburgh's mini-mountain, **Arthur's Seat** (822 ft), views are breathtaking. ⊠ *South of Palace of Holyroodhouse.*

OFF THE BEATEN PATH | **DUDDINGSTON** – Tucked behind Arthur's Seat, and about a one-hour walk from Princes Street via Holyrood Park, this little community, formerly of brewers and weavers, has the interesting Duddingston Kirk with a Norman doorway and a watchtower that was built to keep body snatchers out of the graveyard. The church overlooks Duddingston Loch, popular with bird-watchers, and moments away is an old-style pub called the Sheep's Heid Inn, which offers a variety of beers and the oldest skittle alley in Scotland. ⊠ *Take LRT Bus 42 or 46.*

㉒ **Huntly House.** Dating from 1570, this historic house is now a museum of local history, displaying Scottish pottery and Edinburgh silver and glassware. ⊠ *142 Canongate,* ☎ *0131/529–4143.* ☞ *Free.* ⊙ *Mon.–Sat. 10–5, Sun. (during festival only) 2–5.*

⑱ **John Knox House.** It is not certain that Scotland's severe religious reformer John Knox (1514–72) ever lived here, but mementos of his life are on view inside. This distinctive dwelling offers a glimpse of what Old Town life was like in the 16th century. The projecting upper stories were once commonplace along the Royal Mile, darkening and further closing in the already narrow passage. Look for the initials of former owner James Mossman and his wife, carved into the stonework on the "marriage lintel." Mossman was goldsmith to Mary, Queen of Scots, and was hanged in 1573 for his allegiance to her. ⊠ *45 High St.,* ☎ *0131/556–2647.* ☞ *£1.75.* ⊙ *Mon.–Sat. 10–5 (last admission 4:30).*

⑪ **Kirk of the Greyfriars.** Built (circa 1620) on the site of a medieval monastery, the Gothic Greyfriars church was where the National Covenant, declaring the independence of the Presbyterian Church in Scotland from government control, was signed in 1638. The covenant plunged Scotland into decades of civil war. Informative panels tell the story, and there's a visitor's center on site. ⊠ *Greyfriars Pl.,* ☎ *0131/225–1900.* ☞ *Free.* ⊙ *Easter–Oct., weekdays 10:30–4:30, Sat. 10:30–2:30; Nov.–Easter, Thurs. 1:30–3:30; groups by appointment.*

⑤ **Lawnmarket.** The second of the streets that make up the Royal Mile was formerly the site of the produce market for the city, with, once a week, a special cloth sale of wool and linen. Now it's home to Gladstone's Land (☞ *above*) and the Writers' Museum (☞ *below*). ⊠ *Between Castlehill and High St.*

⑯ **Museum of Childhood.** Even adults enjoy this cheerfully noisy museum—a cacophony of childhood memorabilia, vintage toys, and dolls, as well as a reconstructed schoolroom, street scene, fancy-dress party, and nursery—the first in the world to be devoted solely to the history of childhood. It's two blocks past the North Bridge–South Bridge junction on High Street. ⊠ *42 High St.,* ☎ *0131/529–4142.* ☞ *Free.* ⊙ *Mon.–Sat. 10–5, Sun. (during festival only) 2–5.*

⑩ **National Library of Scotland.** Founded in 1689, this library has a superb collection of books and manuscripts on the history and culture of Scotland and also mounts regular exhibitions. ⊠ *George IV Bridge,* ☎ *0131/226–4531.* ☞ *Exhibitions free.* ⊙ *Mon., Tues., Thurs., Fri. 9:30–8:30, Wed. 10–8:30, Sat. 9:30–1; exhibitions Mon.–Sat. 10–5.*

⑲ **Netherbow Arts Centre.** The gallery and theater here host a regular program of exhibitions and productions. The café serves morning coffee with breakfast home bakes, full lunches, and afternoon teas. ⊠ *43 High St.,* ☎ *0131/556–9579.* ☞ *£1.95.* ⊙ *Mon.–Sat. 10–5 (last admission 4:30), and for evening performances.*

③ **Outlook Tower.** The **Camera Obscura** in this 17th-century tower offers armchair views of the city. The structure was significantly altered in the 1840s and 1850s with the installation of the present system of lenses, which, on a clear day, project an image of the city onto a white concave table. ⊠ *Castlehill,* ☎ *0131/226–3709.* ☞ *£3.85–£3.95.* ⊙ *Apr.–Oct., weekdays 9:30–6, weekends 10–6; Nov.–Mar., daily 10–5.*

㉔ **Palace of Holyroodhouse.** The official residence of the queen when she is in Scotland can be seen through the elaborate wrought-iron gates at the end of Canongate. When the royal family is not in residence, you can take a conducted tour.

The **King James Tower** is the oldest surviving section, containing the rooms of Mary, Queen of Scots, on the second floor, and Lord Darnley's (a.k.a. Henry Stewart, 1545–65) rooms below. Though much has been altered, there are fine fireplaces, paneling, plasterwork, tapestries, and 18th-century furniture throughout. Along the front of the palace, between the two main towers, are the duchess of Hamilton's room and the Adam-style dining room.

Along the southern side of the palace are the **Throne Room** and other drawing rooms now used for social and ceremonial occasions. At the back of the palace is the **King's Bedchamber.** The **Picture Gallery** has a huge collection of portraits of Scottish monarchs (some of the royal figures are invented, and others are imaginary likenesses). All the portraits were painted by a Dutch artist, Jacob De Witt, who signed a contract in 1684 with the Queen's cashkeeper Hugh Wallace that bound him to deliver 110 pictures within two years, for which he received an annual stipend of £120. Surely one of the most desperate scenes in the palace's history is that of the Dutch artist feverishly turning out potboiler portraits at the rate of one a week for two years.

The palace came into existence originally as a guest house for the Abbey of Holyrood, which was founded in 1128 by Scottish king David I (1082–1153). Look for the brass letters SSS set into the road at the beginning of Abbey Strand (the continuation of the Royal Mile beyond the traffic circle). The letters stand for "sanctuary" and recall the days when the former abbey served as a retreat for debtors until 1880, when the government stopped imprisoning people for debt. Curiously, the area of sanctuary extended across what is now Holyrood Park, so debtors could get some fresh air without fear of being caught by their creditors. Oddest of all, however, was the agreement that after debtors checked in at Holyrood they were able to go anywhere in the city on Sunday. This made for great entertainment on Sunday evening as midnight approached: the debtors raced back to Holyrood before the stroke of 12, often hotly pursued by their creditors. The poet Thomas de Quincey (1785–1859) and the comte d'Artois (a.k.a. Charles X, 1757–1836), brother of the deposed King Louis XVIII (1755–1824) of France, were only two of the more exotic of Holyrood's denizens.

After the Union of the Crowns in 1603, when the Scottish Royal Court packed its bags and decamped for England, the building fell into decline. Oliver Cromwell (1599–1658), the Protestant Lord Protector of England who had conquered Scotland, ordered the palace rebuilt after a fire in 1650, but the work was poorly carried out and lasted only until the restoration of the monarchy, after Cromwell's death. When Charles II (1630–85) ascended the British throne in 1660, he ordered Holyrood rebuilt in the architectural style of Louis XIV (alias the Sun King, 1638–1715), and this is the style you see today.

In 1688 an anti-Catholic faction ran riot within the palace, and in 1745, during the last Jacobite campaign, the palace was occupied by Charles Edward Stuart. After the 1822 visit of King George IV (1762–1830), in more peaceable times, the palace sank into decline once again. But Queen Victoria (1819–1901) and her grandson King George V (1865–1936) renewed interest in the palace: The buildings were once more refurbished and made suitable for royal residence. ✉ *Abbey Strand,* ☎ *0131/556-7371, 0131/556-1096 recorded information.* 🎫 *£5.30.* ⏱ *Apr.–Oct., daily 9:30–5:15; Nov.–Mar., daily 9:30–3:45; closed during royal and state visits.*

⑭   **Parliament House.** The seat of Scottish government until 1707, when the crowns of Scotland and England were united, Parliament House is partially hidden by the bulk of St. Giles's. It's now the home of the

Supreme Law Courts of Scotland. Parliament Hall inside is remarkable for its hammer beam roof and its display of portraits by major Scottish artists. ⊠ *Parliament Sq.,* ☎ *0131/225–2595.* ✆ *Free.* ☉ *Weekdays 10–4.*

⑫ **Royal Museum of Scotland and Museum of Scotland.** Occupying an imposing Victorian building on Chambers Street, the Royal Museum of Scotland covers a broad spectrum, from natural history and archaeology to scientific and industrial history. The great Main Hall, with its soaring roof, is architecturally interesting in its own right. A major extension, at press time scheduled to open in late 1998, houses the **Museum of Scotland,** with displays concentrating on Scotland's own heritage. ⊠ *Chambers St.,* ☎ *0131/225–7534.* ✆ *£3 (entry to both museums).* ☉ *Mon. and Wed.–Sat. 10–5, Tues. 10–8, Sun. noon–5.*

④ **Scotch Whisky Heritage Centre.** The mysterious process that turns malted barley and spring water into one of Scotland's most important exports is revealed in this museum. Although whisky-making is not in itself packed with drama, the center manages an imaginative presentation using models and tableaux viewed while riding in low-speed barrel-cars. At one point you'll find yourself inside a huge vat surrounded by bubbling sounds and malty smells. ⊠ *354 Castlehill,* ☎ *0131/220–0441.* ✆ *£4.80.* ☉ *Daily 10–5:30 (last tour 5; extended hrs in summer).*

⑦ **Writers' Museum.** Down a close off Lawnmarket is the Lady Stair's House, built in 1622 and a good example of 17th-century urban architecture. The museum housed here evokes Scotland's literary past with exhibits on Sir Walter Scott, Robert Louis Stevenson (1850–94), and Robert Burns. ⊠ *Off Lawnmarket,* ☎ *0131/529–4901.* ✆ *Free.* ☉ *Mon.–Sat. 10–5, Sun. (during festival only) 2–5.*

New Town

At the dawn of the Scottish Enlightenment, in the 18th century, the city fathers busied themselves with various schemes to improve the capital. By that time Edinburgh's unsanitary environment—created primarily by the crowded conditions in which most people lived—was becoming notorious. The well-known Scots fiddle tune "The Flooers (flowers) of Edinburgh" was only one of many ironic references to the capital's unpleasant atmosphere, which greatly embarrassed the Scot James Boswell (1740–95), biographer and companion of the English lexicographer Dr. Samuel Johnson (1709–84). In his *Journal of a Tour of the Hebrides,* Boswell recalled that on retrieving the newly arrived Johnson from his grubby inn in the Canongate, "I could not prevent his being assailed by the evening effluvia of Edinburgh . . . Walking the streets at night was pretty perilous and a good deal odoriferous . . .."

To help remedy this sorry state of affairs, in 1767 James Drummond, the city's Lord Provost (Scots for mayor), urged the town council to hold a competition to design a new district for Edinburgh. The winner was an unknown young architect named James Craig (1744–95). His plan was for a grid of three main east–west streets, balanced at either end by two grand squares—a symmetry unusual in Britain. These streets survive today, though some of the buildings lining them were altered by later development. Princes Street is the southernmost, with Queen Street to the north and George Street as the axis, flanked by St. Andrew and Charlotte squares.

A Good Walk

Start your walk on **The Mound** ㉖, the sloping street that joins the Old and New towns. Two galleries immediately east of this great linking ramp, the **National Gallery of Scotland** ㉗ and the **Royal Scottish Academy** ㉘, are the work of William Playfair (1789–1857), an architect whose neoclassical buildings contributed greatly to Edinburgh's title, "the Athens of the North."

At the foot of the Mound is Edinburgh's most famous street, **Princes Street** ㉙, abuzz with chain stores on the north side and looking up to the castle to the south. Walk east until you reach the Gothic spire of the **Scott Monument** ㉚. Opposite is that most Edinburgh of institutions, **Jenners** ㉛ department store. **Register House** ㉜, opposite the main post office, marks the eastern end of Princes Street.

The monuments on **Calton Hill** ㉝, growing ever more noticeable ahead as you walk east along Princes Street, can be reached by first continuing along **Waterloo Place** ㉞, the eastern extension of Princes Street, from which you can get to the Regent Bridge. Waterloo Place then continues in a single sweep through the Calton Burial Ground to the screen walling at the base of Calton Hill. On the left you'll see steps that lead to the hilltop. If you're walking and don't feel up to the steep climb, you can take the road farther on to the left, which loops up the hill at a more leisurely pace.

Leaving Calton Hill, you may wish to continue east along Regent Road, perhaps as far as the Burns Monument, to admire the views westward of the castle and of the facade of the former Royal High School (directly above you). Then retrace your steps to the Waterloo Place traffic lights and make your way to **St. Andrew Square** ㉟ by cutting through the St. James Centre shopping mall (across Leith Street) and then through the bus station. After admiring the interior of the Royal Bank of Scotland on the eastern side of the square, walk west along **George Street** ㊱.

The essence of the New Town spirit survives in **Charlotte Square** ㊲, at the western end of George Street, and especially in the **Georgian House** ㊳ and **West Register House** ㊴. To explore further, choose your own route northward, down to the wide and elegant streets centering on **Moray Place** ㊵. Then make your way back eastward along Queen Street to visit the **Scottish National Portrait Gallery** ㊶.

TIMING

This walk could be done in a morning if you start early, but if you want to get the most out of the National Gallery of Scotland and the Scottish National Portrait Gallery, take the whole day and allow at least an hour for each museum. The Portrait Gallery has a good restaurant, so one option is to arrive in time for lunch, then spend the afternoon there.

Sights to See

㉝ **Calton Hill.** Robert Louis Stevenson's favorite view of his beloved city was from the top of this hill, and you will be rewarded, too, if you make the climb. The architectural styles represented by the extraordinary collection of monuments include Gothic—the Old Observatory, for example—and neoclassical. Under the latter falls William Playfair's monument to his talented uncle, the geologist and mathematician John Playfair (1748–1819), as well as his cruciform **New Observatory**. The piece that commands the most attention, however, is the so-called **National Monument**, often referred to as "Edinburgh's [or Scotland's] Disgrace." Intended to copy Athens's Parthenon, this monument for the dead of the Napoleonic Wars was started in 1822 to the specifications of a design by Playfair. But in 1830, only 12 columns later, money ran out, and the columned facade became a monument to high aspirations and poor fund-raising. The tallest monument on Calton Hill is the 100-

ft-high **Nelson Monument,** completed in 1814 in honor of Britain's naval hero Horatio Nelson (1758–1805). The **Burns Monument** is the circular Corinthian temple below Regent Road. Devotees of Robert Burns will want to visit one other grave (☞ Canongate Kirk, *above*)—that of Mrs. Agnes McLehose, or "Clarinda," in the Canongate graveyard. ⊠ *Bounded by Leith St. to the west and Regent road to the south,* ☎ *0131/556–2716.* ◪ *Nelson Monument £2.* ☉ *Apr.–Sept., Mon. 1–6, Tues.–Sat. 10–6; Oct.–Mar., Mon.–Sat. 10–3.*

㊲ Charlotte Square. The New Town's centerpiece opens out at the western end of George Street. The palatial facade—considered one of Europe's finest pieces of civic architecture—on the square's north side was designed by Robert Adam (1728–92), Scotland's most famous neoclassical architect. On the north side is the Georgian House (☞ *below*), and to the west is the West Register House (☞ *below*). ⊠ *Western end of George St.*

NEED A BREAK? You rarely have to wait in line at **Bianco's** (⊠ 9–11 Hope St., ☎ 0131/226–0901), south of the square, for coffee and croissants. It's relaxed, the seats are comfortable, and the coffee, by Edinburgh standards, is very good.

㊱ George Street. With its variety of upmarket shops and handsome Georgian frontages, this is a more pleasant, less crowded street for you to wander along than Princes Street (☞ *below*). The **statue of King George IV,** at the intersection of George and Hanover streets, recalls the visit of George IV to Scotland in 1822. He was the first British monarch to do so since King Charles II, in the 17th century. By the 19th century Scotland was perceived at Westminster, distant English seat of Parliament, as being almost civilized enough for a monarch to visit safely.

The ubiquitous Sir Walter Scott turns up farther down the street. It was at a grand dinner in the **Assembly Rooms,** between Hanover and Frederick streets, that Scott acknowledged having written the *Waverley* novels (the name of the author had hitherto been a secret). You can meet Scott once again, in the form of a plaque just downhill, at 39 Castle Street, where he lived from 1797 until his death in 1832. ⊠ *Between Charlotte and St. Andrew Sqs.*

NEED A BREAK? The little restaurant on the upper floor at **James Thin** bookshop (⊠ 57 George St., ☎ 0131/225–4495) is ideally placed for enjoying a cup of coffee or light lunch while reading your latest vacation purchase.

★ **㊳ Georgian House.** The National Trust for Scotland has furnished the house in period style to show the elegant domestic arrangements of an affluent family of the late 18th century. The hallway was designed to accommodate sedan chairs, in which 18th-century grandees were carried through the streets. The absence of restraining guide ropes is refreshing, but please do not touch the furnishings. ⊠ *7 Charlotte Sq.,* ☎ *0131/225–2160.* ◪ *£4.20.* ☉ *Apr.–Oct., Mon.–Sat. 10–5, Sun. 2–5 (last admission 4:30).*

㉛ Jenners. Edinburgh's equivalent of London's Harrod's department store, Jenners is noteworthy not only for its high-quality wares and good restaurants, but also because of the building's interesting architectural detail—baroque on the outside, with a mock-Jacobean central well inside. It was one of the earliest department stores ever to be established, in 1838. The caryatids decorating the exterior were said to have been placed in honor of the store's predominantly female customers. ⊠ *4–8 Princes St.,* ☎ *0131/225–2442.* ☉ *Mon., Wed., Fri., Sat. 9–5:30, Tues. 9:30–5:30, Thurs. 9–7:30.*

OFF THE
BEATEN PATH

LEITH – Edinburgh's ancient seaport has been revitalized in recent years, with the restoration of those fine commercial buildings that survived an earlier, and insensitive, redevelopment phase. It is worth exploring the lowest reaches of the Water of Leith, an area where pubs and restaurants now proliferate. ⊠ *Reach Leith by walking down Leith St. and Leith Walk, from east end of Princes St. (20- to 30-min brisk walk), or take a bus: LRT Buses 7, 10, 14, 16, 17, 22, 25, 32, 34, 35, 52, or 87, or circle route 2/12.*

㊵ Moray Place. Twelve-sided Moray Place—with its "pendants" Ainslie Place and Randolph Crescent—was laid out in 1822 by the earl of Moray. It is a fine example of an 1820s development, with imposing porticos and a central secluded garden (for residents only). From the start the houses were planned to be of particularly high quality, and the curving facades are still pleasant today. ⊠ *Between Charlotte Sq. and the Water of Leith.*

㉖ The Mound. The Mound originated from the need for a dry-shod crossing of the muddy quagmire left behind when Nor' Loch, the body of water below the castle, was drained (the railway now cuts through this area). The work is said to have been started by a local tailor, George Boyd, who tired of struggling through the mud en route from his New Town house to his Old Town shop. The building of a ramp was under way by 1781, and by the time of its completion, in 1830, "Geordie Boyd's mud brig" (bridge), as the street was first known, had been built up with an estimated 2 million cartloads of earth dug from the foundations of the New Town.

㉗ National Gallery of Scotland. This impressive gallery, renovated in the late 1980s at vast expense to show the William Playfair–designed building in its full glory—original gilding and rich color schemes of reds and greens—has a wide selection of paintings, from the Renaissance to the Post-Impressionist period. Works by Velázquez, El Greco, Rembrandt, Turner, Degas, Monet, and Van Gogh, among others, complement a fine collection of Scottish art. ⊠ *The Mound,* ☎ *0131/ 556–8921.* ▭ *Free.* ☉ *Mon.–Sat. 10–5, Sun. 2–5 (extended hrs during festival); Print Room: weekdays 10–noon and 2–4 by appointment.*

㉙ Princes Street. The north side of this well-planned street is now one long sequence of chain stores whose unappealing modern fronts can be seen in almost any large British town. Luckily the other side of the street is occupied by the well-kept West Princes Street Gardens, which act as a wide green moat to the castle on its rock. ⊠ *Running east–west from Lothian Rd. to Waterloo Pl.*

NEED A
BREAK?

Immediately west of Register House is the **Café Royal** (⊠ 17 W. Register St., ☎ 0131/557–4792), which has good beer and lots of character, with ornate tiles and stained glass contributing to the atmosphere.

㉜ Register House. Scotland's first custom-built archives depository, Register House was partly funded by the sale of estates forfeited by Jacobite landowners, after their last rebellion in Britain (1745–46). Work on the building, designed by Robert Adam, started in 1774. The statue in front is of the first duke of Wellington (1769–1852). ⊠ *Princes St.,* ☎ *0131/535–1314.* ▭ *Free.* ☉ *Mon.–Thurs. 9–4:45, Fri. 9–4:30.*

OFF THE
BEATEN PATH

ROYAL BOTANIC GARDEN – In this 70-acre garden is Britain's largest rhododendron and azalea collection. There is also a convenient cafeteria and a shop on the premises. To reach the gardens, only 10- to 15-minutes' walk from the New Town, walk down Dundas Street, the continuation of Hanover Street, and turn left across the bridge over the Water of Leith, Edinburgh's small-scale river. ⊠ *Inverleith Row,* ☎ *0131/552-7171.* ✉ *Free (donation for greenhouses appreciated).* ◷ *Gardens: Nov.–Jan., daily 9:30–4; Feb. and Oct., daily 9:30–5; Mar. and Sept., daily 9:30–6; Apr.–Aug., daily 9:30–7. Shop, café, and exhibition areas: Mar.–Oct., daily 10–5; Nov.–Feb., daily 10–3:30.*

㉘ Royal Scottish Academy. This most imposing building, with columned facade overlooking Princes Street, is used for the RSA Annual Exhibition of paintings, sculpture, and prints from late April through July. Immediately before the Annual Exhibition, art students have their own exhibition, and the various Scottish societies of artists—watercolorists, landscapists, portraitists—hold exhibitions at other times during the year. ⊠ *Princes St.,* ☎ *0131/225-6671.* ✉ *Fees vary depending on exhibit.* ◷ *Annual Exhibition: late Apr.–July, Mon.–Sat. 10–5, Sun. 2–5.*

㉟ St. Andrew Square. The most notable building on this square, which terminates George Street at its eastward end, is the headquarters of the **Royal Bank of Scotland**; take a look inside at the lavish mid-Victorian decor of the central banking hall. In the distance, at the other end of George Street, on Charlotte Square, you can see the copper dome of the former St. George's Church, now West Register House (☞ *below*). In James Craig's (1744–95) symmetrical plan for the New Town, a matching church was intended for the bank's site, but Sir Lawrence Dundas, a wealthy and influential baronet, somehow managed to acquire the space for his town house. The grand mansion was later converted into the bank. The church originally intended for the site, St. Andrew's, is a little farther down George Street on the right. ⊠ *Royal Bank of Scotland:* ⊠ *St. Andrew Sq.,* ☎ *0131/556-8555.* ✉ *Free.* ◷ *Mon., Wed.–Fri. 9:15–4:45, Tues. 10–4:45.*

㉚ Scott Monument. This unmistakable 200-ft-high Gothic spire looming over Princes Street was built in 1844 in honor of Scotland's most famous author, Sir Walter Scott (1771–1832), author of *Ivanhoe, Waverley,* and many other novels and poems. (Note the marble statue of Scott and his favorite dog.) When Scott died, public sentiment demanded a grand acknowledgment of the work of the then wildly popular writer. After much delay the committee supervising the construction of a suitable memorial announced a competition for its design. (If in doubt about how to proceed with any civic development, the burghers of Edinburgh usually hold a competition.) After the Gothic structure that you now see was chosen, the committee was somewhat dismayed to learn that the design, submitted under a pseudonym, turned out to be not the work of a prestigious architect, but rather that of a carpenter and self-taught draftsman, George Meikle Kemp. A well-traveled man, Kemp incorporated elements of France's Rheims Cathedral into his design for the monument. The monument was undergoing restoration at press time. ⊠ *Princes St.,* ☎ *0131/529-4068.*

OFF THE BEATEN PATH — **SCOTTISH NATIONAL GALLERY OF MODERN ART –** Close to the New Town in a handsome former school building on Belford Road, this magnificent gallery features paintings and sculpture, including works by Pablo Picasso (1881–1973), Georges Braque (1882–1963), Henri Matisse (1869–1954), and André Derain (1880–1954). The gallery also has, rather unexpectedly, an excellent and popular whole foods restaurant in the basement. ⊠ *Belford Rd.,* ☎ *0131/556-8921.* ✉ *Free.* ◷ *Mon.–Sat. 10–5, Sun. 2–5 (extended during the festival).*

㊶ Scottish National Portrait Gallery. A magnificent red sandstone Gothic building on Queen Street houses this must-visit institution. The gallery contains a superb Thomas Gainsborough (1727–88) and portraits by the Scottish artists Allan Ramsay (1713–84) and Sir Henry Raeburn (1756–1823), among many others. ⊠ *Queen St.*, ☎ *0131/556–8921.* ▣ *Free.* ⊙ *Mon.–Sat. 10–5, Sun. 2–5.*

OFF THE
BEATEN PATH

EDINBURGH ZOO – On an 80-acre site on the slopes of Corstorphine Hill, Edinburgh's Zoo offers traditional zoo delights plus animal contact and handling sessions in the main season, as well as its ever-popular Penguin Parade (held daily in summer). ⊠ *Corstorphine Rd., next to Post House Hotel (4 mi west of city),* ☎ *0131/334-9171.* ▣ *£6.* ⊙ *Apr.– Sept., Mon.–Sat. 9–6, Sun. 9:30–6; Mar. and Oct., Mon.–Sat. 9–5, Sun. 9:30–5; Nov.–Feb., Mon.–Sat. 9–4:30, Sun. 9:30–4:30.*

㉞ Waterloo Place. The fine neoclassically inspired architecture on this street was designed as a piece by Archibald Elliot (d. 1823) in 1815. Waterloo Place extends over Regent Bridge, bounded by the 1815 **Regent Arch,** a simple triumphal, Corinthian-column war memorial at the center of Ionic screens bordering the bridge. ⊠ *Eastern extension of Princes St.*

㊴ West Register House. In the middle of the west side of Charlotte Square, the former St. George's Church today fulfills a different role, as an extension of the original Register House on Princes Street. ⊠ *Charlotte Sq.,* ☎ *0131/535–1400.* ▣ *Free.* ⊙ *Mon.–Thurs. 9–4:45, Fri. 9–4:30.*

DINING

As befits a nation's capital, Edinburgh has a cosmopolitan range of restaurants—from Thai to South African, Mexican to Chinese—to suit all tastes. On the whole, restaurants tend to be fairly small to medium size, and it is therefore best to make reservations at the more popular ones, even during the week and definitely at Festival time. You'll find plenty of good restaurants within walking distance of Princes Street, and many more only a short bus or taxi ride away. Take the trouble to seek out those a little farther afield: you will not be disappointed. For bars and pub grub, *see* Nightlife and the Arts, *below.*

It is possible to eat well in Edinburgh without spending a fortune. Even those restaurants that are ranked in the ££££ category could be squeezed into the top of the £££ range, depending on what you order. A service charge of 10% may be added to your bill, though this practice is not adhered to uniformly. If no charge has been added and you are satisfied with the service, a 10% tip is appropriate. Dining hours in Edinburgh are much the same as in the rest of Great Britain, with the main rush at lunchtime from 1 to 2, and at dinner from 8 to 9.

CATEGORY	COST*
££££	over £30
£££	£20–£30
££	£15–£20
£	under £15

*per person for a three-course meal, including VAT and excluding drinks and service

Old Town

French

££££   ✕ **Witchery by the Castle.** The inspiration for this spooky haunt—complete with flickering candlelight—derives from the fact that some 300 years ago hundreds of witches were executed on the Castlehill, barely a few dozen yards from where you will be seated. The lugubrious, cavernous interior is festooned with cauldrons and broomsticks and decorated with cabalistic insignia. There's nothing spooky about the Scottish-accented French food, however, with fine venison, duck, lamb, salmon, and fillet steak among the specialties. There's a £23.95 fixed-price dinner menu. ⊠ *352 Castlehill, Royal Mile,* ☎ *0131/225–5613. Reservations essential. AE, DC, MC, V.*

££–£££ ✕ **Merchants.** On a street running below George IV Bridge and only moments from the Grassmarket, Merchants is competent and reliable. The decor is gently understated, with pinewood floors, crisp white tablecloths, cane chairs, and lots of plants. Light music plays in the background. A sophisticated fixed-price menu (lunch from £6.95, dinner from £15) in French and English has such adventurous moments as veal in dill and coriander; lamb chops with raspberry-and-mint sauce; and herbed roulade of beef filled with prawns and avocado mousse, with orange-and-tarragon vinaigrette. ⊠ *17 Merchant St.,* ☎ *0131/ 225–4009. AE, DC, MC, V.*

£–££ ✕ **Pierre Victoire.** Edinburgh has five branches of this very popular bistro chain. All are fairly chaotic, enjoyable eateries serving healthy portions of French country cooking at low prices. The seafood is fresh and especially good: try the king scallops and smoked salmon with wild-mushroom and martini sauce. ⊠ *38–40 Grassmarket,* ☎ *0131/226– 2442;* ⊠ *10 Victoria St.,* ☎ *0131/225–1721;* ⊠ *8 Union St.,* ☎ *0131/ 557–8451;* ⊠ *5 Dock Pl., Leith,* ☎ *0131/555–6178 (no dinner Sun.);* ⊠ *17 Queensferry St.,* ☎ *0131/226–1890 (no lunch Sun.). MC, V.*

Scottish

£££ ✕ **Jackson's.** Intimate and candlelit in a historic Old Town close, Jackson's offers good Scots fare, including excellent Aberdeen Angus steaks and Border lamb. Seafood and vegetarian specialties are always on the menu. The decor is rustic, with lots of greenery, stone walls, pine farmhouse-style tables and chairs, and fresh flowers. The wine list includes 60 malt whiskies and some Scottish country wines to complete the Scottish experience. ⊠ *2 Jackson Close, 209–213 High St., Royal Mile,* ☎ *0131/225–1793. AE, MC, V.*

£–££ ✕ **Beehive Inn.** One of the oldest pubs in the city, the Beehive snuggles in the Grassmarket, under the majestic shadow of the castle. Some 400 years ago the Beehive was a coaching inn, and outside the pub's doors once stood the main set of city gallows, where numerous executions were held. Now it's a good spot for a quick lunch. The upstairs Rafters restaurant lies hidden in an attractive and spacious attic room, crammed with weird and wonderful junk. Open only for dinner, Rafters features mostly steaks and fish: try the charcoal-grilled trout with Drambuie and oregano sauce, or veal pan fried with thyme and mushrooms. Reservations are advised in summer. ⊠ *18/20 Grassmarket,* ☎ *0131/225–7171. AE, DC, MC, V.*

£–££ ✕ **Doric Tavern.** Beyond this café–bistro bar's rather tatty entrance staircase plastered with posters and playbills, the stripped wood floor, dark wood tables, and navy velvet curtains create a superbly subdued, languid atmosphere. The menu always features a daily special—like roast pigeon salad with raspberry vinegar dressing—and a selection of fresh fish poached with basil and cream. Lunch might present chicken with tarragon or a wild mushroom stir-fry. If you still can't decide, try the fixed-price lunch (£9.45–£11.75) or dinner (£17.25), both excellent values. Be sure to make reservations in summer. ⊠ *15/16 Market St.,* ☎ *0131/225–1084. AE, MC, V.*

Vegetarian

£   ✕ **Banns Vegetarian Cafe.** Just off the Royal Mile in the heart of the
Old Town, Banns serves a tasty range of nonmeat fare in a light and
airy room with sturdy wooden furniture. Enjoy a cup of coffee with a
decadently sinful cake delivered daily by a local French patisserie, or
dine on a phyllo basket of cream cheese, herbs, and vegetables, or en-
chiladas. Allow plenty of time, as service can be slow. ⊠ *5 Hunter Sq.,*
☎ *0131/226–1112. AE, MC, V.*

New Town

Chinese

££   ✕ **Kweilin.** This pleasant family-run restaurant in Edinburgh's sedate
New Town is popular with the city's Chinese community. Among the
traditional Chinese decor are several large paintings depicting scenes
from the Kwangsi province, of which Kweilin is the capital. The suggested menus for two, three, or four diners are a good value, from £10–
£28.50 per person. Two à la carte highlights are the deep-fried crispy
chicken on the bone, and the meat-stuffed eggplant on a hot plate. ⊠
19–21 Dundas St., ☎ *0131/557–1875. AE, MC, V. Closed Mon. except during Dec.*

Eclectic

££   ✕ **The Dome.** The splendid interior of this former bank, with its painted
plasterwork and central dome, provides an elegant backdrop for relaxed dining or just a drink at the central bar, where sophisticated professional types wind down after work. The toasted BLT sandwiches
are almost big enough for two, but if you are feeling hungrier, the eclectic menu offers many other options: try the *penne rigate* (medium-size
pasta tubes scored with lines lengthwise) sautéed in a basil cream
sauce with fresh mussels, or the smoked chicken salad on a bed of wa-
tercress. ⊠ *14 George St.,* ☎ *0131/624–8624. AE, MC, V.*

French

££££   ✕ **Pompadour.** As may be expected of a restaurant named after the
★   king's mistress, Madame de Pompadour, the decor here is inspired by
the court of Louis XV, with subtle plasterwork and rich murals. The
cuisine is also classic French, with top-quality Scottish produce com-
pleting the happiest of alliances. The extensive, well-chosen wine list
complements such dishes as sea bass with crispy leeks and caviar butter sauce, whole lobster with mustard and cheese, or loin of venison
with potato pancakes. This is the place to go if you want a festive night
out. It's more relaxed and informal at lunchtime. ⊠ *Caledonian hotel,
Princes St.,* ☎ *0131/459–9988. Jacket and tie. AE, DC, MC, V. No
lunch weekends.*

Italian

£–££   ✕ **La Lanterna.** This inconspicuous pine-walled and postcard-pinned
★   basement-level trattoria serves wholesome and straightforward pastas—
among them tagliatelle Lanterna (with eggplant, tomato, and an-
chovies in a cheese and cream sauce) and *spaghetti al mare* (spaghetti
with seafood)—and other Italian dishes. The family who runs the business is cheerful; their unaffected approach is popular and packs in the
customers. Seats are comfortable, though tables are set close. It's in
the city center, two minutes from Princes Street. ⊠ *83 Hanover St.,* ☎
0131/226–3090. AE, MC, V. Closed Sun.

£   ✕ **Bar Napoli.** This cellar restaurant with whitewashed walls, green-
and-white checked tablecloths, and open kitchen promises a "genuine
Italian experience." The chef describes his *pizza "rusticana"* (with
tomatoes, mozzarella cheese, fried red peppers, mushrooms, chopped
chicken, artichokes, black olives, and oregano) as his "greatest work

of art," but there is an extensive menu of other pizzas, pasta dishes, antipasti, and ice cream for dessert. ⊠ *75 Hanover St.,* ☎ *0131/225–2600. AE, MC, V.*

Scottish

££££ ✕ **Grill Room.** Set in the Edwardian splendor of the Balmoral Hotel (☞ Lodging, *below*), the Grill Room has established itself at the top end of Edinburgh's dining scene. The Asian-theme room has a luxurious ambience created by a green marble floor, Chinese lacquer wall panels, and an abundance of silver and crystal. The service is formal but relaxed, with no pressure to finish. As its name suggests, the restaurant specializes in grills, but the à la carte menu is extensive. ⊠ *Princes St.,* ☎ *0131/556–2414. Reservations essential. Jacket and tie. AE, DC, MC, V.*

££–£££ ✕ **Martins.** Don't be put off by the typically forbidding northern fa-
★ cade of this restaurant, tucked away in a little back alley between Frederick and Castle streets. All's well in this place for serious eating in an unstuffy atmosphere. The menu emphasizes organically grown local products and wild-caught foods. Typical modern Scottish dishes include fillet of turbot, pan fried with fennel, shiitake mushrooms, and green peppercorn sauce, or charred lamb fillet with couscous, spinach, and an anise sauce. The cheese board, famed far and wide, has a sampling of Scottish and Irish cheeses. Lunches are an excellent value. The wine list includes an excellent choice of half-bottles. Smoking is not permitted. ⊠ *70 Rose St. North La.,* ☎ *0131/225–3106. Reservations essential. AE, DC, MC, V. Closed Sun., and Mon except during Festival. No lunch Sat.*

Thai

££ ✕ **Buntoms Thai Restaurant.** A room in the Linden Hotel was converted into this authentic-looking Thai restaurant by the addition of genuine Thai wall coverings and antiques. You can leave Georgian New Town at the door and be transported halfway around the world with such savory delights as hot-and-sour squid and mushroom salad, seafood with broccoli in oyster sauce, or spiced chicken fried with cashew nuts and onions (one of this restaurant's best offerings). Don't come here if you're on a tight schedule—each dish is prepared fresh, but it's definitely worth the wait. ⊠ *Linden Hotel, 9–13 Nelson St.,* ☎ *0131/557–4344. Reservations essential. AE, DC, MC, V. No lunch Sun.*

Vegetarian

£–££ ✕ **Hendersons.** This was Edinburgh's original vegetarian restaurant long before it was fashionable to offer healthy, meatless creations. Tasty options include eggplant, tomato, and chick-pea curry, or leek and Stilton pie. If you haven't summoned the courage to try an authentic haggis while in Scotland, come here to sample a vegetarian version. The Bistro Bar owned by the same proprietors around the corner on Thistle Street is also open Sunday noon–6. ⊠ *94 Hanover St.,* ☎ *0131/225–2131. AE, DC, MC, V. Closed Sun. (except during festival).*

Haymarket

Cajun

£–££ ✕ **Old Orleans.** A first in Edinburgh: Cajun cooking, served with real Southern panache, plus Mexican and American dishes that include red snapper and swordfish. Smothered turkey, traditional jambalaya, and spareribs (they come with a large bib and finger bowl of hot water) are often on the menu. Decor is typical New Orleans: trellis and metalwork, brass instruments, and travel-related mementos; the music is blues and jazz. There is also a large, mirrored, American-style bar. ⊠ *30 Grindlay St.,* ☎ *0131/229–1511. AE, DC, MC, V.*

Edinburgh Dining and Lodging

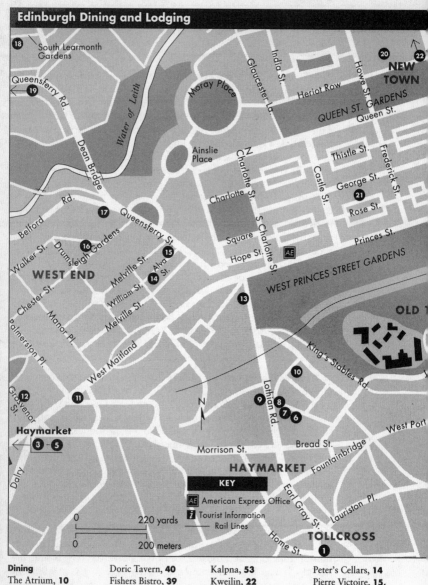

South Learmonth Gardens

Queensferry Rd.

Water of Leith

Moray Place

India St.

Gloucester La.

Heriot Row

Howe St.

NEW TOWN

QUEEN ST. GARDENS

Queen St.

Ainslie Place

Dean Bridge

Rd.

Belford Rd.

Queensferry St.

Walker St.

Drumsleigh Gardens

WEST END

Chester St.

Manor Pl.

Palmerston Pl.

Melville St.

William St.

Melville St.

Alva St.

Charlotte St.

S. Charlotte St.

Square

Hope St.

Thistle St.

George St.

Rose St.

Princes St.

Castle St.

Frederick St.

AE

WEST PRINCES STREET GARDENS

OLD T

King's Stables Rd.

West Maitland

Grosvenor St.

Haymarket

Dalry

Lothian Rd.

N

Morrison St.

Bread St.

West Port

HAYMARKET

Fountainbridge

Earl Gray St.

Lauriston Pl.

Home St.

TOLLCROSS

KEY

AE American Express Office

i Tourist Information

— Rail Lines

0 — 220 yards

0 — 200 meters

Dining

The Atrium, **10**
Banns Vegetarian Cafe, **43**
Bar Napoli, **29**
Beehive Inn, **48**
Buntoms Thai Restaurant, **25**
The Dome, **30**

Doric Tavern, **40**
Fishers Bistro, **39**
Grill Room, **32**
Hendersons, **27**
Howie's, **55**
Indian Cavalry Club, **11**
Jackson's, **41**
Jasmine, **6**

Kalpna, **53**
Kweilin, **22**
La Lanterna, **28**
Malmaison Café Bar & Brasserie, **36**
Martins, **21**
Merchants, **45**
Ndebele, **1**
Old Orleans, **7**

Peter's Cellars, **14**
Pierre Victoire, **15, 34, 37, 44, 47**
Pompadour, **13**
Skippers Bistro, **38**
Thai Orchid, **8**
Witchery by the Castle, **46**

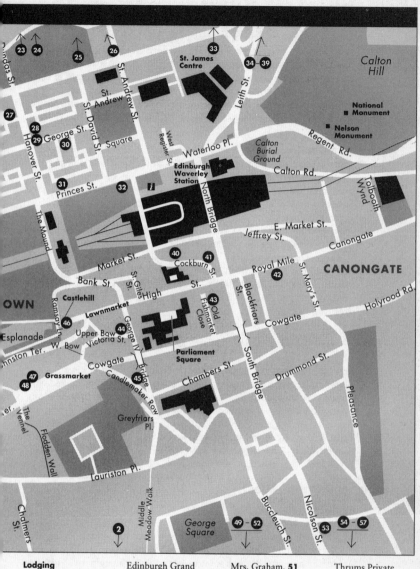

Lodging

Ashdene House, **49**

Balmoral Hotel, **32**

The Bonham, **16**

Caledonian, **13**

Channings, **18**

Classic Guest House, **50**

Crannoch But & Ben, **19**

Drummond House, **26**

Edinburgh Grand Sheraton, **9**

Ellesmere Guest House, **2**

Gloria's Place, **35**

Holiday Inn Crown Plaza, **42**

The Howard, **23**

Jarvis Mount Royal Hotel, **31**

Lodge Hotel, **3**

Malmaison, **36**

Mrs. Graham, **51**

Norton House, **5**

Roselea House, **52**

17 Abercrombie Place, **24**

Sibbet House, **20**

16 Lynedoch Place, **17**

Stakis Edinburgh Grosvenor Hotel, **12**

Stuart House, **33**

Teviotdale House, **54**

Thrums Private Hotel, **57**

Turret Guest House, **56**

22 Murrayfield Gardens, **4**

Chinese

£–££   ✕ **Jasmine.** Seafood is the specialty of this small, friendly, candlelit Cantonese restaurant, with rapid service to deal with the constant stream of customers, even in midweek. The subdued cream decor with wooden screens is relaxing, although tables are quite closely spaced. Delicious dishes include crispy monkfish with honey sauce, baked crabs in black bean sauce, and fried oysters with ginger and spring onions. For two or more people, the set menus are a good value. A take-out menu is available. ⊠ *32 Grindlay St.*, ☎ *0131/229–5757. AE, MC, V.*

Scottish

£££   ✕ **The Atrium.** With its cream-color tented fabric ceiling, smart cream
★   cotton chair covers, and wrought-iron candlesticks and unusual candelabra, the Atrium is a distinctive setting for pre- or post-theater dinner (the Traverse Theatre is right next door). The cuisine's hallmark is the use of typical Scottish ingredients in atypical combinations: curly kale, once the staple of every Scottish rural home, may be married with beef, bacon, and shallots, and salmon is paired with zucchini, red pepper, and Parmesan. The menu changes daily, but there is always a vegetarian option. For a lighter snack, try the upstairs café-restaurant Blue (☎ 0131/221–1222), under the same ownership. ⊠ *10 Cambridge St. (beneath Saltire Ct.)*, ☎ *0131/228–8882. AE, MC, V. Closed Sun. (except during festival) and last 2 wks of Dec. No lunch Sat. (except during festival).*

Thai

£–££   ✕ **Thai Orchid.** The theme is green at this bowfront restaurant, where green walls and brightly colored Thai silks set off Thai statues and gold masks. The food is a genuine taste of Thailand: the first king of Thailand once enjoyed *gaeng masaman* (beef or chicken slow cooked with roasted peanuts and potatoes), and other menu options include *goong nung* (king prawns steamed with lemongrass, white wine, lime juice, and coriander), and *gai yang* (chicken breast marinated with ground rice, garlic, soy sauce, and ground herbs, char grilled and served with sticky rice and chili pepper dip). ⊠ *44 Grindlay St.*, ☎ *0141/228–4438, AE, MC, V. Closed Sun. No lunch Sat.*

West End and Points West

Eclectic

£–££   ✕ **Peter's Cellars.** With a traditional "country cottage" look, complete with wooden booths, flowered curtains, and well-spaced tables, this cellar wine bar-cum-restaurant is casual and relaxing. The food is carefully prepared, though some rather unlikely "imaginative" touches turn up: bacon-wrapped chicken on a bed of haggis! Try the *escalope* (cutlet) of salmon and prawns baked in phyllo pastry on a sweet pepper salsa. ⊠ *11–13 William St.*, ☎ *0131/226–3161. AE, MC, V.*

Indian

£££   ✕ **Indian Cavalry Club.** The menu of this cool and sophisticated Indian restaurant reflects a confident, up-to-date approach. With its steamed specialties, it's almost nouvelle Indian. The Club Tent in the basement serves light meals. ⊠ *3 Atholl Pl.*, ☎ *0131/228–3282. AE, DC, MC, V.*

South Side

African

£   ✕ **Ndebele.** This small, very friendly café—named after the colorful tribe from South Africa and Zimbabwe who have maintained the customs and language of their Zulu ancestors—is ideally placed for a snack before a trip to the Cameo cinema opposite. The wood-paneled, geometric-patterned walls in bright shades of purple and orange are hung with African art. The large range of interesting sandwiches on a choice of breads, the tasty *boerewors* (South African sausage), or smoked ostrich can be eaten on the spot, or ordered out, and there is also a large selection of deli products for sale, including *biltong* (strips of cured, air-dried meat). A small art gallery downstairs has changing exhibitions of African artwork for sale. ⊠ *57 Home St., Tollcross,* ☎ *0131/221–1141 No credit cards.*

French

£–££ ✗ **Howie's.** The steaks at this lively chain of simple neighborhood, French-style bistros are tender Aberdeen beef, and the Loch Fyne herring are sweet-cured to Howie's own recipe. All three restaurants are licensed, but you can bring your own bottle if you want to. All branches are closed Monday lunch, except for Bruntsfield Place. ⊠ *75 St. Leonard's St.,* ☎ *0131/668–2917;* ⊠ *208 Bruntsfield Pl.,* ☎ *0131/ 221–1777;* ⊠ *63 Dalry Rd.,* ☎ *0131/313–3334. AE, MC, V. No lunch Mon.*

Indian

£–££ ✗ **Kalpna.** This vegetarian Indian restaurant is on the city's South Side,
★   close to the university. The unremarkable facade among an ordinary row of shops and the low-key decor enlivened by Indian prints and fabric pictures belies the food—unlike anything you are likely to encounter elsewhere in the city. If you can't decide what you want to eat, order an *anapurna thali,* a sampler tray that here generally comes with curried vegetables complemented with coconut, peas, melt-in-the-mouth halvah, fresh coriander, and a touch of garlic. Kalpna tends to fill up as the evening progresses, so book ahead if you want to eat after 8. ⊠ *2/3 St. Patricks Sq.,* ☎ *0131/667–9890. MC, V. Closed Sun. except in the summer season.*

Leith

French

£–££ ✗ **Malmaison Café Bar and Brasserie.** Freshly made soups, crunchy salads, inventive sandwiches (try the roasted red pepper and pesto), and gooey pastries are the choices in this eatery, part of the stylish Malmaison Hotel (☞ Lodging, *below*) in Edinburgh's rejuvenated dockside area. Extremely popular are the Malmaison fish cakes with chips, buttered spinach, and parsley sauce; if you fancy something more substantial (and more expensive), try the Brasserie (reservations essential), which offers traditional French and modern British cuisine. ⊠ *1 Tower Pl., Leith,* ☎ *0131/555–6868. AE, DC, MC, V.*

Seafood

££   ✗ **Fishers Bistro.** This pub-cum-bistro down on the waterfront in Leith is popular with both locals and visitors (reservations advised). Bar meals are served, but for more comfort and elegance sit in the cozy green-walled dining room. Seafood is a specialty: watch the blackboard for the daily special, perhaps spicy sweet-potato and turnip soup followed by seared swordfish steak with sweet chili pepper sauce. ⊠ *1 The Shore,* ☎ *0131/554–5666. AE, DC, MC, V.*

££   ✗ **Skippers Bistro.** Don't miss this superb seafood restaurant, tucked away in a corner of Leith. It was once a traditional pub and still retains its snug and cluttered ambience, with dark wood, shining brass, and lots of pictures and ephemera. As a starter the delectable home-made fish cakes can't be beat. Main dishes change daily but might feature halibut, salmon, monkfish, or sea bass in delicious and innovative sauces. ⊠ *1A Dock Pl.,* ☎ *0131/554–1018, Reservations essential. AE, MC, V.*

LODGING

If you are planning to stay in Edinburgh during the festival, be sure to reserve several months in advance. Also note that weekend rates in the larger hotels are always much cheaper than midweek rates, so if you want to stay in a plush hotel, come on the weekend.

CATEGORY	COST*
££££	over £120
£££	£90–£120
££	£60–£90
£	under £60

All prices are for a standard double room, including service, breakfast, and VAT.

Old Town

££££ 🏨 **Holiday Inn Crown Plaza.** Although it was built late in the 1980s, this well-located modern hotel blends into its surroundings among the ancient buildings on the Royal Mile. Guest rooms are spacious, neat, and plain—practical rather than luxurious. ⊠ *80 High St., Royal Mile, EH1 1TH,* ☎ *0131/557–9797,* FAX *0131/557–9789. 238 rooms with bath. Restaurant, indoor pool, health club, meeting rooms, parking (fee). AE, DC, MC, V.*

New Town

££££ 🏨 **Balmoral Hotel.** The attention to detail in the elegant rooms and the
★ sheer élan that has re-created the Edwardian heyday of this former grand railroad hotel all contribute to the Balmoral's growing popularity. Staying here, below the impressive clock tower marking the east end of Princes Street, gives you a strong sense of being at the center of Edinburgh life. The hotel's main restaurant is the plush and stylish Grill Room (☞ Dining, *above*). ⊠ *1 Princes St., EH2 2EQ,* ☎ *0131/556–2414,* FAX *0131/557–3747. 189 rooms with bath, 21 suites. 2 restaurants, 2 bars, indoor pool, beauty salon, health club, parking (fee). AE, DC, MC, V.*

££££ 🏨 **Caledonian.** A conspicuous block of red sandstone beyond the west
★ end of West Princes Street Gardens, "the Caley" was built 1898–1902 as the flagship hotel of the Caledonian Railway, and its imposing Victorian decor has been faithfully preserved. The public area has marbled green columns and an ornate stairwell with a burnished-metalwork balustrade. Rooms are exceptionally large and well appointed, and the generous width of the corridors reminds guests that this establishment was designed in a more sumptuous age. ⊠ *Princes St., EH1 2AB,* ☎ *0131/459–9988,* FAX *0131/225–6632. 246 rooms with bath. 2 restaurants, parking (fee). AE, DC, MC, V.*

££££ 🏨 **The Howard.** The Howard, close to Drummond Place, is a classic
★ New Town building, elegant and superbly proportioned. It is also small enough to offer personal attention. You'll like it if you enjoy a swank private club atmosphere. All guest rooms are spacious and furnished with antiques and original works of art, and some overlook the garden. The hotel's acclaimed contemporary restaurant, 36, features innately Scottish dishes with worldly influences. ⊠ *34 Great King St., EH3 6QH,* ☎ *0131/557–3500, 0131/315–2220 reservations,* FAX *0131/557–6515. 15 rooms with bath. Restaurant, free parking. AE, DC, MC, V.*

££££ 🏨 **Jarvis Mount Royal Hotel.** Perched above the ground-floor shops on Princes Street, overlooking Edinburgh Castle and the West Princes Street Gardens, the Mount Royal (and its entrance) is almost hidden between two of the city's major stores (Jenners and Marks & Spencer) and could easily be overlooked. Guest rooms have wood furnishings and pastel colors; the best views are from the rooms at the front of the hotel. ✉ *53 Princes St., EH2 2DG,* ☎ *0131/225–7161,* 𝖥𝖠𝖷 *0131/220–4671. 158 rooms with bath. Restaurant. AE, DC, MC, V.*

££–£££ 🏠 **Drummond House.** Many hotels would be put to shame by the ac-
★ commodations at this top-of-the-heap guest house in the heart of the New Town, within walking distance of the city center. The Georgian terraced house has spacious rooms, sumptuously decorated and furnished with swagged curtains, canopied beds, and antique furniture—all in elegant taste to suit the age of the house. Smoking is not permitted inside Drummond House, but guests can smoke while strolling through the several acres of private gardens across the road, open only to Drummond Place residents and hotel guests. ✉ *17 Drummond Pl., EH3 6PL,* ☎ 𝖥𝖠𝖷 *0131/557–9189. 4 rooms with bath. MC, V.*

££ 🏠 **Gloria's Place.** This luxurious Georgian B&B (built before George Washington was president) is a 20-minute walk from the city center. Well-equipped bedrooms (including direct-dial phone and laptop computer outlets) are complemented by the comfortable sitting room with its wall of books. Smoking is not permitted. ✉ *20 London St., EH3 6NA,* ☎ *0131/557–0216,* 𝖥𝖠𝖷 *0131/556–6445. 3 rooms with bath. MC, V.*

££ 🏠 **17 Abercrombie Place.** An exceptional standard is set at this bed-
★ and-breakfast in the center of the New Town. Stunning views can be had from the top-floor rooms of this Georgian terraced house characterized by shuttered windows and antique furniture and rugs (some used as wall hangings). The host—a keen golfer—and the hostess—a lawyer—both enjoy meeting guests and are very helpful. Dinner can be provided (for guests only) by prior arrangement. This house is unusual for the area, as it has parking spaces for seven cars. ✉ *17 Abercrombie Pl., EH3 6LB,* ☎ *0131/557–8036,* 𝖥𝖠𝖷 *0131/558–3453. 9 rooms with bath or shower. Dining room, free parking. MC, V.*

££ 🏠 **Sibbet House.** The late-18th-century Georgian elegance of this small
★ terraced town house in Edinburgh's New Town has been enhanced by careful attention to drapery, decor, and period antique furniture. Prices are reasonable, it is no-smoking throughout, and breakfasts are traditionally Scottish and sustaining, to say the least. You must eat out in the evenings, but all kinds of restaurants are only a few minutes' stroll away. Three self-catering apartments are also available. This establishment also offers a perk that few others can match—the host plays the bagpipes on request. ✉ *26 Northumberland St., EH3 6LS,* ☎ *0131/556–1078,* 𝖥𝖠𝖷 *0131/557–9445. 4 rooms with bath or shower, 1 suite, 3 apartments. MC, V.*

££ 🏠 **Stuart House.** Within a 15-minute walk from the city center, this
★ B&B is in a Victorian terraced house with some fine plasterwork. The decor suits the structure: bold colors, floral fabrics, and generously curtained windows combine with antique and traditional-style furniture and chandeliers to create an opulent ambience. Smoking is not permitted. ✉ *12 E. Claremont St., EH7 4JP,* ☎ *0131/557–9030,* 𝖥𝖠𝖷 *0131/557–0563. 7 rooms with bath or shower. AE, MC, V.*

Haymarket

££££ 🏠 **Edinburgh Grand Sheraton.** Beyond the reception area and sweeping grand staircase, guest rooms here are well above average size; many are traditional with tartan furnishings and prints of old Edinburgh. The grandest rooms face the castle. This property has two fine restaurants: the brasserie-style Terrace, overlooking Edinburgh Castle and Festival Square, and the intimate Grill Room, serving fine fish, game, and Scottish beef. The hotel's popularity with locals, especially after work and in the evening before and after concerts at Usher Hall, across the street, testifies to its continuing part in Edinburgh's social life. ⊠ *1 Festival Sq., EH3 9SR, ☎ 0131/229–9131, 囲 0131/228–4510. 264 rooms with bath. 2 restaurants, bar, indoor pool, health club, free parking. AE, DC, MC, V.*

West End and Points West

££££   🏨 **The Bonham.** This brand-new contemporary hotel in a traditional town-house space boldly mixes sleek design with state-of-the-art business accommodation. Beyond unassuming white hallways, each room is a unique minimalist concept, with modern pieces from local artists, geometric furnishings, and attractive lighting. The modern restaurant—in chic unadorned style with oversize mirrors and a central catwalk of light—serves Californian twists on Scottish specialties. Leisure and business travelers alike will feel well cared for with the thorough yet unobtrusive service. ⊠ *35 Drumsheugh Gardens EH3 7RN, ☎ 0131/ 226–6050, reservations 0131/623–6060, 囲 0131/226–6080. 50 rooms with bath. Restaurant, meeting rooms. AE, MC, V. Closed Dec. 24–26*

££££   🏨 **Channings.** Five Edwardian terraced town houses make up this in-
 ★   timate, elegant hotel in an upscale West End neighborhood just minutes from the west end of Princes Street. Beyond the clubby, oak-paneled lobby lounge, the quiet guest rooms with restrained colors, antiques, marble baths, and great views of Fife (from those facing north) set a stylish, refined tone. The Brasserie offers excellent value in traditional Scottish and Continental cooking, especially at lunchtime; try the crab cakes with crayfish bisque. ⊠ *15 South Learmonth Gardens, EH4 1EZ, ☎ 0131/315–2226, 0131/332–3232 reservations, 囲 0131/332– 9631. 48 rooms with bath or shower. Restaurant. AE, DC, MC, V.*

££££   🏨 **Norton House.** This magnificent 1861 manor house was once the home of the Usher brewing family and still has the feeling of a private country home. Situated on idyllic grounds on the western outskirts of Edinburgh, the Norton House provides a lovely alternative to downtown lodgings, yet is easily accessible from the city center. The elegant and refurbished reception area is graced by marble pillars; a striking wooden staircase leads to the upper floors. The airy guest rooms are decorated with modern furniture and delicate pastel shades. Guests can choose between two restaurants—the Conservatory, with its fine views of the gardens, offers decent Continental food, and The Gathering serves bistro fare. ⊠ *Ingliston, EH28 8LX, ☎ 0131/333–1275, 囲 0131/333– 5305. 47 rooms with bath. 2 restaurants, bar, airport shuttle, free parking. AE, DC, MC, V.*

££–£££   🏨 **Stakis Edinburgh Grosvenor Hotel.** This attractive, comfortable hotel in the West End comprises several converted terrace houses and is distinguished by an elegant Victorian facade. Guests are pampered as soon as they enter the large reception area, furnished with ample Chesterfield armchairs. The single rooms are fairly small, and the doubles are just adequate. All are brightly decorated with peach curtains and floral bedspreads; the furniture is made of dark wood. First- and second-floor bedrooms have high ceilings with attractive plaster cornices. Just a short walk from the West End's shopping district, the hotel is convenient to the Haymarket railway station. ⊠ *Grosvenor St., EH12 5EF, ☎ 0131/226–6001, 囲 0131/220–2387. 188 rooms with bath. Restaurant, 2 bars. AE, DC, MC, V.*

££   🏨 **Lodge Hotel.** This detached Georgian stone house, a 15-minute
 ★   walk from Princes Street, is easy to find on the main A8 Edinburgh– Glasgow road. Spacious rooms—all no-smoking—are furnished in period style, with swagged curtains and canopied beds, and are stocked with fresh flowers and fruit as well as a decanter of sherry. Downstairs,

there is a cocktail bar and peaceful pink-and-gray sitting room. The dining room has well-spaced tables covered with crisp white cloths and a menu heavy on fresh Scottish produce. ✉ *6 Hampton Terr., West Coates, EH12 5JD,* ☎ *0131/337–3682,* 𝔽𝔸𝕏 *0131/313–1700. 12 rooms with shower. Dining room. MC, V.*

££ 🏠 **16 Lynedoch Place.** You'll find considerate hosts in Andrew and Susie Hamilton (and Gertrude, the lovable dog), who have opened up their beautiful Georgian terraced house as a B&B, a five-minute walk from the center. Rooms (one single and two doubles, all no smoking) are tasteful, with rosy pinks, cool yellows, terra-cotta oranges, and floral patterns. Breakfast is served in a magnificent hunter-green dining room with antiques and family pictures, and Susie goes all out. In a pinch, they will open up the twin and single rooms upstairs for a family. ✉ *16 Lynedoch Pl. EH3 7PY,* ☎ *0131/225–5507,* 𝔽𝔸𝕏 *0131/226–4185. 3 rooms, 1 with bath, 1 with shower. Dining room, library, free parking. MC, V. Closed Dec. 23–27.*

££ 🏠 **22 Murrayfield Gardens.** A handsome, stone detached house with
★ easy parking in an upscale residential area called Murrayfield just a 10-minute bus ride from downtown, this is an impressive B&B on all counts with particularly friendly host and hostess. Warm yellows are used in the elegant decor of the first-floor lounge, sunny dining room, and bedrooms with panoramic views. Dinner can be provided with prior notice. ✉ *22 Murrayfield Gardens, EH12 6DF,* ☎ *0131/337–3569,* 𝔽𝔸𝕏 *0131/337–3803. 3 rooms, 2 with bath and shower, 1 with shower. Dining room, free parking. MC, V. Closed during Christmas, 2 wks Feb.*

£ 🏠 **Crannoch But & Ben.** This tip-top (no-smoking) B&B offers private baths, a comfortable residents' lounge, and good hearty breakfasts. Only 3 mi from the city and on a good bus route, it's also particularly convenient to the airport. ✉ *467 Queensferry Rd., EH4 7ND,* ☎ *0131/ 336–5688. 2 rooms with bath. Free parking. No credit cards.*

South Side

££ 🏠 **Ashdene House.** On a quiet residential street on the South Side, only 10 minutes from the city center by bus, this Edwardian house is a first-class B&B that forbids smoking. Bedrooms are decorated without frills or flounces—just modern furnishings and floral fabrics—but in the downstairs public areas, deep, rich color schemes complement the age of the house. The owners are particularly helpful in arranging tours and evening theater entertainment, and they will recommend local restaurants. There is ample parking on the street and in a lot. ✉ *23 Fountainhall Rd., EH9 2LN,* ☎ *0131/667–6026. 5 rooms with shower. Free parking. No credit cards.*

££ 🏠 **Classic Guest House.** It is easy to find this Victorian terraced house, on a main route from the south into Edinburgh. The decor is modern classic: stripped pine floors throughout, elegant chinoiserie in the dining room, and pastel florals in the warm bedrooms. Smoking is not permitted. Note that three of the four rooms have en suite showers only. ✉ *50 Mayfield Rd., EH9 2NH,* ☎ *0131/667–5847,* 𝔽𝔸𝕏 *0131/662– 1016. 4 rooms with shower or bath. Dining room. MC, V.*

££ 🏠 **Ellesmere Guest House.** Yet another Victorian terraced house, this B&B is close to the King's Theatre and several good restaurants. Its first-class rooms have modern furniture with pleasant pastel floral bedspreads and curtains; one room has a four-poster bed. Guests can relax in the comfortable sitting room, but the owners prefer that they not smoke. Ellesmere is stocked with brochures covering things to do in Edinburgh. ✉ *11 Glengyle Terr., EH3 9LN,* ☎ *0131/229–4823,* 𝔽𝔸𝕏 *0131/229–5285. 6 rooms, 1 with bath, 5 with shower. No credit cards, but dollar checks accepted.*

££   ⊞ **Roselea House.** Another South Side B&B guest house, on the main route from the south, the Roselea is easy to find. The Victorian house is decorated in "a touch of tartan," and there is a sitting room for guests. ⊠ *11 Mayfield Rd., EH9 2NG,* ☎ *0131/667–6115,* FAX *0131/667–3556. 7 rooms with bath or shower. Free parking (for 3 rooms). AE, MC, V.*

££   ⊞ **Thrums Private Hotel.** There is a pleasing mix of the modern and traditional in this detached Victorian house. It is small, cozy, and quiet, yet surprisingly close to downtown. ⊠ *14–15 Minto St., EH9 1RQ,* ☎ *0131/667–5545,* FAX *0131/667–8707. 15 rooms, 8 with bath, 7 with shower. Restaurant, bar, free parking. MC, V.*

£–££   ⊞ **Teviotdale House.** This is a small, family-run and -owned hotel in the genteel South Side. The friendly Covilles are the hosts, and the house is a warm retreat on a tree-lined street away from but within reach of city-center bustle (a 10-minute bus ride). Individually decorated rooms and innovative, appetizing home cooking make this a pleasant, reasonable budget alternative to center-city hotels. The establishment is entirely no-smoking. Note that five of the rooms have en suite showers only. ⊠ *53 Grange Loan, EH9 2ER,* ☎ FAX *0131/667–4376. 7 rooms with bath or shower. Dining room. AE, MC, V.*

£   ⊞ **Mrs. Graham.** It may be difficult to find a parking space on the quiet
★   back street where this Victorian terraced house is situated (South Side/Newington), but it's easy enough to take Bus 3, 31, 69, 80, or 81 here, south from the city center. The spotlessly clean B&B has antique furniture complemented by beautiful kilim rugs and wall hangings. The two rooms share one bath. ⊠ *18 Moston Terr., EH9 2DE,* ☎ *0131/667–3466. 2 rooms without bath. No credit cards. Closed Sept.–Apr.*

£   ⊞ **Turret Guest House.** On a quiet residential street on the South Side, this B&B is close to bus routes as well as the Commonwealth Pool and Holyrood Park. Cheerful and cozy, it has modern furnishings, but many of the building's Victorian cornices, paneled doors, and high ceilings remain. ⊠ *8 Kilmaurs Terr., EH16 5DR,* ☎ *0131/667–6704,* FAX *0131/668–1368. 6 rooms, 4 with shower. MC, V.*

Leith

£££   ⊞ **Malmaison.** Once a seamen's hostel, the Malmaison in the heart of Leith is a new departure for Edinburgh's hotel scene. It offers good value yet stylish digs only 10 minutes by bus from the city center. Public areas are swathed in dramatic black, cream, and taupe color schemes. King-size beds, CD players, and satellite TV are standard in all bedrooms, decorated in a chic, bold modern style. The French theme of the hotel (sister to the Malmaison in Glasgow) is emphasized in the Café Bar and Brasserie (☞ Dining, *above*), serving all day. ⊠ *1 Tower Pl., Leith, EH6 7DB,* ☎ *0131/555–6868,* FAX *0131/555–6999. 60 rooms with bath. Restaurant, bar, café, free parking. AE, DC, MC, V.*

NIGHTLIFE AND THE ARTS

The Arts

The List, available from newsagents throughout the city, *The Day by Day List,* and *Events 1999,* available from the Information Centre (⊠ 3 Princes St., ☎ 0131/557–1700) carry the most up-to-date details about cultural events. *The Scotsman,* an Edinburgh daily, also carries reviews in its arts pages on Monday and Wednesday and daily during the Festival. Tickets are generally available from box offices in advance; in some cases, from certain designated travel agents; or at the door, although concerts by national orchestras often sell out long before the day of the performance.

Dance

Edinburgh has no ballet or modern-dance companies of its own, but visiting companies perform from time to time at the Festival Theatre or Royal Lyceum (☞ *below*).

Festivals

The **Edinburgh International Festival** (⊠ Edinburgh Festival Office, The Festival Centre, Castlehill, EH1 1BW, ☎ 0131/473–2001, FAX 0131/473–2002), August 15–September 4, 1999, the premier arts event of the year, has for more than half a century attracted performing artists of international caliber to a celebration of music, dance, and drama.

The **Edinburgh Festival Fringe** (⊠ Edinburgh Festival Fringe Office, 180 High St., EH1 1QS, ☎ 0131/226–5257 or 0131/226–5259, FAX 0131/220–4205) offers many theatrical and musical events, some by amateur groups (you have been warned), and is more of a grab bag than the official festival. During festival time (same as the International Festival) it's possible to arrange your own entertainment program from morning to midnight and beyond, if you do not feel overwhelmed by the variety available.

The **Edinburgh Film Festival** (⊠ Edinburgh Film Festival Office, at the Filmhouse, 88 Lothian Rd., EH3 9BZ, ☎ 0131/228–4051, FAX 0131/229–5501), August 15–29, 1999, is yet another aspect of this busy summer festival logjam.

The **Edinburgh Military Tattoo** (⊠ Edinburgh Military Tattoo Office, 32 Market St., EH1 1QB, ☎ 0131/225–1188, FAX 0131/225–8627), August 6–28, 1999, may not be art, but it is certainly entertainment. It is sometimes confused with the festival itself, partly because the dates overlap. This celebration of martial music and skills with bands and gymnastics and stunt motorcycle teams is set on the castle esplanade, and the dramatic backdrop augments the spectacle. Dress warmly for late-evening performances. Even if it rains the show most definitely goes on.

If you're a jazz enthusiast, you may delight in the August **International Jazz Festival** (⊠ 116 Canongate, EH8 8DD, ☎ 0131/225–2202). Away from the August–September festival overkill, **Shoots and Roots** (☎ FAX 0131/554–3092), the Edinburgh Folk Festival, takes place over Easter weekend (April 2–5, 1999) and also the third weekend in November (November 19–22, 1999) each year. The two events welcome city-wide performances by Scottish and international folk artists of the very highest renown, with Easter majoring in folk-rock crossover and November focusing on more traditional styles.

In an entirely different vein, the **Edinburgh International Science Festival** (☎ 0131/220–3977), held around Easter each year, aims to make science accessible, interesting, but above all fun. Children's events turn science into entertainment and are especially popular.

Film

Apart from cinema chains, Edinburgh has the excellent two-screen **Filmhouse** (⊠ 88 Lothian Rd., ☎ 0131/228–2688 box office), the best venue for modern, foreign-language, offbeat, or simply less-commercial films. Its diverse monthly program is available from the box office and at a variety of other locations throughout the city (at the Tourist Centre, for example, or in theater foyers).

The **Cameo** (⊠ 38 Home St., ☎ 0131/228–4141) has three extremely comfortable theaters, a bar, and late-night specials (☉ Thurs.–Sat. from 11:30 PM). The family-owned and -run **Dominion** (⊠ Newbattle Terr., ☎ 0131/447–2660) offers one of the most pleasant alternatives to the larger commercial cinemas.

Music

Usher Hall (✉ Lothian Rd., ☎ 0131/228–1155) is Edinburgh's grandest venue, but is currently closed for an extensive renovation. The **Festival Theatre** (✉ 13–29 Nicolson St., ☎ 0131/529–6000) hosts drama as well as concerts, including performances by the Royal Scottish National Orchestra in season. The **Queen's Hall** (✉ Clerk St., ☎ 0131/668–2019) is more intimate in scale and hosts smaller recitals. The **Playhouse** (✉ Greenside Pl., ☎ 0131/557–2692) leans toward popular artists.

The highlight of the year for jazz enthusiasts is the August International Jazz Festival (☞ *above*), but live jazz can also be found in the city throughout the year at venues such as Café Graffiti (☞ *below*). Consult *The List* for information.

Theater

MODERN

The **Traverse Theatre** (✉ 10 Cambridge St., ☎ 0131/228–1404) has developed a solid reputation for stimulating new work—though it has toned down its previously avant-garde approach. The **Netherbow Arts Centre** (✉ 43 High St., ☎ 0131/556–9579) includes modern plays in its program of music, drama, and cabaret. The **Theatre Workshop** (✉ 34 Hamilton Pl., ☎ 0131/226–5425) hosts fringe events during the Edinburgh Festival and modern, community-based theater all year.

TRADITIONAL

Edinburgh has three main theaters. The **Royal Lyceum** (✉ Grindlay St., ☎ 0131/229–9697) shows traditional plays and contemporary works, often transferred from or prior to their London "West End" showings. **Edinburgh Festival Theatre** (✉ 13–29 Nicolson St., ☎ 0131/529–6000) is the city's newest theater and hosts a variety of theatrical and musical entertainment. The **King's** (✉ 2 Leven St., ☎ 0131/229–1201) has a program of contemporary and traditional dramatic works.

The **Playhouse** (✉ Greenside Pl., ☎ 0131/557–2692) hosts mostly popular artists, musical comedies, and dance companies. At Musselburgh, on the eastern outskirts of Edinburgh, the **Brunton Theatre** (✉ Brunton Hall, High St., Musselburgh, ☎ 0131/665–2240) offers a regular program of performances. At the **Church Hill Theatre** (✉ Morningside Rd., ☎ 0131/447–7597), local dramatic societies mount productions of a high standard.

Nightlife

The Edinburgh and Scotland Information Centre above Waverley Market (✉ 3 Princes St., ☎ 0131/557–1700) can supply information on various types of nightlife, especially on spots offering dinner-dances. *The List* provides a lot of information on the music scene.

Bars and Pubs

Abbotsford (✉ 3 Rose St., New Town, ☎ 0131/225–1894) offers an ever-changing selection of five real ales, bar lunches, and lots of Victorian atmosphere. **Cask and Barrel** (✉ 115 Broughton St., New Town, ☎ 0131/556–3132) is a spacious, busy pub in which to sample handpulled ales at the horseshoe bar, reflected in a collection of brewery mirrors. **Cloisters** (✉ 26 Brougham St., Tollcross West End, ☎ 0131/221–9997) is a West End pub priding itself on the absence of music, gaming machines, and any other modern pub gimmicks, and specializing in real ales, malt whiskies, and good food, all at reasonable prices. **Cumberland Bar** (✉ 1–3 Cumberland St., New Town, ☎ 0131/556–9409, closed Sun.) is not to be missed, with 18 ales on tap, wood trim, typical pub mirrors, and a comfy sitting room.

Drum and Monkey (⊠ 80 Queen St., New Town, ☎ 0131/538–8111), with cozy, dark wood booths and a maroon color scheme, is just the place for soup and sandwich lunches with a pint of Old Wallop beer. There is a bistro restaurant downstairs. **Guildford Arms** (⊠ 1 West Register St., east end of Princes St., New Town, ☎ 0131/556–4312) is worth a visit for its interior alone: ornate plasterwork, cornices, friezes, and wood paneling are the setting for some excellent draft ales, including Orkney Dark Island. **Harry's Bar** (⊠ 7B Randolph Pl., New Town, ☎ 0131/539–8100), an Americana-decorated basement bar with disco music, is hugely popular with locals. **Kay's Bar** (⊠ 39 Jamaica St., New Town, ☎ 0131/225–1858) is another friendly, comfortable New Town bar which is a good place for a bar lunch. Don't miss the selection of 50 single malt whiskies in addition to the real ales on draft. **Leslie's Bar** (⊠ 43 Ratcliffe Terr., South Side, ☎ 0131/667–7205) is convenient to the hotels and guest houses of Newington, with superb Victorian decor in its small saloon and public bars.

Madogs (⊠ 38A George St., New Town, ☎ 0131/225–3408) was one of Edinburgh's first all-American cocktail bar-restaurants; it remains popular with professionals after work, with live music most weeknights. The 260-year-old **Malt and Hops** (⊠ 45 The Shore, Leith, ☎ 0131/555–0083), with its own ghost and a choice of real ales, overlooks the waterfront down in Leith. **Milne's Bar** (⊠ 35 Rose St., New Town, ☎ 0131/225–6738) is known as the poets' pub because of its popularity with the Edinburgh literati. Pies and baked potatoes go well with seven real ales and varying guest beers (beers not of the house brewery). Victorian advertisements and photos of old Edinburgh give it an old-time feel. **Southsider** (⊠ 3–7 West Richmond St., South Side, ☎ 0131/667–2003), convenient for the antiques and junk shops of Causewayside, is a busy, sometimes smoky bar popular with locals and students.

Standing Order (⊠ 62–66 George St., New Town, ☎ 0131/225–4460), in a former banking hall with magnificent painted plasterwork ceiling, is one of the popular and expanding J D Wetherspoon chain of pubs priding itself on friendly, music-free watering holes with cheap beer and ample no-smoking areas—you can even lounge in leather armchairs. **Tiles** (⊠ 1 St. Andrew Sq., New Town, ☎ 0131/558–1507, closed Sun.), a converted banking hall, gets its name from the wealth of tiles covering the walls, which are topped by elaborate plasterwork. The large selection of real ales is complemented by a choice of bar meals or a table d'hôte menu specializing in fresh Scottish poultry, game, and fish.

Casinos
The following casinos are private, but membership can be granted with 24 hours' notice. All have American roulette, poker, blackjack, and slot machines and are open 2 PM–4 AM. You must be over 18 years old. **Stanley Berkeley** (⊠ 2 Rutland Pl., ☎ 0131/228–4446). **Stanley Martell** (⊠ 7 Newington Rd., ☎ 0131/667–7763). **The Stanley Edinburgh** (⊠ 5B York Pl., ☎ 0131/624–2121). **Stakis Maybury Casino** (⊠ 5 South Maybury, ☎ 0131/338–4444) has a highly rated restaurant.

Ceilidhs and Scottish Evenings
Several hotels feature traditional Scottish-music evenings in the summer season, including the **Carlton Highland Hotel** (⊠ North Bridge, ☎ 0131/556–7277) and the **King James Thistle Hotel** (⊠ Leith St., ☎ 0131/556–0111), which produces Jamie's Scottish Evening. Contact the hotels for information.

Nightclubs

Many Edinburgh discos offer reduced admission and/or less expensive drinks for early revelers. Consult *The List* for special events.

L'Attaché Nightclub (⊠ Beneath the Rutland Hotel, 1 Rutland St., West End, ☎ 0131/229–3402, closed Sun.–Tues.) features live folk and rock music. **Café Graffiti** (⊠ Mansfield Place Church, E. London St., West End, ☎ 0131/557–8003, closed Sun.–Thurs, except during Edinburgh Festival) books live bands and DJs playing jazz, jazzy funk, Latin, soul, and more. The popular **Club Mercado** (⊠ 36–39 Market St., Old Town, ☎ 0131/226–4224, closed Mon.–Thurs.) offers theme nights covering the full spectrum of musical sounds.

The Honeycomb (⊠ 36–38 Blair St., off High St., Old Town, ☎ 0131/220–4381, closed Mon.–Thurs.) is another hot spot with funky live sounds. **Minus One** (⊠ Carlton Highland Hotel, North Bridge, Old Town, ☎ 0131/556–7277, closed Sun.–Thurs.) specializes in mainstream sounds with a DJ both nights. **The Venue** (⊠ 15 Calton Rd., New Town, ☎ 0131/557–3073) blares varying beats, including techno and progressive house.

Folk Clubs

There are always folk performers in various pubs throughout the city, especially at **The Tron** (⊠ Hunter Sq., ☎ 0131/220–1591) and **The Green Tree** (⊠ Cowgate, ☎ 0131/225–1294). *The List* has details. **Shoots and Roots** (☞ Festivals, *above*), held Easter and in late November, is a traditional and contemporary festival.

OUTDOOR ACTIVITIES AND SPORTS

Edinburgh has joined in the fitness boom of the past decade.

Participant Sports

Biking

Rates in summer are £50 per week up to an 18-speed, and £60 for a mountain bike. Bicycles may be rented at **Sandy Gilchrist Cycles** (⊠ 1 Cadzow Pl., ☎ FAX 0131/652–1760) and **Bike Trax** (⊠ 13 Lochrin Pl., ☎ 0131/228–6333). **Recycling** (⊠ 25–27 Iona St., Leith, ☎ FAX 0131/553–1130 or 0131/467–7775), with the motto "Great Bikes, No Bull," runs a sell-and-buy-back scheme for longer periods (say, more than two weeks), which can save you money, and also offers especially good deals on weekly rates.

Golf

The Tourist Centre will provide local details, and the Scottish Tourist Board offers a free leaflet on golf in Scotland, available from the Edinburgh and Scotland Information Centre (⊠ 3 Princes St., ☎ 0131/557–1700. "SSS" indicates the "standard scratch score," or average score. For information on golfing throughout Scotland, *see* Chapter 2. The following courses are open to visitors.

Braids (⊠ 3 mi south of city, ☎ 0131/447–6666) Course 1, 18 holes, 5,731 yards, SSS 67; Course 2, 18 holes, 4,832 yards, SSS 63. **Bruntsfield Links** (⊠ 2 mi south of city, ☎ 0131/336–4050, FAX 0131/336–5538) 18 holes, 6,407 yards, SSS 71. **Craigentinny** (⊠ 3 mi east of city, ☎ 0131/554–7501) 18 holes, 5,407 yards, SSS 67. **Duddingston** (⊠ 4 mi east of city, ☎ FAX 0131/661–4301) 18 holes, 6,420 yards, SSS 71.

Liberton (⊠ Kingston Grange, 297 Gilmerton Rd., 4 mi south of city, ☎ 0131/664–8580, FAX 0131/666–0853) 18 holes, 5,306 yards, SSS 66. **Lothianburn** (⊠ Biggar Rd., 6 mi south of city, ☎ 0131/445–5067)

18 holes, 5,568 yards, SSS 68. **Portobello** (⊠ Stanley St., 2 mi north of city, ☎ 0131/669–4361) 9 holes, 2,410 yards, SSS 32. **Silverknowes** (⊠ Silverknowes Pkwy., 4 mi northwest of city, ☎ 0131/336–3843) 18 holes, 6,210 yards, SSS 71. **Torphin Hill** (⊠ Torphin Rd., 3 mi west of city, ☎ 0131/441–1100) 18 holes, 4,580 yards, SSS 66.

Health Clubs

Some of the larger Edinburgh hotels have their own fitness centers. Most facilities are free to guests, though there may be a charge for snooker and squash. Unless otherwise stated, the facilities are open to nonguests only through private membership. These include the **Carlton Highland** (⊠ North Bridge, ☎ 0131/556–7277), with pool, gymnasium, snooker, squash, and massage; **Edinburgh Grand Sheraton** (⊠ Lothian Rd., ☎ 0131/229–9131), with pool, gymnasium, and £15/day charge for non-residents; **Royal Scot** (⊠ Glasgow Rd., ☎ 0131/334–9191), with pool, gymnasium, and £10/day charge for nonresidents; and **Forth Bridges Moat House** (⊠ South Queensferry, ☎ 0131/469–9955), with pool, gymnasium, snooker, and squash.

Running and Track Sports

At **Holyrood Park** at almost any time of day or night joggers run the circuit around Arthur's Seat. **Meadowbank Stadium** (⊠ Northeast of the city center, ☎ 0131/661–5351) has facilities for more than 30 different track and indoor sports.

Skiing

Hillend (⊠ Biggar Rd., ☎ 0131/445–4433, ⛷ chairlift £1.10, ☉ Apr.–Aug., weekdays 9:30–9, weekends 9:30–7; Sept.–Mar., Mon.–Sat. 9:30–9, Sun. 9:30–7), on the southern edge of the city, is the longest artificial ski slope in the United Kingdom—go either to ski (equipment can be rented on the spot) or to ride the chairlift for fine city views.

Swimming

The **Royal Commonwealth Pool** (⊠ Dalkeith Rd., ☎ 0131/667–7211 ⛋ £2.35), the largest swimming pool in the city, is part of a complex that includes a fitness center and a cafeteria.

Spectator Sports

Rugby

At Murrayfield Stadium, home of the **Scottish Rugby Union** (☎ 0131/346–5000), Scotland's international rugby matches are played in early spring. During that time of year, crowds of good-humored rugby fans from Ireland and Wales add greatly to the atmosphere in the streets of Edinburgh.

Soccer

Like Glasgow, Edinburgh is soccer-mad, and there is a tense rivalry between the city's two professional teams, the mostly Protestant **Heart of Midlothian Football Club ("Hearts")** based at Tynecastle (☎ 0131/337–6132), and the predominantly Catholic **Hibernian ("Hibs")** club, which plays its home matches at Easter Road (☎ 0131/661–2159).

SHOPPING

Arcades and Shopping Centers

Like most large towns Edinburgh has succumbed to the fashion for "under one roof" shopping. If you dislike a breath of fresh air (or a wonderful view) between shops—or if it's raining—try the upscale **Waverley Market** (⊠ East end of Princes St.), with a fast-food area, designer-label boutiques, and shops that sell Scottish woolens and tweeds, whiskey, and confections. The **St. James Centre** (✉ East end of Princes Street) has unremarkable chain stores. **Cameron Toll** (✉ Bottom of Dalkeith Rd.) shopping center, on the city's South Side, caters to local residents, with food stores and High Street brand names. The newest shopping center at **South Gyle** (✉ On the outskirts of the city near the airport) is based on a typical U.S.-style shopping mall. Here you will find the High Street brand names again, including a huge Marks & Spencer.

Department Stores

In contrast to other major cities, Edinburgh has few true department stores. **Aitken and Niven** (✉ 77–79 George St., ☎ 0131/225–1461) is an Edinburgh institution: a small department store where the well-heeled come to buy upscale clothing, shoes, and accessories. In the city center you will find **Jenners** (✉ 4–8 Princes St., ☎ 0131/225–2442), which specializes in traditional china and glassware and Scottish clothing (upmarket tweeds and tartans) and has a justly famous Food Hall—selling shortbreads and Dundee cakes, honeys and marmalades—as well as a range of high-quality groceries. **Frasers** (✉ West end of Princes St., ☎ 0131/225–2472) is a part of Britain's largest chain of department stores. **John Lewis** (✉ 69 St. James Centre, ☎ 0131/556–9121), specializing in furniture and household goods, pledges that they are "never knowingly undersold." Frasers and John Lewis are not local, independently owned firms, and the goods are similar to those carried in other, United Kingdom–wide branches.

The High Street multiples, **Marks & Spencer** (✉ 54, 91 and 104–106 Princes St., ☎ 0131/225–2301), **British Home Stores** (✉ 64 Princes St., ☎ 0131/226–2621), and so on, are also represented on Princes Street. However, even given the competition, if you plan on a morning or a whole day of wandering from department to department, trying on beautiful clothes, buying crystal or china, or stocking up on Scottish food specialties, with a break for lunch at an in-store restaurant, then Jenners is the store to choose.

Shopping Districts

Despite its renown as a shopping street, **Princes Street** in the New Town may disappoint many visitors with its dull, anonymous modern architecture, average chain stores, and fast-food outlets. It is, however, one of the best spots to shop for tartans, tweeds, and knitwear, especially if your time is limited. One block north of Princes Street, **Rose Street** has many smaller specialty shops; part of the street is a traffic-free pedestrian zone, so it's a pleasant place to browse. The shops on **George Street** tend to be fairly upscale. London names, such as Laura Ashley, Liberty, and Waterstones bookshop, are prominent, though some of the older independent stores continue to do good business.

The streets crossing George Street—Hanover, Frederick, and Castle—are also worth exploring. **Dundas Street,** the northern extension of Hanover Street, beyond Queen Street Gardens, features several antiques shops. **Thistle Street,** originally George Street's "back lane," or service area, has several boutiques and more antiques shops. As may be expected, many of the shops along the **Royal Mile** sell what may be politely or euphemistically described as tourist-ware—whiskies, tartans, and tweeds. Careful exploration, however, will reveal some worthwhile establishments. Shops here also cater to highly specialized interests and hobbies.

Close to the castle end of the Royal Mile, just off George IV Bridge, the specialty shops of **Victoria Street** are contained within a small area.

Follow the tiny West Bow to **Grassmarket** for more specialty stores. North of Princes Street, on the way to the Royal Botanic Garden, **Stockbridge** is an oddball shopping area of some charm, particularly on St. Stephen Street. To get there, walk north down Frederick Street and Howe Street, away from Princes Street, then turn left onto North West Circus Place. **Stafford and William streets** comprise a small, upscale shopping area in a Georgian setting. Walk to the west end of Princes Street and along its continuation, Shandwick Place, then turn right into Stafford Street. William Street crosses Stafford halfway down.

Specialty Shops

Antiques

Antiques dealers tend to cluster together, so it may be easier to concentrate on one area—St. Stephen Street, Bruntsfield Place, Causewayside, or Dundas Street, for example—if you are short of time. **Present Bygones** (⊠ 61 Thistle St., ☎ 0131/226–7646) collects an eclectic mix of items, some antique, some modern, including blue-and-white china, antique samplers, and small furniture. Try **Byzantium** (⊠ 9A Victoria St., ☎ 0131/225–1768) for an eclectic mix of antiques, crafts, clothes— and an excellent coffee shop on the top level.

Books, Paper, Maps, and Games

As a university city and cultural center, Edinburgh is well endowed with excellent bookshops. All keep a wide range of guides and books giving information about every aspect of Edinburgh life, and all have extended opening hours (until 10 PM on certain nights), including Sunday. Some of the most central are **James Thin, the Edinburgh Bookshop** (⊠ 57 George St., ☎ 0131/225–4495; ⊠ 53 South Bridge, ☎ 0131/556– 6743) and **Waterstones** (⊠ 83 George St., ☎ 0131/225–3436; ⊠ 13/ 14 Princes St., ☎ 0131/556–3034; ⊠ 128 Princes St., ☎ 0131/226– 2666).

Try **George Waterstons & Sons, Ltd.** (⊠ 35 George St., ☎ 0131/225– 5690) not only for stationery but also for an excellent selection of small gift items. **R. Somerville of Edinburgh** (⊠ 82 Canongate, ☎ 0131/556– 5225) is a dealer in a large selection of playing cards. **Carson Clark Gallery** (⊠ 181–183 Canongate, ☎ 0131/556–4710) is a specialist in antique maps, sea charts, and prints.

Clothing Boutiques

Edinburgh is home to several top-quality designers (although, it must be said, probably not as many as are found in Glasgow, the country's fashion center), some of whom make a point of using Scottish materials in their creations. **Bill Baber** (⊠ 66 Grassmarket, ☎ 0131/225– 3249) is one of the most imaginative of the many Scottish knitwear designers, and a long way from the conservative pastel "woollies" sold at some of the large mill shops. Well-heeled Edinburgh also has a branch of **D and B by Angela Holmes** (⊠ 37–39 Frederick St., ☎ 0131/ 225–1019), whose distinctive clothing—from silk ball gowns and wedding dresses to flowing corduroy skirts and matching jackets, and pretty cotton print summer dresses—is guaranteed to make you stand out from the crowd. **Judith Glue** (⊠ 60–64 High St., ☎ 0131/558–1866) has brilliantly patterned Orkney knitwear, as well as distinctive crafts, cards, and candles.

If you are shopping for children, especially those who fit the tousled-tomboy mold, try **Baggins** (⊠ 12 Deanhaugh St., Stockbridge, ☎ 0131/315–2011) for practical, reasonably priced clothes made from natural fibers; toys; and fancy dress. All the clothes here are made to the owner's design in the store-workshop. **Burberrys and The Scotch House** (⊠ 39–41 Princes St., ☎ 0131/556–1252) is popular with overseas visitors for its top-quality (if top-price) clothing and accessories. **Something Simple** (✉ 10 William St., ☎ 0131/225–4650) buys clothes for all occasions, including some designer names. **The Extra Inch** (✉ 12 William St., ☎ 0131/226–3303) has a full selection of clothes European size 38 and over.

Coffees and Teas
Kinnels (✉ 36–38 Victoria St., ☎ 0131/220–1150) combines a specialty coffee and tea shop with a relaxed, old-world coffee house, complete with a display of newspapers dating back to the early 1800s.

Hardware
James Gray & Son (✉ 89 George St., ☎ 0131/225–7381) is a long-established, family-owned ironmonger and hardware store that has not forsaken old-fashioned service. Beyond regular household gadgets, you'll find china and giftware.

Jewelry
Joseph Bonnar (✉ 72 Thistle St., ☎ 0131/226–2811) is a specialist in antique jewelry in the heart of the New Town. **Alistir Tait** (✉ 116a Rose St., ☎ 0131/225–4105) offers a collection of high-quality antique and fine jewelry, silver, clocks, and crystal. The jeweler **Hamilton and Inches** (✉ 87 George St., ☎ 0131/225–4898), established in 1866, is a silversmith and goldsmith, worth visiting not only for its modern and antique gift possibilities, but also for its late-Georgian interior, designed by David Bryce in 1834—all gilded columns and elaborate plasterwork.

Linens, Textiles, and Home Furnishings
Go to **And So To Bed** (✉ 22 Howe St., ☎ 0131/225–6998) for a wonderful selection of embroidered and embellished bed linens, cushion covers, and such. **In House** (✉ 28 Howe St., ☎ 0131/225–2888) has designer furnishings and collectibles at the forefront of modern design in the house. The interior design shop **Ampersand** (✉ 18 Victoria St., ☎ 0131/226–2734) stocks a large selection of sundry collectibles, mostly jugs, plates, lamps, and vases, as well as unusual fabric by the meter. **Studio One** (✉ 10–16 Stafford St., ☎ 0131/226–5812) has a well-established and comprehensive inventory of kitchen goods and gift articles. Look into **Hand in Hand** (✉ 3 North West Circus Pl., ☎ 0131/226–3598) for beautiful antique textiles.

Outdoor Sports Gear
If you plan to do a lot of hiking or camping in the Highlands or the Islands, you may want to look over the selection of outdoor clothing, boots, jackets, and heavy- and lightweight gear at **Tiso** (✉ 121 Rose St., ☎ 0131/225–9486).

Scottish Specialties
If you want to identify a particular tartan, several of the shops in Princes Street will be pleased to assist. The **Clan Tartan Centre** (✉ 70–74 Bangor Rd., Leith, ☎ 0131/553–5100) has extensive displays of various aspects of tartanry. For craftware, use as your quality guide the **Edinburgh Old Town Weaving Company** (✉ 555 Castlehill, ☎ 0131/226–1555), where crafts are made on the premises, and you can talk to the craftspeople as they work. The range of items available includes handwoven tartan, kilts, bagpipes, silver, pottery, and Aran knitwear; you can refuel at the Taste of Scotland coffee shop. **Geoffrey (Tailor) Highland Crafts** (✉ 57–59 High St., ☎ 0131/557–0256) can clothe you in full Highland dress, with kilts made in its own workshops. **Edinburgh Crystal** (✉ Eastfield, Penicuik, ☎ 01968/675128) makes fine glassware stocked by many large stores and gift shops in the city center, but you

can also visit its premises (visitor center, restaurant, and shop) in Penicuik (☞ Side Trips from Edinburgh, *below*).

SIDE TRIPS FROM EDINBURGH

The Lothians is the collective name given to the swath of countryside south of the Firth of Forth and surrounding Edinburgh. The 70-mi round-trip exploring the historic houses and castles of West Lothian and the Forth Valley and some territory north of the River Forth can be accomplished in a full day with select stops. Stretching east to the sea and south to the Lowlands from Edinburgh, the sights in Midlothian and East Lothian are no more than one hour from Edinburgh. The inland river valleys, hills, and castles of Midlothian and East Lothian's delightful waterfronts, dunes, and golf links offer a taste of Scotland in close proximity to the capital.

West Lothian and the Forth Valley

West Lothian skirts the edge of the Central Highlands and comprises a good bit of Scotland's central belt. The River Forth snakes across a widening floodplain on its descent from the Highlands, and by the time it reaches the western extremities of Edinburgh it has already passed below the mighty Forth bridges and become a broad estuary. Castles and stately homes sprout thickly on both sides of the Forth.

Cramond

④ At this compact settlement on the coast west of the city (4 mi northwest of city center) you can watch summer sunsets over the Firth of Forth, joined by the River Almond. The river's banks, once the site of mills and industrial works, now offer pleasant leafy walks.

DINING

£–££ ✗ **Cramond Inn.** In this dark village inn dating from the 1600s—once the haunt of Robert Louis Stevenson—you can stop for a pint at the bar or a selection from the small but varied pub menu: red snapper with seafood sauce and new potatoes, chicken with mango chutney and rice, or a steak. ⊠ *Cramond Glebe Rd., Cramond Village,* ☎ *0131/ 336–2035. DC, MC, V.*.

Dalmeny House

The first of the stately homes clustered on the western edge of Edinburgh, **Dalmeny House** is the home of the Earl and Countess of Rosebery. This 1815 Tudor Gothic pile displays among its sumptuous contents the best of the family's famous collection of 18th-century French furniture. Much of this collection was formerly displayed at Mentmore, the country seat 40 mi north of London, which belonged to the present earl's grandfather, Baron Mayer Rothschild (1840–1915). Highlights include the library; the drawing room, with its tapestries and highly wrought French furniture; the Napoleon Room; and the Vincennes and Sevres porcelain collections. ⊠ *B924, by South Queensferry (7 mi west of city center),* ☎ *0131/331–1888.* ⊡ *£3.60.* ☺ *July–early Sept., Sun. 1–5:30, Mon.–Tues. noon–5:30 (last admission 4:45).*

South Queensferry

★ ④ This pleasant little waterside community, a former ferry port 9 mi west of the city, is totally dominated by the **Forth Bridges,** which cross the Firth of Forth here. The **Forth Rail Bridge** was opened in 1890 and is 2,765 yards long, except on a hot summer's day when it expands by about another yard! Its neighbor is the 1,993-yard-long **Forth Road Bridge,** in operation since 1964.

West Lothian and the Forth Valley

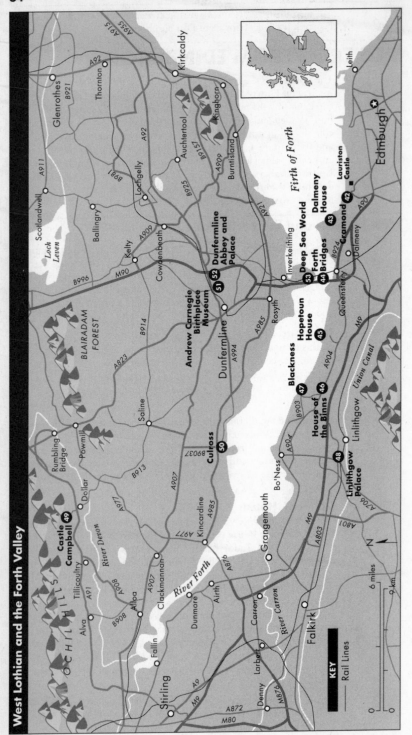

Kirkcaldy

Glenrothes

Thornton

Kinghorn

Auchtertool

Burntisland

Scotlandwell

Ballingry

Lochgelly

Kelty

Loch Leven

Cowdenbeath

Firth of Forth

Lauriston Castle

Dunfermline Abbey and Palace

Dalmeny House

Deep Sea World

51 52

Cramond **42**

Edinburgh

Leith

Inverkeithing

Andrew Carnegie Birthplace Museum

Forth Bridges **53 44**

43

Dunfermline

Rosyth

Queensferry

Hopetoun House **45**

Union Canal

Saline

Blackness

47 46

House of the Binns

Culross **50**

BLAIRADAM FOREST

Linlithgow

Powmill

Rumbling Bridge

Dollar

Bo'Ness

48

Linlithgow Palace

Castle Campbell **49**

Tillicoultry

Alva

River Devon

Grangemouth

O C H I L   H I L L S

Fallin

Clackmannan

Alloa

Dunmore

Airth

River Forth

Kincardine

Carron

River Carron

Falkirk

Stirling

Larbert

Denny

N

KEY

Rail Lines

6 miles

9 km

Hopetoun House

45 The palatial premises of **Hopetoun House,** home of the marquesses of Linlithgow, are considered to be among the Adam family's finest designs. The pile was started in 1699 to the original plans of Sir William Bruce (1630–1710), then enlarged between 1721 and 1754 by William Adam (1689–1748) and his son Robert. There is a notable painting collection, and the house has decorative work of the highest order, plus all the trappings to keep you entertained: a nature trail, a restaurant in the former stables, a museum, and a garden center. Much of the wealth that created this sumptuous building came from the family's mining interests. ⊠ *6 mi west of South Queensferry, off A904,* ☎ *0131/331–2451.* ☑ *£4.70.* ⊙ *Apr.–Sept., daily 10–5:30 (last admission 4:30).*

House of the Binns

46 The 17th-century General Tam Dalyell (circa 1599–1685) transformed a fortified stronghold into a gracious mansion, the **House of the Binns** (the name derives from *ben,* the Scottish word for hill). The present exterior dates from around 1810 and shows a remodeling into a kind of mock fort with crenellated battlements and turrets. Inside there are magnificent plaster ceilings in Elizabethan style. ⊠ *Off A904, 4 mi east of Linlithgow,* ☎ *01506/834255.* ☑ *£3.70.* ⊙ *House: May–Sept., Sat.–Thurs. 1:30–5:30 (last tour 5). Parkland: Apr.–Oct., daily 9:30–7; Nov.–Mar., daily 9:30–4 (last admission 30 mins before closing).*

Blackness

47 The castle of **Blackness** stands like a grounded gray hulk on the very edge of the Forth. A curious 15th-century structure, it has had a varied career as a strategic fortress, state prison, powder magazine, and youth hostel. The countryside is gently green and cultivated, and open views extend across the blue Forth to the distant ramparts of the Ochil Hills. ⊠ *B903, 4 mi northeast of Linlithgow,* ☎ *0131/668–8800.* ☑ *£1.80.* ⊙ *Apr.–Sept., daily 9:30–6; Oct.–Mar., Mon.–Wed. and Sat. 9:30–4, Thurs. 9:30–noon, Sun. 2–4.*

Linlithgow

48 On the edge of Linlithgow Loch stands the splendid ruin of **Linlithgow Palace,** birthplace of Mary, Queen of Scots (1542). Burned, perhaps by accident, by Hanoverian troops during the last Jacobite rebellion in 1746, this impressive shell stands on a site of great antiquity, though nothing for certain survived an earlier fire in 1424. The palace gatehouse is from the early 16th century, and the central courtyard's elaborate fountain dates from around 1535, but the halls and great rooms are cold echoing stone husks. ⊠ *A706, south shore of Linlithgow Loch,* ☎ *0131/668–8800.* ☑ *£2.30.* ⊙ *Apr.–Sept., daily 9:30–6; Oct.–Mar., Mon.–Sat. 9:30–4, Sun. 2–4.*

En Route From the M9 you will begin to gain tempting glimpses of the Highland hills to the northwest and the long humped wall of the Ochil Hills, across the river plain to the north. The **River Carron,** which flows under the M9, gave its name to the *carronade,* a kind of cannon manufactured in Falkirk, a few minutes to the southwest. You will also notice the apocalyptic complex of Grangemouth Refinery (impressive by night), which you may also smell if the wind is right (or wrong!). The refinery processes North Sea crude, but was originally sited here because of the now extinct oil-shale extraction industry of West Lothian, pioneered by a Scot, James "Paraffin" Young. This landscape may not be the most scenic in Scotland, but it has certainly played its role in the nation's industrial history.

Ochil Hills

The scarp face of the Ochil Hills looms unmistakably. It is an old fault line that bears up hard volcanic rocks and contrasts with the softer coal measures immediately around the River Forth. The steep Ochils provided grazing land and water power for Scotland's second-largest textile area. Some mills still survive in the so-called Hillfoots towns on the scarp edge east of Stirling. Several walkers' routes run into the narrow chinks of glens here. Behind Alva is **Alva Glen,** a park near the converted Strude Mill, at the top and eastern end of the little town. A little farther east is the **Ochil Hills Woodland Park,** which provides access to Silver Glen. The **Mill Glen,** behind Tillicoultry (pronounced tilly-*coot*-ree), and its giant quarry, fine waterfalls, and interesting plants is another hiking option for energetic explorers.

Dollar

This *douce* (Scots for well-mannered or gentle) and tidy town below the Ochil Hills slopes lies at the mouth of Dollar Glen. By following signs for **Castle Campbell,** however, you will find a road that angles sharply up the east side of the wooded defile. The narrow road ends in a parking lot from which it's only a short walk to Castle Campbell, high on a great sloping mound in the center of the glen. With the green woods below, bracken hills above, and a view that on a clear day stretches right across the Forth Valley to the tip of Tinto Hill near Lanark, this is certainly the most atmospheric fortress within easy reach of Edinburgh. Formerly known as Castle Gloom, Castle Campbell stands out among Scottish castles for the sheer drama of its setting. The sturdy square of the tower house survives from the 15th century, when this site was first fortified by the 1st earl of Argyll (d. 1493). Other buildings and enclosures were subsequently added, but the sheer lack of space on this rocky eminence ensured that there were never any drastic changes. The castle is associated with the earls of Argyll, as well as with John Knox, the fiery religious reformer, who preached here. It also played a role in the religious wars of the 17th century, having been captured by Oliver Cromwell in 1654 and garrisoned with English troops. ⊠ *Dollar Glen, 1 mi north of Dollar (30 mi northwest of Edinburgh),* ☎ *0131/668–8800.* ◷ *£2.30.* ◷ *Apr.–Sept., daily 9:30–6; Oct.–Mar., Mon.–Wed. and Sat. 9:30–4, Thurs. 9:30–noon, Sun. 2–4.*

Culross

On the muddy shores of the Forth, **Culross** is one of the most remarkable little towns in all of Scotland. It once had a thriving industry and export trade in coal and salt (the coal was used in the salt-panning process). It also had, curiously, a trade monopoly in the manufacture of baking *girdles* (griddles). But as local coal became exhausted, the impetus of the Industrial Revolution passed it by and other parts of the Forth Valley prospered. Culross became a backwater town, and the merchants' houses of the 17th and 18th centuries were never replaced by Victorian developments or modern architecture. In the 1930s, the very new and then very poor National Trust for Scotland started to buy up the decaying properties. With the help of a variety of other agencies, these buildings were conserved and brought to life. Many of the National Trust properties are today lived in by ordinary citizens. A few—the Palace, Study, and Town House—are open to the public. With its mercat cross, cobbled streets, tolbooth, and narrow wynds, Culross is now a living museum of a 17th-century town. ⊠ *25 mi northwest of Edinburgh,* ☎ *0131/226–5922.* ◷ *Palace, Study, and Town House £4.20.* ◷ *Study and Town House: Apr.–Sept., daily 1:30–5; Oct., weekends 11–5; Palace: Apr.–Sept., daily 11–5 (last admission 4).*

Dunfermline

This town 16 mi northwest of Edinburgh was once the world center for the production of damask linen; the **Dunfermline Museum and Small Gallery** (⊠ Viewfield Terr., ☎ 01383/313–838, ◷ Weekdays 11–5;

ring bell) tells the full story, and also has exhibitions of contemporary art and crafts. Today the town is better known as the birthplace of millionaire philanthropist Andrew Carnegie (1835–1919). Undoubtedly Dunfermline's most famous son, Carnegie endowed the town with a library, health and fitness center, spacious park, and, naturally, a Carnegie Hall, still the focus of culture and entertainment. The 1835 weaver's cottage in which Carnegie was born is now the **Andrew Carnegie Birthplace Museum.** Don't be misled by the cottage's exterior. Inside it opens into a larger hall, where documents, photographs, and artifacts tell Carnegie's fascinating life story. You will learn such obscure details as the claim that Carnegie was one of only three men in the United States to be able to translate Morse code by ear as it came down the wire. ⊠ *Moodie St.,* ☎ *01383/724302.* ▨ *£1.50.* ☼ *Apr.– May and Sept.–Oct., Mon.–Sat. 11–5, Sun. 2–5; June–Aug., Mon.– Sat. 10–5, Sun. 2–5; Nov.–Mar., daily 2–4.*

Also in Dunfermline is the **Dunfermline Abbey and Palace.** The abbey complex was founded by Queen Margaret, the English wife of the Scots King Malcolm III (circa 1031–93). Some Norman work can be seen in the present church, where Robert the Bruce (1274–1329) lies buried. The palace grew from the abbey guest house and was the birthplace of Charles I (1600–49). Dunfermline was the seat of the Royal Court of Scotland until the end of the 11th century, and its central role in Scottish affairs is explored by means of display panels dotted around the drafty but hallowed buildings. ⊠ *Monastery St.,* ☎ *0131/668–8800.* ▨ *£1.80.* ☼ *Apr.–Sept., daily 9:30–6; Oct.–Mar., Mon.–Wed. and Sat. 9:30–4, Thurs. 9:30–noon, Sun. 2–4.*

North Queensferry

The former ferry port on the north side of the Forth dropped almost into oblivion after the Forth Road Bridge opened, but was dragged abruptly back into the limelight when the hugely popular **Deep Sea World** arrived in the early 1990s. This sophisticated "aquarium"—for want of a better word—on the Firth of Forth offers a fascinating view of underwater life. Go down a clear acrylic tunnel for a diver's-eye look at more than 5,000 fish, including a posse of 9-ft sharks, and visit the exhibition hall with an audiovisual presentation on local marine life, an Amazon jungle display, and various other creatures. Ichthyophobes will feel more at ease in the adjacent café and gift shop. ⊠ *North Queensferry,* ☎ *01383/411880.* ▨ *£6.15.* ☼ *Apr.–June and Sept.–Oct., daily 10–6; July, Aug., daily 10–6:30; Nov.–Mar., weekdays 11–5, weekends 10–6.*

West Lothian and the Forth Valley A to Z

ARRIVING AND DEPARTING

By Bus: Midland Bluebird (☎ 01324/613777) bus services link most of this area, but working out a detailed itinerary by bus would be best left to your travel agent or guide.

By Car: Leave Edinburgh by Queensferry Road—the A90—and follow signs for the Forth Bridge. Beyond the city boundary at Cramond take the slip road, B924, for South Queensferry, watching for signs to Dalmeny House. From Dalmeny, follow the B924 for the descent to South Queensferry. The B924 continues westward under the approaches to the suspension bridge and then meets the A904. On turning right, onto A904, follow signs for Hopetoun House, House of the Binns, and Blackness Castle. From Blackness, take the B903 to its junction with the A904. Turn left for Linlithgow on the A803. At this point it's best to join the M9, which will speed you westward. Follow Kincardine Bridge signs off the motorway, cross the Forth and take the A977 north from Kincardine, formerly a trading port and distillery center. Take the A907 to Alloa, get on the A908 (marked Tillicoultry) for a short stretch, and then pick up the B908 (marked Alva).

At this point you'll be leaving the industrial northern shore of the Forth behind and entering the Ochil Hills, which you can explore by following the A91 eastward at Alva; squeezed between the gentle River Devon and the steep slopes above, the road continues to Dollar, where you should follow signs to Castle Campbell. From the castle, retrace your route to A91 and turn left. Just a few minutes outside Dollar, turn right onto a minor road (signed Rumbling Bridge). Then turn right onto the A823. Follow A823 through Powmill (signs for Dunfermline); turn right off A823, following the signs for Saline (a pleasant if undistinguished village), and take an unclassified road due south to join the A907. Turn right, and then within a mile go left on the B9037, which leads down to Culross. Take the B9037 east to join the A994, which leads to Dunfermline. From here, follow Edinburgh signs to the A823 and return via North Queensferry and the Forth Road Bridge (toll 40p).

By Train: Dalmeny, Linlithgow, and Dunfermline all have rail stations, and can be reached from Edinburgh Waverley Station. For information, call the **National Train Enquiry Line** (☎ 0345/484950).

VISITOR INFORMATION
The tourist information office in the Mill Trail Visitor Centre (☎ 01259/769696) at **Alva** can provide information on the region's textile establishments as well as a *Mill Trail* brochure, which can lead you to mill shops offering bargain woolen and tweed goods.

Midlothian and East Lothian

In spite of the finest stone carving in Scotland at Rosslyn Chapel, associations with Sir Walter Scott, outstanding castles, and miles of varied rolling countryside, Midlothian, the area immediately south of Edinburgh, for years remained off the beaten tourist path. Perhaps a little in awe of sophisticated Edinburgh to the north and the well-manicured charm of the stockbroker belt of nearby upmarket East Lothian, Midlothian remained quietly preoccupied with its own workaday little towns and dormitory suburbs.

As for East Lothian, it started with the advantage of golf courses of world rank, most notably Muirfield, plus a scattering of stately homes and interesting hotels. Red-pantiled and decidedly middle class, it is an area of glowing grain fields in summer and quite a few discreetly polite STRICTLY PRIVATE signs at the end of driveways. Still, it has plenty of interest for you, including photogenic villages, active fishing harbors, and vistas of pastoral Lowland Scotland, a world away (but much less than an hour by car) from bustling Edinburgh.

Roslin

A pretty little U-shaped miners' village, with its rows of stone-built terraced cottages, Roslin is famous for the extraordinary **Rosslyn Chapel.** Conceived by Sir William Sinclair (circa 1404–80) and dedicated to St. Matthew in 1450, the chapel is outstanding for the quality and variety of the stone carving inside. Covering almost every square inch of stonework are human figures, animals, and plants. The chapel was actually never finished. The original design called for a cruciform structure, but only the choir and parts of the east transept walls were completed. ✉ *Roslin, off A703, 7½ mi south of Edinburgh,* ☎ *0131/ 440–2159.* 💷 *£2.50.* ⏰ *Mon.–Sat. 10–5, Sun. noon–4:45.*

Penicuik

There are fine views of the Pentland Hills beyond this town, but its chief attraction for the tourist is the **Edinburgh Crystal Visitor Centre,**

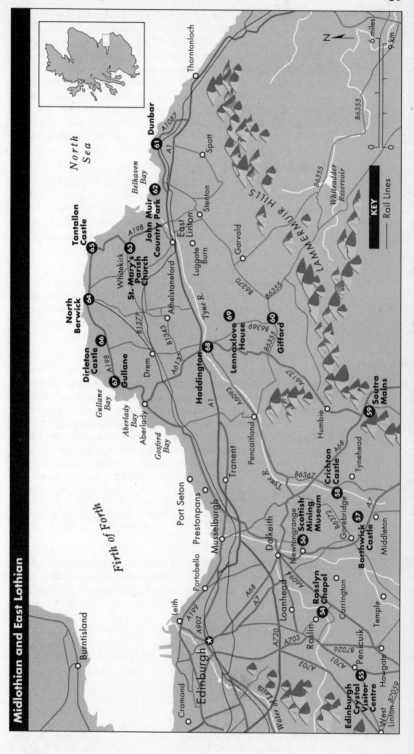

Midlothian and East Lothian

North Sea

Firth of Forth

LAMMERMUIR HILLS

KEY

—— Rail Lines

Thorntonloch

61 Dunbar

Spott

Belhaven Bay

62 John Muir Country Park

Stenton

Whiteadder Reservoir

B6355

65 Tantallon Castle

Whitekirk

63 St. Mary's Parish Church

East Linton

Athelstaneford

Luggate Burn

Garvald

B6370

B6355

B6355

64 North Berwick

B1377

B1343

Tyne R.

69 Lennoxlove House

60 Gifford

B6369

66 Dirleton Castle

A198

Drem

A6137

68 Haddington

A1

A6093

A6137

67 Gullane

Gullane Bay

Aberlady Bay

Aberlady

Gosford Bay

Pencaitland

Humbie

59 Soutra Mains

Port Seton

Tranent

Tyne R.

B6367

A68

Tynehead

58 Crichton Castle

Prestonpans

Musselburgh

Dalkeith

A7

Gorebridge

A702

Portobello

Leith

A199

A902

56 Scottish Mining Museum

Newtongrange

57 Borthwick Castle

Middleton

Burntisland

Cramond

★ Edinburgh

A720

A68

A7

Loanhead

A6094

Roslin

54 Rosslyn Chapel

Carrington

Temple

A703

A702

A701

A7

Penicuik

55 Edinburgh Crystal Visitor Centre

Howgate

West Linton

B7026

B7059

Water of Leith

with crystal pieces and an audiovisual exhibition on the production of crystal. Guided tours reveal the stages involved in the manufacture of cut crystal. In addition, groups of 6–12 people can prebook a VIP tour (adults over 18 only), which has you blow a glass bubble and cut your own piece of glass, later polished and given to you as a keepsake. Advance booking is essential for this tour. The Visitor Centre also has a coffee shop and gift shops. ✉ *Eastfield, Penicuik, 10 mi south of Edinburgh,* ☎ *01968/675128.* ▭ *Center free, tours £2, VIP tour £20.* ⊘ *Mon.–Sat. 9–5, Sun. 11–5. Factory tours: Oct.–Mar., weekdays 9:15–3:30; Apr.–Sept., weekdays 9:15–3:30, weekends 11–2:30 (shorter demonstration tour offered).*

The Pentlands

This unmistakable range of hills immediately south of Edinburgh has the longest artificial ski slope in Britain, at Hillend, and an all-year chairlift that provides magnificent views (even to nonskiers). There are several other access points along the A702 running parallel to the hills—the best is Flotterstone, where you'll find a parking lot, pub, and quiet roads for walking.

DINING

£ ✕ **Old Bakehouse.** Here you will find home-cooked fare in quaint, wood-beamed rooms. Danish open sandwiches are the specialty, but homemade soups and hot main courses are also included on the menu. ✉ *West Linton, southwest of Penicuik on A702,* ☎ *01968/660830. AE, MC, V. Closed Mon. No dinner Tues., Thurs., and Sun.*

Newtongrange

This former mining community 6 mi southeast of Edinburgh is home to the **Scottish Mining Museum,** where, in the buildings of a now-closed colliery, you can learn something about the history of Scotland's coal miners. You can visit various buildings in the complex and view the giant winding engine, and also see a reconstruction of a modern mechanized coalface. Realistic tableaux in the mine's former offices relate the power that the mining company had over the lives of the individual workers in a frighteningly autocratic system that survived well into the 1930s. The mining company owned the houses, shops, and even the pub. Newtongrange was in fact the largest planned mining village in Scotland. The scenery is no more attractive than you would expect, though the green Pentland Hills are still hovering in the distance. ☎ *0131/663–7519.* ▭ *£3.* ⊘ *Mar.–Oct., daily 10–4.*

Borthwick

Set in green countryside with scattered woods and lush hedgerows, the little village of Borthwick, 13 mi southeast of Edinburgh, is dominated by **Borthwick Castle,** which dates from the 15th century and is still occupied (☞ *Lodging, below*). This stark, tall, twin-towered fortress is associated with Mary, Queen of Scots. She came here on a kind of honeymoon with her ill-starred third husband, the earl of Bothwell (circa 1535–78). Their already dubious bliss was interrupted by Mary's political opponents, often referred to as the Lords of the Congregation, a confederacy of powerful nobles who were against the queen's latest liaison and who instead favored the crowning of her young son James. Rather insensitively, they laid siege to the castle while the newlyweds were there. The history books relate that Mary subsequently escaped disguised as a man. She was not free for long, however. It was only a short time before she was defeated in battle and imprisoned. She languished in prison for 21 years before Queen Elizabeth of England (1558–1603) signed her death warrant (1587). Bothwell's fate was equally gloomy: he died insane in a Danish prison.

££££   🏰 **Borthwick Castle.** There are hotels with castle names; and there are hotels inside what once were castles; and then there is Borthwick, first a castle and only second a place where you can stay. This 15th-century fortress was already taking guests half a century before Columbus discovered the Americas. Nowhere else in Scotland offers the extraordinary experience of staying as a part of history. Your "bedchamber," be reassured, is warm and comfortable, fully equipped with bath or shower (the plumbing is not 15th century). You dine, not in a restaurant, but in a magnificent vaulted room, the Great Hall, lit by candles and the gleam of a log fire. ✉ *North Middleton, Midlothian, EH23 4QY,* ☎ *01875/820514,* FAX *01875/821702. 10 rooms, 1 with bath, 9 with shower. AE, DC, MC, V. Closed Jan.–mid-Mar.*

Crichton Castle

58   Like Borthwick Castle, **Crichton Castle** is set in attractive, rolling Lowland scenery, interrupted here and there with patches of woodland. You can reach this castle from Borthwick Castle by taking a peaceful walk through the woods (there are signposts along the way). Crichton was a Bothwell family castle; Mary, Queen of Scots attended the wedding here of Bothwell's sister, Lady Janet Hepburn, to Mary's natural brother, Lord John Stewart. The curious arcaded range reveals diamond-faceted stonework; the particular geometric pattern cut of which is unique in Scotland and is thought to have been inspired by Renaissance styles on the Continent, particularly Italy. The oldest part of the work is the 14th-century keep (square tower). ✉ *B6367, 7 mi southeast of Dalkeith,* ☎ *0131/668–8800.* 🎫 *£1.50.* ☉ *Apr.–Sept., daily 9:30–6.*

En Route   Follow the A68 5 mi south, away from Edinburgh, to the very edge of the Lammermuir Hills. Just beyond the junction with the A6137 you'll
59   come to a spot called **Soutra Mains.** There's a small parking lot here, from which you can enjoy glorious unobstructed views extending northward over the whole of the Lothian plain.

Gifford

60   With its 18th-century kirk and mercat cross, **Gifford** is a good example of a tweedily respectable, well-scrubbed, red-pantile-roofed East Lothian village, 25 mi east of Edinburgh.

Dunbar

In the days before tour companies started offering package deals to the
61   Mediterranean, **Dunbar** was a popular holiday resort. Now a bit faded, the town is lovely for its spacious Georgian-style properties, characterized by the astragals, or fan-shaped windows, above the doors; the symmetry of the house fronts; and the parapeted roof lines. Though not the popular seaside playground it once was, Dunbar, 30 mi east of Edinburgh, does still have an attractive beach and a picturesque harbor.

John Muir Country Park

Taking in the estuary of the River Tyne winding down from the Moor-
62   foot Hills, the **John Muir Country Park** offers varied coastal scenery: rocky shoreline, golden sands, and the mixed woodlands of Tyninghame, teeming with wildlife. Dunbar-born John Muir (1838–1914), whose family emigrated to the United States when he was a child, helped found the Yosemite and Sequoia national parks. Only recently has the work of this early conservationist been acknowledged in his native Scotland. ✉ *28 mi east of Edinburgh.*

Whitekirk

63   The unmistakable red sandstone **St. Mary's Parish Church,** with Norman tower, stands on a site occupied since the 6th century. It was a place of pilgrimage in medieval times because of its healing well. Behind the kirk, in a field, stands a tithe barn. Tithe barns originated in the practice of giving to the church a proportion of local produce, which then required storage space. At one end of the structure is a 16th-century tower house, which at one point in its history accommodated visiting pilgrims. The large three-story barn was added to the tower house in the 17th century. ⊠ *A198; 27 mi east of Edinburgh.* ✉ *Free.* ☉ *Early morning–late evening.*

North Berwick

64 The pleasant little seaside resort of **North Berwick,** 26 mi northeast of Edinburgh, manages to retain a small-town personality even when it's thronged with city visitors on warm summer Sunday afternoons. Munching on ice cream, the city folk stroll on the beach and in the narrow streets or gape at the sailing craft in the small harbor.

65 Rising on a cliff beyond the flat fields east of North Berwick, **Tantallon Castle** is a substantial ruin defending a headland with the sea on three sides. The red sandstone is pitted and eaten by time and sea spray, with the earliest surviving stonework dating from the late-14th century. The fortress was besieged in 1529 by the cannons of King James V (1512–42). (Rather inconveniently, the besieging forces ran out of gunpowder.) Cannons were used again, to deadlier effect, in a later siege during the Civil War in 1651. Twelve days of battering with the heavy guns of Cromwell's General Monk greatly damaged the flanking towers. However, much of the curtain wall of this former Douglas stronghold survives. ⊠ *A198, 3 mi east of North Berwick,* ☎ *0131/668–8800.* ✉ *£2.30.* ☉ *Apr.–Sept.; daily 9:30–6; Oct.–Mar., Mon.–Wed. and Sat. 9:30–4, Thurs. 9:30–noon, Sun. 2–4.*

Dirleton

66 Set right in the center of this small village is the 12th-century **Dirleton Castle,** surrounded by a high outer wall. Within the wall you'll find a 17th-century bowling green, set in the shade of yew trees and surrounded by a herbaceous flower border that comes ablaze with color in high summer. Dirleton Castle was occupied in 1298 by King Edward I of England, as part of his campaign for the continued subjugation of the unruly Scots. ⊠ *A198; 22 mi northeast of Edinburgh,* ☎ *0131/668–8800.* ✉ *£2.30.* ☉ *Apr.–Sept., daily 9:30–6; Oct.–Mar., Mon.–Sat. 9:30–4, Sun. 2–4.*

Gullane

67 Very noticeable along this coastline are the golf courses of East Lothian, laid out wherever there is available links space. **Gullane,** surrounded by them, is ultrarespectable, its inhabitants clad mostly in expensive golfing sweaters. **Muirfield,** venue for the Open Championship, is nearby, as is **Greywalls,** now a hotel (☞ Lodging, *below*), but originally a private house designed by Sir Edwin Lutyens (1869–1944). Apart from golf, at Gullane's beach, well within driving distance of the city, you can enjoy restful summer evening strolls.

LODGING

££££ ☷ **Greywalls.** This is the ideal hotel for a golfing vacation: comfortable, with attentive service and award-winning modern British cuisine that makes the most of local produce. The house itself is an architectural treasure. Edward VII used to stay here, as have Nicklaus, Trevino, Palmer, and a host of other golfing greats. Shades of restful green predominate in the stylish fabrics from the likes of Nina Campbell, Colefax and Fowler, and Osborne and Little. ⊠ *Muirfield, Gullane, EH31 2EG,* ☎ *01620/842144,* ℻ *01620/842241. 23 rooms with bath. Restaurant, putting green, tennis court. AE, DC, MC, V. Closed Nov.–Mar.*

Haddington

One of the best-preserved medieval street plans in the country can be explored in **Haddington,** 15 mi east of Edinburgh. Among the many buildings of architectural or historical interest is the Town House, designed by William Adam in 1748 and enlarged in 1830. A wall plaque at the Sidegate recalls the great heights of floods from the River Tyne. Beyond is the medieval Nungate footbridge, with the Church of St. Mary a little way upstream.

Just to the south of Haddington is **Lennoxlove House,** which displays items associated with Mary, Queen of Scots. A turreted country house, part of it dating from the 15th century, Lennoxlove is a cheerful mix of family life and Scottish history. Housed in the beautifully decorated rooms are collections of portraits, furniture, and porcelain. ⊠ *B6369, 1 mi south of Haddington,* ☎ *01620/823720.* 🖘 *£3.50.* ☉ *Easter–Oct., Wed. and weekends 2–4:30.*

Midlothian and East Lothian A to Z

ARRIVING AND DEPARTING

By Bus: City bus services run out as far as Swanston and the Pentland Hills. **S.M.T./Lowland** (☎ 0131/663–9233) buses run to towns and villages throughout Midlothian and East Lothian. For details of all services, inquire at the St. Andrew Square Bus Station in Edinburgh.

By Car: Leave Edinburgh via the A701 (Liberton Rd.). At the not-very-picturesque community of Bilston, turn left to Roslin on the B7006. From Roslin return to the A701 for Penicuik. From Penicuik, take the A766 to A702, which runs beneath the Pentland Hills to West Linton. Then follow the B7059 and the A701 to Leadburn and then Howgate. Get onto the A6094 for a few minutes, then turn right onto the B6372 and continue past Temple, an attractive village on the edge of the Moorfoot Hills, toward Gorebridge.

At the junction of B6372 with A7, just before Gorebridge, you have a choice. If your interests tend toward social history, turn left and drive 2 mi to reach Newtongrange. If you instead turn right, after a few moments' travel south you will see a sign for Borthwick. Take a left onto an unclassified road off A7, and a few minutes later, Borthwick Castle appears. From Borthwick, take the B6372 and turn right onto the A68. Just beyond the village of Pathhead you'll see signs to Crichton Castle. Having detoured to the castle, follow the A68 south, away from Edinburgh, to the very edge of the Lammermuir Hills. Just beyond the junction with the A6137 at Soutra Mains there's a small parking lot from which to enjoy the view. Make your way back to the A6137 and turn right onto it; turn right again onto the B6355, go through Gifford and head east for the junction with the B6370, which leads to Dunbar.

West of Dunbar, on the way back to Edinburgh, the A1087 leads to the sandy reaches of Belhaven Bay, signposted from the main road, and to the John Muir Country Park. From the park, drive north on the A198 (a right turn off the A1), to reach Whitekirk, Tantallon Castle, and North Berwick. Dirleton, with its own massive castle, and Gullane, surrounded by golf courses, follow. A198 eventually leads to Aberlady, from which you can take the A6137 south to the former county town of Haddington and, by way of the B6369, Lennoxlove House. Return to the A1 at Haddington and head west back to Edinburgh. From Haddington it's about 15 mi back to center city.

By Train: There is no train service in Midlothian. In East Lothian, North Berwick, Drem, and Dunbar have train stations with regular service from Edinburgh. For information, call the **National Train Enquiry Line** (☎ 0345/484950).

EDINBURGH A TO Z

Arriving and Departing

By Bus

Scottish Citylink Coaches (☎ 0990/505050, FAX 0141/332–8055) and **National Express** (☎ 0990/808080) provide bus service to and from London and other major towns and cities. The main terminal, St. Andrew Square Bus Station, is only a couple of minutes (on foot) north of Waverley Station, immediately east of St. Andrew Square. Long-distance coaches must be booked in advance from the booking office in the terminal. Edinburgh is approximately eight hours by bus from London.

By Car

Downtown Edinburgh centers on Princes Street, which runs east–west. Drivers from the east coast will come in on A1, Meadowbank Stadium serving as a landmark. The highway bypasses the suburbs of Musselburgh and Tranent; therefore, any bottlenecks will occur close to downtown. From the Borders the approach to Princes Street is by A7/A68 through Newington, an area offering a wide choice of accommodations. From Newington the east end of Princes Street is reached by North Bridge and South Bridge. Approaching from the southwest, drivers will join the west end of Princes Street (Lothian Rd.) via A701 and A702, and those coming west from Glasgow or Stirling will meet Princes Street from M8 or M9, respectively. A slightly more complicated approach is via M90—from Forth Road Bridge/Perth/east coast; the key road for getting downtown is Queensferry Road, which joins Charlotte Square close to the west end of Princes Street.

By Plane

At present, **Edinburgh Airport** (☎ 0131/333–1000), 7 mi west of city center, offers no transatlantic flights. It does, however, have air connections throughout the United Kingdom—London Heathrow/Gatwick/Stansted/Luton/City, Aberdeen, Birmingham, Bristol, Dundee, East Midlands, Humberside, Kirkwall (Orkney), Leeds/Bradford, Manchester, Norwich, Shetland, Southampton, and Belfast in Northern Ireland—as well as with a number of European cities, including Amsterdam, Brussels, Copenhagen, Dublin, Dusseldorf, Munich, and Paris. There are flights to Edinburgh Airport virtually every hour from London's Gatwick and Heathrow airports; it's usually faster and less complicated to fly through Gatwick (which has excellent rail service from London's Victoria Station). Airlines serving Edinburgh include British Airways, British Midland, KLM UK, BusinessAir, easyJet, Servisair, Sabena, Aer Lingus, and Air France.

Glasgow Airport (☎ 0141/887–1111), 50 mi west of Edinburgh, is now the major point of entry into Edinburgh for transatlantic flights (☞ Glasgow A to Z *in* Chapter 4).

Prestwick Airport (☎ 01292/479822), 30 mi southwest of Glasgow, after some years of eclipse by Glasgow Airport, is beginning to come back into the reckoning, not least because of the activities of Ryanair (☎ 01292/678000), a company that has sparked off a major price war on the Anglo-Scottish routes (e.g., between London and Glasgow/Edinburgh). It offers unbeatable, no-frills, rock-bottom air fares between London Stansted and Prestwick.

BETWEEN EDINBURGH AIRPORT AND THE CITY CENTER

There are no rail links to the city center, despite the fact that the airport sits between two main lines. By bus or car you can usually make it to Edinburgh in a comfortable half hour, unless you hit the morning or evening rush hours (7:30–9 AM and 4–6 PM).

By Bus: Lothian Regional Transport (☎ 0131/555–6363) and **Guide Friday** (☎ 0131/556–2244), run buses between Edinburgh Airport's main terminal building and Waverley Bridge, in center city and within easy reach of several hotels. The buses run every 15 minutes daily (9–5) and less frequently (roughly every hour) during off-peak hours. The trip takes about 30 minutes (about 45 minutes during rush hour). Single fare for Lothian Regional Transport is £3.20, for Guide Friday £3.50.

By Limousine: The following Edinburgh firms provide chauffeur-driven limousines to meet flights at Edinburgh Airport: **David Grieve Chauffeur Drive** (⌧ 9/7 Lower Gilmour Pl., ☎ 0131/229–8666), for about £32; **Little's Chauffeur Drive** (⌧ 33 Corstorphine High St., ☎ 0131/334–2177), £43 plus VAT; and **Sleigh Ltd.** (⌧ 6 Devon Pl., ☎ 0131/337–3171), £44 plus VAT.

By Rental Car: There is a good choice of car rental companies operating from the terminal building (☞ Contacts and Resources, *below*). The cost is from £40 a day, depending on the firm. If you choose to plunge yourself into Edinburgh's traffic system, take care on the first couple of traffic circles (called roundabouts) you encounter on the way into town from the airport—even the most experienced drivers find them challenging. By car the airport is about 7 mi west of Princes Street downtown and is clearly marked from A8. The usual route to downtown is via the suburb of Corstorphine.

By Taxi: These are readily available outside the terminal. The trip takes 20–30 minutes to center city, 15 minutes longer during morning and evening rush hours. The fare is roughly £15. Note that because of a local regulation, airport taxis picking up fares from the terminal are any color, not the typical black cabs, although these also take fares going to the airport.

BETWEEN GLASGOW AIRPORT AND EDINBURGH
By Bus and Train: Scottish Citylink Coaches (☎ 0990/505050) buses leave Glasgow Airport every hour at 10 minutes to the hour and 20 minutes past the hour to travel direct to Edinburgh's St. Andrew Square Bus Station. The trip takes one hour and 10 minutes, and costs about £6.50. A somewhat more pleasant option is to take a cab from Glasgow Airport to Glasgow's Queen Street Train Station (15 minutes, £12–£15) and then take the train to Waverley Station in Edinburgh. Trains leave about every 30 minutes; the trip takes 50 minutes and costs £6.90. Check times on weekends. Another, less expensive alternative—best for those with little luggage—is to take the bus from Glasgow Airport to Glasgow's Buchanan Bus Station, walk five minutes to the Queen Street train station, and catch the train to Edinburgh.

By Taxi: Taxis (☎ 0141/848–4900) from Glasgow Airport to downtown Edinburgh take about 70 minutes and cost around £70–£80.

By Train
Edinburgh's main train hub, **Waverley Station,** is downtown, below Waverley Bridge and around the corner from the unmistakable spire of the Scott Monument. For information, call the **National Train Enquiry Line** (☎ 0345/484950). Travel time from Edinburgh to London by train is as little as 4½ hours for the fastest service.

Edinburgh's other main station is **Haymarket,** about four minutes (by rail) west of Waverley. Most Glasgow and other western and northern services stop here. Haymarket can be slightly more convenient for visitors staying in hotels beyond the west end of Princes Street.

Getting Around

By Bus

Lothian Regional Transport (⊠ 27 Hanover St., ☎ 0131/555–6363, ⊙ Mon.–Sat. 8:30–6; ⊠ Waverley Bridge, ⊙ May–Oct., Mon.–Sat. 8–7:15, Sun. 9–4:30; Nov.–Apr., Tues.–Sat. 9–4:30), operating dark-red-and-white buses, is the main operator within Edinburgh. You can buy tickets on the bus. The Day Saver Ticket (£2.20), allowing unlimited one-day travel on the city's buses, can be purchased in advance. More expensive, and not as good value, is the Tourist Card (£11 for 2 days, £2 each additional day), available in units of 2 to 7 days, which gives unlimited access to buses (except Airlink bus to airport) and includes vouchers for savings on tours and entrance fees. The Rider Card (for which you will need a photo) is valid on all buses for 7 days (Sun.–Sat. night, £10).

S.M.T. (⊠ St. Andrew Square Bus Station, ☎ 0131/663–9233), operating green and cream buses, provides much of the service between Edinburgh and the Lothians and offers day tours around and beyond the city. You will also see other bus companies, including **Eastern Scottish, Lowland Scottish,** and **Midland Scottish**—all part of First Bus Co., along with S.M.T.—and **Fife Scottish,** which operate routes into and out of Edinburgh to other parts of Scotland.

By Car

Driving in Edinburgh has its quirks and pitfalls, but competent drivers should not be intimidated. Metered parking in the center city is scarce and expensive, and the local traffic wardens are a feisty, alert bunch. Note that illegally parked cars are routinely wheel-clamped and towed away, and getting your car back will be expensive. After 6 PM the parking situation improves considerably, and you may manage to find a space quite near your hotel, even downtown. If you park on a yellow line or in a resident's parking bay, be prepared to move your car by 8 AM the following morning, when the rush hour gets under way. Parking lots are clearly signed; overnight parking is expensive and not permitted in all lots.

Princes Street in New Town is usually considered the city center. The street runs east–west; motorists using the A1 east-coast road enter the city from the east end of Princes Street. Using the city bypass, you can reach key points to the west, such as the airport or the Forth Road Bridge (gateway to the north), from many parts of the outskirts and from East Lothian without getting tangled up in downtown traffic.

By Taxi

Taxi stands can be found throughout the downtown area; the following are the most convenient: the west end of Princes Street, South St. David Street, and North St. Andrew Street (both just off St. Andrew Sq.), Waverley Market, Waterloo Place, and Lauriston Place. Alternatively, hail any taxi displaying an illuminated FOR HIRE sign.

By Train

Edinburgh has no urban or suburban rail systems.

Contacts and Resources

Car Rentals

Major companies have booths at the airport. **Avis** (☎ 0131/333–1866). **Alamo** (☎ 0131/344–3250). **Europcar** (☎ 0131/344–3114). **Hertz** (☎ 0131/333–1019).

Consulates

American Consulate General (⊠ 3 Regent Terr., ☎ 0131/556–8315). The London office of the **Canadian High Commission** (☎ 0171/258–6316) can provide local information for visitors.

Emergencies

For **police, ambulance, or fire,** dial ☎ 999. No coins are needed for emergency calls made from pay phones. **Hospital Edinburgh Royal Infirmary** (⊠ 51 Lauriston Pl., ☎ 0131/536–1000) is south of the city center—down George IV Bridge and then to the right.

Guided Tours

EXCURSIONS

Both **Lothian Regional Transport** and **Scotline Tours** (☞ Orientation Tours, *below*) and limousine companies (☞ Between Edinburgh Airport and the City Center, *above*) offer day trips to destinations such as St. Andrews and Fife or the Trossachs and Loch Lomond.

ORIENTATION TOURS

Scottish Tourist Guides (contact Kate Anderson, ⊠ 2/4 Dumbryden Gardens, Edinburgh EH14 2NG, ☎ FAX 0131/453–1297), endorsed by the Scottish Tourist Board, offers knowledgeable guides appropriate for an individual or a group. The tours are wide ranging and flexible.

Lothian Regional Transport (☎ 0131/555–6363) offers an "Edinburgh Classic Tour," a worthwhile introduction to the Old and New Towns. The ticket (🎫 £5.50) is a bargain because it is valid on any other "Classic Tour" bus for the rest of the day. There are frequent departures from Waverley Bridge (outside the rail station) and other points around the city. Open-top buses operate in suitable weather. This is a flexible, show-up-and-hop-on service, meaning that you can get off the bus at any attractions you may want to see more closely. Allow an hour for the complete tour. You can buy tickets from the Lothian Regional Transport offices on Hanover Street or Waverley Bridge, or you can buy them from the driver.

Scotline Tours' (⊠ 87 High St., ☎ 0131/557–0162 8 AM–11 PM for reservations, 🎫 £9) "City Tour" offers a comprehensive introduction to the city, as well as visits to Edinburgh Castle, the High Kirk of St. Giles, and the Palace of Holyroodhouse. Allow at least four hours for the entire tour. Scotline also offers a range of day tours to points beyond the city.

Guide Friday, Ltd. (⊠ Reception Centre, Waverley Station, ☎ 0131/556–2244, 🎫 £6.50) also offers an orientation tour. It runs less frequently than Lothian Regional Transport's equivalent, but you may enjoy riding through the streets of Edinburgh on one of Guide Friday's cheerful open-top, double-decker buses. The commentaries provided tend to be more colorful than accurate. The minimum tour time is one hour, and buses leave from Waverley Bridge.

PERSONAL GUIDES

Scottish Tourist Guides (☎ 0131/453–1297; ☞ Orientation Tours, *above*) can supply guides (in 19 languages) who are fully qualified and will meet clients at any point of entry into the United Kingdom or Scotland.

SPECIAL-INTEREST TOURS

Scottish Tourist Guides (☞ Orientation Tours, *above*) will design tours tailored to your interests; it also offers a special "Nightlife Tour." The **Cadies and Witchery Tours** (⊠ 352 Castlehill, ☎ 0131/225–6745, 🎫 £6.50) operates a "Ghosts and Ghouls" tour through the narrow Old

Town alleyways and closes with costumed guides and other theatrical characters showing up en route.

Robin's Edinburgh Tours (✉ 66 Willowbrae Rd., ☎ 0131/661–0125, 🖭 from £5), run by an Edinburgh native, offers a number of tours every day: "Grand City Tour" 10 AM; "Royal Mile Tour" 11 AM; "Ghosts and Witches" 7 PM; "Dr. Jekyll's Tour" (Apr.–Oct. only) 9 PM.

WALKING TOURS
The **Cadies and Witchery Tours** (☞ *above*), fully qualified members of the Scottish Tourist Guides Association, have since 1983 steadily built a reputation for combining entertainment and historical accuracy in their lively and enthusiastic "Witchery Ghosts and Gore Tour" and "Witchery Murder and Mystery Tour."

Late-Night Pharmacies
You can find out which pharmacy is open late on a given night by looking at the notice posted on every pharmacy-shop door. A pharmacy— or "dispensing chemist"—is easily identified by its sign, showing a green cross on a white background. **Boots** (✉ 48 Shandwick Pl., west end of Princes St., ☎ 0131/225–6757) is open ☉ Monday–Saturday 8 AM– 9 PM, Sunday 10–5.

Lost and Found
To retrieve lost property, try the **Lothian and Borders Police Headquarters** (✉ Fettes Ave., ☎ 0131/311–3131).

Maps
Several excellent city maps are available at bookshops. Particularly recommended: the *Bartholomew Edinburgh Plan*, with a scale of approximately 4 inches to 1 mi, by the once-independent and long-established Edinburgh cartographic company John Bartholomew and Sons, Ltd.

Money
Most city-center banks have a bureau de change (usual banking hours are weekdays 9:30–4:45). The bureau de change at the Tourist Centre, Waverley Market is open daily. There are also bureaux de change at Waverley Rail Station, Edinburgh Airport, and Frasers department store, at the west end of Princes Street.

Post Offices
The post office in the **St. James Centre** (✉ St. Andrew Sq., ☎ 0131/ 556–0478) is the most central and is open Monday 9–5:30, Tuesday– Friday 8:30–5:30, and Saturday 8:30–6. Other main post offices in the city center: (✉ 40 Frederick St.; ✉ 7 Hope St.). Many newsagents also sell stamps.

Travel Agencies
American Express (✉ 139 Princes St., ☎ 0131/225–7881). **Thomas Cook** (✉ 26–28 Frederick St., ☎ 0131/220–4039).

Visitor Information
Edinburgh and Scotland Information Centre (✉ 3 Princes St., ☎ 0131/ 557–1700, 🅵🅰🆇 0131/473–3881, ☉ May, June, and Sept., Mon.–Sat. 9–7, Sun. 10–7; July and Aug., Mon.–Sat. 9–8, Sun. 10–8; Oct.– Apr., Mon.–Sat. 9–6, Sun. 10–6), adjacent to Waverley Station (follow the TIC signs in the station and throughout the city), offers an accommodations service (Book-A-Bed-Ahead) in addition to the more typical services.

Complete information is also available at the **tourist-information desk** (☎ 0131/333–2167, 🅵🅰🆇 0131/335–3576, ☉ Apr.–Oct., Mon.–Sat. 8:30 AM–9:30 PM, Sun. 9:30–9:30; Nov.–Mar., weekdays 9–6, Sat. 9–5, Sun. 9:30–5) at the Edinburgh Airport.

The List, a publication available from city-center bookshops and newsagents, and *The Day by Day List* and **Events 1999** from the Edinburgh and Scotland Information Centre, all list information about all types of events, from movies and theater to sports. *The Scotsman,* a national newspaper published in Edinburgh, is good for both national and international news coverage, as well as for reviews and notices of upcoming events in Edinburgh and elsewhere in Scotland.

4 Glasgow

Cultural and commercial renewal have restored much of Glasgow's style and grandeur from its economically powerful 19th century. A vibrant metropolis with a thriving artistic life and cityscape à la Charles Rennie Mackintosh and Alexander "Greek" Thomson, Scotland's largest city is the 1999 "UK City of Architecture and Design." The "dear green place" is within easy reach of the Clyde Coast to the south and has good transportation links.

I N THE DAYS WHEN BRITAIN still had an empire, Glasgow pronounced itself the Second City of the Empire. The people of Glasgow were justifiably proud of their

By John
Hutchinson

Updated by
Beth Ingpen

city, since it was there that Britain's great steamships, including the 80,000-ton *Queen Elizabeth,* were built. The term *Clyde-built* (from Glasgow's River Clyde) became synonymous with good workmanship and lasting quality. It was also the Glaswegians who built the railway engines that opened up the Canadian prairies, the South African veldt, the Australian plains, and the Indian subcontinent. Scots engineers were to be found wherever there were engines—and so it was perhaps no coincidence that even Captain Kirk on the Starship *Enterprise* had to say, "Beam me up, Scottie" to his engineer.

Scholars have argued for years about what the name Glasgow means (pronounce it to rhyme with *toe* and stress the first syllable), but, generally, "dear green place" is the interpretation that finds most favor today. Most suitable it is, too, for a town that, despite industrialization, has more city parks than anywhere else in Britain, and even the famous River Clyde is now clean enough for trout and salmon.

Glasgow first came into prominence in Scottish history somewhere around 1,400 years ago, and typically for this rambunctious city it was all to do with an argument between a husband and his wife. One of the local chieftains suspected, with some justification, that his wife had been having an affair, so he crept up on the suspect, one of his knights, and took from him a ring that she had rather foolishly given her lover—foolishly, because it had originally been given to her by her husband. The furious husband flung the ring into the River Clyde, then told his wife the next day that he wanted her to wear it that evening. The lady was distraught and called on the local holy man, Mungo, to help. Clearly a useful man to have in a tricky situation, Mungo sent a monk out fishing, and the first bite the monk had was a salmon with the ring in its mouth. Whether the lady learned her lesson or called on Mungo's services regularly after that, history does not relate.

Mungo features in two other legends: one of a pet bird that he nursed back to life, and another of a bush or tree, the branches of which he used to relight a fire. Tree, bird, and the salmon with a ring in its mouth are all to be found on the city of Glasgow's coat of arms, together with a bell that Mungo brought from Rome. Mungo is now the city's patron saint. His tomb is to be found in the mighty medieval cathedral that bears his name.

Glasgow led a fairly quiet existence in the Middle Ages. Its cathedral was the center of religious life, and although the city was made a Royal Burgh in 1175 by King William the Lion, its population was never more than a few thousand. What changed Glasgow irrevocably and laid the foundations for its immense prosperity was the Treaty of Union between Scotland and England in 1707. This allowed Scotland to trade with the essentially English colonies in America, and with their expansion Glasgow prospered. In came cotton, tobacco, and rum; out went various Scottish manufactured goods and clothing. The key to it all in the early days was tobacco, and the prosperous merchants were known as the "tobacco lords." It was they who ran the city, and their wealth laid the foundation stone for the manufacturing industries of the 19th century.

As Glasgow prospered, so her population grew. The dear green place became built over. The original medieval city around the cathedral and High Street expanded westward. The 18th-century Merchant City, today the subject of a great deal of refurbishment, lies just to the south and west of George Square, and the houses of the merchants are even farther westward, along the gridiron pattern of Glasgow's streets up the hill toward Blytheswood Square.

But the city is not known as an 18th-century city; that honor is left to Edinburgh, in the east. Rather, Glasgow is known as one of the greatest Victorian cities in Europe. The population grew from 80,000 in 1801 to more than 700,000 in 1901, and with this enormous growth there developed also a sense of exuberance and confidence that is reflected in its public buildings. The City Chambers, built in 1888, are an extravaganza of marble and red sandstone, a clear symbol of the Victorian merchants' hopes for the future.

Yet, always at the forefront of change, Glasgow boasts, side by side with the overtly Victorian, an architectural vision of the future in the work of Charles Rennie Mackintosh (1868–1928). The Glasgow School of Art, the Willow Tearoom, and the churches and school buildings he designed point clearly to the clarity and simplicity of 20th-century lines.

Today, Glasgow has taken the best of the past and adapted it for the needs of the present day. The dear green places still remain in the city-center parks; the medieval cathedral stands proud, as it has done for 800 years; the Merchant City is revived and thriving; the Victorian splendor has been cleaned of its grime and will look good for many years to come; and the cultural legacy of museums and performing arts lives on stronger than ever. To cap it all, its superb location also makes it an ideal base from which to enjoy day tours of the Scottish countryside. Burns Country, the gardens of Galloway, the islands of the Clyde, Loch Lomond, the Trossachs, and Argyll are only about an hour or so from the city center, as is Edinburgh.

Pleasures and Pastimes

Dining
The restaurants of Glasgow have diversified over the past several years; as a result, you'll find Chinese, Italian, and Indian food in addition to the usual French and Scottish offerings. Glasgow also has a strong café culture: visit one or two to get a feel for this important part of the city. Pubs are also good bets for cheap lunches.

Festivals
It's clear just how strong Glasgow's international reputation is when it comes to cultural events. Glasgow was the 1990 European City of Culture, the first British city to be so designated and is the UK City of Architecture and Design in 1999.

Lodging
Glasgow is now better equipped with hotels of all categories than it has ever been. The city has become a major business destination in the past several years, with the Scottish Conference and Exhibition Centre serving as the hub of activity. There are now some big city-center hotels of both expensive and moderate character, and some good and reasonable small hotels and guest houses with more character in the suburbs convenient to the city by public transport. All the larger hotels have restaurants open to nonguests.

Shopping
The old image of industrial Glasgow has changed considerably in recent years as the city has strenuously shrugged off its poor-cousin-to-Edinburgh label. Glaswegians are clotheshorses, and you'll find some

of the world's best clothes at the many stores and malls that have helped to improve Glasgow's stature as a shopping city. Princes Square is a particularly good place to go if you're looking to enhance your wardrobe (and are willing to break the bank to do it).

EXPLORING GLASGOW

Glasgow is not like Edinburgh, and its layout cannot be read in a single glance. However, the city center is relatively flat and set along a straightforward grid of streets, making for easy walking between the areas around Glasgow Cathedral and Provand's Lordship, High Street, and the Merchant City, once the center of medieval activity. The River Clyde, on which Glasgow's trade across the Atlantic developed, is always at the center of the city—literally cutting the city in half and offering often surprising views across to the buildings on the other side. You will do well to note the often ornate detailing above eye-level.

In the quieter, slightly hillier western part of the city is Glasgow University and that other, "forgotten" side of Glasgow, unjustly perceived as a grimy center of heavy industry.

Numbers in the text correspond to numbers in the margin and on the Glasgow and Glasgow Excursions: Ayrshire and the Clyde Valley maps.

Great Itineraries

To take advantage of Glasgow's wealth of cultural sites and shopping, you could easily plan for four or five days, but in two days you can see the city's greatest hits.

IF YOU HAVE 2 DAYS

Glaswegians are particularly proud of the Burrell Collection in Pollok Country Park, so it should top your list of must-sees. On the first day explore the core of historic Glasgow—the medieval area and Merchant City. Glasgow Cathedral gives a glimpse into history and an impression of St. Mungo. Buchanan Street, including the Princes Square development and the new Buchanan Galleries, has the best shopping. On the second day, see the West End, including the painting, sculpture, and Charles Rennie Mackintosh furniture at the Hunterian Art Gallery. If you have not yet seen the city center parks, venture to Glasgow Green and the art collections at Pollok Country Park and Bellahouston Park. At the end of your days, remember Glasgow's pubs and clubs offer great entertainment till late in the evening.

IF YOU HAVE 5 DAYS

Five days allows enough time to add to the brief tour more of Glasgow's key museums and cultural attractions: the Glasgow Gallery of Modern Art in the city center or the St. Mungo Museum to the east. You could easily take a full day to see the cluster of West End museums by Kelvingrove Park (Kelvingrove Museum and Art Gallery, Hunterian Art Gallery, and Museum of Transport). For a good day trip out of the city, take the hour-long train ride to Wemyss Bay, and from there take the ferry to the Isle of Bute, home to the spectacular Victorian Gothic Mount Stuart house.

IF YOU HAVE 10 DAYS

Ten days based in Glasgow will allow you to thoroughly explore all of its museums (you may well want to visit the Burrell Collection more than once). Shopping in Princes Square can easily occupy at least a morning, while Buchanan Street and Sauchiehall Street will also reward the inveterate shopper. Make time for at least one side trip from the city. Ayrshire and the Clyde Coast need at least two days—possibly three if you want to see everything: Mount Stuart house on the Isle of Bute;

Ayr and Alloway, which will delight Robert Burns enthusiasts; Culzean Castle—its Georgian elegance a sharp contrast to Mount Stuart. Travel up the Clyde Valley to Lanark to spend a morning at New Lanark, the now-restored site of an 18th-century social experiment in improving the lives of mill workers; you will also be able to enjoy beautiful walks along the waterfall-dotted River Clyde here. Biggar will fill an afternoon or more with its fascinating museums, including Moat Park, which has a fine embroidery collection.

Medieval Glasgow and the Merchant City

In this central part of the city there are not only surviving medieval buildings, but also some of the best examples of the architectural confidence and exuberance that so characterized the Glasgow of 100 years ago. Today this revitalized area is enjoying a newfound appreciation.

A Good Walk

George Square ①, the focal point of Glasgow's business district, is the natural starting point for any walking tour. It's in the very heart of Glasgow and is convenient to the Buchanan Street bus and underground stations and parking lot, as well as to the Queen Street railway station. After viewing the **City Chambers** ② on the east side of the square, leave George Square by the northeast corner and head eastward through a not particularly pretty part of the city along George Street, past Strathclyde University. Turn left at High Street, then go up the hill to **Glasgow Cathedral** ③, the **St. Mungo Museum and Cathedral Visitor Center** ④, and the fascinating if macabre **Necropolis** ⑤ burying ground just off Cathedral Square.

Opposite the cathedral, across Castle Street, is **Provand's Lordship** ⑥, Glasgow's oldest house. Retrace your steps down Castle Street and High Street. Look for the Greek goddess Pallas on top of the imposing gray sandstone building on the right, the former Bank of Scotland building, before reaching the Tolbooth Steeple at **Glasgow Cross** ⑦. Continue east along London Road (under the bridge) about a quarter of a mile and you'll come to the **Barras** ⑧ ("barrows," or pushcarts), Scotland's largest indoor market. Turn right down Greendyke Street from London Road to reach **Glasgow Green** ⑨ by the River Clyde, with the **People's Palace** ⑩ museum of social history as its centerpiece.

Go back to Greendyke Street, past the new St. Andrew's Square development—with the magnificent St. Andrew's Church (1750) as its centerpiece—then via Saltmarket northwards to Tolbooth Steeple. Continue westward along Trongate. This is where the powerful "tobacco lords" who traded with the Americas presided. On the right, down Albion Street, are the offices of Glasgow's daily papers, the *Herald* and the *Evening Times*. On the left, jutting out into Trongate, is the Tron Steeple, all that remains of a church burned down in 1793 when a joke by the local chapter of the Hell-Fire Club (young aristocratic troublemakers) got a little out of hand. The rebuilt church has now been converted into the Tron Theatre.

Continue down the Trongate, then turn right on Hutcheson Street. This is Glasgow's **Merchant City,** with many handsome restored Georgian and Victorian buildings. At the end of the street, just south of George Square, look for **Hutcheson's Hall** ⑪, a visitor center and shop for the National Trust for Scotland. Continue up John Street, take a left on Cochrane Street, and a right on South Frederick Street; on the west side of George Square, on the corner with West George Street, is the **Merchants' House** ⑫. Return to Ingram Street and walk down Glassford Street to see, on the right, the Trades House, which has a facade built in 1791 to designs by Robert Adam. Turn right along Wilson Street to reach Virginia Street, another favorite haunt of Glasgow's tobacco merchants. At Number 33, a former tobacco exchange survives, now an indoor shopping center. Nearby, the somewhat faded **Virginia Court** ⑬ echoes those far-off days. Walk northward up Virginia Street back to Ingram Street. To the left you'll have a good view down to the elegant Royal Exchange Square and the Royal Exchange itself. Once a meeting place for merchants and traders, it is now the **Glasgow Gallery of Modern Art** ⑭. Royal Exchange Square leads you westward to the pedestrian-zone shopping area of Buchanan Street. The Princes Square shopping mall on the east side has a particularly good selection of specialty shops.

Make your way down to Argyle Street. Looking to the west, you'll see the large railway bridge supporting the tracks going into **Central Station** ⑮. Pause to look at the lovely iron arcading of Gardner's Warehouse at 36 Jamaica Street. Head north up Union Street and note the extraordinary architecture of Numbers 84–100, the so-called **Egyptian Halls** ⑯, sadly semi-derelict now, of Alexander "Greek" Thomson.

From here continue north to St. Vincent Street and turn right to reach Nelson Mandela Place, also called St. George's Place. Here is the **Scottish Stock Exchange** ⑰, with its ornate "French Venetian"–style exterior. To see a famous example of Alexander Thomson's Greek Revival churches, walk west on St. Vincent Street about eight blocks to Pitt Street to the **St. Vincent's Street Church** ⑱.

TIMING

This walk covers a lot of ground, but can be accomplished comfortably in a day, leaving time to browse in the People's Palace and the Gallery of Modern Art. Aim to start after the morning rush hour, say at 10 AM, and to finish before the evening rush starts, about 4 PM, to avoid the worst of the traffic fumes and hurrying commuters. Remember that the Barras is only open on weekends, and the City Chambers only on weekdays. Many sites are closed Tuesday, when you should avoid taking this walk.

Sights to See

❽ **Barras.** Scotland's largest indoor market, named for the "barrows," or pushcarts formerly used by the stallholders, is a mecca if you're addicted to searching through piles of junk for bargains. The approximately 80-year-old institution, open only on weekends, is made up of nine markets. The atmosphere is always good humored, and you can find just about anything here, in any condition, from old model railroads to cheese rolls. You can reach the Barras by walking from ScotRail's Argyle Street station, or take any of the various buses to Glasgow Cross at the foot of the Gallowgate. ⊠ ¼ mi east of Glasgow Cross, ☎ 0141/552–7258. ⌨ Free. ☉ Weekends 9–5.

⑮ **Central Station.** The depot is known as the Heilanman's Umbrella because it was the point of meeting and shelter for so many Highlanders who had moved to Glasgow in search of better economic opportunities in the last century. ⊠ Bounded by Gordon, Union, Argyle, Jamaica, Clyde, Oswald, and Hope Sts.

★ ❷ **City Chambers.** Dominating the east side of George Square, this splendidly exuberant expression of Victorian confidence, built by William Young, was opened by Queen Victoria (1819–1901) herself in 1888. Among the outstanding features of the interior are the vaulted ceiling of the entrance hall, marble and alabaster staircases, and the banqueting hall, as well as a number of the smaller suites, each furnished in different woods. ⊠ George Sq., ☎ 0141/287–2000. ⌨ Free guided

Glasgow

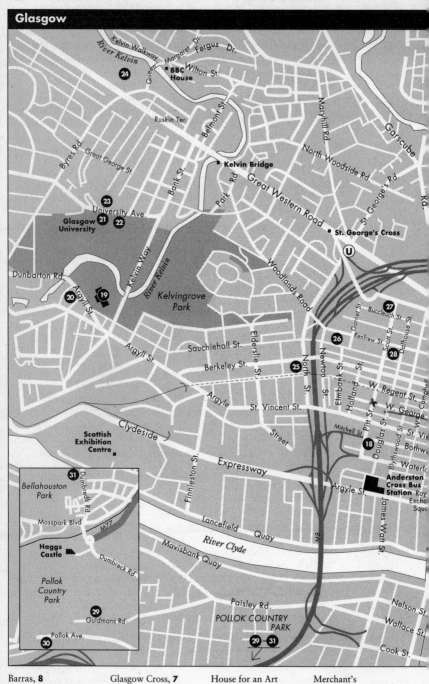

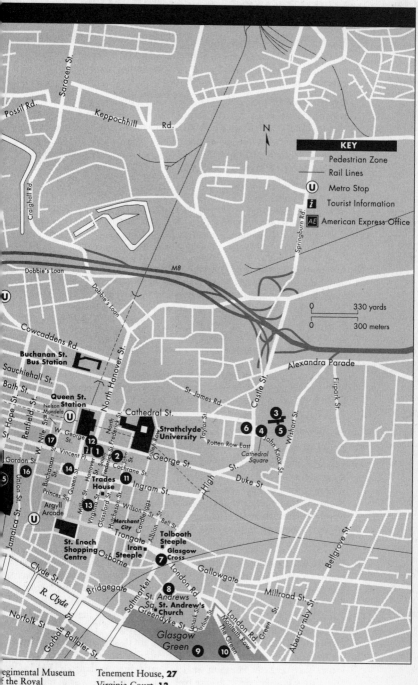

KEY

Pedestrian Zone

Rail Lines

U Metro Stop

i Tourist Information

AE American Express Office

0 | 330 yards
0 | 300 meters

Saracen St.

Possil Rd.

Keppochhill   Rd.

Craighall Rd.

Dobbie's Loan

Dobbie's Loan

M8

Springburn Rd.

N

Cowcaddens Rd.

Buchanan St.
Bus Station

Sauchiehall St.

Bath St.

Hope St.

Renfield St.

Nelson
Mandela
Pl.

Queen St.
Station

Alexandra Parade

St. James Rd.

Cathedral St.

Strathclyde
University

Firpark St.

Castle St.

3

6   4   5

John Knox St.

Wishart St.

Rotten Row East

Cathedral
Square

W. Nile St.

W. George St.

St. Vincent St.

17

12

North Frederick St.

North Hanover St.

Taylor St.

1

2

Cochrane St.

George St.

High   St.

Duke St.

Gordon St.

Union St.

Buchanan St.

Queen St.

14

Miller St.

Hanover St.

Glassford St.

Virginia St.

11

Ingram St.

Rotten Row

Ralley Row

St.

5

16

Princes Sq.

Argyll
Arcade

13

Trades
House

Wilson

Candleriggs

Albion St.

Bell St.

Merchant
City

Jamaica St.

U

Clyde St.

St. Enoch
Shopping
Centre

Trongate

Iron
Steeple

Osborne

Saltmarket

London Rd.

Tolbooth
Steeple

Glasgow
Cross

7

Gallowgate

Millroad St.

Bellgrove St.

Abercromby St.

Bridgegate

Norfolk St.

Gorbals

Ballater St.

R. Clyde

8

St. Andrews
Sq.

St. Andrew's
Church

Greendyke St.

London Rd.

Monteith Row

The Green

Glasgow
Green

9   10

egimental Museum
f the Royal
ighland Fusiliers, **26**

. Mungo Museum
d Cathedral Visitor
enter, **4**

. Vincent's Street
hurch, **18**

ottish Stock
xchange, **17**

tours weekdays at 10:30 and 2:30 (may be closed for occasional civic functions).

⑯ Egyptian Halls. This somewhat dilapidated building was designed and built in 1871 by Victorian architect Alexander "Greek" Thomson (1817–75), who had a penchant for incorporating Egyptian and Greek elements into his work. ⌂ *84–100 Union St.*

❶ George Square. The focal point of Glasgow's business district is lined with an impressive array of statues of worthies from days gone by: Queen Victoria; Scotland's national poet Robert Burns (1759–96); the inventor and developer of the steam engine, James Watt (1736–1819); Prime Minister William Gladstone (1809–98); and towering above them all, Scotland's foremost writer, Sir Walter Scott (1771–1832). The column was intended for George III (1738–1820), after whom the square is named, but his statue was not erected after he was found to be insane toward the end of his reign. On the east side of the square stands the magnificent Italian Renaissance–style **City Chambers** (☞ *above*), and the handsome **Merchants' House** (☞ *below*) fills the corner with West George Street. ⌂ *Between George and St. Vincent Sts.*

★ **❸ Glasgow Cathedral.** An unusual double church, one above the other, and dedicated to Glasgow's patron saint, St. Mungo, the cathedral was begun in the 12th century (consecrated in 1136) and completed about 300 years later. It was spared the ravages of the Reformation, which destroyed so many of Scotland's medieval churches, because the trade guilds of Glasgow regarded it as their own church and defended it. In the lower church is the splendid crypt of St. Mungo, who is sometimes also called St. Kentigern. (Kentigern means "chief word," while Mungo is perhaps a nickname meaning "dear name.") The site of the tomb has been revered since the 6th century, when St. Mungo founded a church here. ⌂ *Cathedral St.,* ☎ *0131/668–8800.* ☞ *Free.* ☼ *Apr.–Sept., Mon.–Sat. 9:30–6, Sun. 2–5; Oct.–Mar., Mon.–Sat. 9:30–4, Sun. 2–4, and for services.*

❼ Glasgow Cross. This crossroads was the very center of the medieval city. The **Mercat Cross** (*mercat* means market), topped by a unicorn, marked the spot where merchants met, where the market was held, and where criminals were executed. Here, too, was the *tron,* or weigh beam, used to check merchants' weights, installed in 1491. The **Tolbooth Steeple** dates from 1626 and served as the civic center and place where travelers entering the city paid tolls. ⌂ *Intersection of Saltmarket, Trongate, Gallowgate, and London Rd.*

⑭ Glasgow Gallery of Modern Art. The newest (1996) of Glasgow's many excellent galleries occupies the former **Royal Exchange** building. Designed by David Hamilton and finished in 1829, the Exchange was a meeting place for merchants and traders; later it became **Stirling's Library.** It incorporates the mansion built in 1780 by William Cunninghame, one of the wealthiest of the "tobacco lords." The modern art, craft, and design collections contained within this handsome building include a strong gathering of Scottish figurative art, works by Scottish artists such as Peter Howson (b. 1958) and John Bellany (b. 1942), and also paintings and sculpture from elsewhere in the world, including Papua New Guinea, Ethiopia, and Mexico. The display scheme is designed to reflect, on each floor, one of the four elements—earth, air, fire, and water—which creates some unexpected juxtapositions and also allows for various interactive exhibits. ⌂ *Queen St.,* ☎ *0141/287–2000.* ☞ *Free.* ☼ *Mon. and Wed.–Sat. 10–5, Sun. 11–5.*

❾ Glasgow Green. Glasgow's oldest park, on the northeast side of the River Clyde, has a long history as a favorite spot for public recreation and political demonstrations. Note the Nelson Column, erected long before London's; the Arch, now the finish line for the thousands of runners of the Glasgow Half Marathon; and the Templeton Business Centre, once a carpet factory, built in the late 19th century in the style of the Doge's Palace in Venice. The most significant building in the park is the **People's Palace** (☞ *below*).

★ ⑪ **Hutcheson's Hall.** Now a visitor center and shop for the National Trust for Scotland, this elegant neoclassical building was designed by David Hamilton (1768–1843) in 1802. The hall was originally a hospice founded by two brothers, George and Thomas Hutcheson; you can see their statues in niches in the facade. ⊠ *158 Ingram St.,* ☎ *0141/ 552–8391.* 🖾 *Free.* ⊙ *Mon.–Sat. 10–5. Closed for public functions, holidays, and Dec. 24–Jan. 6.*

Merchant City. This once run-down area around Hutcheson Street is now being renovated. Among the preserved Georgian and Victorian buildings are elegant designer boutiques. The **City and County Buildings** were built in 1842 to house civil servants; note the impressive arrangement of bays and Corinthian columns.

⑫ **Merchants' House.** This handsome 1874 Victorian building, home to Glasgow's Chamber of Commerce, is topped by a golden sailing ship, a reminder of the importance of trade to Glasgow's prosperity. Inside is a fine **Merchants' Hall,** embellished with stained-glass windows and many portraits. ⊠ *West side of George Sq.,* ☎ *0141/221–8272.* 🖾 *Free.* ⊙ *Hall and anterooms, weekdays 10–noon and 2–5 (unless closed for meetings) or by appointment.*

❺ **Necropolis.** A burying ground since the beginning of recorded history, the Necropolis contains some extraordinarily elaborate Victorian graves, watched over by a statue of John Knox (1514–72). It includes the tomb of 19th-century Glasgow merchant William Miller (1810– 72), author of the "Wee Willie Winkie" nursery rhyme. ⊠ *Behind Glasgow Cathedral.*

★ ❿ **People's Palace.** An impressive Victorian red sandstone building dating from 1894 houses an intriguing museum dedicated to the city's social history; included among the exhibits is one devoted to the ordinary folk of Glasgow, called "The People's Story." Also on show are the writing desk of John McLean (1879–1923), the "Red Clydeside" political activist who came to Lenin's notice, and the famous "banana boots" worn on stage by Britain's—and the world's—most famous Glasgow-born comedian, Billy Connolly (b. 1942). Behind the museum are the well-restored Winter Gardens, a relatively sheltered spot where you can escape the often chilly winds whistling across the green. ⊠ *Glasgow Green,* ☎ *0141/554–0223.* 🖾 *Free.* ⊙ *Mon. and Wed.–Sat. 10–5, Sun. 11–5.*

❻ **Provand's Lordship.** Glasgow's oldest house was built in 1471 by Bishop Andrew Muirhead as a residence for churchmen. Mary, Queen of Scots (1542–87), is said to have stayed here. After her day, however, the house fell into decline and was used alternately as a sweet shop, a soft-drink factory, the home of the city hangman, and a junk shop. It was eventually rescued by the city and turned into a museum. Exhibits show the house as it might have looked in its heyday. ⊠ *Castle St.,* ☎ *0141/552–8819.* 🖾 *Free.* ⊙ *Mon. and Wed.–Sat. 10–5, Sun. 11–5.*

❹ **St. Mungo Museum and Cathedral Visitor Center.** An outstanding collection of artifacts speaks for the many religious groups who've settled throughout the centuries in Glasgow and the west of Scotland. The centerpiece is surrealist Salvador Dalí's (1904–89) magnificent painting, *Christ of St. John of the Cross.* Inside are a gift shop and a café. ⊠ *2 Castle St.,* ☎ *0141/553–2557.* 🎟 *Free.* ☉ *Mon. and Wed.–Sat. 10–5, Sun. 11–5.*

⑱ St. Vincent's Street Church. Dating from 1859, this church, the work of Alexander Thomson, exemplifies his Greek Revival style, replete with Ionic temple, sphinx-esque heads, Greek ornamentation, and rich interior color. ⊠ *Pitt and St. Vincent Sts.*

⑰ Scottish Stock Exchange. Scotland's hub of commerce was built in 1877 in French Gothic style by John Burnet, who was inspired by London's Law Courts in the Strand, designed by William Burges (1827–81). Burges is said to have been flattered rather than perturbed by Burnet's close imitation. ⊠ *7 Nelson Mandela Pl.*

⑬ Virginia Court. Somewhat faded now, Virginia Court is a reminder of the long-gone days of the tobacco merchants who traded with the Americas. Peer through the bars of the gates and note the wagon-wheel ruts still visible in the roadway. Nearby are antiques shops, notably the Virginia Galleries Antiques & Craft (☎ 0141/552–5840), with its pleasant indoor café. ⊠ *Virginia St.*

The West End

Glasgow's West End offers a stellar mix of education, culture, art, and parkland. The neighborhood is dominated by Glasgow University, founded in 1451, making it the third-oldest in Scotland after St. Andrews and Aberdeen, and at least 130 years ahead of the University of Edinburgh. It has thrived as a center of educational excellence, particularly in the sciences. The university buildings are set in parkland, reminding the visitor that Glasgow is a city with more green space per citizen than any other in Europe. It is also a city of museums and art galleries, having benefited from the generosity of industrial and commercial philanthropists and from the deep-seated desire of the city fathers to place Glasgow at the forefront of British cities.

A Good Walk

A good place to start is at the city's main art gallery and museum, **Kelvingrove Museum and Art Gallery** ⑲ in Kelvingrove Park, west of the M8 beltway, at the junction of Sauchiehall (pronounced *socky*-hall) and Argyle streets. There are parking facilities, and plenty of buses go there from downtown. Across Argyle Street in the Old Kelvin Hall exhibition center is the **Museum of Transport** ⑳.

As you walk up Kelvin Way through the trees, the skyline to your left is dominated by the Gilbert Scott building, **Glasgow University**'s ㉑ main edifice. Turn left up University Avenue, past the Memorial Gates, which were erected in 1951 to celebrate the university's 500th birthday. On either side of the road are two important galleries, both maintained by the university. On the south side of University Avenue, in the Victorian part of the university, is the **Hunterian Museum** ㉒. Across University Avenue, in an unremarkable building from the 1970s, is the even more interesting **Hunterian Art Gallery** ㉓.

Here you can either make a small detour north to the Botanic Gardens and return along the banks of the River Kelvin to Kelvingrove Park or go directly through some of Glasgow's elegant 19th-century districts to the extreme northwest of the downtown area, where the rest of the tour resumes. The walk from the university to the **Botanic Gardens** ㉔ is unfortunately not very exciting, but it's worth the effort. Continue along University Avenue and turn right at Byres Road, going as far as Great Western Road and the Grosvenor Hotel. The 40 acres of gardens are across the busy Great Western Road.

After leaving the Botanic Gardens, cross the River Kelvin on Queen Margaret Drive and walk past the BBC Scotland building, just after Hamilton Drive. Turn right, then right again down the steps to the Kelvin Walkway on the north bank of the river. (Farther upstream the Kelvin Walkway connects with the West Highland Way, an official long-distance footpath leading to Fort William, approximately 100 away.) The walkway headed downstream back toward the city center first crosses a footbridge, then passes old mill buildings and goes under Belmont Street and the Great Western Road at Kelvinbridge. At this point it passes Kelvinbridge underground station and goes under the Gibson Street bridge, then back into Kelvingrove Park.

At this point, you can choose to take one of the paths up the hill and explore the stately Victorian crescents and streets of the park area or you can take the lower road past the fountain and head directly back to Sauchiehall Street. Whichever way you choose, you should end up, having walked eastward, at the point where Sauchiehall Street crosses the M8 motorway. Down North Street to your right (southward) you'll see the front of **Mitchell Library** ㉕, the largest public reference library in Europe. Cross the M8 motorway and continue down Sauchiehall Street to the **Regimental Museum of the Royal Highland Fusiliers** ㉖. Turn up Garnet Street and go to the top, then right on Buccleuch (pronounced buck-*loo*) Street. On the left is the **Tenement House** ㉗, a special find tucked away from normal tourist routes. Coming out of the Tenement House, turn east on Buccleuch Street to Scott Street. As you turn south on Scott Street, notice the mural that reflects the name of the area, Garnethill, then turn left onto Renfrew Street to reach Charles Rennie Mackintosh's masterpiece, the **Glasgow School of Art** ㉘. To return to the city center either continue down Scott Street, then east on Sauchiehall Street, or turn south down Blythswood Street, noting the elegant Blythswood Square (1823–29).

TIMING

At least a day is needed for this walk, and even then you will not manage to see all you want to at the Kelvingrove and Hunterian museums; if you anticipate lingering at the museums and galleries, plan at least two days since each could take up an enjoyable day in itself.

Sights to See

㉔ **Botanic Gardens.** Begun by the Royal Botanical Institute of Glasgow in 1842, the displays here include an herb garden, a wide range of tropical plants, and a world-famous collection of orchids. The most spectacular building in the complex is the **Kibble Palace,** built in 1873; it was originally the conservatory of a Victorian eccentric named John Kibble. Its domed, interlinked greenhouses contain tree ferns, palm trees, temperate plants, and the Tropicarium, where you can experience the lushness of a tropical rain forest. Elsewhere on the grounds are more conventional greenhouses, as well as well-maintained lawns and colorful flower beds. ⊠ *Great Western Rd.,* ☎ *0141/334–2422.* 💷 *Free.* ☉ *Gardens: daily 7–dusk; Kibble Palace: daily 10–4:45; other greenhouses: weekdays 10–4:45, Sat. 1–4:45, Sun. noon–4:45. All close at 4:15 in winter.*

NEED A BREAK?

The **Willow Tearoom** (⊠ 217 Sauchiehall St., ☎ 0141/332–0521) has been restored to its original, archetypal Charles Rennie Mackintosh Art Nouveau design, right down to the decorated tables and chairs. The building was designed by Mackintosh in 1903 for Miss Kate Cranston, who ran a chain of tearooms. The tree motifs are echoed in the street address, since *sauchie* is an old Scots word for *willow.*

★ ㉘ **Glasgow School of Art.** This Art Nouveau building—exterior and interior, structure, furnishings, and decoration—forms a unified whole, reflecting the inventive genius of Charles Rennie Mackintosh, who was only 28 years old when he won the competition for its design. Architects and designers from all over the world come to admire it, but because it is a working school of art, general visitor access is sometimes limited. Conducted tours are available. ✉ *167 Renfrew St.,* ☎ *0141/ 353–4500.* 🎫 *£3.50.* ☉ *Tours weekdays 11 AM, 2 PM; Sat. 10:30 AM. Closed last 2 weeks in June.*

OFF THE
BEATEN PATH

QUEEN'S CROSS CHURCH – To learn about the Glasgow-born designer Mackintosh, head for the Charles Rennie Mackintosh Society Headquarters, housed in a church designed by him. Although one of the leading lights in the turn-of-the-century Art Nouveau movement, Mackintosh died in 1928 with his name scarcely known. Today, he is widely confirmed as a brilliant innovator. This off-the-beaten-track center provides a further insight into Glasgow's other Mackintosh-designed buildings, which include Scotland Street School, the Martyrs Public School, the Glasgow School of Art, and reconstructed interiors in the Hunterian Art Gallery. The church is on the corner of Springbank Street at the junction of Garscube Road with Maryhill Road; a cab ride can get you there or a bus heading toward Queen's Cross can be taken from stops along Hope Street. ✉ *870 Garscube Rd.,* ☎ *0141/946-6600.* 🎫 *Free.* ☉ *Weekdays 10:30–5, Sun. 2:30–5 (or by arrangement).*

㉑ **Glasgow University.** The Gilbert Scott Building, Glasgow University's main edifice, was built just over a century ago and is a good example of the Gothic Revival style. **Glasgow University Visitor Centre** has exhibits on the university, a coffee bar, and a gift shop, and is the starting point for guided walking tours of the campus. ✉ *University Ave.,* ☎ *0141/330–5511.* 🎫 *Free; guided tour £1.50.* ☉ *Mon.–Sat. 9:30– 5; May–Sept., also Sun. 2–5. Tours: May–Sept., Wed., Fri., Sat. 11 AM, 2 PM; Oct.–Apr., Wed. 2 PM..*

★ ㉓ **Hunterian Art Gallery.** This gallery, part of Glasgow University, houses William Hunter's (1718–83) collection of paintings (his antiquarian collection is housed in the **Hunterian Museum** nearby, ☞ *below*), together with prints and drawings by Tintoretto (1518–94), Rembrandt (1606–69), Sir Joshua Reynolds (1723–92), and Auguste Rodin (1840–1917), as well as a major collection of paintings by James McNeill Whistler (1834–1903), who had a great affection for the city that bought one of his earliest paintings. Also in the gallery is a replica of Charles Rennie Mackintosh's town house, which used to stand nearby. The rooms are all furnished with Mackintosh's distinctive Art Nouveau chairs, tables, beds, and cupboards, and the walls are decorated in the equally distinctive style devised by him and his wife, Margaret. ✉ *Glasgow University, Hillhead St.,* ☎ *0141/330–5431.* 🎫 *Free.* ☉ *Mon.–Sat. 9:30–5. Mackintosh house closed for lunch 12:30–1:30.*

㉒ **Hunterian Museum.** The city's oldest museum (1807) and part of Glasgow University, the Hunterian houses part of the collections of William Hunter, an 18th-century Glasgow doctor who assembled a staggering quantity of valuable material. (The doctor's art treasures are housed in the **Hunterian Art Gallery** nearby, ☞ *above*.) The museum displays Hunter's hoards of coins, manuscripts, scientific instruments, and archaeological artifacts in a striking Gothic building. ✉ *Glasgow University,* ☎ *0141/330–4221.* 🎫 *Free.* ☉ *Mon.–Sat. 9:30–5.*

★ ⑲ **Kelvingrove Museum and Art Gallery.** Looking like a combination of cathedral and castle, a magnificently ornamented red sandstone edifice dating from the early 20th century contains Glasgow's main museum and art gallery. There has always been debate as to which facade is the front and which is the back. However you enter, Kelvingrove houses what is claimed to be Britain's finest civic collection of British and Continental paintings, with 17th-century Dutch art, a selection from the French Barbizon school, French Impressionism, Scottish art from the 17th century to the present, silver, ceramics, European armor, and even Egyptian archaeological finds. Be sure to pause at Rembrandt's *The Man in Armor.* ⊠ *Kelvingrove Park,* ☎ *0141/287–2000.* ☜ *Free.* ☉ *Mon.–Sat. 10–5, Sun. 11–5.*

Kelvingrove Park. Taking its name from the River Kelvin, which flows through it, this parkland was purchased by the city in 1852. Apart from the abundance of statues of prominent Glaswegians, including Lord Kelvin (1824–1907), the Scottish mathematician and physicist who pioneered a great deal of work in electricity, the park has a massive fountain commemorating a Lord Provost of Glasgow from the 1850s, a duck pond, play area, small open-air theater, and lots of exotic trees. It can be a peaceful retreat from the noise and bustle of the city. ⊠ *Northwest of city center, bounded roughly by Sauchiehall St., Woodlands Rd., and Kelvin Way.*

㉕ Mitchell Library. The largest public reference library in Europe houses more than a million volumes, including what is claimed to be the largest collection on Robert Burns in the world. The library's founder, Stephen Mitchell, who died in 1874 (the same year the library was founded), is commemorated by a bust in the entrance hall. Minerva, goddess of wisdom, looks down from the library's dome, encouraging the library's users and frowning at the drivers thundering along the motorway just in front of her. The western facade (at the back) is particularly beautiful. ⊠ *North St.,* ☎ *0141/287–2931.* ☜ *Free.* ☉ *Mon.–Thurs. 9–8, Fri. and Sat. 9–5.*

★ ㉐ Museum of Transport. Here Glasgow's history of locomotive building is dramatically displayed with full-size exhibits. The collection of Clyde-built ship models is world famous. Anyone who remembers Britain in the 1950s will be able to wax nostalgic at the re-created street scene from that era. ⊠ *Kelvin Hall, 1 Bunhouse Rd.,* ☎ *0141/287–2720.* ☜ *Free.* ☉ *Mon., Wed.–Sat. 10–5, Sun. 11–5.*

㉖ Regimental Museum of the Royal Highland Fusiliers. The history of a famous regiment and the men who served in it is told with exhibits of medals, badges, and uniforms. ⊠ *518 Sauchiehall St.,* ☎ *0141/332–0961.* ☉ *Mon.–Thurs. 9–4:30, Fri. 9–4, weekends by appointment only.*

★ ㉗ Tenement House. This ordinary, simple city-center apartment is anything but ordinary inside: it was occupied from 1911 to 1965 by Miss Agnes Toward, who seems never to have thrown anything away. What is left is a fascinating time capsule, painstakingly preserved with her everyday furniture and belongings. The red sandstone tenement building itself dates from 1892. ⊠ *145 Buccleuch St.,* ☎ *0141/333–0183.* ☜ *£3.* ☉ *Mar.–Oct., daily 2–5 (last admission 4:30).*

Art-Filled Parks West

Just southwest of the city center in the South Side, two of Glasgow's dear green places—Bellahouston Park and Pollok Country Park—have important art collections: Rennie Mackintosh's House for an Art Lover, the Burrell Collection, and Pollok House. A respite from the buzz of the city can also be found in the parks, where you can have a picnic or ramble through greenery and gardens. Both parks are off Paisley Road, about 3 mi southwest of the city center. You can take a taxi

CHARLES RENNIE MACKINTOSH

GLASGOW-BORN architect Charles Rennie Mackintosh (1868–1928) had an extensive influence on European design, but only recently has he been once again acknowledged in his native country as a truly original and creative designer who combined respect for tradition with the excitement of the modern in his own distinctive style.

Mackintosh trained in architecture at Glasgow School of Art, being articled to the Glasgow firm John Hutchison at the age of 16. During his training, his exceptional talent was recognized by the award of various prizes, including two from the Glasgow Institute of Architects (1887) and the Queen's Prize, South Kensington (1889). In 1889 he joined the Glasgow firm Honeyman and Keppie, continuing to win prizes in the following years.

Early influences on his work included the Pre-Raphaelites, James McNeill Whistler (1834–1903), Aubrey Beardsley (1872–98), and Japanese art, but by the 1890s a distinct "Glasgow Style" had been developed by Mackintosh and others. The building for the *Glasgow Herald* newspaper, which he designed in 1893 (and which is now The Lighthouse Centre for Architecture, Design and the City) was soon followed by other major Glasgow buildings: Queen Margaret's Medical College; the Martyrs Public School, tearooms for Catherine Cranston (including the famous Willow Tearooms that can still be seen today; the Hill House, Helensburgh (now owned by the National Trust for Scotland); and Queen's Cross Church (completed in 1899 and now the headquarters of the Charles Rennie Mackintosh Society). The year 1897 saw work started on a new home for the Glasgow School of Art, now recognized as one of his major achievements and which still retains original fittings, furnishings, ornamentation, and documents.

Mackintosh married Margaret Macdonald in 1900, and in later years her decorative work enhanced the interiors of his buildings. Over the next few years he worked abroad as well as in Scotland, being especially successful in Germany and Austria. In 1904 he became a partner in Honeyman and Keppie, and designed Scotland Street School (now a Museum of Education) in the same year. Until 1913, when he left Honeyman and Keppie and moved to England, Mackintosh's various projects included work on buildings and/or interiors over much of Scotland, but especially in the Central Belt: Comrie, Bridge of Allan, Kilmacolm, and many other places. He preferred whenever possible to include interiors—furniture and fittings—as part of his overall design (a talent demonstrated clearly at the Hill House). He believed that building design should be "a total work of art, to the wholeness of which each contrived detail contributes."

Commissions in England after 1913 included a variety of design challenges not confined to buildings, including fabrics, furniture, and even book bindings (for publishers Blackie and Sons). In 1923 Mackintosh settled in France, but returned to London in 1927 and died there in 1928.

Glasgow must be the best place in the world to admire Mackintosh's work: in addition to the buildings mentioned above, most of which can be visited, the Hunterian Art Gallery contains magnificent reconstructions of the principal rooms at 78 Southpark Avenue, Mackintosh's Glasgow home, and original drawings, documents, and records plus the recreation of a room at 78 Derngate, Northampton.

or car, city bus, or a train from Glasgow Central Station to Pollokshaws West Station or Dumbreck.

A Good Tour

Traveling either by car, taxi, bus, or train, start your art exploration at the **Burrell Collection** ㉙, its diverse collections set against nature in a supermodern structure. Repair to the museum's good café-restaurant for a bite, or plan to pack a picnic lunch to enjoy in one of the parks. **Pollok House** ㉚, with the Stirling Maxwell Collection of painting and fine art, is just a few-hundred-yards walk beyond the Burrell. Head north on Haggs Road and Bumbreck Road to Bellahouston Park and Rennie Mackintosh's Art Nouveau **House for an Art Lover** ㉛, based on the architect's entry into an 1901 competition.

TIMING

Allow the good part of a day for seeing the three collections, strolls through the parks, and a picnic or lunch. Note that the House for an Art Lover is usually open on weekends (and some weekdays), and Pollok House and the Burrell Collection are closed Tuesday.

Sights to See

㉙ **Burrell Collection.** Set in Pollok Country Park, a custom-built, ultramodern (1983) yet elegant building of pink sandstone and stainless steel houses 8,000 exhibits of all descriptions, from ancient Egyptian, Greek, and Roman artifacts to Chinese ceramics, bronzes, and jade, to medieval tapestries, stained glass, Rodin sculptures, and exquisite French Impressionist paintings—Degas' *The Rehearsal* and Sir Henry Raeburn's *Miss Macartney* to name a few. The magpie collection was donated to the city in 1944 by eccentric millionaire Sir William Burrell (1861–1958). The exterior and interior were designed with large glass walls so that the items on display could relate to their surroundings: art and nature, supposedly in perfect harmony. It does, however, seem an incongruous setting for Chinese porcelain and the reconstruction of medieval castle rooms. ⊠ *Buses 45, 48, 57 from Union St.,* ☎ *0141/649–7151.* ☞ *Free.* ☉ *Mon., Wed.–Sat. 10–5, Sun. 11–5.*

㉛ **House for an Art Lover.** Set in Bellahouston Park is a "new" Mackintosh house: based on a competition entry Charles Rennie Mackintosh submitted in 1901, but which was never built in his lifetime, it was completed in 1996 and now houses permanent exhibition rooms—containing his designs for various rooms and decorative pieces he and his wife, Margaret, created—and Glasgow School of Art's postgraduate study center. ⊠ *Bellahouston Park, Dumbreck Rd.; Buses 9, 53, 54 from Union St.,* ☎ *0141/353–4770, information 0141/353–4449.* ☞ *£3.50.* ☉ *Weekends 10–5; also occasional weekdays (call for details).*

㉚ **Pollok House.** Dating from the mid-1700s, the classic Georgian Pollok House in Pollok Country Park contains the Stirling Maxwell Collection of paintings, including works by El Greco (1514–1614), Murillo (1617–82), Goya (1746–1828), Signorelli (circa 1445–1523), and William Blake (1757–1827). Fine 18th- and early 19th-century furniture, silver, glass, and porcelain are also on display. The house has fine gardens and looks over the White Cart River and Pollok Park, where, amid mature trees and abundant wildlife, the City of Glasgow's own highland cattle peacefully graze. ⊠ *Pollok Ave.* ☎ *0141/649–7151.* ☞ *Free.* ☉ *Mon., Wed.–Sat. 10–5, Sun. 11–5.*

DINING

Glaswegians are serious about their food and expect good cooking, ample portions, competent service, and value for their money. And thanks to its large and varied ethnic population, Glasgow has an array of foreign restaurants at all prices—from late-night crepe stalls and *pakora* (Indian fried chickpea cakes) bars to elegant restaurants with worldly menus.

Glasgow restaurants tend on the whole to be larger than their Edinburgh counterparts, so getting a table at the restaurant of your choice should usually be no problem, but it is advisable to book for a Friday or Saturday night.

CATEGORY	COST*
££££	over £40
£££	£30–£40
££	£15–£30
£	under £15

per person for a three-course meal, including VAT and excluding drinks and service

Medieval Glasgow and Merchant City

Chinese

££ ✕ **Loon Fung.** There is plenty of space in this popular Cantonese restaurant, which was once a cinema and now seats 200. The pleasant and efficient staff guides you enthusiastically through the house specialties, including the famed dim sum. If you like seafood, try the deep-fried won ton with prawns, crispy stuffed crab claws, or lobster in garlic and cheese sauce. The business lunch and fixed-price dinner are reasonably priced. ⊠ *417 Sauchiehall St.,* ☎ *0141/332–1240. AE, MC, V.*

Eclectic

££–££££ ✕ **Rogano.** This restaurant's Art Deco interior, modeled after the style of the *Queen Mary* liner—bird's-eye maple paneling, chrome trim, and dramatic ocean murals—is enough to recommend it. Portions are generous in the main restaurant, where impeccably prepared specialties include roast rack of lamb and classic seafood dishes such as lobster thermidor. Downstairs in the Café Rogano diner, the brasserie-style food is more modern and imaginative; the menu, which changes monthly, might list clam chowder or Mediterranean grilled swordfish. The theater menu provides early evening and late-night bargains, and the fixed-price lunch menu is popular upstairs. There's also an oyster bar near the entrance. Rogano is patronized by the Glasgow establishment and visiting glitterati, who appreciate, as you will, the extremely good service. ⊠ *11 Exchange Pl.,* ☎ *0141/248–4055. AE, DC, MC, V.*

££–£££ ✕ **Buttery.** This restaurant's exquisite Victorian–Edwardian sur-
★ roundings of dark colors and wood trim are echoed by the staff's period uniforms. The best in Scottish fish, beef, and game is on the international menu; try the fillet of veal with mustard and cheese glaze. There is also a varied vegetarian menu. Service is friendly and the ambience relaxed. ⊠ *652 Argyle St.,* ☎ *0141/221–8188. Reservations essential. AE, DC, MC, V. Closed Sun. No lunch Sat.*

££ ✕ **Drum and Monkey.** This spectacular bar-restaurant in relaxed Victorian surroundings is a popular lunch and after-work meeting place. Snacks and bar meals are tasty: try the hot sandwich with goat cheese, roast red pepper, and pesto on tomato bread. The bistro serves exceptional Scottish–French cuisine: try the asparagus and roast garlic risotto with roast cherry tomatoes, and the potato and smoked-haddock broth. ⊠ *93–95 St. Vincent St.,* ☎ *0141/221–6636. AE, DC, MC, V. Closed Sun. in winter. No dinner Sun. in summer.*

££ ✕ **Brasserie.** A hotel basement (☞ Lodging, *below*) fitted with wooden booths provides a quiet, relaxed environment in which to appreciate a varied British–French menu. Traditional favorites like grilled liver and bacon with caramelized onion, or fish cakes with chips, appear alongside classic French *boeuf en daube* (beef braised in herbs and a red-wine stock). For dessert try the creamed rice pudding with Armagnac prunes. ⊠ *Malmaison hotel, 278 W. George St.,* ☎ *0141/221–6401. Reservations essential. AE, DC, MC, V.*

£–££ ✕ **Café Gandolfi.** Once a Victorian pub, this café's location and decor reflect its trend-setting aspirations. On the edge of the Merchant City, it is now a haven for the design-conscious under-thirty crowd. Wooden tables and chairs carved by Scottish artist Tim Stead are so fluidly shaped it is hard to believe they're inanimate. The café opens early for breakfast, serving croissants, eggs *en cocotte* (casserole-style), and espresso. The rest of the day the menu is filled with interesting soups, salads, local specialties, and Mediterranean favorites. Don't miss the smoked venison or the finnan haddie. Homemade ice cream and good pastries ensure busy afternoons, and evenings are livened up with good beers but less compelling wines. ⊠ *64 Albion St.,* ☎ *0141/552–6813. MC, V.*

£–££ ✕ **78 St. Vincent.** In what was originally the German Embassy—with
★ stone eagles outside and elaborate plasterwork within—maroon velvet drapes, fish wall tiles, and quirky ironwork are now the setting in which to enjoy contemporary Scottish, French-influenced cuisine. Try loin of lamb with a confit of garlic, vegetables, and port, or salmon and scallops with ginger and spring onions *en papillote* (baked in parchment paper). Reservations are advised. ⊠ *78 St. Vincent St.,* ☎ *0141/248–7878. AE, MC, V. No lunch Sun.*

Indian

£ ✕ **Mr. Singh's.** This is one of Glasgow's most popular eateries, serving superb Indian and international cuisine backed by three generations of family experience. The opulent surroundings—gold-painted plaster cornices and large mirrors—combined with Indian waiters in kilts and a menu including curried haggis create a real "Indian with a touch of tartan" ambience. A choice of meats or vegetables can be cooked in a number of deliciously different sauces: try the lamb Mazadar—hot and spicy, with Rèmy Martin—or the pistachio *korma* (curried meat with onions and vegetables). ⊠ *149 Elderslie St.,* ☎ *0141/204–0186 or 0141/221–1452. AE, MC, V.*

Italian

£ ✕ **Fazzi Café Bar.** This inexpensive Italian café-bar, with checkered tablecloths and bentwood chairs set on a tiled floor, is a cheerful place for a quick plateful of gnocchi *alla Emiliana* (with tomato, basil, and cheese sauce), or spinach and ricotta ravioli. The delicatessen at one end sells prepared food to take out. ⊠ *65–67 Cambridge St.,* ☎ *0141/ 332–0941. AE, DC, MC, V.*

Scottish

££–£££ ✕ **Yes.** This stylish restaurant belies its basement location, with care-
★ ful lighting and mirrors setting off the dramatic red, purple, and cream color scheme. Widely spaced tables enhance the relaxed ambience in which to enjoy contemporary Scottish cuisine. Try the "Surprise Menu": an eclectic four-course selection reflecting the best fresh produce available, which might include rack of lamb with a wild mushroom risotto, or seared chicken breast on a bed of spinach. The ground-floor café-bar (£) serves Mediterranean-Italian specialties in flashy digs. ⊠ *22 West Nile St.,* ☎ *0141/221–8044. Reservations essential. AE, DC, MC, V. Closed Sun.*

£ ✕ **CCA Café/Bar.** Attached to the Centre for the Contemporary Arts, this warehouse-style café with oilcloths on the tables, bentwood chairs, and walls bedecked with modern paintings for sale offers a particularly good choice of vegetarian dishes, although meat and fish entrées are also served. Try the leek and mushroom dumplings with tomato and basil sauce, or the tagliatelle with scallops and peat-smoked haddock in spinach and cheese sauce. There's a good wine and beer list

Glasgow Dining and Lodging

Dining

Ashoka West
End, **12**
Bay Tree, **10**
Brasserie, **20**
Buttery, **22**
Café Gandolfi, **29**

CCA Café/Bar, **19**
Cottier's, **8**
Drum and Monkey, **27**
Fazzi Café Bar, **24**
Janssens
Café Restaurant, **11**
Loon Fung, **18**

Mr. Singh's, **16**
Puppet Theatre, **9**
Rogano, **28**
78 St. Vincent, **26**
Two Fat Ladies, **7**
Yes, **25**

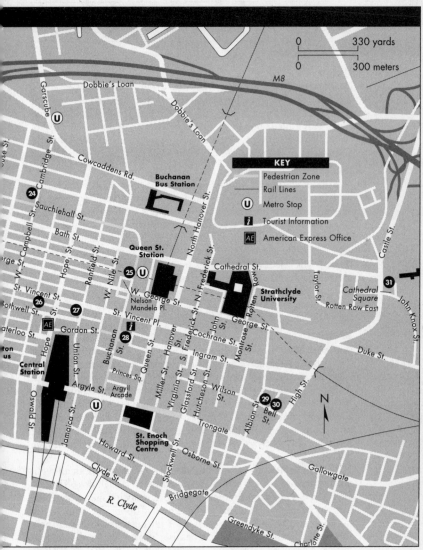

KEY
- Pedestrian Zone
- Rail Lines
- Ⓤ Metro Stop
- ℹ Tourist Information
- AE American Express Office

Lodging

Angus, **14**
Babbity Bowster's, **30**
Cathedral House, **31**
Devonshire Hotel, **2**
Glasgow Hilton, **21**
Kirklee Hotel, **5**

Malmaison, **20**
Number Thirty Six, **13**
One Devonshire Gardens, **3**
The Sandyford, **15**
Sherbrooke Castle Hotel, **23**

Town House, **4**
Victorian House, **17**
White House, **1**
Wickets, **6**

chalked up on the blackboard. ⊠ *350 Sauchiehall St.,* ☎ *0141/332–7864. AE, MC, V.*

West End and Environs

Dutch

£–££   ✕ **Janssens Café Restaurant.** Described as "Amsterdam in Glasgow,"
★   this restaurant has spare but pleasantly relaxing surroundings in which
to enjoy a Continental menu served by a friendly Dutch staff. Pita bread
filled with grilled lamb or gratinéed mussels are typical of the dishes
served, and there are lots of fresh salads. Reservations are advised weekends. ⊠ *1355 Argyle St.,* ☎ *0141/334–9682. MC, V.*

Indian

£   ✕ **Ashoka West End.** This Punjabi restaurant consistently outperforms
★   its many competitors in quality, range, and taste. All portions are large
enough to please the ravenous, but there is nothing heavy-handed
about the cooking here: Vegetable *samosas* (stuffed savory deep-fried
pastries) are crisp and light; the spicing for the lamb, chicken, and prawn
dishes is fresh and fragrant; and the milder kormas are pleasantly
creamy. The selection of breads is superb. The eclectic Eastern decor,
involving a bizarre mixture of plants, murals, rugs, and brass lamps,
and inappropriate Western decor simply emphasize the Ashoka's id-
iosyncracy. Reservations are advised weekends. ⊠ *1284 Argyle St.,* ☎
0800/454817 toll-free. AE, MC, V. No lunch Sat.–Tues.

Scottish

££–£££   ✕ **Puppet Theater.** Down an unprepossessing side street in the West
End is one of Glasgow's most delightful new restaurants. Housed in
a converted Edwardian mews plus striking angled conservatory, the four
dining rooms all have different moods. The contemporary Scottish menu,
with a Mediterranean influence, might offer cream of parsnip and
lentil soup with thyme *chantilly* (whipped cream), followed by breast
of chicken with butternut squash and sweet potato purée. ⊠ *11
Ruthven Lane, off Byres Rd.,* ☎ *0141/339–8444. Reservations essential.
AE, MC, V.*

££   ✕ **Two Fat Ladies.** It's easy to mistake this restaurant for an all-night
grocery because the kitchen can be seen through the window. The dining room has no ornamentation of any sort, just varnished wooden tables, nicotine-yellow walls, and a wooden floor. The cooking, in
modern Scottish style, compensates for the austerity. Fish and shellfish, such as turbot, John Dory, monkfish, and lobster, predominate—
fresh and prepared with imagination and skill. Try the char-grilled king
scallops with garlic and parsley butter. Portions are generous; the salads, colossal. ⊠ *88 Dumbarton Rd.,* ☎ *0141/339–1944. MC, V. Closed
Sun. No lunch Mon.–Thurs.*

South American

£–££   ✕ **Cottier's.** A converted Victorian church with interior decor by Glasgow artist Daniel Cottier is the unusual setting for this theater bar and
restaurant (the Arts Theatre is attached). Red walls and beamed ceilings warm the downstairs bar. Chicken in pumpkin-seed sauce or
Colombian beef and dried fruit stew might be among the South American dishes on the menu. Reservations are advised weekends. ⊠ *93 Hyndland St.,* ☎ *0141/357–5825. AE, MC, V.*

Vegetarian

£   ✕ **Bay Tree.** A small vegetarian haven in the university area, this no-
smoking café serves hearty fare such as peanut and paprika soup or
vegetable and bean hotchpotch, plus a tasty all-day breakfast. The modern paintings on the walls are often for sale. ⊠ *403 Great Western Rd.,*
☎ *0141/334–5898. Reservations not accepted. No credit cards.*

LODGING

CATEGORY	COST*
££££	over £120
£££	£90–£120
££	£50–£90
£	under £50

All prices are for a standard double room, including service, breakfast, and VAT.

Medieval Glasgow and Merchant City

£££–££££ 🏨 **Glasgow Hilton.** You'll be struck by the professionalism at this typical international hotel; Glasgow friendliness permeates the very upscale image. Two themed restaurants, Cameron's, a Highland shooting lodge, and Minsky's, a New York–style deli and carvery, serve superb food, as do the two bars, the Scotch Bar and the colonial-themed Raffles. ⊠ *1 William St., G3 8HT,* ☎ *0141/204–5555,* FAX *0141/204–5004. 319 rooms with bath. 2 restaurants, 2 bars, beauty salon, health club, meeting rooms, free parking. AE, DC, MC, V.*

£££ 🏨 **Malmaison.** In a converted church, the small, modern Malmaison prides itself on personal service: each room has a CD player (suites with CDs, doubles without), robes, and puffy down comforters. The chic art deco decor employs bold colors—eggplant, navy, cream, red—in playful prints and geometric shapes fit for the Little Prince, all balanced out by traditional prints and furniture. In the lobby is a splendid staircase with a wrought-iron balustrade illustrating Napoléon's exploits (the hotel takes its name from his home). The warm Brasserie (☞ Dining, *above*) offers traditional British-French cooking. Café Mal serves savory Italian-Mediterranean pizzas and pasta in an airy terra-cotta-hued room with iron fixtures and a spiral staircase. ⊠ *278 W. George St., G2 4LL,* ☎ *0141/572–1000,* FAX *0141/572–1002. 66 rooms with bath, 8 suites. 2 restaurants, bar, minibars, exercise room, meeting rooms. AE, DC, MC, V.*

££ 🏨 **Babbity Bowster's.** There's a lively atmosphere at this small, intimate hotel in a restored 18th-century town house designed by Robert Adam. Rooms have dark wood Victorian reproductions, white lace bedding, and floral curtains. The first-floor gallery features many works by Glaswegian artists. The teak tables, upholstered chairs, wood floor and gray-and-white colors of the restaurant compliment the handsome hotel. ⊠ *16–18 Blackfriars St., G1 1PE,* ☎ *0141/552–5055,* FAX *0141/552–7774. 6 rooms with shower. Restaurant, bar, café. AE, DC, MC, V.*

££ 🏨 **Cathedral House.** In the heart of old Glasgow, near the cathedral, this small, friendly, freshly decorated hotel is convenient for sightseeing. The café–bar offers a fixed-price lunch, and there's also a restaurant with an à la carte menu that lists interesting Icelandic dishes among more usual fare. ⊠ *28–32 Cathedral Sq., G4 0XA,* ☎ *0141/ 552–3519,* FAX *0141/552–2444. 8 rooms with bath. Restaurant, bar, free parking. AE, DC, MC, V.*

West End and Environs

££££ 🏨 **Devonshire Hotel.** This upscale hotel occupies an elegant terraced mansion, and the native Glasgow hospitality and friendliness contrast sharply with the formality of the sumptuous decor—elegant drapes, marbled pillars, stained glass, and four-poster beds. Frequented by stars when they're in town (Whitney Houston and Bruce Springsteen among them), the hotel strives for excellence in every department, including the modern British cuisine for residents only that makes the most of

Scotland's fish and game. ✉ *5 Devonshire Gardens, G12 0UX,* ☎ *0141/ 339–7878,* FAX *0141/339–3980. 14 rooms with bath. Restaurant. AE, DC, MC, V.*

£££ ☆ ⊞ **One Devonshire Gardens.** This hotel comprises a group of Victorian houses on a sloping tree-lined street 10 minutes west of the city center. Celebrities such as Luciano Pavarotti and Elizabeth Taylor name it as their favorite. Each individually decorated bedroom has rich wallpaper, heavy drapes, and French mahogany furniture; 10 rooms have four-poster beds. The restaurant is equally stylish with a menu that changes daily and specialties that include fillet of venison with potato and turnip gratin, and terrine of chicken and bacon with Cumberland sauce. The wine list is commanding, as are the prices. ✉ *1 Devonshire Gardens, G12 0UX,* ☎ *0141/339–2001,* FAX *0141/337–1663. 27 rooms with bath or shower. Restaurant, free parking. AE, DC, MC, V.*

£££ ⊞ **White House.** This is an unusual Glasgow hotel insofar as it has no dining room. All accommodations at the White House are in self-contained suites, and you can either cook your own food in the fully appointed kitchen, or eat out. The larger suites comprise several linked rooms, and the less expensive have a kitchen area in the sitting room. ✉ *11–13 Clevedon Crescent, G12 0PA,* ☎ *0141/339–9375,* FAX *0141/ 337–1430. 31 suites. AE, DC, MC, V.*

££ ☆ ⊞ **Kirklee Hotel.** In a quiet district of Glasgow near the university, this hotel is small and cozy. Its owners take pride in being friendly and helpful and in keeping the hotel spotless and comfortable. ✉ *11 Kensington Gate, G12 9LG,* ☎ *0141/334–5555,* FAX *0141/339–3828. 9 rooms with bath or shower. AE, DC, MC, V.*

££ ☆ ⊞ **Town House.** A handsome old terraced house in a quiet cul-de-sac, the Town House thrives on repeat business from satisfied guests. The owners are particularly welcoming. The high ceilings, plasterwork, and other original architectural features of the house are complemented by restrained cream-and-pastel–striped decor, stripped pine doors, and plain fabrics. Evening meals are served on request. There is a comfortable sitting room with books and informative leaflets to browse through. ✉ *4 Hughenden Terr., G12 9XR,* ☎ *0141/357–0862,* FAX *0141/339– 9605. 10 rooms with shower. DC, MC, V.*

££ ⊞ **Wickets.** In the heart of Billy Connolly's neighborhood, Partick, this hotel dominates one of the area's few green spaces—the West of Scotland cricket ground. It is a handsome white mansion house with an airy, Continental feel. The rooms are furnished with a cheerful bravado. Its glass-front restaurant looking onto an extensive garden is a rare pleasure in the city. The bar areas are split between the traditional and the artfully Parisienne. Since cricket is not Glasgow's premier sport, Wickets enjoys a tranquil, leafy setting. ✉ *52 Fortrose St., G11 5LP,* ☎ FAX *0141/334–9334. 10 rooms, 8 with bath, 2 with shower. AE, MC, V.*

£–££ ⊞ **Angus.** Another privately run city-center hotel on Sauchiehall Street, the Angus is cozy yet spacious. Its biggest pluses are the friendly staff and their eye for detail. All rooms have been tastefully decorated, creating a Victorian ambience. ✉ *966–970 Sauchiehall St., G3 7TQ,* ☎ *0141/357–5155,* FAX *0141/339–9469. 18 rooms with bath or shower. AE, MC, V.*

£–££ ⊞ **Number Thirty Six.** A Victorian terraced house in the West End, convenient for the Kelvingrove and Hunterian museums and art galleries, this bed-and-breakfast serves a Continental-style breakfast in your room. The house is entirely no-smoking. ✉ *36 St. Vincent Crescent, G3 8NG,* ☎ FAX *0141/248–2086. 5 rooms with bath or shower. No credit cards. Closed Oct.–Mar.*

£ ⊞ **The Sandyford.** With a fine Victorian exterior, this hotel on the west end of famous Sauchiehall Street is convenient to all city-center facilities, including the Scottish Exhibition Centre and many art galleries.

The Sandyford is more an upscale B&B than a hotel, although its rooms are somewhat spartan, with stark white interiors and pine furniture. ✉ *904 Sauchiehall St., G3 7TF,* ☎ *0141/334–0000,* FAX *0141/337–1812. 59 rooms with bath or shower. MC, V.*

£ 🏠 **Victorian House.** This bed-and-breakfast on a quite residential street is only a block away from the Charles Rennie Mackintosh–designed Glasgow School of Art. The plain bedrooms are rather disappointing after the dramatic, dark red decor of the entrance hall and reception area. The staff is welcoming. No meals are served other than breakfast, but there are plenty of restaurants on nearby Sauchiehall Street. ✉ *212 Renfrew St., G3 6TX,* ☎ *0141/332–0129,* FAX *0141/353–3155. 45 rooms, 1 with bath, 36 with shower. MC, V.*

South Side

££–££££ 🏠 **Sherbrooke Castle Hotel.** Come to the Sherbrooke for a flight of Gothic fantasy. Its cavernous rooms hark back to grander times when the South Side of Glasgow was home to the immensely wealthy tobacco barons, whose homes were built with turrets and towers. The spacious grounds are far from the noise and bustle of the city, yet only a 10-minute drive from the city center. Like the tobacco barons, the hotel's proprietor insists on tasteful decor and good traditional cooking. The busy bar is well patronized by locals. ✉ *11 Sherbrook Ave., Pollokshields, G41 4PG,* ☎ *0141/427–4227,* FAX *0141/427–5685. 25 rooms with bath or shower. Restaurant, bar. AE, DC, MC, V.*

NIGHTLIFE AND THE ARTS

Held in the second half of January, **Celtic Connections** (✉ Glasgow Royal Concert Hall, 2 Sauchiehall St., G2 3NY, ☎ 0141/353–4137) is an ever-expanding annual homage to Celtic music, with musicians from Africa, France, Canada, Ireland, and Scotland playing and offering hands-on workshops on such things as harp-making and playing.

The Arts

Concerts

Glasgow's **Royal Concert Hall** (✉ 2 Sauchiehall St., ☎ 0141/287–4000) has 2,500 seats and is the main performance venue of the Royal Scottish National Orchestra, which performs winter and summer. **City Halls** (✉ Candleriggs, ☎ 0141/287–4000) house a wide variety of musical events. The **Henry Wood Hall** (✉ Claremont St., ☎ 0141/226–3868), a former church, is now used for occasional classical concerts and is the administrative base and rehearsal center for the RSNO. The **Scottish Exhibition and Conference Centre** (✉ Finnieston, ☎ 0141/248–3000) is a regular venue for pop concerts.

Dance and Opera

Glasgow is home to the Scottish Opera and Scottish Ballet, both of which perform at the **Theatre Royal** (✉ Hope St., ☎ 0141/332–9000). Visiting dance companies from many countries perform here also. The **Tramway** (✉ 25 Albert Dr., ☎ 0141/287–4000), the city's old museum of transport, is now an exciting venue for opera, drama, and dance.

Film

The **Glasgow Film Theatre** (✉ 12 Rose St., ☎ 0141/332–6535) is an independent public cinema screening the best new-release films from all over the world. The **ABC Film Centre** (✉ Sauchiehall St., ☎ 0141/332–9513), the **Grosvenor** (✉ West End, ☎ 0141/339–4298), and the **Odeon Film Centre** (✉ Renfield St., ☎ 0141/333–9551) show all the latest releases. For details of programs, consult the daily newspapers.

Theater

Tickets for theatrical performances can be purchased at theater box offices or at the **Ticket Center** (⊠ Candleriggs, ☎ 0141/287–4000).

Glasgow offers a plethora of live theater. One of the most exciting is the internationally renowned **Citizen's Theatre** (⊠ 119 Gorbals St., ☎ 0141/429–0022), where productions, and their sets, are often of hair-raising originality. Contemporary works are staged at **Cottier's Arts Theatre** (⊠ 93 Hyndland St., ☎ 0141/287–4000), in a converted church. The **Centre for the Contemporary Arts** (⊠ 350 Sauchiehall St., ☎ 0141/332–7521) not only stages modern plays, but also has exhibitions, films, and musical performances. The **King's Theatre** (⊠ Bath St., ☎ 0141/287–4000) puts on drama, light entertainment, variety shows, musicals, and amateur productions. The **Mitchell** (⊠ Mitchell Library, 6 Granville St., ☎ 0141/227–5033 or 0141/287–4000) mostly accommodates amateur productions, but also hosts lectures and meetings. The **Pavilion** (⊠ Renfield St., ☎ 0141/332–1846) offers family variety entertainment along with rock and pop concerts.

The **Royal Scottish Academy of Music and Drama** (⊠ 100 Renfrew St., ☎ 0141/332–5057) stages a variety of international and student performances. The **Tramway** (⊠ 25 Albert Dr., ☎ 0141/287–4000) is a good venue for drama, as well as dance and opera. The **Tron Theatre** (⊠ 63 Trongate, ☎ 0141/552–4267) houses Scottish and international contemporary theater. The **Arches** (⊠ Midland St., ☎ 0141/287–4000) stages serious and controversial drama from around the world. **Theatre Royal** (⊠ Hope St., ☎ 0141/332–9000) has performances of major drama, including an occasional season of plays by international touring companies.

Nightlife

Consult the fortnightly magazine, *The List,* for up-to-date listings.

Bars and Pubs

Glasgow's pubs were once famous for hard drinkers who demanded few comforts. Times have changed and many pubs have been turned into smart wine bars. For a taste of an authentic Glasgow pub with some traditional folk music occasionally thrown in, go to the Stockwell Street area and search out **The Scotia Bar** (⊠ 112 Stockwell St., ☎ 0141/552–8682), **The Victoria Bar** (⊠ 159 Bridgegate, ☎ 0141/552–6040), or **Clutha Vaults** (⊠ 167 Stockwell St., ☎ 0141/552–7520). Real ale enthusiasts should visit the **Brewery Tap** (⊠ 1055 Sauchiehall St., ☎ 0141/339–8866) or the **Bon Accord** (⊠ 153 North St., ☎ 0141/248–4427). If you visit only one pub in Glasgow, make it the **Horseshoe Bar** (⊠ 17–21 Drury St., ☎ 0141/221–3051), which offers a sepia-tinted sentimental glimpse of all the friendlier Glasgow myths, and serves that cheerful distillation over what is purported to be the world's longest bar. Refurbishment would be a curse on its original tiling, stained glass, and deeply polished woodwork. Almost as intriguing as the decor is the clientele—a complete cross-section of the city's populace. The upstairs lounge (with bargain three-course lunch for £3) serves the steak pie Britain became famous for, and the waitress will ask some pretty pointed questions if you don't finish.

In the center of town the classic Victorian **Drum and Monkey** (⊠ 93 St. Vincent St., ☎ 0141/221–6636, ☞ Dining, *above*) attracts an after-work crowd of young professionals and has live music during the week. **Nico's** (⊠ 375 Sauchiehall St., ☎ 0141/332–5736), designed along the lines of a Paris café, is a favorite with the nearby art school students and young Glaswegian professionals. The best Gaelic pub is **Uisge Beatha** (⊠ 232–246 Woodlands Rd., ☎ 0141/332–0473), pronounced *oos*-ki *bee*-ha, which means "water of life" and is the origin of the word "whiskey" (the term is a phonetic transliteration of the Gaelic word *uisge*). It serves beer from its own Glaschu Brewery, nearby; try the Fraoch (heather beer) in season. There is good live music in the **Halt** (⊠ 160 Woodlands Rd., ☎ 0141/564–1527), which has a mixed-age clientele. In the city center, close to the River Clyde, the **Riverside Club** (⊠ Fox St., off Clyde St., ☎ 0141/248–3144) features traditional *ceilidh* (a mix of country dancing, music, and song pronounced *kay*-lee) bands on Friday and Saturday evenings, and a Tuesday night ceilidh class; get there early—it's very popular.

Nightclubs

As in most of Britain's clubs, electronic music—from house to techno to drum and bass—is par for the course in dance clubs. **The Arches** (⊠ Midland St., ☎ 0141/221–4001, ☉ Fri. 11 PM–3 AM, Sat. 10:30 PM–4 AM) is one of the city's largest arts venues, for both its own and touring theater groups, but on Friday and Saturday nights it thumps with house and techno and welcomes big music names. **Archaos** (⊠ 25 Queen St., ☎ 0141/204–3189, ☉ Tues.–Sun. 11 PM–4 AM), Glasgow's biggest club, has three dance floors blasting house, garage, indie, R& B, soul, and hip-hop music. **The Polo Lounge** (⊠ 84 Wilson St., ☎ 0141/553–1221, ☉ Mon.–Thurs. noon–1 AM; Fri.–Sun. noon–3 AM) is Glasgow's largest gay club, with three bars and two dance floors for 70s, 80s, and 90s sounds, and live jazz on Sunday between 4–6 PM—something for everyone.

OUTDOOR ACTIVITIES AND SPORTS

Biking and Running

The tourist board (☞ Glasgow A to Z, *below*) can provide a list of cycle paths and of the 70 parks and gardens in Glasgow where you can jog around the pathways; many of the parks also have tennis courts and/or bowling greens.

Fishing

With loch, river, and sea fishing available, the area is a mecca for fishermen. Details of fishing permits and locations are available from the tourist board (☞ Glasgow A to Z, *below*).

Golf

Ten municipal courses are operated within Glasgow proper by the local authorities. Bookings are relatively inexpensive, and should be made directly to the course 24 hours in advance to ensure prime tee times (courses open at 7 AM). A comprehensive list of contacts, facilities, and greens fees of the 30 or so other courses near the city is available from the Greater Glasgow and Clyde Valley Tourist Board (☞ Glasgow A to Z, *below,* and Chapter 2).

Kings Park (⊠ Croftpark Ave., ☎ 0141/630–1597) 9 holes, 2,071 yards, SSS 30. **Lethamhill** (⊠ 1240 Cumbernauld Rd., ☎ 0141/770–6220, FAX 0141/770–0520) 18 holes, 5,836 yards, SSS 68. **Linn Park** (⊠ Simshill Rd., ☎ 0141/637–5871) 18 holes, 5,132 yards, SSS 65. **Littlehill** (⊠ Auchinairn Rd., ☎ 0141/772–1916) 18 holes, 6,240 yards, SSS 70. **Ruchill** (⊠ Brassey St., ☎ 0141/946–8793) 9 holes, 2,217 yards, SSS 31.

Health Clubs

There are 19 municipal sports centers in the city, ranging from fairly basic swimming pools to facilities for a wide range of sports. There are also many private clubs, but membership is not usually available to visitors. The best of the council-run sports centers are **Kelvin Hall International Sports Arena** (⊠ Kelvin Hall, Argyle St., ☎ 0141/357–

2525), **Bellahouston Leisure Center** (⊠ 31 Bellahouston Dr., ☎ 0141/427–5454), and **Scotstoun Leisure Centre** (⊠ Danes Dr., Scotstoun, ☎ 0141/959–4000). See the brochure available from the tourist board (☞ Glasgow A to Z, *below*) for details.

The larger hotels in the city also offer a variety of sports and leisure facilities, usually free of charge, to their guests. The following hotels have at least a pool and gym: **Central** (⊠ 99 Gordon St., ☎ 0141/221–9680), **Glasgow Hilton** (⊠ 1 William St., ☎ 0141/204–5555), **Jury Glasgow** (⊠ 2/4 Shelley Rd., Great Western Rd., ☎ 0141/334–8161), **Marriott** (⊠ 500 Argyle St., ☎ 0141/226–5577), **Moat House** (⊠ Congress Rd., ☎ 0141/306–9988), and **Swallow** (⊠ 517 Paisley Rd. West, ☎ 0141/427–3146).

Sailing and Water Sports

The Firth of Clyde and Loch Lomond (each about a 30-minute drive southwest and north of Glasgow, respectively) both offer water-sports facilities for sailing, canoeing, windsurfing, and rowing, with full equipment rental. Details are available from the tourist board (☞ Glasgow A to Z, *below*).

Soccer

The city has been sports-mad, especially for football (soccer), for more than 100 years, and the rivalry between its two main clubs, Rangers and Celtics, is legendary—and often provokes fiercely partisan attitudes on the part of both sets of supporters. Rangers wear blue, are predominantly Protestant, and play at **Ibrox** (pronounced *eye*-brox; ⊠ Edmiston Dr., ☎ 0141/427–8800) to the west of the city. Celtics wear green, are predominantly Roman Catholic, and play in the east at **Celtic Park** (⊠ 95 Kerrydale St., ☎ 0141/556–2611). Matches are played usually on a Saturday in winter, and Glasgow has in total nine different teams playing in the Scottish Leagues. Admission prices start at about £14. Do not go looking for the family-day-out atmosphere of many American football games; soccer remains a fiercely contested game played in relatively primitive surroundings, though Ibrox is an exception to this.

SHOPPING

Arcades and Shopping Centers

As in many other major cities and towns, various centers can be found in and around the city. **St. Enoch's Shopping Centre** (⊠ 55 St. Enoch Sq., ☎ 0141/204–3900) is eye-catching if not especially pleasing. It houses various stores, but most could be found elsewhere. By far the best complex is **Princes Square** (⊠ 48 Buchanan St., ☎ 0141/221–0324), with high-quality shops in an art-nouveau setting, cafés, and restaurants. Look particularly for the Scottish Craft Centre, which has an outstanding collection of work created by some of the best craftspeople in Scotland. The **Buchanan Galleries,** opened in 1998 at the top end of Buchanan Street next to the Royal Concert Hall, has added another high-quality shopping center to Glasgow's shopping scene; its magnet attraction is John Lewis (☞ *below*).

Department Stores

The main department stores are **Debenham's** (⊠ 97 Argyle St., also accessed from the St. Enoch Centre, ☎ 0141/221–0088), with china and crystal as well as women's and men's clothing, and **Frasers**(⊠ 21–45 Buchanan St., ☎ 0141/221–3880), Glasgow's largest and most interesting department store. Frasers is a Glasgow institution, and its wares reflect much of Glasgow's new and traditional images—leading European designer clothes and fabrics combining with home-produced articles, such as tweeds, tartans, glass, and ceramics. The magnificent interior is itself worth a visit, set off by the grand staircase rising to various floors and balconies.

British Home Stores (⊠ 67–81 Sauchiehall St., ☎ 0141/332–0401), **C&A** (⊠ 218 Sauchiehall St., ☎ 0141/333–9441), and **Marks & Spencer** (⊠ 2–12 Argyle St., ☎ 0141/552–4546) are good bets. **John Lewis** (⊠ Buchanan Galleries, Buchanan St.) is a favorite for its good-value mix of clothing and household items.

Shopping Districts

St. Enoch Square, which is also the main underground station, houses the St. Enoch Shopping Centre. On the main, often-crowded pedestrian area of **Argyle Street** you will find all the usual High Street chain stores, such as Debenham's. An interesting diversion off Argyle Street is **Argyll Arcade,** a covered street that has the largest collection of jewelers under one roof in Scotland. This L-shape arcade, built in 1904, houses several locally based jewelers and a few shops specializing in antique jewelry. The other end of the Argyll Arcade leads to **Buchanan Street,** Glasgow's premier shopping street and almost totally a pedestrian area. In addition to household names like Laura Ashley, Burberry's, Jaeger, and Roland Cartier, there are other Buchanan Street shops to look out for.

Merchant City on the edge of the city center is home to many of Glasgow's young and upwardly mobile. Shopping here is expensive, but the area is certainly worth visiting if you are seeking the young Glasgow style. The huge **Barras** (☞ Exploring Glasgow, *above*) indoor market prides itself on selling everything "from a needle to an anchor"; stalls hawk antique (and not-so-antique) furniture, bric-a-brac, student-designed jewelry, and textiles—you name it, it's here. If you're an antiques connoisseur and art lover, a walk along **West Regent Street** is highly recommended, as there are various galleries and antiques shops, some specializing in Scottish antiques and paintings. The area around **West End** and **Byres Road** is dominated by the university, and the shops cater to local and student needs. Take the underground system to Hilllhead station or bus numbers 44 and 59.

Specialty Shops

Antiques and Fine Art
Cyril Gerber Fine Art (⊠ 148 West Regent St, ☎ 0141/221–3095 or 0141/204–0276), specialists in British paintings from 1880 to the present, will export, as will most galleries. The **Compass Gallery** (⊠ 178 West Regent St., ☎ 0141/221–6370) usually has interesting exhibitions in fine and decorative art. **De Courcey's** (⊠ 5–21 Cresswell La.) antiques and crafts arcade has quite a few shops to visit, and a variety of goods, including paintings and jewelry, are regularly auctioned here. De Courcey's is in one of the cobblestone lanes to the rear of Byres Road.

Books and Paper
John Smith & Son (Glasgow) Ltd. (⊠ 57 St. Vincent St., ☎ 0141/221–7472), founded in the mid-18th century, prides itself on being a thoroughly Scottish bookshop, with a super selection of books about Scotland, plus a friendly café upstairs. **Papyrus** (⊠ 374 Byres Rd., ☎ 0141/334–6514; ⊠ 296–298 Sauchiehall St., ☎ 0141/353–2182) has a wide range of designer cards, small gifts, and a good selection of books.

The **Glasgow School of Art** (⊠ 167 Renfrew St., ☎ 0141/353–4526) has The Mackintosh Shop, selling various books, cards, jewelry, and ceramics. Students often sell their work, if you are lucky enough to be visiting during the degree shows in June.

Clothing Boutiques

Glasgow has a fashion-conscious image in Scotland, and a variety of both local and international boutiques can be visited. At Princes Square there are famous designer names like **Katherine Hamnett** (⊠ Unit 38 Princes Sq., ☎ 0141/248–3826), selling pricey women's and men's clothing in classic and modern styles. **Ted Baker** (⊠ Units 24–25 Princes Sq., ☎ 0141/221–9664) stocks men's designer clothing—lots of shirts, ties, and accessories, but no suits—at designer prices. Worth a special mention is the West End's **Strawberry Fields** (⊠ 517 Great Western Rd., ☎ 0141/339–1121), selling a colorful array of children's wear.

Gourmet Foods

Peckham's Delicatessen (⊠ 100 Byres Rd., ☎ 0141/357–1454; ⊠ 43 Clarence Dr., ☎ 0141/357–2909; ⊠ Central Station, ☎ 0141/248–4012) is a Glasgow institution for Continental sausages, cheeses, and everything for a delicious picnic.

Home Furnishings and Textiles

In House (⊠ 24–26 Wilson St., ☎ 0141/552–5902) has top-quality, contemporary designer furniture as well as glassware, china, and textiles. **Casa Fina** (⊠ 1 Wilson St., ☎ 0141/552–6791) stocks stylish modern furniture and giftware. Wander around **Stockwell China Bazaar** (⊠ 67–77 Glassford St., ☎ 0141/552–5781) for a huge array of fine china and earthenware, glass, and ornaments. Items will be packed and sent overseas for you, if required. While in this area you will also find the **National Trust for Scotland**'s shop (⊠ Hutcheson's Hall, 158 Ingram St., ☎ 0141/552–8391). Many items, such as china, giftware, textiles, toiletries, and housewares, for sale are designed exclusively for National Trust properties and are often handmade.

Outdoor Sports Gear

You will find good-quality outerwear at **Tiso Sports** (⊠ 129 Buchanan St., ☎ 0141/248–4877), handy if you are planning some Highland walks.

Scottish Specialties

All the usual Scottish-theme gifts can be found in various locations in Glasgow. Gift items here tend to be a little more interesting and of a higher quality than those found in other, more tourist-oriented areas of the country. **Hector Russell Ltd.** (⊠ 110 Buchanan St., ☎ 0141/221–0217) specializes in Highland outfitting, Scottish gifts, woolens, cashmere, and ladies' fashions.

MacDonald MacKay Ltd. (⊠ 105 Hope St., ☎ 0141/204–3930) makes, sells, and exports Highland dress and accessories for men and custom-made kilts and skirts for women. Glasgow has a definite place in the history of art and design, being most famous for its association with Charles Rennie Mackintosh. For high-quality giftware in his style, **Catherine Shaw** (⊠ 24 Gordon St., ☎ 0141/204–4762; ⊠ 32 Argyll Arcade, ☎ 0141/221–9038) offers a unique selection.

Tobacco

Robert Graham (⊠ 71 St. Vincent St., ☎ 0141/221–6588) tobacconist has a tremendous variety of tobaccos and pipes. Much of Glasgow's wealth was generated by the "tobacco lords" during the 17th and 18th centuries; at Graham's you will experience a little of that colorful history.

SIDE TRIPS FROM GLASGOW

The town of Paisley was once a distinct burgh in its own right, but is now part of the Greater Glasgow suburban area. If your tastes run toward the urban rather than the rural, this town offers plenty of gritty character, largely because of vestiges of its industrial heritage: it was once famous for its shawl manufacturing, and its museum has a fine shawl collection.

Glasgow is also well placed as a touring base for one-day excursions south to the fertile farmlands of Ayrshire, with its Robert Burns connections, the Firth of Clyde, west, and the Clyde Valley southeast of Glasgow. You could do them by car or, in a modified form, by public transportation.

Paisley

32 The industrial prosperity of Paisley came from textiles and, in particular, from the woolen paisley shawl. The internationally recognized Paisley pattern is based on the shape of a palm shoot, an ancient Babylonian fertility symbol brought to Britain by way of Kashmir. The full story of the pattern and of the innovative weaving techniques introduced in Paisley is told in the **Paisley Museum and Art Gallery,** which has a world-famous shawl collection. ⊠ *High St.,* ☎ *0141/889–3151.* ☑ *Free.* ☉ *Mon.–Sat. 10–5.*

The life of the workers in the textile industry is brought to life in **Sma' Shot Cottages,** re-creations of mill workers' houses with displays of linen, lace, and Paisley shawls. An 18th-century weaver's cottage is also open to visitors. ⊠ *11/17 George Pl.,* ☎ *0141/889–1708.* ☑ *Free.* ☉ *Apr.–Sept., Wed. and Sat. 1–5 or by appointment.*

Paisley's 12th-century Cluniac **Abbey** dominates the town center. Almost completely destroyed in 1307 and then rebuilt after the Battle of Bannockburn, the abbey is traditionally associated with Walter Fitzallan, the High Steward of Scotland, who gave his name to the Stewart monarchs of Scotland. Outstanding features include the fine stone-vaulted roof and stained glass of the choir. Paisley Abbey is today a busy parish church. Groups should call ahead. ☎ *0141/889–7654.* ☑ *Free.* ☉ *Mon.–Sat. 10–3:30, and for Sun. services, 11, 12:15, and 6:30.*

Paisley A to Z

ARRIVING AND DEPARTING

By Bus: There are regular services to Paisley from **Buchanan Street Bus Station** (☎ 0141/332–7133).

By Car: Take the M8 westbound and then the A737 clearly signed to Paisley.

By Train: Services run every 5–10 minutes throughout the day from **Glasgow Central Station** (☎ National Train Enquiry Line, 0345/484950).

VISITOR INFORMATION

The **tourist information center** is at the Town Hall (⊠ Abbey Close, ☎ 0141/889–0711, ☉ Apr.–mid-Nov.).

Ayrshire and the Clyde Coast

Robert Burns is Scotland's national and well-loved poet. His birthday is celebrated with speeches and dinners, drinking and dancing (Burns Suppers) on January 25, in a way in which few other countries celebrate a poet. He was born in Alloway, beside Ayr, just an hour or so to the south of Glasgow, and the towns and villages where he lived and loved make an interesting day out from the city.

On your way there, you will travel beside the estuary and Firth of the great River Clyde and be able to look across to Dumbarton and its Rock, a nostalgic farewell point for emigrants leaving Glasgow. The river is surprisingly narrow here, when you remember that the *Queen Elizabeth 2* and the other *Queens* and great ocean liners sailed these waters from the place of their birth. Farther along the coast, the views north and west to Loch Long, Holy Loch, and the Argyll Forest Park are outstanding on a clear day. Two high points of the trip, in addition to the Burns connections, are Mount Stuart House, on the island of Bute, and, south of Ayr, Culzean Castle, flagship of the National Trust for Scotland.

Wemyss Bay

③③ From the old Victorian village of Wemyss Bay there is a ferry service to the Isle of Bute, a favorite holiday spot for Glaswegians earlier this century. The many handsome buildings, especially the station and its covered walkway between platform and steamer pier, with its exuberant wrought ironwork, are a reminder of the grandeur and style of the Victorian era and the generations of visitors who used trains and ferries for their summer holidays. South of Wemyss Bay, you can also look across to the island of Arran, another Victorian holiday favorite, and then the island of Great Cumbrae, a weighty name for a tiny island.

Isle of Bute

③④ The Isle of Bute offers a host of relaxing walks and scenic vistas. **Rothesay,** a faded but appealing resort, is the main town. Bute's biggest
★ draw is spectacular **Mount Stuart,** ancestral home of the marquesses of Bute, about 5 mi south of Rothesay. The massive Victorian Gothic palace built in red sandstone has mind-blowing ornate interiors, including the Marble Hall, with star-studded vault, stained glass, arcaded galleries, and magnificent tapestries woven in Edinburgh in the early 20th century. The collection of paintings and the furniture throughout the house are equally outstanding. ⊠ *Isle of Bute, PA20 9LR,* ☎ *01700/503877.* ⊠ *Joint ticket, house and gardens, £6; gardens only, £3.50.* ☉ *May–mid-Oct., gardens Mon., Wed., Fri.–Sun. 10–5, house 11–4:30; last admission 4.*

DINING AND LODGING

££ ✕☶ **Ardmory House Hotel.** Set in large gardens in a peaceful residential area, this hotel evokes "home away from home" rather than elegance, with beamed ceilings and a cozy bar with an open fire downstairs, and plainly furnished but comfortable bedrooms in muted colors. The staff is exceptionally friendly and attentive. Standard bar meals such as homemade soup, lasagna, or chili are on offer, and the restaurant serves more elaborate inventions—breast of duck with spiced mandarin orange and cherry mulled wine sauce, or salmon on a nest of fettuccine vegetables with saffron butter sauce. ⊠ *Ardmory Rd., Ardbeg, Isle of Bute, PA20 0PG,* ☎ *01700/502346,* ☲ *01700/505596. 5 rooms, 2 with bath, 3 with shower. Restaurant, bar. AE, DC, MC, V.*

Largs

③⑤ At the coastal resort of Largs, the community makes the most of the town's Viking history. It was the site in 1263 of a major battle that finally broke the power of the Vikings in Scotland, and every September a commemorative Viking Festival is held. All year round, **Vikingar!, the Viking Heritage Centre,** tells the story of the Viking influence in Scotland by way of film, tableaux, and displays. ⊠ *Barrfields, Greenock Rd., KA30 8QL,* ☎ *01475/689777.* ⊠ *£3.50.* ☉ *Apr.–Sept., daily 9–6; Oct.–Mar., daily 10–4.*

If you are in Largs on the seafront on a summer's afternoon, take time to look into the **Clark Memorial Church** (☎ 01475/672370), which has a particularly splendid array of Glaswegian arts and crafts stained glass of the 1890s in its windows. Among the studios involved in their design were those of Stephen Adam (1848–1910) and his contemporary Christopher Wall.

☞ ③⑥ Just south of Largs is **Kelburn Castle and Country Park,** the historic estate of the earl of Glasgow. There are walks and trails through the mature woodlands, including the mazelike Secret Forest, which leads deep into the thickets. The adventure center and commando-assault course will wear out overexcited children. (They tell a tale here of rescuing an elderly lady from halfway around the assault course, who commented, "Well, I did think it was rather a *hard* nature trail." Make sure you read the signposts.) ⊠ *Fairlie, Ayrshire, KA29 0BE,* ☎ *01475/ 568685.* ☞ *£4.50.* ◉ *Easter–Oct., daily 10–6; grounds only, Nov.– Easter, daily 11–5.*

Irvine

③⑦ Robert Burns puts in an appearance at Irvine. The Irvine Burns Club is possibly the oldest in the world. He came here to learn to dress flax (the raw material for linen), and the heckling (flax-dressing) shed where he worked and the house where he lived are museums known as the **Glasgow Vennel Museum and Art Gallery.** ⊠ *4 and 10 Glasgow Vennel,* ☎ FAX *01294/275059.* ☞ *Free.* ◉ *June–Sept., Mon., Tues., Thurs.–Sat. 10–1 and 2–5, Sun. 2–5; Oct.–May, Tues., Thurs.– Sat. 10–1 and 2–5.*

Troon

③⑧ The small coastal town of Troon is famous for its international golf course, Royal Troon. You can easily see why golf is so popular here. At times, the whole Ayrshire coast, 60 mi long, seems one endless golf course.

LODGING

£££ ▥ **Piersland House Hotel.** This is set in a late Victorian mansion, formerly the home of a whiskey magnate. All the bedrooms are individually designed and furnished in traditional style. Oak paneling and log fires in the restaurant provide a warm backdrop for traditional Scottish cuisine, including specialties such as beef medallions in pickled walnut sauce. ⊠ *15 Craigend Rd. (just north of Ayr), KA10 6HD,* ☎ *01292/ 314747,* FAX *01292/315613. 28 rooms, 22 with bath, 6 with shower. Restaurant. AE, DC, MC, V.*

GOLF

Royal Troon (⊠ Troon, Ayrshire, ☎ 01292/311555, FAX 01292/318204), a club founded in 1878, has two 18-hole courses: the Old, or Championship, (7,097 yards) and the Portland (6,640 yds.). Access for visitors is limited—call for details.

SHOPPING

Many Glaswegians frequent **Regalia** (⊠ 44–48 Church St., ☎ 01292/ 312162) for its unusual collection of designer outfits for women.

Ayr

③⑨ The commercial port of Ayr is Ayrshire's chief town, a peaceful and elegant place with an air of prosperity and some good shops. Burns was baptized in the Auld Kirk (Old Church) in the town and wrote a humorous poem about the Twa Brigs (two bridges) that cross the river nearby. He described Ayr as a town unsurpassed "for honest men and bonny lasses."

Glasgow Excursions: Ayrshire and the Clyde Valley

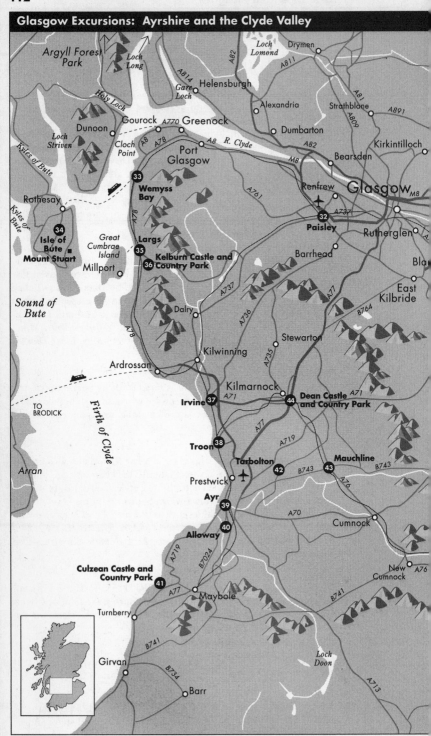

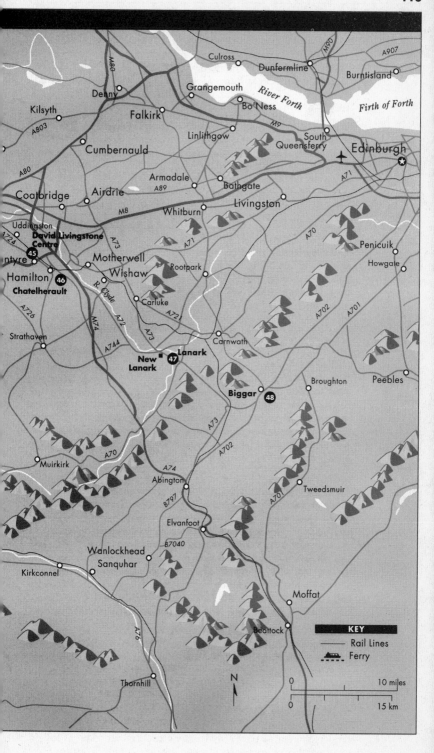

KEY

— Rail Lines

Ferry

0   10 miles

0   15 km

N

④⓪ If you are on the Robert Burns trail, head for **Alloway,** on B7024 in Ayr's southern suburbs. Here, among the many middle-class residences, you will find the one-room thatched **Burns Cottage,** where Scotland's national poet was born in 1759 and which his father built. There is a museum of Burnsiana next door. ☎ 01292/441215. ⌨ £2.50 *(includes admission to Burns Monument, and allows discounted admission to the Tam o' Shanter Experience, ☞ below).* ☼ *Apr.–Oct., daily 9–6; Nov.–Mar., Mon.–Sat. 10–4, Sun. noon–4.*

Find out all about Burns at the **Tam o' Shanter Experience.** Here you can first enjoy a 10-minute audiovisual journey through the life and times of the poet himself, then watch as one of Burns's most famous poems, "Tam o' Shanter," is "brought to life" on a three-screen theatrical set. It is down the road from Burns Cottage and around the corner from Alloway's ruined church. ☎ 01292/443700. ⌨ £2.50 *(includes admission to the Burns Monument, and allows discounted admission to Burns Cottage and museum).* ☼ *Apr.–Sept., daily 9–6; Oct.–Mar., daily 9–5.*

Auld Alloway Kirk is where Tam o' Shanter unluckily passed a witches' revel—with Old Nick himself playing the bagpipes—on his way home from a night of drinking. Tam, in flight from the witches, managed to cross the **Brig o' Doon** (*brig* is Scots for bridge) just in time. His gray mare, Meg, lost her tail to the closest witch. (Any resident of Ayr will tell you that witches cannot cross running water.) The **Burns Monument** (entrance fee included in charge for Burns Cottage and for Tam o' Shanter Experience) overlooks the Brig o' Doon.

DINING

££ ✕ **Fouter's Bistro.** Fouter's is in a long and narrow cellar, yet its white walls and decorative stenciling create an airy ambience. The cuisine is also light and skillful—no heavy sauces here. Try the roast Ayrshire lamb with pan juices and red wine and mint, or sample the "Taste of Scotland" appetizer—smoked salmon, trout, and other goodies. This is modern Scottish cooking at its best, all in a friendly setting. ⌂ *2A Academy St.,* ☎ *01292/261391. AE, DC, MC, V.*

SHOPPING

Ayr has a good mixture of traditional and new shops. Queen's Court, Sandgate, combines small crafts and gift shops. The **Diamond Factory** (⌂ 27 Queen's Ct., ☎ 01292/280476) is a jewelry workshop where you are invited to view craftsmen at work. All jewelry is designed and made on the premises. Rings can be engraved with a family crest, and seal engraving is also undertaken. Particularly coveted are the handmade Celtic wedding bands. The store will export your purchases if you do not have time to wait for completion of the work. The **Mill Shop, Begg of Ayr** (⌂ Viewfield Rd., ☎ 01292/267615) has a good selection of scarves, stoles, plaids, and travel rugs handmade on the premises.

Culzean Castle and Country Park

★ ④① The dramatic cliff-top Culzean Castle and Country Park (pronounced ku-*lain*) is the National Trust for Scotland's most popular property, yet remains unspoiled. The castle, complete with walled garden, is a superb neoclassical mansion designed by Robert Adam (1728–92) in 1777. In addition to its marvelous interiors, the castle contains the National Guest Flat, given by the people of Scotland in appreciation of General Eisenhower's (1890–1969) services during World War II. As president he stayed once or twice at Culzean and his relations still do occasionally. Between visits it is used by the National Trust for Scotland for official entertaining. Approach is by way of rooms evoking the atmosphere of World War II: mementos of Glenn Miller (1904–44), Winston Churchill (1871–1947), Vera Lynn, and other personalities of the era all help create a suitably 1940s mood. ☎ *01655/760269. 🎟 Joint ticket to Country Park and castle, £6.50; Country Park only, £3.50. ⊙ Castle Apr.–Oct., daily 10:30–5:30 (last admission 5 PM), country park daily 9:30–sunset.*

Tarbolton

At Tarbolton you will find the **Bachelors' Club,** a 17th-century house where Robert Burns learned to dance, founded a debating and literary society, and became a Freemason. ☎ *01292/541940. 🎟 £1.60. ⊙ Easter and May–Sept., daily 1:30–5:30; Oct., weekends 1:30–5:30.*

Mauchline

Mauchline also has strong connections with the poet Robert Burns. There is a **Burns House** here, four of his daughters are buried in the churchyard, and **Poosie Nansie's pub,** where he used to drink, is still serving pints today. The village is also famous for making curling stones.

Kilmarnock

This industrial town, home of Johnny Walker whiskey, has more enjoyment for Burns enthusiasts: the Burns Museum and the Dick Institute. If you are looking for something a little different, go to **Dean Castle and Country Park** to enjoy a 14th-century castle with a wonderful collection of medieval arms and armor. Burns also inevitably gets a mention. ⊠ *Off Glasgow Rd.,* ☎ *01563/522702. 🎟 £2.50. ⊙ Daily noon–5 (call for confirmation).*

Ayrshire and the Clyde Coast A to Z

ARRIVING AND DEPARTING

By Bus and Train: Take the bus or train to Largs for Cumbrae; Ardrossan for Arran; Ayr and Kilmarnock for the Burns Heritage Trail; and Troon, Prestwick, and Ayr to play golf. Bus companies also operate one-day guided excursions to this area; for details, contact the tourist information center in Glasgow, **Strathclyde Passenger Transport** (☎ 0141/226–4826), or the **National Train Enquiry Line** (☎ 0345/484950).

By Car: Begin your trip from Glasgow city center westbound on the M8, signposted for Glasgow Airport and Greenock. Join the A8 and follow it from Greenock to Gourock and around the coast past the Cloch lighthouse. Head south on the A78 to the old Victorian village of Wemyss Bay, and take the ferry over to Bute to see Mount Stuart (leave your car behind: a bus service takes you to the house from the ferry). Then continue down the A78 through Largs, Irvine, Troon, and so to Ayr and Alloway. Travel on to Culzean Castle, then return to Ayr and turn eastward on the B743, the Mauchline Road, but before you get there, turn left on a little road to Tarbolton. Return to the B743, visit Mauchline, then head north on A76 to Kilmarnock. Glasgow is only a half hour away on the fast A77.

VISITOR INFORMATION

Ayr (⊠ Burns House, 16 Burns Statue Sq., ☎ 01292/288688). **Irvine** (⊠ New St., ☎ 01294/313886). **Kilmarnock** (⊠ 62 Bank St., ☎ 01563/ 539090). **Largs** (⊠ Promenade, ☎ 01475/673765). **Rothesay** (⊠ 15 Victoria St., Rothesay, Isle of Bute, ☎ 01700/502151). **Troon** (⊠ Municipal Buildings, South Beach, ☎ 01292/317696, ⊙ Easter–Sept.).

Clyde Valley

The River Clyde is (or certainly was) famous for its shipbuilding and heavy industries, yet its upper reaches flow through some of Scotland's most fertile farmlands, rich with tomato crops. It is an interesting area, with ancient castles as well as industrial and social museums that tell the story of manufacturing and mining prosperity.

Blantyre

45 In the not-very-pretty town of Blantyre, look for signs to the **David Livingstone Centre,** a park area around the tiny (tenement) apartment where the great explorer of Africa (1813–73) was born. Displays tell of his journeys, of his meeting with Stanley ("Doctor Livingstone, I presume"), of Africa, and of the industrial heritage of the area. ☎ 01698/823140. 🖼 £2.95. ⊙ Apr.–Sept., Mon.–Sat. 10–5, Sun. 12:30–5; Oct.–Mar., Mon.–Sat. 10:30–3:30, Sun. 12:30–3:30 (call to confirm in winter).

Close to the David Livingstone Centre is **Bothwell Castle,** dating from the 13th century. Its walls are well preserved and stand above the River Clyde. ☎ 0131/668–8800. 🖼 £1.80. ⊙ Apr.–Sept., daily 9:30–6; Oct.–Mar., Mon.–Wed. and Sat. 9:30–4, Sun. 2–4, Thurs. 9:30–noon.

Hamilton

The **Hamilton Mausoleum,** in Strathclyde Country Park near the industrial town of Hamilton, was built in the 1840s as an extraordinary monument to the lavish eccentricities of the dukes of Hamilton (who **46** had more money than sense). Also nearby is **Chatelherault** (pronounced *Shat*-lerro), a unique one-room-deep facade, part shooting lodge, part glorified dog kennel, designed in elegant Georgian style by William Adam, also for the dukes of Hamilton. Within Chatelherault is an exhibition describing life on the estate in all its former glory. ☎ 01698/426213. 🖼 Free. ⊙ Apr.–Sept., Mon.–Sat. 10–5, Sun. noon–5:30; Oct.–Mar., Mon.–Sat. 10–5, Sun. noon–5. Lodge occasionally closed Fri. for functions.

Lanark

47 Set in pleasing, rolling countryside, Lanark is an old, established typical Scottish town. It is now most often associated with its unique neighbor **New Lanark,** a nominated World Heritage Site. New Lanark is distinguished because it was the site of a social experiment. The River Clyde powers its way through a beautiful wooded gorge and its waters were harnessed to drive textile mill machinery before the end of the 18th century. The owner, David Dale (1739–1806), was noted for his caring attitude to the workers, unusual for that era. Later, his son-in-law, Robert Owen (1771–1858), took these social experiments further, founding a benevolent doctrine known as "Owenism," and eventually crossing the Atlantic to become involved in a similar project in Indiana, called New Harmony, which, unlike New Lanark, failed. (Robert Owen's son Robert Dale Owen, 1801–77, helped found the Smithsonian Institution.)

After many changes of fortune the mills eventually closed, but the site has been saved and has a new lease on life with renovated housing and a new hotel, opened in 1998 (☞ *below*). The refurbishment was a success, and those who bought the houses seem able to lead normal lives despite having tourists peering in all day. One of the mills has been converted into an interpretative center, which tells the story of this brave social experiment. Upstream, the Clyde flows through some of the finest river scenery anywhere in Lowland Scotland, with woods and spectacular waterfalls. *Interpretative center:* ☎ 01555/665876. 🖼 £3.75. ⊙ Daily 11–5.

LODGING

££ 🏨 **New Lanark Mill Hotel.** Housed in a converted cotton mill at the 18th-century model village of New Lanark, this new hotel is decorated in a spare, understated style that allows the impressive architecture of barrel-vaulted ceilings and elegant Georgian windows to speak for itself. Set right next to the river in the heart of the village, all attractions—visitor center, shops, Falls of Clyde Wildlife Reserve—are on the doorstep. ⊠ *New Lanark ML11 9DB,* ☎ *01555/661345,* ᴛᴀᴄ *01555/ 665738. 38 rooms, 33 with bath and shower, 5 with shower; 8 cottages. MC, V.*

SHOPPING

Lanark offers an interesting selection of shops within walking distance of each other. **McKellar's the Jewellers** (⊠ 41 High St., ☎ 01555/661312) has a good range of Charles Rennie Mackintosh–inspired designs in gold and silver. **Strands** (⊠ 2 Broomgate, ☎ 01555/665757) carries a wide variety of yarns and knitwear, including Aran designs and one-of-a-kind creations by Scottish designers. **The Lanark Gallery** (⊠ 116–118 North Vennel, ☎ 01555/662565) displays paintings, pottery and ceramics, and sculptures, all by Scottish artists.

Biggar

A pleasant stone-built town, Biggar is a rewarding place to spend an hour or two, out of all proportion to its size. **Gladstone Court Museum** offers a fascinating portrayal of life in the town, with reconstructed Victorian shops, a bank, a telephone exchange, and a school. ⊠ *Gladstone Ct.,* ☎ *01899/221050.* ᴀᴄ *£1.80.* ◷ *Apr.–Oct., Mon.–Sat. 10–12:30 and 2–5, Sun. 2–5.*

For Biggar's geology and prehistory, plus an interesting embroidery collection (including samplers and fine patchwork coverlets), visit the **Moat Park Heritage Centre,** also in the town center, in a former church. ⊠ *Moat Park Church, Moat Park,* ☎ *01899/221050.* ᴀᴄ *£2.40.* ◷ *Easter–mid-Oct., Mon.–Sat. 10–5, Sun. 2–5.*

Just down the street from Moat Park is the **Gasworks,** built in 1839, a fascinating reminder of the efforts once needed to produce gas for light and heat. ⊠ *National Museums of Scotland,* ☎ *01899/221050.* ᴀᴄ *£1.* ◷ *June–Sept., daily 2–5.*

Also near Moat Park Heritage Centre is the **Greenhill Covenanters' House,** a farmhouse with Covenanting relics, 17th-century furnishings, costume dolls, and rare farm breeds. ⊠ *Moat Park,* ☎ *01899/221050.* ᴀᴄ *£1.* ◷ *Easter–early Oct., daily 2–5.*

Biggar Puppet Theatre regularly presents performances by Purves Puppets. Between performances, two hands-on, half-hour tours are available, led by the puppeteers. One tour goes backstage with the puppets being demonstrated on stage, the other is of the puppet museum. The theater also has games and a picnic area. ⊠ *B7016, east of Biggar,* ☎ *01899/220631.* ᴀᴄ *Performances: £4.40.* ◷ *Mon.–Sat. 10–5; Easter–Sept., also Sun. 2–5. Call for additional opening times and details.*

At Biggar, you are near the headwaters of the Clyde, on the moors in the center of southern Scotland. The Clyde flows west toward Glasgow and the Atlantic Ocean, while the Tweed, only a few miles away, flows east toward the North Sea. There are fine views around Biggar: to Culter Fell and to the Border Hills in the south.

DINING AND LODGING

£££–££££ ✕▥ **Shieldhill.** This foursquare Norman manor has stood on this spot since 1199, though it was greatly enlarged in 1560. It is in an ideal location for touring the Borders—just 27 mi from Edinburgh and 31 mi from Glasgow. The rooms are named after great Scottish battles—Culloden, Glencoe, Bannockburn—and are furnished with great comfort (miles of Laura Ashley fabrics and wallpaper). ⊠ *Quothquan, near Biggar, ML12 6NA,* ☎ *01899/220035,* ᴛᴀᴄ *01899/221092. 12 rooms with bath or shower. Restaurant. MC, V.*

Clyde Valley A to Z

ARRIVING AND DEPARTING

By Bus: Bus services run out of Glasgow to Hamilton and Lanark (Lanark Sun. only). Inquire at the **Buchanan Street Bus Station** (☎ 0141/332–7133) for details.

By Car: Take A724 heading east out of Glasgow, south of the river through Rutherglen toward Hamilton. It is not a very pretty road, but in Blantyre look for signs to the David Livingstone Centre. From Blantyre, take the main road to Hamilton. Then travel on the A72 past Chatelherault toward Lanark. You pass the ruins of medieval Craignethan Castle, lots of greenhouses for tomatoes, plant nurseries, and gnarled old orchards running down to the Clyde. Before reaching Lanark, follow the signs down a long winding hill, to New Lanark. A72 continues south of Lanark to join A702 near Biggar. At the end of a full day of touring you can return to Glasgow the quick way by joining the M74 from the A744 west of Lanark (the Strathaven road). Or take a more scenic route through Strathaven (pronounced *stra-ven*) itself, A726 to East Kilbride, and enter Glasgow from south of the river.

By Train: Service runs from Glasgow Central Station to Hamilton and Lanark (for details, call the **National Train Enquiry Line,** ☎ 0345/484950). There are no trains to Biggar, but there is a connecting bus from Hamilton to Biggar.

VISITOR INFORMATION

Biggar (✉ 155 High St., ☎ 01899/221066). **Hamilton** (✉ Road Chef Services, M74 Northbound, ☎ 01698/285590). **Lanark** (✉ Horsemarket, Ladyacre Rd., ☎ 01555/661661).

GLASGOW A TO Z

Arriving and Departing

By Bus

Glasgow's bus station is at **Buchanan Street** (☎ 0141/332–7133). The main intercity operators are **National Express** (☎ 0990/808080) and **Scottish Citylink**(☎ 0990/505050), which serve a wide variety of towns and cities in Scotland, Wales, and England, including London (journey time from London is approximately 8½–9 hours); there is also service to Edinburgh. Buchanan Street is close to the underground station of the same name and to Queen Street station.

By Car

If you come to Glasgow from England and the south of Scotland you will probably approach the city from the M6, M74, and A74. The city center is clearly marked from these roads. From Edinburgh the M8 leads to the city center and is the motorway that cuts straight across the city center and into which all other roads feed. From the north either the A82 from Fort William or the A/M80 from Stirling also feed into the M8 in Glasgow city center. From then on, you only have to know your exit: exit 16 serves the north of the city center, exit 17/18 leads to the northwest and Great Western Road, and exit 18/19 takes you to the hotels of Sauchiehall Street, the Scottish Exhibition Centre, and the Anderston Centre.

By Plane

Glasgow Airport (information, ☎ 0141/887–1111; tourist information desk and accommodations-booking service, ☎ 0141/848–4440), about 7 mi west of the city center on the M8 to Greenock, offers internal Scottish and British services, European and transatlantic scheduled services, and vacation-charter traffic. Most major European carriers fly into Glasgow, offering frequent and convenient connections (some via airports in England) to Amsterdam, Brussels, Copenhagen, Frankfurt, Madrid, Malta, Milan, Paris, Reykjavík: the destinations are being updated all the time so phone the airport for up-to-date information. There are frequent shuttle services from London, as well as regular flights from Birmingham, Bournemouth, Bristol, East Midlands, Leeds/Bradford, Manchester, Southampton, Isle of Man, and Jersey. There are also flights from Wales (Cardiff) and Ireland (Belfast, Carrickfinn, Dublin, and Londonderry).

Local Scottish connections can be made to Aberdeen, Barra, Benbecula, Campbeltown, Inverness, Islay, Kirkwall, Shetland (Sumburgh), Stornoway, and Tiree.

Airlines operating through Glasgow Airport to Europe and the rest of the United Kingdom include **Aer Lingus** (☎ 0645/737747), **Air Malta** (☎ 0181/785–3177), **Air UK** (☎ 0345/666777), **Bright Air** (☎ 0845/309–8098), **British Airways** and **British Airways Express** (☎ 0345/222111), **British Midland** (☎ 0345/554554), **Business Air** (☎ 0500/340146), **easyJet** (☎ 0990/292929), **Euro Scot** (☎ 0870/607–0809), **Icelandair** (☎ 0171/388–5599), **Lufthansa** (☎ 0345/737747), **Manx** (☎ 0345/256256), **Sabena** (☎ 0345/125254), and **SAS Wideroe** (☎ 0345/090900).

Scheduled services to and from North America are provided by **Air Canada** (☎ 0990/247226), **American Airlines** (☎ 0345/789789), **British Airways** (☎ 0345/222111), and **Continental** (☎ 0800/776464).

Prestwick Airport (☎ 01292/479822), on the Ayrshire coast about 30 mi southwest of Glasgow and for some years eclipsed by Glasgow Airport, is beginning to come back into the reckoning, not least because of the activities of **Ryanair** (☎ 01292/678000), a company that has sparked a major price war on the Anglo-Scottish routes (e.g., between London and Glasgow/Edinburgh). It offers unbeatable, no-frills, rock-bottom air fares between London Stansted and Prestwick. **Gill Airways** (☎ 01292/678000) also flies out of Prestwick, serving Belfast (Northern Ireland).

BETWEEN GLASGOW AIRPORT AND CENTER CITY
Though there is a railway station about 2 mi from Glasgow Airport (✉ Paisley Gilmour St.), most people travel the short distance to the city center by bus or taxi. Journey time is about 20 minutes except at rush hour.

By Bus: Express buses run from Glasgow Airport (bus depot 2, outside departures lobby) to near the Central railway station and to the **Buchanan Street Bus Station** (☎ 0141/332–7133). There is service every 15 minutes throughout the day (every half-hour in winter). The fare is £2.50.

By Limousine: Most of the companies that provide chauffeur-driven cars and tours will also do limousine airport transfers. Companies that are currently members of the Greater Glasgow and Clyde Valley Tourist Board are **Charlton Chauffeur Drive** (☎ 0141/445–1777), **Charter** (☎ 0141/942–4228), **Corporate Travel** (☎ 0141/639–8057), **Little's** (☎ 0141/883–2111), **Peter Holmes** (☎ 0141/954–4455), and **Robert Neil** (☎ 0141/641–2125).

By Car: The drive from Glasgow Airport into the city center is normally quite easy, even if you are used to driving on the right. The M8 motorway runs beside the airport (junction 29) and takes you straight into Glasgow city center. Thereafter Glasgow's streets follow a grid pattern, at least in the city center, but a map is useful and can be supplied by the rental company.

By Taxi: Metered taxis are available at the terminal building. The fare should be about £12.

BETWEEN PRESTWICK AIRPORT AND CENTER CITY

By Bus: An hourly coach service operates to Glasgow, but takes much longer than the frequent train service.

By Car: The city center is reached via the fast A77 in about 40 minutes (longer in rush hour).

By Taxi: Metered taxi cabs are available at the airport. The fare to Glasgow is about £25.

By Train: There is a rapid half-hourly train service (hourly on Sundays) direct from the terminal building.

By Train

Glasgow has two main rail stations: **Central** and **Queen Street.** Central is the arrival and departure point for trains from London Euston (journey time is approximately 5 hours), which come via Crewe and Carlisle in England, as well as via Edinburgh from Kings Cross. It also serves other cities in the northwest of England and towns and ports in the southwest of Scotland. These include Kilmarnock, Dumfries, Ardrossan (for the island of Arran), Gourock (for Dunoon), Wemyss Bay (for the island of Bute, Rothesay), and Stranraer (for Ireland). Queen Street Station has connections to Edinburgh (journey time 50 minutes) and onward by the east coast route to Aberdeen or south via Edinburgh to Newcastle, York, and London Kings Cross. Other services from Queen Street go to Stirling, Perth, and Dundee; northward to Inverness, Kyle of Lochalsh, Wick, and Thurso; along the Clyde to Dumbarton and Balloch (for Loch Lomond); and on the scenic West Highland line to Oban, Fort William, and Mallaig. Oban and Mallaig have island ferry connections. For details, contact the **National Train Enquiry Line** (☎ 0345/484950).

A regular bus service links Queen Street and Central stations. Both of these are close to stations on the Glasgow underground. At Queen Street go to Buchanan Street, and at Central go to St. Enoch. Black city taxis are available at both stations.

Getting Around

Glasgow city center—the area defined by the M8 motorway to the north and west, the River Clyde to the south, and Glasgow Cathedral to the east—is relatively compact, and if you are staying in this area you should make some of your excursions on foot. Glaswegians themselves walk a good deal, and the streets are designed for pedestrians (some are for pedestrians only). The streets are relatively safe even at night (but you should be sensible), and good street maps are available from bookstores and the helpful tourist-information center (☞ Visitor Information, *below*). Most of the streets follow a grid plan; if you get lost, though, just ask a local—they are famous for being friendly.

To go farther afield, to the West End (the university, the Transport Museum, Kelvingrove Museum and Art Gallery, or the Hunterian Museum) or to the south (the Burrell Collection), some form of transportation is required. Glasgow is unusual among British cities in having an integrated transport network, and information about all options is available from **Strathclyde Passenger Transport (SPT) Travel Centre** (⊠ St. Enoch Sq., ☎ 0141/226–4826).

By Bus

The many different bus companies cooperate with the underground and ScotRail to produce the Family Day Tripper Ticket (☞ £12.50), which is a great way to get around the whole area from Loch Lomond to Ayrshire. Tickets are a good value and are available from **Strathclyde Passenger Transport (SPT) Travel Centre** (✉ St. Enoch Sq., ☎ 0141/226–4826) and at main railway and bus stations.

By Car

A car is not necessary in the city center. Though most of the newer hotels have their own parking lots, parking in the city center can be very trying. More convenient are the park-and-ride schemes at underground stations (Kelvinbridge, Bridge Street, and Shields Road) that will bring you into the city center in a few minutes. The West End museums and galleries have their own parking lots, as does the Burrell. Remember, parking wardens are constantly on patrol, and you will be fined (upwards of £26) if you park illegally. Multistory parking garages are open 24 hours a day at the following locations: Anderston Centre, George Street, Waterloo Place, Mitchell Street, Cambridge Street, and Buchanan Street. Rates at the individual garages vary between £1 and £2 per hour.

By Subway

As befits the Second City of the Empire, Glasgow is the only city in Scotland that has a subway, or underground, as it's called here. It was built at the end of the last century and takes the simple form of two circular routes, one going clockwise and the other counterclockwise. All trains will eventually bring you back to where you started, and the complete circle takes 24 minutes. This extremely simple and effective system operated relatively unchanged in ancient carriages (cars) until the 1970s when it was entirely modernized. The tunnels are pretty small, so the trains themselves are tiny (by London standards), and this, together with the affection in which the system is held and the bright orange paintwork of the trains, gives it the nickname the Clockwork Orange.

Flat fares (☎ 65p) and the **Heritage Trail** one-day pass (☎ £2) are available. Trains run regularly Monday to Saturday, with a limited Sunday service, and connect the city center with the West End (for the university) and the city south of the River Clyde. Look for the orange U signs marking the 15 stations. Further information is available from **Strathclyde Passenger Transport Travel Centre** (✉ St. Enoch Sq., ☎ 0141/226–4826).

By Taxi

Metered taxis (usually black and of the London type) can be found at taxi ranks all over the city center. Most have radio dispatch, so they can be called very easily. Dial ☎ 0141/332–6666 or 0141/332–7070. Some have also been specially adapted to take wheelchairs. In the street, a taxi can be hailed if it is displaying its illuminated FOR HIRE sign. A typical ride from city center to the West End or South Side costs £1–£2.

By Train

In addition to the underground, the Glasgow area has an extensive network of suburban railway services. They are still called the Blue Trains by local people, even though most of them are now orange. Look for signs to LOW LEVEL TRAINS at Queen Street and Central stations. For further information and a free map, call **Strathclyde Passenger Transport Travel Centre,** (✉ St. Enoch Square, ☎ 0141/226–4826) or the National Train Enquiry Line (☎ 0345/484950). Details are also available from the tourist board.

Contacts and Resources

Car Rentals

Costs vary according to the size of the car, but average about £30–£40 per day.

Alamo (⊠ Glasgow Airport, ☎ 0141/848–1166; ⊠ Prestwick Airport, ☎ 01292/671222). **Avis** (⊠ 161 North St., ☎ 0141/221–2827; ⊠ Glasgow Airport, ☎ 0141/887–2261; ⊠ Prestwick Airport, ☎ 01292/477218). **Budget Rent-a-Car** (⊠ 101 Waterloo St., ☎ 0141/226–4141; ⊠ Glasgow Airport, ☎ 0141/887–0501). **Eurodollar** (⊠ 76 Lancefield Quay, ☎ 0141/204–1051; ⊠ Glasgow Airport, ☎ 0141/887–7915). **Europcar** (⊠ 556 Pollokshaws Rd., ☎ 0141/423–5661; ⊠ Glasgow Airport, ☎ 0141/887–0414; ⊠ Prestwick Airport, ☎ 01292/678198). **Hertz** (⊠ 106 Waterloo St., ☎ 0141/248–7736; ⊠ Glasgow Airport, ☎ 0141/887–2451).

Discount Admission Tickets

The **Scottish Explorer Ticket,** available from any staffed Historic Scotland property, and many tourist information centers, allows visits to HS properties over a 7-day (☐ £12.50) or 14-day (☐ £17) period. The **Touring Ticket,** issued by the National Trust for Scotland (☎ 0131/226–5922), is also available for 7 (£16) or 14 (£24) days and allows access to all National Trust for Scotland properties. It is available from the National Trust for Scotland or main tourist information centers (☞ *below*).

Doctors and Dentists

Your hotel receptionist or B&B host will be the best person to ask for the names of local doctors who will treat visitors. Most dentists will treat visitors by appointment. A full list can be found in the Yellow Pages telephone directory. Emergency dental treatment can be obtained from the **Glasgow Dental Hospital** (⊠ 378 Sauchiehall St., ☎ 0141/211–9600 weekdays from 9–3).

Emergencies

Dial ☎ 999 from any telephone (no coins are needed for emergency calls from public telephones) to obtain assistance from the **police, ambulance, fire brigade, mountain rescue, or coast guard.** Twenty-four-hour accident and emergency services are provided at **Glasgow Royal Infirmary** (⊠ Castle St., ☎ 0141/211–4000), near the cathedral. Accident and emergency facilities are also available at **Glasgow Western Infirmary** (⊠ Dumbarton Rd., ☎ 0141/211–2000), near the university; **Southern General Hospital** (⊠ 1345 Govan Rd., ☎ 0141/201–1100) on the south side of the Clyde Tunnel; and **Stobhill Hospital** (⊠ 133 Balornock Rd., ☎ 0141/201–3000) near the Royal Infirmary and Bishopriggs.

Guided Tours

BOAT TOURS

Cruises are available on Loch Lomond and to the islands in the Firth of Clyde; details are available from the tourist board. Contact **Waverley** paddle steamer (☎ 0141/221–8152) June through August; **Clyde Marine Cruises** (Greenock, ☎ 01475/721–281) May to September.

HELICOPTER TOURS

Bond Air Services (☎ 0141/226–4261) swoop over downtown Glasgow and the immediate environs as far as Loch Lomond, taking off from the helipad at the Scottish Exhibition Centre. Trips normally last 20–30 minutes and cost between £80 and £120.

ORIENTATION TOURS

Discovering Glasgow bus tours leave daily in summer from the west side of George Square. The Greater Glasgow and Clyde Valley Tourist Board (☞ Visitor Information, *below*) can give further information and arrange reservations. Details of longer tours northward to the Highlands and islands can be obtained from the tourist board or Strathclyde Passenger Transport Travel Centre, St. Enoch Square (☞ Getting Around, *above*).

PERSONAL GUIDES AND WALKING TOURS
In each case your first contact should be the tourist board, where you can find out about special walks on a given day. The **Scottish Tourist Guides Association** (☎ FAX 0131/453–1297) also offers an all-around service.

SPECIAL-INTEREST
The Scottish Tourist Guides Association (☎ FAX 0131/453–1297) can tailor a tour to suit you. Standard fixed fees apply. **Classique Sun Saloon Luxury Coaches** (☎ 0141/889–4050) operates restored coaches from the '50s, '60s, and '70s on tours to the north and west. The following Glasgow companies run regular bus tours around the region: **Scott Guide Tours** (☎ 0141/204–0444); **Southern Coaches** (☎ 0141/876–1147); and **Weirs Tours** (☎ 0141/944–6688). **Little's Chauffeur Drive** (⊠ 1282 Paisley Rd. W, Glasgow, ☎ 0141/883–2111) also offers personally tailored car-and-driver tours, both locally and throughout Scotland.

Several chauffeur-driven limousine companies (☞ Between the Airport and City Center, *above*) also provide tours of the city center and beyond.

Taxi firms also arrange tours of the city. They vary from one to three hours, usually at a fixed price: one hour £14, two hours £26, three hours £30. They can be booked in advance, and you can be picked up and dropped off where you like. Contact the **Taxi Owners Association** (☎ 0141/332–7070, ✆ £13/hr or meter reading, whichever is greater) or the **Taxi Cab Association** (☎ 0141/332–6666, ✆ £11/hr).

Late-Night Pharmacies
Pharmacies in Glasgow operate on a rotating basis for late-night opening (hours are posted in storefront windows). **Munro Pharmacy** (⊠ 693 Great Western Rd., ☎ 0141/339–0012) is open daily 9–9.

Post Office
Although there is a **main post office** (⊠ St. Vincent St., ☎ 0141/204–3688), there are many smaller post offices around the city.

Travel Agencies
American Express (⊠ 115 Hope St., ☎ 0141/221–4366). **Thomas Cook** (⊠ 15–17 Gordon St., ☎ 0141/221–6611).

Visitor Information
The **Greater Glasgow and Clyde Valley Tourist Board** (⊠ 11 George Sq., near Queen Street Station, ☎ 0141/204–4400, FAX 0141/221–3524) offers a comprehensive tourist information service. At this location there is also an accommodations-booking service, bureau de change, and ticket office for the theater, city bus tours, guided walks, boat trips, and extended coach tours around Scotland. Books, maps, and souvenirs are sold. The office is open Monday–Saturday 9–6 and, May to September, Monday–Saturday 9–8 and Sunday 10–6. The tourist board's branch office at the airport is open Monday–Saturday 7:30–5, Sunday 7:30–3:30.

Information about goings-on around town can be found in the Greater Glasgow and Clyde Valley Tourist Board's own publications, as well as in *The List* and the *Herald* and *Evening Times* newspapers.

5 The Borders and the Southwest

Dumfries, Galloway

Great rolling hills, gentle moors, wooded river valleys, and farmland stretch south from Lothian, crowned by Edinburgh, to the border. Hilly and sparsely populated, the Dumfries and Galloway region, south of Glasgow and divided from England by the Solway Firth, is a riot of green pastures, somber forests, and radiant gardens, where the palm, in places, is as much at home as the pine.

By Gilbert
Summers

IF YOU ARE COMING TO SCOTLAND from any point south of the border with England, the Borders is the first region you will encounter. Let it be said straightaway that although the border has no checkpoints or customs outposts, the Scottish tourist authorities firmly promulgate the message that it is indeed Scottish land you are on once you cross the border. All the idiosyncracies that distinguish Scotland—from the myriad names for beer, to the seemingly unpredictable Monday local holidays—start as soon as one reaches the first Scottish signs by the main roads north.

Although most visitors inevitably pass this way, the Borders and especially Galloway to the west are unfortunately overlooked. So strong is the tartan-ribboned call of the Highlands that many visitors rush past, pause for breath at Edinburgh, then plunge northward, thus missing a scenic portion of upland Scotland.

The Borders and the Dumfries and Galloway regions have as broad a selection of stately homes and fortified castles as you will encounter in Scotland (with the possible exception of Grampian). Galloway, west of the town of Dumfries and the surrounding area called Dumfrieshire, has the advantage of a coastline facing south, made even more appealing by the North Atlantic Drift (Scotland's part of the Gulf Stream), which bathes the coastal lands with warmer water. With its coastal farmlands giving way to woodlands, high moors, and some craggy hills, Galloway may not be the Highlands, but it gives a convincing impression to those seeking the authentic Scotland.

Pleasures and Pastimes

Biking
In the rural farming areas and upland stretches you will have a wide choice of quiet side roads to avoid the heavy traffic on "A" routes, the main arteries. The Craik Forest is typical of Forestry Commission properties, with mountain bike routes and trails in the network of forestry access roads.

Dining
The Borders is reasonably well served by hotels ranging from budget to luxury, and most good restaurants are, with very few exceptions, found within hotels rather than as independent establishments. Despite being slightly off the beaten tourist path, the region of Dumfries and Galloway offers a good selection of relatively inexpensive options for dining, though once again most are within hotels.

CATEGORY	COST*
££££	over £40
£££	£30–£40
££	£15–£30
£	under £15

*per person for a three-course meal, including VAT and excluding drinks and service.

Fishing
This region is a fisherman's paradise. The Solway Firth is noted for sea angling, notably at Isle of Whithorn, Port William, Portpatrick, Stranraer, and Loch Ryan. The wide range of game fishing opportunities extends from the expensive salmon beats of the River Tweed, sometimes called the Queen of Scottish Rivers, to undiscovered hill lochans. You can buy permits at tourist offices, tackle shops, newsstands, and post offices.

Lodging

In the Borders you'll have a wide range of price categories to choose from, ranging from top-quality hotels to quaint bed-and-breakfasts. Dumfries and Galloway tends to be a little cheaper, and here farmhouse B&Bs are good options. You're likely to get a hearty farm breakfast, but keep in mind that many of these B&Bs are *working* farms, where early morning activity and the presence of animals are an inescapable part of the scene.

CATEGORY	COST*
££££	over £120
£££	£90–£120
££	£50–£90
£	under £50

Prices are for a standard double room, including service, breakfast, and VAT.

Shopping

The Borders in particular has a fairly affluent population, which is reflected in the variety of upscale shops in Peebles, for example, where there are more deluxe stores than might be expected. The Borders is well-known for its knitwear industry, and mill shops are in abundance. Throughout the Borders region also look for the specialty peppermint or fruit-flavored boiled sweets—Jethart Snails, Hawick Balls, Berwick Cockles, and Soor Plums—which, with tablet (a solid caramel-like candy) and fudge, are available at most local confectioners.

Exploring the Borders and the Southwest

The best way to explore the region is to get off the main arterial roads—the A1, A697, A68, A7, M74/A74, and A75—onto the little back roads. You may occasionally be delayed by a herd of cows on their way to the milking parlor, but this is often far more pleasant than, for example, tussling on the A75 with heavy-goods vehicles rushing to make the Irish ferries.

The Scottish Borders is largely characterized by upland moors and hills, with fertile, farmed, and forested river valleys. The textile towns of the Borders have plenty of personality—Border folk are sure of their own identity and are fiercely partisan toward their own native towns. The Southwest, often known as Dumfries and Galloway, shares the upland characteristics and, if anything, has a slightly wilder air (the highest hill in Dumfries and Galloway is the Merrick, 2,765 ft). Easygoing and peaceful, towns are usually very attractive, with wide streets and colorful frontages.

Numbers in the text correspond to numbers in the margin and on the Borders and the Southwest maps.

Great Itineraries

To visit all the places described in the Borders would certainly take more than one day. To travel at a leisurely pace and spend time at some of the grand mansions noted, you could easily allow three days, although the total driving distance between each town is not great: In the Borders there are several points of interest quite close to one another.

Owing to the high ground and forests at the heart of Dumfries and Galloway, a linear itinerary that keeps largely to the coast might be best. Once again, distances between towns are not large, but traveling on narrow country roads can take a little longer than you might expect. If you particularly enjoy sketching or taking photographs, this is not an area to be rushed, in which case three days is the minimum time

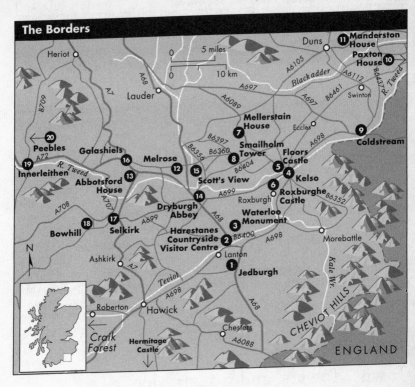

The Borders

to allow to sample an abbey or two and see the settings of Dumfries and Galloway towns.

IF YOU HAVE 2 DAYS

Jedburgh ① is the best orientation place to get an idea of how important the Border abbeys were. If you cross the border to the west, then head for somewhere like **Kirkcudbright** ㉜ for a flavor of Dumfries and Galloway. In short, if you only have two days, then you will have to choose between the Borders and the Southwest.

IF YOU HAVE 5 DAYS

Plan to divide your time between the Borders (three days) and Dumfries and Galloway (two days); you will have to be selective about which abbeys and stately homes to make more than a quick visit to. Jedburgh Abbey in **Jedburgh** ① is a must-see, as is Melrose Abbey in **Melrose** ⑫. Melrose Abbey also has gardens to enjoy, several museums, and famous stately homes nearby, including **Abbotsford House** ⑬, home of Sir Walter Scott. Finish up at **Peebles** ⑳, where you should allow plenty of time to shop.

In Dumfries and Galloway, two days will give you time to visit **Sweetheart Abbey** ㉗ in New Abbey, then **Arbigland Gardens** ㉘ in Kirkbean, an excellent example of the lush gardens for which the area is famous. Try to fit in Castle Douglas and **Threave Gardens** ㉛, with the nearby gaunt Threave Castle, on a river island and reached by boat, to provide a gritty contrast. **Kirkcudbright** ㉜ is also worth even a quick visit for its artistic connections.

IF YOU HAVE 10 DAYS

In five days in the Borders, such jewels as **Floors Castle** ⑤, **Mellerstain House** ⑦, and **Paxton House** ⑩ can all be enjoyed (though you may get stately home indigestion), and you will also have time to admire the views and soak up the historic atmosphere at **Smailholm Tower** ⑧ or **Dryburgh Abbey** ⑭. One of the most unlikely attractions, Robert Smail's Printing Works at **Innerleithen** ⑲, is also one of the most historically interesting, and it is close to Traquair House, reported to be the oldest lived-in house in Scotland. You will also have time for an essential shopping visit to **Peebles** ⑳.

Five days in Dumfries and Galloway will also minimize the problem of choosing what to see—you'll have time for nearly everything. Still, at the top of your list should be **Threave Gardens** ㉛, Threave Castle, and **Kirkcudbright** ㉜. You should spend some time exploring the hills above Gatehouse of Fleet, with its **Cardoness Castle** ㉝ and heritage center, meander around the southern coastline, penetrate the wild and wooded **Glen Trool** ㊱, and travel deep into the Machars to **Whithorn** ㊳, a site of early religious importance. You will even be able to see **Castle Kennedy Gardens** ㊵ and **Logan Botanic Gardens** ㊷ to complete your Galloway gardens experience.

When to Tour the Borders and the Southwest

Because many properties are privately owned and are closed from early autumn until early April, the area is less well suited to off-season touring than some other parts of Scotland. The region does look magnificent in autumn, however, especially along the wooded river valleys of the Borders. Late spring is the time to see the rhododendrons of the gardens in Dumfries and Galloway.

THE BORDERS
Towns, Towers, and Countryside

This area never possessed the high romance of the Gaelic-speaking clans in the Highlands to the north, but it did have (and still has) powerful Border families, whose ancestry is soaked in the bloodshed that occurred along this once very real frontier between Scotland and her more opportunist neighbor to the south.

Border folk take great pride in the region's heritage as Scotland's main woolen-goods manufacturing area. To this day the residents possess a marked determination to defend their towns and communities. We can all be thankful, however, that the changing times have allowed them to reposition their priorities: Instead of guarding against southern raiders, they now concentrate on maintaining a fiercely competitive rugby team for the popular intertown rugby matches. The Borders is a stronghold of this European counterpart to American football.

Border communities are also re-establishing their identities through the curious affairs known as the Common Ridings. Long ago it was essential that each town be able to defend its area, and over the centuries this need has become formalized in mounted gatherings to "ride the boundaries." The observance of the tradition lapsed in certain places but has been revived. Leaders and attendants are solemnly elected each year, and Borderers who now live away from home make a point of attending their town's event. (You are welcome to watch and enjoy the excitement of clattering hooves and banners proudly displayed, but this is essentially a time for the native Borderers.) The Common Ridings possess at least as much authenticity and historic significance as the concocted Highland Games, so often taken to be the essence of Scotland. The little town of Selkirk, in fact, claims its Common Riding to be the largest mounted gathering anywhere in Europe.

The Borders towns cluster around and between the two great regional rivers, the Tweed and the Teviot. They encompass all four of the great ruined Border abbeys. The monks in these long-abandoned religious foundations were the first to work the fleeces of their sheep flocks, hence laying the foundation for what is still the area's main industry.

Jedburgh

1 *50 mi south of Edinburgh, 95 mi southeast of Glasgow.*

The town of Jedburgh (*-burgh* is always pronounced *burra* in Scots) was for centuries the first major Scottish target of invading English armies. In more peaceful times it developed textile mills, most of which have since perished. The large landscaped area around the town's tourist information center was once a mill but now provides an encampment for the modern armies of tourists. The past still clings to this little town, however. The ruined abbey dominates the skyline and is compulsory visiting if you are interested in acquiring a feeling of the former role of the Border abbeys.

★ Still impressive, though it is now only a roofless shell, **Jedburgh Abbey** was destroyed by the English earl of Hertford's forces in 1544–45, during the destructive time known as "the Rough Wooing." This was the English king Henry VIII's (1491–1547) armed attempt to persuade the Scots that it was a good idea to unite the kingdoms by the marriage of his young son to the infant Mary, Queen of Scots. (The Scots disagreed and sent Mary to France instead.) The full story is explained in vivid detail at the **Jedburgh Abbey Visitor Centre,** which provides information on interpreting the ruins. Only ground patterns and foundations remain of the once-powerful religious complex. ⊠ *High St.,* ☎ *0131/668–8800.* ⊡ *£2.80.* ⊙ *Apr.–Sept., daily 9:30–6; Oct.–Mar., Mon.–Sat. 9:30–4, Sun. 2–4.*

There is much else to see in Jedburgh, including **Mary, Queen of Scots House.** This *bastel* (from the French *bastille*) was the fortified town house in which, some say, Mary stayed before embarking on her famous 20-mi ride to visit her wounded lover, the earl of Bothwell, at **Hermitage Castle** (☞ Off the Beaten Path, *below*). An interpretative center in the building relates the tale. ⊠ *Queen St.,* ☎ *01835/863331.* ⊡ *£2.* ⊙ *June–Sept., 10–4:30; Mar.–May and Oct.–Nov., Mon.–Sat. 10–5, Sun. noon–4:30.*

Jedburgh Castle Jail re-creates life in a Howard Reform Prison, with prison cells to inspect. The history of the Royal Burgh of Jedburgh is told through room settings in period style, costumed figures, and audiovisuals. ⊠ *Castlegate,* ☎ *01835/863254.* ⊡ *£1.25.* ⊙ *Mid-Mar.–mid-Nov., daily 10–4..*

2 Just a few miles north of Jedburgh, the **Harestanes Countryside Visitor Centre** conveys life in the Borders. The Discovery Room has changing displays on the countryside, wildlife, and crafts, plus you'll find a wooden games and puzzles room, and a tearoom and gift shop. Outside are a play area, marked trails, and guided walks. ⊠ *Monteviot, at the junction of A68 and B6400,* ☎ *01835/830306.* ⊡ *Free.* ⊙ *Apr.–Oct., daily 10–5.*

3 In view on the skyline is the **Waterloo Monument,** a pencil-thin tower that is another reminder of the whims and power of the landowning gentry: A marquis of Lothian built the monument in 1815, with the help of his tenants, in celebration of the victory of Wellington at Waterloo. If you have time, you can walk to the tower from the Harestanes Countryside Visitor Centre (1 hour). ⊠ *Off B6400, 5 mi north of Jedburgh.*

OFF THE
BEATEN PATH

HERMITAGE CASTLE – To appreciate Mary, Queen of Scots's famous 20-mi ride to visit her wounded lover, the earl of Bothwell (circa 1535–78), travel southwest from Jedburgh to this, the most complete remaining example of the bare and grim medieval border castles, full of gloom and foreboding. Restored in the early 19th century, it was built in the 14th century (replacing an earlier structure) to guard what was at the time one of the important routes from England into Scotland. The original owner, Lord Soulis, notorious for diabolical excess, was captured by the local populace, who wrapped him in lead and boiled him in a cauldron, or so the tale goes. The castle lies on an unclassified road between the A7 and B6399, about 10 mi south of Hawick, in the desolate Borders hills. ⊠ *Liddesdale,* ☎ *0131/668–8800.* ⌑ *£1.50.* ☉ *Apr.–Sept., daily 9:30–6.*

Lodging

£–££   🖼 **Larkhall Burn.** Your accommodations will be in one of a series of
★   modern, terraced cottages set on a sunny hillside high above the rooftops of Jedburgh. The interiors of these units are decorated in pastel shades and floral fabrics. You can order your meals to be delivered from a restaurant in town, or use the well-equipped kitchen. Larkhall Burn provides more comfort than many hotels, including maid service, and at a competitive price—only £20 per person a night. The minimum stay is two nights. ⊠ *Jedburgh, TD8 6AX,* ☎ ☎ *01835/862313. 6 cottages with baths. MC, V.*

£   🖼 **Spinney Guest House.** Made up of two unpretentiously converted and modernized farm cottages, this B&B offers the highest standards for the price. Two log cabins each sleep three, with self-catering or B&B service. ⊠ *Langlee, TD8 6PB,* ☎ *01835/863525,* ☎ *01835/864883. 3 rooms with bath or shower, 2 log cabins. No credit cards. Closed mid-Nov.–Feb.*

Kelso

❹ *12 mi northeast of Jedburgh.*

One of the most charming Borders burghs, Kelso is often described as having a Continental flavor—some visitors think it resembles a Belgian market town. The town has a broad, paved Market Square and fine examples of Georgian and Victorian Scots town architecture.

Kelso Abbey is the least intact ruin of the four great Border abbeys—just a bleak fragment of what was once the largest of the group. On a main nvasion route, the abbey was burned three times in the 1540s alone, on the last occasion by the English Earl of Hertford's forces in 1545 when the garrison of 100 men and 12 monks were butchered and the structure all but destroyed. ⊠ *Bridge St.,* ☎ *0131/668–8800.* ⌑ *Free.* ☉ *Apr.–Sept., daily 9:30–6; Oct.–Mar., Mon.–Sat. 9:30–4, Sun. 2–4.*

On the bank of the River Tweed, just 2 mi northwest of Kelso, stands
★ **❺** the palatial **Floors Castle.** Ancestral home of the duke of Roxburghe, the castle was built by William Adam (1689–1748) in 1721 and modified with mock-Tudor touches by William Playfair (1789–1857) in the 1840s. A holly tree in the deer park marks the place where King James II (1430–60) was killed in 1460 by an exploding cannon. ⊠ *A6089,* ☎ *01573/223333.* ⌑ *Joint ticket for castle and grounds, £4.50; grounds only, £2.* ☉ *Easter–Sept., daily 10–4.*

❻ Do not confuse the comparatively youthful Floors Castle with **Roxburghe Castle,** nearby. Only traces of rubble and earthworks remain of this ancient structure. The modern-day village of **Roxburgh** is young; the original Roxburgh, one of the oldest burghs in Scotland, has virtually disappeared, though its name lives on in the duke's title and in the name of the old county of Roxburghshire. ⊠ *Off the A699, 4 mi southwest of Kelso.*

❼ If you are a devotee of ornate country houses, you are well served in the Borders. Begun in the 1720s, **Mellerstain House** was finished in the 1770s by Robert Adam (1728–92) and is considered to be one of his finest creations. Sumptuous plasterwork covers almost all interior surfaces, and there are outstanding examples of 18th-century furnishings. The beautiful terraced gardens are as renowned as the house. ⊠ *Off A6089, 7 mi northwest of Kelso,* ☎ *01573/410225.* 🎟 *£4.50.* ☉ *House: Easter and May–Sept., Sun.–Fri. 12:30–5; restaurant: Easter and May–Sept., Sun.–Fri. 11:30–5:30.*

★ ❽ In the hills south of Mellerstain sits a characteristic Borders structure that certainly contrasts with the luxury of Mellerstain House. **Smailholm Tower** stands uncompromisingly on top of a barren, rocky ridge. Built solely for defense, this 16th-century Border *peel* (small fortified tower common to this region) offers memorable views. If you let your imagination wander in this windy spot, you can almost see the flapping pennants and rising dust of an advancing raiding party and hear the anxious securing of doors and bolts. Sir Walter Scott found this an inspiring spot. His grandfather lived at nearby Sandyknowe Farm (not open to the public), and the young Scott visited the tower often during his childhood. ⊠ *Off B6404, 8 mi west of Kelso,* ☎ *0131/668–8800.* 🎟 *£1.80.* ☉ *Apr.–Sept., daily 9:30–6.*

Lodging

££–£££ 🏨 **Edued House Hotel.** Ninety percent of the guests are return visitors
★ to this large, appealing hotel on the banks of the River Tweed, close to Kelso's grand abbey and old Market Square. The open fire in the hall, sporting paintings, and cozy armchairs impart a homey feeling. The restaurant's three glass walls afford views of the garden and river; the Scottish fare here includes fresh local vegetables, salmon from the River Tweed, Aberdeen Angus beef, and homemade ice cream and traditional puddings. ⊠ *Bridge St., TD5 7HT,* ☎ *01573/224168,* 🅵🅰🆇 *01573/226319. 32 rooms with bath or shower. Restaurant, golf privileges, horseback riding, fishing. MC, V. Closed late Dec.–early Jan.*

Coldstream

❾ *9 mi east of Kelso.*

Three miles west of Coldstream, the England-Scotland border comes down from the hills and runs beside the Tweed for the rest of its journey to the sea. Coldstream itself, like Gretna (☞ *below*), was once a marriage place for runaway couples from the south at a time when the marriage laws of Scotland were more lenient than those of England (a plaque on the former bridge tollhouse recalls this fact). It is also celebrated in military history: in 1659, General Monck raised a regiment of foot guards here on behalf of his exiled monarch Charles II (1630–85). Known as the Coldstream Guards, the successors to this regiment have become an elite corps in the British army.

The **Coldstream Museum,** in the Coldstream Guards' former headquarters, investigates the history of the community of Coldstream, past and present. A special exhibition recalls the history of the Coldstream Guards. ⊠ *Market Sq.,* ☎ *01890/882630.* 🎟 *£1.* ☉ *Apr.–Sept., Mon.–Sat. 10–4, Sun 2–4. Oct., Mon.–Sat 1–4.*

The stretch of the Tweed near Coldstream is lined with dignified houses and gardens. The best known house is **The Hirsel,** where a complex of farmyard buildings now serves as a crafts center and museum, with interesting walks on the extensive grounds. It's a favorite spot for bird-watchers, and superb rhododendrons bloom here in late spring. The house itself is not open to the public. ⊠ *A697, immediately west of Coldstream,* ☎ *01890/882834.* ☜ *Free (parking charge: Easter–Sept. £2, Oct.–Easter £1).* ☉ *Grounds: daily sunrise–sunset; museum and crafts center: weekdays 10–5, weekends noon–5.*

⑩ If you are spending a lot of time in the area, you could tour northeast from Coldstream to see more stately mansions. **Paxton House** is a comely Palladian mansion with interiors designed by Adam, and Chippendale and Trotter furniture. The splendid Regency picture gallery is an out-station of the National Galleries of Scotland and contains a magnificent collection of paintings. The garden is delightful, with an ice house, squirrel hide, and a restored boathouse with a museum of salmon net fishing; a craft shop and a tearoom are adjacent to the house. ⊠ *Paxton, 15 mi northeast of Coldstream (take A6112 and B6461),* ☎ *01289/386291.* ☜ *Joint ticket for house and garden, £4; garden only, £2.* ☉ *House and garden: Easter–Oct., daily 11–5; tearoom: daily 10–5:30.*

⑪ **Manderston House** is a good example of the grand, no-expense-spared Edwardian country house. The family who built it made their fortune selling herring to Russia. An original 1790s Georgian house on the site was completely rebuilt 1903–5 to the specifications of John Kinross. The staircase is silver plated (thought to be unique) and was modeled after the Petit Trianon at Versailles. There is also much to see downstairs in the kitchens, and outside, among a cluster of other buildings, is the one-of-a-kind marble dairy. The house is reached by traveling farther northwest from Coldstream along the A6112 to Duns, then taking the A6105 east. ⊠ *2 mi east of Duns,* ☎ *01361/882636.* ☜ *Joint ticket for house and grounds: £5; grounds only: £3.* ☉ *Mid-May–Sept., Thurs. and Sun. 2–5:30.*

Lodging

££ 🍴 **Wheatsheaf Hotel and Restaurant.** A country inn on the main street of Swinton, midway between Coldstream and Duns, the Wheatsheaf offers outstanding food in both the black-beamed bar and the restaurant. The sheer class of the Scottish cuisine, whether the meal is beef, salmon, or venison, has won widespread praise, yet neither the food nor the small but carefully chosen wine list is overpriced. If you do not want to leave after your meal, stay in one of the four country-style bedrooms. ⊠ *Wheatsheaf Hotel, Swinton, TD11 3JJ,* ☎ FAX *01890/860257. 6 rooms, 4 with bath or shower. Restaurant. MC, V. Closed last 2 wks in Feb. and last wk in Oct.*

Melrose

⑫ *15 mi west of Coldstream.*

In the center of the handsome community of Melrose sits **Melrose Abbey,** another of the four Borders abbeys. "If thou would'st view fair Melrose aright, go visit it in the pale moonlight," wrote Scott in *The Lay of the Last Minstrel,* and so many of his fans took the advice literally that a sleepless custodian begged him to rewrite the lines. Today the abbey is still impressive: a red sandstone shell with slender windows in the Perpendicular style and some delicate tracery and carved capitals, carefully maintained. Among the carvings high on the roof is one of a bagpipe-playing pig. An audio tour is included in the admission price. ⊠ *Main Sq.,* ☎ *0131/668–8800.* ☜ *£2.80.* ☉ *Apr.–Sept., daily 9:30–6; Oct.–Mar., Mon.–Sat. 9:30–4, Sun. 2–4.*

Next to Melrose Abbey is the National Trust for Scotland's (☞ Threave Gardens, *below*) **Priorwood Gardens,** which specializes in flowers for drying. Next to the gardens is an orchard with some old apple varieties. Dried flowers are on sale in the shop. ⊠ *Main Sq..* ☜ *£1.* ☉ *Apr.–Sept., Mon.–Sat. 10–5:30, Sun. 1:30–5:30; Oct.–Dec. 24, Mon.–Sat. 10–4, Sun. 1:30–4.*

The renovated **Melrose Station,** a poignant survivor of the old **Waverley Route,** a railroad which until 1969 ran between Edinburgh and Carlisle, is now used as offices, with a restaurant (☎ 01896/822546, closed Mon. and Tues.; no dinner Wed. and Sun.) on the ground floor serving morning coffee, light lunches, and complete evening meals.

The **Trimontium Exhibition,** in the Square displays artifacts from the largest Roman settlement in Scotland, which was at nearby Newstead. Tools and weapons, a blacksmith's shop, pottery, and scale models of the fort are included in the display. A guided 5-mi, 4-hour walk to the site takes place each Thursday afternoon; phone for details. ⊠ *Ormiston Institute, the Square, Melrose* ☎ 01896/822651. ☜ *£1.30.* ☉ *Apr.–Oct., daily 10:30–4:30 (Sat. and Sun. closed 12:30–1:30).*

Teddy Melrose, a teddy bear museum, tells the story of British teddy bears from the early 1900s. There is, of course, a collector's bear shop. ⊠ *High St.,* ☎ 01896/822464. ☜ *£1.50.* ☉ *Daily 10–5.*

★ ⑬ Two miles west of Melrose stands **Abbotsford House,** home of Sir Walter Scott (1771–1832). In 1811, already an established writer, Scott bought a farm on this site named Cartleyhole, which was a euphemism for the real name, Clartyhole (*clarty* means muddy or sticky in Scots). The name was surely not romantic enough for Scott, who renamed the property and eventually had it entirely rebuilt in the Romantic style, emulating several other Scottish properties. The resulting pseudomonastic, pseudobaronial mansion became the repository for the writer's collection of Scottish memorabilia and historic artifacts. The library holds some 9,000 volumes. Scott died here in 1832. Today the house is owned by his descendants. ⊠ *B6360,* ☎ 01896/752043. ☜ *£3.50.* ☉ *Mid-Mar.–Oct., Mon.–Sat. 10–5, Sun. 2–5; June–Sept., also Sun. 10–5.*

★ ⑭ Sir Walter's final resting place and the most peaceful and secluded of the Borders abbeys, **Dryburgh Abbey** is situated on gentle parkland in a loop of the Tweed. The abbey suffered from English raids until, like Melrose, it was abandoned in 1544. The style is transitional, a mingling of rounded Romanesque and pointed early English. The side chapel, where the Haig and Scott families lie buried, is lofty and pillared, detached from the main buildings. ⊠ *Off A68, 4 mi southeast of Melrose,* ☎ 0131/668–8800. ☜ *£2.30.* ☉ *Apr.–Sept., daily 9:30–6; Oct.–Mar., Mon.–Sat. 9:30–4, Sun. 2–4.*

★ ⑮ There is no escaping Sir Walter in this part of the country: 3 mi north of Dryburgh is **Scott's View,** possibly the most photographed rural view in the south of Scotland. (Perhaps the only view that is more often used to summon a particular interpretation of Scotland is Eilean Donan Castle, far to the north.) You arrive at this peerless vista by taking the B6356 north from Dryburgh. A poignant tale is told about the horses of Scott's funeral cortege: on their way to Dryburgh Abbey they stopped here out of habit as they had so often in the past. The sinuous curve of the River Tweed, the gentle landscape unfolding to the triple peaks of the **Eildons,** then rolling out into shadows beyond, is certainly worth seeking.

SIR WALTER SCOTT

SIR WALTER SCOTT (1771–1832) was born in College Wynd, Edinburgh. Though trained as a lawyer, it is as a prolific writer that he is best remembered today. His works, usually Scottish in setting and character, were wildly popular in his own day, yet also stand as major historical novels. As part of the Romantic movement in Britain, (the English poets William Wordsworth and Samuel Taylor Coleridge were his near contemporaries) Scott wrote of Scotland as a place of Highland wildness and clan romance, shaping outsiders' perceptions of Scotland in a way which to a certain extent even survives today.

As a young boy recovering from illness, Scott was sent to his grandfather's farm near Smailholm in the Borders, where he first heard the stirring tales of Border history. After qualifying as an advocate in 1792, and his marriage in 1797 to Margaret Charlotte Charpentier, daughter of a French refugee, Scott began seriously to devote his spare time to writing. "The Lay of the Last Minstrel," a romantic poem published in 1805, brought him fame and was soon followed by further romantic verse narratives.

In 1811, Scott bought the house that was to become Abbotsford, his Borders mansion near Melrose, which he rebuilt and which gradually became a storehouse of Scottish history: Bonnie Prince Charlie's *quaich* (drinking bowl), library ceiling plaster casts from Rosslyn Chapel, Rob Roy's broadsword, an entrance porch copied from Linlithgow Palace—all can still be seen today among a wealth of other artifacts.

Scott started on his series of Waverley Novels in 1814, at first anonymously, and by 1820 had produced *Waverley, Guy Mannering, The Antiquary, Tales of My Landlord* (three series), *Rob Roy*. Between 1820 and 1825, a further 11 titles followed, including *Ivanhoe* and *The Pirate* (which was partly written during a voyage around Scotland with lighthouse-builder Robert Stevenson, grandfather of novelist Robert Louis Stevenson). Many of his verse narratives and novels focused on real life settings, in particular the Trossachs, west of Stirling, which rapidly became, and still remain, extremely popular with visitors.

In 1826, Ballantyne's publishing house, in which Scott was a partner, went bankrupt and Scott took it as a matter of honor that he should personally clear the debts. His copious output from then until 1832 included, in addition to further novels, a *Life of Napoleon* and translations of German work. Scott's health started to fail under the pressure of work, and he died on September 21, 1832.

Apart from his writing, Scott is also remembered as the discoverer, in 1819, of the Honours of Scotland (the crown, scepter, and sword of state of the Scottish monarchs), which had been wrapped up, dumped in the bottom of a chest in Edinburgh Castle, and forgotten since 1707, when Scotland lost her independence. Today these historic symbols of Scotland's sovereignty are on display in the castle. Abbotsford can be visited in the summer season, and other houses associated with Scott can be seen (from the outside only) in Edinburgh: 25 George Square, his father's house, and 39 Castle Street. The site of his birthplace in College Wynd is marked with a plaque. The most obvious structure associated with Scott is the Scott Monument in Princes Street, a Gothic rocket ship with a statue of Scott and his pet dog as passengers.

OFF THE
BEATEN PATH

THIRLESTANE CASTLE – At the children's nursery in this 17th-century castle, children are allowed to play with Victorian-style toys and masks and to dress up in costumes. Thirlestane is on the A68 10 mi north of Melrose. ⊠ *Lauder,* ☎ *01578/722430.* ✉ *Joint ticket for castle and grounds: £4; grounds only: £1.50.* ⊙ *Easter week, May, June, and Sept., Mon., Wed., Thurs., and Sun. 2–5; July–Aug., Sun.–Fri. noon–5 (grounds open noon–6). Last admission to house and grounds 4:30.*

Dining and Lodging

£–££
★

✗ **Marmion's Brasserie.** This cozy restaurant has outstanding country-style Scottish cuisine. It is a great place to stop for lunch after a visit to nearby Abbotsford or Dryburgh Abbey. Try the honey-and-orange lamb, or the Stilton-stuffed mushrooms. ⊠ *Buccleuch St.,* ☎ *01896/ 822245. AE, MC, V. Closed Sun.*

££££
🏨 **Dryburgh Abbey Hotel.** Right next to the abbey ruins, this civilized hotel is surrounded by beautiful scenery and has a restaurant (no smoking) specializing in traditional Scottish fare. The restrained decor and earthy, muted colors throughout create a peaceful atmosphere in keeping with the location. ⊠ *St. Boswells, TD6 0RQ,* ☎ *01835/ 822261,* ℻ *01835/823945. 38 rooms with bath. Restaurant (jacket and tie), golf privileges. AE, MC, V.*

£££
🏨 **Burts Hotel.** Built in 1772, this quiet hotel in the center of Melrose retains a considerable amount of its period style, updated with modern conveniences. It has a particularly welcoming bar, with a cheerful open fire and a wide selection of fine malt whiskies, ideal for a quiet dram before or after a meal in the elegant dining room, which has dark-green striped wallpaper, high-back upholstered chairs, and white linen tablecloths. Cannon of venison and roast duck terrine are typical entrées on the Scottish menu, which has Continental overtones. The bedrooms and public areas are individually decorated with reproduction antiques and floral pastels. Shooting and fishing can be arranged. ⊠ *Market Sq., TD6 9PN,* ☎ *01896/822285,* ℻ *01896/822870. 20 rooms with bath or shower. Restaurant. AE, DC, MC, V.*

Galashiels

⓯ *5 mi northwest of Melrose.*

A gray stone and busy Borders town, Galashiels is still active with textile mills and knitwear shops. At the **Lochcarron of Scotland Cashmere and Wool Centre** is a museum of the town's history and industry; visitors can go on a mill tour and learn about the manufacture of tartans and tweeds. ⊠ *Nether Mill,* ☎ *01896/752091.* ✉ *£2.50.* ⊙ *Oct.–May, Mon.–Sat. 9–5; June–Sept., also Sun. noon–5. Guided tours Mon.– Thurs. 10:30, 11:30, 1:30, 2:30; Fri. 10:30 and 11:30.*

Dating from 1583, **Old Gala House,** a short walk from the town center, is the former home of the lairds of Galashiels. It is now a museum with displays on the building's history and the town of Galashiels, and also a contemporary art gallery and exhibition space. ⊠ *Scott Crescent,* ☎ *01750/20096.* ✉ *Free.* ⊙ *Apr.–Sept., Tues.–Sat. 10–4; Oct., Tues.–Sat. 1–4.*

Lodging

££
🏨 **Woodlands House Hotel.** This Gothic revival–style hotel, chintz-hung and traditionally furnished, has stunning views over Tweeddale, the tree-lined, lush green valley of the River Tweed. The main restaurant specializes in fresh seafood and hearty Scottish cuisine, while Sanderson's Steakhouse is named after a former owner of the house whose portrait gazes down on diners; bar meals are also served. ⊠ *Windy-*

knowe Rd., TD1 1RG, ☎ FAX *01896/754722. 10 rooms with bath and shower. 3 restaurants, golf privileges, horseback riding, fishing. MC, V.*

Shopping
Lochcarron of Scotland Cashmere and Wool Centre (☞ *above*) has a wide selection of woolens and tweeds.

Selkirk

⑰ *7 mi south of Galashiels.*

Selkirk is a hilly outpost with a smattering of antiques shops and an assortment of bakers selling the Selkirk Bannock (fruited sweet bread-cake) and other cakes—evidence of Scotland's incurable sweet tooth. Sir Walter Scott was sheriff (county judge) of Selkirkshire from 1800 until his death in 1832, and his statue stands in Market Place. **Sir Walter Scott's Courtroom,** where he presided, contains a display examining Scott's life, his writings, and his time as sheriff, and includes an audiovisual presentation. ⊠ *Market Pl.,* ☎ *01750/20096.* 🎫 *£1.* ☉ *Apr.–Sept., Mon.–Sat. 10–4; June–Aug., also Sun. 2–4; Oct., Mon.–Sat. 1–4..*

Tucked off the main square in Selkirk, **Halliwell's House Museum** was once an ironmonger's shop, now re-created downstairs. Upstairs, an exhibit tells the town's tale, with useful background information on the Common Ridings and an audiovisual presentation. ⊠ *Market St.,* ☎ *01750/20096.* 🎫 *Free.* ☉ *Apr.–June and Sept.–Oct, Mon.–Sat. 10–5, Sun. 2–4; July–Aug., daily 10–6.*

⑱ Another of the stately homes in the Borders, 19th-century **Bowhill** houses an outstanding collection of works by Gainsborough (1727–88), Van Dyck (1599–1641), Canaletto (1697–1768), Reynolds (1723–92), and Raeburn (1756–1823), as well as porcelain and period furniture. Note the house itself is open in July only; the grounds and playground have more friendly hours. ⊠ *Off A708, 3 mi west of Selkirk,* ☎ FAX *01750/22204.* 🎫 *Joint ticket for house and grounds/playground: £4; grounds/playground only: £1.* ☉ *House: July, daily 1–4:30; grounds/playground: May–June and Aug., Sat.–Thurs. noon–5; July, daily noon–5.*

Innerleithen

⑲ *15 mi northwest of Selkirk.*

The main reason to come to the linear community of Innerleithen is **Robert Smail's Printing Works.** The fully operational, restored print shop with reconstructed waterwheel will fascinate adults and older children, who can try their hand at typesetting. ⊠ *7/9 High St.,* ☎ *01896/830206.* 🎫 *£2.40.* ☉ *Easter and May–Sept., Mon.–Sat. 10–1 and 2–5, Sun. 2–5; Oct., Sat. 10–1 and 2–5, Sun. 2–5 (last admission 45 mins before closing, morning and afternoon).*

Near the town is **Traquair House,** said to be the oldest continually oc-cupied house in Scotland. Secret stairs, intricate embroidery, a bed used by Mary, Queen of Scots, in 1566, more than 3,000 books, and a maze are just a few of the discoveries. Ale is still brewed in the 18th-century brewhouse here, and is recommended! ⊠ *Traquair, near Innerleithen,* ☎ *01896/830323.* 🎫 *£4.50.* ☉ *Apr.–May and Sept., daily 12:30–5:30; June–Aug., daily 10:30–5:30; Oct., Fri.–Sun. 12:30–5:30 (last admission 5:30).*

Lodging
££££ 🏠 **Traquair House.** Stay in the private quarters at Traquair to experi-ence the unique atmosphere of this ancient house for yourself. The Blue

Room and the Pink Room, furnished with antiques and with chintz-draped canopied beds, offer a most relaxing environment, as does the 18th-century Lower Drawing Room, where you can savor a glass of the house's own ale. ☒ *Innerleithen, Peeblesshire, EH44 6PW,* ☎ *01896/830323,* FAX *01896/830639. 2 rooms with bath. MC, V. Closed Dec.–Feb.*

Shopping

The **Mill Shop** (☒ Walkerburn, 2 mi east of Innerleithen, ☎ 01896/870619) has a large mill shop offering a wealth of styles, and an adjacent museum of woolen textiles.

Peebles

🔟 *6 mi west of Innerleithen.*

Thanks to its excellent, though pricey, shopping, Peebles gives the impression of catering primarily to well-to-do, leisured country gentlefolk. Architecturally the town is nothing out of the ordinary, a very pleasant Borders burgh (do not miss the splendid dolphins ornamenting the bridge crossing the River Tweed).

Lodging

££££ 🏨 **Cringletie House.** Surrounded by an old-fashioned walled garden
★ whose produce is used in the restaurant, this property—with turrets and crow-step gables in traditional Scottish baronial style—is personally supervised by the family of owners. From the spacious, elaborately ceilinged first-floor drawing room you can enjoy pretty views of the valley. The simple yet comfortably furnished bedrooms are a prelude to the hotel's major achievement: its food. Locals also flock to the restaurant for such upscale Scottish fare as roast duckling with red currant and cassis sauce. Afternoon tea served in the conservatory is especially recommended. ☒ *Eddleston, EH45 8PL,* ☎ *01721/730233,* FAX *01721/730244. 13 rooms with bath. Restaurant, putting green, tennis court, croquet. AE, MC, V.*

££££ 🏨 **Peebles Hydro.** Not only does it have something for everyone, but
★ it has it in abundance: archery, snooker, pony trekking, squash, a whirlpool, and a sauna are just a few of the diversions the hotel offers. The elegant Edwardian building, reminiscent of a French château, is set on 30 acres. High ceilings give the public areas an airy, spacious ambience. Bedrooms are comfortably furnished, though room sizes and decorative standards can vary. The restaurant features a Scottish menu with local salmon, lamb, and beef. ☒ *EH45 8LX,* ☎ *01721/720602,* FAX *01721/722999. 137 rooms with bath. Restaurant, pool, tennis court, health club, bicycles, baby-sitting, children's programs (ages infant–16), playground, laundry service. AE, DC, MC, V.*

£££ 🏨 **Park Hotel.** This hotel, on the banks of the River Tweed at the northern tip of the Ettrick Forest, offers comfort and tranquility. Rooms have striped or floral wallpaper and pastel fabrics. The restaurant (jacket and tie) serves superior Scottish cuisine, many of the dishes based on local salmon and trout. ☒ *Innerleithen Rd., EH45 8BA,* ☎ *01721/720451,* FAX *01721/723510. 24 rooms with bath. Restaurant. AE, DC, MC, V.*

£ 🏨 **Drummore.** This hillside B&B, set in an acre of wild gardens full of bird life, is well-positioned both for touring the Borders and for visiting Edinburgh. The house is modern and clean, and the guest lounge has a vast picture window that overlooks the River Tweed. ☒ *Venlaw High Rd., EH45 8RL,* ☎ *01721/720336,* FAX *01721/723004. 2 rooms with bath. MC, V. Nov.–Mar.*

Outdoor Activities and Sports

BIKING

Scottish Border Trails (✉ Drummore, Venlaw High Rd., Peebles, EH45 8RL, ☎ 01721/720336) rents bicycles and also organizes cycling and walking holidays, including lodging.

Shopping

You can easily spend a day browsing on High Street and in the courts and side streets leading off it, temptations awaiting at every turn.

GIFTS

Head to Toe (✉ 43 High St., ☎ 01721/722752) stocks natural beauty products of all descriptions and a variety of linens—from lace doilies to patchwork quilts; dried flowers; and porcelain pieces. If you need a rest after all that shopping, repair to **The Country Shop** (✉ 56 High St., ☎ 01721/720630), a gift store with souvenirs aplenty and a coffee shop upstairs, replete with views over the town and bustling High Street.

HARDWARE

Scott's Hardware Store (✉ 48 High St., ☎ 01721/720262) has every kind of tool, implement, fixture, fitting, and garden gadget (even mousetraps) spread in glorious array over floors, walls, and ceiling.

JEWELRY

Among many craftspeople and jewelers on High Street is **Keith Walter** (✉ 28 High St., ☎ 01721/720650), a gold- and silversmith who makes items on the premises and stocks jewelry made by other local designers.

GALLOWAY HIGHLANDS

Galloway is the name given to the southwest portion of Scotland, west of the main town of Dumfries. The area's terrain is diverse—from its gentle coastline and breezy uplands to areas gradually disappearing below blankets of conifers. Use caution when negotiating the A75: although this main trunk road has been improved in recent years, you are liable to find aggressive trucks bearing down on you as these commercial vehicles race for the Irish ferries at Stranraer and Cairnryan. (Anything as environmentally sensible as a direct east–west railway link was closed years ago.) Trucks notwithstanding, once you are off the main roads, Dumfries and Galloway offers some of the most pleasant touring roads in Scotland—though the occasional herd of cows on the way to be milked is a potential hazard.

Gretna

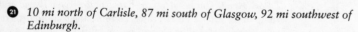 10 mi north of Carlisle, 87 mi south of Glasgow, 92 mi southwest of Edinburgh.

Gretna and **Gretna Green** are, quite simply, an embarrassment to native Scots. What else can you say about a place that advertises "amusing joke weddings," as does one of the visitor centers here? The reason for all these strange goings-on is tied to the reputation the community received as a refuge for runaway couples from England, who once came north to take advantage of Scotland's less-strict marriage laws. This was the first place they reached on crossing the border. At one time anyone could perform a legal marriage in Scotland. Often the village blacksmith did the honors, presumably because he was conveniently situated near the main road.

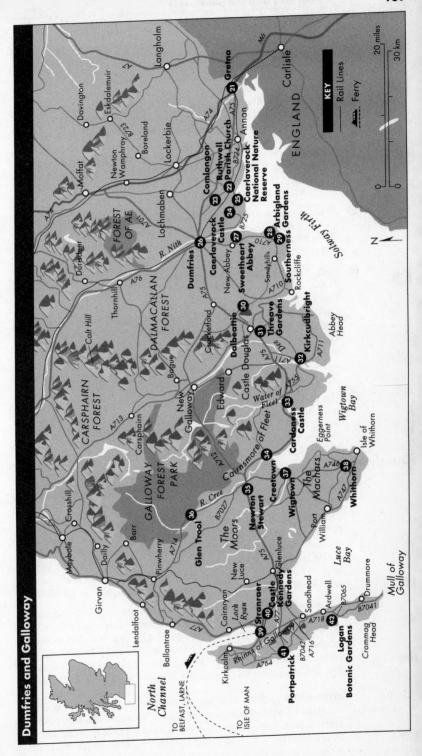

Dumfries and Galloway

KEY
— Rail Lines
⛴ Ferry

20 miles
30 km

N

ENGLAND

Carlisle

Langholm

Gretna 21

Davington

Eskdalemuir

Boreland

Newton Wamphray

Lockerbie

Moffat

Annan

Ruthwell Parish Church 22

Comlongon 23

Caerlaverock National Nature Reserve

FOREST OF AE

Lochmaben

24 25 Caerlaverock Castle

27 Arbigland Gardens 28

29 Southerness Gardens

Solway Firth

Duisdeer

Durisdeer

R. Nith

26 Dumfries

New Abbey

Sweetheart Abbey

Sandyhills

Rockcliffe

Thornhill

Colt Hill

DALMACALLAN FOREST

Bogue

Crocketford

30 Dalbeattie

Threave Gardens

31 Castle Douglas

Kirkcudbright

Abbey Head

CARSPHAIRN FOREST

Carsphairn

New Galloway

Edward

Castle Douglas

Water of Fleet

32

Dee

33 Cardoness Castle

Eggerness Point

Wigtown Bay

Cairnsmore of Fleet

34

Isle of Whithorn

GALLOWAY FOREST PARK

R. Cree

The Moors

35 Newton Stewart

Creetown 37

Wigtown 37

The Machars

38 Whithorn

Maybole

Crosshill

Barr

Glen Trool 36

New Luce

A75

Port William

Dailly

Girvan

Pinwherry

Glenluce

Lendalfoot

Ballantrae

Cairnryan

Loch Ryan

Stranraer 40

39

Castle Kennedy Gardens

Sandhead

Ardwell

Luce Bay

Drummore

Mull of Galloway

Crommag Head

Kirkcolm

Rhins of Galloway

Portpatrick 41

42 Logan Botanic Gardens

North Channel

TO BELFAST, LARNE

TO ISLE OF MAN

Ruthwell

21 mi west of Gretna, 83 mi south of Glasgow, 88 mi southwest of Edinburgh.

The landscape is not impressive around the flat fields of the Upper Solway Firth, but as you progress west you'll find more of interest. Inside **㉒** **Ruthwell Parish Church** is the 8th-century **Ruthwell Cross,** a Christian sculpture admired for the quality of its carving. Considered an idolatrous monument, it was destroyed by the Scottish authorities in 1640 but was later reassembled. Near the church in Ruthwell is the **Savings Bank Museum,** which tells the story of the savings-bank movement, founded by the Reverend Doctor Henry Duncan in 1810. ⊠ *6½ mi west of Annan,* ☎ *01387/870640.* ⚑ *Free.* ◷ *Apr.–Sept., daily 10–1 and 2–5; Oct.–Mar., Tues.–Sat. 10–1 and 2–5.*

㉓ At nearby Clarencefield, **Comlongon,** a more recent mansion house, adjoins a well-preserved 15th-century border keep. You can also avail of the B&B at the castle. ⊠ *B724, 8 mi west of Annan, DG1 4NA,* ☎ *01387/870283.* ⚑ *£3.* ◷ *Mar.–Nov., daily 10–6.*

★ ㉔ Built in a triangular design unique in Britain, moated **Caerlaverock Castle** stands overlooking a nature reserve on a coastal loop of the B725. This 13th-century fortress has solid-sandstone masonry and an imposing double-tower gatehouse. King Edward I of England (1239–1307) besieged the castle in 1300, when his forces occupied much of Scotland as the Wars of Independence commenced. The castle suffered many times in Anglo-Scottish skirmishes, as the video presentation attests. ⊠ *Off B725, 7 mi west of Ruthwell,* ☎ *01387/770244.* ⚑ *£2.30.* ◷ *Apr.–Sept., daily 9:30–6; Oct.–Mar., Mon.–Sat. 9:30–4, Sun. 2–4.*

㉕ The **Caerlaverock National Nature Reserve** is a treat for bird-watchers, who can observe wintering wildfowl from blinds and a visitor center. ⊠ *Off B725, east of Caerlaverock Castle,* ☎ *01387/770275.* ⚑ *Free.* ◷ *Year-round.*

Dumfries

㉖ *15 mi northwest of Ruthwell, 76 mi south of Glasgow, 81 mi southwest of Edinburgh.*

The town of Dumfries, where Scotland's national poet Robert Burns (1759–96) spent the last years of his short life, is a no-nonsense, red-sandstone community. The **River Nith** meanders through Dumfries, and the pedestrian-only town center makes shopping a pleasure (the A75 now bypasses the town). The town also contains Robert Burns's favorite pub (the Globe Inn), the house he lived in, and his mausoleum.

Not surprisingly, in view of its close association to the poet, Dumfries has a **Robert Burns Centre,** housed in a sturdy former mill overlooking the river. The center has an audiovisual program and an extensive exhibit on the life of the poet. ⊠ *Mill Rd.,* ☎ *01387/264808.* ⚑ *Free (small charge for audiovisual show).* ◷ *Apr.–Sept., Mon.–Sat. 10–8, Sun. 2–5 (café, daily 11–4); Oct.–Mar., Tues.–Sat. 10–1 and 2–5.*

OFF THE
BEATEN PATH

DRUMLANRIG CASTLE – This ornate red-sandstone structure was built on the site of an earlier Douglas stronghold in Nithsdale. The 17th-century castle contains Louis XIV furniture and a valuable collection of paintings by Leonardo da Vinci (1452–1519), Holbein (1497–1543), Rembrandt (1606–69), and others. There's also a bird of prey center with falconry displays, crafts workshops, a playground, gift shop, and tearoom. ⊠ *Near Thornhill, about 15 mi northwest of Dumfries off A76,* ☎ *01848/ 330248.* ⚑ *Joint ticket for castle and park: £6; park only: £3.* ◷ *Cas-*

tle: May–mid-Aug., daily 11–5 (last entry 4:15); guided tours 12–4; country park, gardens, and adventure playground: May–Aug., daily 11–5.

MUSEUM OF SCOTTISH LEAD MINING – Reached by taking the Mennock Pass through rounded moorland hills, this museum—devoted to one of Scotland's lesser-known industries—is at Wanlockhead, at Scotland's highest elevation a fairly bleak village. There are underground trips for the stout-hearted. The Miners' Library not only shows how the miners educated themselves, but offers a genealogical computer database. ✉ *Goldscaur Rd., Wanlockhead, on B797 northeast of Sanquhar, 27 mi northwest of Dumfries.* ☎ *01659/74387.* 🎫 *£3.50.* ☉ *Apr.–Oct., daily 11–4:30 (last guided tour at 4); Nov.–Apr., by appointment only.*

Nightlife and the Arts

THE ARTS

Gracefield Arts Centre (✉ Edinburgh Rd., ☎ 01387/262084) has public art galleries and studios with a constantly changing exhibition program. **The Dumfries and Galloway Arts Festival** is usually held at the end of May at several venues throughout the region. The **Robert Burns Centre Film Theatre** (✉ Mill Rd., ☎ 01387/264808) features special-interest, foreign, and other films not widely released.

Outdoor Activities and Sports

BIKING

Cycles can be rented from **Greirson and Graham** (✉ 10 Academy St., ☎ 01387/259483).

Shopping

GIFTS AND CRAFTS

Dumfries is the main shopping center for the region, with all the big-name chain stores as well as specialty shops. **Greyfriars Crafts** (✉ 56 Buccleuch St., ☎ 01387/264050) has mainly Scottish goods, including glass, ceramics, and jewelry.

If you are visiting Drumlanrig Castle (☞ Off the Beaten Path, *above*), do not miss the **crafts center** (☎ 01848/331555, ☉ open May–Aug., daily 9–5; Sept.–Apr., by appointment) in the stable block, chock full of all types of crafts, including leather goods, blown-glass pieces, landscape and portrait works, stainless steel jewelry and cutlery, stained glass, and pottery.

POSTCARDS

For a souvenir that's easier to pack, try **David Hastings** (✉ Marying, Shieldhill, Lockerbie DG11 1SG, ☎ 01387/710451; visitors by appointment), which has more than 100,000 old postcards.

New Abbey

7 mi south of Dumfries, 83 mi south of Glasgow, 88 mi southwest of Edinburgh.

➋⁷ The village of New Abbey has at its center **Sweetheart Abbey,** which provides a mellowed red and roofless backdrop to the village. It was founded in 1273 by Devorgilla Balliol, in memory of her husband, John. The couple's son, also named John (1250–1315), was the puppet king installed in Scotland by Edward of England when the latter claimed sovereignty over Scotland. After John's appointment the Scots gave him a scathing nickname that would stay with him for the rest of his life: *Toom Tabard,* meaning "Empty Shirt." ✉ *A710 at New Abbey,* ☎ *0131/668–8800.* 🎫 *£1.20.* ☉ *Apr.–Sept., daily 9:30–6; Oct.–Mar., Mon.–Wed. and Sat. 9:30–4, Thurs. 9:30–noon, Sun. 2–4.*

Kirkbean

5 mi south of New Abbey, 88 mi south of Glasgow, 94 mi southwest of Edinburgh.

㉘ A little community (blink and you've missed it) set in a bright green landscape is the setting for **Arbigland Gardens**; follow signs from the village. The son of a former gardener of Arbigland, whose name was John Paul, left Scotland and became the founder of the U.S. Navy. This seafaring son, John Paul Jones (1747–92), returned to his native coast in a series of daring raids in 1778. A museum will brief you on the history. The gardens tended by Jones's father are typical of the area: lush and sheltered, with blue water visible through the protecting trees; the walled garden dating from 1745 is currently being restored, with plantings of roses typical of the 18th century. ⊠ *Off A710, by Kirkbean,* ☎ *01387/880613.* ▣ *£2.* ⊙ *Apr.– June and Sept., Tues.–Sun. 10–5; July–Aug., daily 10–5 (closed Mon. except bank holidays).*

Southerness

㉙ *3 mi south of Kirkbean, 91 mi south of Glasgow, 97 mi southwest of Edinburgh.*

The road to Southerness ends in a welter of recreational vehicles and trailer homes in the shadow of one of Scotland's earliest lighthouses, built in 1749 by the port authorities of Dumfries who were anxious to make the treacherous River Nith approaches safer.

En Route   The road turns west and becomes faintly Riviera-like. You can take a brisk walk from Sandyhills to Rockcliffe, two of the sleepy coastal communities overlooking the creeping tides and endless shallows of the Solway coast.

Dalbeattie

㉚ *12 mi northwest of Southerness, 89 mi south of Glasgow, 95 mi southwest of Edinburgh.*

Like the much larger Aberdeen far to the northeast, Dalbeattie's buildings were constructed with local gray granite from the town's quarry. The predominance of granite, with its well-scrubbed gray glitter, makes Dalbeattie atypical of Galloway towns, whose house fronts are predominantly painted in pastels.

Lodging

££   🏠 **Auchenskeoch Lodge.** This quaint and informal Victorian shooting
★   lodge, now a country-house hotel, has three bedrooms and delicious food (for residents only). The chintz furnishings have a comfortable, faded elegance. Many of the vegetables and herbs used in the set menu—prepared to a high standard in traditional Scottish style—are grown on the 20 acres of gardens and woodland surrounding the house. The sitting room houses crammed bookshelves and an open fire, and in the games room is a full-size billiards table. A private loch, turf and gravel maze, and croquet lawn provide outdoor entertainment. ⊠ *By Dalbeattie, DG5 4PG,* ☎ ℻ *01387/780277. 3 rooms with bath or shower. Croquet. MC, V. Nov.–Easter.*

Outdoor Activities and Sports

HORSEBACK RIDING

Barend Properties Riding School and Trekking Centre (⊠ Sandyhills, by Dalbeattie, Kirkcudbright, ☎ 01387/780663) helps you to a "horse-high" view of the beautiful coast and countryside of this region.

Castle Douglas

6 mi west of Dalbeattie, 94 mi south of Glasgow, 99 mi southwest of Edinburgh.

★ ③① Although it is a pleasant town with a long main street where the home bakeries vie for business, Castle Douglas's main interest is its proximity to **Threave Gardens.** As Scotland's best-known charitable conservation agency, the National Trust for Scotland cares for several garden properties. This horticultural undertaking demands the employment of many gardeners—and it is at Threave that the gardeners train, thus ensuring there is always some fresh development or experimental planting here. This gives lots of vigor and interest to the sloping parkland around the mansion house of Threave. There is a good visitor center as well. ⊠ *South of A75, 1 mi west of Castle Douglas,* ☎ *01556/502575.* 🔲 *£4.* ⊙ *Gardens: daily 9:30–sunset; walled garden and greenhouses: daily 9:30–5; visitor center, exhibition, and shop: Apr.–Oct., daily 9:30– 5:30; restaurant: 10–5.*

Threave Castle (not to be confused with the mansion house in Threave Gardens) is a few minutes away by car and is signposted from the main road. To get there you must leave your car in a farmyard (trying to pretend you don't have the feeling you're intruding) and walk the rest of the way. Reassured by the Historic Scotland signs (because Threave is being cared for by the national government), you make your way down to the reeds by the river on an occasionally muddy path. At the edge of the river you can then ring a bell, and, rather romantically, a boatman will come to ferry you across to the great stone tower looming from a marshy island in the river. Threave was an early home of the Black Douglases, the earls of Nithsdale, and lords of Galloway. The castle was dismantled in the religious wars of the mid-17th century, though enough of it remains to have housed prisoners from the Napoleonic Wars of the 19th century. ⊠ *North of A75, 3 mi west of Castle Douglas,* ☎ *0131/668–8800.* 🔲 *£1.80 (includes ferry).* ⊙ *Apr.–Sept., daily 9:30–6.*

Outdoor Activities and Sports

BIKING

You can rent cycles from **Ace Cycles** (⊠ Church St., Castle Douglas, ☎ FAX 01556/504542).

WATER SPORTS

The **Galloway Sailing Centre** (⊠ Loch Ken, ☎ FAX 01644/420626) rents dinghies, windsurfing equipment, and canoes. It also runs residential sailing, windsurfing, and canoeing courses.

Shopping

BOOKS

It is well worth the short drive north from Castle Douglas (A75 then B794) to visit **Benny Gillies Books, Maps and Prints** (⊠ 31–33 Victoria St., Kirkpatrick Durham, ☎ 01556/650412), which stocks an outstanding selection of hand-colored antique maps and prints featuring areas throughout Scotland.

GIFTS

The Posthorn (⊠ 26–30 St. Andrew St., ☎ 01556/502531) consists of two shops specializing in gift items, including the figurines made by Border Fine Art.

JEWELRY

Galloway Gems (⊠ 130–132 King St., ☎ 01556/503254) not only has silver jewelry, but also stocks mineral specimens, polished stone slices, and art materials.

Kirkcudbright

㉜ *11 mi southwest of Castle Douglas, 103 mi south of Glasgow, 109 mi southwest of Edinburgh.*

Kirkcudbright is an 18th-century town of unpretentious houses, some of them color-washed in pastel shades and roofed with the blue slates of the district. For much of this century it has been known as an artists' town, and its L-shaped main street is full of crafts and antiques shops. Conspicuous in the town center is **MacLellan's Castle,** the shell of a once-elaborate castellated mansion dating from the early 16th century. ⊠ *Off High St.,* ☎ *0131/668–8800.* ▣ *£1.20.* ⊙ *Apr.–Sept., daily 9:30–6.*

The 17th-century **Broughton House** was once the home of the artist E. A. Hornel (he was one of the "Glasgow Boys" of the early 20th century). Many of his paintings hang in the house, which is furnished in period style and contains an extensive library specializing in local history. There is also a Japanese garden. ⊠ *12 High St.,* ☎ FAX *01557/ 330437.* ▣ *£2.40.* ⊙ *Apr.–Oct., daily 1–5:30 (last admission 4:45).*

The delightfully old-fashioned **Stewartry Museum,** stuffed with all manner of local paraphernalia, allows you to putter and absorb as much or as little as takes your interest in the display cases. ⊠ *St. Mary St.,* ☎ *01557/331643.* ▣ *£1.50.* ⊙ *Oct.–Apr., Mon.–Sat. 11–4; May, Mon.–Sat. 11–5; June and Sept., Mon.–Sat. 11–5, Sun. 2–5; July– Aug., Mon.–Sat. 10–6, Sun. 2–5.*

The **Tolbooth Arts Centre,** in the old tolbooth, gives a history of the town's artists' colony and its leaders E. A. Hornel, Jessie King, and Charles Oppenheimer, and displays some of their paintings as well as works by modern artists and craftspeople. ⊠ *High St.,* ☎ *01557/ 331556.* ▣ *£1.50.* ⊙ *Oct.–Apr., Mon.–Sat. 11–4; May, Mon.–Sat. 11–5; June and Sept., Mon.–Sat. 11–5, Sun. 2–5; July–Aug., Mon.– Sat. 10–6, Sun. 2–5.*

Gatehouse of Fleet

9 mi west of Kirkcudbright, 108 mi southwest of Glasgow, 114 mi southwest of Edinburgh.

㉝ A peaceful, pleasant backwoods sort of place, Gatehouse of Fleet has a castle guarding its southern approach from the A75. **Cardoness Castle** is a typical Scottish tower house, severe and uncompromising. The 15th-century structure once was the home of the McCullochs of Galloway, then later the Gordons. ⊠ *A75, 1 mi southwest of Gatehouse of Fleet,* ☎ *0131/668–8800.* ▣ *£1.80.* ⊙ *Apr.–Sept., daily 9:30–6; Oct.–Mar., Sat. 9:30–4, Sun. 2–4.*

The **Mill on the Fleet** heritage center is a converted cotton mill in which you can learn the history behind this pretty little town's involvement in this industry. As you go around, you wear a hard hat with earphones that pick up individual room commentaries—a little disconcerting at first. The tearoom serves light lunches and delicious home-baked goods. ⊠ *High St.,* ☎ *01557/814099.* ⊙ *Easter–Oct., daily 10–5:30.*

Lodging

£££–££££ 🏨 **Cally Palace.** This hotel was once a private mansion (built in 1759). Many of the public rooms in the Georgian building retain their original grandeur, which includes elaborate plaster ceilings and marble fireplaces. The bedrooms are individually decorated and well equipped. The house is surrounded by 150 acres of gardens, loch, and parkland, including an 18-hole golf course, and has an indoor leisure center with pool, solarium, and sauna. Scottish produce stars in the French-influenced restaurant in such dishes as poached salmon with hollandaise sauce. The staff is exceptionally friendly and prepared to spoil you. ✉ *DG7 2DL,* ☎ *01557/814341,* 𝔉𝔸𝔛 *01557/814522. 56 rooms with bath. Restaurant, bar, indoor pool, hot tub, sauna, 18-hole golf course, putting green, tennis court, croquet, fishing. MC, V. Closed Jan. and Feb.*

£ 🏠 **High Auchenlarie Farmhouse.** This working beef farm, set high on a hillside overlooking Wigtown Bay, offers B&B and, for a small additional charge, evening meals. ✉ *DG7 2HB,* ☎ *01557/840231. 3 rooms with bath or shower. No credit cards. Closed Nov.–Feb.*

Shopping

There is a well-stocked gift and crafts shop at the **Mill on the Fleet** heritage center (✉ High St., ☎ 01557/814099). The merchandise shop at **Galloway Lodge Preserves** (✉ 24–28 High St., ☎ 𝔉𝔸𝔛 01557/ 814357) stocks its marmalades and mustards, plus Scottish pottery.

En Route If you single-mindedly pursue the suggested policy of avoiding the A75, then your route will loop to the northwest. Take a right by the Anwoth Hotel in Gatehouse of Fleet, where the signpost points to Gatehouse Station. This route will provide you with a taste of the Dumfries and Galloway hinterland. Beyond the wooded valley where the Water of Fleet runs (local rivers are often referred to as "Water of . . ."), dark hills and conifer plantings lend a brooding, empty air to this lonely stretch.

Creetown

34 *12 mi west of Gatehouse of Fleet, 95 mi southwest of Glasgow, 112 mi southwest of Edinburgh.*

The low-ground community of Creetown is noted for its **Gem Rock Museum.** The museum has an eclectic mineral collection, a dinosaur egg, and an entertaining demonstration of the various colors with which some rocks fluoresce. ✉ *A75,* ☎ *01671/820357.* 🔲 *£2.75.* ⊗ *Easter–Sept., daily 9:30–6; Oct.–Nov., daily 10–4; Dec.–Feb., weekends 10–4; Mar.–Easter, daily 10–4 and by appointment; last admission 30 mins before closing.*

Shopping

The **Creetown Gem Rock Museum** (✉ Creetown, ☎ 01671/820357) sells extraordinary mineral and gemstone crystals—both loose and in settings—in its gift shop.

Newton Stewart

35 *8 mi northwest of Creetown, 89 mi southwest of Glasgow, 108 mi southwest of Edinburgh.*

The solid and bustling little town of Newton Stewart makes a good touring base for the western region of Galloway. One possible excursion to the north from Newton Stewart takes you to the **Galloway Forest Park.** Take the A714 north from town along the wooded valley of the **River Cree,** with a nature reserve, the Wood of Cree, on the far bank.

★ **36** After about 10 mi turn right at the signpost for **Glen Trool.** This road leads you toward the hills that have thus far been the backdrop for the woodlands. Watch for another sign for Glen Trool. Follow this little road through increasingly wild woodland scenery to its terminus at a parking lot. Only after you have left the car and climbed for a few minutes onto a heathery knoll does the full, rugged panorama become apparent. With high purple-and-green hilltops shorn rock-bare by glaciers, a dark, winding loch, and thickets of birch trees sounding with birdcalls, the setting almost looks more highland than the real Highlands to the north. Glen Trool is one of Scotland's best-kept secrets. Note **Bruce's Stone,** just above the car park, marking the site where Scotland's champion Robert the Bruce (King Robert I, 1274–1329) won his first victory, in 1307, in the Scottish Wars of Independence.

En Route   The **Machars** is the name given to the triangular promontory south of Newton Stewart. This is an area of gently rolling farmlands, yellow gorse hedgerows, rich grazings for dairy cattle, and a number of stony prehistoric sites. Most of the glossy, green expanse is used for dairy farming. Fields are bordered by dry *stane dykes* (dry walling) of sharp-edge stones, and small hills and hummocks give the area its characteristic frozen-wave look, a reminder of the glacial activity that shaped the landscape.

Wigtown

㊲ *8 mi south of Newton Stewart, 96 mi southwest of Glasgow, 114 mi southwest of Edinburgh.*

The sleepy hamlet of Wigtown has a broad main street and colorful housefronts. Down by the muddy shores of Wigtown Bay there's a monument to the Wigtown Martyrs, two women who were tied to a stake and left to drown in the incoming tide during the anti-Covenant witch hunts of 1685. Much of Dumfries and Galloway's history is linked with Border feuds, but even more with the ferocity of the so-called Killing Times, when the Covenanters were persecuted for their belief that the king should be second to the church, and not vice versa. Wigtown, like several other places in the region, is dominated by a hilltop Covenanters' Monument, a reminder of the old persecutions.

Whithorn

㊳ *11 mi south of Wigtown, 107 mi southwest of Glasgow, 125 mi southwest of Edinburgh.*

The Machars are well known for their early Christian sites. The road that is now the A746 was a pilgrim's way and a royal route that ended at **Isle of Whithorn** (which is not, in fact, quite an island), a place that early Scottish kings and barons sought to visit at least once in their lives. The pilgrimage was often prescribed as a penance, but these pleasant shores impose no penance today. The goal was St. Ninian's chapel, the 4th-century cell of Scotland's premier saint. Some pilgrims made for Whithorn village and others for the sandspit "isle." Both places claimed to be the site of the original "Candida Casa" of the saint. As you approach Whithorn's 12th-century priory, observe the royal arms of pre-1707 Scotland—that is, Scotland before the Union with England—carved and painted above the arch of the *pend* (covered way).

The **Whithorn Dig and Visitor Centre** explains the significance of what is claimed to be the site of the earliest Christian community in Scotland. The museum includes a collection of early Christian crosses. The dig site itself is beside the shell of the priory. ✉ *Main St., Whithorn,* ☎ *01988/500508.* 🎫 *£2.70.* ☉ *Apr.–Oct., daily 10:30–5 (last tour 4:30).*

Lodging

£££   🏨 **Corsemalzie House.** This attractive 19th-century mansion is set on 40 acres of peaceful grounds behind the fishing village of Port William, west of Whithorn. Sporting pursuits are the hotel's main draw, with shooting, sea and game fishing, and golf on tap. The restaurant features a Scottish menu with hearty venison stew or steak Auld Alliance (with red-wine sauce), and the public rooms and bedrooms are in keeping with the country-house style of the hotel. ✉ *Corsemalzie, Port William, Newton Stewart, Wigtownshire, DG8 9RL,* ☎ *01988/860254,* FAX *01988/860213. 15 rooms with bath or shower. Golf privileges, fishing. AE, MC, V. late-Jan.–Feb.*

Stranraer

39 *34 mi northwest of Whithorn, 89 mi southwest of Glasgow via A77, 133 mi southwest of Edinburgh.*

Stranraer is the main ferry port (if you happen to make a purchase in one of its shops, you may wind up with some Irish coins in your change). It is not a very scenic place itself, but nearby is a high point of this region.

★ **40** Three miles east of Stranraer, **Castle Kennedy Gardens** surround the shell of the original Castle Kennedy, which was burned out in 1716. The present property owners, the earl and countess of Stair, live on the grounds, at Lochinch Castle, built in 1864 (not open to the public). Pleasure grounds dispersed throughout the property were built by the second earl of Stair in 1733. The earl was a field marshal and used his soldiers to help with the heavy work of constructing banks, ponds, and other major landscape features. When the rhododendrons are in bloom, the effect is kaleidoscopic. There is also a pleasant tearoom. ✉ *North of A75, 3 mi east of Stranraer,* ☎ *01776/702024.* ✉ *£2.* ☾ *Apr. (or Easter if earlier)–Sept., daily 10–5.*

Dining

£ ✕ **Eynhallow Hotel.** A traditional pub with shining brasses, open fire, and peach and brown color scheme, the Eynhallow is a good bet for its homecooked bar lunches (noon–2:30) and bar suppers (6–11). ✉ *Eynhallow, DG9 8SQ.* ☎ *01581/400256. MC, V.*

Portpatrick

41 *8 mi southwest of Stranraer, 97 mi southwest of Glasgow, 143 mi southwest of Edinburgh.*

The holiday town of Portpatrick lies across the Rhinns of Galloway from Stranraer. Once an Irish ferry port, Portpatrick's exposed harbor eventually proved too risky for larger vessels. Today the village is the starting point for Scotland's longest official long-distance footpath, the **Southern Upland Way,** which runs a switchback course for 212 mi to Cockburnspath, on the eastern side of the Borders. Just south of Portpatrick are the lichen-yellow ruins of 16th-century **Dunskey Castle,** accessible by a clifftop path.

The southern half of the **Rhinns of Galloway** has a number of interesting places to visit, all easily reached from Portpatrick. Among them is **Ardwell House Gardens,** a pleasant retreat on a domestic scale. ✉ *Ardwell,* ☎ *01776/860227.* ✉ *£1.50.* ☾ *Apr.–Sept., daily 10–5.*

If you wish visit the southern tip of the Rhinns of Galloway, called the **Mull of Galloway,** follow the B7065/B7041 until you run out of land. The cliffs and seascapes here are rugged, and there is a lighthouse and a bird reserve.

★ **42** Spectacular for garden lovers and close to Ardwell are the **Logan Botanic Gardens,** a specialist garden of Edinburgh's **Royal Botanic Garden.** The Logan Gardens feature plants that enjoy the prevailing mild climate, especially tree ferns, cabbage palms, and other Southern Hemisphere exotica. ✉ *Off B7065 at Port Logan,* ☎ *01776/860231.* ✉ *£3.* ☾ *Mar.–Oct., daily 9:30–6.*

THE BORDERS AND THE SOUTHWEST A TO Z

Arriving and Departing

By Bus

From the south the main bus services use the M6 or A1, with appropriate feeder services into the hinterland; contact **Scottish Citylink** (☎ 0990/505050) or **National Express** (☎ 0990/808080). There are also bus links from Edinburgh and Glasgow. Contact **Lowland Omnibuses** (☎ 01896/752237) or **Stagecoach Western Scottish** (☎ 01563/525192, 01387/253496, or 01776/704484).

By Car

The main route into both the Borders and Galloway from the south is the M6, which deteriorates into the less-maintained A74 north of the border (it is currently being upgraded). This road gives the choice of the leisurely A7 (signed off from the A74) northeastward through Hawick toward Edinburgh or the A75 and other parallel routes westward into Dumfries and Galloway and to the ferry ports of Stranraer and Cairnryan.

There are, however, a number of alternative routes: starting from the east, the A1 brings you from the English city of Newcastle to the border in about an hour. The A1 has the added attraction of Berwick-Upon-Tweed, on the English side of the border. Moving west, the A697, which leaves the A1 beside Alnwick (in England) and crosses the border at Coldstream, is a leisurely back-road option with a view of the countryside. The A68 offers probably the most scenic route to Scotland: after climbing to Carter Bar, it reveals a view of the rolling blue Border hills and windy skies before dropping into the ancient town of Jedburgh, with its ruined abbey.

By Ferry

P&O European Ferries runs a service from Larne in Northern Ireland to Cairnryan several times daily, with a crossing time of 2 hours, 15 minutes. Details are available from P&O at Cairnryan (✉ Stranraer, DG9 8RF, ☎ 0990/980777). **Seacat** (☎ 0990/523523) operates a fast-speed catamaran service four times a day, taking only 90 minutes to cross from Belfast to Stranraer.

By Plane

The nearest Scottish airports are at Edinburgh and Glasgow (☞ Chapters 3 and 4).

By Train

The Borders are not well served by rail. You can use services from London Euston, in England, to Glasgow; these trains stop at Carlisle, just south of the border, and some stop at Lockerbie. There are also direct trains from Carlisle to Dumfries, stopping at Gretna Green. On the east coast some services stop at Berwick-Upon-Tweed, just south of the border. For more information, call the **National Rail Enquiry Line** (☎ 0345/484950).

Getting Around

By Bus

Bus services in the area include **Stagecoach Western Scottish** (☎ 01563/525192, 01387/253496, or 01776/704484), which serves towns and villages in Dumfries and Galloway, and **Lowland Omnibuses** (☎ 01896/752237), which offers Reiver Rover (✉ £26.50 weekly, £7.50 daily, children half-price) and Waverley Wanderer (✉ £31.50 weekly, £10.50

daily, children half-price) flexible tickets that provide considerable savings for travel in the Borders.

By Car

A solid network of rural roads allows you to avoid the A1 in the eastern Borders, as well as the A75, which runs along the Solway coast east to west linking Dumfries and Stranraer. Both roads carry heavy traffic, partly because of the poor rail connections.

By Train

Train travel is not very practical in the Borders. In fact the **Scottish Borders Rail Link** is nothing of the kind: it's actually a bus service linking Hawick, Selkirk, and Galashiels with rail services at Carlisle. In Dumfries and Galloway you can pick up connecting trains from Carlisle to Stranraer, which also has a direct link to Ayr and Glasgow. There is also a service twice daily between Dumfries and Stranraer. (Both the Borders and the Southwest suffered badly in the shortsighted contraction of Britain's rail network in the 1960s.) Contact the **National Train Enquiry Line** (☎ 0345/484950) for further details.

Contacts and Resources

Emergencies

For **police, fire, or ambulance,** dial ☎ 999 from any telephone. No coins are needed for emergency calls from public telephone booths.

Fishing

Scottish Borders Angling Guide is the best way to find your way around the many Borders waterways. *Fishing in Dumfries and Galloway* covers the southwest. The tourist boards for Dumfries and Galloway and the Borders (☞ Visitor Information, *below*) carry these and other publications (including a comprehensive information pack). In short, finding suitable water in this area is quite easy.

Golf

There are more than 30 courses in Dumfries and Galloway and 19 in the Borders. The Freedom of the Fairways Pass (5-day, £70; 3-day, £46) allows play on all 19 Borders courses, and is available from the Scottish Borders Tourist Board. The Gateway to Golf Pass (5-day, £95; 3-day, £65) is accepted by most of the clubs in Dumfries and Galloway and is available from the Dumfries and Galloway Tourist Board. Both tourist boards (☞ Visitor Information, *below*) supply comprehensive leaflets.

Guided Tours

ORIENTATION

The bus companies mentioned above also run a variety of orientation tours in the area. In addition, tours are run by **Galloway Heritage Tours** (✉ Rosemount Guest House, The Front, Kippford, ☎ 01556/620214).

SPECIAL-INTEREST

The area is primarily covered through Edinburgh- or Glasgow-based companies (☞ Chapters 3 and 4). **James French** (✉ French's Garage, Coldingham, ☎ 01890/771283) runs coach tours in the summer season. **Ramtrad Holidays** (✉ 54 Edinburgh Rd., Peebles, ☎ FAX 01721/720845) offers chauffeur-driven tours tailored to customers' requirements, and also golf and fishing packages.

Late-Night Pharmacies

All towns in the region have at least one pharmacy. Pharmacies are not found in rural areas, where general practitioners often dispense medicines. The police will provide assistance in locating a pharmacist in an emergency.

Visitor Information

Dumfries and Galloway: **Dumfries** (✉ Whitesands, ☎ 01387/253862, FAX 01387/245555); **Gretna Gateway** (✉ Off the M74 northbound at Gretna, ☎ 01461/338500, FAX 01461/338700). The Borders: **Jedburgh** (✉ Murray's Green, ☎ 01835/863435, FAX 01835/864099); **Peebles** (✉ High St., ☎ 01721/720138, FAX 01721/724401).

Seasonal information centers are at Castle Douglas, Coldstream, Dalbeattie, Eyemouth, Galashiels, Gatehouse of Fleet, Gretna Green, Hawick, Kelso, Kirkcudbright, Langholm, Melrose, Moffat, Newton Stewart, Sanquhar, Selkirk, and Stranraer.

6 Fife and Angus

St. Andrews, Dundee

The sunniest and driest part of Scotland, Fife is an area of sandy beaches, fishing villages, and windswept cliffs, hills, and glens. On the east coast is the ancient university and golf town of St. Andrews, with its romantic stone houses and seaside ruins. The glens of Angus—Dundee's hinterland—provide scenic hiking terrain along secluded hill passes that penetrate the massif and lead to high, empty, wild places.

By Gilbert
Summers

THE REGIONS OF FIFE AND ANGUS sandwich Scotland's fourth-largest—and often overlooked—city, Dundee. This is typical eastern-seaboard country: open beaches, fishing villages, and breezy cliff-top walkways. Scotland's east coast has only light rainfall throughout the year; northeastern Fife, in particular, may claim the record for the most sunshine and the least rainfall in all Scotland, which all adds to the enjoyment when you're touring the East Neuk (*neuk,* pronounced nyook, is Scots for corner) or exploring St. Andrews's nooks and crannies.

The particular charm of Angus is its variety: in addition to its seacoast and pleasant Lowland market centers, there's also a hinterland of lonely rounded hills with long glens running into the typical Grampian Highland scenery beyond. One of Angus's interesting features, which it shares with the eastern Lowland edge of Perthshire, is its fruit-growing industry. Seen from roadside or railway, what at first sight appear to be sturdy grapevines on field-length wires turn out to be soft-fruit plants, mainly raspberries. The chief fruit-growing area is Strathmore, the broad vale between the northwesterly Grampian mountains and the small coastal hills of the Sidlaws behind Dundee. Striking out from this valley—the heart of the Angus region—visitors can make a number of day trips to uplands or seacoast.

Pleasures and Pastimes

Dining

With its affluent population, St. Andrews supports several upmarket hotel restaurants. Because it is also a university town and popular tourist destination, there are also many good-value cafés and bistro-style restaurants. Not far away at Peat Inn is a restaurant that many would claim to be one of the very best in Scotland. The coastal communities can also serve up fine seafood, in particular at Anstruther. In some of the West Fife towns, such as Kirkcaldy and Dunfermline, and in Dundee, you will find restaurants serving not only traditional Scottish fare, but also ethnic food (Italian, Indian, and Chinese are popular), in addition to numerous small cafés of all kinds. Bar lunches are becoming the rule in large and small hotels throughout the region, and in seaside places the "carry oot" (to go) meal is an old tradition.

CATEGORY	COST*
££££	over £40
£££	£30–£40
££	£15–£30
£	under £15

per person for a three-course meal, including VAT and excluding drinks and service

Golf

Every golfer's ambition is to play at St. Andrews, and once you are in Fife the ambition is easily realized. Five St. Andrews courses are open to visitors (all are part of the St. Andrews Club). There are more than 40 other courses in the region. Most offer golf to the visitor by the round or the day. Many of the area's hotels offer golfing packages or will arrange a day of golf (☞ Chapter 2).

Lodging

If you're staying in Fife, the obvious base is St. Andrews, with ample accommodations of all kinds. Other towns also offer a reasonable selection, and you will find good hotels and guest houses at Dunfermline and Kirkcaldy. Along the coastal strip and in the Howe of Fife between

Strathmiglo and Cupar there are some superior country-house hotels, many with their own restaurants.

CATEGORY	COST*
££££	over £120
£££	£90–£120
££	£50–£90
£	under £50

All prices are for a standard double room, including service, breakfast, and VAT.

Shopping

St. Andrews, with its university and its world-renowned golfing facilities, attracts enough affluent people to sustain some smaller specialty shops. Dundee is an important retail shopping center for the northern part of Angus, but the choices for shoppers here are similar to those found in most large towns (department stores, such as Marks and Spencer, predominate).

Exploring Fife and Angus

Fife lies north of the Firth of Forth, stretching far up the Forth Valley (which is west and a little north of Edinburgh), with St. Andrews on its eastern coast. Northwest of Fife, the city of Dundee and its rural hinterland, Angus, stretch still farther north and west towards the foothills of the Grampian mountains.

Numbers in the text correspond to numbers in the margin and on the Fife Area, St. Andrews, and Angus Area maps.

Great Itineraries

This is not a huge area, so getting around is straightforward. Treat it as a series of excursions off the main north–south artery, the A90/M90, which leads from Edinburgh to Aberdeen. Fife has a pleasant but not spectacular rural hinterland—in fact, it feels a long way from the hills. Angus is different, with a strong sense of a looming massif always to the north. To explore it, take your pick of the Angus Glens—especially Glens Prosen or Clova or—farthest north—Esk—all beautifully out of the way. They represent probably one of the most overlooked corners of Scotland.

IF YOU HAVE 2 DAYS

Two days allows you to sample the extremes of the area in every sense. Make your way to 🏠 **St. Andrews** ①–⑦ to take in this most attractive of Scottish east coast Lowland towns. Next day travel north of 🏠 **Dundee** ⑱ to visit **Kirriemuir** ㉖, a typical Angus town with "Peter Pan" connections, and **Glamis** ㉘, for its castle—and perhaps penetrate the hills via the Glens of Angus west of Kirriemuir.

IF YOU HAVE 5–6 DAYS

This allows plenty of time to spend two or three days sampling not just 🏠 **St. Andrews** ①–⑦, but also the rest of the East Neuk, the easternmost corner with its characteristic pantile-roofed fishing villages—**Crail** ⑧, Anstruther with its **Scottish Fisheries Museum** ⑨, **Pittenweem** ⑩ and, just inland, **Kellie Castle** ⑪—strung along the south-facing coast. Also worth exploring are the inland communities of **Falkland** (its **palace** ⑬ was once a royal hunting lodge), **Cupar** ⑮, close to **Hill of Tarvit House** ⑯, and the **Fife Folk Museum** ⑰ at 🏠 **Ceres** (for a real treat, have a meal and stay overnight at the Peat Inn). If you golf, then you could allocate a day on a golf course as well. Likewise, in Angus, you could first travel along the breezy coast toward **Arbroath** ㉑ and **Montrose** ㉒, where the sharply contrasting Adam-designed **House of Dun** ㉓ and an-

Fife Area

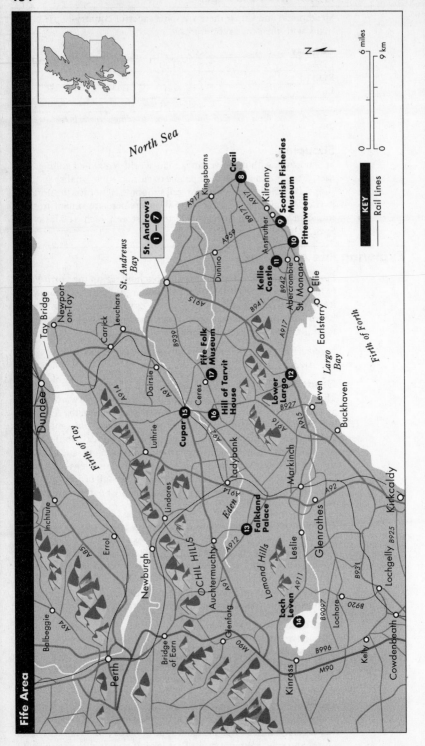

North Sea

Tay Bridge

Newport-on-Tay

St. Andrews Bay

St. Andrews 1—7

Kingsbarns A917

Crail 8

Scottish Fisheries Museum 9

Kilrenny

Anstruther B9171

Pittenweem 10

11

A942 Kellie Castle

B942

Abercrombie

St Monans

Elie

Leven

Dunino

A959

A915

Leuchars

Carrick

Dundee

B939

Dairsie

A91

Ceres

Fife Folk Museum 17

Hill of Tarvit House 16

15 Cupar

Luthrie

A914

Lindores

A92

Firth of Tay

Inchture

Errol

A85

Newburgh

Glenfarg

OCHIL HILLS

Auchtermuchty

A91

Lomond Hills

Falkland Palace 13

A912

Leslie

A911

Loch Leven 14

B9097

B996

Kinross

M90

Kelty

Cowdenbeath

Lochore

B920

B9171

Lochgelly B925

Kirkcaldy

Glenrothes

A92

B931

Markinch

Ladybank

A91

Eden

A916

Lower Largo 12

B927

Buckhaven

Largo Bay

Earlsferry

Firth of Forth

Bridge of Earn

Perth

A94

Balbeggie

KEY

Rail Lines

6 miles

9 km

N

In case you want to see the world.

At American Express, we're here to make your journey a smooth one. So we have over 1,700 travel service locations in over 120 countries ready to help. What else would you expect from the world's largest travel agency?

do more

http://www.americanexpress.com/travel

Travel

In case you want to be welcomed there.

We're here to see that you're always welcomed at establishments everywhere. That's why millions of people carry the American Express® Card — for peace of mind, confidence, and security, around the world or just around the corner.

do more®

Cards

In case you're running low.

We're here to help with more than 118,000 Express Cash locations around the world. In order to enroll, just call American Express before you start your vacation.

do more

Express Cash

And just in case.

We're here with American Express® Travelers Cheques and Cheques *for Two*.® They're the safest way to carry money on your vacation and the surest way to get a refund, practically anywhere, anytime.
Another way we help you...

do more®

Travelers Cheques

cient **Edzell Castle** ㉕ lie within easy reach. Staying overnight near 🏨 **Forfar** ㉗ would bring the inland communities of **Kirriemuir** ㉖, **Glamis** ㉘, and **Meigle** ㉙, with its outstanding collection of early medieval sculpture, within easy reach the next day.

When to Tour Fife and Angus

Spring in the Angus glens can be quite captivating, with the high tops still snow-covered. Similarly, the moorland colors of autumn are appealing. (In autumn and winter, some hotels in rural Angus get busy with foreign sportsmen intent on marauding the local wildfowl.) However, it has to be said that Fife and Angus are really spring and summer destinations—unless you simply like wandering about enjoying scenery.

AROUND FIFE

In its western parts, Fife still bears the scars of heavy industry, especially coal mining. Yet these signs are less evident as you move farther east: northeastern Fife, around the university-and-golf town of St. Andrews, seems to have played no part in the industrial revolution; the residents instead earned a livelihood from the grain fields or from the sea. Fishing has been a major industry, and in the past a string of Fife ports traded across the North Sea. Today the legacy of Dutch-influenced architecture—crow-step gables and distinctive town houses, for example—is still plain to see and gives these East Neuk villages a distinctive charm.

St. Andrews is unlike any other Scottish town. Once Scotland's most powerful ecclesiastical center, seat also of the country's oldest university, and then, much later, the very symbol and spiritual home of golf, the town has a comfortable, well-groomed air, sitting almost smugly apart from the rest of Scotland.

St. Andrews

52 mi northeast of Edinburgh, 83 mi northeast of Glasgow.

Scotland's golf mecca, St. Andrews is, after Edinburgh, one of the most visited places in Scotland. The center of this compact town retains its original medieval street plan of three roughly parallel streets—North, Market, and South—leading away from the city's earliest religious site, near the cathedral.

The local legend about the founding of St. Andrews has it that a certain St. Regulus, or Rule, acting under divine guidance, carried relics of St. Andrew by sea from Patras in Greece. He was shipwrecked on this Fife headland and founded a church. The holy man's name survives in the square-shaped **St. Rule's Tower,** consecrated in 1126 and the oldest surviving building in St. Andrews. You can enjoy dizzying views of town from the top of the tower, accessed via a steep set of stairs. Near the tower is the city **cathedral,** today only a ruined, poignant fragment of what was formerly the largest and most magnificent church in Scotland. Work on it began in 1160, and consecration was finally celebrated in 1318, after several setbacks. The cathedral was subsequently damaged by fire and repaired, but finally fell into decay in the 16th century, during the Reformation. Only ruined gables, parts of the nave south wall, and other fragments survive. The on-site museum helps you interpret the remains and gives a sense of what the cathedral must once have been like. ✉ *Off Pends Rd.,* ☎ *0131/668-8800.* 🎫 *Joint ticket to cathedral and castle (☞ below) £3.50, cathedral only £1.80.* ☉ *Apr.–Sept., daily 9:30–6; Oct.–Mar., Mon.–Sat. 9:30–4, Sun. 2–4.*

St. Andrews

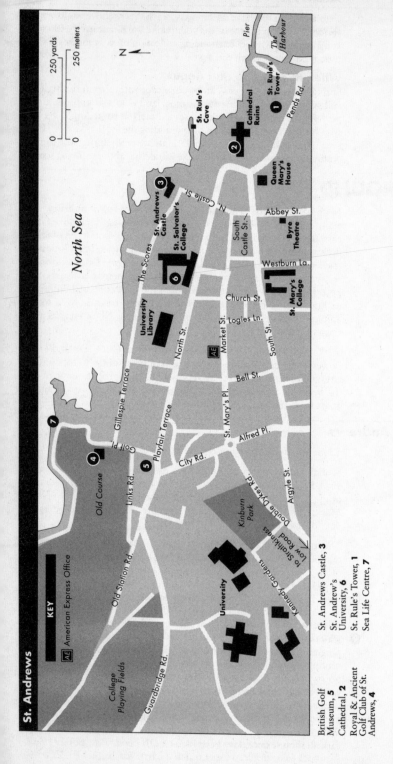

North Sea

Pier

The Harbour

St. Rule's Cave

Cathedral Ruins

1 St. Rule's Tower

Pends Rd.

2

Queen Mary's House

3 St. Andrews Castle

N. Castle St.

Abbey St.

St. Salvator's College

South Castle St.

Byre Theatre

6 University Library

Westburn La.

The Scores

Church St.

St. Mary's College

North St.

Logies Ln.

Market St.

AE

South St.

Bell St.

Gillespie Terrace

Playfair Terrace

St. Mary's Pl.

7

4

Golf Pl.

5

City Rd.

Alfred Pl.

Argyle St.

Old Course

Links Rd.

Old Station Rd.

Kinburn Park

Double Dykes Rd.

to Strathkinness low Road

Kennedy Gardens

American Express Office

KEY

AE American Express Office

College Playing Fields

Guardbridge Rd.

University

250 yards

250 meters

N

British Golf Museum, **5**

Cathedral, **2**

Royal & Ancient Golf Club of St. Andrews, **4**

St. Andrews Castle, **3**

St. Andrew's University, **6**

St. Rule's Tower, **1**

Sea Life Centre, **7**

❸ Directly north of the cathedral on the shore stands **St. Andrews Castle,** which was started at the end of the 13th century. Although now a ruin, the remains include a rare example of a bottle dungeon, cold and gruesome, in which many a prisoner spent their last hours. Even more atmospheric is the castle's mine and countermine. The former was a tunnel dug by besieging forces in the 16th century; the latter, a tunnel dug by castle defenders in order to meet and wage battle below ground. You can stoop and crawl into this narrow passageway—an eerie experience, despite the addition of electric light. The visitor center has a good audiovisual presentation on the castle's history. ⊠ *End of North Castle St.,* ☎ *0131/668–8800.* ✉ *Joint ticket to cathedral and castle £3.50, castle only £2.30.* ☼ *Apr.–Sept., daily 9:30–6; Oct.–Mar., Mon.–Sat. 9:30–4, Sun. 2–4.*

❹ The **Royal & Ancient Golf Club of St. Andrews** on The Scores, the ruling house of golf worldwide, is the spiritual home of all who play or follow the game. Its clubhouse on the dunes—a dignified building, more like a town hall than a clubhouse and open to club members only—is adjacent to St. Andrews's famous **Old Course** (☞ Outdoor Acclivities and Sports, *below*). The town of St. Andrews prospers on golf, golf schools, and golf equipment (the manufacture of golf balls has been a local industry for more than 100 years), and the Old Course is associated with the greatest players of the game.

❺ Just opposite the Royal & Ancient Golf Club is the **British Golf Museum,** which explores the centuries-old relationship between St. Andrews and golf and displays a variety of golf memorabilia. ⊠ *Golf Pl.,* ☎ *01334/478880.* ✉ *£3.75.* ☼ *Mid-Apr.–mid-Oct., daily 9:30–5:30; mid-Oct.–mid-Apr., Thurs.–Mon. 11–3.*

❻ St. Andrews is also the home of Scotland's oldest university. Founded in 1411, **St. Andrew's University** now consists of two stately old colleges in the middle of town and some modern buildings on the outskirts. A third weather-worn college, originally built in 1512, has become a girls' school. The handsome university buildings can be explored on guided walks, sometimes led by students in scarlet gowns. ☎ *01334/462158.* ☼ *Tours twice daily July–early Sept.*

❼ At the **Sea Life Centre** sea lions, penguins, and many other forms of marine life inhabit various aquariums and pool gardens designed to simulate their natural habitats. ⊠ *The Scores, West Sands,* ☎ *01334/474786.* ✉ *£4.25.* ☼ *July and Aug., daily 10–7; Sept.–June, daily 10–5.*

Only a few minutes (about 6 mi) northwest of St. Andrews's famous Old Course on the A919, **Leuchars** has a 12th-century church with some of the finest Norman architectural features to be seen anywhere in Scotland. Note in particular the blind arcading (arch shapes on the wall) and the beautifully decorated chancel and apse.

Dining and Lodging

££ ✗ **Grange Inn.** On a breezy hilltop overlooking St. Andrews, the Grange Inn offers old-fashioned charm with polished brass, low lights, and open fires. Of the three dining areas, two (no-smoking) have superb views over St. Andrews. The delicious specials on the modern Scottish menu might include monkfish with pesto, braised duck with red cabbage, or gravlax with sweet dill mustard. There is also an extensive wine list. ⊠ *Grange Rd.,* ☎ *01334/472670. AE, DC, MC, V. Closed Mon. and Tues., and Nov.–Mar.*

££££ ✗▥ **Rufflets Country House Hotel.** This creeper-covered country house just outside St. Andrews is surrounded by 10 acres of formal and informal gardens. All the rooms are handsomely decorated and comfortable, with the amenities one would expect of a top-class hotel. Dinner is served in the roomy Garden Restaurant, famous for its use of local produce to create memorable Scottish dishes. Recommended are the Tay salmon and fillet of Aberdeen Angus beef. ⊠ *Strathkinness Low Rd., KY16 9TX,* ☎ *01334/472594,* FAX *01334/478703. 25 rooms with bath or shower. Restaurant, bar. AE, DC, MC, V.*

£ 🏠 **Aslar Guest House.** A Victorian terraced house is central for shops, golf courses, and historic attractions such as the castle. All rooms are individually decorated—one with a four-poster bed—have private bathrooms or shower rooms (unusual for B&Bs); evening meals are not served. ⊠ *230 North St. KY16 9AF,* ☎ *01334/473460,* FAX *01334/ 477540. 5 rooms, 4 with bath, 1 with shower. MC, V.*

£ 🏠 **University of St. Andrews.** For accommodation within walking distance of all the town's attractions, it's hard to better the university for value and convenience. Room sizes—mainly singles—vary from adequate in the new building to happily spacious in the old building. The newer rooms have private bathrooms. ⊠ *79 North St., KY16 9AJ,* ☎ *01334/462000,* FAX *01334/462500. 153 rooms, 72 with shower. Restaurant, bar, lounge, coin laundry. MC, V. Closed early Sept.–May.*

Nightlife and the Arts

PUBS

Chariots (⊠ The Scores), inside the Scores Hotel, is popular with locals in their thirties and forties. With open fires and dark wood paneling, the **Grange Inn** (☞ Dining and Lodging, *above*) has a pleasant old-style, traditional feel.

THEATER

Byre Theatre (⊠ Abbey St., ☎ 01334/476288) has a resident repertory company. A brand-new theater is currently under construction and is due for completion in late 1999.

Outdoor Activities and Sports

GOLF

The following five St. Andrews courses (all are part of the St. Andrews Links Trust) are open to visitors. For details of availability—there is usually a waiting list—contact the **Reservations Department** (⊠ Links Management Committee, Pilmour Cottage, St. Andrews, KY16 9SF, ☎ 01334/466666, FAX 01334/477036), or phone the Golf Line (☎ 01334/477685) for an expert answer to all your golfing queries.

Eden Course (1914) 18 holes, 6,112 yards, SSS 70. **Jubilee Course** (1897) 18 holes, 6,805 yards, SSS 73. **New Course** (1895) 18 holes, 6,604 yards, SSS 72. **Old Course** (15th century) 18 holes, 6,566 yards, SSS 72, handicap certificate required. **Strathyrum Course** (1993) 18 holes, 5,094 yards, SSS 64.

Shopping

Douglas Renton (⊠ 72 South St., ☎ 01334/476334) is the best place in the region, if not in all Scotland, for Oriental rugs and carpets of all colors, patterns, and sizes—many of them antiques. **The St Andrews Pottery Shop** (⊠ Church Sq., between South St. and Market St., ☎ 01334/477744) sells decorative and domestic stoneware, porcelain, ceramics, and enamel jewelry. **Bonkers** (⊠ 80 Market St., ☎ 01334/ 473919) has a huge selection of clothing, clocks, books, cards, pottery, and gift items. **St. Andrews Fine Art** (⊠ 84A Market St., ☎ 01334/474080) is the place to go for Scottish paintings from 1800 to the present (oils, watercolors, drawings, and prints).

Crail

★ ❽ *10 mi south of St. Andrews via A917.*

One of numerous East Neuk fishing communities along the Fife coast, the town of Crail has a picturesque Dutch-influenced town house, or *tolbooth,* which contains the oldest bell in Fife, cast in Holland in 1520. Full details on the heritage and former trading links of this tiny port can be found in the **Crail Museum and Heritage Center.** ⊠ *62 Marketgate,* ☎ *01333/450869.* ✉ *Free.* ☻ *Easter wk and June–Sept., Mon.–Sat. 10–1 and 2–5, Sun. 2–5; after Easter wk–end of May, weekends and public holidays 2–5.*

Anstruther

4 mi southwest of Crail.

★ ❾ Anstruther's picturesque waterfront (larger than Crail's) has a few shops brightly festooned with children's pails and shovels as a gesture to seaside vacationers. Facing Anstruther harbor is the **Scottish Fisheries Museum,** housed in a colorful cluster of buildings, the earliest of which dates from the 16th century. This museum illustrates the difficult life of Scottish fishermen, past and present, through documents, artifacts, ship models, paintings, and tableaux. (These displays, complete with the reek of tarred rope and net, have been known to induce nostalgic tears in not a few old deckhands.) There are also floating exhibits at the quayside. ⊠ *Anstruther harbor,* ☎ *01333/310628.* ✉ *£3.50.* ☻ *Apr.–Oct., Mon.–Sat. 10–5:30, Sun. 11–5; Nov.–Mar., Mon.–Sat. 10–4:30, Sun. 2–4:30 (last admission 45 minutes before closing).*

Dining

££ ✕ **The Cellar.** Specializing in fish, but offering a selection of Scottish
★ beef and lamb as well, the Cellar is devoted to serving top-quality ingredients cooked simply in modern Scottish style and preserving all the natural flavor. The crayfish-and-mussel bisque is famous, and the wine list reflects high standards. Entered through a small courtyard, the restaurant is charmingly furnished in an unpretentious, old-fashioned style. It is popular with the locals, but its fame is even more widespread. ⊠ *24 East Green,* ☎ *01333/310378. AE, MC, V.*

Nightlife and the Arts

The **Dreel Tavern** (⊠ 16 High St., ☎ 01333/310727) is a 16th-century coaching inn famous for its hand-drawn ales.

Outdoor Activities and Sports

The back roads of Fife make pleasant biking terrain. Bicycles can be rented from **East Neuk Outdoors** (⊠ Cellardyke Park, ☎ 01333/311929), which also has archery, rappeling, orienteering, and canoeing equipment.

Pittenweem

❿ *1½ mi southwest of Anstruther.*

The working harbor at Pittenweem is backed by many examples of East Neuk architecture. Look for the crow-step gables (the stepped effect on the ends of the roofs), the white *harling* (Scots for rough-casting, the rough mortar finish on walls), and the red pantiles (S-shaped in profile). The "weem" part of the town's name comes from the Gaelic *uaime,* or cave. This town's particular cave is **St. Fillan's Cave,** which contains the shrine of St. Fillan, a 6th-century hermit who lived therein. It's up a close (alleyway) behind the waterfront. ⊠ *Cove Wynd, near harbor,* ☎ *01333/311495 (St. John's Episcopal Church for information).* ✉ *40p.* ☻ *Tues.–Sat. 10–5, Sun. noon–5.*

⓫ For a break from this nautical atmosphere follow B942 inland to **Kellie Castle.** Dating from the 16th and 17th centuries and restored in Victorian times, the castle stands among the grain fields and woodlands of northeastern Fife. The castle is surrounded by four acres of pretty

gardens. ✉ B9171, 3 mi northwest of Pittenweem, ☎ 01333/720271.
🎫 Joint ticket to castle and gardens £3.70, gardens only £1. ⊙ Castle Easter and May–Sept., daily 1:30–5:30; Oct., weekends 1:30–5:30 (last admission 4:45), garden and grounds daily 9:30–sunset.

Lower Largo

⑫ 10 mi west of Pittenweem.

The main claim to fame of Lower Largo is that it was the birthplace of Alexander Selkirk (1676–1721), the Scottish sailor who was the inspiration for Daniel Defoe's (1660–1731) Robinson Crusoe (1719). His statue can be seen above the doorway of the house where he was born in Main Street.

Shopping

At nearby Upper Largo, in a converted barn, **Scotland's Larder** (✉ Upper Largo, ☎ 01333/360414) is a shop (and restaurant) that sells a huge assortment of Scottish preserves, baked goods, and seasonal produce— anything from shortbread to smoked salmon, Dundee cakes to oysters. It also offers tastings, talks, and cooking demonstrations, all of which show off the savory foods of Scotland.

Glenrothes

9 mi west of Lower Largo.

A modern planned town, Glenrothes is notable for its public murals and sculptures.

Shopping

The **Balbirnie Craft Centre** (✉ near Balbirnie House, ☎ 01592/758759), in an 18th-century stable mews, is a peaceful setting in which to buy items made by craftspeople who live on the premises. Their work includes furniture, silver, jewelry, paintings and picture framing, glassblowing, sculpture, and leather goods.

Falkland

★ 5 mi north of Glenrothes via A92 and A912.

★ ⑬ One of the loveliest communities in all Fife, Falkland is a royal burgh of twisting streets and crooked stone houses. The town is dominated by **Falkland Palace,** a former hunting lodge of the Stuart monarchs and one of the earliest examples in Britain of the French Renaissance style. Overlooking the main street is the palace's most impressive feature— the south range of walls and chambers, rich with Renaissance buttresses and stone medallions, built for King James V (1512–42) in the 1530s by French masons. He died here, and the palace was a favorite resort of his daughter, Mary, Queen of Scots (1542–87). Behind the palace are gardens that contain a most unusual survivor: a "royal" tennis court (not at all like its modern counterpart) built in 1539 and still in use. ✉ Falkland, ☎ 01337/857397. 🎫 Joint ticket to palace and gardens £4.80, gardens only £2.40. ⊙ Apr.–Oct., Mon.–Sat. 11–5:30, Sun. 1:30–5:30 (last admission to palace 4:30, to garden 5).

Loch Leven

⑭ 10 mi southwest of Falkland via A911.

Scotland's largest Lowland loch, Loch Leven is famed for its fighting trout. The area is also noted for its birdlife, particularly its wintering wildfowl. On the southern shore overlooking the loch, **Vane Farm Nature Reserve,** a visitor center run by the Royal Society for the Protec-

tion of Birds, is informative about Loch Leven's
Farm, Rte. B9097, just off M90 and B996, ☎ 0157.
⊙ Apr.–Dec., daily 10–5; Jan.–Mar., daily 10–4.

Cupar

⑮ *21 mi northwest of Loch Leven via M90 and A91.*

⑯ Cupar is a busy market town with a variety of shops. On rising ground
near the town is the National Trust for Scotland's **Hill of Tarvit House.**
A 17th-century mansion, the house was later altered in the high-
Edwardian style in the late 1890s–1900s by the Scottish architect Sir
Robert Lorimer (1864–1929). Inside the house are fine collections of
antique furniture, Chinese porcelain, bronzes, tapestries, and Dutch
paintings. There is also a tearoom. ⊠ *2 mi south of Cupar off A916,*
☎ *01334/653127.* ☒ *Joint ticket to house and gardens £3.70, gar-*
dens only £1. ⊙ *House Easter and May–Sept., daily 1:30–5:30; Oct.,*
weekends 1:30–5:30 (last admission 4:45); tearoom 12:30–close; gar-
den and grounds Apr.–Oct., daily 9:30–9; Nov.–Mar., daily 9:30–4:30.

☾ Just outside Cupar at the **Scottish Deer Centre,** red deer can be seen at
close quarters on ranger-guided tours. There are also nature trails, a
winery, falconry displays, an adventure playground (a wood and tire
fortress not suited for young children), five shops, and a coffee bar. ⊠
A91, near Rankelour Farm, ☎ *01337/810391.* ☒ *£2.95.* ⊙ *Easter–*
Oct., daily 10–6; Nov.–Easter, daily 10–5.

OFF THE
BEATEN PATH
DAIRSIE BRIDGE – A few minutes east of Cupar at Dairsie, an unclassified road goes off to the right from the A91 and soon runs by the River
Eden. Dairsie Bridge over the river is 450 years old and has three
arches. Above the trees rises the spire of Dairsie Church, dating from
the 17th century, and the stark ruin of Dairsie Castle, often overlooked,
stands gloomily over the river nearby. With wild-rose hedges, grazing
cattle, and pheasants calling from the woody thickets, this is the very
essence of rural, Lowland Fife, yet it's only about 15 minutes from the
Old Course.

Outdoor Activities and Sports
Cupar Sports Centre (⊠ Carselogie Rd., ☎ 01334/412290) has a
swimming pool, sports hall, fitness rooms, squash, and steam bath.

Shopping
Margaret Urquhart (⊠ 13–17 Lady Wynd, ☎ 01334/652205) attracts customers from as far away as Edinburgh and Glasgow and stocks
a wide range of British and international designer clothing names.

Ceres

3 mi southeast of Cupar via A916 and B939, 9 mi southwest of St.
Andrews.

⑰ To learn more about the history and culture of rural Fife, visit the **Fife**
Folk Museum at Ceres. The life of local rural communities is reflected
in artifacts and documents, all housed in suitably authentic buildings
that include a former weigh house and adjoining weavers' cottages. ⊠
Town center, ☎ *01334/828250.* ☒ *£2.* ⊙ *Easter and mid-May–Oct.,*
Sat.–Thurs. 2–5.

Dining and Lodging
££££ ✕ ⌂ **Peat Inn.** This popular inn and modern Scottish–style eatery is
★ best known for its outstanding restaurant, generally considered one of
the finest in Scotland. Mouthwatering entrées such as a salad of warm
venison liver, smoked bacon, wild mushrooms, and truffles, or a sauté

ecology. ☒ Vane
7/86235. 🖅 £2.

monkfish with spiced pork and apple justify the high
nch is slightly cheaper. For either you may have to book
. In a detached building there are eight comfortable dou-
ing this a French-style restaurant with rooms. ☒ Jct.
6 mi southwest of St. Andrews, KY15 5LH. ☎ 01334/
34/840530. 8 suites. Restaurant, bar. AE, DC, MC,
nd Mon.

DUNDEE AND ANGUS

The industrial city of Dundee, famed historically for its economic re-
liance on "jute, jam, and journalism," contrasts dramatically with the
farmlands and glens of its rural hinterland and the coastal links northward. Peaceful back roads in this area are uncluttered; the main road
from Perth/Dundee to Aberdeen—the A90—requires special care, with
its mix of fast cars, lorries, and unexpectedly slow farm traffic.

Dundee

🔞 *14 mi northwest of St. Andrews, 58 mi north of Edinburgh, 79 mi northeast of Glasgow.*

Dundee's urban renewal program—its determination to shake off its
grimy industrial past—was motivated in part by the arrival of the **RRS
(Royal Research Ship)** *Discovery,* the vessel used by Captain Robert Scott
(1868–1912) on his polar explorations. The steamer was originally built
and launched in Dundee; now it's a permanent tourist exhibit. A visitor center and onboard exhibition allow visitors to sample life as it
was aboard the intrepid *Discovery.* ☒ *Discovery Point, Discovery
Quay,* ☎ 01382/201245. 🖅 *£4.50.* ☉ *Apr.–Oct., Mon.–Sat. 10–5,
Sun. 11–5; Nov.–Mar., Mon.–Sat. 10–4, Sun. 11–4.*

At Victoria Dock, the frigate **Unicorn,** a 46-gun wooden warship, lies
berthed. The *Unicorn* has the distinction of being the oldest British-
built warship afloat (the fourth-oldest in the world), having been
launched at Chatham, England, in 1824. Onboard models and displays
offer a glimpse into the history of the Royal Navy. ☒ *Victoria Dock
(just east of Tay Rd. Bridge),* ☎ 01382/200900 or 200893. 🖅 *£3.*
☉ *Mid-Mar.–Oct., daily 10–5; Nov.–mid-Mar., weekdays 10–4 (last
admission 30 mins before closing).*

On dry land, in a former jute mill the **Verdant Works** houses a multi-
faceted exhibition on the story of jute and Dundee's historical involvement in the jute trade. Restored machinery, audiovisuals, and
tableaux all re-create vividly the hard, noisy life of the jute worker. ☒
West Hendersons Wynd, ☎ 01382/225282. 🖅 *£3.25.* ☉ *Apr.–Oct.,
Mon.–Sat. 10–5, Sun. 11–5; Nov.–Mar., Mon.–Sat. 10–4, Sun. 11–4.*

Dundee's principal museum and art gallery is **The McManus Galleries,**
which has displays on a range of subjects, including local history,
trade, and industry. ☒ *Albert Sq.,* ☎ 01382/432020. 🖅 *Free.* ☉ *Mon.
11–5, Tues.–Sat. 10–5.*

The **Barrack Street Museum** specializes in natural history, with exhibitions on the wildlife and geology of Angus and the Highlands. The
museum also displays the skeleton of the famous Tay Whale, immortalized by Scotland's worst poet, William MacGonagall, born in Dundee
in 1830. ☒ *Barrack St. and Meadowside,* ☎ 01382/432067. 🖅 *Free.*
☉ *Mon. 11–5, Tues.–Sat. 10–5.*

The **University Botanic Gardens** are a well-landscaped collection of native and exotic plants. Also on the premises are tropical and temperate greenhouses and a visitor center. ☒ *Riverside Dr.,* ☎ 01382/

Angus Area

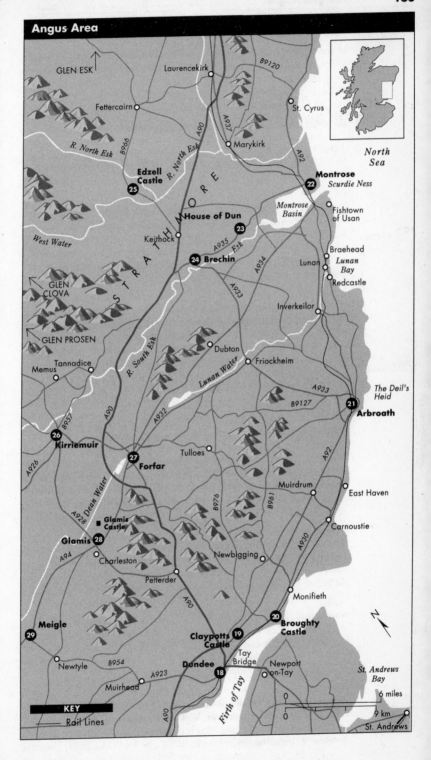

GLEN ESK

Laurencekirk

Fettercairn

St. Cyrus

R. North Esk

B966

A937

A90

Marykirk

North
Sea

Edzell
Castle
25

House of Dun

Montrose **22**
Scurdie Ness

STRATHMORE

Montrose
Basin

Fishtown
of Usan

Keithock

A935

Braehead

Lunan
Bay

West Water

24 Brechin

A934

Lunan

Redcastle

GLEN
CLOVA

A933

Inverkeilor

GLEN PROSEN

R. South Esk

Dubton

The Deil's
Heid

Memus

Tannadice

A932

Lunan Water

Friockheim

A933

B9127

21
Arbroath

26
Kirriemuir

A90

Tulloes

B976

B961

A92

A926

27
Forfar

Muirdrum

East Haven

A928 Dean Water

Carnoustie

28 Glamis
Castle

A930

Glamis

Charleston

Newbigging

Petterden

29
Meigle

A90

Monifieth

Newtyle

B954

A94

20
Broughty
Castle

Claypotts **19**
Castle

Dundee **18**

Tay
Bridge

Newport
on-Tay

St. Andrews
Bay

A923

Muirhead

Firth of Tay

0   6 miles

0   9 km

A90

St. Andrews

KEY

— Rail Lines

566939. ☎ £1.50. ☼ Mar.–Oct., Mon.–Sat. 10–4:30, Sun. 11–4; Nov.–Feb., Mon.–Sat. 10–3, Sun. 11–3.

⑲ In the eastern suburbs of Dundee, away from the surviving Victorian architecture of the city center, are two castles of interest. **Claypotts Castle** is a well-preserved 16th-century tower house laid out on a Z-plan. ✉ *South of A92 (3 mi east of city center),* ☎ *0131/668–8800.* ☎ *£ 1.* ☼ *Call for opening times.*

⑳ Built to guard the Tay estuary, **Broughty Castle** is now a museum focusing on fishing, ferries, and the history of the town's whaling industry. There is also a display of arms and armor. ✉ *Broughty Ferry (4 mi east of city center),* ☎ *01382/776121.* ☎ *Free.* ☼ *Oct.–June, Mon. 11–1 and 2–5, Tues.–Thurs. and Sat. 10–1 and 2–5; July–Sept. also Sun. 2–5.*

Dundee is ringed by country parks that offer ample sports and leisure activities. **Crombie Country Park** has a reservoir with extensive woodlands in 250 acres, as well as wildlife blinds, nature trails, a children's play park, picnic areas, and a display-and-interpretation center staffed by a ranger. ✉ *Off Rte. B961 (7 mi northwest of Newbigging),* ☎ *01241/860360.* ☎ *Free.* ☼ *Daily 9–dusk.*

Lodging

££££ 🏨 **Kinnaird.** A luxurious country house set in extensive grounds above the Tay valley northwest of Dundee, Kinnaird has elegant, individually decorated bedrooms with king-size beds and antique furniture. Reception rooms welcome you with open fires and fresh flowers. Two dining rooms offering imaginative Scottish cuisine round out the memorable experience. The management does not allow families with children younger than 12. ✉ *Kinnaird Estate PH8 0LB,* ☎ *01796/482440,* FAX *01796/482289. 9 rooms with bath or shower. 2 restaurants, 2 tennis courts, bowling, croquet, fishing. AE, MC, V.*

Nightlife and the Arts

DISCOS

Dundee has several discos: **De Sthils** (✉ S. Ward Rd., ☎ 01382/200066), **Fat Sam's Disco** (✉ 31 S. Ward Rd., ☎ 01382/228181), **Arthur's** (✉ St. Andrews Lane, ☎ 01382/221061), **The Coliseum** (✉ Brown St., ☎ 01382/221176), and **Mardi Gras** (✉ 21 S. Ward Rd., ☎ 01382/205551).

FILM

ABC (✉ Seagate, ☎ 01382/225247 or 01382/226865) screens mainstream films. **Odeon Cinema** (✉ Stack Leisure Park, ☎ 01382/400855) shows recent releases. **Steps Film Theatre** (✉ Wellgate Centre, ☎ 01382/434037) plays less-mainstream films and current releases.

MUSIC

Bonar Hall (✉ Park Pl., ☎ 01382/345466) hosts classical, jazz, and rock concerts, as well as chamber music. **Caird Hall** (✉ City Sq., ☎ 01382/434940) is one of Scotland's finest concert halls, staging a wide range of music. **West Port Bar** (✉ Henderson's Wynd, ☎ 01382/200993) offers folk music on Monday.

THEATER

Dundee Repertory Theatre (✉ Tay Sq., ☎ 01382/223530) is in an award-winning complex that includes an exhibition gallery, and is home to a resident theater group as well as a dance company. Both offer diverse programs. **Little Theatre** (✉ Victoria Rd., ☎ 01382/225835) presents a wide variety of performances, especially modern theatrical works by local and visiting groups. **Whitehall Theatre** (✉ Bellfield St., ☎ 01382/322684) offers a variety of choices, including Scottish shows, light opera, and variety and musical entertainments.

Outdoor Activities and Sports

Dundee Olympia Leisure Centre (⊠ Earl Grey Pl., ☎ 01382/434888) has four swimming pools, a diving pool, sauna, water slides, exercise equipment, and a restaurant.

Shopping

COFFEE AND TEA

J. Allan Braithwaite (⊠ 6 Castle St., ☎ 01382/322693) offers 13 freshly roasted coffees and more than 30 blended teas, including mango and apricot. (Remember that such specialty teas can usually be taken home without import restriction if you purchase them as gifts.)

JEWELRY

There are several good jewelers in Dundee. **Rattray & Co.** (⊠ 32 Nethergate, ☎ 01382/227258) has been in business for more than 140 years. **Stephen Henderson the Jeweller** (⊠ 1 Union St., ☎ 01382/221339) has a good selection of silver and pewter Ortak jewelry from Orkney, *skean dhus* (ornamental Highlander daggers), and *quaichs,* a small dish with handles traditionally used for whiskey tasting.

KITCHENWARE

The Cookshop (⊠ 27 Wellgate Centre, ☎ 01382/221256) stocks an enormous variety of cooking equipment and other kitchenware.

SHOPPING MALL

The modern covered shopping mall in Dundee, the **Wellgate Shopping Centre** (⊠ off Panmure St., ☎ 01382/225454), is the place to visit if you're looking for the major retail chains.

Arbroath

㉑ *15 mi north of Dundee via A92.*

In the holiday resort and fishing town of Arbroath traditional boat-building can be seen. Arbroath has several small curers and processors, with shops offering the town's most famous delicacy, "Arbroath smokies"—whole haddock gutted and lightly smoked.

Arbroath Abbey, founded in 1178, in town center, is unmistakable and seems to straddle whole streets, as if the town were simply ignoring the redstone ruin in its midst. Surviving today are remains of the church, as well as one of the most complete examples in existence of an abbot's residence. From here in 1320 a passionate plea was sent by King Robert the Bruce (1274–1329) and the Scottish church to Pope John XXII (circa 1245–1334) in far-off Rome. The pope had until then sided with the English kings, who adamantly refused to acknowledge Scottish independence. The Declaration of Arbroath stated firmly, "For as long as but a hundred of us remain alive, never will we on any conditions be brought under English rule. It is in truth not for glory, nor riches, nor honours that we are fighting, but for freedom—for that alone, which no honest man gives up but with life itself." Some historians describe this plea (originally drafted in Latin) as the single most important document in Scottish history. The pope advised English King Edward II (1284–1327) to make peace, but warfare was to break out along the border from time to time for the next 200 years. ⊠ *Arbroath town center,* ☎ *0131/668–8800.* ☞ *£1.80.* ☼ *Apr.–Sept., daily 9:30–6; Oct.–Mar., Mon.–Sat. 9:30–4, Sun. 2–4.*

Arbroath was the shore base for the construction of the Bell Rock lighthouse on a treacherous, barely exposed offshore rock in the early 19th century. A signal tower was built to facilitate communication between the mainland and the builders working offshore. The **Signal Tower Mu-**

seum in the tower now tells the story of the lighthouse, built by Robert Stevenson (1772–1850) in 1811. (The name Stevenson is strongly associated with the building of lighthouses throughout Scotland, though the most famous son of that family is remembered for another talent. In fact, Robert Louis Stevenson, 1850–94, gravely disappointed his family by choosing to become a writer instead of an engineer.) The museum also houses a collection of items related to the history of the town, its folk life, and the local fishing industry. ⊠ *Ladyloan (west of harbor)*, ☎ 01241/875598. ⌇ *Free.* ☉ *Sept.–June, Mon.–Sat. 10–5; July–Aug., also Sun. 2–5.*

Nightlife and the Arts

Arbroath dances at **Club Metro** (⊠ Queen's Dr., ☎ 01241/872338). For a good pint, seek out the **Foundry Bar** (⊠ E. Mary St., ☎ 01241/872524), a spartan bar frequented by locals and enlivened by impromptu music sessions—customers often bring along their fiddles and accordions, and all join in.

Outdoor Activities and Sports

Arbroath Sports Centre (⊠ Keptie Rd., ☎ 01241/872999) has a swimming pool, squash courts, games hall, and a gymnasium. The **Saltire Leisure Centre** (⊠ Montrose Rd., ☎ 01241/431060) has fitness rooms, sauna, and exercise equipment.

Montrose

❷❷ *14 mi north of Arbroath via A92.*

A handsome, unpretentious town with a museum and a selection of shops, Montrose is also noted for its beach. Behind Montrose the River Esk forms a wide estuary known as the Montrose Basin. The **Scottish Wildlife Trust** (⊠ Montrose Basin, ☎ 01674/676336) operates a nature reserve here, with a good number of geese, ducks, and swans.

The National Trust for Scotland's leading attraction in this area, the ★ ❷❸ **House of Dun** overlooks the Montrose Basin. This 1730s mansion, built by architect William Adam (1689–1748), is particularly noted for its ornate plasterwork. ⊠ *A935 (4 mi west of Montrose)*, ☎ 01674/810264. ⌇ *Joint ticket to house and garden £3.70, garden only £1.* ☉ *House Easter and May–Sept., daily 1:30–5:30; Oct., weekends 1:30–5:30 (last admission 5); restaurant 11–close; garden and grounds daily 9:30–sunset.*

Outdoor Activities and Sports

Montrose Sports Centre (⊠ Marine Ave., ☎ 01674/676211) is an indoor sports center with a gymnasium.

Brechin

❷❹ *10 mi west of Montrose.*

The small market town Brechin, in Strathmore, has a cathedral that was founded about 1200 and contains an interesting selection of antiquities. The town's 10th-century **Round Tower** is one of only two on mainland Scotland (they are more frequently found in Ireland). It was originally built for the local Culdee monks.

Nightlife and the Arts

Flicks (⊠ 7–9 High St., ☎ 01356/624313) has a mix of live bands and DJs, and attracts young people (older than 18) from a wide area.

Edzell

6 mi north of Brechin via B966.

★ ㉕ **Edzell Castle,** an impressive ruin from the 16th century built in the local red sandstone, is nestled among the Grampian foothills. This structure was originally a typical Scottish fortified tower, but was later transformed into a house that gave some degree of domestic comfort as well as protection from the elements. The simple "L" shape of the original building was extended, and a pleasance, or walled garden, was added in 1604. This formal garden, along with unique heraldic and symbolic sculptures, survives today. ⊠ *Off B966,* ☎ *0131/668–8800.* 🖅 *£2.30.* ⊘ *Apr.–Sept., daily 9:30–6; Oct.–Mar., Mon.–Wed. and Sat. 9:30–4, Thurs. 9:30–noon, Sun. 2–4.*

OFF THE
BEATEN PATH

WHITE AND BROWN CATERTHUNS – The remains of Iron Age hill forts crown two rounded hills southwest of Edzell Castle. Lovers of wild places will enjoy the drive to the Caterthuns from Edzell (if in doubt at junctions, turn left), especially the climb up the narrow road (from Balrownie to Pitmudie) that passes between the two hills; along the way there are magnificent views southward to the patterned fields of Strathmore. Marked paths run up to each fort (both are now officially protected sites) from the main road. The White Caterthun, so called because of the pale quartzite rock that was used to build its now-tumbled ramparts, is the better preserved of the two.

En Route You can rejoin the hurly-burly of the A90 for the journey back southward, though the more pleasant route leads southwestward using minor roads (there are several options) along the face of the Grampians, following the fault line that separates Highland and Lowland at this point. The **Glens of Angus** extend north from various points on Route A90. Known individually as the glens of Isla, Prosen, Clova, and Esk, these long valleys run into the high hills of the Grampians and offer a choice of clearly marked walking routes (those in Glen Clova are especially appealing).

Kirriemuir

㉖ *20 mi southwest of Edzell.*

Kirriemuir stands at the heart of Angus's red sandstone countryside and was the birthplace of the writer and dramatist Sir James Barrie (1860–1937), most well known abroad as the author of *Peter Pan.* **Barrie's House,** now in the care of the National Trust for Scotland, has upper floors furnished as they might have been in Barrie's time, with manuscripts and personal mementos displayed. The outside washhouse is said to have been Barrie's first theater. Next door, at 11 Brechin Road, is an exhibition on "The Genius of J. M. Barrie" that gives literary and theatrical background. ⊠ *9 Brechin Rd.,* ☎ *01575/572646 or 01575/572353.* 🖅 *£2.* ⊘ *Easter and May–Sept., Mon.–Sat. 11–5:30, Sun. 1:30–5:30; Oct., Sat. 11–5:30, Sun. 1:30–5:30 (last admission 5).*

Dining

£ ✕ **Drovers Inn.** Set in the heart of the Angus farmlands, the Drovers
★ is a rare find in Scotland, having more of the feeling of an English country pub. Plain but friendly surroundings, decorated with old farm implements and historic photographs, are the setting for simple bar food, homemade pies, and nourishing soups, and a restaurant serving a Scottish menu of venison, *cloutie* (fruit pudding boiled or steamed in a cloth) dumplings, and other delights. It's popular with locals; on weekends it's best to make reservations, even for bar meals. ⊠ *Memus, near Kirriemuir,* ☎ *01307/860322. MC, V.*

Forfar

㉗   *7 mi east of Kirriemuir.*

Forfar goes about its business of being the center for a farming hinterland, without being preoccupied about tourism. This means it is an everyday, friendly, pleasant enough Scottish town, bypassed by the A90 on its way north.

Dining and Lodging

££   ✕🖪 **Royal Hotel.** In the center of Forfar, this former coaching inn has been fully modernized, and is a welcoming base for exploring or golfing. Bedrooms are well equipped, though some in the most modern part of the hotel are rather small. All are decorated in a green-and-peach color scheme, with stained wood finishes and floral fabrics. The public rooms have retained their 19th-century charm. The leisure complex has a pool, gym, and roof garden. The restaurant turns out well-cooked, international standard fare—fish and chips, lasagna—served by a friendly staff. ⊠ *Castle St., DD8 3AE,* ☎ ℻ *01307/462691. 19 rooms with bath or shower. Restaurant, indoor pool, sauna, exercise room. AE, DC, MC, V.*

£   🖪 **Redroofs.** This former cottage hospital, now a hospitable private
★   home, offers superb bed-and-breakfast accommodations in spacious surroundings, set among trees. Guests can also use a characterful sitting room decorated with curios collected by the owners on their travels. Evening meals can be provided by prior arrangement. ⊠ *Balgavies, DD8 2UE,* ☎ ℻ *01307/830268. 3 rooms, 1 with shower. No credit cards.*

Glamis

★   **㉘**   *5 mi southwest of Forfar, 6 mi south of Kirriemuir via A928.*

Set in pleasantly rolling countryside is the village of Glamis, site of the **Angus Folk Museum.** This museum village is made up of a row of 19th-century cottages with unusual stone-slab roofs; exhibits focus on the crafts and tools of domestic and agricultural life in the region during the past 200 years. ⊠ *Off A94,* ☎ *01307/840288.* 🖭 *£2.40.* ⊙ *Easter and May–Sept., daily 11–5; Oct., weekends 11–5 (last admission 4:30).*

One of Scotland's best-known castles, because of its association with
★   the present Royal Family, is **Glamis Castle.** This was the childhood home of the current Queen Mother and the birthplace of Princess Margaret. The property of the earls of Strathmore and Kinghorne since 1372, the castle was largely reconstructed in the late 17th century; the original keep, which is much older, is still intact. One of the most famous rooms in the castle is Duncan's Hall, the legendary setting for Shakespeare's (1564–1616) *Macbeth* (1605–06). Guided tours offer visitors a look at fine collections of china, tapestries, and furniture. Other visitor facilities include shops, a produce stall, and licensed restaurant. ⊠ *A94, 1 mi north of Glamis,* ☎ *01307/840393.* 🖭 *Joint ticket to castle and grounds £5.20, grounds only £2.40.* ⊙ *Apr.–June and Sept.–late Oct, daily 10:30–5:30; July and Aug., daily 10–5:30 (last tour at 4:45); groups by private appointment at other times.*

Meigle

㉙   *7 mi southwest of Glamis, 15 mi west of Dundee.*

The **local museum** at Meigle, in the wide swathe of Strathmore, has a magnificent collection of some 25 sculptured monuments from the Celtic Christian period (8th to 10th centuries), nearly all of which were found in or around the local churchyard. This is one of the most notable collections of medieval work in Western Europe. ⊠ *A94,* ☎ *0131/ 668–8800.* ☑ *£1.50.* ☉ *Apr.–Sept., daily 9:30–6.*

FIFE AND ANGUS A TO Z

Arriving and Departing

By Bus

From Edinburgh's St. Andrew Square Bus Station and Glasgow's Buchanan Street Bus Station, services run into Fife and Angus. There are hourly services to Dundee from both Glasgow and Edinburgh operated by **Scottish Citylink** (☎ 0990/505050). **Stagecoach/Fife Scottish** (☎ 01383/621249) serves Fife and St. Andrews.

By Car

The M90 motorway from Edinburgh takes you to within a half hour of St. Andrews and Dundee. Travelers coming from Fife can use the A91 and the A914, then cross the Tay Bridge to reach Dundee, though the quickest way is to use the M90/A90. Travel time from Edinburgh to Dundee is about one hour, from Edinburgh to St. Andrews, 1½ hours.

By Plane

Glasgow Airport (☞ Chapter 4), 50 mi west of Edinburgh, is now a major point of entry for international flights. Passengers landing in Glasgow have easy access to Edinburgh and Fife and Angus. **Edinburgh Airport** (☞ Chapter 3), 7 mi west of downtown Edinburgh, offers connections throughout the United Kingdom, as well as with a number of cities on the Continent.

By Train

ScotRail stops at Kirkcaldy, Markinch (for Glenrothes), Cupar, Leuchars (for St. Andrews), Dundee, Arbroath, and Montrose. For details of services, call the **National Train Enquiry Line** (☎ 0345/484950).

Getting Around

By Bus

A local network provides service from St. Andrews and Dundee to many of the smaller towns throughout Fife and Dundee. The fare for the Kirkcaldy–St. Andrews run is £3.30; St. Andrews–Dundee, £2; Perth–Montrose, £6.30. For information about routes and fares call **Fife Scottish** (☎ 01592/642394), **Scottish Citylink** (☎ 0990/505050), or **Strathtay Scottish** (☎ 01382/228345).

By Car

Fife is an easy area to get around and presents no major obstacles. Most of the roads are quiet and uncongested. The most interesting sights are in the east, which is served by a network of cross-country roads. Angus is likewise an easy region to explore, being serviced by a main fast road— the A90—which travels through the middle of the Strathmore valley and then on to Aberdeen; another, gentler road—the A92—that runs to the east near the coast; and a network of rural roads between the Grampians and Route A90.

By Train

For the main towns with stations in this area, *see* Arriving and Departing, *above.*

Contacts and Resources

Car Rentals

Arnold Clark (⊠ East Dock St., Dundee, ☎ 01382/225382). **Avis** (c/o DIS, ⊠ Old Glamis Rd., Dundee, ☎ 01382/832264). **Hertz** (⊠ 18 Marketgate, Dundee, ☎ 01382/223711).

Doctors and Dentists

Consult your hotel, a tourist information center, or the yellow pages of the telephone directory for listings of local doctors and dentists.

Emergencies

For **police, fire, or ambulance,** dial ☎ 999 from any telephone. No coins are needed for emergency calls made from public telephone booths.

Guided Tours

ORIENTATION

Travel Greyhound (✉ Commercial St., Dundee, ☎ 01382/202655) offers a variety of general orientation tours of the main cities and the region from late July to early August. **Fisher Tours** (✉ West Port, Dundee, ☎ 01382/227290) has tours all year both within and outside the region; one of their most popular tours is "Lochs and Glens."

SPECIAL-INTEREST

Links Golf Tours (✉ 7 Pilmour Links, St. Andrews, ☎ 01334/478639, FAX 01334/474086) offers tours tailored to individual requirements.

Late-Night Pharmacies

Late-night pharmacies are not found outside the larger cities. In St. Andrews, Dundee, and other larger centers, pharmacies use a rotating system for off-hours and Sunday prescription service. Consult the listings displayed on pharmacy doors for the names and addresses of pharmacies that provide service outside regular hours. In an emergency the police can help you contact a pharmacist. Note that in rural areas general practitioners may also dispense medicine.

Visitor Information

Arbroath (✉ Market Pl., ☎ 01241/872609). **Dundee** (✉ 4 City Sq., ☎ 01382/434664). **Glenrothes** (✉ Rothes Halls, Rothes Sq., ☎ 01592/754954). **Kirkcaldy** (✉ 19 Whytescauseway, ☎ 01592/267775). **Leven** (✉ The Beehive, Durie St., ☎ 01333/429464). **St. Andrews** (✉ 70 Market St., ☎ 01334/472021).

Smaller tourist information centers operate seasonally in the following towns: Anstruther, Brechin, Carnoustie, Crail, Cupar, Forfar, Kirriemuir, and Montrose.

7 The Central Highlands

Stirling, Loch Lomond and the Trossachs, Perthshire

Perth and Stirling are easily accessible gateways to the rugged, spectacular Central Highlands stretching north from Glasgow. This may not be the fabled Highlands of the north, but you're among wild country—lush, green woodlands and wandering lochs. In the Trossachs and the west, deep lochs—including Loch Lomond— shimmer at the foot of hills cloaked in birch, oak, and pine.

By Gilbert
Summers

THE CENTRAL HIGHLANDS CONSIST of the counties of Perthshire and Stirlingshire. Today the old county seats of Perth and Stirling, respectively, still play important roles as the primary administrative centers in the area. Both lie on the edge of a Highland region that offers reliable road and rail connections to the central belt of Scotland. You can judge just how near the area is to the well-populated Midland Valley by looking out from the ramparts of Edinburgh Castle: the Highland hills—which meander around the Trossachs and above Callander—are clearly visible. Similarly, the high-tower blocks of some of Glasgow's peripheral housing developments are noticeable from many of the higher peaks, notably Ben Lomond.

In fact, the Lowland–Highland contrast is pronounced in this region. Geologists have designated a prominent boundary between the two distinct landscapes as the Highland Boundary Fault. This geological divide also marked the boundary between Scotland's two languages and cultures, Gaelic and Scots, with the Gaels ensconced northwest behind the mountain barrier. In the Central Highlands the fault runs through Loch Lomond, close to Callander, to the northeast above Perth, and into the old county of Angus.

As early as 1794 the local minister in Callander, on the very edge of the Highlands, wrote: "The Trossachs are often visited by persons of taste, who are desirous of seeing nature in her rudest and unpolished state." What these early visitors came to see was a series of lochs and hills, whose crags and slopes were hung harmoniously with shaggy birch, oak, and pinewoods. The tops of the hills are high but not too savage (real wilderness would have been too much for these fledgling nature lovers). The Romantic poets, especially William Wordsworth (1770–1850), sang the praises of such locales. Though Wordsworth is most closely associated with the Lake District in England, his travels through Scotland and the Trossachs inspired several poems. But it was Sir Walter Scott (1771–1832) who definitively put this Highland-edge area on the tourist map by setting his dramatic verse narrative, *Lady of the Lake,* written in 1810, firmly in the physical landscape of the Trossachs. Scott's verse was an immediate and huge success, and visitors flooded in to trace the events of the poem across the region. Today visitors continue to flock here, though few can quote a line of his poem.

If the Trossachs have long attracted those with discriminating tastes, then much of the same sentimental aura has attached itself to Loch Lomond. This is Scotland's largest loch in terms of surface area. By looking at the map, you will see that the loch is narrow to the north and broad in the south. The hard rocks to the north confine it to a long thin ribbon, and the more yielding Lowland structures allow it to spread out and assume a softer, wider form. Thus Lowland fields and lush hedgerows quickly give way to dark woods and crags—all this just a half hour's drive from the center of Glasgow. The song, "The Banks of Loch Lomond," said to have been written by a Jacobite prisoner incarcerated in Carlisle, England, seems to capture a particular style of Scottish sentimentality, resulting in the popularity of the "bonnie, bonnie banks" around the world, wherever Scots are to be found.

Finally, remember that even though the Central Highlands are easily accessible, there is still much high, rough country in the region. Ben Lawers, near Killin, is the ninth-highest peak in Scotland, and the moor of Rannoch is as bleak and empty a stretch as can be seen anywhere in the northlands. But if the glens and lochs prove to be too lonely or intimidating, it's a short journey to the softer and less harsh Lowlands.

Pleasures and Pastimes

Biking

The big attraction for cyclists is the dedicated Glasgow–Killin cycleway. This runs along former railroad track beds, as well as otherwise private and some quiet minor roads, to reach well into the Central Highlands by way of the Trossachs and Callander. Away from the cycleway, the main roads can be busy with holiday traffic.

Dining

Central Highlands restaurants have been continually improving for the past several years. Regional country delicacies—loch trout, river salmon, mutton, and venison—are now found regularly on even modest menus; this was extremely rare 20 years ago. The urban areas south and southwest of Stirling, in contrast, lack refinement in matters of eating and drinking. Here you will find simple low-built pubs, often crowded and noisy, but serving substantial food at lunchtime (eaten balanced on your knee, perhaps, or at a shared table). Three sturdy courses at one of these pubs will cost you about £10.

CATEGORY	COST*
££££	over £40
£££	£30–£40
££	£15–£30
£	under £15

*per person for a three-course meal, including VAT and excluding drinks and service

Fishing

There are several fishing options in the area, including coarse and game fishing, loch and river fishing, and sea angling. There are statutory fishing seasons for salmon and sea trout (January 15–October 15 on Tay River system). Coarse fishing for grayling, pike, perch, and roach on the Earn River System is reserved February–October. In some cases, Sunday fishing is illegal. Tourist information centers have publications, updated annually, that show the best locations.

Golf

There are many excellent courses in the region (☞ Chapter 2). Tourist information centers can supply details of local courses.

Hiking

Hill walking and "Munro-bagging" (climbing up all the mountains more than 3,000 ft high) are popolar, so even in the wilder parts of the Highlands, you will find locals able to give advice on routes. For high-level routes, it is essential to be properly supplied with boots and safety equipment. Tourist information centers carry information on a variety of local routes. The publications *Walk Loch Lomond and the Trossachs* or *Walk Perthshire* are invaluable for hikers and trekkers and are available at bookshops or tourist information centers.

Lodging

In Stirling and Callander, as well as in the small towns and villages throughout the region, you will find a selection of tourist accommodations out of all proportion to the size of the communities. (The industrial towns are the exceptions.) Standards of less-expensive establishments have improved in recent years and are still improving. The grand hotels, though few, were brought into existence by the carriage trade of the 19th century, when travel in Scotland was the fashion. The level of service at these places has, by and large, not slipped. You will also find many country hotels, however, that match the grand hotels in comfort.

CATEGORY	COST*
££££	over £120
£££	£90–£120
££	£50–£90
£	under £50

Prices are for a standard double room, including service, breakfast, and VAT.

Nightlife and the Arts

The nightlife in the area tends toward *ceilidhs* (participatory song, music, and dance) and Scottish concerts. Folk evenings in a number of hotels are also popular. In general, local pubs are friendly and down-to-earth, with locals who don't mind talking to visitors about what to see and do.

Shopping

Perth has been known, since Roman times, for its freshwater Scottish pearls, and in Stirling, High Street stores compete with long-established local firms. In smaller towns and villages, the selection is more limited but the relaxed pace makes for pleasant shopping.

Exploring the Central Highlands

The main towns of Stirling and Perth serve as roadway hubs for the area, making both places natural starting points for Highland tours. Stirling itself is worth covering in some detail on foot. The successive waves of development of this important town can easily be traced— from castle and Old Town architecture to Victorian developments and urban and industrial sprawl.

The Trossachs are a short distance from Stirling, all easily covered in a loop. You can get to Loch Lomond from either Glasgow or Stirling, and there are two other routes to take. The main road up the west bank (A82) is not recommended for leisurely touring. Do use this road, however, if you are on your way to Oban, Kintyre, or Argyll. Loch Lomond is best seen from one of two cul-de-sac roads: by way of Drymen at the south end, up to Rowardennan or, if you are pressed for time, west from Aberfoyle to reach Loch Lomond near its northern end, at Inversnaid. Visitors should note that in the Trossachs, the road that some maps show going all the way around Loch Katrine is a private road belonging to the Strathclyde Water Board and is open only to walkers and cyclists.

Getting around Perthshire is made interesting by the series of looped tours accessible from the A9, a fast main artery. Exercise caution while driving the A9 itself, however: there have been many auto accidents in this area. Although the entire route can be completed in a single day, travelers with some time on their hands who seek a little spontaneity can choose from a variety of accommodations in villages along the way.

Numbers in the text correspond to numbers in the margin and on the Central Highlands and Stirling maps.

Great Itineraries

This is excellent touring country. The glens, in some places, run parallel to the lochs, including those along Lochs Earn, Tay, and Rannoch, making for satisfying loops and round trips.

IF YOU HAVE 2 DAYS
There is enough to see in ⊞ **Stirling** ①–⑱ to take up at least a day. The second day, cover the **Trossachs** loop, which includes **Loch Venachar** ㉔, Loch Achray, and **Loch Katrine** ㉕, **Dunblane** ⑲, **Doune** ⑳, **Callander** ㉑, and **Aberfoyle** ㉖.

IF YOU HAVE 6 DAYS
Spend a day in ⊞ **Stirling** ①–⑱. (Don't overlook the Mill Trail country, east of Stirling, if you are shopping for Scottish woolens.) Then cover the route for the **Trossachs** and **Loch Lomond** ㉙; visit the historic towns of **Dunblane** ⑲ and **Doune** ⑳, staying overnight at ⊞ **Callander** ㉑ to explore the fine country northward toward **Balquhidder Glen** ㉓. Spend a day in the Trossachs around ⊞ **Loch Venachar** ㉔ and **Loch Katrine** ㉕, and take a boat ride to see the landscape at its best. The next day, travel to **Drymen** ㉘ for a morning around Loch Lomond before driving into Perthshire. Spend a night at ⊞ **Auchterarder** ㊼ with its antiques shops, or travel straight to ⊞ **Perth** ㉚, where you should base yourself for two or three days while exploring Perthshire. Go west for **Crieff** ㊺ and **Drummond Castle** ㊻, or north for Highland resort towns such as **Dunkeld** ㉞, with its cathedral; **Pitlochry** ㉟, close to the historic **Pass of Killiecrankie** ㊲ and impressive **Blair Castle** ㊳; and **Aberfeldy** ㊵. Between Pitlochry and Aberfeldy, make time for the bleak landscapes of **Loch Rannoch** ㊴—a great contrast to the generally pastoral Perthshire countryside.

When to Tour the Central Highlands

The Trossachs and Loch Lomond can get quite busy in high summer. This area is also a good choice for off-season touring. You are near enough to the Lowland edge to take advantage of any good weather in winter to enjoy the dramatic Highland light; fall colors are also spectacular.

STIRLING

26 mi northeast of Glasgow, 36 mi northwest of Edinburgh.

In some ways, Stirling is like a smaller version of Edinburgh. Its castle, built on a steep-sided plug of rock, dominates the landscape, and its Esplanade offers views of the surrounding valley-plain of the River Forth. The city is rich in historic heritage—the Stewart monarchs held court here from time to time, as they did in Edinburgh—and plans various cultural events, including a summer program of open-air historical tableaux.

Exploring Stirling

The historic part of town is tightly nestled around the castle—everything is within easy walking distance. You might want to get a taxi out to Bannockburn Heritage Center or the National Wallace Monument, which are on the town's outskirts, but still walkable for the fit person.

A Good Tour

Stirling is one of Britain's great historic towns. An impressive proportion of the old town walls remain and can be seen from Dumbarton Road, as soon as you step outside the tourist information center. On Corn Exchange Road there is a modern statue of Robert MacGregor (1671–1734), better known as Rob Roy, notorious cattle dealer and drover, part-time thief and outlaw, Jacobite (most of the time), and hero of Sir Walter Scott's namesake novel (1818). In 1995 Hollywood discovered this local folk legend with the film *Rob Roy,* starring actor Liam Neeson. Rob is practically inescapable if you visit Callander and the

The Central Highlands

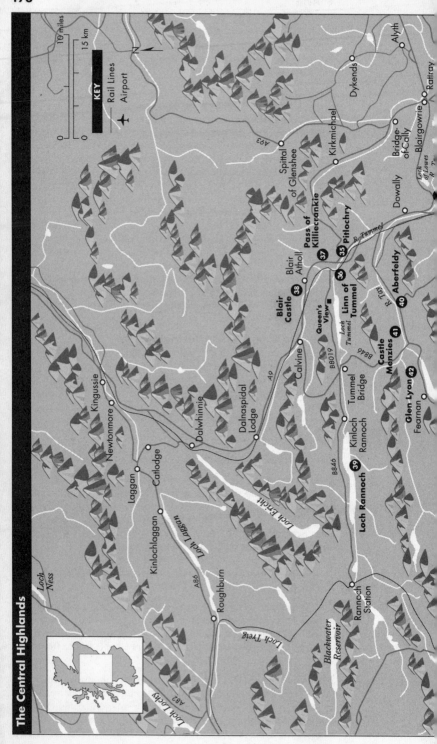

0 — 10 miles

0 — 15 km

Loch Ness

Kingussie

Newtonmore

Laggan

Catlodge

Kinlochlaggan

Roughburn

Dalwhinnie

Dalnaspidal Lodge

Loch Laggan

Loch Ericht

A86

A82

A9

Loch Lochy

Loch Treig

Blackwater Reservoir

Rannoch Station

Loch Rannoch **39**

Kinloch Rannoch

B846

B846

Tummel Bridge

B8019

Calvine

Blair Atholl

Blair Castle **38**

Pass of Killiecrankie **37**

Pitlochry **35**

36

Queen's View

Loch Tummel

Linn of Tummel

R. Tummel

R. Garry

Spital of Glenshee

A93

Kirkmichael

Dowally

Aberfeldy **40**

Castle Menzies **41**

Glen Lyon **42**

Fearnan

R. Tay

R. Lyon

Loch of Lowes

Bridge of Cally

Blairgowrie

Rattray

Dykends

Alyth

R. Tay

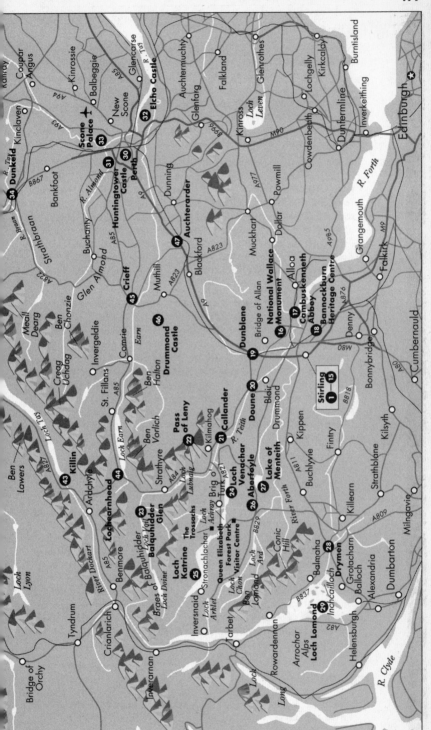

Trossachs, where he had his home. Along Dumbarton Road to the west is the **Smith Art Gallery and Museum** ①.

Near Rob Roy's statue, a gentle but relentless uphill path known as the **Back Walk** ② eventually leads to the town's most famous and worthwhile sight—Stirling Castle. On Academy Road is the Old High School, built in 1854 on the site of the former Greyfriars Monastery and now the Stirling Highland Hotel (☞ Dining and Lodging, *below*). Two fine examples of Scottish domestic architecture, now used for private housing, stand near the junction of Academy Road and Spittal Street, **Darrow House** ③ and **Spittal House.**

Another typical town house stands on St. John's Street, uphill from Darrow House and sometimes known as **Bothwell Ha** ④. The former military detention barracks behind Bothwell Ha is now known as the **Old Town Jail** ⑤, describing life in a 19th-century Scottish prison. Adjacent to the Old Town Jail is Erskine Marykirk, a neoclassical church built in 1824 that now houses a youth hostel (☞ Dining and Lodging, *below*). At the top of St. John's Street is the medieval **Church of the Holy Rude** ⑥. The nearby **Guildhall** ⑦ was built as almshouses in 1639. Within the **cemetery** ⑧, beyond the Church of the Holy Rude, are some unusual monuments.

You are almost at the castle, to which you have been making your way uphill since the start of the walk: at this point, you will appreciate **Stirling Castle's** ⑨ splendid strategic position. The **Royal Burgh of Stirling Visitor Centre** ⑩ stands beside to Stirling Castle Esplanade. After exploring the castle, walk downhill toward the heart of the old town of Stirling, recently the subject of a massive renovation program. Along Castle Wynd is a series of interesting buildings, the most important of which is **Argyll's Lodging** ⑪, now fully restored after a considerable period of neglect. The long and ornate facade of the distinctively Renaissance **Mar's Wark** ⑫ extends along the street frontage opposite Argyll's Lodging.

When you stand in front of Mar's Wark and look downhill, you gaze into the heart of the old town. One of its most notable structures is the **Tolbooth** ⑬ on Broad Street. The Mercat Cross, where proclamations were made, stands nearby, as does the **Cornerstone Gallery** ⑭ occupying Mar Place House, a Georgian town house saved from dereliction and painstakingly restored. Continue downhill to reach the more modern part of Stirling, with its variety of shopping, or walk a few minutes down from the castle (via Barn Road, Castlehill, and Lower Bridge Street) to see the medieval **Old Stirling Bridge** ⑮. Drive north-northeast down Causewayhead Road from the castle to get to the **National Wallace Monument** ⑯, commemorating Scotland's great freedom fighter. Due east of the castle and most easily reached from the monument are the ruins of **Cambuskenneth Abbey** ⑰, in an idyllic riverside setting. The historic battlesite of **Bannockburn Heritage Centre** ⑱—rather incongruously set in the middle of a housing development—is south of town, off Glasgow Road (A80).

TIMING

Stirling is a compact town, and this tour, though with many sights to admire, can be done at speed in a day, or in a more leisurely fashion during two days.

Sights to See

⑪ **Argyll's Lodging.** A nobleman's town house built in three phases from the 16th century onward, this building is actually older than the name it bears—that of Archibald, ninth earl of Argyll (1629–85), who bought it in 1666. It was for many years a military hospital, then a

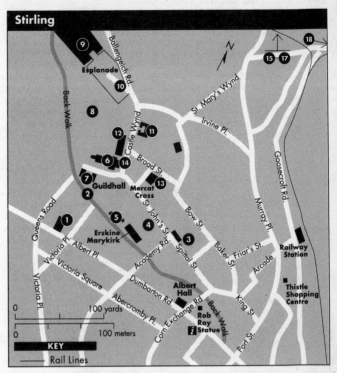

youth hostel. It has now been refurbished to show how the nobility lived in 17th-century Stirling. Specially commissioned reproduction furniture and fittings are based on the original inventory of the house's contents at that time. ⊠ *Castle Wynd,* ☎ *0131/668–8800.* ⊡ *£4.50, including admission to Stirling Castle.* ☉ *Apr.–Sept., daily 9:30–5:15; Oct.–Mar., daily 9:30–4:15.*

② Back Walk. The Back Walk will take you along the outside of the city's walls, past a watchtower and the grimly named Hangman's entry, carved out of the great whinstone boulders that once marked the outer defenses of the town. One of several access areas is off Dumbarton Road, opposite the tourist information center. ⊠ *Runs from Dumbarton Rd. to the Castle Rock.*

★ ⑱ Bannockburn Heritage Centre. In 1298, the year after William Wallace's victory, Robert the Bruce (1274–1329), materialized as the nation's champion, and the last bloody phase of the Wars of Independence began. Bruce's rise resulted from the uncertainties and timidity of the great lords of Scotland (ever unsure of which way to jump and whether to bow to England's demands). This tale is recounted at the Bannockburn Heritage Centre, hidden among the sprawl of housing and commercial developments on the southern edge of Stirling. This was the site of the famed Battle of Bannockburn in 1314. In Bruce's day, the Forth had a shelved and partly wooded floodplain. He chose the site cunningly, noting the boggy ground on the lower reaches in which the heavy horses of the English would founder. The atmosphere has been re-created within the center by means of an audiovisual presentation, models, and costumed figures, and an arresting mural depicting the battle in detail (look closely for some particularly unsavory goings-on). ⊠ *Off M80,* ☎ *01786/812664.* ⊡ *£2.40.* ☉ *Mar. and Nov.–Dec. 23, daily 11–3; Apr.–Oct., daily 10–5:30.*

④ Bothwell Ha. Said to have been owned by the earl of Bothwell, Mary, Queen of Scots' (1542–87) third husband, this hall ("ha" means "hall" in Scots) dates to the 16th century. ⊠ *St John's St. Closed to the public.*

⑰ Cambuskenneth Abbey. On the south side of the Abbey Craig, the scanty remains of 13th-century abbey lie in a sweeping bend of the River Forth, with the dramatic outline of Stirling Castle as a backdrop. Important meetings of the Scottish Parliament were once held here, and King Edward I (1239–1307) of England visited in 1304. The abbey was looted and damaged during the Scots Wars of Independence (1307–14). The reconstructed tomb of King James III (1452–88) can be seen near the outline of the high altar. ⊠ *Ladysneuk Rd.,* ☎ *0131/668–8800.* ⊠ *Free.* ☉ *Daily 9–6.*

⑧ Cemetery. The most notable among many unusual monuments in the cemetery near the Church of the Holy Rude are the **Star Pyramid** of 1858 and the macabre, glass-walled **Martyrs Monument,** erected in memory of two Wigtownshire girls who were drowned in 1685 for their Covenanting faith. The castle dominates the foreground and from **Ladies' Rock,** a high perch within the cemetery, there are excellent views of the looming fortress. ⊠ *Top of St. John St..*

⑥ Church of the Holy Rude. The nave of this handsome church survives from the 15th century, and a portion of the original medieval timber roof can also be seen. The church has the distinction of being the only church in Scotland still in use that witnessed the coronation of a Scottish monarch, James VI (1566–1625) in 1567. ⊠ *St. John St..*

⑭ Cornerstone Gallery. This complex, housed in the handsome Georgian Mar Place House, is in three parts: a gallery with changing exhibitions of Scottish contemporary work—sculpture, pottery, paintings—and displays of quality Scottish prints; a conservatory tearoom; and a shop with upscale Scottish gifts (☞ Shopping, *below*). ⊠ *Mar Pl.,* ☎ *01786/ 474444.* ⊠ *Free.* ☉ *Apr.–Oct., daily 10–6 (open later at height of summer season); Nov.–Mar., Mon.–Sat. 10–5, Sun. 11–5.*

③ Darrow House. Dating from the 17th century, this house displays the characteristic crowstep gables, dormer windows, and projecting turnpike stair of the period. ⊠ *Spittal St.*

⑦ Guildhall. Built as Cowane's Hospital in 1639 for *decayed breithers* (unsuccessful merchants), this building has above its entrance a small, cheery statue of the founder himself, John Cowane, that is said to come alive on Hogmanay Night (December 31) to walk the streets with the locals and join in their New Year's revelry. ⊠ *St. John's St. View from outside only.*

⑫ Mar's Wark. This distinctive windowless and roofless ruin is the stark remains of a Renaissance palace built in 1570 by Lord Erskine (d. 1572), earl of Mar, as well as Stirling Castle governor. Its name means Mar's work or building. Look for the armorial carved panels, the gargoyles, and the turrets flanking a railed-off *pend* (archway). Mar's Wark was sieged and severely damaged during the 1745 Jacobite rebellion, but its admirably worn shell survives. ⊠ *Castle Wynd,* ☎ *0131/668– 8800. View from outside only.*

⑯ National Wallace Monument. It was near Old Stirling Bridge that the Scottish freedom fighter William Wallace (1270–1305) and a ragged army of Scots won a major victory in 1297. The 1995 movie *Braveheart,* directed by and starring Mel Gibson, was based on Wallace's life, and attendance here has soared as a result of the film. A more accurate version is told in an exhibition and audiovisual presentation at this pencil-thin museum on the Abbey Craig. Up close, this Victorian shrine to William Wallace, built between 1856 and 1869, becomes less slim and soaring, revealing itself to be a substantial square tower with a creepy spiral stairway. To reach the monument, follow Bridge of Allan signs (A9) northward, crossing the River Forth by Robert Stephenson's (1772–1850) New Bridge of 1832, next to the historic old one. The National Wallace Monument is signposted at the next traffic circle. ⊠ *Abbey Craig,* ☎ *01786/472140.* ☞ *£3.* ⊙ *Mar.–May and Oct., daily 10–5; June and Sept., daily 10–6; July–Aug., daily 9:30–6:30; Feb. and Nov., weekends 10–4.*

⑮ Old Stirling Bridge. North of Stirling Castle, on the edge of town, this 15th-century bridge is now only for pedestrian use. ⊠ *Off Drip Rd. (A84).*

❺ Old Town Jail. The original town jail, now restored, tells the story of life in a 19th-century Scottish prison. Furnished cells, models, exhibitions, and staff—appropriately dressed as prisoners, wardens, and prison reformers—bring the past vividly to life. ⊠ *St. John's St..* ☎ *01786/450050.* ☞ *£2.75.* ⊙ *Apr.–Sept., daily 9:30–5:30; Oct.–Mar., daily 9:30–4.*

⑩ Royal Burgh of Stirling Visitor Centre. Standing at the foot of the Castle Esplanade, this visitor center houses a shop and exhibition hall with an audiovisual production on the town and surrounding area. ⊠ ☎ *01786/462517.* ☞ *Free.* ⊙ *Apr.–June and Sept.–Oct., daily 9:30–6; July–Aug., daily 9–6:30; Nov.–Mar., daily 9:30–5.*

❶ Smith Art Gallery and Museum. Founded in 1874 with the bequest of a local collector, this is a good example of a community art gallery that offers a varied exhibit program of paintings and sculpture. ⊠ *Albert Pl., Dumbarton Rd.,* ☎ *01786/471917.* ☞ *Free.* ⊙ *Tues.–Sat. 10:30–5, Sun. 2–5.*

★ **❾ Stirling Castle.** Its magnificent strategic position made Stirling Castle the grandest prize in the Scots Wars of Independence in the late 13th and early 14th centuries. The Battle of Bannockburn in 1314 was fought within sight of its walls, and the victory by Robert the Bruce yielded both the castle and freedom from English subjugation for almost four centuries.

King Robert's daughter, Marjory, married Walter, the High Steward of Scotland. Their descendants included the Stewart dynasty of Scottish monarchs (Mary, Queen of Scots, was a Stewart, though she preferred the French spelling, *Stuart*). The Stewarts were mainly responsible for many of the works that survive within the castle walls today. They made Stirling Castle their court and power base, creating fine Renaissance-style buildings that were not completely obliterated, despite subsequent reconstruction for military purposes.

The castle is entered through its outer defenses, which consist of a great curtain wall and batteries that date from 1708, built to bulwark earlier defenses by the main gatehouse. From this lower square the most conspicuous feature is the **palace,** built by King James V (1512–42) between 1538 and 1542. This edifice shows the influence of French masons in the decorative figures festooning the ornately worked outer walls. Overlooking the upper courtyard is the **Great Hall,** built by King James IV (1473–1513) in 1503. Before the Union of Parliaments in 1707, when the Scottish aristocracy sold out to England, this building had been used as one of the seats of the Scottish Parliament. After 1707 it sank into decline, becoming a riding school, then a barracks. Today, a slow restoration is underway.

Among the later works built for regiments stationed here, the **King's Old Building** stands out; it is a 19th-century baronial revival on the site of an earlier building. The oldest building on the site is the **Mint**, or **Coonzie Hoose**, perhaps dating from as far back as the 14th century. Below is an arched passageway leading to the westernmost section of the ramparts, the **Nether Bailey.** You'll have the distinct feeling here that you are in the bow of a warship sailing up the *carselands* (valley-plain) of the Forth Valley, which fans out before the great superstructure of the castle. Among the gun platforms and the crenellations of the ramparts, this is the place to ponder the strategic significance of Stirling. To the south lies the hump of the Touch and the Gargunnock Hills (part of the Campsie Fells), diverting would-be direct routes from Glasgow and the south. For centuries all roads into the Highlands across the narrow waist of Scotland led to Stirling. If you look carefully northward, you can still see the Old Stirling Bridge (☞ *above*), once the lowest and most convenient place to cross the river. For all these geographic reasons, the castle here was perhaps the single most important fortress in Scotland. ✉ *Castlehill*, ☎ *0131/668–8800.* 🖭 *£4.50, including admission to Argyll's Lodging.* ⏱ *Apr.–Sept., daily 9:30–5:15; Oct.–Mar., daily 9:30–4:15.*

⓭ **Tolbooth.** Built in 1705, the Tolbooth has a traditional Scottish steeple and gilded weathercock. For centuries the Burgh Court handed down sentences here. ✉ *Broad St.*

Dining and Lodging

££   ✕ **Heritage.** This elegant 18th-century establishment is run by a French family. The decor is all fanlights and candles; the menu features French classics such as *filet au poivre* (pepper beef steak) and *magret de canard* (duck breast). ✉ *16 Allan Park*, ☎ *01786/473660. MC, V.*

£–££   ✕ **Cross Keys Hotel.** A stone-walled dining room adds atmosphere to this restaurant's varied, traditionally Scottish menu. ✉ *Main St., Kippen (A811, west of Stirling)*, ☎ 𝖥𝖠𝖷 *01786/870293. MC, V.*

£££–££££   ✕🖼 **Stirling Highland Hotel.** The attractive building this hotel occupies was once the Old High School, and many original architectural features have been retained. Furnishings are old-fashioned, with solid wood, tartan, florals, and low-key, neutral color schemes. The hotel has two restaurants: the Italian Rizzio's and the traditional Scottish Scholars, with especially outstanding seafood. ✉ *Spittal St., FK8 1DU*, ☎ *01786/475444*, 𝖥𝖠𝖷 *01786/462929. 78 rooms with bath, 2 suites. 2 restaurants, piano bar. AE, DC, MC, V.*

££   🖼 **Terraces Hotel.** This central hotel with plenty of parking is a good base for exploring Stirling and the region. A comfortable Georgian town house, it is comparatively small, with friendly and attentive service. ✉ *4 Melville Terr., FK8 2ND*, ☎ *01786/472268*, 𝖥𝖠𝖷 *01786/450314. 17 rooms with bath or shower. Restaurant. AE, DC, MC, V.*

£–££   🖼 **Castlecroft.** Tucked beneath Stirling Castle, with fine views over the
★   plain of the River Forth toward the Highland hills, this warm and comfortable modern house has a particularly helpful host who is full of local information. ✉ *Ballengeich Rd., Stirling, FK8 1TN*, ☎ *01786/474933.* 𝖥𝖠𝖷 *01786/466716. 6 rooms with shower. MC, V.*

£–££   🖼 **West Plean.** This handsome house is part of a working farm, with a walled garden and woodland walks. Well-cooked food and spacious rooms make this bed-and-breakfast an excellent bargain. ✉ *Denny Rd., FK7 8HA*, ☎ 𝖥𝖠𝖷 *01786/812208. 3 rooms with bath or shower. No credit cards.*

£   🖼 **Lochend Farm.** Extensive views, wholesome farm cooking, and a pleasantly relaxing pace are the hallmarks of this peaceful working farm. Only 5 mi from the M9/M80, southwest of Stirling, it also makes a good touring base. The traditionally furnished (and very comfortable) bedrooms have washbasins and share a bathroom. ✉ *Carronbridge, Denny, Stirlingshire, FK6 5JJ,* ☎ *01324/822778. 2 rooms without bath. No credit cards.*

£ 🛏 **Stirling Youth Hostel.** Built within the shell of a former church, the hostel offers high-grade four- and six-bed rooms (and a few doubles) with en suite bath facilities. Use of the television room, the dining room, and the self-catering, fully equipped kitchen is included in the bargain price of £11.50 (£12.50 in July and August) per person, including breakfast. ✉ *Erskine Marykirk, St. John's St., FK8 1DU,* ☎ *01786/473442,* 📠 *01786/445715. 128 beds. MC, V.*

Nightlife and the Arts

The **Macrobert Arts Centre** (✉ Stirling University, ☎ 01786/461081) has a theater, art gallery, and studio with programs that range from films to pantomime.

Shopping

Books

In the Old Town, **McCutcheons** (✉ 30 Spittal St., ☎ 01786/461771) will keep lovers of antiquarian books happy for an hour or two with its huge range of titles, including books on every aspect of Scotland.

Ceramics

South of Stirling, at Larbert, don't miss **Barbara Davidson's pottery studio** (✉ Muirhall Farm, Larbert, ☎ 01324/554430, 🕐 Mon.–Sat. 10–5, Sun. noon–5), run by one of the best-known potters in Scotland, in an 18th-century farm setting. In July and August you can even try throwing your own pot for a small fee.

Knitwear

East of Stirling is **Mill Trail** country, along the foot of the Ochil Hills. A leaflet from a tourist information center will lead you to the delights of a real mill shop and low mill prices—even on cashmere—at Tillicoultry, Alva, and Alloa.

Scottish Specialties

The **Cornerstone Gallery** (✉ Mar Pl., ☎ 01786/474444) includes a shop with traditional but exceptionally high-quality Scottish and other British gifts, including tartan items, heraldic crests, and collectors' chess sets. **R. R. Henderson Ltd.** (✉ 6–8 Friars St., ☎ 01786/473681) is a "Highland outfitters," selling tartans, woolens, and accessories and offering a made-to-measure kilt service.

THE TROSSACHS AND LOCH LOMOND

Inspired by the views of mountainous terrain seen from the ramparts of Stirling Castle, you can use this route to explore areas west and north to the Highland line. Distances are not great if you go by car. If you travel the classic Trossachs loop, you will share the route with plenty of day-trippers from the central belt.

Dunblane

★ ⑲ *7 mi north of Stirling.*

The oldest part of Dunblane—with its twisting streets and mellow town houses—huddles around the square and churchyard where the partly restored ruins of **Dunblane Cathedral** stand. King David built the existing structure in the 13th century on the site of St. Blane's tiny 8th-century cell. It is contemporary with the Border abbeys (☞ Chapter 5), but more mixed in its architecture—part early English and part Norman. Dunblane ceased to be a cathedral, as did most others in Scotland, at the time of the Reformation in the mid-16th century. ☎ 0131/668–8800. ☞ *Free.* ☉ *Apr.–Sept., daily 9:30–6; Oct.–Mar., Mon.– Sat. 9:30–4, Sun. 2–4; and for services.*

Dining and Lodging

££££ ✕🏨 **Cromlix House Hotel.** This Victorian hunting lodge's period atmosphere is enhanced by cherished furniture and paintings, the original conservatory, and the library. The restaurant offers country-house decor and a choice of two elegant dining rooms. Specialties include game and lamb from the hotel estate. Try the delicious cheese and potato terrine as a starter, followed by beef with pickled walnuts. ⊠ *Kinbuck, on B8033, 3 mi northeast of Dunblane, 10 mi northeast of Stirling, FK15 9JT,* ☎ *01786/822125,* 🖷 *01786/825450. 6 rooms with bath, 8 suites. Restaurant, tennis court, fishing, library. AE, DC, MC, V. Closed Jan.*

Doune

★ ⑳ *5 mi west of Dunblane via A820.*

The Highland-edge community of Doune was once a center for pistol making. No self-respecting Highland chief's attire was complete without a prestigious and ornate pair of pistols. Today, Doune is more widely known as the site of one of the best-preserved medieval castles in Scotland. **Doune Castle** looks like an early castle is supposed to look: grim and high walled, with echoing stone vaults and numerous drafts. Construction of the fortress began in the early 15th century on a now-peaceful riparian tract. The best place to photograph this squat, great-walled fort is from the bridge, a little way upstream, which carries the A84 west. The castle is signposted left as you enter the town from the Dunblane road. ⊠ *Off A84,* ☎ *0131/668–8800.* ☞ *£2.30.* ☉ *Apr.–Sept., daily 9:30–6; Oct.–Mar., Mon.–Wed. and Sat. 9:30–4, Thurs. 9:30– noon, Sun. 2–4.*

Callander

㉑ *8 mi northwest of Doune via A84.*

A traditional Highland-edge resort, Callander bustles throughout the year—even on Sunday during off-peak times—simply because it is a gateway to Highland scenery within easy reach of Edinburgh and Glasgow. As a result, there is plenty of window-shopping here, plus nightlife in pubs and a good choice of accommodations.

Callander's **Rob Roy and Trossachs Visitor Centre,** housed in the former St. Kessog's Church, provides another encounter with the famed Rob Roy MacGregor. As defender of the downtrodden and scourge of the authorities, MacGregor is known as a tartan Robin Hood. A much revered Highland hero, he died peacefully at his home in 1734. You can learn more about his high jinks in a high-tech account—replete with displays and tableaux—in the modern visitor center. ⊠ *Ancaster Sq.,* ☎ *01877/330342.* ☞ *£2.50.* ☉ *Jan.–Feb., weekends 10–4; Mar.–May and Oct.–Dec., daily 10–5; June and Sept., daily 9:30–6; July–Aug., daily 9–7.*

A walk is signposted from the east end of the main street to the **Bracklinn Falls,** over whose lip Sir Walter Scott once rode a pony to win a bet. Another walk goes through the woods up to the **Callander Crags,** with views of the Lowlands as far as the Pentland Hills behind Edinburgh. (This walk is for the fit and well-shod only.)

Callander is the gateway to the Trossachs, but since it is on the main road, the A84, it also attracts overnight visitors on their way to Oban, Fort William, and beyond. All this traffic enters the proper Highlands just north of Callander, where the thickly clad slopes squeeze both the road and rocky river into the narrow **Pass of Leny.** An abandoned railway—now a pleasant walking or bicycling path—also goes through the pass, past **Ben Ledi mountain** and **Loch Lubnaig.**

Through the Pass of Leny and beyond Strathyre, with its extensive forestry-commission plantings, within a 20-minute drive of Callander, is **Balquhidder Glen** (pronounced *bal*-whidd-*er*), a typical Highland glen that runs westward. Note its characteristics, seen throughout the north: a flat-bottomed, U-shape profile formed by prehistoric glaciers; extensive forestry plantings replacing much of the natural woodlands above; a sprinkling of farms; and farther up the glen, new hill roads bulldozed into the slopes to provide access for shepherds and foresters. Note also the boarded-up look of some of the houses, many of which are second homes for affluent residents of the south. The glen is also where **Loch Voil** and **Loch Doune** spread out, adding to the stunning vistas. This area is often known as the Braes (Slopes) of Balquhidder and was once the home of the MacLarens and the MacGregors. Rob Roy MacGregor's grave is signposted beside Balquhidder village itself. The site of his house, now a private farm, is beyond the parking lot at the end of the road up the glen.

The glen has no through road, although in earlier times local residents were familiar with hill passes to the north and south. There still exists, for example, a right-of-way from the churchyard where Rob Roy is buried, through the plantings in Kirkton Glen and then on to open windy grasslands and a blue *lochan* (little lake). This path eventually drops into the next valley, Glen Dochart, and rejoins the A84.

Dining and Lodging

£   ✕ **Pip's Coffee House.** Just off the main street, this cheerful little place offers light meals, soups, and salads, as well as Scottish home baking, and more substantial three-course meals in the evenings (April–October). There is also a small picture gallery with plenty of Scottish material to browse through. ✉ *Ancaster Sq.,* ☎ *01877/330470.* ⏰ *10–5 (extended hours Apr.–Oct.). MC, V. Closed Wed. Oct.–Mar.*

£££–££££   ✕▣ **Roman Camp.** This former hunting lodge, dating from 1625, has ★   20 acres of gardens with river frontage, yet is within easy walking distance of Callander's town center. Private fishing on the River Teith is another plus, as are the sitting rooms and the library, which, with their numerous antiques, are more reminiscent of a stately family home than a hotel. The restaurant has high standards, with a good reputation for its salmon, trout, and other seafood, cooked in an imaginative, modern Scottish style. ✉ *Callander, Perthshire, FK17 8BG,* ☎ *01877/ 330003,* ☒ *01877/331533. 14 rooms with bath or shower. Restaurant, library. AE, DC, MC, V.*

Outdoor Activities and Sports

BIKING

You can rent bicycles from **Wheels/Trossachs Backpackers** (✉ Invertrossachs Rd., Callander, Perthshire, FK17 8HW, ☎ 01877/331100); this friendly firm can also help with route planning and offers hostel accommodation, organized walks, and canoe trips.

GOLF

The golf course at **Callander** (✉ Aveland Rd., ☎ 01877/330090) was designed by Tom Morris and has a scenic, upland feel, with fine views and a tricky moorland layout. The course is 18 holes, 5,125 yards, par 66.

Shopping

A vast selection of woolens is on display at three mill shops in and near Callander. All the stores, which are part of the Edinburgh Woollen Mill Group, offer overseas mailing and tax-free shopping: **Kilmahog Woollen Mill** (☎ 01877/330268), **Trossachs Woollen Mill** (✉ North of town at Trossachs turning, ☎ 01877/330178), and **Callander Woollen Mill** (✉ Main St., ☎ 01877/330273).

Uniquely Scottish is the stoneware of **Mounter Pottery** (✉ Ancaster Sq. La., ☎ 01877/331052), which you can see being made.

The Trossachs

10 mi west of Callander via A84 and A821 (to the Trossachs parking lot at Loch Katrine, taken to be the center of the Trossachs).

With their harmonious scenery of hill, loch, and wooded slopes, the Trossachs have been a tourist mecca since the late 18th century, at the dawn of the age of the Romantic poets. Influenced by the writings of Sir Walter Scott, early visitors who strayed into the Highlands from the central belt of Scotland admired this as the first "wild" part of Scotland they encountered. The Trossachs represent the very essence of what the Highlands are supposed to be: birchwood and pine forests; vistas down lochs where the woods creep right to the water's edge; and in the background, peaks that rise high enough to be called mountains, though they're not as high as those to the north and west. The Trossachs are almost, but not quite, a Scottish visual cliché. They're popular right through the year, drawing not only first-time visitors from all around the world, but also Edinburghers and Glaswegians out for a Sunday drive.

㉔ The A821 runs west along with the first and gentlest of the Trossachs lochs, **Loch Venachar.** The sturdy gray stone buildings, with a small dam at the Callander end, control the water that feeds into the River Teith (and, hence, into the Forth) to compensate for the Victorian tinkerings with the water supply. Within a few minutes the road becomes muffled in woodlands, and twists gradually down to **Brig o' Turk.** (*Turk* is Gaelic for the Scots *tuirc,* meaning wild boar, a species that has been extinct in this region since about the 16th century.)

West of Brig o' Turk stretches **Loch Achray,** dutifully fulfilling expectations of what a verdant Trossachs loch should be: small, green, reedy meadows backed by dark plantations, rhododendron thickets, and lumpy, thickly covered hills. The parking lot by Loch Achray is where you begin the ascent of steep, heathery **Ben An.** To enjoy the best Trossachs' views, you will need a couple of hours and good lungs.

★ ㉕ At the end of Loch Achray, a side road turns right into a narrow pass, leading to **Loch Katrine,** the heart of the Trossachs. During the time of Sir Walter Scott, the road here was narrow and almost hidden by the overhanging crags and mossy oaks and birches. Today it ends at a slightly anticlimactic parking lot with a shop, café, and visitor center. To see the finest of the Trossachs lochs properly, you must—even for just a few minutes—go westward on foot. The road beyond the parking lot (open only to Strathclyde Water Board vehicles) is well-paved and level. Loch Katrine's water is taken by aqueduct and tunnel to Glasgow—a Victorian feat of engineering that has ensured the purity of the supply to Scotland's largest city for more than a hundred years. Not readily visible from the parking lot, the steamer SS *Sir Walter Scott* embarks on cruises of Loch Katrine every summer. Take the cruise if time permits, as the shores of Katrine remain undeveloped and impressive. This loch is the setting of Scott's narrative poem, *Lady of the Lake,*

BONUS MILES MAKE GREAT SOUVENIRS.

Earn Miles With Your MCI Card.

Take the MCI Card along on this trip and start earning miles for the next one. You'll earn frequent flyer miles on all your calls and save with the low rates you've come to expect from MCI. Before you know it, you'll be on your way to some other international destination.

Sign up for MCI by calling 1-800-FLY-FREE

Earn Frequent Flyer Miles.

Is this a great time, or what? :-)

Easy To Call Home.

1. To use your MCI Card, just dial the WorldPhone access number of the country you're calling from.
2. Dial or give the operator your MCI Card number.
3. Dial or give the number you're calling.

# Austria (CC) ♦	022-903-012
# Belarus (CC)	
From Brest, Vitebsk, Grodno, Minsk	8-800-103
From Gomel and Mogilev regions	8-10-800-103
# Belgium (CC) ♦	0800-10012
# Bulgaria	00800-0001
# Croatia (CC) ★	0800-22-0112
# Czech Republic (CC) ♦	00-42-000112
# Denmark (CC) ♦	8001-0022
# Finland (CC) ♦	08001-102-80
# France (CC) ♦	0-800-99-0019
# Germany (CC)	0800-888-8000
# Greece (CC) ♦	00-800-1211
# Hungary (CC) ♦	00▼800-01411
# Iceland (CC) ♦	800-9002
# Ireland (CC)	1-800-55-1001
# Italy (CC) ♦	172-1022
# Kazakhstan (CC)	8-800-131-4321
# Liechtenstein (CC) ♦	0800-89-0222
# Luxembourg	0800-0112
# Monaco (CC) ♦	800-90-019
# Netherlands (CC) ♦	0800-022-9122
# Norway (CC) ♦	800-19912
# Poland (CC) ÷	00-800-111-21-22
# Portugal (CC) ÷	05-017-1234
Romania (CC) ÷	01-800-1800
# Russia (CC) ÷ ♦	
To call using ROSTELCOM ■	747-3322
For a Russian-speaking operator	747-3320
To call using SOVINTEL ■	960-2222
# San Marino (CC) ♦	172-1022
# Slovak Republic (CC)	00-421-00112
# Slovenia	080-8808
# Spain (CC)	900-99-0014
# Sweden (CC) ♦	020-795-922
# Switzerland (CC) ♦	0800-89-0222
# Turkey (CC) ♦	00-8001-1177
# Ukraine (CC) ÷	8▼10-013
# United Kingdom (CC)	
To call using BT ■	0800-89-0222
To call using C&W ■	0500-89-0222
# Vatican City (CC)	172-1022

Flying to France on Friday? Get Francs from Chase on Thursday. Call Currency To Go at 935-9935 for overnight delivery.

r pounds for London. Or Deutschmarks for Düsseldorf. Or any of 75 foreign currencies. Call **Chase Currency To Go**[SM] **at 935-9935** in area codes 212, 718, 914, 516 and Rochester, N.Y.; all other area codes call 1-800-935-9935. We'll deliver directly to your door.* Overnight. And there are no exchange fees. Let Chase make your trip an easier one.

CHASE. The right relationship is everything.[SM]

CLOSE-UP: HOLLYWOOD COMES IN FOR THE KILT

THE RECENT SUCCESS OF movies such as *Rob Roy* and *Braveheart* has virtually created a new genre—the so-called kilt movie. In 1996, Scotland became hot, its scenery a greater than ever attraction to Hollywood. So what if big chunks of *Braveheart* were actually filmed in Ireland?

Not that there is anything new about Scotland as a dramatic backdrop. In 1922, a silent film described at the time as "the first Scottish epic" featured Rob Roy and a cast of two thousand. It was shot partly around Loch Lomond, onetime homeland of the real-life Rob Roy MacGregor (1671–1734). As defender of the downtrodden and scourge of the authorities, MacGregor is known as a tartan Robin Hood. In 1953 Rob Roy's adventures again made it to the screen, in Walt Disney's *The Sword and the Rose,* starring Richard Todd.

The 1995 *Rob Roy,* starring Liam Neeson, was shot at and around Glen Nevis and Glencoe, both near Fort William; the gardens of Drummond Castle near Crieff; and Crichton Castle near Edinburgh. Another 1995 release, and winner of the Academy Award for that year's Best Picture, Mel Gibson's huge blockbuster, *Braveheart,* is the story of Scotland's first freedom-fighter, Sir William Wallace (circa. 1270–1305). It also uses the spectacular craggy scenery of Glen Nevis

The Prime of Miss Jean Brodie (1969), based on the Muriel Spark novel, starred Dame Maggie Smith in the title role. She won an Academy Award for Best Actress for her performance as an eccentric teacher who reigns over an Edinburgh girls' school. (Pauline Kael praised her for being "very funny—snobbish, full of affectations, and with a jumble shop of a mind.")

Filmed in Edinburgh (as well as in London), it is a Scottish classic. Even Greyfriars Bobby—the Skye terrier who watched over his master's grave at Greyfriars for 14 years, beginning in 1858, and who was made a citizen of Edinburgh—had his moment on the silver screen, in the eponymous 1961 Walt Disney film.

Mel Gibson's *Hamlet* (1990) was filmed at Dunnottar Castle at Stonehaven in the east. Looking further back, *Highlander* (1986) with Christopher Lambert and Sean Connery, also used the spectacular crags of Glencoe, along with the prototypical Scottish castle, Eilean Donan—almost a visual cliché in Scottish terms. Starring Peter Riegert and Burt Lancaster, *Local Hero* (1983) put together the best of east and west coast Scotland. The village of Pennan, an hour north of Aberdeen, huddles below spectacular cliffs and became Ferness, the village threatened by oil developments. The village phone box, which plays an important part in the film, has been carefully preserved. (And, yes, you can see the Aurora Borealis—the Northern Lights—from it, sometimes.) In fact, the phone box has become something of a local landmark.

Trainspotting (1996), based on the namesake novel by Irvine Welsh, is about heroin addicts in an economically depressed Edinburgh. Although it was produced in Britain, it found a large North American audience. *Small Faces* (1995), written and directed by Gillies MacKinnon, tells the harrowing story of gangland violence in Glasgow in 1968. And with the story of Robert the Bruce about to be released and a Macbeth in the making, it looks like Scotland will remain fertile ground for moviemakers for some time to come.

—Gilbert Summers

and Ellen's Isle is named after his heroine. ⊠ *Trossachs Pier,* ☎ *01877/ 376316.* 🎫 *£4.95.* ⊙ *Cruises Apr.–late Oct., daily at 11, 1:45, and 3:15.*

Dining and Lodging

££ ✕ **Byre Restaurant.** Adjoining Dundarroch Country House (☞ *below*), this is a well-run pub and restaurant just beyond Brig o' Turk, with dark beams and loosely defined Victorian decor, as well as attentive, friendly service. It's a lunchtime haven, particularly on a wet day in the woodlands, but also offers a full evening menu. Savory Scottish offerings include roasted venison. Call ahead in winter, when hours are limited. ⊠ *Brig o' Turk,* ☎ *01877/376292. MC, V.*

££ 🏨 **Dundarroch Country House.** This Victorian country house, set on 14 acres, offers first-class accommodations furnished with antiques, paintings, and tapestries in a warm, relaxing atmosphere. The mountain views from the guest rooms are stunning. ⊠ *Brig o' Turk, Trossachs, Perthshire, FK17 8HT,* ☎ *01877/376200,* 📠 *01877/376202. 3 rooms with bath or shower. MC, V. Closed Nov.–Mar.*

Outdoor Activities and Sports

The **Highland Boundary Fault Walk** (⊠ Forestry Commission, Aberfoyle, Stirlingshire, FK8 3UX, ☎ 01877/382383) runs along the Highland boundary fault edge, offering superb views of both the Highlands and Lowlands, 6 mi south of the Trossachs on A821.

En Route   After going back through the pass to the main A821, turn right and head south to higher moorland blanketed with conifer plantations (some of which have near-mature timber planted about 60 years ago by the Forestry Commission). The conifers hem in the views of Ben Ledi and Ben Venue, which can be seen over the spiky green waves of trees as the road snakes around heathery knolls and hummocks. There is another viewpoint at the highest point here, indicated by a small parking lot on the right. Soon the road swoops off the Highland edge and leads downhill. Near the start of the descent, the **Queen Elizabeth Forest Park Visitor Centre** can be seen on the left. The center features displays on the life of the forest, a summer-only café, some fine views over the Lowlands to the south, and a network of footpaths. The Trossachs end here.

Aberfoyle

㉖ *11 mi south of Loch Katrine.*

You are unlikely to want to linger in the small resort town of Aberfoyle, with its range of souvenir shops, unless you have children with
Ⓒ you. The **Scottish Wool Centre** tells the story of Scottish wool "from the sheep's back to your back." The Sheep Amphitheatre has live specimens of the main breeds, and in the Textile Display Area, you can try spinning and weaving. There is also a Kids' Farm (with lambs and kids) and Sheepdog Training School (weekends in summer only). The shop stocks a huge selection of woolen garments and knitwear. Live sheep shows (four each day) are held in summer. ⊠ *Off Main St., Aberfoyle, Stirlingshire,* ☎ *01877/382850.* 🎫 *£2.50.* ⊙ *Apr.–Sept., daily 9:30– 6; Oct.–Mar., daily 10–5.*

㉗ A short distance to the east of Aberfoyle is the **Lake of Menteith.** The tiny island of **Inchmahome** on the loch was a place of refuge for the young Mary, Queen of Scots, in 1547.

From Aberfoyle, you can take a trip to see the more enclosed northern portion of **Loch Lomond** (☞ Loch Lomond, *below*). During the off-season, the route has an untamed and windswept air when it extends beyond the shelter of trees. Take the B829 (signposted Inversnaid and

Stronachlachar), which runs west from Aberfoyle and offers outstanding views of **Ben Lomond,** especially in the vicinity of **Loch Ard.** The next loch, where the road narrows and bends, is **Loch Chon,** dark and forbidding. Its ominous reputation is further enhanced by the local legend: the presence of a dog-headed monster prone to swallowing passersby. Beyond Loch Chon, the road climbs gently from the plantings to open moor with a breathtaking vista over **Loch Arklet** to the **Arrochar Alps,** the name given to the high hills west of Loch Lomond. Hidden from sight in a deep trench, Loch Arklet is dammed to feed Loch Katrine. Go left at the road junction (a right will take you to Stronachlachar) and take the open road along Loch Arklet. These deserted green hills were once the rallying grounds of the Clan Gregor. Near the dam on Loch Arklet, on your right, **Garrison Cottage** recalls the days when the government had to billet troops here to keep the MacGregors in order. From Loch Arklet, the road zigzags down to **Inversnaid,** where you will see a hotel, house, and parking lot, with Loch Lomond stretching out of sight above and below. The only return to Aberfoyle is by retracing the same route.

Outdoor Activities and Sports

BIKING

Rent bicycles from **Trossachs Cycle Hire** (✉ Trossachs Holiday Park, ☎ 01877/382614).

WALKING

The long-distance walkers' route, the **West Highland Way,** which runs 95 mi from Glasgow to Fort William, follows the bank of Loch Lomond at Inversnaid. Take a brief stroll up the path, particularly if you are visiting during the spring, when the oak tree canopy is filled with birdsong. You may get an inkling why Scots get so romantic about their bonnie, bonnie banks.

Drymen

28 *11 mi southwest of Aberfoyle via A81 and A811.*

Drymen is a respectable and cozy town in the Lowland fields, with shops, tea shops, and pubs catering to the well-to-do Scots who have moved here from Glasgow.

For the most outstanding Loch Lomond view from the south end, drive west from Drymen and take just a few minutes to clamber up bracken-covered **Duncryne Hill.** If here at sunset, you may be rewarded by a spectacular sight. You can't miss this unmistakable dumpling-shaped hill, south of Gartocharn on the Drymen–Balloch road, the A811.

Shopping

The Rowan Gallery (✉ 36 Main St., ☎ FAX 01360/660996) shows original paintings and prints, specializing in Scottish scenes, but also has a fine selection of Scottish crafts, cards, books, and jewelry.

Loch Lomond

29 *3 mi west of Drymen via B837 signposted Rowardennan and Balmaha, 14 mi west of Aberfoyle.*

At the little settlement of **Balmaha,** the versatile recreational role filled by Loch Lomond is clear: cruising craft are at the ready, hikers appear out of woodlands on the West Highland Way, and day-trippers stroll at the loch's edge. The heavily wooded offshore islands look alluringly close. One of the best ways to explore them is to take a cruise or rent a boat (☞ *below*). The island of **Inchcailloch** (*inch* is *innis,* Gaelic for island), just offshore, can be explored in an hour or two. Pleasant pathways thread through oak woods planted in the 18th century, when the bark was used by the tanning industry.

Behind Balmaha is **Conic Hill,** a wavy ridge of bald heathery domes above the pine trees. You can note from your map how Inchcailloch and the other islands line up with it. This geographic line is indicative of the Highland Boundary Fault, which runs through Loch Lomond and the hill.

If you want to take in even more of Loch Lomond, a road that ends in a cul-de-sac continues northwest to **Rowardennan,** with the loch seldom more than a narrow field's length away. Where the drivable road ends, in a parking lot crunchy with pinecones, you can ramble along one of the marked lochside footpaths, or make your way toward not-so-nearby Ben Lomond.

Dining and Lodging

££££ ✕🏨 **Cameron House.** This luxury hotel offers a mix of top-quality hotel
 ★   and country-club facilities on the shores of Loch Lomond. Bedrooms are decorated in modern pastel shades with high-quality reproductions of antique furniture. The outstanding restaurant serves Scottish-French cuisine of the highest order, in rich Victorian surroundings. There's also an American-theme diner called Breakers. ⊠ *Loch Lomond, Alexandria, Dumbartonshire, G83 8QZ,* ☎ *01389/755565,* FAX *01389/759522. 96 rooms with bath. 2 restaurants, bar, 2 pools, golf privileges, health club, squash, fishing. AE, DC, MC, V.*

Outdoor Activities and Sports

MacFarlane and Son (⊠ Boatyard, Balmaha, Loch Lomond, ☎ 01360/870214) runs cruises on Loch Lomond. They also operate a mail boat (🕐 July–Aug., Mon.–Sat. 11.30; Apr.–June and Sept.–Oct., Mon., Thurs., and Sat. 11.30; Nov.–Mar., Tues. and Thurs. 10:50) to the islands, which takes passengers. You can even rent a rowboat from Mac-Farlane's if you prefer to do your own exploration. From Tarbet on the western shore, **Cruise Loch Lomond** (⊠ Boatyard, Tarbet, ☎ 01301/702356) runs tours all year. From Balloch there are the *Lomond Duchess* and *Lomond Maid* (⊠ Balloch Marina, Riverside, ☎ 01389/751481).

Shopping

Thistle Bagpipe Works (⊠ Luss, Dunbartonshire G83 8NX, ☎ FAX 01436/860250), on the western shore of Loch Lomond, will let you commission your own made-to-order set of bagpipes. You can also order a complete Highland outfit: kilt, jacket, and so forth.

PERTHSHIRE

Although Perth has an ancient history, it has been rebuilt and recast innumerable times, and sadly, no trace remains of the pre-Reformation monasteries that once dominated the skyline. In fact, modern Perth has swept much of its colorful history under a grid of bustling shopping streets. The town serves a wide rural hinterland and has a well-off air, making it one of the most interesting shopping towns, aside from Edinburgh and Glasgow.

Perth's rural hinterland is grand in several senses. On the Highland edge, prosperous-looking farms are scattered across heavily wooded countryside, and even larger properties are screened by trees and parkland. All this changes as the mountain barrier is penetrated, giving rise to grouse moors and deer forest (where forest is used in the Scots sense of, paradoxically, open hill). Parts of Perthshire are quite remote without ever losing their cozy feel.

Perth

🔟 *36 mi northeast of Stirling, 43 mi north of Edinburgh, 61 mi northeast of Glasgow.*

Some say Perth took its name from a Roman camp, Bertha, on the shores of the Tay. Whatever the truth, this strategic site has been occupied continuously for centuries, even before its becoming a Royal Burgh in 1210. Perth has long been a focal point in Scottish history, and several critical events took place here, including the assassination of King James I of Scotland (1394–1437) and John Knox's (1513–72) preaching in St. John's Kirk in 1559. (Knox's sermon undoubtedly stirred his congregation; afterward, they went rampaging through the town, igniting the Reformation in Scotland.) Later, the 17th-century religious wars in Scotland saw the town occupied, first by the marquis of Montrose (1612–50), then later by Oliver Cromwell's (1599–1658) forces. Perth was also occupied by the Jacobites in the 1715 and 1745 rebellions. Perth's attractions—with the exception of the shops—are scattered and take time to reach on foot. Some, in fact, are far enough away to necessitate the use of a car, bus, or taxi.

St. John's Kirk, dating from the 15th century, escaped the worst excesses of the Reformation mob and is now restored. ⊠ *St. John St.,* ☎ *01738/626159.* ⊙ *Weekdays 10–2 and 2–4 and for Sun. services.*

The **Perth Art Gallery and Museum** has a wide-ranging collection of natural history, local history, and archaeology, plus a rotating exhibit program. ⊠ *George St.,* ☎ *01738/632488.* ⊡. ⊙ *Mon.–Sat., 10–5.*

On the North Inch of Perth, look for **Balhousie Castle** and the **Regimental Museum of the Black Watch.** Some will tell you the Black Watch was a Scottish regiment whose name is a reference to the color of its tartan. An equally plausible explanation, however, is that the regiment was established to keep an undercover watch on rebellious Jacobites. *Black* is the Gaelic word *dubh,* meaning, in this case, hidden or covert, used in the same sense as the word blackmail. ⊠ *Facing North Inch Park (entrance from Hay St.),* ☎ *0131/310–8530.* ⊡ *Free.* ⊙ *May–Sept., Mon.–Sat. 10–4:30; Oct.–Apr., weekdays 10–3:30. Last Sat. in June.*

The nearby Round House is home to the **Fergusson Gallery,** displaying a selection of 6,000 works—paintings, drawings, prints—by the Scottish artist J. D. Fergusson (1874–1961). ⊠ *Marshall Pl.,* ☎ *01738/ 441944.* ⊡ *Free.* ⊙ *Mon.–Sat. 10–5.*

Off the A9 west of town is **Caithness Glass,** where, from the viewing gallery, you can watch glassworkers creating silky-smooth bowls, vases, and other glassware. There is also a small museum, restaurant, and shop. ⊠ *Inveralmond, Perth,* ☎ *01738/637373.* ⊡ *Free.* ⊙ *Factory weekdays 9–4:30, shop Easter–mid-Oct., Mon.–Sat. 9–5, Sun. 10–5; mid-Oct.–Easter, Mon.–Sat. 9–5, Sun. noon–5.*

㉛ A modest selection of castles is within easy reach of Perth. **Huntingtower Castle,** a curious double tower that dates from the 15th century, is associated with an attempt to wrest power from the young James VI in 1582. Some early painted ceilings survive, offering the vaguest hint of the sumptuous decor once found in many such ancient castles that are now reduced to bare and drafty rooms. ⊠ *Off A85,* ☎ *0131/ 668–8800.* ⊡ *£1.80.* ⊙ *Apr.–Sept., daily 9:30–6; Oct.–Mar., Mon.– Wed. and Sat. 9:30–4, Thurs. 9–noon, Sun. 2–4.*

㉜ **Elcho Castle** is a fortified mansion on the east side of Perth. It is the abandoned 15th-century seat of the earls of Wemyss, and now only a shell. ⊠ *On River Tay,* ☎ *0131/668–8800. View from outside only.*

★ 🖐 ㉝ **Scone Palace** is much more cheerful and vibrant than Perth's other castles. The palace is the present home of the earl of Mansfield and is open to visitors. Although it incorporates various earlier works, the palace today consists mainly of a 19th-century theme, featuring mock castellations that were fashionable at the time. There is plenty to see if you have an interest in the acquisitions of an aristocratic Scottish family: magnificent porcelain, furniture, ivory, clocks, and 16th-century needlework. A coffee shop, restaurant, gift shop, and play area are on site, and the extensive grounds have a pinetum.

The palace has its own mausoleum nearby, on the site of a long-gone abbey, on **Moot Hill**, the ancient coronation place of the Scottish kings. To be crowned, they sat on the Stone of Scone, which was seized in 1296 by Edward I of England (1239–1307), Scotland's greatest enemy, and placed in the coronation chair at Westminster Abbey in London. It was returned to Scotland in November 1996 and is now on view in Edinburgh Castle. Some Scots hint darkly that Edward was fooled by a substitution, and that the real stone is hidden, waiting for Scotland to regain its independence. ✉ *Braemar Rd.,* ☎ *01738/552308.* 💷 *£5.20.* ☼ *Easter–Oct., daily 9:30–5:15 (last admission 4:45).*

🖐 Near Perth, **Fairways Heavy Horse Centre** has Clydesdale horses for day rides. You can tour the center's stables and exercise fields. ✉ *Glencarse Village,* ☎ *01738/860888.* 💷 *Tours £2.* ☼ *Daily 10–5.*

Dining and Lodging

£££ ✕🏨 **Parklands.** A stylish Georgian town house overlooking lush woodland—an ideal setting for this top-quality hotel—Parklands is perhaps best known for its cuisine, featuring Scottish fish, game, and beef. The restrained decor and modern furniture are in keeping with the subdued but elegant ambience. ✉ *2 St. Leonard's Bank, PH2 8EB,* ☎ *01738/622451,* FAX *01738/622046. 14 rooms with bath. 2 restaurants. AE, DC, MC, V.*

££ ✕🏨 **Sunbank House Hotel.** You'll find this early Victorian gray stone
★ mansion in a fine residential area near Perth's Branklyn Gardens. A lesson in traditional style, it offers solid, unpretentious comforts along with great views over the River Tay and the city. The restaurant specializes in locally raised meats and game, imaginatively prepared Continental style with some Scottish overtones. ✉ *50 Dundee Rd., PH2 7BA,* ☎ *01738/624882,* FAX *01738/442515. 9 rooms with bath or shower. Restaurant. MC, V.*

Nightlife and the Arts

The Victorian **Perth Repertory Theatre** (✉ High St., Perth, ☎ 01738/621031) offers a variety of plays and musicals. In the summer it is the main venue for the Perth Festival of the Arts. **Perth City Hall** (☎ 01738/624055) is the main venue for musical performances of all types.

Shopping

CLOTHING

A comprehensive selection of sheepskins, leather jackets, and hand-knit Aran sweaters is sold at **C & C Proudfoot** (✉ 104 South St., ☎ 01738/632483).

GLASS AND CHINA

Perth is an especially popular hunting ground for china and glass: **William Watson & Sons** (✉ 163–167 High St., ☎ 01738/639861) has sold exquisite bone china and cut crystal since 1900 and can pack your purchase safely for shipment overseas. At **Caithness Glass** (✉ Inveralmond, off A9 at northern town boundary, ☎ 01738/637373), you can buy all types of glassware in the factory shop.

Perth proffers an unusual buy: Scottish freshwater pearls from the River Tay, in delicate settings, some of which take their theme from Scottish flowers. The Romans coveted these pearls. If you do, too, then you can make your choice at **Cairncross Ltd., Goldsmiths** (⊠ 18 St. John's St., ☎ 01738/624367), where you can also admire a display of some of the more unusual shapes and colors of pearls. Antique jewelry and silver (including Scottish items) can be found at **Timothy Hardie** (⊠ 25 St. John's St., ☎ 01738/633127). **Whispers of the Past** (⊠ 15 George St., ☎ 01738/635472) has a collection of linens, old pine, and jewelry.

SCOTTISH SPECIALTIES

The Perthshire Shop (⊠ Lower City Mills, W. Mill St., ☎ 01738/ 627958) sells ties and scarves in Perthshire's own tartan, Scottish cook books, and oatmeal products made at this working Victorian water mill.

Dunkeld

34 *14 mi north of Perth.*

At Dunkeld, Thomas Telford's sturdy river bridge of 1809 carries the road into town. In Dunkeld you will find that the National Trust for Scotland not only cares for grand mansions and wildlands but also actively restores smaller properties. Its "Little Houses" project can be seen in the square off the main street, opposite the fish-and-chips shop. All the houses on the square were rebuilt after the 1689 Battle of Killiecrankie (☞ *below*) when, after its victory, the Jacobite army marched south and was defeated here.

The ospreys that frequent Speyside's Loch Garten in summer get so much attention from conservation societies that they sometimes overshadow **Loch of Lowes,** a Scottish Wildlife Trust reserve near Dunkeld. Here the domestic routines of the osprey, one of Scotland's conservation success stories, can be observed in relative comfort. ⊠ *Off A923 northeast of Dunkeld,* ☎ *01350/727337.* ☉ *Apr.–Sept., daily 10–5.*

Shopping

Dunkeld Antiques (⊠ Tay Terr., ☎ 01350/728832), facing the river as you cross the bridge, stocks everything from large items of furniture down to ornaments and jewelry, books, and prints. At the **Highland Horn and Deerskin Centre** (⊠ City Hall, Atholl St., ☎ 01350/727569), you can purchase stag antlers and cow horns shaped into walking sticks, cutlery, and tableware. Deerskin shoes and moccasins, a range of small leather goods made from deerskin, and a specialist malt whisky collection of more than 200 different malts are also sold. The center has a worldwide postal service and a tax-free shop.

Pitlochry

35 *15 mi north of Dunkeld.*

A typical central Highland resort, always full of leisurely hustle and bustle, Pitlochry has wall-to-wall souvenir and gift shops, large hotels recalling even more-laid-back days, and a mountainous golf course. Most Scottish dams have salmon passes or ladders of some kind, enabling the fish to swim upstream to their spawning grounds. In Pitlochry, the **Pitlochry Dam and Fish Ladder,** just behind the main street, leads into a glass-paneled pipe so that the fish can observe the visitors.

For those with a whisky-tasting bent, Pitlochry also is home to **Edradour Distillery,** which claims to be the smallest single-malt distillery in Scotland (but then, so do others). ⊠ *2½ mi east of Pitlochry,* ☎ *01796/*

472095. ✉ *Free.* ☉ *Tour and tastings Mar.–Oct., Mon.–Sat. 9:30–5, Sun. noon–5, shop also Nov.–Feb., Mon.–Sat. 10:30–4.*

㊱ The **Linn of Tummel,** a series of marked walks along the river and through tall, mature woodlands, is a little north of Pitlochry. Above the Linn, the new A9 is raised on stilts and gives an exciting view of the valley. The

★ **㊲** **Pass of Killiecrankie,** set among the oak woods and rocky river just north of the Linn of Tummel, was a key strategic point in the Central Highlands: a famous battle was won here in the Jacobite rebellion of 1689. The National Trust for Scotland's **visitor center** at Killiecrankie explains the significance of this, the first attempt to restore the Stewart monarchy. The battle was noted for the death of the Jacobite leader, John Graham of Claverhouse (1649–89), also known as Bonnie Dundee, who was hit by a stray bullet; the rebellion fizzled out after that. To reach Killiecrankie from Pitlochry, stay on the old A9, heading north. ✉ *Off A9,* ☎ FAX *01796/473233.* ✉ *£1.* ☉ *Apr.–Oct., daily 10–5:30.*

Only a few minutes farther north from the Pass of Killiecrankie sits

★ **㊳** **Blair Castle.** Thanks to its historic contents and its war-torn past, this castle is one of Scotland's most highly rated. Painted white and turreted, Blair Castle was home to successive dukes of Atholl and their family, the Murrays, until the death of the 10th duke. Its ownership and care have now passed to a charitable trust. One of the many fascinating details in the interior is a preserved piece of flooring that still bears marks of the red-hot shot fired through the roof during the 1745 Jacobite rebellion—the last occasion in Scottish history that a castle was besieged. The castle holds not only military artifacts—historically, the duke was allowed to keep a private army, the Atholl Highlanders—but also a fine collection of furniture and paintings. Outside, a Victorian walled garden has been restored, and there are extensive parklands backed by high, rounded hills. ✉ *From Pitlochry, take the A9 to Blair Atholl and follow signs,* ☎ *01796/481207.* ✉ *£5.50.* ☉ *Apr.–late Oct., daily 10–6 (last admission at 5).*

㊴ Also easily reached from Pitlochry is **Loch Rannoch,** which, with its shoreline of birch trees framed by dark pines, is the quintessential Highland loch. The road ends at Rannoch, where you meet the West Highland railroad line on its way across Rannoch Moor to Fort William. Fans of Robert Louis Stevenson (1850–94), especially of *Kidnapped* (1886), will not want to miss the last, lonely section of road. Stevenson describes the setting: "The mist rose and died away, and showed us that country lying as waste as the sea; only the moorfowl and the peewees crying upon it, and far over to the east a herd of deer, moving like dots. Much of it was red with heather, much of the rest broken up with bogs and hags and peaty pools . . ."

Apart from the blocks of alien conifer plantings in certain places, little here has changed. To reach this atmospheric locale, take the B8019 at the Linn of Tummel north of Pitlochry, then the B846 at Tummel Bridge.

Nightlife and the Arts

Pitlochry Festival Theatre (✉ Pitlochry, ☎ 01796/472680, ☎ FAX 01796/473054) presents six plays each season and features eight Sunday concerts. The theater is open from May to early October.

Aberfeldy

㊵ *15 mi southwest of Pitlochry.*

Aberfeldy is a sleepy town that is popular as a tourist base. Aberfeldy Bridge (1733), with five arches and a humpback, was designed by William

④ Adam (1689–1748).West of Aberfeldy, on the opposite bank of the River Tay, stands **Castle Menzies.** This Z-plan 16th-century fortified tower house is now the setting for the **Clan Menzies' Museum.** ☎ *01887/ 820982.* ⌂ *£3.* ⊙ *Apr.–mid-Oct., Mon.–Sat. 10:30–5, Sun. 2–5 (last admission at 4:30).*

④ **Glen Lyon** is one of central Scotland's most attractive glens; it comprises a rushing river, forests, high hills on both sides, prehistoric sites complete with legendary tales, and the typical *big hoose* (big house) hidden on private grounds. There is even a dam at the head of the loch, as a reminder that little of Scotland's scenic beauty is unadulterated. You can reach the glen by a high road from Loch Tay: take the A827 to Fearnan, then turn north to Fortingall. The **Fortingall yew,** in the churchyard near the Fortingall Hotel, wearily rests its great limbs on the ground. This tree is thought to be more than 3,000 years old. Legend has it that Pontius Pilate was born beside it, while his father served as a Roman legionnaire in Scotland. After viewing the yew, turn west into Glen Lyon.

Outdoor Activities and Sports

Loch Tay Boating Centre (✉ Carlin and Brett, Pier Rd., Kenmore, ☎ 01887/830291) has cabin cruisers, fishing boats, and canoes from April to October.

En Route Between Aberfeldy and Killin, take the north-bank road by Loch Tay, the A827, which offers fine views west along Loch Tay toward Ben More and Stobinian, and north to Ben Lawers.

Killin

④ *24 mi southwest of Aberfeldy, 39 mi north of Stirling, 45 mi west of Perth.*

A village with an almost alpine flavor, known for its modest but surprisingly diverse selection of crafts and woolen wares, Killin is also noted for its scenery. The **Falls of Dochart,** white-water rapids overlooked by a pine-clad islet, are at the west end of the village. By the Falls of Dochart you will find the **Breadalbane Folklore Centre,** with its canter through the heritage and folk tales of the area. The most curious of these are the "healing stones of St. Fillan"—water-worn stones that have been looked after lovingly for centuries for their supposed curative powers. ✉ *Killin,* ☎ *01567/820254.* ⌂ *£1.* ⊙ *Mar.–June and Sept.–Oct., daily 10–5; July–Aug., daily 9–6; Nov.–Dec. and Feb., weekends 10–4 (call to confirm hours in winter).*

Across the River Dochart and near the golf course sit the ruins of **Finlarig Castle,** built by Black Duncan of the Cowl, a notorious Campbell laird. The castle can be visited at any time.

Lodging

£–££ 🏠 **Lodge House.** Few other guest houses in Scotland can match the mountain views from this 100-year-old property; it's certainly worth the short drive (about 15 miles) west from Killin to Crianlarich. Informal and cozy, the guest house is successful thanks to what the Scots call good "crack"—conviviality, in this case between host and guests. The food (for resident guests only) is good Scots fare: haggis, salmon, and oatcakes. The bedrooms are plain and unfussy, but more than adequate. You may wish to walk along the riverbank after dinner, or have a wee dram in the tiny bar instead. ✉ *Lodge House, Crianlarich, Perthshire, FK20 8RU,* ☎ *01838/300276. 6 rooms with bath or shower. MC, V.*

Outdoor Activities and Sports

If you want to explore the northern end of the Glasgow–Killin cycle-way, rent a bicycle from **Killin Outdoor Centre and Mountain Shop** (⊠ Main St., Killin, ☎ FAX 01567/820652).

En Route   Southwest of Killin the A827 joins the main A85. By turning south over the watershed, you will see fine views of the hill ridges behind Killin. The road leads into Glen Ogle, "amid the wildest and finest scenery we had yet seen . . . putting one in mind of prints of the Khyber Pass," as Queen Victoria (1819–1901) recorded in her diary when she passed this way in 1842.

Lochearnhead

44   *8 mi south of Killin, 37 mi west of Perth, 31 mi northwest of Stirling.*

The settlement of Lochearnhead is set, as its name suggests, on the shore of **Loch Earn.** To the east are good views of the long, gray screes of Ben Vorlich southward across the loch.

Outdoor Activities and Sports

Lochearnhead Water Sports Centre (⊠ Loch Earn, ☎ 01567/830330) rents sailboats, canoes, and sailboards for wind surfing, and offers instruction for water-sports enthusiasts, from novices to experts.

En Route   Between Lochearnhead and Crieff, the road passes through lush Perthshire estates and farmlands, reminiscent of the Lowlands. The little communities of St. Fillans and Comrie punctuate the route; the higher hills can always be seen to the north.

Crieff

45   *19 mi east of Lochearnhead.*

The hilly town of Crieff offers walks with Highland views from **Knock Hill** above the town. Tours of the **Glenturret Distillery** can be undertaken if you have not already discovered the delights of whisky distilling. There are also two restaurants offering award-winning "Taste of Scotland" menus, an audiovisual presentation entitled "The Water of Life," and the "Spirit of the Glen" exhibition. It is signposted on the west side of the town. ☎ 01764/656565. 🎫 £3.50. ⊙ Mar.–Dec., Mon.–Sat. 9:30–6, Sun. noon–6 (last tour 4:30); Jan.–Feb., weekdays 11:30–4 (last tour 2:30).

Just south of Crieff is a paperweight manufacturer, part of a complex called the **Crieff Visitors Centre.** Adjacent to the complex is a small pottery factory and a restaurant. During the week there are surprisingly interesting tours of the factory grounds, where you can see Thistle hand-painted pottery, intricate millefiori glass, and lamp-work Perthshire paperweights being made. ⊠ A822, south of Crieff, ☎ 01764/654014. 🎫 Free (£1 charge for pottery factory tour). ⊙ Daily 9–5:30 (restricted hours during winter; call ahead).

46   **Drummond Castle,** southwest of the town, has an unusual formal Italian garden. ⊠ Off Crieff–Muthill Rd., ☎ 01764/681257. 🎫 Gardens £3. ⊙ Easter weekend and May–Oct., daily 2–6 (last admission at 5).

Shopping

Crieff is a center for china and glassware. **Stuart Crystal** (⊠ Muthill Rd., ☎ 01764/654004), a factory shop, sells Stuart crystal, but also Waterford and Wedgwood wares. Also visit the **Crieff Visitors Centre** (☞ above).

Auchterarder

47 *11 mi southeast of Crieff, 15 mi southwest of Perth, 21 mi northeast of Stirling.*

Famous for the **Gleneagles Hotel** (☞ Dining and Lodging, *below*), Auchterarder also has a flock of antiques shops.

Dining and Lodging

££££ ✕🖼 **Auchterarder House Hotel.** Secluded and superbly atmospheric,
★ this is a wood-paneled, richly furnished Victorian country mansion. The plush, exuberantly styled dining room, filled with glittering glassware, is an appropriate setting for the unusual and creative use of many locally produced foods by a Masterchef of Great Britain, winner of an annual U.K. TV series competition. ✉ *On B8062 at Auchterarder, 15 mi southwest of Perth, PH3 1DZ,* ☎ *01764/663646,* 𝔽𝔸𝕏 *01764/ 662939. 15 rooms with bath. Restaurant, golf privileges, croquet. AE, DC, MC, V.*

££££ ✕🖼 **Gleneagles Hotel.** One of Britain's most famous hotels, Gleneagles is the very image of modern grandeur. Like a vast, secret palace, it stands hidden in breathtaking countryside amid world-famous golf courses. Recreation facilities are nearly endless, and there are three restaurants: the Strathearn, for à la carte and table d'hôte; the Clubhouse Grill (at the 18th hole of the King's Course), for à la carte; and the Gallery Brasserie, by the swimming pool. All this, plus a shopping arcade, Champneys Health Spa, the Gleneagles Mark Phillips Equestrian Centre, the British School of Falconry, Gleneagles Jackie Stewart Shooting School, the Golf Academy, and the Off-road at Gleneagles driving school, make a stay here a luxurious and unforgettable experience. ✉ *Auchterarder, near Perth, PH3 1NF,* ☎ *01764/662231,* 𝔽𝔸𝕏 *01764/ 662134. 234 rooms with bath. 3 restaurants, sauna, golf privileges, tennis court, exercise room. AE, DC, MC, V.*

THE CENTRAL HIGHLANDS A TO Z

Arriving and Departing

By Bus

A good network of buses connects with the central belt via Edinburgh and Glasgow. Express services also link the larger towns in the Central Highlands with all main towns and cities in England. Contact **Scottish Citylink** (☎ 0990/505050) or **National Express** (☎ 0990/808080).

By Car

You will find easy access to the area from the central belt of Scotland via the motorway network. The M9 runs within sight of the walls of Stirling Castle, and Perth can be reached via the M90 over the Forth Bridge.

By Plane

Perth and Stirling can be reached easily from **Edinburgh** and **Glasgow** airports (☞ Chapters 3 and 4) by train, car, or bus.

By Train

The Central Highlands are linked to Edinburgh and Glasgow by rail, with through routes to England (some direct-service routes from London take fewer than five hours). A variety of "Savers" ticket options are available, although in some cases on the ScotRail system, the discount fares must be purchased before your arrival in the United Kingdom. Contact the **National Train Enquiry Line** (☎ 0345/484950) for details.

Getting Around

By Bus

The following companies organize reliable service on a number of convenient routes: **Scottish Citylink** (⊠ Leonard St. bus station, Perth, ☎ 01738/626848), **Midland Bluebird Bus Services** (⊠ Goosecroft Rd. bus station, Stirling, ☎ 01786/446474), and **Stagecoach** (⊠ Ruthvenfield Rd., Inveralmond Industrial Estate, Perth, ☎ 01738/629339).

By Car

There is an adequate network of roads, and the area's proximity to the central belt speeds road communications. The Scottish Tourist Board's touring map is useful.

By Train

The **West Highland Line** runs through the western portion of the area. Services also run to Stirling, Dunblane, Perth, and Gleneagles; destinations on the Inverness–Perth line include Dunkeld, Pitlochry, and Blair Atholl. Contact the **National Train Enquiry Line** (☎ 0345/484950) for details.

Contacts and Resources

Arnold Clark (⊠ St. Leonard's Bank, Perth, ☎ 01738/638511). **Avis** (⊠ 54–56 Victoria St., Perth, ☎ 01738/442646). **Europcar** (⊠ 26 Glasgow Rd., Perth, ☎ 01738/636888).

Doctors and Dentists

Local practitioners will usually treat visitors. Information is available from tourist information centers, or from your hotel receptionist or bed-and-breakfast host. Names of doctors can also be found in the Yellow Pages telephone directory.

Emergencies

For **police, fire, or ambulance,** dial ☎ 999 from any telephone. No coins are needed for emergency calls from telephone booths.

Perth Royal Infirmary (⊠ Tullylumb, Perth, ☎ 01738/623311). **Stirling Royal Infirmary** (⊠ Livilands Gate, Stirling, ☎ 01786/434000). **Vale of Leven Hospital** (⊠ Main St., Alexandria, ☎ 01389/754121).

Guided Tours

ORIENTATION

The bus companies listed in Getting Around By Bus (☞ *above*) offer a number of general orientation tours. Inquire at the nearest tourist information center, where tour reservations can usually be booked.

SPECIAL-INTEREST

There are many taxi and chauffeur companies offering tailor-made tours by the day or week; the nearest tourist information center is your best source for detailed, up-to-date information. Do not miss the opportunity to take a boat trip on a Scottish loch, especially in the Trossachs (Loch Katrine) and Loch Lomond; (☞ *above*) or consult a tourist information center.

Late-Night Pharmacies

Late-night pharmacies are found only in the larger towns and cities. In an emergency, the police will help you find a pharmacist. In rural areas, general practitioners may also dispense medicine.

Visitor Information

Aberfeldy (⊠ The Square, ☎ 01887/820276). **Alva** (⊠ Mill Trail Visitor Centre, West Stirling St., ☎ 01259/769696). **Auchterarder** (⊠ 90 High St., ☎ 01764/663450). **Blairgowrie** (⊠ 26 Wellmeadow, ☎

01250/872960). **Crieff** (✉ Town Hall, High St., ☎ 01764/652578).
Drymen (✉ The Square, ☎ 01360/660068). **Kinross** (✉ Service Area
Junction 6 M90, ☎ 01577/863680). **Perth** (✉ 45 High St., ☎ 01738/
638353). **Pitlochry** (✉ 22 Atholl Rd., ☎ 01796/472215). **Stirling** (✉
41 Dumbarton Rd., ☎ 01786/475019; ✉ Royal Burgh of Stirling Visitor Centre, ☎ 01786/479901).

Seasonal tourist information centers are also open (generally April–
October) in the following towns: Aberfoyle, Balloch, Callander, Dumbarton, Dunblane, Dunkeld, Helensburgh, Inveralmond, Killin, Pirnhall,
Tarbert, Tarbet, and Tyndrum. All are clearly marked with the standard I sign in white on a blue background.

8 Aberdeen and the Northeast

The glittering granite city of Aberdeen, Scotland's third largest, is a main port of North Sea oil operations. The terrain changes from coastline—some of the United Kingdom's wildest shorelines of high cliffs and sandy beaches—to farmland, to forests, to hills. The Grampian mountains and the Cairngorms, of heather and forest, granite peaks and deep glens, beckon hill walkers and skiers. Brooding castles and whisky distilleries also dot the land.

BECAUSE OF ITS GEOGRAPHIC ISOLATION the granite city of Aberdeen has, throughout its history, been
a fairly autonomous place. Even now it is perceived
by many inhabitants of the United Kingdom as lying almost out of reach
in the north. In reality, this northeastern locale is only 90 minutes' flying time from London or—thanks to recent road improvements—a little more than two hours by car from Edinburgh. Its magnificent,
confident 18th- and early 19th-century city center amply rewards exploration, and there are also many surviving buildings from earlier centuries to seek out.

By Gilbert
Summers

Yet even if Aberdeen vanished from the map of Scotland, an extensive
portion of the Northeast would still be worth exploring. The area's
chief scenic attraction lies in the gradual transition from high mountain
plateau—by a series of gentle steps through hill, forest, and farmland—
to the Moray Firth and North Sea coastline where the word *unadulterated* is redefined. The coastline includes some of the United Kingdom's
most perfect wild shorelines, both sandy and sheer cliff. The Grampian
Mountains to the west contain some of the highest ground in the
United Kingdom, in the area of the Cairngorms. But the Grampian hills
also have shaped the character of the folk who live in the Northeast.
In earlier times, the massif made communication with the South somewhat difficult. As a result, native Northeasterners still speak the rich-
est Lowland Scottish (*not* Gaelic, which is an entirely different language).

Nowhere else in Scotland is there such an eclectic selection of castles,
offering you an opportunity to touch the fabric of Scotland's story. There
are so many that in one part of the region a Castle Trail has been assembled, leading you to fortresses like the ruined medieval Kildrummy
Castle, which once controlled the strategic routes through the valley
of the River Don. Later work, such as Craigievar, a narrow-turreted
castle resembling an illustration from a fairy-tale book, reflects the changing times of the 17th century, when defense became less of a priority.
Later still, grand mansions, such as Haddo House, with its symmetrical facade and elegant interiors, surrender any defensive need entirely
and instead make statements about their owner's status and power.

As a visitor to Scotland, you can be sure of one thing: no matter where
you are, a whisky distillery can't be far off. Morayshire, in the northwestern part of this region, where the distilling is centered in the valley of the River Spey and its tributaries, is no exception. Just as the
Loire in France has famous vineyards clustered around it, the Spey has
famous single-malt distilleries. Instead of Muscadet, Chinon, Vouvray,
or Pouilly-sur-Loire, there's Glenfiddich, Glen Grant, Tamdhu, or
Tamnavulin. As well as being sweeter and less peaty than some of the
island malts, eastern or Speyside malts have the further advantage of
having generally easier-to-pronounce brand names.

Pleasures and Pastimes

Biking

Northeast Scotland is superb biking country, with networks of minor
roads and farm roads crisscrossing rolling fields. It's also now possible to bicycle on a variety of rails-to-trails routes—former railway track
beds converted to bicycle and pedestrian pathways. The Buchan line,
from Aberdeen to Fraserburgh and Peterhead, is a good route.

Dining

Partly in response to the demands of spendthrift oilmen, the number
of restaurants in Aberdeen has grown during the past several years,

and the quality of the food has improved. Elsewhere in the region you are never far from a good pub lunch or a hotel high tea or dinner.

CATEGORY	COST*
££££	over £40
£££	£30–£40
££	£15–£30
£	under £15

per person for a three-course meal, including VAT and excluding drinks and service

Fishing

With major rivers such as the Dee, Don, Deveron, and Ythan, as well as popular smaller rivers such as the Ugie, plus loch and estuary fishing, this is one of Scotland's leading game-fishing areas. Details of beats, boats, and permit prices can be obtained from local tourist information centers. Some local hotels offer fishing packages or, at least, can organize permits. Prices vary widely, depending on the fish and individual river beat.

Golf

The Northeast has more than 50 golf clubs, some of which have championship courses (☞ Chapter 2). Tourist information centers can supply leaflets appropriate to their area. All towns and many villages have their 9- and 18-hole municipal links, at which you pay £5–£10 per round. The more prestigious clubs charge up to £60 a day and expect you to book by letter or to bring a letter of recommendation from a member.

Lodging

The Northeast has some splendid country hotels with log fires and rich furnishings, where you can also be sure of eating well if you have time for a leisurely meal. Note that in Aberdeen many hotels offer competitive room rates on weekends.

CATEGORY	COST*
££££	over £120
£££	£90–£120
££	£50–£90
£	under £50

All prices are for a standard double room, including service, breakfast, and VAT.

Shopping

Aberdeen, serving a large and fairly prosperous hinterland, has the widest choice of shopping in the region. Elgin, a smaller center, also has some shops of interest. Because of the fishing and farming prosperity, plus new money from oil and even newer money from people moving from the south, there are a few shopping surprises in some of the smaller towns as well.

Skiing

The area's main skiing development is at **Glenshee** (☎ 013397/41320), just south of Braemar, though the season can be brief here. Visitors accustomed to long alpine runs and extensive choice will find the runs here short, unlike the lift lines. **The Lecht** (☎ 01975/651440) lies at even lower altitude, also within easy reach of the area, and is mainly suitable for beginners. The development at **Cairngorm** (☎ 01479/861261) by Aviemore is also nearby (☞ Chapter 10). There is an artificial "dry" slope at **Alford** (☎ 019755/63024).

Exploring Aberdeen and the Northeast

Once you have spent time in Aberdeen, you may be inclined to venture west into Deeside, with its Royal connections and looming mountain backdrop, and then pass over the hills into the "castle country" to the north. You might head farther west to touch on Speyside and "whisky country," before meandering back east and south along the pristine coastline at the northeasternmost tip of Scotland.

Union Street is the center of Aberdeen, and through traffic from the north and northwest is signposted through Aberdeen beyond its east end and to the harbor. Through traffic from the south is signposted around Anderson Drive, from where all the main routes into the Grampian hinterland are also signposted: for example, the Deeside and Donside routes, the main Inverness A96, as well as coastal routes to the north. Outside Aberdeen, the Castle and Whisky trails are generally well marked.

Numbers in the text correspond to numbers in the margin and on the Royal Deeside, Aberdeen, and the Northeast maps.

Great Itineraries

Remember that Grampian is not a huge area, albeit one with great variety. Overall, to get a real flavor of this most authentic of Scottish regions, make sure you sample both the coastline and the mountains.

IF YOU HAVE 2 DAYS

Spend a day touring in Royal Deeside and take in a castle. **Balmoral** ㉙ may not be your best bet, as there are more worthwhile castle experiences, such as **Drum** ㉒, **Crathes** ㉓, and **Braemar** ㉚. Stay overnight in ▣ **Aberdeen** ①–⑳, then on the following day, explore the coastline north from Aberdeen toward **Fraserburgh** ㊾, with its memorable Lighthouse Museum, and west toward **Banff** ㊿, where there is a splendid collection of pictures at Duff House.

IF YOU HAVE 4 DAYS

Downtown ▣ **Aberdeen's** ①–⑳ silver granite certainly deserves a little time. Then travel from Aberdeen into Speyside for its distilleries: **Dufftown** ㊲, and north via **Craigellachie** ㊳ and **Aberlour** ㊴ to ▣ **Elgin** ㊵. Spend a morning exploring Elgin before moving east along the coast to stay overnight in ▣ **Fordyce** ㊽ or ▣ **Banff** ㊿. Visit the magnificent Duff House gallery in Banff, before traveling east along a spectacular coastline (take the B9031 from Macduff) to **Fraserburgh** ㊾ for Scotland's Lighthouse Museum; return to Aberdeen. If you have time on the last day, see a castle or two: **Drum** ㉒ or **Crathes** ㉓ on Deeside; **Haddo House** ㊶ or **Fyvie Castle** ㊷ northwest of **Ellon** ㊴; or loop northwestward for **Corgarff** ㉜, the ruined castle at ▣ **Kildrummy** ㉝, fairy-tale **Craigievar** ㉟, or **Castle Fraser** ㊱.

When to Tour Aberdeen and the Northeast

Because the National Trust for Scotland tends to close its properties in the winter, many of the Northeast's castles are not suitable for off-season travel, though you can always see them from the outside. The Lighthouse Museum, Duff House, Macduff Marine Aquarium, and some of the distilleries are open much of the year, but May and June are probably the best times to visit.

ABERDEEN, THE SILVER CITY

In the 18th century, local granite quarrying produced a durable silver stone that would be used to build the Aberdonian structures of the Victorian era. Thus granite was used boldly—in glittering blocks, spires,

Royal Deeside

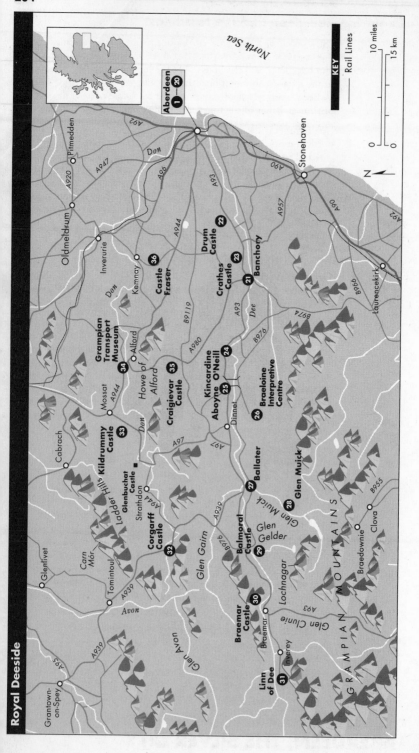

KEY

— Rail Lines

North Sea

Aberdeen ① ⑳

Pitmedden
Oldmeldrum
Inverurie
Kemnay
Castle Fraser ㊱
Alford
Grampian Transport Museum ㉞
Howe of Alford
Mossat
Craigievar Castle ㉟
Kincardine O'Neill ㉔
Aboyne ㉕
Dinnet ㉖
Braeloine Interpretive Centre
Drum Castle ㉒
Crathes Castle ㉓
Banchory ㉑
Dee
Stonehaven
Laurencekirk
Cabrach
Kildrummy Castle ㉝
Ladder Hills
Strathdon
Glenbuchat Castle
Corgarff Castle ㉜
Carn Mór
Ballater ㉗
Glen Muick ㉘
Glen Muick
Glen Gelder
Balmoral Castle ㉙
Lochnagar
Glenlivet
Tomintoul
Avon
Glen Avon
Glen Gairn
Braemar Castle ㉚
Braemar
Inverey
Linn of Dee ㉛
Glen Clunie
Clova
Braedownie
GRAMPIAN MOUNTAINS
Grantown-on-Spey

10 miles

15 km

columns, and parapets—to build downtown Aberdeen. It remains one of the United Kingdom's most distinctive urban environments, although some would say it depends on the weather and the brightness of the day. The mica chips embedded in the rock are a million mirrors in sunshine. In rain and heavy clouds, however, their sparkle is snuffed out.

The North Sea has always been an important feature of Aberdeen: in the 1850s the city was famed for its fast clippers, sleek sailing ships that raced to India for cargoes of tea. In the late 1960s the course of Aberdeen's history was unequivocally altered when oil and gas were discovered in the North Sea. Aberdeen at first seemed destined to become an oil-rich boomtown, and throughout the 1970s the city was overcome by new shops, new office blocks, new hotels, new industries, and new attitudes. Fortunately, some innate local caution has helped the city to retain a sense of perspective and prevented it from selling out entirely.

Exploring Aberdeen

Aberdeen centers on Union Street, but the street's role as the main shopping street has been diluted by the arrival of three large shopping malls nearby. Still, there are many fine survivors of the Victorian and Edwardian streetscape. Old Aberdeen is very much a separate area of the city, north of the modern city center and clustered around St. Machar's Cathedral and the many fine buildings of the University of Aberdeen.

A Good Tour

Start your walk at the eastern end of **Union Street** ①, Aberdeen's equivalent to Princes Street in Edinburgh. Some hints of an older Aberdeen have survived and add to the city's charm. Indeed here, within the original old town, is the Castlegate. The actual castle once stood somewhere behind the Salvation Army Citadel (1896), an imposing baronial granite tower whose design was inspired by Balmoral Castle. On the north side of Castle Street stands the 17th-century **Tolbooth** ②, a reminder of Aberdeen's earliest days. The impressive **Mercat Cross** ③, always the symbolic center of a Scottish medieval burgh, stands just beyond King Street. Turn north down Broad Street to reach **Marischal College** ④, which dominates the top end of the street with its glittering granite frontage.

A survivor from an earlier Aberdeen can be found opposite Marischal College, beyond the concrete supports of St. Nicholas House (of which the tourist information center is a part): **Provost Skene's House** ⑤ was once part of a closely packed area of town houses and is now a museum portraying civic life. Just around the corner in Upperkirkgate, at the lowest point, are two modern shopping malls—the St. Nicholas Centre on the left, the Bon-Accord Centre on the right. Until recent years George Street, at the foot of the hill here, was a bustling shopping street. But not even Aberdeen, in its far northern perch, exempted itself from the British trend toward chain-store anonymity, and it thus demolished traditional stonework to accommodate the chains. If you do enter the portals of the Bon-Accord Centre, you will eventually emerge at the truncated George Street.

Upperkirkgate becomes Schoolhill where, as the slope eases off at the top, there is a complex of silver-toned buildings in front of which stands a statue of General Charles Gordon (1833–85), the military hero of Khartoum (1885). Interestingly, he is not the Gordon recalled in **Robert Gordon's University** ⑥ behind the statue. The University's next door neighbor is **Aberdeen Art Gallery** ⑦, which plays an active role in Aberdeen's cultural life and is a popular rendezvous for locals.

206

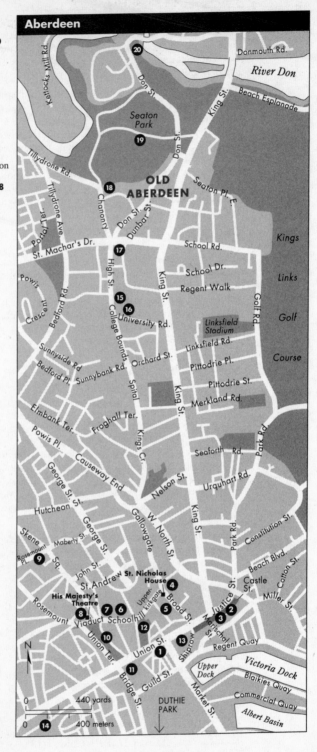
Aberdeen

A library, church, and nearby theater on **Rosemount Viaduct** ⑧ are collectively known by all Aberdonians as Education, Salvation, and Damnation: the silvery and handsome Central Library and St. Mark's Church, and the restored Edwardian His Majesty's Theatre. If you're taking photographs you can choose an angle that includes the statue of Scotland's first freedom fighter, Sir William Wallace (1270–1305), in the foreground pointing majestically to Damnation. **Rosemount Celebration Centre** ⑨, great for kids, is off Rosemont Viaduct on Rosemount Place.

Union Terrace ⑩, a 19th-century development, runs back toward Union Street. Smug cats seated primly on its parapet decorate **Union Bridge** ⑪, at the junction of Union Terrace with Union Street. Here you should turn left, across the bridge, to find **St. Nicholas Kirk** ⑫ a few minutes farther down Union Street. It is set in a peaceful green churchyard, screened from Union Street by a colonnaded facade (1829) and popular with office workers for lunchtime picnics in summer.

You are now almost back at your starting point on Castle Street, but turn right, opposite Broad Street, and head down Ship Row to enjoy the Aberdeen Maritime Museum, housed partly in **Provost Ross's House** ⑬ (1593) and partly in a magnificent modern glass extension. Below Ship Row is the harbor, which contains some fine architecture from the 18th and 19th centuries. Explore it if time permits and you don't mind the background traffic. Also close to your starting point, and an essential place to visit if you have children with you, is **Satrosphere** ⑭, a hands-on exhibition of science and technology that makes science come alive. It's up off the west end of Union Street, but worth the 15-minute walk.

The second part of your city walk is best accomplished by first getting on a bus travelling north from a stop near Marischal College, or up King Street, off the Castlegate, to reach **Old Aberdeen. College Bounds** ⑮ has handsome 18th- and 19th-century houses, cobbled streets, and paved sidewalks. **King's College** ⑯ was founded in 1494 and is now part of the University of Aberdeen. This street has some fine restored Georgian houses, including the **Town House** ⑰. Behind the Town House the modern intrusion of St. Machar's Drive destroys some of the old-town ambience, but the atmosphere of the old town can be savored again by a stroll down the Chanonry, past the elegant houses once lived in by the officials connected with the cathedral nearby. Today, they house mainly university staff.

North on the Chanonry, **St. Machar's Cathedral** ⑱ was built in AD 580, but nothing remains of the original foundation. Much of what you see dates from the 15th and 16th centuries. Beyond St. Machar's Cathedral lies **Seaton Park** ⑲, full of daffodils in spring. Until the early 19th century, the only route out of Aberdeen to the north was over the River Don on the **Brig o'Balgownie** ⑳ (1314), found at the far end of Seaton Park—a 15-minute walk.

TIMING

Depending on how many places you want to look into en route, and how long you stay in each, you can either devote a day to each half of this walk, or spend a long morning in the center of Aberdeen, then take a bus out to Old Aberdeen after a late lunch, and do the tour in a (long) day.

Sights to See

❼ **Aberdeen Art Gallery.** This popular gallery, which locals take great pride and pleasure in, houses a wide-ranging collection—from the 18th century to contemporary work—of paintings, prints and drawings, sculpture, porcelain, costume, and much else. It also hosts frequent important temporary exhibitions. ⊠ *Schoolhill*, ☎ *01224/646333*. 🎫 *Free.* ⊙ *Mon.– Sat. 10–5; Sun. 2–5.*

⑳ Brig o'Balgownie. Until 1827, the only way out of Aberdeen to the north was over the River Don on this single-arch bridge. It dates from 1314 and is thought to have been built by Richard Cementarius, Aberdeen's first provost. ⊠ *Seaton Park.*

⑮ College Bounds. Handsome 18th- and 19th-century houses line this cobbled street with paved sidewalks. ⊠ *Old Aberdeen.*

★ **⑯ King's College.** Founded in 1494, King's College is now part of the University of Aberdeen. Its **Chapel**, which was built around 1500, has an unmistakable flying (or crown) spire. The fact that it has survived at all was due to the zeal of the principal, who managed to defend his church against the destructive fanaticism that swept through Scotland during the Reformation, when the building was less than a century old. Today the renovated chapel plays an important role in university life. The tall oak screen that separates the nave from choir, the ribbed wooden ceiling, and the stalls constitute the finest medieval wood carving to be found anywhere in Scotland. The University's **Visitor Centre** on High Street will tell you more about the university. ⊠ *College Bounds.*

★ **❹ Marischal College.** Founded in 1593 by the earl Marischal as a Protestant alternative to the Catholic King's College in Old Aberdeen, the two colleges combined to form Aberdeen University in 1860. (The earls Marischal held hereditary office as keepers of the king's mares.) The original university buildings on this site have undergone extensive renovations and the present facade was built in 1891. The spectacularly ornate work is set off by the gilded flags, and this turn-of-the-century creation is still the second-largest granite building in the world. Only the Escorial in Madrid is larger. The main part of the building, no longer needed by the university, is at present the subject of various plans, one being to turn it into a hotel. The **Marischal Museum** exhibits artifacts and photographs relating to the heritage of the Northeast. ⊠ *Broad St.,* ☎ *01224/273131.* 🎫 *Free.* ⊙ *Museum weekdays 10–5, Sun. 2–5.*

❸ Mercat Cross. Built in 1686 and restored in 1820, the Mercat Cross, always the symbolic center of a Scottish medieval burgh, stands just beyond King Street. Along its parapet are 12 portrait panels of the Stewart monarchs.

Old Aberdeen. Once an independent burgh, near the River Don, but swallowed up by the expanding main city before the end of the 19th century, Old Aberdeen still retains a certain degree of character and integrity. ⊠ *Between King's College and St. Machar's Cathedral.*

★ 🐾 **⑬ Provost Ross's House.** Dating from 1593, this building now houses the **Aberdeen Maritime Museum**, which tells the story of the city's involvement with the sea, from early inshore fisheries by way of tea clippers to the North Sea oil boom. It is a fascinating place for grade-schoolers, with its ship models, paintings, and equipment associated with the fishing, local shipbuilding, and North Sea oil and gas industries. ⊠ *Provost Ross's House, Ship Row,* ☎ *01224/337700.* 🎫 *Free.* ⊙ *Mon.–Sat. 10–5, Sun. 11–5.*

❺ Provost Skene's House. *Provost* is Scottish for mayor, and this former mayor's domestic dwelling was once part of a closely packed area of town houses. Steeply gabled and built of rubble, it survives in part from 1545. It is now a museum portraying civic life, with restored furnished period rooms and a painted chapel. ⊠ *Guestrow off Broad St.,* ☎ *01224/641086.* ☐ *Free.* ⊙ *Mon.–Sat. 10–5.*

❻ Robert Gordon's University. Built in 1731, this was originally called Robert Gordon's Hospital and was used to educate poor boys. It became an independent school later and then an institute of technology, before gaining university status in 1992. ⊠ *Schoolhill..* ⊙ *View from outside only.*

❾ Rosemount Celebration Centre. This houses an activities-based heritage museum and learning center called Jonah's Journey, based on life in a 2,000-year-old Israelite village. The center has costumes, spinning and weaving, mosaic making, puppet plays, and jigsaw puzzles. ⊠ *Rosemount Pl.,* ☎ *01224/620111.* ☐ *£3.* ⊙ *Mon.–Sat. 10–noon, Sun. 2:30–4:30.*

❽ Rosemount Viaduct. Three buildings on this bridge are collectively known by all Aberdonians as Education, Salvation, and Damnation. Silvery and handsome, the **Central Library** and **St. Mark's Church** date from the last decade of the 19th century, and **His Majesty's Theatre** (1904–08) has been restored inside to its full Edwardian splendor (☞ Nightlife and the Arts, *below*).

⑱ St. Machar's Cathedral. Originally founded in AD 580, nothing remains of the original structure. It is said that St. Machar was sent by St. Columba to build a church on a grassy platform near the sea, where a river flowed in the shape of a shepherd's crook. This spot fit the bill. Much of the existing building dates from the 15th and 16th centuries. The central tower collapsed in 1688, reducing the building to half its original length. The twin octagonal spires on the western towers date from the first half of the 16th century. The nave is thought to have been rebuilt in red sandstone in 1370, but the final renovation was completed in granite by the middle of the 15th century. Along with the nave ceiling, the twin spires were finished in time to take a battering in the Reformation, when the barons of the Mearns stripped the lead off the roof of St. Machar's and stole the bells. The cathedral suffered further mistreatment—including the removal of stone by Oliver Cromwell's (1599–1658) English garrison in the 1650s—until a 19th-century scheme restored the church to its former grandeur. ⊠ *Chanonry,* ☎ *01224/485988.* ⊙ *Daily 9–5.*

⑫ St. Nicholas Kirk. The Mither Kirk, as this, the original burgh church, was known, is curiously not within the bounds of the early town settlement: that was located to the east, near the end of present-day Union Street. During the 12th century, the port of Aberdeen flourished and room could not be found for the church within the settlement. Its earliest features are the pillars—supporting a tower built much later—and its clerestory windows: Both date from the original 12th-century structure. St. Nicholas was divided into east and west kirks at the Reformation, followed by a substantial amount of renovation from 1741 on. Some early memorials and other works have survived. ⊠ *Union St.* ⊙ *Weekdays 10–1, Sun. for services.*

⑭ Satrosphere. This hands-on exhibition of science and technology makes science come alive. Children (and adults) of even the most unscientific bent will love it. ⊠ *19 Justice Mill La.,* ☎ *01224/213232.* ☐ *£3.90.* ⊙ *Apr.–early Oct., Mon.–Sat. 10–5, Sun. 1:30–5; mid-Oct.–Mar., Mon. and Wed.–Fri. 10–4, Sat. 10–5, Sun. 1:30–5.*

⑲ Seaton Park. With its spring daffodils, tall trees, and herbaceous, boldly colored borders, this park is typical of Aberdeen's exceptionally high standards of civic horticulture; the city is a frequent prizewinner in the "Britain in Bloom" contest each year. ⊠ *Don St., Old Aberdeen.*

② Tolbooth. From this building, the city was governed for 200 years. It was also the burgh court and jail: narrow, winding stairs lead to dank stone cells where "Jacobite prisoner" William Baird tells his story. Many other exhibits show the evolution of the city's government, and crime and punishment since medieval times. ⊠ *Castle St.,* ☎ *01224/621167.* 🎫 *Free.* ☉ *Tues.–Sat. 10–5, Sun 2–5.*

⑰ Town House. This Georgian work, plain and handsome, uses parts of an earlier building from 1720. ⊠ *High St., Old Aberdeen.*

⑪ Union Bridge. Built in the early years of the 19th century, as was much of Union Street, this bridge has a gentle rise—or descent, if you are traveling east—and the street is carried on a series of blind arches. The north side of Union Bridge is the most obvious reminder of the grand thoroughfare's artificial levels. (Despite appearances, you'll discover you're not at ground level.) Much of the original work remains. ⊠ *Union St..*

① Union Street. This great thoroughfare is to Aberdeen what Princes Street is to Edinburgh: the central pivot of the city plan and the product of a wave of enthusiasm to rebuild the city in a contemporary style in the early 19th century.

⑩ Union Terrace. In the 19th-century development of Union Terrace stands a statue of Robert Burns (1759–96), addressing a daisy. Behind Burns are the **Union Terrace Gardens,** faintly echoing Edinburgh's Princes Street Gardens in that they separate the older part of the city, to the east, from the 19th-century development of Union Terrace and points west (as well as Union Street itself). Most of the buildings on Union Terrace around the grand-looking Caledonian Hotel are late Victorian, when exuberance and confidence in style was at its height.

OFF THE
BEATEN PATH

DUTHIE PARK AND WINTER GARDENS – A great place to feed the ducks, Duthie Park also has a boating pond and trampolines, carved wooden animals, and playgrounds. In the very attractive (and warm!) Winter Gardens are fish in ponds, free-flying birds, turtles, and terrapins among the luxuriant foliage and flowers. The park lies close beside Aberdeen's other river, the Dee. ⊠ *Polmuir Rd., Riverside Dr., about 1 mi south from city center* 🎫 *Free.* ☉ *Entertainment in summer only, gardens daily 10–dusk.*

Dining and Lodging

£££ ✕ **Silver Darling.** Situated right on the quayside, the Silver Darling is
★ one of Aberdeen's most acclaimed restaurants. It specializes, as its name suggests, in fish. The style is French provincial, and an indoor barbecue guarantees flavorful grilled fish and shellfish. ⊠ *Pocra Quay, Footdee,* ☎ *01224/576229. Reservations essential. AE, DC, MC, V. Closed Sun. No lunch Sat.*

££–£££ ✕ **Brasserie Gerard's.** On a side street moments from the upmarket west end of Union Street, Gerard's is a long-established part of the Aberdeen dining scene. Classic French cuisine is ably prepared with local produce—fish and red meats in particular. Try the seafood thermidor, with king prawns, scallops, and monkfish served with creole rice. Nouvelle cuisine this is not, but it's satisfying, and the fixed-price lunch is an especially good value. The relaxed, softly lit setting includes a flagstone-floored garden room, with greenery and tile or marble tables. ⊠ *50 Chapel St.,* ☎ *01224/639500. AE, DC, MC, V.*

££££ 🏨 **Marcliffe at Pitfodels.** The spacious, old country house hotel in the
★ West End benefits from the skills and experience of leading Scottish hotelier Stewart Spence. The combination of old and new in the indi-

vidually decorated rooms is impressive—some have reproduction antique furnishings, others are more modern. There are two restaurants: an informal conservatory dining area and the Invery, offering international fare with a Scottish flavor. ⊠ *N. Deeside Rd., Pitfodels, AB15 9YA,* ☎ *01224/861000,* ℻ *01224/868860. 42 rooms with bath. 2 restaurants. AE, DC, MC, V.*

££–££££ 🏨 **Caledonian Thistle Hotel.** Well-situated and offering pleasant views over city gardens, one of the larger hotels in the Granite City is generally considered to be one of the best, but seems to be resting on its laurels lately, in need of a refurbishment. Rooms are decorated in traditional style, and the pleasant restaurant serves tasty dishes from a menu best described as eclectic Scottish. ⊠ *Union Terr., AB10 1WE,* ☎ *01224/640233,* ℻ *01224/641627. 80 rooms, 77 with bath, 3 with shower. 2 restaurants, bar, coffee shop. AE, DC, MC, V.*

££ 🏨 **Atholl Hotel.** One of Aberdeen's many splendid silver granite properties, the Atholl Hotel is turreted and gabled and set within a leafy residential area to the west of the city. Rooms are done in rich, dark colors; the best views are from the top floor; the larger rooms are on the first floor. The restaurant prepares traditional Scottish dishes like lamb cutlets and roast rib of beef. ⊠ *54 Kings Gate, AB15 4YN,* ☎ *01224/323505,* ℻ *01224/321555. 35 rooms with bath or shower. Restaurant. AE, DC, MC, V.*

££ 🏨 **Craighaar Hotel.** Perhaps because it's convenient to the airport, the Craighaar is popular with businesspeople. But what makes it stand out is the personal service—this is the kind of place where the staff remember your name. The comfortable restaurant serves cuisine with a Scottish slant: Orkney oysters, smoked trout, crab claws, gourmet scampi, and char-grilled steaks. Guest rooms are cheerful with bright floral prints. The gallery suites—split-level rooms—are outstanding. ⊠ *Waterton Rd., Bucksburn, AB21 9HS,* ☎ *01224/712275,* ℻ *01224/716362. 55 rooms with bath or shower. Restaurant, bar. AE, DC, MC, V.*

££ 🏨 **Palm Court.** This sister hotel to the Craighaar (☞ *above*) offers the same high standards of accommodation and service. Traditional Scottish meals are served in the Conservatory, where your attention may well be distracted from a plate of delicious, freshly prepared salmon or roast chicken by the wealth of intriguing decorative artifacts surrounding you. Rooms, though not especially spacious, are well equipped and attractively furnished with warm, floral color schemes. ⊠ *81 Seafield Rd., AB15 7YU,* ☎ *01224/310351,* ℻ *01224/312707. 24 rooms with bath. Restaurant, bar. AE, DC, MC, V.*

Nightlife and the Arts

As you would expect, Aberdeen is the nightlife hot spot and cultural center of the region. In part because of the oil-industry boom, Aberdeen has a fairly lively nightlife scene, though much of it revolves around pubs and hotels; theaters, concert halls, arts centers, and cinemas are also well represented. The principal newspapers—the *Press and Journal* and the *Evening Express*—and *Aberdeen Leopard* magazine can fill you in on what's going on anywhere in the Northeast. Outside Aberdeen a number of small-town local papers list events under the "What's On" heading. Aberdeen's tourist information center (☞ Visitor Information *in* Aberdeen and the Northeast A to Z, *below*) has a monthly "What's On" with a full calendar, as well as contact telephone numbers.

The Arts

ARTS CENTERS

The Lemon Tree (⊠ 5 W. North St., ☎ 01224/642230) features an innovative and international program of dance, stand-up comedy, folk, jazz, rock and roll, and art exhibitions. **Aberdeen Arts Centre** (✉ 33 King St., ☎ 01224/635208) is a theater and concert venue where experimental plays, poetry readings, exhibitions by local and Scottish artists, and many other arts-based presentations can be enjoyed. At **Haddo House** (✉ off B9005 near Methlick, ☎ 01651/851770), 20 mi north of Aberdeen, the Haddo House Arts Trust runs a wide-ranging program of events, from opera and ballet to Shakespeare, Scots-language plays, and puppetry.

CONCERT HALL

The Music Hall (✉ Union St., ☎ 01224/641122) presents seasonal programs of concerts by the Scottish National Orchestra, the Scottish Chamber Orchestra, and other major orchestras and musicians. Its wide-ranging program of events also includes folk concerts, crafts fairs, and exhibitions.

DANCE

His Majesty's Theatre (✉ Rosemount Viaduct, ☎ 01224/641122) and **Aberdeen Arts Centre** (✉ 33 King St., ☎ 01224/635208) are regular venues for dance companies. Contact the box offices for details of current productions.

FESTIVALS

The **Aberdeen International Youth Festival** (box office, ✉ Music Hall, Union St., ☎ 01224/641122) in August has worldwide recognition and attracts youth orchestras, choirs, dance, and theater companies from many countries. During the festival, many companies take their productions to other venues in the Northeast. The October **Aberdeen Alternative Festival** (☎ 01224/635822) offers an eclectic mix of arts-based events at venues throughout the city.

FILM

The following cinemas show general release films. **ABC** (✉ Union St., ☎ 01224/590201). **Capitol** (✉ 431 Union St., ☎ 01224/583141). **Odeon** (✉ Justice Mill La., ☎ 01224/587160). **Virgin Multiplex** (✉ Queen's Links, ☎ 01224/550502).

OPERA

Both **His Majesty's Theatre** (✉ Rosemount Viaduct, ☎ 01224/641122) and **Haddo House Arts Trust** (✉ off B9005 near Methlick, ☎ 01651/851770) present operatic performances throughout the year; call for details or inquire at the tourist information center.

THEATER

His Majesty's Theatre (✉ Rosemount Viaduct, ☎ 01224/641122) is one of the most beautiful theaters in Britain. Live shows are presented throughout the year, many of them in advance of their official opening in London's West End.

Nightlife

CASINO

If you're interested in trying your luck at the gaming tables, you can place bets at the **Stakis Regency Casino** (✉ 61 Summer St., ☎ 01224/645273; membership with 24 hours' notice).

DISCOS

Most clubs in Aberdeen do not allow jeans or athletic shoes, and it's advisable to check beforehand that a particular disco is not closed for a private function. **Cotton Club** (✉ 491 Union St., ☎ 01224/581858). **De Niro's** (✉ 120 Union St., ☎ 01224/640641). **Franklyn's** (✉ Justice Mill La., ☎ 01224/212817). **Hotel Metro** (✉ 17 Market St., ☎ 01224/583275). **The Ministry** (✉ 16 Dee St., ☎ 01224/211661). **Club**

Latino (✉ 70–78 Chapel St., ☎ 01224/642112). **The Palace Nightclub** (✉ Bridge Pl., ☎ 01224/581135). **Zig-Zag** (✉ 2 Diamond St., ☎ 01224/641580).

MUSIC CLUBS

The Lemon Tree (✉ 5 W. North St., ☎ 01224/642230), with a wide-ranging music program, is the main rock venue and stages frequent jazz events. There is jazz on Saturday night at the **Masada Continental Lounge** (✉ Rosemount Viaduct, ☎ 01224/641587).

Outdoor Activities and Sports

Biking
The tourist information center can provide a leaflet of suggested cycle tours. Rates for bicycle rentals vary, depending on the type of bike. An average rate for a mountain bike is £12 a day. You can rent bicycles at **Alpine Bikes** (✉ 70 Holburn St., ☎ 01224/211455), which has a tandem bike available, and **Outdoor Gear** (✉ 88 Fonthill Rd., ☎ FAX 01224/573952).

Golf
The following courses in and around Aberdeen are open to visitors: **Balgownie, Royal Aberdeen Golf Club** (☎ 01224/702221) 18 holes, 6,372 yards, SSS 70 (☞ Chapter 2). **Balnagask** (✉ St. Fitticks Rd., ☎ 01224/871286) 18 holes, 5,986 yards, SSS 69. **Hazlehead** (☎ 01224/321830): Course 1, 18 holes, 6,204 yards, SSS 70; course 2, 18 holes, 5,742 yards, SSS 67; course 3, 9 holes, 2,770 yards, SSS 34.

Murcar (✉ Bridge of Don, ☎ 01224/704354) 18 holes, 6,241 yards, SSS 71. **Westhill** (☎ 01224/742567) 18 holes, 5,849 yards, SSS 69.

Health Clubs
Balmedie Leisure Centre (✉ Eigie Rd., Balmedie, ☎ 01358/743725). **Bon-Accord Swimming and Leisure Centre** (✉ Justice Mill La., Aberdeen, ☎ 01224/587920). **Kincorth Sports Centre** (✉ Corthan Dr., Aberdeen, ☎ 01224/879759). **Sheddocksley Sports Centre** (✉ Springhill Rd., Aberdeen, ☎ 01224/692534). **Westdyke Leisure Centre** (✉ 4 Westdyke Ave., Skene, ☎ 01224/743098).

Shopping

Aberdeen's shopping scene is in the throes of change. For generations, residents from nearby would come into Aberdeen for the day—the city is a kind of large-scale market town. Their chief delight would be to stroll the length of Union Street and perhaps take in George Street as well. Now this pattern is changing, thanks mainly to the modern and faceless shopping developments (pleasant enough in an anonymous way), the Trinity Centre (Union St.), and the St. Nicholas and Bon-Accord Centres (George St.), which have taken the emphasis away from Union Street.

Department Stores
Most of the larger national-name department stores are to be found in the shopping malls or along Union Street. However, note the spacious **John Lewis** store (✉ George St., reached via Bon Accord Centre, ☎ 01224/625000, closed Mon.), which closely resembles a double-decker sandwich, its filling illuminated and the crusts left on. It has a good-value, wide-ranging stock of clothing, household items, giftware, and much more.

Specialty Shops
Smaller specialty shops are still to be found, particularly in the **Chapel Street–Thistle Street** area at the west end of **Union Street** and on the

latter's north side, which has a series of interesting small retailers well worth discovering.

ANTIQUES

Colin Wood (✉ 25 Rose St., ☎ 01224/643019) is the place to go for antiques, maps, and prints.

BOOKS

At the **Aberdeen Family History Shop** (✉ 164 King St., ☎ 01224/646323) you can browse through a huge range of publications related to local history and genealogical research. For a small membership fee, the Aberdeen & North East Family History Society will undertake some research on your behalf.

GIFTS

Nova (✉ 20 Chapel St., ☎ 01224/641270), where the locals go for gifts, stocks major U.K. brand names, such as Liberty of London, Dartington Glass, and Crabtree and Evelyn, as well as a wide range of Scottish silver jewelry.

SCOTTISH SPECIALTIES

Harlequin (✉ 65 Thistle St., ☎ 01224/635716) stocks a large selection of embroidery and tapestry kits, designer yarns, and expensive, colorful knitwear. If you're looking for bargains, try the **Crombie Woollen Mill** (✉ Grandholm Mills, Woodside, off the A96, ☎ 01224/483201) on the edge of town; a particularly good value is the men's overcoats bearing the high-quality Crombie name.

TOYS

Aberdeen shops catering to children include **The Toy Bazaar** (✉ 45 Schoolhill, ☎ 01224/640021), which stocks a range of toys for children preschool age and up. **The Early Learning Centre** (✉ Bon-Accord Centre, George St., ☎ 01224/624188) specializes in toys with educational value.

ROYAL DEESIDE AND CASTLE COUNTRY

Deeside, the valley running west from Aberdeen down which the River Dee flows, earned its "Royal" appellation when discovered by Queen Victoria. To this day, where royalty goes, lesser aristocracy and freshly minted millionaires from across the globe follow. In fact, it is still the aspiration of many to own a grand shooting estate in Deeside. In a sense this yearning is understandable since piney hill slope, purple moor, and blue river intermingle most tastefully here, as you will see from the main road. Royal Deeside's gradual scenic change adds a growing sense of excitement as the road runs deeper and deeper into the Grampians.

There are castles along the Dee and to the north, an area that is indeed known as "castle country," and that well illustrates the gradual geological change in the Northeast: uplands lapped by a tide of farms. Although best toured by car, much of this area is accessible either by public transportation or on tours from Aberdeen.

Banchory

㉑ *19 mi west of Aberdeen via A93.*

Banchory is an immaculate place with a pinkish tinge to its granite. It is usually bustling with ice-cream-eating city strollers, out on a day trip from Aberdeen. If you visit in autumn and have time to spare, drive out to the **Brig o'Feuch** (pronounced fyooch, the "ch" as in loch). Here, salmon leap in season, and the fall colors and foaming waters make for an attractive scene.

22 East of town, and passed on the way from Aberdeen, are two castles for castle hoppers to explore. The first is **Drum Castle,** an ancient foursquare tower that dates from the 13th century, with later additions. Note the rounded corners of the tower, said to make battering-ram attacks more difficult. Nearby, fragments of the ancient Forest of Drum still stand, dating from the early days when Scotland was covered by great woodlands of oak and pine. ⊠ *Off A93, 10 mi west of Aberdeen,* ☎ *01330/811204.* 🏛 *Castle and garden £4.20, grounds and garden £2.* ☉ *Castle Easter and May–Sept., daily 1:30–5:30 (last admission at 4:45); Oct., weekends 1:30–5:30; garden of historic roses Easter and May–Sept., daily 10–6; Oct., weekends 10–6; grounds daily 9:30–dusk.*

23 **Crathes Castle** was once home of the Burnett family. Keepers of the Forest of Drum for generations, the family acquired lands here by marriage and later built a new castle, completed in 1596. Crathes is in the care of the National Trust for Scotland; the trust also looks after the grand gardens, with their calculated symmetry and clipped yew hedges. Sample the tasty home baking in the tearoom. ⊠ *Off A93, 3½ mi east of Banchory,* ☎ *01330/844525.* 🏛 *Castle £2, grounds or garden £2, grounds and garden £4, castle, grounds, and garden £4.80.* ☉ *Castle Apr.–Oct., daily 11–5:30 (last admission at 4:45), garden and grounds daily 9–dusk.*

Dining and Lodging

£££–££££ ✕🏨 **Banchory Lodge.** With the River Dee running past just a few yards away at the bottom of the garden, the Banchory Lodge, a fine example of a 17th-century country house, is an ideal spot for anglers. The lodge has retained its period charm, and tranquility is the keynote here. Rooms, with bold colors and tartan or floral fabrics, are individually decorated. The restaurant has high standards for its Scottish cuisine with French overtones; try the fillet of salmon, roast duckling, or guinea fowl with wild berries. ⊠ *Kincardineshire, AB31 5HS,* ☎ *01330/822625,* 🗚 *01330/825019. 22 rooms with bath. Restaurant, fishing. AE, DC, MC, V.*

Kincardine O'Neill

24 *9 mi west of Banchory.*

The ruined **kirk** in the little village of Kincardine O'Neill was built in 1233 and once sheltered travelers: it was the last hospice before the Mounth, the name given to the massif that shuts off the south side of the Dee Valley. Beyond Banchory (and the B974), no motor roads run south until you reach Braemar (A93), though the Mounth is crossed by a network of tracks used in former times by Scottish soldiers, invading armies (including the Romans), and cattle drovers. Photography buffs won't want to miss the bridge at **Potarch,** just to the east.

Aboyne

25 *5 mi west of Kincardine O'Neill.*

Aboyne is a pleasant, well laid-out town, with a village green (unusual for Scotland) that is the setting for an annual Highland Games. There is, however, not a great deal to detain the visitor here, except a good coffee shop.

26 The **Braeloine Interpretive Centre** in Glen Tanar beyond Aboyne has a natural history display, café, picnic area, and walks. ⊠ *Glen Tanar (cross River Dee, take right on B976, and left into the glen),* ☎ *013398/86072.* ☉ *Daily 10–5 (extended hours in summer).*

Dining

£   ✕ **At the Sign of the Blackfaced Sheep.** Filled rolls, soups, salads and delicious home-baked goods are served here, but another good reason to visit is the range of up-scale gifts and paintings that can be purchased in this coffee and crafts shop. ⊠ *Ballater Rd., Aboyne, AB34 5HT,* ☎ *013398/87311. DC, MC, V.*

En Route   Look for a large granite boulder next to the A93 on which is carved YOU ARE NOW ENTERING THE HIGHLANDS. You may find this piece of information superfluous, given the quality of the scenery.

Ballater

㉗   *12 mi west of Aboyne, 43 mi west of Aberdeen.*

The handsome holiday resort of Ballater, once noted for the curative properties of its local well, has profited from the proximity of the royals, nearby at Balmoral (☞ *below*). You might be amused by the array of BY ROYAL APPOINTMENT signs proudly hanging from many of its various shops (even monarchs need bakers and butchers). If you get a chance, take time to stroll around this neat community—well laid out in silver-gray masses. Note that the railway station now houses the tourist information center and a display on the former glories of this Great North of Scotland branch line, closed in the 1960s along with so many others in this country.

★ **㉘**   As long as you have your own car, you can capture the feel of the eastern Highlands, yet still be close to town. Start your expedition into **Glen Muick** (Gaelic for pig, pronounced "mick") by crossing the River Dee and turning upriver on the south side, shortly after the road forks, into this fine Highland glen. The native red deer are quite common throughout the Scottish Highlands, but Glen Muick is one of the very best places to see them in abundance, with herds grazing the flat valley floor. Beyond the lower glen, the prospect opens to reveal not only grazing herds, but also fine views of the battlement of cliffs edging the mountain called Lochnagar.

㉙   The enormous parking lot is indicative of the popularity of **Balmoral Castle,** the rebuilt castle modified by Prince Albert (1819–61) in 1855 for Queen Victoria (1819–1901). Balmoral's visiting hours depend on whether the royals are in residence (usually August). In truth, there are more interesting and historic buildings to explore, as the only part of the castle on view is the ballroom, with an exhibition of Royal artifacts. However, there are also extensive gardens and grounds to explore. ⊠ *A93 7 mi west of Ballater,* ☎ *013397/42334.* ☎ *£3.50.* ☺ *Good Friday–May, Mon.–Sat. 10–5; June–July, daily 10–5 (last admission 4).*

Dining and Lodging

££££   ✕▥ **Stakis Royal Deeside Hotel.** This magnificent country-house hotel, just outside Ballater on a hillside overlooking the River Dee, really does manage to keep everyone happy. Hotel guests are cosseted in luxurious surroundings and kept busy at the nearby leisure facilities. An even better value are the pine lodges set among the trees around the hotel. These self-catering cottages are geared for families and fitted with every kind of labor-saving appliance. There is also a solid choice of on-site restaurants, including the top-quality Oaks for modern Scottish à la carte cuisine, and The Clubhouse poolside brasserie. ⊠ *Ballater, AB35 5XA,* ☎ *013397/55858,* ℻ *013397/55447. 38 rooms with bath, 6 suites. 2 restaurants, 2 indoor pools, wading pool, beauty salon, hot tub, sauna, tennis court, exercise room, Ping-Pong, squash. AE, DC, MC, V.*

£££ ✕⊞ **Balgonie Country House.** A tranquil Edwardian country house in three acres of gardens overlooking Ballater's golf course, Balgonie delivers top-quality food and accommodation at real value-for-money prices. Bedrooms are all individually decorated in soft greens, blues, or pinks, with either antique furniture or, in the attic rooms, specially designed modern Swedish-style fitted furniture. The dining room is a peaceful setting for a four-course menu of Scottish specialties cooked in classic French style. ⊠ *Braemar Pl., Ballater, AB35 5NQ,* ☎ FAX *013397/55482. 9 rooms with bath. AE, MC, V. Closed Jan. and Feb.*

££–£££ ✕⊞ **Darroch Learg Hotel.** Amid tall trees on a hillside, the Darroch Learg is everything a Scottish country-house hotel should be, with the added bonus that the charming town of Ballater is moments away. Built in the 1880s as a country residence, the hotel exudes charm. Most guest rooms are decorated with mahogany furniture and designer fabrics in rich colors. The Scottish cuisine in the conservatory restaurant is sophisticated but also substantial, with the rich flavors of local beef and fish. ⊠ *Braemar Rd., Ballater, Aberdeenshire, AB35 5UX,* ☎ *013397/ 55443,* FAX *013397/55252. 18 rooms with bath or shower. Restaurant. AE, DC, MC, V.*

Shopping

The **McEwan Gallery** (⊠ on A939, 1 mi west of Ballater, ☎ 013397/ 55429) displays a good range of fine paintings, watercolors, prints, and books (many with a Scottish or golf theme) in an unusual house built by the Swiss artist Rudolphe Christen in 1902. For a low-cost gift you could always see what is being boiled up at **Dee Valley Confectioners** (⊠ Station Sq., ☎ 013397/55499). You can buy Scottish designer knitwear at **Goodbrand Knitwear** (⊠ 1 Braemar Rd., ☎ 013397/ 55947). At either of **Countrywear**'s two shops (⊠ 15 and 35 Bridge St., ☎ 013397/55453), you'll find everything you need for Highland country living, including fishing tackle, shooting accessories, cashmere, tweeds, and that flexible garment popular in Scotland between seasons: the bodywarmer.

En Route Continuing west into Highland scenery, further pine-framed glimpses appear of the "steep frowning glories of dark Lochnagar," as it was described by the poet Lord Byron (1788–1824). Lochnagar (3,786 ft) was made known to a wider audience than hillwalkers by the Prince of Wales, who published a children's story, "The Old Man of Lochnagar."

Braemar

17 mi west of Ballater, 60 mi west of Aberdeen, 51 mi north of Perth via A93.

③⓪ The village of Braemar is dominated by **Braemar Castle** on its outskirts, dating from the 17th century, with defensive walls built later in the plan of a pointed star. At Braemar (the braes, or slopes, of the district of Mar) the standard, or rebel flag, was first raised at the start of the spectacularly unsuccessful Jacobite rebellion of 1715. Thirty years later, during the last rebellion, Braemar Castle was strengthened and garrisoned by Hanoverian (government) troops. ⊠ *Braemar,* ☎ *013397/ 41219; 013397/41224 off-season.* ☞ *£2.50.* ☉ *Easter–Oct., Sat.–Thurs. 10–6.*

Braemar is also associated with the **Braemar Highland Gathering** held every September. Although it's one of many such events celebrated throughout Scotland, Braemar's gathering is distinguished by the presence of the royal family. You can find out more about the Braemar Highland Gathering at the **Braemar Highland Heritage Centre,** in a converted stable block in the middle of Braemar. It tells the history of the village with displays and a film, and also has a gift shop. ⊠ *The Mews, Mar Rd.,* ☎ *013397/41944.* ☞ *Free.* ⊙ *Daily 9–5 (extended hours in summer).*

Although the main A93 slinks off to the south from Braemar, a little unmarked road will take you farther west into the hilly heartlands. In fact, even if you do not have your own car, you can still explore this area by catching the post bus that leaves from Braemar Post Office once a day. The road offers you delectable views over the winding River Dee and the blue hills before passing through the tiny hamlet of Inverey and crossing a bridge at the **Linn of Dee.** *Linn* is a Scots word meaning rocky narrows, and the river's rocky gash here is deep and roaring. Park beyond the bridge and walk back to admire the sylvan setting of river and woodland, replete with bending larch bows and deep, tranquil pools with salmon glinting in them.

★ ③①

Dining and Lodging

£££   ✕🏠 **Invercauld Arms Thistle.** This handsome stone-built Victorian hotel in Braemar center makes a good base for exploring Royal Deeside. The welcoming entrance lounge, with plush sofas and elegant velvet chairs, leads to beautifully restored public rooms with attractive plasterwork and prints and to comfortable guest rooms with floral drapes and reproduction antique furniture. The restaurant serves an international cuisine with Scottish overtones, not least in the use of local fish, game, lamb, and beef. Dishes might include Aberdeen Angus steak with tomato and wild mushroom sauce or chicken with bean sprouts and water chestnuts with oyster sauce. ⊠ *Braemar, AB35 5YR,* ☎ *013397/41605,* 🆉 *013397/41428. 68 rooms with bath and shower. Restaurant, bar. AE, DC, MC, V.*

Outdoor Activities and Sports

Braemar has a tricky golf course laden with foaming waters. Erratic duffers take note: The compassionate course managers have installed, near the water, poles with little nets on the end for those occasional shots that may go awry.

En Route   From Braemar, retrace the A93 as far as Balmoral. From Balmoral, look for a narrow road going north, signposted B976. Be careful on the first twisting mile through the trees. Soon you will emerge from scattered pines into the open moor in upland Aberdeenshire. Behind is the massif of Lochnagar again, and to the west are snow-tipped domes of the big Cairngorms. Roll down to a bridge and go left on the A939, which comes in from Ballater. Another high moor section follows: as the road leaves the scattered buildings by the bridge, see if you can spot the roadside inscription to the company of soldiers who built the A939 in the 18th century.

Corgarff Castle

③② *23 mi northeast of Braemar, 14 mi northwest of Ballater.*

Eighteenth-century soldiers paved a military highway, now the A939, north from Ballater to Corgarff Castle, a lonely tower house with another star-shaped defensive wall—a curious replica of Braemar Castle (☞ *above*). Corgarff was built as a hunting seat for the earls of Mar in the 16th century. After an eventful history that included the wife of a later laird being burned alive in a family dispute, the castle ended its career as a garrison for Hanoverian troops. The troops also had the responsibility of trying to prevent illegal whisky distilling, at one time a popular hobby in these parts. ⊠ *Signposted off A939,* ☎ *0131/668–8800.* ⊙ *Apr.–Sept., daily 9:30–6; Oct.–Mar., Sat. 9:30–4, Sun. 2–4.*

En Route If you return east from Corgarff Castle to the A939/A944 junction and make a left onto the A944, the thorough castle signposting will tell you that you are on the **Castle Trail.** The A944 meanders along the River Don to the village of Strathdon, where a great mound by the roadside— on the left—turns out to be a *motte,* or the base of a wooden castle, built in the late 12th century. Surviving mottes are significant in terms of confirming the history of Scottish castles, but it is difficult for visitors to become enthusiastic about a great grassed-over heap, no matter what its historic content. The A944 then joins the A97 (go left) and just a few minutes later a sign points to Glenbuchat Castle, a plain Z-plan tower house.

Kildrummy

18 mi northeast of Corgarff, 23 mi north of Ballater, 22 mi north of Aboyne.

★ ③③ **Kildrummy Castle** is significant because of its age (13th century) and because it has ties to the mainstream medieval traditions of European castle building. It shares features with Harlech and Caernarfon in Wales, as well as with Continental sites, such as Château de Coucy near Laon, France. Kildrummy had undergone several expansions at the hands of England's King Edward I (1239–1307) when, in 1306, back in Scottish hands, the castle was besieged by King Edward I's son. The defenders were betrayed by a certain Osbarn the Smith, who had been promised a large amount of gold by the English forces. They gave it to him after the castle fell, pouring it molten down his throat, or so the ghoulish story goes. Kildrummy's prominence came to an end after the collapse of the 1715 Jacobite uprising. It had been the rebel headquarters and was consequently dismantled. ☎ *0131/668–8800.* ✆ *£1.80.* ⊘ *Apr.–Sept., daily 9:30–6.*

Kildrummy Castle Gardens behind the castle—with a separate entrance from the main road—are built in what was the original quarry for the castle. This sheltered bowl within the woodlands has a broad range of shrubs and alpine plants and a notable water garden. If the weather is pleasant, it makes for a nice place to pause and plan the next stage of your journey. ✉ *A97,* ☎ *019755/71203 or 019755/71277.* ✆ *£2.* ⊘ *Apr.–Oct., daily 10–5 (call to confirm opening times late in season).*

Dining and Lodging

££££ ✕⊞ **Kildrummy Castle Hotel.** A grand late-Victorian country house, this hotel offers an attractive blend of a peaceful setting, attentive service, and sporting opportunities. Oak paneling, beautiful plasterwork, and gentle color schemes create a serene environment, enhanced by the views of Kildrummy Castle Gardens (☞ *above*) next door. The award-winning Scottish cuisine features local game and seafood. ✉ *Kildrummy, by Alford, Aberdeenshire, AB33 8RA,* ☎ *019755/71288,* 𝔽𝔸𝕏 *019755/71345. 16 rooms with bath or shower. Restaurant, golf privileges, fishing. AE, MC, V.*

Alford

9 mi east of Kildrummy, 28 mi west of Aberdeen.

A plain and sturdy settlement in the Howe (Hollow) of Alford, this town gives those visitors who have grown somewhat weary of castle ③④ hopping a break: it has a museum instead. The **Grampian Transport Museum** specializes in road-based means of locomotion. One of its more unusual exhibits is the *Craigievar Express,* a steam-driven creation invented by the local postman to deliver mail more efficiently. ✉ *Alford,* ☎ *019755/62292.* ✆ *£3.* ⊘ *Apr.–Oct., daily 10–5.*

★ ㉟ Two of the finest castles on the Castle Trail are near Alford. **Craigievar**'s historic structure represents one of the finest traditions of local castle building. It also has the advantage of having survived intact, much as the stonemasons left it in 1626, with its pepper-pot turrets and towers, the whole slender shape covered in a pink-cream pastel. It was built in relatively peaceful times by William Forbes, a successful merchant in trade with the Baltic Sea ports (hence he was also known as Danzig Willie). Centuries of care and wise stewardship have ensured that the experience proffered you today is as authentic as possible. ⊠ *5 mi south of Alford on A980,* ☎ *013398/83635.* ☒ *£5.80; grounds only £1.* ☉ *Castle May–Sept., daily 1:30–5:30 (last admission at 4:45), grounds daily 9:30–sunset.*

㊱ The massive **Castle Fraser** is the largest of the castles of Mar. Although this building shows a variety of styles reflecting the taste of its owners from the 15th to the 19th centuries, its design is typical of the cavalcade of castles that exist here in the northeast. It has the further advantages of a walled garden, picnic area, and tearoom. ⊠ *8 mi east of Alford off A944,* ☎ *01330/833463.* ☒ *£4.20.* ☉ *Castle Easter, May–June, and Sept., daily 1:30–5:30; July–Aug., daily 11–5:30; Oct., weekends 1:30–5:30 (last admission at 4:45), gardens daily 9:30–6, grounds daily 9:30–sunset.*

THE NORTHEAST

This route starts inland, traveling toward Speyside—the valley or strath of the River Spey—famed for its whisky distilleries, which it promotes in yet another signposted trail. Whisky distilling is not an intrinsically spectacular process. It involves pure water, malted barley, and, sometimes, peat smoke, then a lot of bubbling and fermentation, all of which causes a range of extremely odd smells. The end result is a prestigious product with a fascinating range of flavors that you either enjoy immensely or not at all.

Instead of assiduously following the Whisky Trail, just dip into it and blend it with some other aspects of the lower end of Speyside—the county of Moray. Whisky notwithstanding, Moray's scenic qualities, low rainfall, and other reassuring weather statistics are also worth remembering. The suggested route then ranges widely to sample the seaboard of the Northeast, including some of the best, but least-known, coastal scenery in Scotland.

Dufftown

★ ㊲ *54 mi from Aberdeen via A96 and A920 (turn west at Huntly).*

On one of the Spey tributaries, Dufftown was planned in 1817 by the earl of Fife. One of the most famous malt whiskies of all, the market leader is distilled at **Glenfiddich Distillery.** The independent company of William Grant and Sons Limited was the first distillery to realize the tourist potential of the distilling process. It subsequently built an entertaining visitor center in addition to offering tours. In short, if you do intend to visit a distillery, it may as well be Glenfiddich, especially because it probably offers the most complete range of on-site activities, from floor malting to bottling. In fact, it is the only Speyside distiller that bottles on the premises. The audiovisual show and displays in the visitor center are also worthwhile, and the traditional stone-walled premises with the typical pagoda-roofed malting buildings have a pleasant period ambience. You don't have to like whisky to come away feeling you've learned something about a leading Scottish export.

The Northeast

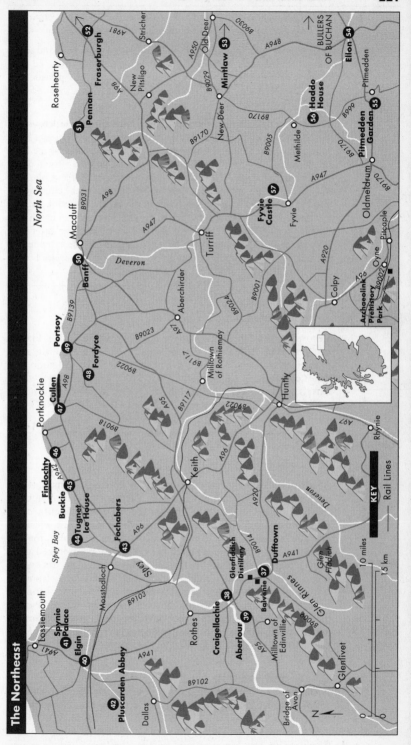

North Sea

Rosehearty
Fraserburgh **52**
Stricher
New Pitsligo
New Deer
Old Deer
Mintlaw **53**
BULLERS OF BUCHAN
Ellon **54**
Pitmedden
Pennan **51**
Haddo House **56**
Methilde
Pitmedden Garden **55**
Oldmeldrum
Macduff
Fyvie Castle **57**
Fyvie
Banff **50**
Deveron
Turriff
Aberchirder
Pitcaple
Oyne
Archaeolink Prehistory Park
Portsoy **49**
Colpy
Portknockie
Cullen **47**
Fordyce **48**
Milltown of Rothiemay
Findochty **46**
Huntly
Buckie **45**
Keith
Rhynie
KEY — Rail Lines
Spey Bay
Tugnet Ice House **44**
Fochabers **43**
Dufftown
Glen Fiddich
Deveron
Lossiemouth
Mosstodloch
Glenfiddich Distillery
Balvenie **37**
10 miles
15 km
Spynie Palace **41**
Elgin **40**
Craigellachie **38**
Rothes
Aberlour **39**
Milltown of Edinville
Glen Rinnes
Pluscarden Abbey **42**
Dallas
B9102
Bridge of Avon
Glenlivet

A981 A98 A950 B9029 B9030 A948 B9999 B9000 B9170 B9005 B9170 A947 B9999 B9170 B9002 A920 A96 A947 A98 B9031 A947 B9139 B9002 B9001 B9023 A97 B9117 B911 A95 B9018 A941 A942 A98 A96 A920 A96 B9014 A941 A95 B9009 B9103 A941 A96 B9170 A920 A97 A98

✉ *North of Dufftown on A941,* ☎ *01340/820373.* 🎟 *Free.* ☼ *Mon.– Fri. 9:30–4:30; Easter–mid-Oct., also Sat. 9:30–4:30, Sun. noon–4:30.*

On a mound just above Glenfiddich Distillery is a grim, gray, and squat curtain-walled castle, **Balvenie.** This fortress, which dates from the 13th century, once commanded the glens and passes toward Speyside and Elgin. ✉ *Dufftown,* ☎ *0131/668–8800.* 🎟 *£1.20.* ☼ *Apr.–Sept., daily 9:30–6.*

In the center of Dufftown, the conspicuous battlemented **clock tower**— the centerpiece of the planned town and a former jail—houses a local museum open in summer. **Mortlach Church,** set in a hollow by the Dullan Water, is thought to be one of the oldest Christian sites in Scotland, perhaps founded by St. Moluag, a contemporary of St. Columba, as early as AD 566. Note the weathered Pictish cross in the churchyard and the even older stone under cover in the vestibule, with a strange Pictish elephantlike beast carved on it. Though much of the church was rebuilt after 1876, some early work survives, including three lancet windows from the 13th century and a leper's squint (a hole extended to the outside of the church so that lepers could hear the service but be kept away from the rest of the congregation).

Craigellachie

38   *4 mi northwest of Dufftown via A941.*

Renowned as an angling resort on the Spey, Craigellachie, like so many Speyside settlements, is sometimes enveloped in the malty reek of the local industry. As you arrive in the village, you will notice the huge **Cooperage** (✉ Dufftown Rd., ☎ 01340/871108), the place where barrels are made and repaired. The Spey itself is crossed by a handsome suspension bridge, designed by Thomas Telford (1757–1834) in 1814 and now bypassed by the modern road.

Aberlour

39   *2 mi southwest of Craigellachie via A95.*

Aberlour, often marked as Charlestown of Aberlour on maps, is another handsome little burgh, essentially Victorian in style, though actually founded in 1812 by the local landowner. Glenfarclas, Cragganmore, and Aberlour are the names of the noted local whiskies; if you're interested in something nonalcoholic, take a look at the **Village Store.** After the owners retired in 1978, the shop was locked away intact, complete with stock. In the late 1980s, new owners discovered they had bought a time capsule—a range of products dating from the early decades of the present century—as well as all the paraphernalia, books and ledgers, accounts, and notes of a country business. Part of the premises is now a gift shop, but the remainder is preserved for visitors to enjoy, with stock of a bygone era on the shelves. ✉ *76 High St.,* ☎ *01340/871243.* 🎟 *Free.* ☼ *Feb.–Dec., Mon.–Sat. 10–5, Sun. 1:30–5.*

Dining and Lodging

£   ✕ **Old Pantry.** This corner restaurant, overlooking Aberlour's pleasant, tree-shaded central square, serves everything from a cup of coffee to a four-course spread. ✉ *The Square,* ☎ *01340/871617.* MC, V.

££–£££   ✕▣ **Minmore House.** Former home of George Smith, founder of the
★   Glenlivet Distillery, Minmore, a 25-minute drive from Aberlour, retains a strong private-house feel. Faded chintz in the drawing room (where afternoon tea is served) and a paneled library (now housing a bar with nearly 100 malt whiskies) are complemented by very comfortable

guest rooms (one, allegedly, with a ghost) with an eclectic mix of antiques. The restaurant serves exceptional modern Scottish dishes, including Highland lamb with a mint and honey glaze. The Speyside Way long-distance footpath passes below the house, and the area is famous for bird-watching—you might sight buzzards, peregrines, or maybe even a golden eagle. Take the A95 south from Aberlour, then turn left on the B9008 at Bridge of Avon. ⊠ *Glenlivet, Ballindalloch, Banffshire, AB37 9DB,* ☎ *01807/590378,* ℻ *01807/590472. 10 rooms with bath. Restaurant, bar. MC, V. Closed mid.-Oct.–Apr.*

Elgin

⓵ *16 mi north of Aberlour via A941, 69 mi northwest of Aberdeen, 41 mi east of Inverness via A96.*

As the center of the fertile Laigh (low-lying lands) of Moray, Elgin has been of local importance for centuries. Like Aberdeen, it is self-supporting and previously remote, sheltered by great hills to the south and lying between two major rivers, the Spey and the Findhorn. Beginning in the 13th century, Elgin became an important religious center, a cathedral city with a walled town growing up around the cathedral and adjacent to the original settlement. Left in peace for at least some of its history, Elgin prospered and became, by the early 18th century, a mini-Edinburgh of the north and a place where country gentlemen came to spend the winter. It even echoed Edinburgh in the wide-scale reconstruction of the early 19th century: much of the old town was swept away in a wave of rebuilding, giving Elgin the fine neoclassical buildings that survive today.

The old street plan of the town survived almost intact until this century, when it succumbed to the modern madness of demolishing great swaths of buildings for the sake of better traffic flow: Elgin suffered from its position on the Aberdeen–Inverness main road. However, the central main street plan and some of the older little streets and wynds (alleyways) remain. Visitors can also recall Elgin's past by observing the arcaded shop fronts—some of which date from the late 17th century—on the main shopping street.

At the center of Elgin, the most conspicuous, positively unavoidable building is **St. Giles Church,** which divides High Street. The grand four-square building built in 1828 exhibits the style known as Greek Revival: note the columns, the pilasters, and the top of the spire, surmounted by a representation of the Lysicrates Monument. Past the arcaded shops at the east end of High Street, you can see the **Little Cross** (17th century), which marked the boundary between the town and the cathedral grounds. Near the Little Cross, the **Elgin Museum** (♡ summer months only) has an especially interesting collection of dinosaur relics.

★ Cooper Park, a short distance to the southeast across the modern bypass road, is home to a magnificent ruin, **Elgin Cathedral,** consecrated in 1224. The cathedral's eventful story included devastation by fire: a 1390 act of retaliation by Alexander Stewart (circa 1343–1405), the Wolf of Badenoch. The illegitimate son-turned-bandit of King David II (1324–71) had sought revenge for his being excommunicated by the bishop of Moray. The cathedral was rebuilt but finally fell into disuse after the Reformation in 1560. By 1567, the highest authority in the land at the time, the regent earl of Moray, had stripped the lead from the roof to pay for his army. Thus ended the career of the religious seat known as the Lamp of the North. Some traces of the cathedral settlement survive, although they have been drastically altered: the gateway Pann's Port and the Bishop's Palace. ☎ *0131/668–8800.* 🎫 *£1.80,* *combined admission with Spynie Palace £2.80.* ○ *Apr.–Oct., daily 9:30–6; Nov.–Mar., Mon.–Wed. and Sat. 9:30–4, Thurs. 9:30–noon, Sun. 2–4.*

④ Just northwest of Elgin is **Spynie Palace,** the large 15th-century former headquarters of the bishops of Moray. It has now fallen into ruin and decay, though the top of the tower has good views over the Laigh of Moray. Find it by turning right off the main A941 Elgin–Lossiemouth road. ☎ *0131/668–8800.* ☞ *£1.80, combined admission with Elgin Cathedral £2.80.* ○ *Apr.–Oct., daily 9:30–6; Nov.–Mar., Sat. 9:30–4, Sun. 2–4.*

Given the general destruction caused by the 16th-century religious upheaval of the Reformation, abbeys in Scotland tend to be ruinous and
④ deserted, but at **Pluscarden Abbey** the monks' way of life continues. Originally a 13th-century foundation, the religious community abandoned their abbey after the Reformation. The third marquis of Bute bought the remains in 1897 and initiated a repair and restoration program that continues to this day. Monks from an abbey near Gloucester, England, returned here in 1948, and today the abbey is an active religious community. ✉ *6 mi southwest of Elgin, off B9010.* ☞ *Free.* ○ *Daily 5 AM–8:30 PM.*

Dining and Lodging

££££ ✕▣ **Mansion House Hotel.** This Scots baronial mansion complete with tower is set on the River Lossie. The rooms are individually decorated; all provide comfort and pleasant surroundings. The Scottish cuisine in the restaurant includes dishes such as brochette of monkfish and salmon with lime and butter sauce, or breast of pheasant with port sauce; vegetarians are also well catered to. ✉ *The Haugh, IV30 1AW,* ☎ *01343/548811,* ℻ *01343/547916. 23 rooms with bath. Restaurant, bar, indoor pool, beauty salon, sauna, exercise room. AE, DC, MC, V.*

Nightlife and the Arts

Moray Playhouse (✉ High St., Elgin, ☎ 01343/542680) shows mainstream releases.

Shopping

Elgin has, in addition to the usual range of High Street stores, **Gordon and MacPhail** (✉ 58 South St., ☎ 01343/545110), an outstanding delicatessen and wine merchant that, in addition to wine, stocks a breathtaking range of otherwise scarce malt whiskies. This is a good place to shop for gifts for those foodies among your friends. **Johnstons of Elgin** (✉ Newmill, ☎ 01343/554099) has a worldwide reputation for its luxury fabrics, including cashmere. The bold color range is particularly appealing.

Fochabers

④ *9 mi east of Elgin.*

Just before reaching Fochabers, you will see the works of a major local employer, Baxters of Fochabers, a family-run firm with an international reputation for fine foods. From Tokyo to New York, upmarket stores stock their soups, jams, chutneys, and other gourmet products—all of which are made here, close to the River Spey. Factory tours yield glimpses of impeccably attired staff stirring great vats of boiling marmalade and other concoctions. The **Baxters Visitors Centre** also offers a video presentation, a re-creation of the Baxters' first grocery shop, as well as a real shop stocking Baxters' goods (among other products), the Best of Scotland shop (specializing in Scottish goods), a store selling quality cooking utensils, cooking demonstrations, and two restaurants that offer an assortment of delectables. ✉ *1 mi west of Fochabers,*

☎ *01343/820666. ✉ Free; small charge for cooking demonstrations.
🕐 Daily 10–5:30 (extended hours in summer), guided tours Mon.–
Thurs. 10–11:30 and 12:30–4, Fri. 10–11:30 and 12:30–2 (excluding 1 wk Apr., 2 wks June–July, 1 wk Aug.).*

Once over the Spey bridge, you will find that Fochabers itself has a symmetrical village green. Perhaps this pleasing, mellow ambience attracts the antiques dealers to Fochabers, their wares ranging from near-junk to designer pieces. Through one of the antiques shops, you can enter the **Fochabers Folk Museum,** a converted church that has a fine display of rural items, ranging from carts and carriages to interesting farm implements. ☎ *01343/821204. ✉ Free. 🕐 Winter, daily 9:30–1 and 2–5; summer, daily 9:30–1 and 2–6.*

Consider diverting onto the road that runs south directly opposite the Fochabers Folk Museum. Leaving the houses behind for well-hedged country lanes, you will discover a Forestry Commission sign to the **Earth Pillars.** These curious eroded sandstone pillars are framed by tall-trunked pines and overlook a wide prospect of the lower Spey Valley.

Another option is to take the B9108 from Fochabers to the mouth of the River Spey. Here, by a storm beach with a high swell of smooth-washed pebbles, the river enters the sea. Nearby is the **Tugnet Ice House,** once the centerpiece of the local salmon fishing industry. Before the days of mechanical refrigeration, the salmon were stored in icy chambers. The ice was gathered in the winter and lasted in its insulated cellars throughout the fishing season. Now a museum housed in the ice house tells the story. ✉ *Spey Bay,* ☎ *01309/673701. ✉ Free. 🕐 May–Sept., daily 11–4.*

Shopping

This is the place for antiques hunters, with several antiques shops all within a few yards of each other on the main street. Try **Sylvan Antiques** (✉ 23 High St., ☎ 01343/820814) for pottery and bric-a-brac; **Antiques (Fochabers)** (✉ Hadlow House, The Square, ☎ 01343/820838) for kitchenware and furniture; and **Pringle Antiques** (✉ High St., ☎ 01343/820362) for small furniture, pottery, glassware, and jewelry. If you are interested in local artwork, **Just Art** (✉ 64 High St., ☎ 01343/820500) is a fine gallery with high-quality ceramics and paintings. **Balance Natural Health** (✉ 59 High St., ☎ 01343/821443) stocks homeopathic remedies, potpourris, and the like. At **The Quaich** (✉ 85 High St., ☎ 01343/820981), you can stock up on gifts, then sit with a cup of tea and a home-baked snack.

Buckie

8 mi east of Fochabers via A98 and A942.

The fishing port of Buckie and its satellite villages are gray and workaday, with plenty of Victorian architecture added to the original end-on-to-the-sea fishermen's cottages. The **Buckie Drifter** maritime museum, housed in premises designed to be reminiscent of an old fishing drifter, is a hands-on visitor center that tells the story of the herring industry and of Buckie's development as a herring port. Upstairs, you enter a 1920s quayside scene, with a replica steam drifter that you can board, and barrels you can pack with herring. ✉ *Freuchny Rd., off Commercial Rd.,* ☎ *01542/834646. ✉ £2.50. 🕐 Apr.–Oct., Mon.–Sat. 10–5, Sun. noon–5.*

The **Peter Anson Gallery** shows a selection of watercolor works also related to the development of the fishing industry. The gallery is housed in a room accessed through the library. ✉ *Cluny Pl.,* ☎ *01542/832121. ✉ Free. 🕐 Weekdays 10–8, Sat. 10–noon.*

Dining

£££–££££ ✕ **Old Monastery.** On a broad, wooded slope set back from the coast
★   near Buckie, with westward views as far as the hills of Wester Ross,
          the Old Monastery was once a Victorian religious establishment. This
          theme carries through to the restrained decor of the Cloisters Bar and
          the Chapel Restaurant, with its hand stenciling. The local specialties—
          the freshest fish, venison, and Aberdeen Angus beef—make up the Scot-
          tish menu, or you can opt for such dishes as pan-fried, oatmeal-crusted
          chicken breast with a mustard cream sauce. There is a no-smoking din-
          ing room. This is quite simply the best for miles around. ✉ *Drybridge,
          Buckie,* ☎ FAX *01542/832660. AE, MC, V. Closed Sun., Mon., 3 wks
          in Jan., and 2 wks in Nov.*

En Route You will find a string of other fishing communities down by the shore,
          running east. These salty little villages paint a colorful scene with their
          gable-ended houses and fishing nets set out to dry amid the rocky shore-
          line.

Findochty

🟡46 *2 mi east of Buckie on A942.*

The residents of Findochty are known for their fastidiousness and cre-
ativity in painting their houses, taking the fine art of housepainting to
a new level. Some residents even paint the mortar between the stonework
a different color. This small town also has a harbor with a faint echo
of the Mediterranean about it.

Cullen

★ 🟡47 *3 mi east of Findochty.*

You will see some wonderfully painted homes again at Cullen, in the
old fishermen's town below the railway viaduct. But the real attractions of this little resort are its white-sand beach and the fine view west
toward the Bowfiddle Rock (the reason for its name is obvious on sight).
A stroll along the beach reveals the shape of the fishing settlement below
and the planned town above. Cullen and its shops are far enough away
from major town superstores to survive on local, intermittent trade;
most unusual for a town of its size, Cullen has a full range of specialty
shops—galleries and gift shops, butchers, an ironmonger, baker, hab-
erdasher, and a locally famous ice-cream shop among them—and several hotels and cafés.

Dining and Lodging

££ ✕🏨 **Seafield Arms Hotel.** A former coaching inn built in 1822, this hotel
offers high standards in every area: service, decor, and food. Deep, rich
colors prevail, and comfort and friendliness are the keynotes. The
restaurant, with its deep blue walls and tartan carpet, offers an extensive
à la carte Scottish menu featuring local seafood, game, beef, and lamb.
✉ *Seafield St., AB56 2SG,* ☎ *01542/840791,* FAX *01542/840736. 25
rooms with bath or shower. Restaurant, bar. AE, MC, V.*

Fordyce

🟡48 *5 mi east of Cullen.*

The conservation village of Fordyce lies among the barley fields of Banffshire like a small slice of rural England gone far adrift. You can stroll
by the churchyard, picnic on the old bleaching green (an explanatory
notice board tells you all about it), or visit a restored 19th-century carpenter's workshop.

Lodging

£ ⭐ 🔳 **Academy House.** This top-of-the-range bed-and-breakfast offers accommodation in what was once the headmaster's house for the local secondary school. Traditional decor and some well-chosen antique furniture decorate the spacious, well-proportioned rooms. Evening meals are served on request. ⊠ *School Rd., Fordyce, AB45 2SJ,* ☎ *01261/ 842743. 3 rooms without bath. No credit cards.*

Portsoy

㊾ *6 mi east of Cullen.*

The little town of Portsoy has a much more ancient layout than many Northeast communities. It can boast Moray Firth's oldest harbor, built in the 17th century. Once a North Sea trading port and later participating in the 19th-century fishing boom, the community thereafter fell into a decline. But thoughtful conservation programs have revitalized much of Portsoy's old fabric.

Shopping

Portsoy Marble (⊠ The Marble Workshop, Shorehead, ☎ 01261/ 842404) stocks not only marble items—eggs, platters, and so on—but also local pottery, books, cards, knitwear, and ornaments. (Portsoy marble, which can have a greenish or reddish tone, even found its way to France's Versailles Palace.)

Banff

㊿ *36 mi east of Elgin, 47 mi north of Aberdeen.*

Midway along the northeast coast, overlooking Moray Firth and the estuary of the River Deveron, Banff is a fishing town of considerable elegance that feels as though it is a million miles from tartan-clad Scotland. Part Georgian, like Edinburgh's New Town, and part 16th-century small burgh, like Culross, Banff is an exemplary east-coast salty town, with its tiny harbor and fine Georgian domestic architecture. It is also within easy reach of plenty of unspoiled coastline—cliff and rock to the east at Gardenstown (known as Gamrie) and Pennan, or beautiful little sandy beaches westward toward Sandend or Cullen.

The jewel in Banff's crown is the grand mansion of **Duff House,** a splendid William Adam-designed baroque mansion that has been restored as an outstation of the National Galleries of Scotland. Many fine paintings are displayed in rooms furnished to reflect the days when the house was occupied by the Dukes of Fife. There is also a good tearoom and an enticingly stocked shop in the basement. ☎ *01261/818181.* 🔳 *£3.* ☉ *Apr.–Sept., daily 11–4; Oct.–Mar., Thurs.–Sun. 11–4.*

Across the river in Banff's twin town, Macduff, on the shore east of the harbor, stands **Macduff Marine Aquarium.** A 250,000-gallon central tank and many smaller display areas and touch pools feature the sea life of the Moray Firth and North Atlantic. ⊠ *High Shore,* ☎ *01261/ 833369.* 🔳 *£2.75.* ☉ *Daily 10–5.*

Lodging

££ 🔳 **Eden House.** Surrounded by woodland, this Georgian mansion house set high above the River Deveron has magnificent views and makes an elegant but comfortable base from which to explore the coast east of Inverness. Since it is also the home of the proprietors, you are likely to feel like a houseguest rather than a room number. Tennis, billiards, fishing, and shooting can all be arranged, and numerous golf courses are within easy reach. Relax in the evening surrounded by carefully chosen antiques. Dinner (resident guests only) might include local seafood, Deveron salmon, game, or Scottish beef. ⊠ *AB45 3NT,* ☎ *01261/821282,* FAX *01261/821283. 5 rooms, 3 with bath or shower. No credit cards.*

Pennan

51 *12 mi east of Banff.*

A huddle of houses tucked below a crescent of grassy cliffs, Pennan shot to minor fame as the setting for some of the filming of *Local Hero,* which starred Burt Lancaster. The phone box and the inn featured in the film are still there. Pennan is set in a remote cliff coastline about as far from the tourist trail as is possible. Find it off B9031 between Macduff, east of Banff, and Fraserburgh.

Fraserburgh

52 *27 mi east of Banff, 47 mi north of Aberdeen.*

The gray-toned, workaday port of Fraserburgh has two great surprises for visitors. The **beach** should not be missed: its sands sweep away out of sight, backed by wind-sculpted dunes, and it is often to-
★ tally unoccupied save by seabirds. Past the harbor you will find **Scotland's Lighthouse Museum** at the northeasternmost point of Scotland, overlooked by a 16th-century castle that was converted into the first lighthouse to be built by the Commissioners for Northern Lights in the 1780s. The museum tells the story of Scotland's lighthouses, vital in the development of the country's maritime history. Highlights include the displays of astonishingly beautiful lenses, which would be the envy of any interior designer, and the tour of the lighthouse itself, right up to the top. ⊠ *Kinnaird Head, Fraserburgh,* ☎ *01346/511022.* 🖼 *£2.50.* ☉ *Apr.–Oct., Mon.–Sat. 10–6, Sun. 12:30–6; Nov.–Mar., Mon.–Sat. 10–4, Sun. 12:30–4.*

Mintlaw

53 *13 mi south of Fraserburgh.*

It can seem to the casual visitor that Mintlaw consists of little except a few houses and a traffic circle. However, here in Aden Country Park, the **Northeast Scotland Agricultural Heritage Centre** tells through videos the moving story of life on the land and the hard toil of the farming folk who battled to tame the ground of the Northeast. Housed in a handsome courtyard of former farm buildings, implements, tableaux, models, and displays create a vivid impression. Aden Country Park is also an important recreational resource for the locals, with trails that meander throughout the park's 230 acres. ⊠ *Off A92, west of Mintlaw,* ☎ *01771/622857.* 🖼 *Free.* ☉ *May–Sept., daily 11–4:30; Apr., Oct., and early Nov., weekends noon–4:30 (last admission 4).*

West of Mintlaw at **Deer Abbey** are the remains of a Cistercian monastery founded in 1218. ⊠ *Old Deer,* ☎ *0131/668–8800.* 🖼 *Free.* ☉ *At all times.*

Ellon

54 *14 mi south of Mintlaw.*

Formerly a market center on what was then the lowest bridging point of the River Ythan, Ellon is a small town at the center of a rural hinterland and a bedroom suburb of Aberdeen.

It is also well-placed for visiting several more of "castle country's" splendid properties. West of Ellon, at Pitmedden, is a unique re-creation by

⑤⑤ the National Trust for Scotland of a 17th-century garden: **Pitmedden Garden** is best visited in high summer, from July onward, when annual bedding plants form intricate formal patterns of the garden plots. The 100-acre estate also has a variety of woodland and farmland walks, as well as the Museum of Farming Life. ☎ *01651/842352.* 🖾 *£3.70.* ☉ *May–Sept., daily 10–5:30 (last admission at 5).*

⑤⑥ Created as the home of the earls and marquesses of Aberdeen, **Haddo House**—designed by William Adam (father of Robert, 1689–1748)—is now cared for by the National Trust for Scotland. Built in 1732, the elegant mansion has a light and graceful design, with curving wings on either side of a harmonious, symmetrical facade. The Chapel has a stained-glass window by Sir Edward Burne-Jones (1833–98). 🖾 *Off B999, northwest of Ellon,* ☎ *01651/851440.* 🖾 *£4.20.* ☉ *House Easter and May–Sept., daily 1:30–5:30; Oct., weekends 1:30–5:30 (last admission at 4:45); garden and park daily 9:30–dusk.*

In an area rife with castles, many are distinguished within their own categories: Craigievar for untouched perfection, Corgarff for sheer ⑤⑦ loneliness, Haddo House for elegance. Perhaps **Fyvie Castle** stands out in its own category: most complex. Five great towers built by five successive powerful families turned a 13th-century foursquare castle into an opulent Edwardian statement of wealth. There's an array of superb paintings on view, including 12 Raeburns (1756–1823), as well as myriad sumptuous interiors and walks on the castle grounds. Fyvie is praised for its sheer impact, if you like your castles oppressive and gloomy. 🖾 *Off A947 between Oldmeldrum and Turriff, 18–20 mi northwest of Ellon,* ☎ *01651/891266.* 🖾 *£4.20.* ☉ *Castle Apr. (or Easter if earlier)–June and Sept., daily 1:30–5:30; July–Aug., daily 11–5:30; Oct., weekends 1:30–5:30 (last admission at 4:45); grounds daily 9:30–dusk.*

OFF THE BEATEN PATH

BULLERS OF BUCHAN – On a stretch of windy cliff and cove coastline—once used by smugglers—the sea has cut through a cave, collapsing its roof and forming a great rocky cauldron, fearsome in bad weather. The Bullers of Buchan is an impressive sight, worth seeing if you like your sights austere and elemental, but not if you're vertigo-prone. Approach the cliff edge with great care. 🖾 *Off A952/A975 northeast of Ellon.*

ARCHAEOLINK PREHISTORY PARK– A strange, grass-covered dome rises from the hillside halfway between Huntly and Aberdeen. This example of modern architecture houses an exhibition about far older structures: the many stone circles, symbol stones, and other prehistoric monuments that are scattered in seeming abundance all over this part of the Northeast. Dedicated to the "exploration of life before history," Archaeolink also includes open-air structures such as a replica of an Iron Age farm. 🖾 *Off A96 at Oyne,* ☎ *01464/851500.*

ABERDEEN AND THE NORTHEAST A TO Z

Arriving and Departing

By Ferry

There is a summer (June–August) ferry service between Aberdeen, Lerwick (Shetland), and Bergen (Norway). It is operated by **P&O Ferries** (contact via 🖾 Box 5, Jamieson's Quay, Aberdeen, ☎ 01224/572615) and is subject to annual review; if you plan to use this route, check that the service will be running.

By Bus

Long-distance coach service operates to and from most parts of Scotland, England, and Wales. Contact **National Express** (☏ 0990/808080) or **Scottish Citylink** (☏ 0990/505050).

By Car

It is now possible to travel from Glasgow and Edinburgh to Aberdeen on a continuous stretch of the A90/M90, a fairly scenic route that runs up Strathmore, with a fine hill view to the west. The coastal route, the A92, is a more leisurely alternative, with its interesting coastal resorts and fishing villages. The most scenic route, however, is probably the A93 from Perth, north to Blairgowrie and into Glen Shee. The A93 then goes over the Cairnwell Pass, the highest main road in the United Kingdom. (This route is not recommended in the winter months when snow can make driving over high ground difficult.)

By Plane

Aberdeen Airport (☏ 01224/722331)—serving both international and domestic flights—is in Dyce, 7 mi west of the city center on the A96 (Inverness). The terminal building is modern (expanded in recent years because of Dyce's prominent role in North Sea oil-rig communications) and generally uncrowded.

Airlines linking Aberdeen with Europe include **KLM U.K.,** with flights to Amsterdam (the Netherlands), and Bergen and Stavanger (Norway); **SAS (Scandinavian Airlines),** serving Stavanger; **British Airways,** serving Paris via Manchester; and **Business Air,** with flights to Esbjerg (Denmark). An extensive network of domestic flights linking Aberdeen with most major U.K. airports is operated by **British Airways, British Midland, Brymon, Business Air, easyJet, KLM U.K.,** and **Gill Air.** Consult the individual airlines or your travel agent for arrival and departure times (airport information desk).

Note the direct Amsterdam–Aberdeen link enabling transatlantic passengers to visit Scotland's northeast by first flying from the United States to Amsterdam and then flying on to Aberdeen with Air U.K.; this can actually be faster than traveling to Aberdeen from other parts of Scotland or England.

BETWEEN THE AIRPORT AND CITY CENTER

By Bus: Grampian Transport's (☏ 01224/650000) number 27 bus operates between the airport terminal and Union Street in the center of Aberdeen. Buses (📧 fare £1.30) run frequently at peak times, less often in midday and evenings; the journey time is approximately 40 minutes.

By Car: The drive to the center of Aberdeen is easy via the A96 (which can be busy in the rush hour).

By Train: Dyce is on **ScotRail's** Inverness–Aberdeen route. The rail station is a short taxi ride from the terminal building. The ride by rail into Aberdeen from Dyce takes 12 minutes. Trains run approximately every two hours. If you intend to visit the western part of the area first, it is possible to travel northwest, away from Aberdeen, by rail, direct to Elgin via Inverurie, Insch, Huntly, and Keith. For information contact the **National Train Enquiry Line** (☏ 0345/484950).

By Train

Travelers can reach Aberdeen directly from Edinburgh (2½ hours), Glasgow (3 hours), and Inverness (2½ hours). See ScotRail time-table for full details, or call the **National Train Enquiry Line** (☏ 0345/484950). There are also London–Aberdeen routes that go through Edinburgh and the east-coast main line.

Getting Around

Aberdeen is not a large city. Its center is Union Street, the main thoroughfare running east–west. Anderson Drive is an efficient ring road on the western side of the city; inexperienced drivers should be extra careful on its many traffic circles. In general, road signs are clear and legible, and parking near the center of Aberdeen is no worse than in any other U.K. city, though the park-and-ride facility clearly signposted on the northern outskirts of Aberdeen at the Bridge of Don is recommended.

By Bus

Grampian Transport (☎ 01224/650000) operates services throughout the city. There is an inquiry kiosk on St. Nicholas Street, outside Marks and Spencers department store, and timetables are available at the kiosk or from the tourist information center at St. Nicholas House nearby.

By Car

Aberdeen is a compact city with good signing. Union Street is the axis and tends to get crowded with traffic. It is better to leave your car in one of the parking garages (arrive early to get a space) and walk around. Alternatively, make use of the convenient park-and-ride scheme at the Bridge of Don, north of the city. Street maps are available from the tourist information center or from newsagents and booksellers. Around the Northeast roads are generally not busy, but speeding and erratic driving can be a problem on the main A roads. The rural side roads are a pleasure to drive.

By Taxi

Taxi stands can be found throughout the center of Aberdeen: along Union Street, at the railway station at Guild Street, at Back Wynd, and at Regent Quay. Taxis are mostly black, though variations in beige, maroon, or white exist.

Contacts and Resources

Camping

Most of the population centers in the area have campsites; contact tourist offices for information (☞ Visitor Information, *below*). It is possible to camp on private land, but you must obtain the permission of the landowner first. Except for the more remote upland areas, "wild land" camping is better pursued farther west.

Car Rentals

Alamo (⊠ at Airport Skean Dhu Hotel, ☎ 01224/770955). **Arnold Clark** (⊠ Girdleness Rd., ☎ 01224/249159). **Avis** (⊠ Aberdeen Airport, ☎ 01224/722282; ⊠ 16 Broomhill Rd., ☎ 01224/574252). **Budget Rent a Car** (⊠ Great Northern Rd, Kittybrewster, ☎ 01224/488770). **Eurodollar** (⊠ 46 Summer St., ☎ 01224/626955). **Europcar** (⊠ Aberdeen Airport, ☎ 01224/770770; ⊠ 121 Causeway End, ☎ 01224/631199). **Hertz** (⊠ Aberdeen Airport, ☎ 01224/722373; ⊠ Railway Station, ☎ 01224/210748). **Kenning** (⊠ 240 Market St., ☎ 01224/591966). **Mitchell Self-Drive** (⊠ 35 Chapel St., ☎ 01224/642642). **Watson's Self-Drive** (⊠ 114–126 Hutcheon St., ☎ 01224/625625).

Emergencies

For **fire, police, or ambulance,** dial ☎ 999 from any telephone. No coins are needed for emergency calls made from public telephone booths. **Grampian Police** (⊠ Force Headquarters, Queen St., Aberdeen, ☎ 01224/639111). There is a lost property office here. **Aberdeen Royal Infirmary** (⊠ Accident and Emergency Department, Foresterhill, Aberdeen, ☎ 01224/681818). **Dr. Gray's Hospital, Elgin** (⊠ Accident

and Emergency Department, at end of High St. on A96, ☎ 01343/
543131, ext. 77310).

Doctors and Dentists
The **Grampian Health Board** (✉ Primary Care Department, Wool-
manhill, ☎ 01224/681818, ext. 55537) can help you find a doctor or
dentist; or consult your hotel receptionist, bed-and-breakfast proprietor, or the Yellow Pages telephone book.

Guided Tours
ORIENTATION
City tours are available on most days between June and mid-September.
Grampian Transport (☎ 01224/650000), **Grampian Coaches** (operated
by Grampian Transport, ☎ 01224/650024), **Bluebird Northern** (☎
01224/212266), and **McIntyre's Coaches** (☎ 01224/493112) all operate
tours encompassing the Northeast coastline and countryside. Some of
the tours are of general interest, others are based on one of the area's
various trails: Malt Whisky, Coastal, Castle, or Royal.

PERSONAL GUIDES
The **Scottish Tourist Guides Association** (✉ Mrs. Jess Lumsden, Kingsfield House, Kingsfield Rd., Kintore, Inverurie, AB51 0UD, ☎ FAX
01467/632366) can supply experienced personal guides, including for-
eign-language-speaking guides if necessary.

The following firms offer chauffeur-driven limousines to take clients
on tailor-made tours: **Alamo Chauffeur Drive** (☎ 0990/993000 or
01224/770955) and **Scotland Scene Ltd.** (☎ 01309/676563).

WALKING TOURS
The **Scottish Tourist Guides Association** (☞ *above*) organizes an "Old
Aberdeen" walk from mid-May through August on Wednesday evenings
and Sunday afternoons.

Late-Night Pharmacies
Notices on pharmacy doors will guide you to the nearest open pharmacy at any given time. The police can provide assistance in an emergency.

Anderson Pharmacy (✉ 34 Holburn St., ☎ 01224/587148) and **Boots
the Chemists Ltd.** (✉ Bon Accord Centre, George St., ☎ 01224/
626080), both in Aberdeen, keep longer hours than most. There also
is an in-store pharmacist at **Safeway Food Store** (✉ 215 King St., ☎
01224/624398).

Visitor Information
Aberdeen (✉ St. Nicholas House, Broad St., ☎ 01224/632727); this
tourist information center has a currency exchange and supplies information on all of Scotland's Northeast. **Banchory** (✉ Bridge St., ☎
01330/822000). **Braemar** (✉ The Mews, Mar Rd., ☎ 013397/41600).
Elgin (✉ 17 High St., ☎ 01343/542666).

In summer, also look for tourist information centers in Aboyne, Alford, Ballater, Banff, Crathie, Dufftown, Forres, Fraserburgh, Huntly,
Inverurie, Stonehaven, and Tomintoul.

9 Argyll and the Isles

With long sea lochs carved into the mountainous interior, Argyll is a beguiling interplay of water and land— mossy woods and hills rich from the rainy Atlantic weather. The Kintyre peninsula is a wonderland of sea views and early monuments. Mull's Tobermory, with its brightly painted houses, has a Mediterranean feel. Islay, synonymous with whiskey, produces seven distinct, peaty malts. Arran is the Scots' outdoor playground.

By Gilbert
Summers

THIS POPULAR AND ALLURING REGION in western
Scotland, divided in two by the long peninsula of
Kintyre, is characterized by a splintered, complex
seaboard. The west is an aesthetic delight, though it catches the moist—
and that's a euphemism—Atlantic weather systems. The same holds
true for the Great Glen area to the north. But an occasionally wet foray
is the price you pay for the glittering freshness of oak woods and
bracken-covered hillsides, and for the bright interplay of sea, loch, and
rugged green peninsula.

Kintyre also separates the islands of the Firth of Clyde (including
Arran), from the islands of the Inner Hebrides, the largest of which
are Mull, Islay, and Jura. You could spend all your time touring these
larger islands, but keep in mind that there are plenty of small islands
that can also be explored—the captivating gem, Colonsay, between Islay
and Mull, for example. Coming from the mainland, you cannot avoid
the touring center of Oban, an important ferry port with a main road
leading south into Kintyre.

Pleasures and Pastimes

Biking

As a popular vacation destination and a ferry gateway, Oban gets a
lot of bike traffic. Main routes to and from town are busy, and there
are few side roads. Arran is a popular island for cycling, with a large
number of bicycle-rental shops. Island roads may be single-track, so
wear high-visibility clothing, especially in the busy summer months,
and be *sure* to bring rain gear.

Dining

This part of Scotland is not usually considered a great gastronomic center, though it does have some restaurants of distinction. Still, the ingredients used in dishes are of good quality and are locally produced:
fish, fresh from the sparkling lochs and sea, could hardly be better. Beef,
lamb, and game are also common. In the rural districts, your best bet
is to choose a hotel or guest house that can provide a decent evening
meal as well as breakfast.

CATEGORY	COST*
££££	over £40
£££	£30–£40
££	£15–£30
£	under £15

*per person for a three-course meal, including VAT and excluding drinks and
service*

Fishing

Local fishing literature, available at tourist offices, identifies at least
50 fishing sites on lochs and rivers for game fishing and at least 20 coastal
settlements suited to sea angling.

Golf

The area has about two dozen golf courses, notably the fine coastal
links, of which Machrihanish near Campbeltown is the most famous.

Lodging

Accommodations in Argyll and the isles range from château-like hotels to modest inns. The traditional provincial hotels and small coastal
resorts have been modernized and equipped with all the necessary
comforts, yet they retain their sense of personalized service and the charm
that comes with older buildings. Apart from these, however, your

choices are more limited, and your best overnight option is usually a modest guest house offering bed, breakfast, and an evening meal.

CATEGORY	COST*
££££	over £120
£££	£90–£120
££	£50–£90
£	under £50

All prices are for standard double room, including service, breakfast, and VAT.

Shopping

Although great shopping is not what lures visitors to this predominantly rural area, there are several interesting crafts outlets. On Islay, in particular, you can sample and purchase fine island whiskies.

Exploring Argyll and the Isles

On mainland-based tours, Loch Fyne tends to get in the way. It is a long haul around the end of this fjordlike sea loch to reach Inveraray. Ferry services provided by Caledonian MacBrayne (☞ Getting Around *in* Argyll and the Isles A to Z, *below*) make all kinds of interisland tours possible and can shorten mainland distances. From Ardrossan, southwest of Glasgow, you can reach the island of Arran, then take a short ferry crossing west to Kintyre. You can continue to the islands of Islay and Jura, and from there a ferry can take you northeast to Oban. All the ferries transport cars and pedestrians.

Numbers in the text correspond to numbers in the margin and on the Argyll and the Isles map.

Great Itineraries

You could easily spend a week here, wandering across the islands. It will take you a day to get around Mull, for instance, especially if you are visiting castles, or it can take even longer if you go to Iona. Arran, too, by the time you have driven around it and gone to Brodick, is more than just a day trip. Overall, allow yourself a good chunk of time, particularly if the weather looks settled. Mainland areas, such as Inveraray, and Oban and its environs, have places of interest that can easily swallow up the day.

IF YOU HAVE 2 DAYS

Make your way to **Inveraray** ⑥, via Loch Lomond and the Rest and Be Thankful pass (A83). Continue south via **Crarae Gardens** ⑧ then on south, taking A816 north at Lochgilphead for the **Crinan Canal** ⑩, then go north on A816 for 35 mi to overnight at ⚜ **Oban** ①. The next day, follow the A85 east from Oban, taking in **Dunstaffnage Castle** ② and **Kilchurn Castle** ⑤, before returning to the Loch Lomond/Glasgow area.

IF YOU HAVE 4 DAYS

Starting from Ardrossan in Ayrshire, take the ferry to ⚜ **Brodick** ⑯ on the island of Arran and tour the island, visiting **Brodick Castle and Country Park** ⑱. Take the ferry from **Lochranza** ㉓ for Claonaig, crossing the Kintyre peninsula to Kennacraig. Then, go south to the island of **Gigha** ⑭. Next, return north to the ⚜ **Crinan Canal** ⑩ area. Go north to **Oban** ①, make an excursion to Mull for **Iona** ㊳, ⚜ **Tobermory** ㊶, and **Torosay Castle** ㊱, then return to Oban or go farther north, via the Fishnish to Lochaline ferry.

IF YOU HAVE 7 DAYS

This noncircular route provides a good flavor of the islands. As with the four-day itinerary above, start from Ardrossan in Ayrshire and take the ferry to ⚜ **Brodick** ⑯. Stay overnight on Arran and tour the island,

Argyll and the Isles

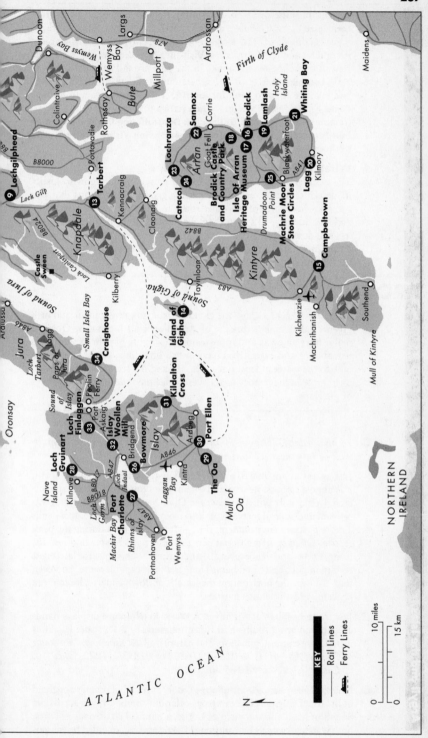

visiting **Brodick Castle and Country Park** ⑱. Take the ferry from **Lochranza** ㉓ for Claonaig, crossing the Kintyre peninsula to Tarbert, then visit the island of 🎬 **Islay** ㉖–㉝, staying two nights for its whiskey, island life, and nature reserves. Visit Jura, and **Craighouse** ㉞, as well. Return to the mainland to take in the area around Knapdale, staying at 🎬 **Lochgilphead** ⑨ for at least one night. Go north to 🎬 **Oban** ① and take the ferry to Mull for **Iona** ㉟, 🎬 **Tobermory** ㊶, and **Torosay Castle** ㊱, staying two nights. Then return to Oban to explore the attractions along the A85 to the east: **Dunstaffnage Castle** ②, **Bonawe Iron Furnace** ③, **Cruachan Dam Power Station Visitor Centre** ④, and **Kilchurn Castle** ⑤.

When to Tour Argyll and the Isles

The mainland part of this area is near enough to Glasgow to justify its description as a year-round touring ground. This means that you can take advantage of the quiet roads in late autumn or early spring and still find a good selection of accommodations, but if the weather lets you down, you can get back to the main cities with little difficulty. Avoid the islands in winter, when howling gales and frigid temperatures prevail.

AROUND ARGYLL

Take time to get to know the characteristic mix of grandeur and lush greenery that makes this bit of Argyll special. Inevitably, Oban, a major ferry gateway and route center, will figure in your explorations hereabouts, and even if you have only a little time, you should try to take to the water at least once. The sea and the sea lochs have played a vital role in the history of the west, since the time of the war galleys of the clans.

Oban

① *96 mi north of Glasgow, 50 mi south of Fort William, 118 mi southwest of Inverness, 125 mi northwest of Edinburgh.*

Just as it is impossible to avoid Fort William when touring the north, it is almost impossible to avoid Oban when touring this part of Scotland. Unlike Fort William, however, Oban has a fairly characterful waterfront and several ferry excursions from which to choose. It also has a more pleasant environment, though it does get busy during the peak season. Oban is a traditional Scottish resort where you find *ceilidhs* (song, music, and dance festivals) and tartan kitsch, as well as late-night revelry in pubs and hotel bars. There is an inescapable sense, however, that just over the horizon, on the islands or down Kintyre, loom more peaceful and authentic environs.

☼ Just south of Oban at Kilninver, **A World in Miniature** displays handcrafted miniature rooms and furniture made to a 1½ scale. Facilities include a restaurant, gift shop, and nature trail. ⊠ *Kilninver, 7 mi south of Oban, PA34 4UT,* ☎ *01852/316202 or 01852/316272.* 🎫 *£2.50.* ☼ *Easter–Oct., daily 10–5:30.*

② North of Oban stands **Dunstaffnage Castle,** once an important stronghold of the MacDougalls. The ramparts offer outstanding views across the **Sound of Mull** and the **Firth of Lorne**, a nautical crossroads of sorts, once watched over by Dunstaffnage Castle and commanded by the galleys (in Gaelic, *birlinn*) of the Lords of the Isles. ⊠ *Just off A85,* ☎ *0131/668–8800.* 🎫 *£1.80.* ☼ *Apr.–Sept., daily 9:30–6.*

From Dunstaffnage Castle, you should be able to see **Connel Bridge,** less than a mile farther east. This elegant structure once carried a branch railway along the coast, but it has since surrendered to the all-conquering automobile. Below the bridge, in the shadow of the girders, the **Falls of Lora** foam, given the right tidal conditions. Upstream is fjordlike **Loch Etive** (with cruises from Oban); the water leaving this deep, narrow loch foams and fights with the incoming tides, creating turbulence and curious cascades under the bridge.

Dining and Lodging

££££ ✕⊞ **Isle of Eriska.** Top-quality at prices to match, this hotel on its own island 10 mi north of Oban is reached by a short bridge from the mainland. The baronial-style, rather severe-looking granite facade belies the luxurious welcome within: spacious rooms with every detail carefully considered for your comfort. The restaurant serves sublime, innovative Scottish cuisine from local products: try the scallop and zucchini timbale with squat lobsters, artichoke, and champagne butter sauce. Take a stroll after your meal to catch sight of seals and otters offshore, or herons and badgers on the grounds. ✉ *Ledaig, by Oban, Argyll PA37 1SD,* ☎ *01631/720371,* FAX *01631/720531. 17 rooms with bath or shower. Restaurant, indoor pool, 6-hole golf course, 1 tennis court, health club. AE, MC, V. Closed Jan.–Feb..*

£££ ⊞ **Manor House Hotel.** Once the home of the duke of Argyll, this 1780 stone house on the shore, just outside Oban, is now a hotel with great views of the sea. The reception and public areas are furnished with many genuine antiques, the bedrooms with reproductions. Bedcovers and curtains are in country-house style using floral fabrics. The restaurant serves Scottish and French dishes, including lots of local seafood and game in season, complemented by a carefully chosen wine list. It's within easy walking distance of downtown Oban and the bus, train, and ferry terminals. ✉ *Gallanach Rd., Oban, Argyll, PA34 4LS,* ☎ *01631/562087,* FAX *01631/563053. 11 rooms with bath. Restaurant. AE, MC, V. Closed Mon. and Tues. (Nov.–Feb.).*

££ ⊞ **Kilchrenan House.** A fully refurbished Victorian house only a few minutes' walk from the town center, this is a high-grade bed-and-breakfast, with rooms offering views out to sea and to the islands. ✉ *Corran Esplanade, Oban, Argyll, PA34 5AQ,* ☎ FAX *01631/562663. 10 rooms, 7 with bath, 3 with shower. MC, V. Closed Nov.–Mar.*

££ ⊞ **Ronebhal Guest House.** Loch Etive and the mountains beyond can be seen from this stone house east of Oban. Although Connel is on the main road, Ronebhal is set back within its own grounds. It offers B&B in spacious surroundings. ✉ *Connel, Argyll, PA37 1PJ,* ☎ FAX *01631/710310. 6 rooms with shower. MC, V. Closed Nov.–Mar.*

£ ⊞ **Dungrianach.** This aptly named B&B ("the sunny house on the hill")
★ is set in woodland with superb views of the ocean and islands, yet it is only a few minutes' walk from Oban's ferry piers and town center. Both rooms in this late Victorian house have private facilities and are decorated with reproduction antiques. ✉ *Pulpit Hill, Oban, Argyll, PA34 4LX,* ☎ FAX *01631/562840. 2 rooms, 1 with bath, 1 with shower. No credit cards. Closed Oct.–Mar.*

Nightlife and the Arts

The **Highland Discovery Centre** (✉ George St., Oban, ☎ 01631/562444) shows feature films and also has a theater for plays.

Outdoor Activities and Sports

Rent bicycles from **Oban Cycles** (✉ 9 Craigard Rd., Oban, ☎ 01631/566996).

Shopping

Caithness Glass Oban (✉ Railway Pier, ☎ FAX 01631/563386), a factory shop for Caithness Glass, is a good place to buy a memento of

Scotland to treasure. Especially lovely are the paperweights with swirling colored patterns.

OFF THE
BEATEN PATH **SEA-LIFE CENTRE –** This outstanding place for children (and adults) provides a fascinating display of marine life, including shoals of herring, sharks, rays, catfish, and seals. The restaurant offers morning coffee with homemade scones, a full lunch menu (which might include oysters, homemade soup, fish pie, or baked potatoes with various fillings), and afternoon teas. Drive south from Glencoe village on A828. ⊠ *Barcaldine, Connel, Argyll,* ☎ *01631/720386.* ☒ *£5.50.* ☉ *Jan.–mid-Feb., weekends 10–5; mid-Feb.–Jun. and Sept.–Nov., daily 10–6; July, Aug., daily 9–7; first 2 wks of Dec., weekends 10–5; Christmas and New Year's, 10–5.*

Taynuilt

12 mi east of Oban.

❸ At Taynuilt, the **Bonawe Iron Furnace** is signposted. No industrial activity takes place there now, but once the peaceful wooded slopes overlooked the smoky glow of furnaces burning local timber to make charcoal. The furnaces played a central role in the iron-smelting industry, which flourished here between 1753 and 1876. Today, Historic Scotland cares for the well-preserved buildings. ⊠ *Bonawe,* ☎ *0131/668–8800.* ☒ *£2.30.* ☉ *Apr.–Sept., daily 9:30–6.*

★ **❹** Through the narrow Pass of Brander is the **Cruachan Dam Power Station Visitor Centre.** If you want to go underneath **Ben Cruachan,** the mountain seen from Dunstaffnage Castle—but lost to view at close proximity—stop at the visitor center for instructions. A horseshoe-shaped series of peaks, Ben Cruachan has a man-made dam within its confines. Water flows from the dam to Loch Awe, the loch to the west, turning turbines along the way. You can learn about this at the visitor center and on a brief minibus trip down a tunnel into a huge cavern-cum-turbine hall. Be sure to take this trip, which will take you under several cubic miles of mountain. ⊠ *off A85, 18 mi east of Oban,* ☎ *01866/822673.* ☒ *£3.* ☉ *Apr.–mid-Nov., daily 9–4:30.*

Shopping
Inverawe Fisheries and Smokery (☎ 01866/822446) produces smoked salmon and other fish to eat on the premises or take out. The fish may be impractical to take home, but it's delicious for picnics.

Lochawe

18 mi east of Oban.

Lochawe is a scattered loch-side community squeezed between the broad shoulder of Ben Cruachan and Loch Awe itself. The road gets busy in peak season, filled with people trying to park by Lochawe Station. Cruises on Loch Awe and to Kilchurn Castle start here, aboard the *Lady Rowena* **Steam Launch,** an Edwardian peat-fired steamboat. Reservations may be made on the spot or in advance. ⊠ *Lochawe Station,* ☎ *01838/200440 or 01838/200449.* ☒ *£4.25 per hr.*

★ **❺** Near Lochawe is **Kilchurn Castle,** a ruined fortress at the eastern end of Loch Awe. The castle was built by Sir Colin Campbell (d. 1493) of Glenorchy in the 15th century and rebuilt in the 17th century. The Campbells had their original power base in this area. Park on the south side of the A85 about a mile northeast of Lochawe, at the tip of Loch Awe, and cross the railway line, then walk across the grassy flats to the airy vantage points (complete with informative signs) amid the towers; from there you'll see fine panoramas. ⊠ *1 mi northeast of Lochawe,* ☎ *0131/668–8800.* ☞ *£1.* ☼ *Apr.–Sept., daily 9:30–6; Oct.–Mar., Mon.–Sat. 9:30–4, Sun. 2–4.*

Near Dalmally, just east of Lochawe, the **Duncan Ban Macintyre Monument** was erected in honor of this Gaelic poet (1724–1812), sometimes referred to as the Robert Burns of the Highlands. The view from here is one of the finest in Argyll, taking in Ben Cruachan and the other peaks nearby, as well as Loch Awe and its scattering of islands. To find it from Dalmally, follow an old road running southwest toward the banks of Loch Awe. At the road's highest point, often called Monument Hill, you'll see the round, granite monument.

En Route The A819 between Lochawe and Inveraray initially runs alongside Loch Awe, the longest loch in Scotland, but soon leaves its pleasant banks, turning south to join the A83. The A83 carries traffic from Glasgow and Loch Lomond by way of the high pass of the Rest and Be Thankful. (Many visitors come up the loch and head west by the A83.) The Rest and Be Thankful is perhaps its most scenic point—an aptly named, almost-Alpine pass among high green slopes and gray rocks. For information on Loch Lomond, *see* Chapter 7.

Inveraray

★ ❻ *21 mi south of Lochawe, 61 mi north of Glasgow, 29 mi west of Loch Lomond.*

On the approaches to Inveraray, note the ornate 18th-century bridgework that carries the road along the loch-side. This is the first sign that Inveraray is not just a higgledy-piggledy assembly of houses. In fact, much of Inveraray was designed as a planned town for the third duke of Argyll in the mid-18th century. The present Campbell duke's seat is **Inveraray Castle,** a grayish-green, turreted stone castle that can be seen through the trees on the right. Like Inveraray town, the castle was built around 1743. Much of this powerful family's history can be seen on a tour. ☎ *01499/302203.* ☞ *£4.50.* ☼ *July and Aug., Mon.–Sat. 10–5:45, Sun. 1–5:45; Apr.–June and Sept.–mid-Oct., Mon.–Thurs. and Sat. 10–1 and 2–5:45, Sun. 1–5:45.*

The **Combined Operations Museum** sits close to Inveraray Castle, a reminder that this sleepy place among the hills was an important wartime training area. ⊠ *Cherry Park,* ☎ *01499/500218.* ☞ *£2.* ☼ *Apr.–mid-Oct., Mon.–Thurs. 10–5:30, Sun. 1–5:30 (last admission at 5).*

The **Inveraray Jail** is one of the latest generation of visitor centers. The old town jail and courtroom now house realistic courtroom scenes, period cells, and much other paraphernalia that enable the visitor to glimpse life behind bars in Victorian times. There is also a Scottish crafts shop within the jail. ⊠ *Inveraray,* ☎ *01499/302381.* ☞ *£4.30.* ☼ *Apr.–Oct., daily 9:30–6; Nov.–Mar., daily 10–5 (last admission 1 hr before closing).*

Also in Inveraray is the **Arctic Penguin,** a 1911 lightship and a rare example of a riveted iron vessel. She now houses exhibits and displays on the maritime heritage of the River Clyde and Scotland's west coast. ☎ *01499/302213.* ☞ *£2.50.* ☼ *Apr.–Oct., daily 10–6; Nov.–Mar., daily 10–5.*

Ardkinglas Woodland Garden is home to one of Britain's finest collections of conifers, set off by rhododendron blossoms in early summer. Find it around the head of Loch Fyne about 4 mi east of Inveraray. ⊠ *Cairndow,* ☎ *01499/600263.* ☞ *£2.* ☼ *Daily.*

At **Loch Fyne Oysters,** you can purchase these delicious shellfish to take away (or the company can supply by mail order), or sit down and consume a dozen with a glass of white wine. ⊠ *Clachan Farm, Cairndow, Argyll,* ☎ *01499/600236.*

★ ❼ A glimpse of 18th-century lifestyles can be seen at the **Auchindrain Museum.** Formerly a communal tenancy farm, this 18th-century cooperative venture has been restored. The old bracken-thatched or iron-roofed buildings provide information about early farming life in the Highlands. There is also an interpretation center and shop. ⊠ *A83, 5 mi south of Inveraray,* ☎ *01499/500235.* ▣ *£3.* ☉ *Apr.–Sept., daily 10–5.*

★ ❽ Well worth a visit are the **Crarae Gardens,** occasionally likened to a wild valley in the Himalayas. Magnolias and azaleas give the area a moist and lush atmosphere, undoubtedly aided by the local rainfall. There are paths through the plantings that will suit hikers of every fitness level. ⊠ *off the A83, about 10 mi southwest of Inveraray,* ☎ *01546/886614 or 01546/886388.* ▣ *£2.50.* ☉ *Daily 9–6 (restricted to daylight hours in winter); visitor center Easter–Oct., daily 9–6.*

Dining and Lodging

££–£££ ✕▥ **Creggans Inn.** This traditional inn overlooking Loch Fyne on its eastern shore, 21 mi from Inveraray, dates to the 17th century. You can enjoy an appetizing lunch or supper in the bar, or a more formal dinner in the inn's cozy dining room, which serves local produce and seafood, including Loch Fyne oysters. The bedrooms vary in size from large to rather small, all individually decorated in traditional Scottish style. The staff is friendly and hospitable. ⊠ *Strachur, Argyll, PA27 8BX,* ☎ *01369/860279,* ▣ *01369/860637. 19 rooms, 17 with bath, 2 with shower. Restaurant. AE, DC, MC, V.*

Lochgilphead

❾ *26 mi south of Inveraray.*

The area's main town is at its aesthetic best when the tide is in: Loch Gilp, really a bite out of Loch Fyne, reveals a muddy shoreline at low tide. However, the neat little town with its well-kept, colorful frontages along the main street is well worth a visit.

❿ The **Crinan Canal** was opened in 1801 to enable fishing vessels to avoid the long haul around the south-stretching Kintyre peninsula and reach the Hebridean fishing grounds more easily. At the western end of the canal it drops to the sea in a series of lochs. This area can be a busy spot, with yachting enthusiasts strolling around and frequenting the coffee shop beside the Crinan Hotel. To reach Crinan, take the A816 Oban road north from Lochgilphead for about a mile and turn left.

⓫ To capture a glimpse of early Scottish history, visit **Dunadd Fort.** Follow a track to a rocky hump that rises out of the level ground around Crinan; you will find—by clambering up the rock—a basin, a footprint, and an outline of a boar carved on the smooth upper face of the knoll. This breezy refuge was once the capital of the early kingdom of Dalriada, founded by the first wave of Scots who migrated from Ireland around AD 500. ⊠ *West off A816, 4 mi northwest of Lochgilphead,* ☎ *0131/668–8800.* ▣ *Free.* ☉ *Daily.*

A number of early monuments are along the road between Dunadd and **Kilmartin,** a small village dotted with finely carved medieval grave slabs and crosses. Keep a sharp lookout: from the road you can see a number of even earlier monuments—notably burial cairns and stone circles dating from the Bronze Age and earlier. A leaflet giving further details is available locally.

⑫ A tower house called **Carnasserie Castle** has the distinction of having belonged to the writer of the first book printed in Gaelic. The writer, John Carswell, bishop of the isles, translated a text by the Scottish reformer, John Knox, into Gaelic and published it in 1567. ⊠ *Off A816, 9 mi north of Lochgilphead.,* ☎ *0131/668–8800.* ☲ *Free.* ☉ *Daily.*

Dining and Lodging

££££
★
✕🏨 **Crinan Hotel.** This turn-of-the-century property, overlooking the picturesque Crinan Canal and the Sound of Jura, has been extensively refurbished. The friendly and helpful Frances Macdonald, an artist and one of the owners, has put her artistic skills to great use in the interior design of the hotel. Two restaurants offer both Scottish cuisine and the freshest local seafood: the Westward Room serves dinner in a luxurious, country-mansion setting, where you are surrounded by antiques and floral arrangements; the rooftop Loch 16 has a nautical theme, and superb sunsets accompany the award-winning seafood. ⊠ *Near Lochgilphead, PA31 8SR,* ☎ *01546/830261,* 🅵🅰🆇 *01546/830292. 22 rooms, 21 with bath, 1 with shower. 2 restaurants, coffee shop, boating, fishing. AE, DC, MC, V.*

Outdoor Activities and Sports

Explorers can take off from **Castle Riding Centre and Argyll Trail Riding** (⊠ Brenfield, Ardrishaig, Argyll, ☎ 01546/603274), south of Lochgilphead, with highly qualified trail guides leading you along routes throughout Argyll; instruction in jumping and eventing is also offered here.

Shopping

At the **Highbank Porcelain Pottery** (⊠ Highbank Industrial Estate, Lochgilphead, ☎ 01546/602044), you can watch slip casting, hand painting, and firing on a tour (☲ £2) of the workshop, then buy the products (including reasonably priced seconds) at the shop; the shop also stocks ceramic giftware from other potteries.

OFF THE
BEATEN PATH

CASTLE SWEEN – The oldest stone castle on the Scottish mainland (12th century) sits on a rocky sea edge, about 15 mi southwest of Lochgilphead. The castle is reached by an unclassified road from Crinan, which offers outstanding views of the Paps of Jura across the sound. There are also some temptingly deserted white sand beaches here.

SEIL AND EASDALE ISLANDS – The "Bridge over the Atlantic" leads to the island of Seil. This crossing is less spectacular than it sounds—the island is so close to the mainland that a single-span bridge, built in 1791, carries the road across. From Seil, visitors are ferried to neighboring Easdale Island. Once Easdale and Seil were known as the slate islands: extensive quarrying for roofing materials was undertaken on both isles. The B844 leads to these islands, west off the A816 at Kilninver, 40 mi north of Lochgilphead, 17 mi south of Oban.

Kintyre Peninsula

52 mi (to Campbeltown) south of Lochgilphead.

⑬ **Tarbert,** in Gaelic, means a place of portage—there are other Tarberts scattered throughout the Highlands—and a glance at the map tells you why: this little town, with a workaday waterfront, has grown up on the narrow neck of land between East and West Loch Tarbert. Long ago, boats were carried across the land to avoid looping all the way around the peninsula.

Tairbeart Heritage Centre will tell you more about the history of this area; it is just a two-minute drive south of the village ⊠ *Tarbert, Argyll, PA29 6SX,* ☎ *01880/820190.* ☲ *£3.* ☉ *Daily 10–sunset.*

⑭ The **Island of Gigha** is a delectable Hebridean island, barely 5 mi long, sheltered in a frost-free, sea-warmed climate between Kintyre and Islay. The **Achamore House Gardens** benefit from the climate to display lush shrubberies with spectacular azalea displays in late spring. It is possible to take the ferry from Tayinloan (a 20-minute trip), walk to the gardens, and return to the mainland, all on a short day trip. ☎ 01583/505267. ➤ *Gardens £2, ferry £4.15 per person plus £16 per car.* ☉ *Gardens daily 10–dusk, ferry May–early Oct., daily 9–5, hourly on the hour; mid-Oct.–Apr., daily 9:15–4:30, hourly on the hour.*

⑮ **Campbeltown** is a fairly substantial town with whiskey distilling and fishing among its day-to-day activities. It has a reasonable choice of shops—so don't feel you have to stock up on items, such as film, farther up the peninsula.

Famous in song, the **Mull of Kintyre** is, in reality, a narrow road to the lighthouse beyond Campbeltown at the tip of Kintyre. The road crosses moors and sheep pastures. There is a parking place before the road suddenly dips to reach the lighthouse tower, which is well down the steep slope that tilts toward the sea. Do not go down the hill; the best sunset views are from the adjacent moors, from which you can see Ireland clearly.

Outdoor Activities and Sports

Machrihanish (☎ 01586/810277), near Campbeltown, is the most famous golf course in this area, and deservedly popular; book well ahead, especially for weekends. There are two courses: 18-hole, 6,228 yards, par 70; 9-hole, 2,395 yards, par 34.

Shopping

Campbeltown is the center for local shopping on the Kintyre peninsula; here you will find **Oystercatcher Crafts and Gallery** (✉ 10 Hall St. and 2–4 Main St., ☎ 01586/553070), with original paintings, art materials, wood carvings, gifts, and cards.

A couple of miles north of Campbeltown, at Carradale, is **Wallis Hunter Design** (✉ The Steading, ☎ ℻ 01583/431683), which makes gold and silver jewelry. Clachan is the home of **Ronachan Silks** (✉ Ronachan Farmhouse, ☎ 01880/740242), which produces distinctive jewel-colored scarves, cushion covers, kimonos, and caftans.

ARRAN

Many Scots, especially those from Glasgow and the west, are well disposed toward Arran, which reminds them of unhurried childhood holidays. In fact, some of its cafés and boarding houses still exude a 1950s mood—a pleasant reminder of the days when Scots all took their holidays in Scotland. Only a few decades ago, the Clyde estuary was the coastal playground for the majority of the populace living in Glasgow and along Clydeside. Their annual holiday comprised a trip by steamer to any one of a number of Clyde coast resorts, known as going *doon the watter* (down the water, the estuary of the Clyde). Today the masses go to Spain, but, as with other parts of the Clyde, the island of Arran has for a long time been associated with the healthy outdoor life.

To get to Arran, take the ferry from Ardrossan. During the ride, stroll on deck and note the number of fellow travelers wearing hiking boots. They're ready for the delights of Goat Fell, an impressive peak (2,868 ft) that gives the island one of the most distinctive profiles of any in Scotland. The cone of Goat Fell with its satellites serves as an eye-catching backdrop to the northwest, as the ferry approaches Brodick. As you will have seen while crossing, the southern half of Arran is less mountainous: the Highland Boundary Fault crosses just to the north of Brodick Bay.

Exploring on Arran is easy: the A841 road encircles the island and makes it difficult to get lost.

Brodick

⑯ *1 hour by ferry from Ardrossan.*

The largest township on the island, Brodick is really just a village, with a frontage spaciously set back from a promenade and beach.

⑰ Brodick is the site of the **Isle of Arran Heritage Museum,** which documents the life of the island from ancient times to the present century. A number of buildings, including a cottage and *smiddy* (blacksmith's), have period furnishings and displays on prehistoric life, geology, farming, fishing, and many other aspects of the island's heritage. ⊠ *Rosaburn, Brodick,* ☏ *01770/302636.* 🖾 *£2.* ⊗ *Apr.–Oct., Mon.–Sat. 10–5, Sun. 11–4.*

In **Glen Rosa,** visitors can walk through a long glen that offers a glimpse of the wild ridges that call so many outdoor enthusiasts to the island. To get there, go just beyond the Isle of Arran Heritage Museum and find the junction where the String Road cuts across the island. Drive up the String Road a short way to a signpost and turn right into the glen. The road soon becomes undrivable, but park the car and walk a little way up the glen.

★ **⑱** Arran's most important draw for those other than the outdoor enthusiasts is **Brodick Castle and Country Park,** on the north side of Brodick Bay, its red sandstone cosseted by trees and parkland. Now, under the auspices of the National Trust for Scotland, this former seat of the dukes of Hamilton has a number of rooms open to the public. The furniture, paintings, silver, and sporting trophies are opulent in their own right, but the real attraction is the garden with its brilliantly colored rhododendrons, particularly in late spring and early summer. Though there are many unusual varieties, you will find the ordinary yellow variety unmatched for its scent: your initial encounter with them is comparable to hitting a wall of perfume. Leave time to visit the Servant's Hall, where an award-winning restaurant serves morning coffee (with hot scones—try the date and walnut!), a full lunch menu that changes daily, and afternoon teas with home-baked goods, including the bread. Eat out on the terrace on a fine day, with chaffinches clamoring for crumbs. ⊠ *Slightly less than a mile north of Brodick pier,* ☏ *01770/302202.* 🖾 *£4.80, gardens only £2.40.* ⊗ *Castle Easter–Oct., daily 11:30–5 (last admission at 4:30), garden and country park daily 9:30–dusk.*

A pleasant walk to **Corriegills** offers fine views over Brodick Bay. It is signed from the A841 just to the south of Brodick.

Dining and Lodging

££–£££
★
✕🔀 **Kilmichael Country House Hotel.** At the head of Glen Cloy, just outside Brodick, is this 300-year-old mansion, built by the Fullerton family on land granted to them by Robert the Bruce. Now an outstanding small hotel, it is furnished in Georgian oak antiques, Sanderson fabrics, and light, sunny colors. At one end of the blue-and-yellow sitting room, in what was once a private chapel, is a stained-glass window showing the Fullerton family crest. Cuisine in the hotel's restaurant is also exceptional: salmon en croûte with dill sauce, duck with kumquats, and salad of pigeon with walnuts and smoked bacon are examples of

the marriage of fresh Scottish produce and international flair. ⊠ *Brodick, Isle of Arran, KA27 8BY,* ☎ *01770/302219,* ℻ *01770/302068. 9 rooms with bath. Restaurant. MC, V.*

Outdoor Activities and Sports

BIKING

Rent bicycles from **Brodick Boat and Cycle Hire** (⊠ The Beach, ☎ 01770/302009) or **Brodick Cycles** (⊠ Opposite Village Hall, ☎ 01770/302460).

HORSEBACK RIDING

Explore Arran on horseback with **Cloyburn Equestrian Centre** (⊠ Brodick, Arran, ☎ 01770/302800).

Shopping

Arran's shops are particularly well stocked with island-produced goods. **Duchess Court Shops** (⊠ The Pier, Brodick, ☎ 01770/302731) include **Something Special** for scented items, such as candles, as well as glass ornaments and designer pottery; **The Nature Shop** for nature-oriented books and gifts; and **The Home Farm Kitchen Shop** for locally made mustards and other preserves, together with kitchenware. Also at the Home Farm is the Island Cheese Company, with Arran-made cheese such as blue cheese and a wide selection of other handmade British cheeses.

Lamlash

🔟 *4 mi south of Brodick.*

Lamlash, with views offshore to steep-flanked Holy Island, has a breezy seaside holiday atmosphere—like the whole island. To reach the highest point accessible by car, go through the village and turn right beside the bridge, onto Ross Road, which climbs steeply from a thickly planted valley, Glen Scorrodale, and yields fine views of Lamlash Bay.

Shopping

Patterson Arran Ltd. (⊠ The Old Mill, Lamlash, ☎ 01770/600606) is famous for its mustards, preserves, and marmalades.

Lagg

🔟 *10 mi southwest of Lamlash via the Ross Road.*

This little community with an inn in a hollow beneath the sheltering trees sits peacefully by the banks of the Kilmory Water.

En Route Continuing east on the A841 along the bottom end of the island, past white-painted farmhouses and cottages, you'll have views across gently tilting fields to the steep hump of Ailsa Craig, offshore in the Firth of Clyde. Cheese connoisseurs will be pleased to know the creamery at Torrylinn makes Arran Cheddar from local milk. Beyond Kildonan the road twists north; the trees extend to the sea edge, where gannets seem to dive through the branches.

Whiting Bay

🔟 *8 mi east of Lagg.*

Whiting Bay has a string of hotels and well-kept property along the seafront.

Outdoor Activities and Sports

Rent bicycles from **Whiting Bay Cycle Hire** (⊠ Elim, Silverhill, Whiting Bay, ☎ 01770/700382).

Shopping

Crafts of Arran (✉ Whiting Bay, ☎ 01770/700251) prides itself on stocking crafts including silverware, porcelain, pottery, and wooden items produced in Arran.

En Route Northward from Brodick, the road is built along a raised beach platform, a common phenomenon in Scotland, caused by the lifting of the land after its burden of ice melted at the end of the Ice Age. Large, round boulders rest on softer sandstones in certain places on the shore. These stones, called *erratics,* were once carried by glaciers off the granite mountains that loom in the distance to your left as you approach Corrie.

Corrie

11 mi north of Brodick.

Corrie is a sparse, spread-out settlement with stores that sell the ubiquitous pottery and crafts items.

Outdoor Activities and Sports

Rent bicycles from **Spinning Wheels** (✉ The Trossachs, Corrie, ☎ 01770/810640).

Shopping

Corriecraft and Antiques (✉ Corrie, ☎ 01770/810661) sells crafts—though they may come from different parts of Scotland—and a carefully chosen mix of small antiques and curios.

Sannox

㉒ *2 mi north of Corrie.*

At Sannox, a locale consisting of another cluster of houses, there is a sandy bay of ground granite, washed down from the mountainous interior. There are also outstanding views of the rugged hills of the interior, particularly the steep pyramid of **Cir Mhor.** You can enjoy a good coastal walk from North Sannox.

Lochranza

㉓ *6 mi north of Sannox.*

The well-situated settlement of Lochranza is one more community that focuses on crafts. It is sheltered by the bay of Loch Ranza, which spills in shallows up the flat-bottomed glacial glen. The village is set off by a picturesque ruin: **Lochranza Castle,** situated on a low sand spit. It's said to have been the landing place of Robert the Bruce, who returned from Rathlin Island in 1307 to start the campaign that won Scotland's independence. ☎ *0131/668–8800.* ✑ *Free.* ☉ *Weekdays, 9–5.*

South of Lochranza, the raised beach backed by a cliff continues to make a scenic platform for the road. There are fine views across the **㉔** Kilbrannan Sound to the long rolling horizon of Kintyre. At **Catacol,** immediately after the Catacol Bay Hotel, sit the **Twelve Apostles,** a row of fishermen's houses, identical except for differences in the window shapes (so they can be recognized from offshore).

Machrie

11 mi south of Lochranza.

Near the scattered homesteads of Machrie—which has a popular **㉕** beach—a Historic Scotland sign points to the **Machrie Moor Stone Circles,** which are just about a mile farther along, although on foot it feels a bit more than that. A well-surfaced track will take you to a grassy moor by a ruined farm, where you will see small, rounded, granite-boulder circles and much taller, eerie red-sandstone monoliths. The lost and lonely stones out in the bare moor are very atmospheric and well worth a walk to see, if you like solitude. The Machrie area is littered with these sites: chambered cairns, hut circles, and standing stones dating from the Bronze Age.

Outdoor Activities and Sports
Even novices can enjoy guided rides on a mount from **Cairnhouse Riding Centre** (✉ Blackwaterfoot, Arran, ☎ 01770/860466).

Shopping
The **Old Byre Showroom** (✉ Auchencar Farm, ☎ 01770/840227) sells sheepskin goods, locally hand-knit "jumpers" (sweaters), designer knitwear, leather goods, and tweeds.

En Route　Continuing to Blackwaterfoot, you can return to Brodick by the String Road; turn left by the Kinloch Hotel, up the hill. There are more fine views of the granite complexities of Arran's hills: gray notched ridges beyond brown moor and, past the watershed, a vista of Brodick Bay. From this high point the road rolls down to Brodick.

ISLAY AND JURA

Islay has a personality distinct from that of the rest of the Hebrides. The western half, in particular, has large farms rather than crofts. Many of Islay's best beaches—as well as wildlife and historical preserves—are also in its western half, in contrast to the southeast area, which is mainly an extension of Jura's inhospitable quartzite hills. A number of distilleries—the source of the island's delectable malt whiskies—provide jobs for the locals. Islay is also known for its wildlife, especially its birds, including the rare chough—a crow with red legs and beak—and, in winter, its barnacle geese.

Although it is possible to meet an Islay native in a local pub, such an event is statistically less likely on Jura, with its one road, one distillery, one hotel, and six sporting estates. In fact, visitors have a better chance of bumping into one of the island's red deer, which outnumber the human population by at least 20 to 1. The island has a much more rugged look than Islay, with its profiles of the Paps of Jura, a hill range at its most impressive when basking in the rays of a west-coast sunset.

Bowmore

㉖ *11 mi north of Port Ellen.*

Bowmore is compact and about the same size (population 1,000) as the ferry port of Port Ellen, but slightly better suited as a base for touring. Bowmore, which gives its name to the whiskey made in the distillery (founded 1779) by the shore, is a tidy town. Its grid pattern was laid out in 1768 by the local landowner Daniel Campbell of Shawfield. Bowmore's Main Street stretches from the pier head to the commanding parish church, built in 1767 in an unusual circular design—so the devil could not find a corner to hide in. The town has a selection of accommodations and restaurants despite its small size.

Dining and Lodging
££　✕🏠 **Harbour Inn.** The cheerfully noisy public bar in the inn is frequented by locals and off-duty distillery workers who are happy to rub elbows with visitors and exchange island gossip. The superb restaurant serves morning coffee, lunch, and dinner, with both the bistro-style lunch menu and the "modern Scottish" dinner menu also available at the bar. Local lobster, crab and prawns, and island lamb and beef feature

prominently on both menus. Each of the four bedrooms has been decorated to a different theme (Victorian Garden, Captain's Cabin, Tartan, and Seaside). ⊠ *Main St., Bowmore,* ☎ *01496/810330,* FAX *01496/810990. 4 rooms with shower. Restaurant. MC, V.*

Shopping

On Islay you'll be spoiled by the sheer number of distilleries from which to choose a holiday purchase. Their delicious products, characterized by a peaty taste, can be purchased at off-license shops on the island, at local pubs, or at those distilleries that have shops. Most of them welcome visitors by appointment, some having a small charge for a tour, which is redeemable against a purchase of whiskey.

Distilleries: Bowmore (⊠ School St., Bowmore, ☎ 01496/810441). **Bunnahabhain** (⊠ Port Askaig, ☎ 01496/840646). **Caol Ila** (⊠ Port Askaig, ☎ 01496/840207). **Isle of Jura** (⊠ Craighouse, Jura, ☎ 01496/820240). **Lagavoulin** (⊠ Port Ellen, ☎ 01496/302250). **Laphroaig** (⊠ Port Ellen, ☎ 01496/302418).

En Route Traveling north out of Bowmore (signposted Bridgend), the road skirts the sand flats at the head of Loch Indaal. To reach Port Charlotte, follow the loch shores all the way past Bruichladdich, which, like Bowmore, is the name of a malt whiskey as well as a village with a distillery.

Port Charlotte

㉗ *11 mi west of Bowmore via A846/A847.*

At Port Charlotte, above the road on the right, in a converted *kirk* (church), is the **Museum of Islay Life,** a haphazard but authentic and informative display of times past. ☎ *01496/850358.* 🎫 *£1.60.* ☉ *Apr.–Oct., Mon.–Sat. 10–5, Sun. 2–5.*

From Port Charlotte a loop road allows for further exploration into the wilder landscape of the **Rhinns of Islay.** At the southern end are the scattered cottages of **Portnahaven** and its twin, **Port Wemyss.** To reach them, take the A847 south from Port Charlotte. You can return by the bleak, unclassified road that loops westward and passes by the recumbent stone circle at Coultoon and the chapel at Kilchiaran, before reaching Port Charlotte.

En Route To get a glimpse of Islay's peerless western seascapes, make a left onto the B8018, north of Bruichladdich. After about 2 mi, turn left again onto a little road that meanders past Loch Gorm and ends close to Machir Bay and its superb (and probably deserted) sandy beach. Soon after you turn around to go back, make a right, which will lead you to the derelict kirk of Kilchoman. In the kirkyard are some interesting grave slabs and two crosses of late-medieval times, from the Iona school of carving. (There was another Scottish "school" in Kintyre.) They are a wonderful introduction to the island's wealth of stone carvings. From Kilchoman turn right and then left to circle Loch Gorm, pausing as the road all but touches the coast at Saligo. It's worth a stroll (beyond the former wartime camp) to enjoy the view of some fine seascapes, especially if the westerlies are piling up high breakers on the rock ridges. On the return journey east, turn right at the B8018, then left on the B8017. Take a left at Aoradh Farm onto a minor road that runs north along the west side of Loch Gruinart.

Loch Gruinart

㉘ *7 mi northeast of Port Charlotte, 8 mi north of Bowmore.*

You will be inevitably drawn to the long reaches of Loch Gruinart. Dunes flank its sea outlet, and pale beaches rise out of the falling tides. Traveling north up its western shore, the road soon brings you to **Cill Naoimh** (Kilnave). Kilnave's ruined chapel is associated with a dark tale in which a group of wounded Maclean clansmen were defeated in a nearby battle with the Maconalds in 1598. The Macleans sought sanctuary in the chapel; their pursuers set its roof aflame, and the clansmen perished within. In the graveyard is a weathered 8th-century carved cross.

If you appreciate wide skies, crashing waves, and lonely coast, the best view of Loch Gruinart is northwards up its eastern shore. From the far dunes of the headland, held together with marram grass, there are views of the islands of **Colonsay** and **Oronsay** across Hebridean waters, on which plumes and fans of white spray rise from hidden reefs. The priory on the island of Oronsay, with its famous carved cross, is barely distinguishable. To witness this peerless scenery, return to the B8017 from visiting Kilnave, cross the flats at the head of the loch, and then go left up its eastern shore. Park before a gate, where the road deteriorates, and continue on foot.

The Oa

㉙	*13 mi south of Bowmore.*

The southern peninsula of the Oa is a region of caves rich in tales of smuggling. At its tip, the Mull of Oa, there is a monument recalling the 650 men who lost their lives when the troopships *Tuscania* and *Otranto* went down nearby in 1918. To get here, take the long straight of the A846 that passes the island airport just inland from the endless sandy curve of Laggan Bay. Before you reach Port Ellen, go straight ahead to a minor road to Imeraval, then make a right at a junction and then a left.

Port Ellen

㉚	*11 mi south of Bowmore.*

The sturdy community of Port Ellen was founded in the 1820s, with much of its architecture still dating to the 19th century. It has a harbor, a few shops, and some inns, but not enough commercial development to mortgage its personality.

The road eastward from Port Ellen passes communities bearing several more names known to the malt-whiskey connoisseur: the whiskey of the **Laphroaig distillery**—which offers tours—is perhaps one of the most distinctive of the local whiskies, with a tangy, peaty, seaweed/iodine flavor. This distillery is a little less than a mile along the road to Ardbeg from Port Ellen. ☎ *01496/302418.* 🎫 *Free.* ☉ *Tours by appointment.*

From Port Ellen, it is also possible to experience one of the highlights of Scotland's Celtic heritage. Passing through a pleasantly rolling, partly wooded landscape northeastward, take a narrow road signposted from Ardbeg. This leads to a ruined chapel with surrounding kirkyard, in which stands the finest carved cross anywhere in Scotland: the 8th-
★ **㉛** century **Kildalton Cross.** Carved from a single slab of epidiorite rock, this ringed cross is encrusted on both sides with elaborate designs in the style of the Iona school. Interesting early grave slabs from the 12th and 13th centuries can also be seen in the kirkyard.

Outdoor Activities and Sports
Ballivicar Pony Trekking (✉ Ballivicar Farm, Port Ellen, ☎ 01496/302251) takes riders on trips along nearby beaches and into the surrounding countryside.

Bridgend

3 mi north of Bowmore via A846 (follow signs for Port Askaig).

★ ㉜ Bridgend itself is a tiny little community beside the main road, but hardly a mile beyond is a sign for the **Islay Woollen Mill** (☞ Shopping, *below*). Set in a wooded hollow by the river, the mill has a fascinating selection of working machinery to inspect.

Shopping

The **Islay Woollen Mill** has a shop selling high-quality products that are woven on site. All the tartans and tweeds worn in the film *Braveheart* were woven here. Beyond the usual tweed lengths, there is a distinctive range of hats, caps, and clothing made from the mill's own cloth. ✉ *Bridgend,* ☎ *01496/810563.* 🖃 *Free.* ⊙ *Mon.–Sat. 10–5.*

Loch Finlaggan

㉝ *7 mi northeast of Bridgend; take a side road (to the left) 1 mi beyond Ballygrant, then drive through a gate.*

At first sight, there is not a great deal to see at Loch Finlaggan. But the little island on the loch, with its scanty traces of early buildings, was the council seat of the Lords of the Isles. This former western power base of the Clan Donald threatened the sovereignty of the Stewart monarchs of Scotland in its heyday; the ruins are a reminder of how independent the Highlands were in those times. A cottage **interpretative center** is nearby, with an exhibition relating to the ongoing excavations of the island ruins. ☎ *01496/840644.* 🖃 *Small fee.* ⊙ *Apr.–Sept., Sun., Tues., and Thurs. 2:30–5.*

Lodging

££ 🏠 **Kilmeny Farmhouse.** There are fine views over the surrounding countryside from this white-painted traditional farmhouse, on a working farm. It offers B&B accommodations with an evening meal, if desired. Home baking and homemade preserves make breakfast a special treat. ✉ *Ballygrant, Isle of Islay, PA45 7QW,* ☎ 🖷 *01496/840668. 3 rooms with bath or shower. No credit cards.*

Port Askaig

3 mi northeast of Loch Finlaggan via A846.

Tiny Port Askaig is the ferry port for Jura; it is just a cluster of cottages by the pier. Uphill, just outside the village, a side road travels along the coast, giving impressive views of Jura on the way. At the road's end, the **Bunnahabhain Distillery** (☎ 01496/840646) sits on the shore. You must make a reservation to visit the distillery.

Dining and Lodging

££ ✕🏠 **Port Askaig Hotel.** This modernized drovers' inn by the roadside, with grounds extending to the shore, overlooks the Sound of Islay and the island of Jura and is convenient to the ferry terminal. Accommodations are comfortable without being luxurious, and the traditional Scottish food is well prepared, using homegrown produce. ✉ *Port Askaig, Isle of Islay, Argyll, PA46 7RD,* ☎ *01496/840245,* 🖷 *01496/ 840295. 8 rooms, 6 with bath. Restaurant, 2 bars. No credit cards.*

Jura

5 minutes by ferry from Port Askaig.

Having crossed the Sound of Islay, you will find it easy to choose which road to take—Jura only has one. Apart from the initial stretch it is all single-lane. The A846 starts off below one of the many raised beaches, then climbs across poor moorland, providing scenic views across the Sound of Jura. The ruined **Claig Castle,** on an island just offshore, was built by the Lords of the Isles to control the sound. Beyond the farm buildings of Ardfin is **Jura House** in the woodlands, with its sheltered garden walks and fine views. Teas are served from June to August, weekdays 10–4. ☎ *01496/820315.* ⌷ *Gardens £2.* ☉ *Daily 9–5.*

Beyond Jura House the road turns northward across open moorland with scattered forestry blocks and the faint evidence, in the shape of parallel ridges, of the original inhabitants' lazy beds or strip cultivation. The original settlements were cleared with the other parts of the Highlands when the island became more of a sheep pasture and deer forest. The community of **Craighouse** is home to the island's only distillery (☎ 01496/820240), producing Isle of Jura malt whiskey.

The aptly named **Small Isles Bay** has a superb strip of beach to the north of Craighouse. As the road climbs away from the bay, the little cottage above the creek is a reminder of the history of this island—the cottage is the only survivor of a village with a population of 56 that was destroyed in Highland Clearances in 1841. Ironically, a sheep *fank* (fold) farther up the creek shows what happened to the stones of the demolished cottages. Although the landscapes of Jura seem devoid of life, they are, in fact, populated with many ghosts, most of which are missed by the casual visitor.

Beyond the River Corran the road climbs, offering austere views of the Paps, with their long quartzite screes, and of the fine, though usually deserted, anchorage in the scoop of **Lowlandman's Bay.** The next section of road is more hemmed in and runs to **Lagg,** formerly a ferry-crossing point on the old cattle-driving road between here and Feolin. Beyond Lagg, the sea views are blocked by conifer plantings. Views of fjordlike **Loch Tarbert,** westward to the left, are at their best next to the forestry plantation a little farther on. At this point the road leads through a stretch of rough, uninhabited landscape. A gate and cattle grid by **Ardlussa** to the north mark the start of a Site of Special Scientific Interest—a government-agency designation for rare plants and/or insects—in a shady oak wood. The coast here is rocky and unspoiled. Choose your own picnic site, but be sure to park sensibly—the road is very narrow. Yellow flag (a Scottish iris), bracken, strands of crisp seaweed on the salty grass, and background birdsong from the mossy woods make this an idyllic stretch when the sun shines. Try not to be too loud, so you won't distract the area's resident otter population.

The last house you will see is at **Lealt,** where you cross the river. Shortly beyond this point the tarmac ends rather abruptly, with a turning space cut into the hill. Ordinary cars should not attempt to go any farther on the remainder of this trail, though Jeeps, Rovers, and other high-clearance vehicles can make it through. With an ordinary car, you have no choice but to retrace your route to the ferry pier Feolin. The track beyond the surfaced road continues for another 5 mi to **Kinuachdrach,** a settlement that once served as a crossing point to Scarba and the mainland. The coastal footpath to Corryvreckan lies beyond, over the bare moors. This area has two enticements: the first, for fans of George Orwell (1903–50), is the house of **Barnhill,** where the author wrote *1984;* the second, for wilderness enthusiasts, is the whirlpool of the **Corryvreckan** and the unspoiled coastal scenery.

Dining and Lodging

££ ✕⌷ **Jura Hotel.** In spite of its monopoly, this hotel set in pleasant gardens genuinely welcomes its guests and can be relied on for high-quality accommodations and good, simple food cooked using local ingredients. ✉ *Craighouse, PA60 7XU,* ☎ *01496/820243,* FAX *01496/ 820249. 17 rooms, 11 with bath or shower. Restaurant. AE, DC, MC, V.*

THE ISLE OF MULL

It's possible to spend a long weekend on Mull and not meet a single resident who was born north of Manchester, England. Though Mull certainly has an indigenous population, the island is often referred to as the Officers' Mess because of its popularity with retired military personnel. Visitors make their way across the Ross of Mull to Iona, cradle of Scottish Christianity and ancient burial site of the kings of Scotland.

Craignure

③⑤ *40-minute ferry crossing from Oban, 15-minute ferry crossing to Fishnish (5 mi northwest of Craignure) from Lochaline.*

Craignure, little more than a pier with some houses, is close to Mull's two best-known castles, Torosay and Duart. Reservations are accepted (and advised in summer) from Oban; the ferry from Lochaline to Fishnish, just northwest, runs in summer only and takes no reservations.

★ **③⑥** **Torosay Castle** has the novelty of a steam-and-diesel service on a narrow-gauge railway, which takes 20 minutes to run from the pier at Craignure to Torosay's grounds. Scottish baronial in style, Torosay has a friendly air. You have the run of much of the house, which is full of intrigue and humor by way of idiosyncratic information boards and informal family albums. The main feature of the castle's gardens—a gentle blend of formal and informal—is its Italian statue walk. ✉ *Off the A849, about 1 mi southeast of Craignure,* ☎ *01680/812421.* 💷 *Castle and gardens £4.50, train £2.30.* ☉ *Castle Easter–mid-Oct., daily 10:30–5:30 (last admission at 5), gardens Easter–mid-Oct., daily 9–7; mid-Oct.–Easter, daily dawn–dusk.*

③⑦ If you're energetic you can take a long walk along the shore from Torosay to **Duart Castle.** The not-so-energetic can drive the 3 mi from Craignure. This ancient Maclean seat was ruined by the Campbells in 1691 but bought and restored by Sir Fitzroy Maclean in 1911. One display depicts the wreck of the *Swan,* a Cromwellian vessel sunk offshore in the mid-17th century and currently being excavated by marine archaeologists. If you're driving to Duart, use the A849, then turn off left round the shore of Duart Bay. ✉ *3 mi southeast of Craignure,* ☎ *01680/ 812309.* 💷 *£3.50.* ☉ *May–mid-Oct., daily 10:30–6.*

Lodging

£ 🏠 **Inverlussa.** Idyllically set beside a stream close to Loch Spelve, this warm, friendly, modern guest house makes a good touring base for Mull. Tranquil green, blue, or cream color schemes in the bedrooms, pine furniture, and an open fire in the lounge create a relaxing environment, and there is a choice of restaurants and pubs close by for evening meals. ✉ *By Craignure, Argyll PA65 6BD,* ☎ FAX *01680/812436. 3 rooms, 1 with shower. No credit cards. Closed Nov.–Mar.*

En Route Traveling from Craignure to Fionnphort, the double-lane road narrows as it goes southwest, touched by sea inlets at Lochs Don and Spelve. Gray and green are the most prevalent colors of the interior, with vivid grass and high rock faces in Glen More. These stepped-rock faces, the by-product of ancient lava flows, reach their highest point in Ben More, the only island *munro* outside Skye. (A munro is a Scottish mountain more than 3,000 ft high.) Its high, bald slopes are prominent by the time you reach the road junction at the head of Loch Scridain. Stay on the A849 for a pleasant drive the length of the Ross of Mull, a wide promontory with scattered settlements. There are good views to the right of the dramatic cliff ramparts of Ardmeanach, the stubbier promontory to the north: the National Trust for Scotland cares for the rugged stretch of coast known as The Burg, which is home to a 40 million-year-old fossil tree (at the end of a long walk from the B8035, signposted west off the A849). The A849 continues through the village of Bunessan and eventually ends in a long parking lot opposite the houses of Fionnphort.

Fionnphort

36 mi west of Craignure.

The vast parking space at the small village of Fionnphort is made necessary by the popularity of the nearby island of Iona, which does not allow cars. Ferry service is frequent in summer months.

Iona

★ ❸ *5 minutes by ferry from Fionnphort.*

The fiery and argumentative Irish monk, Columba, chose Iona for the site of a monastery in AD 563 because it was the first place he landed from which he could not see Ireland. Christianity had been brought to Scotland (Galloway) by Saint Ninian in 397, but until Saint Columba's church was founded, the word had not spread widely among the ancient northerners, called Picts. Iona was the burial place of the kings of Scotland until the 11th century. It survived repeated Norse sackings and finally fell into disuse around the time of the Reformation. Restoration work began at the turn of this century, and later, in 1938, the **Iona Community** was founded. Today the restored buildings, including the abbey, serve as a spiritual center under the jurisdiction of the Church of Scotland. The ambience of the complex is a curious amalgam of the ancient and the earnest. But beyond the restored cloisters the most mystifying aspect of all is the island's ability to absorb visitors and still feel peaceful; most people only make the short walk from the ferry pier by way of the nunnery to the abbey. ☎ 01681/700404. ⊙ *Abbey gift and bookshop Apr.–Oct., Mon.–Sat. 10–5, Sun. noon–4, abbey coffeehouse Apr.–Oct., Mon.–Thurs. and Sat. 11–4:30, Fri. and Sun. noon–4:30.*

Shopping

Iona has one or two pleasant surprises for shoppers, the biggest being the **Old Printing Press Bookshop** (⊠ Beside the St. Columba Hotel), an excellent antiquarian and secondhand bookshop. The shop at the **Abbey** (☎ 01681/700404) is also worth a visit for its selection of Celtic-inspired gift items.

Carsaig

❸ *20 mi east of Fionnphort via A849 and an unclassified road.*

On your return to Mull, retrace your route eastward, then turn south for a side trip to the remote south coast. From the pier head toward the tiny settlement of Carsaig (look for a sign on the right as you approach the head of Loch Scridain). A rough path meanders west below lava cliffs to the impressive **Carsaig Arches.** Taking on the arches is a separate excursion reserved for the agile.

En Route   Turning west onto the B8035 at Loch Scridain, the road rises away from the loch to the conifer plantations and green slopes of Gleann Seilisdeir.

The main road through the glen breaches the stepped cliffs and drops to the shore, offering inspiring views of the island of Ulva guarding Loch na Keal. This stretch of the B8035, with splinters of rock from the heights strewn over it in places, feels remote. The high ledges eventually give way (not literally) to vistas of the screes of Ben More. Continue to skirt the coast by way of the B8073, and you will enjoy a succession of fine coastal views with Ulva in the foreground. Beyond Calgary Bay the landscape is gentler, as the road leads to the village of Dervaig.

Dervaig

40 *42 mi north of Carsaig, 27 mi northwest of Craignure.*

Just before the village of Dervaig, the **Old Byre Heritage Centre** is signposted. An audiovisual presentation on the history of Mull plays here (every hour on the half hour); there is also a crafts shop and a restaurant, where the wholesome catering certainly will be appreciated by weary travelers, particularly those who enjoy thick and hearty homemade soups. ⊠ *Dervaig PA75 6QR,* ☎ *01688/400229.* ☞ *£2.* ☉ *Easter–Oct., daily 10:30–6:30 (last admission at 6).*

In Dervaig the **Mull Little Theatre** (☞ Nightlife and the Arts, *below*) offers a varied program and claims the record as the smallest professional theater in the United Kingdom.

Dining and Lodging

£££ ✕🏠 **Druimard Country House.** From this handsome Victorian house on the outskirts of the village, there are loch and glen views over the River Bellart. The restaurant is elegantly furnished and offers an original menu with several vegetarian options (dinner is included in the room rate). Roast loin of venison on a bed of red cabbage with game sauce and medallions of local monkfish topped with Provençale bread crumbs on a pool of two pepper sauces are two popular dishes. Rooms are individually decorated with Laura Ashley wallpaper and fabrics and antique Victorian oak and mahogany furniture. ⊠ *Dervaig, Isle of Mull, Argyll, PA75 6QW,* ☎ 🅵🅰🆇 *01688/400345. 6 rooms with bath or shower. Restaurant. MC, V. Closed Nov.–Mar.*

Nightlife and the Arts

Mull Little Theatre (⊠ Dervaig, Isle of Mull, ☎ 01688/400267) is Britain's smallest professional playhouse—43 seats—and presents a number of productions throughout the season.

Tobermory

41 *5 mi east of Dervaig.*

Founded as a fishing station, Tobermory gradually declined, hastened by the arrival of the railroad station at Oban, which took away fishing traffic. However, the brightly painted crescent of 18th-century buildings around the harbor, which is now a popular mooring with yachtsmen, gives Tobermory a Mediterranean look.

Dining and Lodging

££–£££ ✕🏠 **Western Isles Hotel.** This traditional resort hotel set high above the town has superb views from many of its rooms. All the spacious bedrooms are individually decorated with floral fabrics, elegant canopies above many of the beds, and touches of tartan; the terra-cotta lounge and airy conservatory bar both offer comfort and relaxation. Two restaurants serve Indian and Far Eastern cuisine, and a Taste of Scotland with local fish, seafood, game, and lamb. ⊠ *Tobermory, Argyll PA75 6PR,* ☎ *01688/302012.* 🅵🅰🆇 *01688/302297. 24 rooms with bath, 1 suite. 2 restaurants, bar. AE, MC, V.*

Outdoor Activities and Sports

Rent bicycles from **On Yer Bike** (⊠ Salen, Aros, Isle of Mull, ☎ 01680/ 300501).

En Route   The route to the ferry lies southward on the A848, which yields pleas-ant, though unspectacular, views across to Morven on the mainland. On the coast just beyond Aros, across the river flats, stands the ruined 13th-century Aros Castle. The road continues through Salen to either Fishnish, for the ferry to Lochaline, or Craignure, for the ferry to Oban.

ARGYLL AND THE ISLES A TO Z

Arriving and Departing

By Bus

Daily bus service from Glasgow Buchanan Street Station to mid-Argyll and Kintyre is available through **Scottish Citylink** (☎ 0990/505050).

By Car and Ferry

The A85 reaches Oban, the main ferry terminal for Mull, and the A83 rounds Loch Fyne and heads down Kintyre to reach Kennacraig, the main ferry terminal for Islay. Farther down the A83 is Tayinloan, the ferry departure point for Gigha. Brodick (Arran) is reached from Ardrossan on the Clyde coast (A8/A78 from Glasgow). All ferries take pedestrians and cars. For information on ferry times, contact **Caledonian MacBrayne** (CalMac, main office, ⊠ Ferry Terminal, Gourock, ☎ 01475/650100, 0990/650000 reservations).

By Plane

Although the nearest full-service airport for the entire area is in Glas-gow (☞ Chapter 4), there are two airports within Argyll and the isles. Both **Campbeltown** (on the mainland Kintyre peninsula) and the island of **Islay** are served Monday to Saturday by **British Airways Express** (☎ 0345/222111) from Glasgow.

By Train

Oban and Ardrossan are the main rail stations. For details of services, telephone the **National Train Enquiry Line** (☎ 0345/484950). All trains connect with ferries.

Getting Around

By Bus

The following companies operate in the area: **B. Mundell Ltd.** (⊠ Islay, ☎ 01496/840273). **Bowman's Coaches** (⊠ Mull, ☎ 01680/812313). **C. MacLean** (⊠ Jura, ☎ 01496/820221). **Oban & District Buses** (⊠ Oban and Lorne, ☎ 01631/562856). **Western Buses** (⊠ Arran, ☎ 01770/ 302000). **West Coast Motor Service** (⊠ Mid-Argyll and Kintyre, ☎ 01586/552319).

By Car and Ferry

Negotiating this area is easy except in peak season (July and August), when the roads around Oban may be congested. There are some single-lane roads, especially on the east side of the Kintyre peninsula and on the islands. Car-ferry services to and from the main islands are oper-ated by **Caledonian MacBrayne** (CalMac, main office, ⊠ Ferry Terminal, Gourock; ☎ 01475/650100, 0990/650000 reservations). An Island Hop-scotch ticket reduces the cost of island-hopping excursions. **Western Ferries** (☎ 01369/704452) operates the Islay–Jura ferry service.

By Train

Aside from the main line to Oban, with stations at Dalmally, Loch Awe, Falls of Cruachan (request stop), Taynuilt, and Connel Ferry, there is no train service. You can travel from the pier head at **Craignure** on **Mull** to **Torosay Castle,** a distance of about a half mile, by narrow-gauge railway.

Contacts and Resources

Doctors and Dentists

Information is available from your hotel, the local tourist information center, and the police, or look under "Doctors" or "Dentists" in the Yellow Pages telephone directory.

Emergencies

For **police, fire, or ambulance,** dial ☎ 999 from any telephone. No coins are needed for emergency calls from public telephone booths. There is an emergency room at **Lorne and Islands District General Hospital** (✉ Glengallen Rd., Oban, ☎ 01631/567500).

Guided Tours

ORIENTATION

Many of the bus companies listed in (☞ Getting Around by Bus, *above*) offer orientation tours.

SPECIAL-INTEREST

Bowman's Coaches (✉ Mull, ☎ 01680/812313) offers trips to Mull, Staffa, and Iona from Oban, from March to October. **Gordon Grant Marine** (✉ Staffa Ferries, Isle of Iona, ☎ 01681/700338) offers a "Three Isle" excursion to Mull, Iona, and Staffa, and also trips to the Treshnish Isles and to Staffa, from Mull. Other boat cruises are available on **Loch Etive Cruises** (✉ from Taynuilt near Oban, ☎ 01866/ 822430, or call tourist information center at Oban). **Sea Life Surveys** (from Dervaig on Mull, ☎ 01688/400223) offers four-hour day trips, and three, five-, and seven-day packages where you can assist with an ongoing whale and dolphin survey. **MacDougall's Tours** (✉ Oban, ☎ 01631/562133) runs half- and full-day touring and sailing expeditions to Mull and Iona. **Turas Mara** (✉ Penmore Mill, Dervaig, Isle of Mull, ☎ ℻ 01688/400242) runs daily excursions from Oban and Mull to Staffa, Iona, and the Treshnish Isles.

Late-Night Pharmacies

Late-night pharmacies are not found in rural areas, although most towns will have a pharmacy keeping normal shop hours. In an emergency the police will provide assistance in locating a pharmacist. In rural areas general practitioners may also dispense medicines.

Visitor Information

Bowmore, Islay (✉ The Square, ☎ 01496/810254). **Brodick, Arran** (✉ The Pier, ☎ 01770/302140, ℻ 01770/302395). **Campbeltown** (✉ Mackinnon House, The Pier, ☎ 01586/552056). **Craignure, Mull** (✉ The Pierhead, ☎ 01680/812377). **Dunoon** (✉ 7 Alexandra Parade, ☎ 01369/703785, ℻ 01369/706085). **Inveraray** (✉ Front St., ☎ 01499/302063). **Lochgilphead** (Apr.–Oct., ☎ 01546/602344). **Oban** (✉ Boswell House, Argyll Sq., ☎ 01631/563122, ℻ 01631/564273). **Tarbert** (Apr.–Oct., ☎ 01880/820429). **Tobermory, Mull** (☎ 01688/ 302182).

10 Around the Great Glen

Inverness, Loch Ness, Speyside, Fort William

The Great Glen cuts through the Southern Highlands from Inverness to Fort William—two of the Highlands' best areas for lodging and shopping—and is rimmed by Scotland's tallest mountains and fine glens. The lochs of the Great Glen include Scotland's most famous, Loch Ness. Ben Nevis is Britain's highest peak and easily reached from Fort William, behind which is Glen Nevis, another scenic treat.

THE ANCIENT RIFT VALLEY of the Great Glen is a dramatic feature on the map of Scotland, giving the impression that the top half of the country has slid

By Gilbert
Summers

southwest. Geologists confirm that this actually occurred, having matched granite from Strontian in Morvern, west of Fort William, with the same rocks found at Foyers, on the east side of Loch Ness, some 65 mi away. The Great Glen, with its sense of openness, lacks the grandeur of Glencoe or the Torridons, but the highest mountain in the United Kingdom, Ben Nevis (4,406 ft), looms over its southern portals, and spectacular scenery lies within a short distance of the main glen.

Though it's the capital of the Highlands, Inverness has the flavor of a Lowland town, its winds blowing in a sea-salt air from the Moray Firth. Inverness is also home to one of the world's most famous monster myths: in 1933, during a quiet news week for the local paper, the editor decided to run a story about a strange sighting of something splashing about in Loch Ness. More than 60 years later the story lives on, and the dubious Loch Ness phenomenon continues to keep cameras trained on the deep waters, which have an ominous tendency to create mirages in still conditions. The loch also has the greatest volume of water of any Scottish loch.

Fort William, without a monster on its doorstep, makes do with Ben Nevis and the Road to the Isles, a title sometimes applied to the breathtakingly scenic route to Mallaig, which is best seen by rail. On the way, road and rail routes pass Loch Morar, the country's deepest body of water, which lays claim to its own monster, Morag.

Away from the Great Glen to the north lie the heartlands of Scotland, a bare backbone of remote mountains. The great hills that loom to the south can be seen clearly on either side of Strathspey, the broad valley of the River Spey, an area also commonly known as Speyside.

Pleasures and Pastimes

Beaches
The most extensive beaches are at Nairn, with miles of clean, golden sand. The best-known are at Morar, home of the famous white-and-silver sands.

Biking
The Great Glen itself has a very busy main road, not recommended for cyclists, along the west bank of Loch Ness via Drumnadrochit. The B862/B852, which runs by the east side of Loch Ness, has less traffic and is a better bet for cyclists. There are plans to expand off-road routes for cyclists in this area—one option is the tow path of the Caledonian Canal. To the east, there is a good network of back roads around Inverness and toward Nairn. The A9, however, on either side of Aviemore, is not recommended for cyclists.

Dining
No doubt about it, there are some fine places with superb cuisine in this area, with a wealth of country house hotels to choose from, as well as an excellent seafood restaurant in Fort William.

CATEGORY	COST*
££££	over £40
£££	£30–£40
££	£15–£30
£	under £15

*per person for a 3-course meal, including VAT and excluding drinks and service

Fishing

The Great Glen is laced with rivers and lochs where you can fly-fish for salmon and trout. The fishing seasons are as follows: salmon, early February through September or early October (depending on the area); brown trout, March 15 to September 30; sea trout, May through September or early October; rainbow trout, no statutory-close season. Sea angling from shore or boat is also possible. Tourist information centers (☞ Visitor Information *in* Around the Great Glen A to Z, *below*) can provide information on locations, permits, and fishing rights (which differ from those in England and Wales).

Golf

As is the case with most of Scotland, there is a broad selection of courses, especially toward the eastern end of this area. Nairn, with two courses, is highly regarded among Scottish players (☞ Chapter 2).

Lodging

The main centers, Inverness, Fort William, and Aviemore, have plenty of accommodations in all price ranges. Since this is such an old, established vacation area, there are few places where you'd have trouble finding a room for a night. However, the area is quite busy in peak season.

CATEGORY	COST*
££££	over £120
£££	£90–£120
££	£50–£90
£	under £50

Prices are for a standard double room, including service, breakfast, and VAT.

Nightlife and the Arts

Do not visit this area expecting to have a big-city choice of late-night activities. With the exception of Inverness, evening entertainment revolves around pubs and hotels. The *ceilidh,* a small, informal, musical get-together, and "Scottish Evening," a staged performance of tartan-clad Highland dancers, are the most popular forms of entertainment offered to visitors.

Walking

The Great Glen area is renowned for its hill-walking opportunities, but if you head for the hills you should be fit and properly outfitted. Remember that on Ben Nevis, a popular route even for inexperienced hikers, it can snow on the summit plateau at any time of the year—Ben Nevis is a large and dangerous mountain.

Exploring the Great Glen

The first possible route centers on Inverness, moving east into Speyside, then west down the Great Glen. The second route, originating in Fort William, takes in the special qualities of the birch-knoll and blue island West Highland views. There are many romantic and historic associations with this area. It was here where the rash adventurer Prince Charles Edward Stuart (1720–88) arrived for the final Jacobite rebellion of 1745–46, and it was from here that he departed after the last battle.

Numbers in the text correspond to numbers in the margin and on the Great Glen Area map.

Great Itineraries

The road between Fort William and Mallaig, though narrow and winding, is one of the classic routes of Scottish touring, and is popularly known as the Road to the Isles. Similarly, the Great Glen road is a vital coast-to-coast link. The fact that it passes by a loch with a "monster" phenomenon is just a happy coincidence.

IF YOU HAVE 2 DAYS

Both ⛯ **Inverness** ① and ⛯ **Fort William** ㉛ have a choice of loops running from them. Base yourself anywhere around Fort William, so that you can take in the spectacular scenery of **Glencoe** ㉙ and Glen Nevis, and also at least glimpse the western seaboard toward **Mallaig** ㉟.

IF YOU HAVE 4 DAYS

Spend two days at one of two bases at each end of the Great Glen, say, ⛯ **Inverness** ① or ⛯ **Nairn** ④ at the north end, and ⛯ **Fort William** ㉛ or ⛯ **Ballachulish** ㉚ at the south end. This will give you adequate time to see this chunk of Scotland. The first day, travel to Nairn from Inverness, and from Nairn go southward via **Cawdor Castle** ⑥ and **Lochindorb Castle** to **Grantown-on-Spey** ⑧. Then follow the Spey as far as you feel like, via **Boat of Garten** ⑨, with its ospreys in spring and early summer; **Aviemore** ⑫ and its mountain scenery; and **Kingussie** ⑮, where the Highland Folk Museum does a good job of explaining what life was really like before modern domestic and agricultural equipment made things easy. The next day, explore Loch Ness, traveling down the eastern bank as far as **Fort Augustus** ㉒, and returning up the western bank via **Drumnadrochit** ㉔; if you have time on a long summer evening, divert northward at Drumnadrochit to discover beautiful glens Affric and Cannich, before returning to Inverness. The third day, travel to ⛯ **Fort William** ㉛, taking in the **Caledonian Canal** ㉑ and **Commando Memorial** ⑳. Spend a day doing the suggested loop to **Mallaig** ㉟ and back through **Glenfinnan** ㊲ to Fort William, or go straight to **Arisaig** ㉞ and take an unforgettable day cruise among the Small Isles.

IF YOU HAVE 7 DAYS

This is plenty of time to visit all the places in the Great Glen area. Base yourself at ⛯ **Inverness** ① or ⛯ **Nairn** ④ for two nights, then spend a night at ⛯ **Kingussie** ⑮ and a night at ⛯ **Drumnadrochit** ㉔ or ⛯ **Whitebridge** ㉖. Moving west to the Fort William area, either stay in ⛯ **Fort William** ㉛ itself, or go farther west to the excellent accommodations of ⛯ **Arisaig** ㉞ for two nights. Either base will allow for exploration of the suggested circular route, a day at sea among the Small Isles, and a half-day or day amid the grandeur of **Glencoe** ㉙, or Glen Nevis behind Fort William. You may also want to make excursions farther north and west.

When to Tour the Great Glen

This is a spring and autumn kind of area, for summer contends with pesky midges, and winter brings raw chill. However, in summer, if the weather is settled, it can be very pleasant in the far west, perhaps on the Road to the Isles, toward Mallaig. Early spring is a good time to sample Scottish skiing at Nevis Range or Glencoe.

SPEYSIDE AND LOCH NESS

Inverness itself is not really a town to linger in, unless you need to do some shopping. Because Jacobite tales are interwoven with landmarks throughout this entire area, you should first learn something about this thorny but colorful period of Scottish history. One of the best places to do this is at Culloden, just east of Inverness, where a major battle ended in final defeat for the Jacobites. Other areas to concentrate on are the inner Moray Firth moving down into Speyside, before moving west into the Great Glen. Loch Ness is just one of the attractions hereabouts, both natural and man-made. In the Great Glen and Speyside,

Around the Great Glen

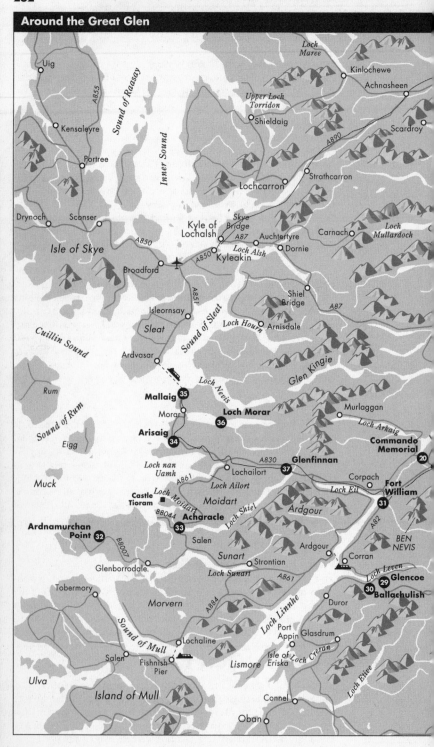

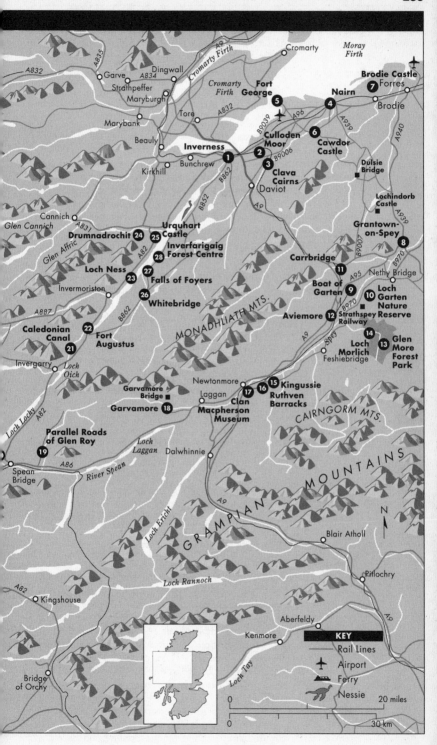

Moray Firth

Cromarty

Cromarty Firth

A9

A832

Garve
Dingwall
Strathpeffer
Maryburgh

A835
A834

Brodie Castle
7
Forres

Fort George
5
Nairn
4
Brodie

A832

Cromarty Firth

Marybank

Tore

A96

Culloden Moor

Cawdor Castle
6

A939

A940

Beauly

B9039

Inverness
1
Bunchrew

2
3
Clava Cairns

Kirkhill

B862

Daviot

Dulsie Bridge

B9006

A9

Lochindorb Castle

A939

Cannich

Glen Cannich

A831

Urquhart Castle

Drumnadrochit
24
25

Grantown-on-Spey
8

B9007

Glen Affric

A82

Inverfarigaig Forest Centre
28

Carrbridge

A95

Nethy Bridge

B970

Loch Ness
23
27
Falls of Foyers

Whitebridge
26

11

Boat of Garten
9
10
Loch Garten Nature Reserve

B970

Invermoriston

B862

MONADHLIATH MTS.

Aviemore
12
Strathspey Railway

A887

Caledonian Canal

22
Fort Augustus

A9

Spey

14
Loch Morlich
13
Glen More Forest Park

21

Feshiebridge

Invergarry

Loch Oich

Garvamore Bridge

Newtonmore

CAIRNGORM MTS.

Loch Locky

A82

Garvamore
18

Laggan

15
Kingussie
Ruthven Barracks

17
16

Clan Macpherson Museum

Parallel Roads of Glen Roy
19

Loch Laggan

Dalwhinnie

GRAMPIAN
MOUNTAINS

Spean Bridge

A86

River Spean

Loch Ericht

Blair Atholl

Kingshouse

A82

Loch Rannoch

Pitlochry

A9

Aberfeldy

Bridge of Orchy

Kenmore

Loch Tay

N

KEY

Rail Lines

Airport

Ferry

Nessie

0   20 miles

0   30 km

the best sights are often hidden from the main road, an excellent reason to favor peaceful rural byways and avoid, as far as possible, the busy A82 (down Loch Ness's western shore), and the A96 and A9, which carry much of the eastern traffic in the area.

Inverness

❶ *176 mi north of Glasgow, 109 mi northwest of Aberdeen, 161 mi northwest of Edinburgh.*

Inverness seems designed for the tourist, with its banks, souvenirs, high-quality woolens, and well-equipped tourist information center. Compared with other Scottish towns, however, Inverness has less to offer visitors who have a keen interest in Scottish history. Throughout its past, Inverness was burned and ravaged by one or another of the restive Highland clans competing for dominance in the region. Thus, a decorative wall panel here, and a fragment of tower there are all that remain amid the modern shopping facilities and 19th-century downtown developments.

One of Inverness's few historic landmarks is the **castle** (the local Sheriff Court), nestled above the river. The present structure is Victorian, built after a former fort was blown up by the Jacobites in the 1745 campaign.

★ **❷** At **Culloden Moor,** on a sleety April day in 1746, an army of 5,000 Jacobites, under Prince Charles Edward Stuart, also called Bonnie Prince Charlie, faced 9,000 well-armed British troops, under the command of the prince's distant cousin, General Willian Cumberland (1721–65). The latter became known in Scotland as Butcher Cumberland because of the atrocities committed by his men after the battle ended. The story of the encounter, of how the ill-advised, poorly organized, and exhausted rebel army was swept aside by superior British firepower, is illustrated in the visitor center by a moving audiovisual presentation. ⊠ *5 mi east of Inverness via B9006,* ☎ *01463/790607.* ☞ *£3.* ⊙ *Site daily, visitor center Apr.–Oct., daily 9–6; Nov.–Dec. and Feb.–Mar., daily 10–4.*

❸ Not far from Culloden, on a narrow road southeast of the battlefield, are the **Clava Cairns,** dating from the Bronze Age. In a cluster among the trees, these stones and monuments form a large ring with passage graves, which consist of a central chamber below a cairn, reached via a tunnel. Placards explain the graves' significance.

Dining and Lodging

££££   ✕🏨 **Dunain Park Hotel.** You receive individual attention in this 18th-century mansion set in six acres of wooded gardens. A log fire awaits you in the living room, a good place to sip a drink and browse through books and magazines. Antiques and traditional decor make the bedrooms equally cozy and attractive. The restaurant offers French-influenced Scottish dishes— saddle of venison in port sauce and boned quail stuffed with pistachios—served on bone china with crystal glasses. ⊠ *Dunain, 2½ mi southwest of Inverness on A82, IV3 6JN,* ☎ *01463/ 230512,* 🖷 *01463/224532. 14 rooms with bath. Restaurant, indoor pool, sauna. AE, DC, MC, V.*

££–££££   ✕🏨 **Bunchrew House.** This turreted mansion, on the banks of the Beauly Firth, abounds with handsome wood paneling. The dining room is particularly attractive, with fine antique furniture, and the lounge and comfortable bedrooms are decorated with velvet and chintz. The restaurant serves French-influenced Scottish cuisine, using the best Aberdeen Angus beef, local salmon, and game. The extensive grounds are delightful for a predinner stroll, and the views of the Firth are superb. ⊠ *Bunchrew, Inverness-shire, IV3 6TA,* ☎ *01463/234917,* ℻ *01463/710620. 11 rooms with bath. Restaurant. AE, MC. V.*

££–££££ ✕⛉ **Kingsmills Hotel.** A rambling mansion set in four acres of gardens on the edge of a golf course, the Kingsmills is about 1 mi from the center of Inverness. It's a great place for families: children under 14 stay for free, and the heated indoor pool and extensive leisure facilities offer plenty to do. The bedrooms are particularly spacious, comfortable, and well equipped. The restaurant serves well-prepared and reliable steaks, seafood tagliatelle, and game pâté. ⊠ *Culcabock Rd., IV2 3LP,* ☎ *01463/237166,* ℻ *01463/225208. 80 rooms with bath. Restaurant, indoor pool, golf privileges, 3-hole golf course, health club. AE, DC, MC, V.*

££ ✕⛉ **Priory Hotel.** A haven in Beauly center, about 10 mi west of Inverness, the Priory is a comfortable, traditional-style hotel—with cheerful patterned carpets and modern furnishings—notable for the warmth of its staff and its excellent food. In the restaurant, Scottish tradition, in the form of satisfying game, steaks, and seafood, is tempered with imaginative sauces: try the pork flamed with calvados with cream and apple. It's all that a good hotel should be, and rarely is, at reasonable prices. ⊠ *The Square, Beauly, IV4 7BX,* ☎ *01463/782309,* ℻ *01463/782531. 35 rooms with bath or shower. Restaurant. AE, DC, MC, V.*

££ ⛉ **Ballifeary House Hotel.** This well-maintained Victorian property is within easy reach of downtown Inverness. The particularly helpful proprietors offer high standards of comfort and service. Rooms are individually decorated with modern furnishings, and the downstairs has reproduction antiques. ⊠ *10 Ballifeary Rd., IV3 5PJ,* ☎ *01463/235572,* ℻ *01463/717583. 5 rooms with bath or shower. No smoking. No children under 12. MC, V. Closed Nov.–Mar.*

£–££ ⛉ **Clach Mhuilinn.** This modern family home is set in a pretty garden
★ and has good parking facilities. It offers bed-and-breakfast of a very high standard. ⊠ *7 Harris Rd., IV2 3LS,* ☎ *01463/237059.* ℻ *01463/242092. 2 rooms with shower. No smoking. MC, V. Closed Dec.–Feb.*

£ ⛉ **Atholdene House.** This family-run, 19th-century stone villa offers a friendly welcome and modernized accommodations. Evening meals can be provided for guests on request. The bus and railway stations are a short walk away. ⊠ *20 Southside Rd., IV2 3BG,* ☎ ℻ *01463/233565. 9 rooms, 7 with shower. No credit cards.*

£ ⛉ **Daviot Mains Farm.** A 19th-century farmhouse, 5 mi south of Inverness on the A9, provides the perfect setting for home comforts and
★ traditional Scottish cooking for guests only; lucky ones may find wild salmon on the menu in the dining room. ⊠ *Daviot Mains, IV1 2ER,* ☎ *01463/772215,* ℻ *01463/772099. 3 rooms, 2 with bath or shower. MC, V.*

£ ⛉ **Easter Dalziel Farm.** This 210-acre working farm offers plenty of interest for guests staying one night or longer. The Victorian farmhouse, with its log fire, home baking, evening meals by arrangement, and pretty gardens, is a welcome change from impersonal hotels. Rooms have antique mahogany, oak, or pine furniture and floral fabrics; tapestries stitched by the owner are displayed throughout the house. ⊠ *Dalcross, Inverness, IV1 2JL,* ☎ ℻ *01667/462213. 3 rooms without bath. MC, V.*

Nightlife and the Arts

BARS AND LOUNGES

Inverness has an array of bars and lounges. **Gunsmith's** (⊠ Union St., ☎ 01463/710519) is a traditional pub offering bar meals. **DJ's Café Bar** (⊠ High St.) serves everything from breakfast to late-night cocktails.

Scottish Showtime (✉ Cummings Hotel, Church St., Inverness, ☎ 01463/232531) offers Scottish cabaret from June to September of the tartan-clad dancer and bagpipe/accordion variety.

Eden Court Theatre (✉ Bishops Rd., Inverness, ☎ 01463/221718) offers not only drama, but also a program of music, film, and light entertainment, and an art gallery.

Outdoor Activities and Sports

Inverness Golf Club (☎ FAX 01463/239882) welcomes visitors. **Torvean Golf Course** (✉ Inverness, ☎ 01463/711434) is open to visitors paying a greens fee.

Shopping

Although Inverness has the usual High Street stores and department stores—including Arnott's and Marks and Spencer—the most interesting goods are to be found in the specialty outlets in and around town.

The Riverside Gallery (✉ 11 Bank St., ☎ 01463/224781) sells paintings and prints of Scottish landscapes, natural history, and sporting themes. For contemporary art there's **art.tm** (✉ 20 Bank St., ☎ 01463/712240, formerly the Highland Printmakers' Workshop), which doubled in size in 1998 and now aims to present the best of contemporary arts and crafts.

Highland Aromatics (✉ Drumchardine, Kirkhill, ☎ 01463/831625), in a converted church, makes sweet-smelling soaps, perfumes, colognes, and other toiletries with the scents of the Highlands. **Highland Wineries** (✉ Moniack Castle, Kirkhill, ☎ 01463/831283) creates wines from Scottish ingredients, such as birch sap, and also makes jams, marmalade, and other preserves.

Duncan Chisholm and Sons (✉ 49 Castle St., ☎ 01463/234599) specializes in Highland dress, tartans, and Scottish crafts. Mail-order and made-to-measure services are available. **James Pringle Ltd.** (✉ Holm Woollen Mills, Dores Rd., ☎ 01463/223311) has a shop stocked with a vast selection of cashmere, lamb's wool, and Shetland knitwear, tartans, and tweeds. **Hector Russell Kiltmakers** (✉ 4/9 Huntly St., ☎ 01463/222781) explains the history of the kilt, shows them being made, and then gives you the opportunity to buy from a huge selection, or have a kilt made-to-measure. The firm offers overseas mail-order.

Nairn

❹ *17 mi east of Inverness via B9006/B9091, 92 mi west of Aberdeen.*

Although Nairn has the air of a Lowland town, it is actually part of the Highlands. A once-prosperous fishing village, Nairn has something of a split personality. King James VI (1566–1625) once boasted that there was a town in his kingdom so large that the residents at either end of town spoke different languages. He was referring to the fact that in past centuries, Nairn's fisherfolk spoke Lowland Scots by the sea, while the uptown farmers and crofters spoke Gaelic.

The fishing boats have since moved to larger ports, but Nairn's historic flavor has been preserved in the **Nairn Fishertown Museum,** a hall crammed with artifacts, photographs, and model boats. This is an informal museum in the best sense, where the volunteer staff is full of information and eager to talk. ✉ *Laing Hall, King St.,* ☎ *01667/453331.*

✉ *50p.* ☼ *June–Sept., Mon.–Sat. 2:30–4:30, also Wed. and Fri. 6:30 PM–8:30 PM.*

Two contrasting defensive structures lie within easy reach of Nairn. As a direct result of the battle at Culloden, the nervous government in London ordered the construction of a large fort on a promontory reaching into the Moray Firth: **Fort George** was started in 1748 and completed some 20 years later. It survives today as perhaps the best-preserved 18th-century military fortification in Europe. A visitor center and a number of tableaux at the fort portray the 18th-century Scottish soldier's way of life, as does the **Regimental Museum of the Queen's Own Highlanders.** To reach the fort take the B9092 north off A96 west of Nairn. ✉ *Ardersier,* ☎ *0131/668–8800.* ✉ *Fort £3, museum free.* ☼ *Apr.–Sept., daily 9:30–6; Oct.–Mar., Mon.–Sat. 9:30–4, Sun. 2–4 (last admission 45 mins before closing).*

★ ❻ Southwest of Nairn is **Cawdor Castle** (☞ Outdoor Activities and Sports, *below*). Shakespeare's (1564–1616) Macbeth was Thane of Cawdor, but the sense of history that exists within these turreted walls is more than fictional. Cawdor is a lived-in castle, not an abandoned, decaying structure. The earliest part of the castle is the 14th-century central tower; the rooms contain family portraits, tapestries, fine furniture, and paraphernalia reflecting 600 years of history. Outside the castle walls are sheltered gardens and walks. ✉ *Cawdor, off B9090, 5 mi southwest of Nairn,* ☎ *01667/404615.* ✉ *Castle £5.20, garden and grounds £2.80.* ☼ *May–mid-Oct., daily 10–5.*

★ ❼ East of Nairn at Brodie is **Brodie Castle,** in the care of the National Trust for Scotland and widely regarded as one of the "best" in the United Kingdom. The original medieval castle was rebuilt and extended in the 17th and 19th centuries. Fine examples of late-17th-century plasterwork are preserved in the Dining Room and Blue Sitting Room. ✉ *Brodie, by Nairn.* ☎ *01309/641371.* ✉ *£4.20.* ☼ *Castle Apr.–Sept., Mon.–Sat. 11–5:30, Sun. 1:30–5:30; Oct., Sat. 11–5:30, Sun. 1:30–5:30 (last admission 4:30), grounds daily 9:30–sunset.*

Dining and Lodging

£££ ✕▥ **Clifton House.** Original works of art cover the walls of this unique
★ hotel, antique furniture graces its rooms, and antique silver gleams in the dining room. The hotel is also licensed as a theater, and each year (Sept.–Apr.) you can enjoy excellent theatrical and musical performances. The restaurant is famous for its classic Scottish cuisine—the lamb cutlets, and duck *à l'orange* (sautéed with oranges and orange liqueur) are particularly good—and the wine list is probably the longest in the area. ✉ *Viewfield St., Nairn,* ☎ *01667/453119,* ℻ *01667/452836. 12 rooms with bath. 2 restaurants. AE, DC, MC, V. Closed Dec. and Jan.*

££ ▥ **Carnach House Hotel.** An overnight at this elegant stone mansion on seven acres of lawns and woodland is an experience, thanks to the pleasant setting, nice rooms, good food, and caring service—it's a fun stay at a reasonable price. ✉ *Delnies, Nairn, IV12 5NT,* ☎ *01667/452094,* ℻ *01667/452994. 8 rooms, 5 with bath, 3 with shower. Restaurant, bar. AE, MC, V.*

Nightlife and the Arts

Clifton House (☞ Dining and Lodging, *above*) at Nairn runs a program of concerts, recitals, and plays from September through April.

Outdoor Activities and Sports

GOLF

Nairn's courses, which welcome visitors, are highly regarded by golfers: indeed, the Walker Cup is to be held here in September 1999. They're very popular, so be sure to book far in advance at the **Nairn Dunbar Golf Club** (☎ 01667/452741) and **Nairn Golf Club** (☎ 01667/453208). For additional information on golfing, *see* Chapter 2.

WALKING

Cawdor Castle Nature Trails has five walks through some of the most beautiful and varied woodlands in Britain. ⊠ *Cawdor Castle (Tourism) Ltd., Cawdor Castle, Nairn, near Inverness, IV12 5RD,* ☎ *01667/ 404615.* ⊡ *£2.80.* ☉ *May–mid-Oct.*

Shopping

Do not miss **Nairn Antiques** (⊠ St. Ninian Pl., near the traffic circle, ☎ 01667/453303) for a wide selection of antique jewelry, glassware, furniture, pottery, prints, and some unusual giftware. Visit **Brodie Country Fare** (⊠ Brodie, east of Nairn, ☎ 01309/641555), only if you are feeling flush: unusual knitwear, quality designer clothing and shoes, gifts, and toys are very covetable, but *not* cheap. You'll also find a food store and delicatessen stocking only the highest quality produce (rather like a miniature Harrods Food Hall, or Fortnum and Mason). Finally, there is an excellent and surprisingly cheap restaurant. Not surprisingly this establishment is extremely popular with the locals.

OFF THE BEATEN PATH

DULSIE BRIDGE AND LOCHINDORB CASTLE – If Cawdor has inspired you to seek the wild Highlands, use the unclassified roads southeast of Cawdor to find a classic Highland "edge" landscape, where the open moor contrasts with the improved upland pasture and thickets of birch and fir. As you take to the higher ground, look for the longest views back over the Firth—you should still just barely be able to see Fort George in the distance. Follow what was the former military road built in the 1750s to service the garrison. Look for the point where the road crosses the River Findhorn by a narrow span, the Dulsie Bridge. Just beyond the bridge, on the right, is a parking place and kissing gate. If you park and go through the gate, a walk of a few yards brings you to a viewpoint over the birch-scattered rocky confines of the river.

Shortly after Dulsie Bridge, turn right off the unclassified road onto the B9007. Shakespeare's Thane of Cawdor met the three prophesying witches on a bare moor very much like this one. Rolling folds of marbled purple and brown are broken here and there by a roofless cottage. Follow the sign (pointing east) for a view of the lonely ruin of Lochindorb Castle. What appears to be a walled enclosure fills and surrounds an entire island on Lochindorb loch. This 13th-century stronghold was the former power base of Alexander Stewart, the Wolf of Badenoch and marauding earl of Buchan (circa 1343–1405), who damaged Elgin Cathedral. The castle was eventually dismantled by a 15th-century Thane of Cawdor, on orders of the king. Lochindorb's iron *yett* (gate) is now on view at Cawdor Castle.

Grantown-on-Spey

❽ *24 mi south of Nairn via A939, 7 mi southeast of Lochindorb Castle via unclassified road and A939.*

The sturdy settlement of Grantown-on-Spey, set amid tall pines that flank the River Spey, is a classic Scottish planned town. This means it is a community that was planned and laid out by the local landowner, in this case Sir James Grant in 1776. It has handsome buildings in silver granite and some good shopping for Scottish gifts.

Shopping

Speyside Heather Centre (⊠ Skye of Curr, ☎ 01479/851359) has 200–300 varieties of heather for sale (some in sterile planting material). The company can supply heather plants by mail-order overseas. There is also a crafts shop, floral-art sundries, antiques shop, and a tearoom. **The Four Seasons** (✉ 82 High St., Grantown-on-Spey, ☎ 01479/872911) is a well-stocked, high-quality gift and kitchenware shop specializing in local crafts.

Boat of Garten

❾ *11 mi southwest of Grantown via B970.*

In the peaceful village of Boat of Garten, the scent of pine trees mingles with an equally evocative smell: this is the terminus of the **Speyside Railway,** and the oily scent of smoke and steam hang faintly in the air near the authentically preserved train station. From here there's a 5-mi train trip to Aviemore, offering a chance to wallow in nostalgia and enjoy superb views of the high and often white domes of the Cairngorms.

❿ The **Loch Garten Nature Reserve,** administered by the Royal Society for the Protection of Birds (RSPB), is just outside Boat of Garten, about 1 mi to the east. This sanctuary achieved fame when the osprey, a bird that was facing extinction in the early part of this century, returned to breed here. Instead of cordoning off the nest site, conservation officials encouraged visitors by constructing a blind for bird-watching. Now thousands of bird lovers visit annually to get a glimpse of the domestic arrangements of this fish-eating bird, which has since bred in many other parts of the Highlands. ☎ *01479/831694 or 01463/715000.* ▭ *£2.* ☉ *Osprey observation post May–Aug., daily 10–6, other areas of reserve daily year-round.*

⓫ In **Carrbridge,** just north of Boat of Garten, you'll find the **Landmark Highland Heritage and Adventure Park,** an early pioneer in the move toward more sophisticated visitor attractions. It has a 3-D audiovisual presentation on the story of the Caledonian Forest; a permanent exhibition; a display on forestry with a working steam-powered sawmill and a Clydesdale horse to haul the logs; a forestry workshop, where you can try out forest skills, such as cross-cut sawing; a bookshop; and restaurant. Outdoors are nature trails, a treetop trail, and a giant fire tower to climb up, as well as plenty of diversions for children, such as a Wild Forest maze, terrifying (children love them) Wild Water coasters (incredibly steep water slides you go down on a kind of sled—if you are crazy enough), and an adventure playground. Reach Carrbridge on the quiet B9153—keep off the A9. ✉ *Carrbridge,* ☎ *01479/841613.* ▭ *£3.50–£6.20.* ☉ *Apr.–mid-July, daily 10–6; mid-July– Aug., daily 10–7:30; Sept.–Oct., daily 10–6; Nov.–Mar., daily 10–5.*

Aviemore

⓬ *6 mi southwest of Boat of Garten via B970.*

Once a quiet junction on the Highland Railway, Aviemore now has all the brashness and concrete boxiness of a year-round holiday resort. A resort environment translates into a lot of things to do, however, and here you can swim, curl, skate, see a movie, dance, and shop.

The Aviemore area is a versatile walking base, but you must be dressed properly for high-level excursions onto the near-arctic plateau. Visitors interested in skiing and rugged hiking can follow the B970 from Aviemore, in the **Glen More Forest Park,** past **Loch Morlich,** to the high parking lots on the exposed shoulders of the **Cairngorm Mountains.** The chairlifts take you even higher, during and after the ski season, for extensive views of the broad valley of the Spey. But be forewarned: it can get very cold above 3,000 ft, and weather conditions can change rapidly even in the middle of summer. ✉ *Off B9152,* ☎ *01479/861261.* 🎫 *£5 for chairlift.* ☉ *Daily, weather permitting.*

While you are on the high slopes, you may see the reindeer herd that was introduced here in the 1950s. By inquiring at the **Cairngorm Reindeer Centre,** by Loch Morlich, you can accompany the keeper on his daily rounds. ✉ *Loch Morlich, Glen More Forest Park,* ☎ 🖷 *01479/861228.* 🎫 *Reindeer Centre £4, paddocks £1.50.* ☉ *Reindeer Centre daily 10–5 (or dusk), rounds (subject to weather conditions) Apr.–Oct., daily 11 and 2:30, Nov.–May, daily 11.*

★   The place that best sums up Speyside's piney ambience is probably **Loch an Eilean.** A converted cottage on the **Rothiemurchus Estate** (☎ 01479/810858) houses a visitor center (the area is a National Nature Reserve). The estate also offers a lot of diversions, including fly-fishing for salmon and trout, guided walks, safari tours, off-road driving, and clay-pigeon shooting.

Shopping
The **Cairngorm Whisky Centre,** with more than 500 malt whiskies, has one of the largest selections in the world. There is a tasting room to help you make your choice. ✉ *Aviemore, on the road to the Cairngorms,* ☎ 🖷 *01479/810574.* 🎫 *Tasting room £3.50.* ☉ *Daily 9:30–4:30 (longer hrs in summer).*

Kingussie

🅱 *13 mi southwest of Aviemore.*

The village of Kingussie (pronounced Kin-*yoo*-see) is of interest primarily for its **Highland Folk Museum.** The interior exhibits are housed in what was an 18th-century shooting lodge, its paneled and varnished ambience still apparent. Displays include 18th-century furniture, clothing, and implements. Outside, various types of Highland buildings have been reconstructed. In summer, local weavers and other artisans demonstrate Highland crafts. You can wander around the grounds freely or see the highlights of the museum on a guided tour. ✉ *Kingussie,* ☎ *01540/661307.* 🎫 *£3.* ☉ *Apr.–Oct., Mon.–Sat. 10–6, Sun. 2–6; Nov.–Mar., weekdays 10–3.*

🆖 **Ruthven Barracks,** which from a distance looks like a ruined castle on a mound, is redolent with tales of the '45 (as the last Jacobite rebellion is often called). The defeated Jacobite forces rallied here after Culloden, but then abandoned and blew up the government outpost they had earlier captured. You'll see it as you approach Kingussie. ✉ *B970, ½ mi south of Kingussie,* ☎ *0131/668–8600.* 🎫 *Free.* ☉ *At all times.*

The rounded **Monadhliath Mountains** (*monadhliath* is Gaelic for gray moors) loom northward over Kingussie and Strathspey (the valley of the River Spey), separating Speyside from the Great Glen. The Monadhliath are less often explored by hikers than the Cairngorms, which form Speyside's southern side.

Dining and Lodging
££££ ✕🏨 **The Cross.** Meals are superb and the wine list extensive. This is
★   an award-winning "restaurant with rooms" in the French style. Dinner, which could be fillet of local venison with port and red currants, or scallop mousse with a prawn and basil sauce, is included in the price of your room. Bedrooms—all with king-size beds—are individually decorated, and may have a balcony, canopied bed, or an antique dressing table. ✉ *Tweed Mill Brae, Kingussie, Inverness-shire, PH21 1TC,* ☎

01540/661166, FAX *01540/661080. 9 rooms with bath. Restaurant. MC,*
V. Closed Dec.–Feb. No dinner Tues.

£–££ ✗▦ **Osprey Hotel.** This friendly hotel in the village of Kingussie is an
ideal base for skiing and hiking. Rooms have old or antique furniture
and floral wallpaper. An impressive wine list complements the much
praised cuisine, which might include such dishes as breast of duck with
grape and red wine sauce or monkfish with Bloody Mary sauce. ✉
Kingussie, Inverness-shire, PH21 1EN, ☎ FAX *01540/661510. 8 rooms
with bath. Restaurant. AE, DC, MC, V.*

Newtonmore

3 mi southwest of Kingussie.

⑰ Newtonmore is home of the **Clan Macpherson Museum.** One of many
clan museums scattered throughout the old homelands, the Macpherson Museum displays a number of interesting artifacts associated with
the '45 rebellion, as well as those of clan chiefs of the even more distant past. ✉ *Newtonmore,* ☎ *01540/673332.* ▭ *Free (donation box).*
⊙ *Apr.–Oct., Mon.–Sat. 10–5, Sun. 2:30–5 (open at other times by
appointment).*

A few miles southwest of Newtonmore on the A86 at **Laggan,** where
the main road crosses the young River Spey, an unclassified road runs
⑱ west up the glen to **Garvamore.** If you are not pressed for time, it's
worth taking this road to view the **Garvamore Bridge** (about 6 mi north
of the junction, at the south side of Corrieyairack Pass). This dual-arched
bridge was built in 1735 by English General Wade (1673–1748), who
had been charged with the task of improving Scotland's roads by a British
government concerned that its troops would not be able to travel the
Highlands quickly enough to quell an uprising.

En Route The A86 hugs the western shore of **Loch Laggan.** This was the route
chosen by later road builders than General Wade, to avoid the high
Corrieyairack Pass. Still quite narrow in a few places, this stretch of
the A86 is to be enjoyed. It offers superb views of the mountainous
heartlands to the north, where high peaks loom, and to the south, over
the silvery spine of hills known as the **Grey Corries,** culminating with
views of **Ben Nevis.**

Roybridge

34 mi west of Newtonmore.

In the tiny community of Roybridge you'll find a cul-de-sac diversion
⑲ to the so-called **Parallel Roads of Glen Roy:** three curious terraces, parallel and level, cut across the hillsides on both sides of the glen. Their
levelness hints of their origins as former shorelines of lochs dammed
by ice that melted in stages at the end of the last Ice Age. ✉ *Unclassified road off A86 at Roybridge.*

Spean Bridge

3 mi west of Roy Bridge.

Uphill and beyond the little village of Spean Bridge, easily visible from
⑳ the road, is the arresting and dignified **Commando Memorial.** The rugged
glens and hills of this area were a training ground for elite forces during World War II. Today, three battle-equipped figures on a high stone
plinth overlook the panorama, and the veterans and younger generations who visit follow their gaze.

Laggan

30 mi north of Spean Bridge via A82.

㉑ Traveling north up the Great Glen takes you parallel to Loch Lochy (on the eastern shore) and over the **Caledonian Canal** at Laggan Locks. From this beautiful spot, which offers stunning vistas of lochs, mountains, and glens in all directions, you can look back on the impressive profile of Ben Nevis. The canal, which links the lochs of the Great Glen— Loch Lochy, Loch Oich, and Loch Ness—owes its origins to a combination of military as well as political pressures that emerged at the time of the Napoleonic Wars with France. (Mostly, the British needed a better and faster way to get naval vessels from one side of Scotland to the other.) The great Scottish engineer Thomas Telford (1757–1834) surveyed the route in 1803. The canal, which took 19 years to complete, has 29 locks and 42 gates. Because Telford took advantage of the three lochs that lie in the Great Glen, which have a combined length of 45 mi, only 22 mi of canal had to be constructed to connect the lochs and complete the waterway from coast to coast.

Dining and Lodging

££–£££ ✕▥ **Glengarry Castle Hotel.** This rambling, pleasantly old-fashioned mansion makes a good touring base; Invergarry is just south of Loch Ness and within easy reach of the Great Glen's best sights. Rooms have traditional Victorian decor; some have superb views over Loch Oich. The food is in traditional Scottish style; try the poached salmon with hollandaise or the loin of lamb with rosemary. The grounds include the ruins of Glengarry Castle, a seat of the MacDonnell clan. The hotel entrance is south of the A82–A87 road junction. ✉ *Invergarry, Inverness-shire, PH35 4HW,* ☎ *01809/501254,* ⅏ *01809/501207. 26 rooms with bath. Restaurant, tennis court, fishing. MC, V. Closed Nov.–Mar.*

Fort Augustus

㉒ *53 mi north of Laggan.*

The best place to see the locks of the Caledonian Canal in action is at Fort Augustus, at the southern tip of Loch Ness. Fort Augustus itself was captured by the Jacobite clans during the 1745 rebellion. Later the fort was rebuilt as a Benedictine abbey. In the village center, considerable canal activity takes place at a series of locks that rise from Loch Ness.

From the B862, just east of Fort Augustus, you'll get your first good
㉓ long view of the formidable and famous **Loch Ness,** which has a greater volume of water than any other Scottish loch and a maximum depth of more than 800 ft. Early travelers who passed this way included English lexicographer Dr. Samuel Johnson (1709–84), and his guide and biographer, James Boswell (1740–95), who were on their way to the Hebrides in 1783. They remarked at the time about the condition of the population and the squalor of their homes. Another early travel writer, Thomas Pennant (1726–98), noted that the loch kept the locality frost-free in winter. Even General Wade came here, his troops blasting and digging a road up much of the eastern shore. None of these observant early travelers ever made mention of a monster. Clearly, they had not read the local guidebooks.

En Route A more leisurely alternative to the fast-moving traffic on the busy A82 to Inverness, and one that combines monster-watching with peaceful road touring, is to take the B862 from Fort Augustus and follow the east bank of Loch Ness. The B862 runs around the end of Loch Ness, then climbs into moorland and forestry plantation. Fine views of Fort

Augustus can be seen by climbing a few yards up and to the right, onto the moor; here you'll be able to see above the conifer spikes. The half-hidden track beside the road is a remnant of the military road built by General Wade. Loch Ness quickly drops out of sight, but is soon replaced by the peaceful, reedy Loch Tarff.

Drumnadrochit

㉔ *21 mi north of Fort Augustus via A82.*

If you're in search of the infamous beast Nessie, at Drumnadrochit you will find the **Official Loch Ness Monster Exhibition,** which presents the facts and the fakes, the photographs, the unexplained sonar contacts, and the sincere testimony of eyewitnesses. It's then up to you to make up your own mind. ⌧ *Drumnadrochit,* ☎ *01456/450573 and 01456/ 450218.* ⌧ *£4.50..* ☉ *Mar.–May, daily 9:30–4:30; June and Sept., daily 9:30–5:30; July–Aug., daily 9–7:30; Oct., daily 9:30–5; Nov.–Feb., daily 10–3 (last admission 1 hr before closing). Off-season opening times vary; call ahead.*

㉕ **Urquhart Castle,** near Drumnadrochit, is a favorite Loch Ness monster–watching spot. This plundered fortress stands on a promontory overlooking the loch, as it has since the Middle Ages. Because of its central and strategic position in the Great Glen line of communication, the castle has a complex history involving military offense and defense, as well as its own destruction and renovation. The castle was begun in the 13th century and was destroyed before the end of the 17th century to prevent its use by the Jacobites. The ruins of what was one of the largest castles in Scotland were plundered for building material. Today swarms of bus tours pass through after investigating the Loch Ness phenomenon. ⌧ *2 mi southeast of Drumnadrochit,* ☎ *0131/668– 8800.* ⌧ *£3.50.* ☉ *Apr.–Sept., daily 9:30–6; Oct.–Mar., daily 9:30– 4 (last admission 45 minutes before closing).*

Dining and Lodging

££–£££ ✕🏠 **Polmaily House.** This country house is on the northern edge of
★ Loch Ness (the house has sailing on the loch), amid lovely parkland. Books, log fires, and a helpful staff contribute to an atmosphere that is warmer and more personal than that found at grander, more expensive hotels, and families are sincerely welcomed. The restaurant is noted for its traditional British cuisine, which takes advantage of fresh Highland produce. Tay salmon in pastry with dill sauce, roast rack of lamb with rosemary, and cold smoked venison with melon, are examples of some flavorful dishes, cooked modern British style. ⌧ *Drumnadrochit, IV3 6XT,* ☎ *01456/450343,* 𝔽𝔸𝕏 *01456/450813. 12 rooms with bath, 2 suites. Restaurant, indoor pool, tennis court, croquet, horseback riding, boating, fishing. MC, V.*

£–££ 🏠 **Borlum Farmhouse.** Spectacular views over Loch Ness are the outstanding feature of this guest house on a working farm. The rooms are individually decorated with antique furniture, and breakfasts are well cooked. ⌧ *Drumnadrochit, Inverness, IV3 6XN,* ☎ 𝔽𝔸𝕏 *01456/450358. 6 rooms, 2 with bath. No smoking. MC, V.*

OFF THE
BEATEN PATH
GLENS AFFRIC AND CANNICH – Two outstanding mountain landscapes, those of Glens Affric and Cannich, are toward the northern end and to the west of the Great Glen. These two glens offer a cross section of typical remote Highland landscape, yet are accessible. Glen Cannich is constricted by crags and birch-clad slopes before opening into a broad valley with a hydroelectric dam at its far end. Glen Affric is even more aesthetically appealing, with oak woodlands and hay fields in the lower reaches, and, higher up, wild lochs (also dammed) and pine forests,

similar to the Trossachs, but on a grander scale. Take the A831 west from Drumnadrochit to Cannich village, then turn left onto the respective minor road for each glen.

Whitebridge

㉖ *12 mi north of Fort Augustus via B862.*

The B862 follows the line of the former military route and shows appropriate military precision nearly all the way to Whitebridge, where a handsome single-arch Wade bridge (look for it on your right) has been restored. Just before the bridge is the **Whitebridge Hotel,** a former Kingshouse, one of a chain of inns built by the government in the 18th century to service the military roads. The Kingshouse name is still used by a few of Scotland's hotels.

En Route Beyond Whitebridge the small banks on either side of the road are thought to have survived from the military's original work in 1726; thus you find yourself traveling one of the earliest roads in the Highlands. Take the B852, left at the junction beyond Whitebridge, to regain the shores of Loch Ness by way of some fine woodlands.

Foyers

3 mi north of Whitebridge, 21 mi southwest of Inverness.

㉗ At Foyers, almost back at Loch Ness, a sign outside the general store will direct you to the **Falls of Foyers.** Steep paths, strewn with pine cones, lead to a site where a thin waterfall streams into a dark pot and then down a ravine. The original volume of the falls was much reduced shortly before the turn of the century, when the power generated here was harnessed for the first commercial application of hydroelectricity (1896), in an aluminum-smelting plant on a site by Loch Ness.

㉘ The road meanders pleasantly north from Foyers, offering some views of the loch on the way to **Inverfarigaig** and the **Inverfarigaig Forest Centre.** The center has several displays on forestry activities, plus a number of trails leading into the woodlands. ✉ *Inverfarigaig,* ☎ *01320/366322.* 🎫 *Free.* ☉ *Easter–mid-Oct., daily 9:30–7.*

TOWARD THE SMALL ISLES

Fort William has enough points of interest—a museum, exhibits, and shopping—to compensate for its less-than-picturesque milieu. The town's primary purpose is to serve the west Highland hinterland; its role as a tourist stop is secondary. Since this is a relatively wet part of Scotland, and since Fort William itself can always be explored if it rains, strike west toward the coast if the weather looks settled: on a sunny day, the Small Isles—Rum, Eigg, Canna, and Muck—look as blue as the sea and sky together. From here you could also visit Skye via the ferry at Mallaig, or take a day cruise from Arisaig to the Small Isles for a glimpse of traffic-free island life. South of Fort William, Ballachulish and Glencoe are within easy striking distance.

Glencoe

㉙ *92 mi north of Glasgow, 44 mi northwest of Edinburgh.*

Glencoe, where great craggy buttresses loom darkly over the road, has a special place in the folk memory of Scotland: it was the site of an infamous massacre in 1692, still remembered in the Highlands for the treachery with which soldiers of the Campbell clan, acting as government militia, treated their hosts, the MacDonalds. According to Highland code, in his own home a clansman should give shelter even to his sworn enemy. In the face of bitter weather, the Campbells were accepted as guests by the MacDonalds. Apparently acting on orders from the British government, the Campbells turned on their hosts, committing murder "under trust." The National Trust for Scotland's **visitor center** at Glencoe (at the western end of the glen) tells the story of the massacre and also offers excellent displays on local geology. ☎ *01855/ 811307.* ✆ *50p.* ☉ *Apr.–mid-May and Sept.–Oct., daily 10–5; mid-May–Aug., daily 9:30–5:30 (last admission 30 mins before closing).*

Outdoor Activities and Sports

The **Glencoe ski development** (☎ 01855/851226), at the east end of the glen, once had a formidable reputation in Scotland: if you could ski there, you could ski anywhere, because of a frequent combination of severe weather and icy runs, as well as fairly primitive facilities. Things have improved in recent years. Although the black runs are still very challenging, there are now extensive, well-maintained beginner and intermediate runs on the lower plateau. There's also a good restaurant.

Ballachulish

③⓪ *1 mi west of Glencoe, 15 mi south of Fort William, 39 mi north of Oban.*

Ballachulish, once a slate-carrying community, acts as gateway to the western approaches to Glencoe. There is a Glencoe village as well. On a little peninsula north of the main road, which is actually reclaimed land using the slate spoils from the old quarry, you will find a hotel and visitor center complex, **Highland Mystery World** (☞ Dining and Lodging, *below*), which promises a journey into the Highland environment of old, where the spirit world and the mythical world are portrayed as they appeared to our ancestors. You can also enjoy real-life snacks and meals here. ✉ *Ballachulish,* ☎ *01855/821582.* ✆ *£4.95.* ☉ *Apr.–Oct., daily 10–5.*

Dining and Lodging

££££ ✕▥ **Airds Hotel.** This former ferry inn, dating from the 17th century, has some of the finest views in all of Scotland. Set in a peaceful village midway between Ballachulish and Oban, the long white building, backed by trees, has a friendly feel to it. Quilted bedspreads and family mementos make you feel right at home. Shooting and fishing trips can be arranged. The restaurant serves Scottish cuisine, including venison and grouse. Dinner is included in the room rate. ✉ *Port Appin, Argyll, PA38 4DF,* ☎ *01631/730236,* ⅎ⅏ⅉ *01631/730535. 12 rooms with bath. Restaurant. MC, V.*

£££ ✕▥ **Holly Tree Hotel.** Railway buffs should enjoy this converted Edwardian railway station, complete with some of its original fixtures and fittings. The spacious restaurant is on the carefully extended former platform. You may see seals in Loch Linnhe from your dinner table, along with memorable sunsets over the Ardgour mountains. The emphasis is on fresh, locally raised pigeon, venison, lamb, scallops, and salmon. Bedrooms are modern and well equipped, if on the small side. ✉ *Kentallen, on A828, south of Ballachulish,* ☎ *01631/740292,* ⅎⅉ⅏ *01631/740345. 10 rooms with bath or shower. Restaurant. MC, V.*

££–£££ ✕▥ **Isles of Glencoe Hotel.** An excellent base for families, this hotel is ★ right next to Highland Mystery World, and also has its own leisure facilities including a toy corner. Everything from menus to staff attitudes makes children welcome, but adults will not feel neglected. The decor is modern, with streamlined fitted furniture in the bedrooms and plenty of original landscape paintings. The cuisine—a choice of well-cooked beef, chicken, fish, and game dishes—aims not to be original and inventive, but to satisfy after a hard day's sightseeing, and it succeeds to perfection. In keeping with its youth-friendly atmosphere, there is also a separate children's menu. ⊠ *Ballachulish, PA39 4HL,* ☎ *01855/ 811602,* FAX *01855/811770. 39 rooms with bath. Restaurant, pool, sauna, playground. MC, V.*

Fort William

③ *15 mi north of Ballachulish, 69 mi southwest of Inverness, 108 mi northwest of Glasgow, 138 mi northwest of Edinburgh.*

As its name suggests, Fort William originated as a military outpost, first established by Cromwell's General Monk in 1655 and refortified by George I (1660–1727) in 1715 to help combat an outbreak by the turbulent Jacobite clans. It remains the southern gateway to the Great Glen and to the far west, and is a bustling, tourist-oriented place. The **West Highland Museum,** in the town center, explores the theme of Prince Charles Edward Stuart and the 1745 rebellion. Included in the museum's folk exhibits is a tartan exhibit. ⊠ *Cameron Sq.,* ☎ FAX *01397/702169.* ☞ *£2.* ☼ *June and Sept., Tues.–Sat. (and bank holidays) 10–5; July–Aug., Mon.–Sat. 10–5 and Sun. 2–5; Oct.–May, Tues.–Sat. 10–4, Sun. 2–5.*

Scotland's (and Britain's) highest mountain, the 4,406-ft **Ben Nevis,** looms over Fort William less than 4 mi from Loch Linnhe, an inlet of the sea. Although a hike to its summit is a rewarding experience, hikers should be fit and well prepared—food and water, compass, first-aid kit, whistle, hat, gloves, and warm clothing for starters—as the unpredictable weather can make it a hazardous hike.

A huge collection of gemstones, crystals, and fossils, including a 26-pound uncut emerald, is displayed at **Treasures of the Earth,** in a converted church at Corpach on A830 near Fort William. ☎ *01397/ 772283.* ☞ *£3.* ☼ *July–Sept., daily 9:30–7; Oct.–Dec. and Feb.–June, daily 10–5; Jan., by appointment.*

Dining and Lodging

£–££ ✕ **Crannog Scottish Seafoods.** Set conspicuously on a small pier pro-
★ jecting over the waters of Loch Linnhe, the Crannog has transformed Fort William dining. The sight of a fishing boat drawing up to the pier side to land its catch straight into the restaurant kitchen, says all that needs to be said about the freshness of the seafood. Sitting at a window seat—pine predominates in fixtures and fittings—with the sun going down behind the steep hills on the far side of the loch, is a special treat. The chef's deft touch ensures that the fresh flavors are not overwhelmed. ⊠ *Crannog Scottish Seafoods, Town Pier, Fort William,* ☎ *01397/705589. MC, V.*

££££ ✕🏨 **Inverlochy Castle.** A red-granite Victorian castle, Inverlochy stands in 50 acres of woodlands in the shadow of Ben Nevis, with striking Highland landscape on every side. Dating from 1863, the hotel retains all the splendor of its period, with a fine frescoed ceiling, crystal chandeliers, a handsome staircase in the Great Hall, paintings and hunting trophies everywhere, and plush, comfortable bedrooms. The restaurant is exceptional—a lovely room with wonderful cuisine. Many specialties use local produce, such as roast saddle of roe deer or wood pigeon consommé, with orange soufflé as the final touch. ⊠ *Torlundy (3 mi northeast of Fort William on A82), PH33 6SN,* ☎ *01397/702177,* FAX *01397/702953. 17 rooms with bath. Restaurant, tennis court, croquet, fishing, billiards. AE, MC, V. Closed Jan.–Feb.*

££ 🏨 **Ashburn House.** A Victorian house on its own grounds, but only a 5-minute walk from downtown, offers luxury at B&B prices. Chintz-draped bedrooms in shades of pink and blue are complemented by the conservatory lounge with stunning loch views, and a delightful Victorian-corniced dining room in which to enjoy home-baked oven scones for breakfast. This establishment is no-smoking throughout. ✉ *Achintore Rd. Fort William PH33 6RQ,* ☎ FAX *01397/706000. 7 rooms with bath or shower. AE, MC, V. Closed Dec.*

££ ⊡ **Crolinnhe.** An elegant Victorian house with colorful gardens, over-
★ looking Loch Linnhe yet only a 10-minute walk from town, Crolinnhe is an exceptionally comfortable B&B. Antique and high-quality reproduction furniture is set off by pastel walls and bold-toned curtains, with each bedroom individually decorated. The breakfasts are among the best you will taste in any establishment in any price range in Scotland. ✉ *Grange Rd., Fort William, PH33 6JF,* ☎ *01397/702709. 4 rooms with bath or shower. No credit cards. Closed Nov.–Mar.*

Nightlife and the Arts

McTavish's Kitchens (✉ High St., Fort William, ☎ 01397/702406) offers Scottish cabaret in the summer season, of the tartan-clad dancer and bagpipe-accordion variety.

Outdoor Activities and Sports

BIKING

Bicycles can be rented from **Off Beat Bikes** (✉ 117 High St., Fort William, ☎ FAX 01397/704008).

GOLF

The 18-hole golf course at **Fort William** (☎ 01397/704464) welcomes visitors.

HIKING

This area, especially around Glencoe and Ben Nevis, is very popular with hikers, but you should try it only if fit and properly outfitted. The tourist information center (☞ Visitor Information *in* Around the Great Glen A to Z, *below*) can offer guidance on low-level routes. Several excellent guides are available locally; they can and should be consulted for high-altitude routes. Be advised that **Ben Nevis** is a large and dangerous mountain, where snow can fall on the summit plateau any time of the year.

SKIING

Nevis Range (✉ Fort William, ☎ 01397/705825), the newest of Scotland's ski areas, is a fashionable and modern development on the flanks of Aonach Mor, offering good and varied skiing, as well as superb views of Ben Nevis. There are runs for all ability levels and a gondola system, unique in Scotland.

Shopping

The majority of shops here are along High Street, which in summer attracts ever-present, bustling crowds intent on stocking up for excursions to the west. **Ben Nevis Woollen Mill** (✉ Belford Rd., ☎ 01397/704244), at the north end of town, is a major supplier of tartans, woolens, and tweeds, and has a restaurant. **The Granite House** (✉ High St., ☎ 01397/703651) stocks Scottish contemporary jewelry, china and crystal giftware, wildlife sculptures, folk music CDs, unusual ethnic clothing, and cards.

Scottish Crafts and Whisky Centre (✉ 135–139 High St., ☎ 01397/704406) has the usual range of souvenirs, but it also sells homemade chocolates and a vast range of malt whiskies, including miniatures and limited edition bottlings. **Treasures of the Earth** (✉ Corpach, ☎ 01397/772283) has a shop that stocks an Aladdin's Cave assortment of gemstone jewelry, crystal ornaments, mineral specimens, polished stones, fossils, and books on related subjects. It's a treasure trove of unusual gifts.

En Route   Travel down the eastern side of Loch Linnhe to Corran, where a frequent ferry shuttles cars and foot passengers across the loch to Ardgour. (From the map you will see you can avoid the ferry by driving
around the head of Loch Eil, but it's not a particularly scenic route.)
From Ardgour, the two-lane A861 runs south along Loch Linnhe before turning into Glen Sanda, crossing the watershed, and running down
to the long shores of Loch Sunart. This is a typical west Highlands sea
loch: orange kelp marks the tide lines, and herons stand muffled and
miserable, wondering if it is worth risking a free meal at the local fish
farm. As for the fish farms themselves, you will become accustomed
to their floats and cages turning up in the foreground of every sea-loch
view. The farms were originally hailed as the savior of the Highland
economy because of the number of jobs they created, but questions are
now being raised about their environmental effects, and the market for
their product is threatened by Scandinavian imports. At the little village of Salen, either turn north immediately, or divert west to Ardnamurchan Point.

Ardnamurchan Point

   32 *55 mi west of Fort William via A861 and B8007.*

   Along a narrow road blindly curving partly through thickets of rhododendrons, the westernmost point of mainland Scotland is reached at
   Ardnamurchan Point. The Ardnamurchan peninsula is a must-see if
   you love unspoiled coastal scenery. Here you'll find small farming
   communities and vacation homes.

Acharacle

   ★ **33** *3 mi north of Salen.*

   On the way north to Acharacle (pronounced ach-*ar*-ra-kle with a Scots
   "ch"), you'll pass through deep-green plantations and moorland lily
   ponds. This spread-out settlement, backed by the hills of Moidart, lies
   at the shallow and reedy western end of **Loch Shiel;** the north end is
   more dramatic and sits deep within the rugged hills.

   A few minutes north of Acharacle—where the main road turns sharply
   right—a narrow road goes left, overhung in places by mossy trees, to
   emerge at **Castle Tioram.** This ruined fortress dominates a bracken-green
   islet, barely anchored to the mainland by a sand spit. The castle was
   once the home of the chief of the MacDonalds of Clan Ranald, but
   the last chief burned the castle to prevent its falling into the hands of
   his enemies, the Campbells, during the 1715 Jacobite rebellion. This
   fragment of Scottish history guards the south channel of Loch Moidart.
   The castle changed ownership in 1997 and its future is under discussion. ⊠ *Reached by an unclassified road north of A861.* ⊠ *Free.* ☉
   At all times.

En Route   Traveling between Acharacle and Arisaig, you'll reach the upper sandy
   shores of Loch Moidart by climbing on the A861 over a high moorland pass. On the next ascent, from Loch Moidart, you'll be rewarded
   with stunning sea views. The sea coast is reached by the mouth of Loch
   Ailort (pronounced *eye*-ort), and there are plenty of places to pull off
   among the boulders and birch scrub and sort out the view of the islands. In the distance you'll be able to spot Eigg, a low island marked
   by the dramatic black peak of An Sgurr. Beyond Eigg is the larger Rum,
   with its range of hills, the Norse-named Rum Coullin, looming cloud-
   capped over the island. Loch Ailort itself is another picturesque inlet,
   now cluttered with the garish floats of fish cages. You meet the main

road again at the junction with the A830, the main road from Fort William to Mallaig. Turn left here. The breathtaking seaward views continue to distract you from the road beside Loch nan Uamh (from Gaelic meaning cave, and pronounced oo-am). This loch is associated with Prince Charles Edward Stuart's nine-month stay on the mainland, during which he gathered a small army, marched as far south as Derby in England, alarmed the king, retreated to unavoidable defeat at Culloden in the spring, and then spent a few months as a fugitive in the Highlands. A cairn by the shore marks the spot where the prince was picked up by a French ship. Prince Charles never returned to Scotland.

Arisaig

34 *27 mi north of Acharacle.*

Considering its small size, Arisaig offers a surprising choice of high-quality options for dining and lodging. To the north of Arisaig, the road cuts across a headland to reach a stretch of coastline where silver sands glitter with the mica in the local rock; clear water, blue sky, and white sand lend a tropical flavor to the beaches—when the sun shines.

Try to visit at least a couple of the **Small Isles: Rum, Eigg, Muck,** and **Canna,** from Arisaig. Contact **Murdo Grant** (⊠ Arisaig Marine, Arisaig, Inverness-shire, PH39 4NH, ☎ 01687/450224), who runs a service from the harbor at Arisaig. The MV *Shearwater,* a former naval inshore minesweeper, delivers supplies and mail as well as visitors to the diminutive island communities. What sets Grant's operation apart from the tourism-oriented excursions is that it offers visitors a glimpse of island life from a working vessel going about its summer routine.

Dining and Lodging

££££ ✕🏠 **Arisaig House Hotel.** This secluded and grand Victorian mansion offers tranquility and some marvelous scenery, including views of Loch nan Uamh. The bedrooms are plush and restful, with soft pastels, original moldings, and antique furniture. The cuisine showcases fresh local produce, such as seafood or venison cooked in the modern British style: try the local scallops and prawns with fresh basil and coriander or the spring lamb with fresh herbs. A 9-hole golf course is at Traigh, 6 mi north. ⊠ *Beasdale, by Arisaig (13 mi south of Mallaig on A830, west of Glenfinnan), PH39 4NR,* ☎ *01687/450622,* 🅵🅰🆇 *01687/450626. 12 rooms with bath or shower, 2 suites. Restaurant, 9-hole golf course, croquet, boating, fishing, billiards, library. No children under 10. MC, V. Closed Nov.–Mar.*

££ ✕🏠 **Arisaig Hotel.** An old coaching inn close to the water, with magnificent views of the Small Isles, this hotel offers a slightly more modest environment than Arisaig House. The inn has retained its provinciality with simple decor and home cooking. High-quality local ingredients are used here to good advantage; locally caught lobster, langoustines, and crayfish are specialties, as are proper puddings, such as fruit crumbles. ⊠ *Arisaig, PH39 4NH,* ☎ *01687/450210,* 🅵🅰🆇 *01687/450310. 13 rooms with bath or shower. Restaurant, recreation room. MC, V.*

££ ✕🏠 **Old Library Lodge and Restaurant.** This guest house, a converted barn on the waterfront, has a fine restaurant, giving you another reason to believe that the village of Arisaig is unusually well endowed with good places to eat at all price levels. Local produce is prepared in a French bistro style, served in a whitewashed, airy dining room. The bedrooms are very comfortable, with flowery duvets and cozy armchairs. ⊠ *Arisaig, PH39 4NH,* ☎ *01687/450651,* 🅵🅰🆇 *01687/450219. 6 rooms, 4 with bath, 2 with shower. Restaurant. AE, MC, V. Closed Nov.–Mar.*

Outdoor Activities and Sports

Bespoke Highland Tours (⊠ The Bothy, Camusdarach, by Arisaig, Inverness-shire, ☎ 01687/450272) rents bicycles and arranges tours of the Great Glen and the Highlands.

Mallaig

㉟ *8 mi north of Arisaig, 44 mi northwest of Fort William.*

After the approach along the coast, the workaday fishing port of Mallaig itself is anticlimactic. It has a few shops, and there is some bustle by the quayside when fishing boats unload or the Skye ferry departs: this is the departure point for the southern ferry connection to the Isle of Skye, the largest island of the Inner Hebrides. Mallaig is also the starting point for day cruises up the Sound of Sleat, which separates Skye from the mainland. For cruises, which operate all year, contact **Bruce Watt Sea Cruises** (⊠ Western Isles Guest House, Mallaig, PH41 4QG, ☎ 01687/462320). The sound offers views into rugged Knoydart and its long, fjordlike sea lochs, **Lochs Nevis and Hourn.** The area to the immediate north and west, beyond Loch Nevis, one of the most remote in Scotland, is often referred to as the Rough Bounds of Knoydart. In Mallaig itself, the **Heritage Centre** has exhibits, films, photographs, and models on all aspects of the local history. ⊠ *Station Rd.,* ☎ *01687/462085. Call for admission and hours of operation.*

Beside the harbor, **Mallaig Marine World** shows you what goes on beneath the surface of the Sound of Sleat: live fish and shellfish, and a display on the local fishing traditions are among the attractions here. ⊠ *The Harbour,* ☎ *01687/462292.* 🎫 *£2.75.* ☉ *June–Aug., daily 9:30–9; Sept.–May, daily 9:30–5:30 (call to confirm hours in winter).*

㊱ A small, unnamed side road leads east just south of Mallaig, to an even smaller road that will bring you to **Loch Morar,** the deepest of all the Scottish lochs (more than 1,000 ft); the next deepest point is miles out into the Atlantic, beyond the continental shelf. Apart from this short public road, the area around the loch is all but roadless.

Glenfinnan

㊲ *26 mi southeast of Mallaig.*

Glenfinnan, perhaps the most visitor-oriented stop on the route between Mallaig and Fort William, has the most to offer if you're interested in Scottish history. Here the National Trust for Scotland has capitalized on the romance surrounding the story of the Jacobites and their intention of returning a Stuart monarch and the Roman Catholic religion to a country that had become staunchly Protestant. In Glenfinnan, in 1745, the sometimes-reluctant clans joined forces and rallied to Prince Charles Edward Stuart's cause.

The raising of the prince's standard is commemorated by the **Glenfinnan Monument** (an unusual tower on the banks of Loch Shiel), and the story of his campaign is told in the nearby visitor center. Note that the figure at the top of the monument is of a Highlander, not the prince. The view down Loch Shiel from the Glenfinnan Monument is one of the most photographed views in Scotland. ⊠ *A830,* ☎ *01397/722250.* 🎫 *£1.50.* ☉ *Visitor center Apr.–mid-May and Sept.–Oct., daily 10–5; mid-May–Aug., daily 9:30–6.*

As impressive as the Glenfinnan Monument (if you've tired of the Jacobite "Will He No Come Back Again" sentiment) is the curving railway viaduct that stretches across the green slopes behind the monument. The **Glenfinnan Viaduct,** 21 spans and 1,248 ft long, was in its time the wonder of the Highlands. The railway's contractor, Robert MacAlpine, known as Concrete Bob by the locals, pioneered the use of mass concrete for viaducts and bridges when his company built the Mallaig extension, which opened in 1901.

The train is the most relaxing way to take in the landscape of birch- and bracken-covered wild slopes; **rail services** (☎ 01397/703791) run all year on the stretch of line between Fort William and Mallaig, with the possibility of steam engines operating in summer.

AROUND THE GREAT GLEN A TO Z

Arriving and Departing

By Bus

There is a long-distance **Scottish Citylink**(☎ 0990/505050) service from Glasgow to Fort William. Inverness is also well served from the central belt of Scotland; for info, call the Inverness coach station (☎ 01463/233371).

By Car

As in all areas of rural Scotland, a car is a great asset for exploring the Great Glen and Speyside, especially since the best of the area is away from the main roads. The fast A9 brings you to Inverness in roughly three hours from Glasgow or Edinburgh, even if you take your time.

By Plane

Inverness Airport (✉ Dalcross, ☎ 01463/232471) has flights from London, Edinburgh, Glasgow, and Amsterdam, and a wide range of internal flights covering the Highlands and islands. Flights are operated by **British Airways** (☎ 0345/222111), **KLM U.K.** (☎ 0990/074074), and **easyJet** (☎ 0990/292929). Fort William has bus and train connections with Glasgow, so **Glasgow Airport** (☎ 0141/887–1111) can be an appropriate access point (☞ Chapter 4).

By Train

The area is well served by trains. There are connections from London to Inverness and Fort William (including overnight sleeper service), as well as reliable links from Glasgow and Edinburgh. For information call the **National Train Enquiry Line** (☎ 0345/484950).

Getting Around

By Bus

There is limited service available in the Great Glen area and some local service running from Fort William. **Highland Country Buses** (☎ 01397/702373) operates buses down the Great Glen, around Fort William, and in the Lochaber area, and also a service from Fort William south to Oban. A number of post-bus services will help get you to the more remote corners of the area. The timetable is available from the **Royal Mail** (✉ 7 Strothers La., Inverness, IV1 1AA, ☎ 01463/256273).

By Car

You can use the main A9 Perth–Inverness road (via Aviemore) to explore this area or use one of the many other smaller roads (some of them old military roads) to explore the much quieter east side of Loch Ness. The same applies to Speyside, where a variety of options open up away from the A9, especially through the pinewoods by Coylumbridge and Feshiebridge, east of the main road. Mallaig, west of Fort William, also has improving road connections, but the road is still narrow and winding in many places and rail remains the most enjoyable way to experience the rugged hills and loch scenery between these two places. In Morvern, the area across Loch Linnhe southwest of Fort William, you may encounter single-lane roads, which require slower speeds and concentration.

By Train

Though the Great Glen has no rail connection (in Victorian times Fort William and Inverness had different lines built by companies that could not agree), this area has the **West Highland line**, which links Fort William to Mallaig; a trip on this scenic line is highly recommended. There is also train service between Glasgow (Queen Street) and Inverness, via Aviemore, which gives access to the heart of Speyside. For information call the **National Train Enquiry Line** (☎ 0345/484950).

Contacts and Resources

Car Rentals

Europcar Ltd. (✉ The Highlander Service Station, Millburn Rd., Inverness, ☎ 01463/235337). **Hertz** (✉ Dalcross Airport, Inverness, ☎ 01667/462652).

Emergencies

For **police, fire, coast guard, or ambulance,** dial ☎ 999 from any telephone. No coins are needed for emergency calls from phone booths.

Belford Hospital (✉ Belford Rd., Fort William, ☎ 01397/702481). **Raigmore Hospital** (✉ Perth Rd., Inverness, ☎ 01463/704000). **Town and County Hospital** (✉ Cawdor Rd., Nairn, ☎ 01667/452101).

Guided Tours

ORIENTATION

From Fort William, **ScotRail** (☎ 01397/703791) runs services on the outstandingly beautiful West Highland Line to Mallaig. **Caledonian MacBrayne** (☎ 01475/650100) runs scheduled service and cruises to Skye, the Small Isles, and Mull from Mallaig. **Arisaig Marine** (☎ 01687/450224) operates highly recommended Hebridean day cruises on the MV (motor vessel) *Shearwater* to the Small Isles at Easter, and daily from May to September, when trips also go to Skye. Also available for charter from Arisaig Marine is a fast twin-engine motor yacht, which can take up to 12 passengers for go-where-you-please cruises around the Small Isles and farther afield.

From Inverness, **Macdonald's Tours** (✉ 65 Fairfield Rd., Inverness, ☎ 01463/240673) offers coach tours during the summer season.

SPECIAL-INTEREST

From Inverness, **Highland Insight Tours and Travel** (☎ 01463/831403) offers personalized touring holidays and full-day or half-day tours that cater to any interest. **James Johnson** (☎ 01463/790179) will drive you anywhere, but he has a particularly good knowledge of the Highlands and islands, including the Outer Isles. **Jacobite Cruises Ltd.** (✉ Tomnahurich Bridge, Glenurquhart Rd., Inverness, ☎ 01463/233999) runs morning and afternoon cruises on Loch Ness to Urquhart Castle, and boat and coach excursions to the Monster Exhibition.

Macaulay Charters (✉ 12 Pict Ave., Inverness, ☎ FAX 01463/717337) provides trips by boat from Inverness, offering you the chance to see dolphins in their breeding area. An unusual option from Inverness is a day trip to Orkney: **John o'Groats Ferries** (☎ 01955/611353) offers day tours from Inverness to Orkney, daily from June to August.

Late-Night Pharmacies

Pharmacies are not common away from the larger towns. In an emergency, the police will assist you in locating a pharmacist. In Inverness,

Kinmylies Pharmacy (⊠ 1 Charleston Ct., Kinmylies, ☏ 01463/ 221094) is open weekdays until 6 and Saturdays until 5:30. The pharmacy at the **Scottish Co-Op** superstore (⊠ Milton of Inshes, Perth Rd., outside Inverness, ☏ 01463/712188), is open Monday to Wednesday 9–8, Thursday and Friday 9–9, Saturday 9–6, and Sunday 10–6. In Fort William, **Boots the Chemist** (⊠ High St., ☏ 01397/705143) is open weekdays 8:45–6, Saturday 8:45–5:30. For Sunday openings, consult a doctor (☞ Emergencies, *below*).

Visitor Information
Aviemore (⊠ Grampian Rd., ☏ 01479/810363). **Fort William** (⊠ Cameron Centre, Cameron Sq., ☏ 01397/703781). **Inverness** (⊠ Castle Wynd, ☏ 01463/234353).

Other tourist information centers, open seasonally, include those at Ballachulish, Carrbridge, Daviot Wood (A9), Fort Augustus, Grantown-on-Spey, Kilchoan, Kingussie, Mallaig, Nairn, Ralia (A9), Spean Bridge, and Strontian.

11 The Northern Highlands

Red sandstone, black gabbro, and silver-gray gneiss, scoured by now-vanished glaciers, are the building blocks of the region—from the long rolling moors of Caithness to the jagged profile of the Cuillin Hills of Skye. Drive through Glen Torridon or walk through the bare-bones landscape around Lochinver, and the last Ice Age doesn't seem so long ago.

By Gilbert
Summers

THE OLD COUNTIES OF ROSS AND CROMARTY (sometimes called Easter and Wester Ross), Sutherland,
and Caithness constitute the most northern portion
of mainland Scotland. The population is sparse, mountains and moorland limit the choice of touring routes, and distances are less important than whether the winding, hilly roads you sometimes encounter
are two lanes or one. On a map, this area seems far from major urban
centers, but it is easy to get to. Inverness has an airport with direct links
to London, Edinburgh, Glasgow, and even Amsterdam, and you can
reach destinations such as the fishing town of Ullapool in an hour by
car from Inverness. In fact, much of the western seaboard is easily accessible from the Northern Highlands.

The area contains some of Scotland's most intriguing scenery. Much
of Sutherland and Wester Ross, for example, is comprised of a rocky
platform of Lewisian gneiss, certainly the oldest rocks in Britain,
scoured and hollowed by glacial action into numerous lochs. On top
of this rolling wet moorland landscape sit strangely shaped quartzite-
capped sandstone mountains, eroded and pinnacled.

Many of the place-names in this region reflect its early links with Scan-
dinavia. Sutherland, the most northern portion of mainland Scotland,
was once the "southern land" of the Vikings. Scotland's most northern point, Cape Wrath, got its name from the Viking's word *hvarth*,
(turning point) and Laxford, Suilven, and dozens of other names in the
area have Norse rather than Gaelic derivations.

The islands of Skye and especially the Outer Hebrides, which are now
often referred to as the Western Isles, are the stronghold of the Gaelic
language. Skye is famous for its misty mountains called the Cuillins,
and the Outer Hebrides have some of Scotland's finest beaches.

Pleasures and Pastimes

Biking
The landscapes are great, but the open and rugged terrain has not favored the development of a network of rural back roads. Be prepared
to meet holiday traffic at peak season, especially on the mainland. Some
side roads (and even, in the far northwest, some main roads) are single-
track and narrow, meaning there will be traffic coming the other way
between passing places. High-visibility clothing is advised.

Dining
In an area with such a low population, the choice of restaurants is a
bit more restricted in comparison with other parts of Scotland. But reliable country houses and inns serving hearty, traditional Highland fare
are to be found.

CATEGORY	COST*
££££	over £40
£££	£30–£40
££	£15–£30
£	under £15

*per person for a three-course meal, including VAT and excluding drinks and
service*

Fishing
The possibilities for fishing are endless here, as a glance at the loch-
littered map of Sutherland suggests. Trout-fishing permits on several hill
lochans should be available at local post offices, shops, and hotels. Inquire
at your accommodation or at the nearest tourist information center.

Golf

There are only about 15 courses in the area, with almost no courses on the west coast, although Gairloch Golf Club has its enthusiasts. The best-known club in the area is Royal Dornoch on the east coast north of Inverness. Were it not for its northern location, the club, sometimes described as the "St. Andrews of the north," could be a candidate for the Open Championship. For more information, *see* Chapter 2.

Lodging

This region of Scotland has some good modern hotels and some charming inns but not many establishments in the more expensive categories. You will often find that the most enjoyable accommodations are low-cost guest houses (often family run), offering bed-and-breakfast. Dining rooms of country-house lodgings frequently reach the standard of top-quality restaurants.

CATEGORY	COST*
££££	over £120
£££	£90–£120
££	£50–£90
£	under £50

All prices are for a standard double room, including service, breakfast, and VAT.

Nightlife

The nightlife here is confined mainly to hotels and pubs. *Ceilidhs* (song, music, and dance), dances, and concerts take place on a sporadic basis and are advertised locally. During the **Highland Festival** (☎ 01463/711112) in late May–early June, a wide range of cultural activity takes place in the region.

Orienteering

In early August 1999, the **World Orienteering Championships** take place in the Northern Highlands, which will certainly provide a challenging map-reading environment. For details, contact the local tourist office (☎ 01997/423019).

Pony Trekking

Pony trekking was invented to give the sturdy Highland ponies a job to do when they weren't carrying dead deer off the hills during the "stalking" (deer hunting) season. Treks last from two hours to a whole day, and ponies suit all ages and levels of experience.

Shopping

As in Argyll and the Western Isles, shopping in the Northern Highlands tends to be more interesting for the variety of crafts available rather than for the number and types of shops. After all, the population of the area is scattered, and the locals usually travel to the larger population centers, as well as to Inverness, for shopping. In the Outer Hebrides, the specialty to look for is Harris tweed, woven by individuals working at home, and available either directly from the weaving shed or at local crafts shops.

Exploring the Northern Highlands

From Inverness (☞ Chapter 10), gateway to the Northern Highlands, roads fan out like the spokes of a wheel to join the coastal route around the rim of mainland Scotland. Many roads here are single track, and you pause at passing places to allow ongoing traffic to pass. There simply are no roads into the wilder areas, and few roads at all—so you are bound to be sharing the roads with heavy trucks and buses. Ferry services are generally very reliable, weather permitting.

CLANS, TARTANS AND TARTANITIS

WHATEVER THE ORIGINS of the clans—some with Norman roots, intermarried into Celtic society; some of Norse origin, the product of Viking raids on Scotland; others traceable to the monastic system; yet others possibly descended from Pictish tribes—by the 13th century the clan system was at the heart of Gaelic tribal culture. By the 15th century the clan chiefs of the Scottish Highlands were a threat even to the authority of the Stewart monarchs.

The word "*clann*" means family or children in Gaelic, and it was the custom for clan chiefs to board out their sons among nearby families, a practice that helped to bond the clan unit and create strong allegiances: the chief became "father" of the tribe and was owed loyalty by lesser chiefs and ordinary clansmen.

The clan chiefs' need for strong men-at-arms, fast-running messengers, and bards for entertainment and the preservation of clan genealogy was the probable origin of the Highland Games still celebrated in many Highland communities each year and which are an otherwise rather inexplicable mix of sport, music, and dance.

Gradually, by the 18th century, increasing knowledge of Lowland agricultural improvements, and better roads into the Highlands that improved communication of ideas and "southern" ways, began to weaken the clan system: fine clothes, French wines, even a Lowland education, became more common in chiefly households. Even without the defeat at Culloden the clan system had begun to lose its tight grip on the Highlands.

Tartan's own origins as a part of the clan system are disputed; the Gaelic for striped cloth is "*breacan*"—piebald or spotted—so even the word itself is not Highland. However, it is indisputable that in the days before mass manufacture, when cloth was spun, woven, and dyed using plant-based dyestuffs, each neighborhood would have different dyestuffs—bilberry, iris, bramble, water lily—and therefore colors, available. In this way, particular combinations of colors and favorite patterns of the local weavers could become associated with a particular area and therefore clan, but were not in any sense a clan's "own by exclusive right."

Between 1746 and 1782, the wearing of tartan was generally prohibited. When the ban was lifted, many recipes for dyes, and weaving patterns, had been forgotten. In addition, chemical dyes and mechanization began to take away the production of cloth and its coloring from particular neighborhoods.

It took the influence of Sir Walter Scott, with his Romantic, and fashionable, view of Highland history, to create the "modern myth" of clans and tartan. Sir Walter engineered George IV's visit to Scotland in 1822, which turned into a tartan extravaganza. The idea of one tartan or group of tartans "belonging" to one particular clan was created at this time—literally created, with new patterns and colorways being dreamt up and "assigned" to particular clans. Queen Victoria and Prince Albert, with their passion for all things Scottish and for tartan in particular at Balmoral, reinforced the "tartan culture" later in the century, and it persists, on and off, to this day.

It is considered more "proper" in some circles to wear the "right" tartan, i.e. that of your clan, if you can find a clan connection with the help of expertise at Scotland's Clan Tartan Centre, 70–74 Bangor Road, Leith, Edinburgh.

Numbers in the text correspond to numbers in the margin and on the Northern Highlands and Skye and the Outer Hebrides maps.

Great Itineraries

The quality of the northern light and the sheer ambience of the landscapes add to the touring adventure. Above all, don't rush things. And take a good look at how multiple-journey ferry tickets—the Island Hopscotch, for example—can help you stay flexible (☞ Getting Around by Car and Ferry *in* The Northern Highlands A to Z, *below*).

IF YOU HAVE 2 DAYS

In only two days, you should stay on the mainland and take in the western seaboard, particularly around 🔢 **Shieldaig** ㉑ and **Glen Torridon** ㉒ or between 🔢 **Ullapool** ③ and 🔢 **Lochinver** ⑥.

IF YOU HAVE 5 DAYS

If the weather looks settled, then head for Skye, which needs two days at least if you are going to take in some of its attractions as well as enjoy the scenery. Base yourself at 🔢 **Portree** ㉗. You could then hop over from Uig in the north of Skye to 🔢 **Tarbert** ㊸ in the Western Isles for **Calanais Standing Stones** ㊶, the **Arnol Black House** ㊳, and some deserted beaches, returning to 🔢 **Ullapool** ③ in the north, and travelling to Inverness via **Strathpeffer** ①. Otherwise, stay on the mainland and do the entire north of Scotland loop, staying overnight at 🔢 **Ullapool** ③, 🔢 **Scourie** ⑧, 🔢 **Thurso** ⑪, 🔢 **Wick** ⑬, or 🔢 **Dornoch** ⑰.

IF YOU HAVE 8 DAYS

Tackle the north of Scotland coastal loop counterclockwise, taking the ferry at 🔢 **Ullapool** ③ for 🔢 **Stornoway** ㊱ and the Western Isles, returning to the mainland via the ferry from 🔢 **Tarbert** ㊸ to Uig on Skye, then over the Skye Bridge.

When to Tour the Northern Highlands

There is no best season to tour this area, though you should avoid the depth of winter, with its short days. The earlier in the spring or later in the autumn you go, the greater the chances of your encountering the elements in their extreme form. But although you may not want to take a western sea passage in a gale, the area is spectacular in all seasons.

THE NORTHERN LANDSCAPES

Wester Ross and Sutherland

The northern landscapes offer some of the most distinctive mountain profiles in all of Scotland, although the coastal rim roads are more interesting than the cross-country routes. In recent years, an influx of newcomers from other parts of the United Kingdom has led to improvements in the choices in lodging and dining.

The essence of Caithness, the area at the top of Scotland, is space, big skies, and distant blue hills beyond endless rolling moors. There is a surprising amount to see and do on the east coast beyond Inverness—so make sure you allow enough time to see the visitor centers and croft houses open to view.

Strathpeffer

❶ *19 mi northwest of Inverness via A9, A835, and A834.*

At the former Victorian spa town of Strathpeffer you can take a walk to admire Victorian "holiday houses" and a Pictish stone carved with a lifelike eagle, or enjoy a toy museum in the former railway station.

Not far from Strathpeffer are the tumbling **Falls of Rogie** (signposted off the A835), where an interestingly bouncy suspension bridge leaves you with a fine view of the splashing waters below.

En Route Follow the A835 through Garve and on across the bare backbone of Scotland. As the road begins to drop down from the bleak lands of the interior, look for Braemore junction and continue on the A835. Shortly after, as you draw closer to the woods, you'll see the Corrieshalloch Gorge parking lot on the left.

Lodging

🏠 **Craigvar.** Host Margaret Scott is a delight and keeps plenty of tourist leaflets to keep you busy. The rooms at this Georgian house are prettily decorated; the so-called Beige Room is actually white and cream, with a swag of dried hydrangea above the bed. Idiosyncratic pictures—from 18th-century portraits to Japanese-style still lifes—hang on the walls. The Blue Room is replete with a four-poster bed and Victorian bath. ✉ *The Square, Strathpeffer, Ross-shire IV14 9DL,* ☎ *01997/421622,* ℻ *01997/421796. 3 rooms, 1 with bath, 2 with shower. V.*

Corrieshalloch Gorge

★ ➋ *39 mi west of Strathpeffer.*

For a touch of vertigo, the Corrieshalloch Gorge is not to be missed. A burn draining the high moors plunges 150 ft into a 200-ft-deep, thickly wooded gorge. There is a suspension-bridge viewpoint and an atmosphere of romantic grandeur, like an old Scottish print come to life.

Ullapool

➌ *5 mi west of Corrieshalloch Gorge, 238 mi north of Glasgow.*

Set by the shores of salty **Loch Broom,** Ullapool was founded in 1788 as a fishing station to exploit the local herring stocks. In recent years the fishing activity here has included "klondyking," the direct purchase of fish from local boats by large Eastern European factory ships. Ullapool has a cosmopolitan air and comes alive when the Lewis ferry docks and departs.

North and west from Ullapool lies the strange landscape of Wester Ross, with the little mountain Stac Polly, resembling a ruined fortress, and the humps of Suilven. At **Knockan,** about 15 mi north of Ullapool, a nature trail along a cliff illuminates some of the interesting local geology, as well as the area's flora and fauna. If this jaunt sounds too energetic, a more restful alternative may be to stay on the road and enjoy the
➍ good views of the mountains in the **Inverpolly National Nature Reserve.**

Dining and Lodging

£–££££ ✕🏠 **Ceilidh Place.** This hostelry is extremely comfortable, and about as far away in style as you can get from a major chain hotel. You can while away the hours on deep luxurious sofas in the first-floor sitting room—which overlooks the bay—and borrow one of the many books scattered throughout. Rooms have cream bedspreads and rich, warm color schemes. The inn's restaurant specializes in seafood and vegetarian food (try the Highland smoked lamb with honey and mustard dressing, monkfish and prawn brochettes, or pasta with zucchini and mushrooms in creamy garlic sauce), and ceilidhs and other musical events are held here frequently. A cheaper alternative is the bunkhouse across the road. ✉ *W. Argyle St., Ullapool, IV26 2TY,* ☎ *01854/612103,* ℻ *01854/612886. 26 rooms, 10 with bath or shower. Restaurant. AE, DC, MC, V.*

The Northern Highlands and Skye

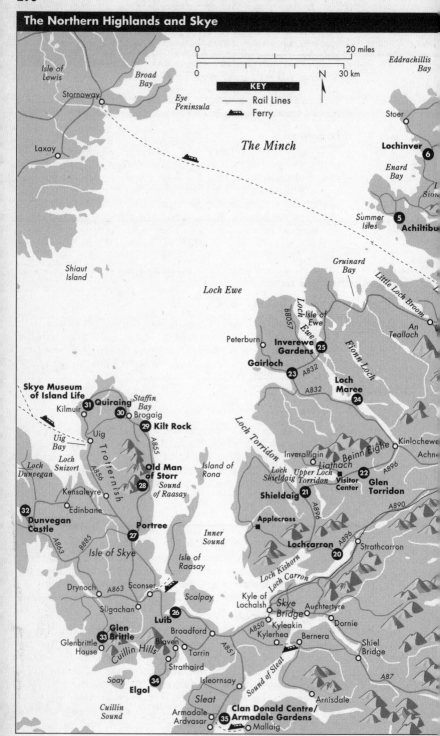

KEY
— Rail Lines
⛴ Ferry

0 — 20 miles
0 — 30 km

N

Isle of Lewis

Stornoway

Broad Bay

Eye Peninsula

Laxay

The Minch

Eddrachillis Bay

Stoer

Lochinver 6

Enard Bay

Shiant Island

Summer Isles

5 Achiltibu...

Gruinard Bay

Little Loch Broom

Loch Ewe

Isle of Ewe

An Teallach

Peterburn

Inverewe Gardens 25

Loch Ewe

B8057

Gairloch 23 A832

A832

Fionn Loch

Loch Maree 24

Skye Museum of Island Life

Kilmuir 31 **Quiraing** 30

Staffin Bay
Brogaig
29 **Kilt Rock**

Uig

Uig Bay

A855

Loch Snizort

Trotternish

A856

Old Man of Storr 28

Sound of Raasay

Island of Rona

Loch Torridon

Inveralligin **Beinn Eighe**

Liathach

Kinlocheve...

Achn...

Loch Dunvegan

Kensaleyre

Edinbane

32 **Dunvegan Castle**

A863

B885

Isle of Skye

27 **Portree**

Sconser

Inner Sound

Isle of Raasay

Scalpay

Loch Shieldaig *Upper Loch Torridon*

Visitor Center 22

Glen Torridon

A896

Shieldaig 21

Applecross

Lochcarron 20

Strathcarron

A890

Loch Kishorn

Loch Carron

Kyle of Lochalsh

Skye Bridge

Auchtertyre

Dornie

Drynoch A863

Sligachan

Luib 26

Broadford

Kyleakin

Kylerhea

Bernera

Shiel Bridge

Glen Brittle 33

Glenbrittle House

Blaven

Torrin

Cuillin Hills

Strathaird

A851

A850

A896

A87

Soay

Elgol 34

Isleornsay

Sleat

Sound of Sleat

Arnisdale

Cuillin Sound

Armadale
Ardvasar

35 **Clan Donald Centre/ Armadale Gardens**

Mallaig

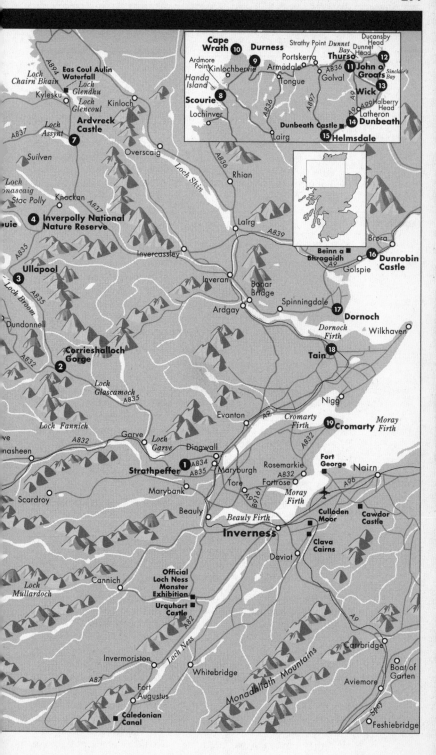

Nightlife and the Arts

Ceilidh Place (☞ Dining and Lodging, *above*) frequently presents ceilidhs and has a regular program of musical and dramatic productions—chamber music, folk music, and opera all find a place here.

En Route   Drive north of Ullapool and there is a strong sense of passing into a different kind of landscape. You won't find the broad flanks of great hills that hem you in here, as you do, say, in the Great Glen or Glen Coe. Instead, the mountains rear out of the hummocky terrain and seem to shift their position, hiding behind one another in a slightly bewitching way. Even their names seem different from those of the *bens* (mountain peaks or high hills) elsewhere: Cul Mor, Cul Beag, Stac Polly, Canisp, Suilven, some owing their origins to Norse words rather than to undiluted Gaelic—a reminder of the Vikings who used to sail this northern seaboard.

Achiltibuie

⑤ *25 mi northwest of Ullapool.*

A spread-out line of crofts, many now owned by newcomers, marks the approach to Achiltibuie. Offshore are the **Summer Isles,** romantic enough in theory, but in reality bleak and austere. In Achiltibuie there's a **smokehouse** that serves succulent smoked cuts of venison and other delicacies. The **Hydroponicum** is a huge glass house that looks out of place but is effective in producing giant strawberries.

En Route   A single-lane unclassified road winds north from Achiltibuie, through a wild though harmonious landscape of bracken and birch trees, heather and humped-hill horizons, with outstanding sea views on the second half of the route. Do not fall victim to the breathtaking landscape, however: the road has several blind curves that demand special care. Along this road, you will be near what is perhaps Scotland's most remote bookshop. Just before Inverkirkaig is a parking lot next to the River Kirkaig, and a short stroll away is Achins Book and Craft Shop (☞ Shopping in Lochinver, *below*; look for signs by the river bridge).

Lochinver

⑥ *18 mi north of Achiltibuie via unclassified road, 38 mi north of Ullapool via A835/A837.*

Lochinver is a charming community with a few dining and lodging options. Behind the town the mountain Suilven rises abruptly. This unusual monolith is best seen from across the water, however. Take the cul-de-sac, **Baddidarach Road,** for the finest photo opportunity.

Bold souls spending time at Lochinver may enjoy the interesting single-lane B869 **Drumbeg loop** to the north of Lochinver—it has several challenging hairpin turns along with breathtaking views. (The junction is just north of the River Inver bridge on the outskirts of the village, signed Stoer and Clashnessie.) Just beyond the scattered community of Stoer, a road leads west to **Stoer Point Lighthouse.** If you're an energetic walker, you can hike across the short turf and heather along the cliff top for fine views east toward the profiles of the northwest mountains. There is also a red-sandstone sea stack to view: the **Old Man of Stoer.** This makes a pleasant excursion on a long summer evening. If you stay on the Drumbeg section, there is a particularly tricky hairpin turn in a steep dip that may force you to take your eyes off the fine view of Quinag, yet another of Sutherland's shapely mountains.

❼ Beside Loch Assynt, on the road east from Lochinver, stand the abandoned ruins of **Ardvreck Castle.** This was a clan MacLeod stronghold, built in the 15th century.

Lodging

£ 🖭 **Linne Mhuirich.** This modern croft house B&B is set in the middle of open country surrounded by superb mountain and loch scenery. Rooms have pine furniture and tartan or floral fabrics. Smoking is not permitted throughout the property. ✉ *Unapool Croft Rd., Kylesku, via Lairg, Sutherland, IV27 4HW,* ☎ *01971/502227. 2 rooms, 1 with bath. No credit cards.* ⊗ *May–Oct.*

Shopping

Highland Stoneware (✉ Baddidarroch, Lochinver, ☎ 01571/844376) manufactures tableware and decorative items with hand-painted designs of Highland wildflowers, animals, and landscapes. In the showroom you can browse and purchase wares.

At Inverkirkaig, just south of Lochinver, do not miss **Achins Book and Craft Shop** (✉ Inverkirkaig, ☎ 01571/844262, ⊗ daily 9:30–6) for Scottish books on natural history, hill walking, fishing, and crafts as well as a well-chosen variety of crafts: knitwear, tweeds, and pottery. Its pleasant coffee shop is open Easter through October, daily 10–5.

OFF THE BEATEN PATH — **EAS COUL AULIN WATERFALL** – This is the longest waterfall in the United Kingdom. At the head of Loch Glencoul, the falls have a 685-ft drop. A rugged hike leads to the falls; in summer, cruises offer a less taxing alternative. The falls are located 3 mi southeast of the Kylesku Bridge off the A894; contact the tourist information center in Ullapool or Lochinver for more information.

Scourie

❽ *28 mi north of Lochinver.*

Scourie is a small settlement catering to visitors—fishermen especially—with a choice of local accommodations. It also makes a good base for a trip to the bird sanctuary on the island of Handa.

Dining and Lodging

££ ✕🖭 **Eddrachilles Hotel.** This long-established, traditional inn has one of the best views of any hotel in Scotland—across the islands of Eddrachillis Bay (which can be explored by boat from the hotel). The hotel sits on 320 acres of private moorland and is just south of the Handa Island bird sanctuary. The bedrooms are modern and comfortable, and each is outfitted with tea- and coffee-making facilities. The chef uses local produce to prepare meals cooked in straightforward Scottish style, with the emphasis on fish and game: try the saddle of venison or the poached salmon. ✉ *Badcall Bay, Scourie IV27 4TH,* ☎ *01971/ 502080,* 🕱 *01971/502477. 11 rooms with bath or shower. Restaurant, bar. MC, V. Closed Nov.–Feb.*

En Route From Scourie northward, the A894/A838 traverses the most northerly landscapes, with the empty quarter below Cape Wrath on the western side. You can sample this by way of a hike to Sandwood Bay, at the end of the B801, beyond the fishing port of Kinlochbervie. Sandwood has rock stacks and a white beach and also its own ghost, said to frequent a cottage (or bothy) near the shore— truly a haunting area.

Durness

❾ *55 mi north of Lochinver.*

Durness is strung along the north-facing coast, the sudden patches of greenness hereabouts caused by the richer limestone outcrops among the acid moorlands. The limestone's most spectacular feature is **Smoo Cave,** a cave system hollowed out of the limestone by water action. Boat tours run daily from April to September (reservations advised since there's a limit of six per tour, lasting 20 minutes). The seasonal tourist information center (✉ Sango, ☎ 01971/511259) has full information.

❿ If you have made it this far north, you will probably want to go all the way to **Cape Wrath** at the northwest tip of Scotland. You can't drive your own vehicle, though, as a small boat (May–September) ferries only people across the Kyle of Durness, a sea inlet, from Keoldale then a minibus takes you to the lighthouse. The highest mainland cliffs in Scotland lie between the Kyle and Cape Wrath. These are the 800-ft **Cleit Dubh** (the name means "black cleft" in Gaelic and comes from the Old Norse *klettr* (crag).

En Route The north coast road along the top of Scotland is both attractive and severe. It runs, for example, round the head of Loch Eriboll, which was a World War II convoy assembly point and was usually referred to as "Loch 'orrible" by the crews. Yet it has its own desolate charm. There are little beaches and bays to explore along this road, and the landscape gradually softens as you journey east.

Thurso

⓫ *74 mi east of Durness.*

The town of Thurso is hard to categorize. Quite substantial for a community so far north, since the 1950s its development has been related to the atomic reactor (Britain's first) along the coast at Dounreay—situated there, presumably, to be as far away from the seat of government in London as possible. There is not much to see in the town itself, though there are fine beaches, particularly to the east at Dunnet Bay. Many people make the trip to the truly most northern point of mainland Britain at **Dunnet Head,** with its fine views to Orkney.

Lodging

£££   🏨 **Forss Country House Hotel.** Surrounded by woodland 4 mi west of Thurso, despite its stark, gray exterior, this house dating from 1810 offers a most welcoming environment as a base for fishing (guide service and instruction provided) or touring. Restrained decor with plain, soft-toned walls and spare, dark-wood antique and reproduction furniture, log fires, and sturdy Scottish cuisine add up to a highly recommended place to stay. ✉ *Forss, about 4 mi west of Thurso, KW14 7XY,* ☎ *01847/861201,* ᶠᴬˣ *01847/861301. 10 rooms, 9 with bath, 1 with shower. Restaurant, golf privileges, fishing. AE, MC, V. Closed Dec. 25 and Jan. 1.*

£   🏨 **Murray House.** This Victorian town house in the center of Thurso offers B&B of a very high standard, including baths in two of its bedrooms. ✉ *1 Campbell St., Thurso, KW14 7HD,* ☎ *01847/895759. 4 rooms, 2 with bath, 2 with shower. No credit cards.*

Outdoor Activities and Sports

Bikes can be hired from **The Bike Shop** (✉ 35 High St., Thurso, ☎ ᶠᴬˣ 01847/896124 or 01847/894223), whose help are also happy to advise on routes.

John o'Groats

⑫ *21 mi east of Thurso via A836.*

The windswept little outpost of John o'Groats is usually taken to be the most northern community in the Scottish mainland, though that is not strictly accurate, as an exploration of the little network of roads between Dunnet Head and John o'Groats will confirm. However, John o'Groats has some high-quality crafts shops and should be visited. Go east to **Duncansby Head** for spectacular views of cliffs and sea stacks by the lighthouse—and puffins, too, if you know where to look.

Nightlife and the Arts

The **Lyth Arts Centre,** between Wick and John o'Groats, is set in an old country school. From April to November each year, it hosts frequent performances by quality touring music and theater companies (it forms part of the circuit of British Arts Centres). In July and August there are also local and touring exhibitions of contemporary fine art. ⊠ *Lyth, 4 mi off A9,* ☎ *01955/641270.* ☒ *Performances £8, concessions £5, exhibitions £1.50.* ☉ *July–Aug. daily, exhibitions 10–6; Apr.–Nov., performances at 8 PM.*

Outdoor Activities and Sports

Wildlife cruises are operated from John o'Groats harbor by **John o'Groats Ferries.** The 1½-hour trip takes passengers into the Pentland Firth, to Duncansby Stacks, and the island of Stroma, and offers spectacular cliff scenery and bird life. ☎ *01955/611353.* ☒ *£12.* ☉ *Cruise mid-June–Aug., daily 2:30 PM.*

Wick

⑬ *17 mi south of John o'Groats, 22 mi southeast of Thurso via A882.*

Wick is a substantial town that was built on its fishing industry. For details on how this town grew, visit the **Wick Heritage Centre**—it's run by local people in part for the local community, and they are real enthusiasts. ⊠ *18 Bank Row,* ☎ *01955/605393 or 01955/603385.* ☒ *£2.* ☉ *June–Sept., Mon.–Sat. 10–5 (last admission 4:15).*

The gaunt, bleak ruins of **Castle Sinclair** and **Castle Girnigoe** teeter on a cliff top to the north of Wick. The **Northlands Viking Centre,** which highlights the role of Scandinavian settlers in this area, has models of the Viking settlement at Freswick and of a Viking long ship, and artifacts such as coins. ⊠ *The Old School, Auckengill,* ☎ *01955/607771.* ☒ *£1.40.* ☉ *June–Sept., daily 10–4.*

Lodging

£ ⌂ **Greenvoe.** This B&B is a well-appointed modern house, fresh and beautifully maintained, with unfussy, functional, and comfortable bedrooms. A delicious, generous breakfast is included in the room rate, and late-night snacks are a hospitable touch. Smoking is prohibited. ⊠ *George St., Wick, Caithness, KW1 4DE,* ☎ *01955/603942. 3 rooms without bath. No credit cards. Closed last 2 wks Dec.*

Shopping

Perhaps the best-known purveyor of crafts in the area is **Caithness Glass** (⊠ Wick Industrial Site, Wick Airport, ☎ 01955/602286). Producing a distinctive style of glassware and paperweights (most of the better gift shops stock Caithness Glass), the factory has tours of the glass-blowing workshops and a shop stocking the full product range.

Dunbeath

⑭ *21 mi south of Wick.*

As the moors of Caithness roll down to the sea at Dunbeath, the **Dunbeath Heritage Centre** is an old school that the local community—concerned that their past should be recorded—turned into a museum. It displays photographs and domestic and crofting artifacts that relay the history of the area from the Bronze Age to the oil age, and it's particularly helpful to those researching their family histories. ⊠ *Dunbeath,* ☎ *01593/731233.* ⊠ *£1.50.* ☉ *Apr.–Sept., Mon.–Sat. 10–5, Sun. 11–6.*

Just north of Dunbeath, the **Laidhay Croft Museum** feels, appropriately, more like a private home than a museum. It was built around 1842, comprises a longhouse and barn—animals and people lived under the same long roof—and is furnished as it would have been during its working life. ⊠ *Dunbeath,* ☎ *01593/731244.* ⊠ *£1.* ☉ *Easter–Oct., daily 10–6.*

Helmsdale

⑮ *15 mi south of Dunbeath.*

At Helmsdale, the **Timespan Heritage Centre,** a thought-provoking mix of displays, artifacts, and audiovisual materials, portrays the history of the area, from the Stone Age to the 1869 gold rush in the Strath of Kildonan. ⊠ *Helmsdale,* ☎ *01431/821327.* ⊠ *£3.* ☉ *Apr.–June and Sept.–Oct., Mon.–Sat. 9:30–5, Sun. 2–5 (last admission 1 hr before closing); July–Aug., Mon.–Sat. 9:30–6, Sun. 2–6.*

Nearby, at **Baile an Or (Gold Town),** on the site of the 1869 gold rush, panning is still possible, using pans supplied by **Strathullie Local and Scottish Crafts.** ⊠ *Dunrobin St., Helmsdale,* ☎ FAX *01431/821343.* ⊠ *£2 a day to hire pan, sieve, and trowel.* ☉ *Daily, 9–5:30.*

Golspie

18 mi south of Helmsdale.

Golspie is a little coastal town with a number of shops and accommodations, though it has the air of a place that visitors just pass through. **⑯** The Scottish home of the dukes of Sutherland is **Dunrobin Castle,** which is one of the largest houses in the Highlands and is open to visitors. ⊠ *Golspie (on the A9),* ☎ *01408/633177.* ⊠ *£5.* ☉ *Apr.–May and Sept.–Oct., Mon.–Sat. 10:30–4, Sun. noon–4; June–Aug., daily 10:30–5.*

Shopping

The **Orcadian Stone Company** (⊠ Main St., Golspie, ☎ 01408/633483) makes stone products (including giftware made from local Caithness slate), jewelry, incised plaques, and prepared mineral specimens. There is also a geological exhibition.

En Route Traveling south on the A9, you'll see the controversial statue of the first duke of Sutherland, like some Eastern Bloc despot, on Beinn a Bragaidh (Ben Braggie), the hilltop to the west. Many people feel strongly that it should be removed, as the "improving" policies of the duke were ultimately responsible for the brutality associated with the Sutherland Clearances of 1810–20. This was a kind of ethnic cleansing when thousands of native Gaels were evicted from settlements in the interior and forced to emigrate or settle at sites on the coast.

Dornoch

⑰ *10 mi south of Golspie.*

A town of mellow sandstone and tiny, rose-filled gardens, with a 13th-century cathedral, Dornoch is noted for its golf—you may hear it referred to as "the St. Andrews of the north." Visit the **Town Jail Craft Centre,** which occupies the former town jail; here you can watch weavers at work weaving tartan cloth. There's also an exhibition of prison life in past times, just to remind you of the building's origins. ⊠ *Castle St.,* ☎ FAX *01862/810555.* ✉ *Free.* ⊙ *Easter–Sept., daily 9–5; Oct.–Easter, weekdays 10–1 and 2–4.*

Dining and Lodging

££ ✕🏨 **Dornoch Castle Hotel.** A genuine castle, once the palace of the Bish-
★ ops of Caithness and set right in the center of Dornoch, this hotel is a delightful blend of the very old (late-15th-century castle) and the more modern (rooms in the 1974 wing). The lounge is a relaxing Adamesque room of soft green and cream, and the bedrooms wear pastel stripes and floral fabrics. This is not a luxury hotel, but it is clean and comfortable, with friendly staff and satisfying, well-cooked Scottish food: try the crisp-battered cod fillet with seasonal vegetables. ⊠ *Dornoch, Sutherland IV25 3SD,* ☎ *01862/810216,* FAX *01862/810981. 17 rooms with bath or shower. AE, MC, V. Nov.–mid-Mar.*

£–££ 🏨 **Highfield.** In its own grounds on the edge of town, no-smoking Highfield delivers deluxe B&B accommodations in a modern family home. ⊠ *Evelix Rd., Dornoch, IV25 3HR,* ☎ FAX *01862/810909. 3 rooms with bath and shower. No credit cards.*

Outdoor Activities and Sports

Were it not for its northern location, **Royal Dornoch** (☎ 01862/810219, 18 holes, 6,185 yards, par 70) would undoubtedly be a candidate for the British Open Championship. It is a superb, breezy, and challenging links course, praised by the world's top golfers. For more information, *see* Chapter 2.

Shopping

The **Town Jail Craft Centre** (⊠ Castle St., Dornoch, ☎ FAX 01862/810555) is a textile-and-crafts center where you can buy tartans woven on the premises.

Tain

⑱ *11 mi south of Dornoch.*

Over the Dornoch Firth—there is a bridge—lies Tain, another attractive community and once a place of pilgrimage of the Scottish kings. The ruins of **St. Duthac's Chapel,** built from 1065 to 1256, mark the site of the birthplace of St. Duthac, an early missionary to the Picts. The chapel was a pilgrimage site for centuries.

The **Pilgrimage Visitor Centre** (under the theme of "Tain through Time") has a slightly tedious audiovisual presentation in the center, as well as a much more interesting tape tour and museum. ⊠ *Tower St.,* ☎ FAX *01862/894089.* ✉ *£3.*

Cromarty

⑲ *42 mi south of Tain via A9 and B9163, 23 mi north of Inverness via A832, B9161, A9.*

Set at the tip of the Black Isle, a pleasant mixture of woods and farmland, Cromarty is a good example of a Scottish eastern seaboard town, with narrow, winding streets and old cottages interspersed with a few

Georgian mansions, the town houses of landowners living 200 years ago. Thanks to the conversion of the **Cromarty Courthouse** into a visitor center, you can learn all about life in an 18th-century Scottish *burgh* (a town with trading rights). Take a self-guided walking tour of the town—the center's cassette and headphones will keep you on track. ✉ *Church St.,* ☎ *01381/600418.* 🎟 *£3.* ⊙ *Mar. and Nov.–Dec., daily noon–4; Apr.–Oct., daily 10–5; Jan.–Feb. by appointment only.*

Hugh Miller's Cottage is close to Cromarty Courthouse. Hugh Miller (1802–56) was a 19th-century stonemason, theologian, and self-taught geologist who advanced the science of geology by his fossil discoveries in Scotland. The whitewashed and thatched cottage (in National Trust for Scotland's care) dates from 1711, when it was built by Miller's great-grandfather. It contains an exhibition on Miller's life and work, and it is decorated in period style. ✉ *Church St.,* ☎ *01381/ 600245.* 🎟 *£2.* ⊙ *May–Sept., Mon.–Sat. 11–1 and 2–5, Sun. 2–5.*

THE TORRIDONS

The Torridons have a grand and wild air that feels especially remote, yet it is not much more than an hour from Inverness before you reach Kinlocheweg at the east end of Glen Torridon. The western end is equally spectacular. There are plenty of opportunities to enjoy mountain panoramas as well as walks and trails.

En Route   The A890 is a single-lane road in some stretches, with plenty of open vistas across the deserted heart of northern Scotland.

Lochcarron

㉒ *66 mi west of Inverness via A9/A835/A832/A890.*

Lochcarron is a village strung along the shore without a recognizable center. It does, however, function as a local hub for shopping, garage facilities, and so on.

Shopping
The premises of **Lochcarron Weavers** (✉ Mid Strone, Lochcarron, ☎ 01520/722212) are open to the public: weavers can be seen at work, producing pure-wool worsted tartans that can be bought on site or at the firm's other outlets in the area. East of Lochcarron, at Achnasheen, is the **Highland Line Craft Centre** (✉ center of Achnasheen, ☎ 01445/ 720227), where silver and gold jewelry is made. You can watch the silversmiths; their products are available in the shop on the premises.

En Route   Driving north by the A896, you pass **Rassal Ash Wood,** on your right. The lushness of the fenced-in area within this small nature reserve is a reminder of what Scotland might have been had sheep and deer not been kept here in such high numbers. The combined nibbling of these animals ensures that Scotland's natural tree cover does not regenerate without human intervention.

Shieldaig

㉓ *16 mi northwest of Lochcarron.*

Just west of the southern coast of Upper Loch Torridon is Shieldaig, a village that sits in an attractive crescent overlooking a loch of its own, **Loch Shieldaig.** For an atmospheric evening foray, walk north toward Loch Torridon at the northern end of the village, by the church. The path is fairly well made, though hiking shoes are recommended. You will find exquisite views and tiny rocky beaches.

★ ㉒ The scenic spectacle of **Glen Torridon** lies east of Shieldaig. Some say that Glen Torridon has the finest mountain scenery in Scotland. It consists mainly of the long gray quartzite flanks of **Beinn Eighe** (rhymes with *say*), which make up Scotland's oldest national nature reserve, and **Liathach** (*leea*-gach), with its distinct ridge profile that looks like the keel of an upturned boat. At the end of the glen the National Trust for Scotland operates a **visitor center** that explains the ecology and geology of the area. ☎ 01445/791221. ✉ *Audiovisual display and deer museum £1.50.* ☺ *Countryside center May–Sept., Mon.–Sat. 10–5, Sun. 2–5, estate, deer park, and deer museum year-round, daily 9–5.*

Dining and Lodging

££££ ✕▥ **Loch Torridon Hotel.** Once a shooting lodge, and right on the shore of Loch Torridon with forest and mountains rising behind, the hotel provides a real Highland welcome. Log fires, handsome plasterwork ceilings, mounted stag heads, and traditional furnishings set the mood downstairs, and bedrooms are decorated in restrained pastel shades with antique mahogany furniture. The restaurant makes elaborate use of local seafood, salmon, beef, lamb, and game, and the cellar keeps many fine wines. ✉ *Torridon, by Achnasheen, Wester Ross, IV22 2EY,* ☎ *01445/791242,* ℻ *01445/791296. 21 rooms, 20 with bath, 1 with shower. Restaurant. AE, MC, V.*

OFF THE BEATEN PATH

APPLECROSS – The tame way to reach Applecross, a small community facing Skye, is by a coastal road from near Shieldaig; the exciting route turns west off the A896 a few miles farther south. A series of hairpin turns corkscrews up the steep wall at the head of a corrie (a glacier-cut mountain valley), over the Bealach na Ba (Pass of the Cattle). There are spectacular views of Skye from the bare plateau on top, and you can boast afterward that you have been on what is probably Scotland's highest drivable road. The village of Applecross itself is pleasant but not riveting.

Gairloch

㉓ *38 mi north of Shieldaig.*

This region's main center, with some shops and accommodations, Gairloch has one further advantage: lying just a short way from the mountains of the interior, this small oasis often escapes the rain clouds that sometimes cling to the high summits. Guests can enjoy a game of golf here and perhaps stay dry, even when the nearby Torridon hills are deluged. In the village is the **Gairloch Heritage Museum,** with exhibitions covering prehistoric times to the present. ✉ *Achtercairn,* ☎ *01445/712287.* ✉ *£2.50.* ☺ *Apr.–Oct., Mon.–Sat. 10–5.*

Southeast of Gairloch stretches one of Scotland's most scenic lochs,
★ ㉔ **Loch Maree.** The harmonious environs of the loch, with its tall Scots pines and the mountain Slioch looming as a backdrop, witnessed the destruction of much of the tree cover in the 18th century. Iron ore was shipped in and smelted using local oak to feed the furnaces. Oak now grows here only on the northern limits of the range. Scottish Natural Heritage has an **information center** and nature trails by the loch side. Red deer sightings are virtually guaranteed; locals say the best place to spot another local denizen, the pine marten, is around the trash containers in the parking turnoffs. Further on, look for the sign for **Victoria Falls,** a waterfall named after the queen who visited them.

★ ㉕ The highlight of this area for most travelers is **Inverewe Gardens,** 6 mi northeast of Gairloch. The reputation of the gardens at Inverewe, in spite of their comparatively remote location, has grown steadily through the years. The main attraction lies in the contrast between the bleak coastal headlands and thin-soiled moors and the lush plantings of the garden behind its dense shelterbelts. These are proof of the efficacy of the warm North Atlantic Drift, part of the Gulf Stream, which takes the edge off winter frosts. (Inverewe is sometimes described as sub-tropical, but this is an inaccuracy that irritates the head gardener; do not expect coconuts and palm trees here.) There is also a licensed restaurant, offering light lunches and a selection of cakes and biscuits. ⊠ *Poolewe,* ☎ *01445/781200.* 🎫 *£4.80.* ⊙ *Gardens mid-Mar.–Oct., daily 9:30–9; Nov.–mid-Mar., daily 9:30–5, visitor center mid-Mar.–Oct., daily 9:30–5:30, guided walks with the head gardener Apr.–Sept., weekdays at 1:30, restaurant mid-Mar.–Oct., daily 10–5.*

Dining and Lodging

££–£££ ✕🏨 **Dundonnell Hotel.** Set on the roadside by Little Loch Broom, east of Gairloch, this excellent hotel has been a family-run enterprise since 1962 and has cultivated a solid reputation for hospitality and cuisine. The bedrooms are decorated in a fresh, modern style, with light, floral curtains and bedspreads and contemporary furnishings. Many bedrooms and public rooms have stunning views of pristine hills and lochs. The Taste of Scotland menu features homemade soups, fresh seafood, and desserts well worth leaving room for. ⊠ *Dundonnell, near Garve, Ross-shire,* ☎ *01854/633204,* 🆅🆇 *01854/633366. 30 rooms with bath. Restaurant, bar. AE, MC, V.*

Outdoor Activities and Sports

Gairloch Golf Club (☎ 01445/712407, 9 holes, 1,942 yards, SSS 62), one of few on this stretch of coast, has its enthusiasts.

En Route The road between Gairloch and the Corrieshalloch Gorge initially offers coastal scenery with views of Gruinard Bay and its white beaches, then woodlands around Dundonnell and Loch Broom. Soon the route traverses wild country: the toothed ramparts of the mountain An Teallach (pronounced *tyel* lach, with Scots *ch,* of course) can be seen on the horizon. The moorland route you travel is known chillingly as Destitution Road. It was commissioned in 1851 to give the local folk (long vanished from the area) some way of earning a living after the failure of the potato crop; it is said the workers were paid only in food. At Corrieshalloch, the A832 joins the A835 for Inverness.

SKYE, THE MISTY ISLAND

Skye ranks near the top of most visitors' priority lists: The romance of Prince Charles Edward Stuart (1720–88), Bonnie Prince Charlie, the misty Cuillin Hills, and its nearness to the mainland all contribute to its popularity. You can tour comfortably around the island in two or three days. Orientation is easy: follow the only roads around the loops on the northern part of the island. There are some stretches of single-lane road, but none pose a problem.

Luib

㉖ *15 mi west of Kyle of Lochalsh via Skye Bridge and A850.*

At Luib, note the **Old Skye Crofter's House,** with its traditional thatch and 19th-century furnishings.

En Route The hills north have a reddish hue—they comprise the Red Cuillin, the gentler companions of the Black Cuillins, which swing spectacularly into view on the approaches to Sligachan. Turning away from the hills, the road goes north through tranquil scenery.

Portree

㉗ *19 mi north of Luib.*

The population center of the island, Portree is not overburdened by historical features, but it's a pleasant center clustered around a small and sheltered bay, and it makes a good touring base.

Dining and Lodging

££–£££ ✕⌂ **Cuillin Hills Hotel.** Set just outside Portree, this gabled hotel has many rooms with outstanding views over Portree Bay toward the Cuillin Hills. Bedrooms are individually decorated in bold floral patterns, and there is a choice of public rooms. The seafood dishes in the restaurant are especially tasty: try the local prawns, lobster, or scallops, or glazed ham carved from the bone. ⊠ *Portree, Isle of Skye,* ☎ *01478/612003,* ℻ *01478/613092. 25 rooms with bath or shower. Restaurant, bar. AE, MC, V.*

££ ✕⌂ **Rosedale Hotel.** Right on the harbor, the Rosedale offers modern style accommodations and delicious modern Scottish cooking within converted 19th-century buildings. The menu might include breast of duck with cranberries and parsnip puree, or pasta rolls with smoked haddock and lemon butter. ⊠ *Beaumont Crescent, Portree, IV51 9DF,* ☎ *01478/613131,* ℻ *01478/612531. 23 rooms with bath or shower. AE, MC, V. Closed Oct.–mid-May.*

Shopping

Skye Original Prints (⊠ Portree, ☎ 01478/612544) stocks original prints by local artist Tom Mackenzie. **Skye Batiks** (⊠ Portree, ☎ 01478/613331; ⊠ Armadale, ☎ 01471/844396) dyes fabrics with Celtic motifs for wall hangings and cotton and linen clothing at reasonable prices.

Trotternish Peninsula

16 mi north of Portree via A855.

As the road goes north from Portree, cliffs rise to the left. They are actually the edge of an ancient lava flow, set back from the road, that runs for miles as your rugged companion. In some places the hardened lava has created spectacular features, including a curious pinnacle
㉘ called the **Old Man of Storr.** The A855 travels past neat white crofts
㉙ and forestry plantings to **Kilt Rock.** Everyone on the Skye tour circuit stops here to peep over the cliffs (there is a safe viewing platform) for a look at the curious geology of the cliff edge: bands of two different types of rock have a folded, pleated effect just like a kilt.

★ **㉚** The spectacular **Quiraing** dominates the horizon 5 mi past Kilt Rock. For a closer view of the strange pinnacles and rock forms, make a left onto a small road at **Brogaig** by **Staffin Bay.** There is a parking lot near the point where this road breaches the ever-present cliff line, though you will have to be physically fit to walk back toward the Quiraing itself, where the rock formations and cliffs are most dramatic. The trail is on uneven, stony ground, and it's a steep scramble up to the rock formations. In ages past, stolen cattle were hidden deep within the Quiraing's rocky jaws.

㉛ The main A855 reaches around the top end of Trotternish, to the **Skye Museum of Island Life** at Kilmuir, where you can see the old farming ways brought to life. Included in the displays and exhibits are documents and photographs, reconstructed interiors, and implements. Flora Macdonald, helpmate of Bonnie Prince Charlie, is buried nearby. ⊠ *Kilmuir, Isle of Skye,* ☎ ℻ *01470/552206.* 🎟 *£1.75.* ☉ *Easter–Oct., Mon.–Sat. 9:30–5:30.*

The west coast of Trotternish is pleasant, as the route carries you back to Portree.

Dunvegan Castle

32 *22 mi west of Portree.*

In a commanding position above a sea loch, Dunvegan Castle has been the seat of the chiefs of Clan Macleod for more than 700 years. Though greatly changed over the centuries, a gloomy ambience prevails, and there is plenty of family history on display, notably the fascinating "Fairy Flag"—a silk banner, thought to be originally from Rhodes or Syria and believed to have magically saved the clan from danger. The banner's powers are said to suffice for only one more use. ⊠ *Dunvegan,* ☎ *01470/521206.* ☜ *Garden only £3.50, castle and garden £5.* ☉ *Mid-Mar.–Oct., daily 10–5:30 (last admission 5).*

Shopping

For wood-fired stoneware, try **Edinbane Pottery** (⊠ Edinbane, ☎ 01470/582234), 8 mi east of Dunvegan. **Skye Silver** (⊠ The Old School, Colbost, ☎ 01470/511263), west of Dunvegan, designs gold and silver jewelry with a Celtic theme.

Glen Brittle

★ **33** *26 mi southwest of Portree.*

Spectacular mountain scenery can be enjoyed in Glen Brittle, with some fine views of the Cuillin ridges—not a place for the ordinary walker (there are many dangerous ridges and steep faces). Glen Brittle extends off the A863 on the west side of the island.

Elgol

40 mi southwest of Portree via A881.

A small cul-de-sac resembling Glen Brittle leads from **Broadford** to one of the finest views in Scotland. This road passes through **Strath Suardal** and little **Loch Cill Chriosd** (Kilchrist) by a ruined church. If there are cattle wading in the loch and the light is soft—typical of Skye—then this place takes on the air of a romantic Victorian oil painting. Skye marble, with its attractive green veining, is produced from the marble quarry at **Torrin.**

34 Breathtaking views of the mountain **Blaven** can be appreciated as the A881 continues to **Elgol,** a gathering of crofts along the suddenly descending road, which ends at a pier. You can admire the heart-stopping profile of the Cuillin peaks from the shore or, at a point about halfway down the hill, find the path that goes toward them across the rough grasslands.

Outdoor Activities and Sports

Broadford Bicycle Hire (⊠ Fairwinds, Elgol Rd., Broadford, ☎ 01471/822270), rents bicycles year-round.

Shopping

Craft Encounters (⊠ Broadford, ☎ 01471/822754) stocks an array of Skye crafts, including pottery and jewelry.

Armadale

43 mi south of Portree, 5 mi (ferry crossing) west of Mallaig.

35 At Armadale the popular **Clan Donald Centre and Armadale Gardens** tell the story of the Macdonalds and their proud title: the Lords of the

Isles. In the 15th century they were powerful enough to threaten the authority of the Stuart monarchs of Scotland. There is also a major exhibition in a restored part of the castle, as well as extensive gardens and nature trails. ✉ *Armadale, ½ mi north of Armadale Pier,* ☎ *01471/ 844305 or 01471/844227.* 🎫 *£3.50.* ☉ *Clan Donald Centre Apr.– Oct., daily 9:30–6 (last entry 5), gardens year-round.*

Dining and Lodging

£££–££££   ✕🏨 **Kinloch Lodge.** Just a few miles up the road from Armadale, this hotel offers elegant comfort on the edge of the world. Run by Lord and Lady Macdonald with flair and considerable professionalism, Kinloch Lodge is a supremely comfortable country house, with warm, restful lounges with antiques, chintz fabrics, book cases, and family photographs. Snug bedrooms are individually decorated with quilted bedspreads and pastel wallpaper. Lady Macdonald is now offering cooking demonstrations in the new wing off the main lodge. Dinner is served at 8 PM in the handsome dining room, and you choose from the small menu that changes daily and features such savory dishes as spicy tomato soup with avocado cream; roast duck with apple and calvados purée and green peppercorn sauce; and for dessert, dark chocolate nemesis. ✉ *Isleornsay, Sleat, IV43 8QY,* ☎ *01471/833333,* FAX *01471/833277. 15 rooms with bath. Restaurant, fishing, helipad. AE, MC, V. Closed Dec.–Feb.*

Outdoor Activities and Sports

The Skye Ferry Filling Station (✉ Ardvasar, ☎ 01471/844249) rents bicycles in summer.

Shopping

Ragamuffin (✉ Armadale Pier, ☎ 01471/844217) specializes in designer knitwear and clothing. **Harlequin Knitwear** (✉ Duisdale, Sleat, ☎ 01471/833321) sells colorful wool sweaters created by local designer Chrissy Gibbs.

OUTER HEBRIDES (WESTERN ISLES)

The Outer Hebrides—the Western Isles in common parlance—stretch about 130 mi from end to end and lie about 50 mi from the Scottish mainland. This splintered archipelago extends from the pugnacious Butt of Lewis in the north to the 600-ft Barra Head on Berneray in the south, whose lighthouse has the greatest arc of visibility in the world. The Isle of Lewis and Harris is the northernmost and largest of the group. The island's only major town, Stornoway, is situated on a big, nearly landlocked harbor on the east coast of Lewis and is probably the most convenient starting point for a driving tour of the islands if you're approaching the Western Isles from the Northern Highlands.

Just south of the Sound of Harris is North Uist, rich in monoliths, chambered cairns, and other reminders of a prehistoric past. Though it is one of the smaller islands in the chain, Benbecula, sandwiched between North and South Uist and sometimes referred to as the Hill of the Fords, is in fact less bare and neglected looking than its bigger neighbors to the north. South Uist, once a refuge of the old Catholic faith, is dotted with ruined forts and chapels; in summer its wild gardens burst with riots of Alpine and rock plants. Eriskay and a scattering of islets almost block the 6-mi strait between South Uist and Barra, the southernmost major formation in the Outer Hebrides, an isle you can walk across in an hour.

Harris tweed is available at many outlets on the islands, including some of the weavers' homes; keep an eye out for signs directing you to weavers' workshops. Note that on the islands Sunday is strictly observed as a day of rest, and nearly all shops and visitor attractions are closed.

Stornoway

36 *2½-hr ferry trip from Ullapool.*

The port capital for the Outer Hebrides is Stornoway on Lewis. The **An Lanntair Gallery** offers a varied program of contemporary and traditional exhibitions that change monthly, as well as frequent musical and theatrical events emphasizing traditional Gaelic culture. ⊠ *Town Hall, S. Beach St., Stornoway,* ☎ *01851/703307.* 🎫 *Free.* 🕑 *Mon.– Sat. 10–5:30.*

Lodging

£ 🏠 **Ravenswood.** On a quiet residential street just a few minutes' walk from the harbor and town center, the house dates from the turn of the century. A stay reveals high-quality B&B accommodation, with a residents' lounge and attractive gardens. ⊠ *12 Matheson Rd., Stornoway, Lewis, HS87 2LR,* ☎ *01851/702673. 3 rooms, 2 with bath or shower. No credit cards.*

Nightlife and the Arts

An Lanntair Gallery (☎ 01851/703307), in the Town Hall, conducts an eclectic program of monthly exhibitions and evening events.

Outdoor Activities and Sports

Hire bicycles from **Alex Dan Cycle Centre** (⊠ 67 Kenneth St., Stornoway, ☎ 01851/704025).

En Route   The best road to use to explore the territory north of Stornoway is the A857, which runs first across the island to the northwest and then to the northeast all the way to Port of Ness (about 30 mi).

Port of Ness

30 mi north of Stornoway.

The stark, windswept community of Port of Ness cradles a small harbor squeezed in among the rocks, overlooked by **Harbour View,** a small gallery and café. At the northernmost point of Lewis stands the 37 **Butt of Lewis Lighthouse,** designed by David and Thomas Stevenson of the prominent engineering family, whose best-known member was the novelist Robert Louis Stevenson (1850–94). The lighthouse was first lit in 1862. The adjacent cliffs provide a good vantage point for viewing seabirds, whales, and porpoises. The lighthouse is just a few minutes northwest of Port of Ness along the B8014.

Shopping

At **Borgh Pottery** (⊠ Fivepenny House, Borve, on the road to Ness, ☎ 01851/850345) you can buy attractive hand-thrown studio pottery made on the premises, including lamps, vases, platters, mugs, dishes, and candleholders.

Arnol

21 mi southwest of Port of Ness, 16 mi northwest of Stornoway.

In the small community of Arnol, look for signs off the A858 for the 38 **Arnol Black House,** a well-preserved example of an increasingly rare type of traditional Hebridean home. Once common throughout the islands (as recently as 50 years ago), these dwellings were built without mortar and thatched on a timber framework without eaves. Other characteristic features include an open central peat hearth and the absence

ATLANTIC OCEAN

Isle of Lewis
and Harris

Butt of Lewis
Lighthouse **37**

Butt of
Lewis

Port of
Ness

A857

Tolsta

Arnol Black
House

Barvas

38

Arnol

39 Shawbost School
Museum

Shawbost

Garenin

40 Dun
Carloway

East Loch Roag
Loch
Roag

Valtos

Callanish

Brenish

41 Calanais
Standing
Stones

MORSGAIL
FOREST

L E W I S

A859

Stornoway

36 Stornoway

Tiumpan
Head

B895

Eye
Peninsula

TO
ULLAPOOL

Amhuinnsuidhe

FOREST OF
HARRIS

Seaforth
Island

Amhuinnsuidhe
Castle **44**

B887

42 Rhenigidale

Traigh Luskentyre

45 Tarbert

Loch
Seaforth

Luskentyre

43 Tarbert

H A R R I S

A859

Northton
Leverburgh

Sound of Harris

46 St. Clement's
Church

Rodel

North Uist

Newtonferry
(Port nan Long)
47

Balranald
Nature Reserve
50

Trinity
Temple

48

49

Bayhead

A865

A867 Lochmaddy

Barpa Langass
Chambered Cairn

Clachan-a-Luib

Grimsay

A865

Reuval Hill

51

Benbecula

Our Lady
of the Isles

Loch Druidibeg
National **52**
Nature Reserve

A865

Sandwick

Ormaclete Castle

53 Howmore

Flora Macdonald's
birthplace

Kildonan

54

South Uist

Lochboisdale

Sea of
Hebrides

Uig

Trotternish

Isle of
Skye

The Minch

Eriskay

Barra

Eoligarry

Cille Bharra **56**

Traigh Moor

55 Castlebay

Kisimul
Castle

Berneray

Barra Head

TO
OBAN

N

KEY

Ferry Lines

0 ——— 10 miles
0 ——— 15 km

of a chimney—hence the sooty atmosphere and the designation "black." On display inside are many of the house's original furnishings. To reach Arnol from Port of Ness, go back south on the A857 and pick up the A858 at Barvas. ⊠ *Arnol,* ☎ *0131/668–8800.* ☑ *£1.80.* ☉ *Apr.–Sept., Mon.–Sat. 9:30–6; Oct.–Mar., Mon.–Thurs. and Sat. 9:30–4.*

Shawbost

5 mi south of Arnol.

㊴   Shawbost is home of the **Shawbost School Museum.** This museum came to life as a result of the so-called Highland Village Competition in 1970, during which school pupils gathered artifacts and contributed to displays aimed at illustrating a past way of life in Lewis. ⊠ *Shawbost,* ☎ *01851/710213.* ☑ *Donation.* ☉ *Apr.–Nov., Mon.–Sat. 9–6.*

Carloway

8 mi south of Shawbost.

㊵   The scattered community of Carloway is dominated by **Dun Carloway,** one of the best-preserved Iron Age *brochs* (circular stone towers) in Scotland. The mysterious circular defensive tower of the Dun Carloway broch was built about 2,000 years ago, possibly as protection against seaborne raiders. The interpretative center explains more about the broch and its setting. ⊠ *Carloway,* ☎ *0131/668–8800.* ☑ *Free.* ☉ *At all times.*

Up a side road north from Carloway at **Garenin,** an old "black house" village is gradually being brought back to life.

Callanish

10 mi southeast of Carloway.

㊶   At Callanish (Calanais) are the **Calanais Standing Stones,** lines of megaliths rated second only to Stonehenge in England. Probably positioned in several stages between 3000 and 1500 BC, this grouping is made up of an avenue of 19 monoliths extending northward from a circle of 13 stones, with other rows leading south, east, and west. It's believed they may have been used for astronomical observations. The site is accessible at any time. The **visitor center** (☎ 01851/621422) has an exhibition on the stones, a shop, and a tearoom. The restored black house next to the gate leading to the stones houses the **Callanish Stones Tearoom** (☎ 01851/621373), a more interesting atmosphere in which to take refreshment or browse among the crafts on display.

Rhenigidale

㊷   *36 mi south of Callanish, 33 mi south of Stornoway.*

Considered to be the most isolated inhabited village in Harris, Rhenigidale was for a long time accessible only by sea or via a rough hill path. A road completed in the early 1990s offers fine views high above Loch Seaforth, and now links the village with the rest of Scotland.

Tarbert

㊸   *11 mi south of Rhenigidale.*

Tarbert is the main port of Harris, with one or two shops and accommodations. About 10 mi northwest of Tarbert on the B887 stands

㊹   **Amhuinnsuidhe Castle** (the name is almost impossible to pronounce— try avun-*shooee*), a turreted structure built in the 1860s by the earls of Dunmore as a base for fishing and hunting in the North Harris deer forest.

45 **Traigh Luskentyre,** roughly 5 mi southwest of Tarbert, is a spectacular example of Harris's tidy selection of beaches—2 mi of yellow sands adjacent to **Traigh Seilebost** beach, with superb views northward to the hills of the Forest of Harris.

Lodging

££–£££ **Ardvourlie Castle.** A former Victorian hunting lodge, Ardvourlie is
★ set in splendid isolation amid the dramatic mountain scenery of Harris, an ideal habitat for hill walking. The decor is bold, idiosyncratic, and entirely in keeping with the High Victorian atmosphere of the castle. The country-house hospitality is perpetuated by the well-stocked library and roaring fires. The cooking (for resident guests only) is along traditional lines and is of a high standard, favoring fresh local produce and, often, wild game. ⊠ *Isle of Harris, 15 mi north of Tarbert, signed off the A859, HS3 3AB,* ☎ *01859/502307,* FAX *01859/502348. 4 rooms, 3 with bath, 1 with shower. Restaurant, library. No credit cards.*

Northton

16 mi south of Tarbert

This little community has two attractions: **The McGillivray Centre** (☎ 01859/502011 for details) focuses on the life and work of William McGillivray, a noted naturalist with strong links to Harris. **Co Leis Thu?** (⊠ The Old Schoolhouse, Northton HS3 3JA, ☎ FAX 01859/520258) is a family history resource center offering a genealogical research service, publications, and exhibitions.

Rodel

20 mi south of Tarbert.

At the southernmost point of Harris is the community of Rodel. Here
46 you'll find **St. Clement's Church,** a cruciform church standing on a hillock. It was built around 1500 and contains the magnificently sculptured tomb (1528) of the church's builder, Alasdair Crotach, MacLeod chief of Dunvegan Castle. An arched recess contains sculpted panels showing, among other scenes, a galley in full sail, a hunting scene with deer, and St. Michael and Satan weighing souls. There are also other effigies and carvings within this building, the most impressive pre-Reformation church in the Outer Hebrides.

North Uist

8 mi south of Rodel via ferry from Leverburgh, Harris.

47 At **Newtonferry (Port nan Long),** by Otternish and the ferry pier for the Leverburgh (Harris) ferry service, stand the remains of what was reputed to be the last inhabited broch in North Uist, **Dun an Sticar.** This defensive tower, reached by a causeway over the loch, was home to Hugh Macdonald, a descendant of MacDonald of Sleat, until 1602.

48 The ruins of **Trinity Temple (Teampull na Trionaid),** a medieval college and monastery said to have been founded in the 13th century by Beathag, daughter of Somerled, the progenitor of the Clan Donald, can be seen 8 mi southwest of Lochmaddy, off the A865. ☜ *Free.*

49 The **Barpa Langass Chambered Cairn,** dating from the third millennium BC, is the only chambered cairn in the Western Isles known to have retained its inner chamber fully intact. It sits very close to the A867 on the stretch between Lochmaddy and Clachan.

㊿ The **Balranald Nature Reserve,** administered by the Royal Society for the Protection of Birds (RSPB), is home to large numbers of waders and seabirds, including red-necked phalarope, living in a varied habitat of loch, marsh, *machair* (grasslands just behind the beach), and sandy and rocky shore. The reserve can be viewed anytime (guided walks by an RSPB warden April–September), but visitors are asked to keep to the paths during breeding season (March to July) so as not to disturb the birds. It is on the western side of North Uist, about 3 mi northwest of Bayhead, which you can reach via A865. ✉ *Visitor Centre at Goular,* ☎ *01463/715000 or 0131/557–3136.* 🎫 *Free.* ☉ *Daily.*

Outdoor Activities and Sports
Uist Outdoor Centre (✉ Lochmaddy, North Uist, ☎ 01876/500480) offers a wide range of activities, from rock climbing to diving, from walking to offshore island trips.

South Uist

34 mi south of Newtonferry via Grimsay, Benbecula, and three causeways.

You can travel the length of South Uist along route A865, making short treks off this main road on your way to Lochboisdale on the southeastern coast of the island. At Lochboisdale you can get ferries to Barra, the southernmost principal island of the Outer Hebrides, or to Oban on the mainland.

㉑ About 5 mi south of the causeway from Benbecula, atop Reuval Hill, stands the 125-ft-high statue of the Madonna and Child known as **Our Lady of the Isles.** The work of sculptor Hew Lorimer, the statue was erected in 1957 by the local Catholic community. A few miles south **㉒** of Reuval Hill, to the west of A865, you will come to the **Loch Druidibeg National Nature Reserve.** One of only two remaining British native—nonmigrating—populations of greylag geese make their home here in a fresh and brackish loch environment. (Stop at the warden's office for full information about access.)

A few miles south of Howmore, just west of A865, stand the ruins of **㉓** **Ormaclete Castle,** built in 1708 for the chief of the Clan Ranald, but accidentally destroyed by fire in 1715 on the eve of the Battle of Sheriffmuir, during which the chief was killed. **Kildonan Museum and Heritage Centre** (✉ Kildonan, ☎ 01878/710343) focuses on local history, archaeology, and culture and has a craft shop and tearoom. At Gearraidh Bhailteas (just west of A865 near Milton), you can see the ruins **㉔** of **Flora Macdonald's birthplace.** South Uist's most famous daughter, Flora, helped the Young Pretender Prince Charles Edward Stuart avoid capture and was feted as a heroine afterward.

Shopping
Hebridean Jewelry (✉ Garrieganichy, Lochdar, ☎ 01870/610288) makes decorative jewelry and framed pictures; the owners also run a crafts shop.

Barra

1 hr 50 mins by ferry from Lochboisdale.

Barra is an island with a rocky east coast and a west coast of sandy **㉕** beaches. **Kisimul Castle,** the largest ancient monument in the Western Isles, is on an islet in Castlebay, Barra's principal harbor. Kisimul was the stronghold of the Macneils of Barra, noted for their lawlessness and piracy. The main tower dates from about AD 1120. A restoration that was completed in 1970 was started by the 45th clan chief, an American architect. The present (46th) chief is a lawyer in Chicago. *Contact tourist information center for opening times and admission prices.*

Craigston Museum, in a thatched cottage at Baile ne Creige (Craigston), displays artifacts of local crofting life. (It's open only during the main summer season.) At Eolaigearraidh (Eoligarry), the departure point for the passenger ferry to South Uist, you can view **Cille Bharra,** the ruins of the church dedicated to the saint who gave his name to the island. The restored **Chapel of St. Mary** stands near part of a medieval monastery and cemetery.

Barra's airport is at the north end of the island on a simple stretch of sand known as **Traigh Moor** (the Cockle Strand)—which is washed twice daily by the tides. The departure and arrival times for the daily flights to and from Glasgow, Benbecula, and Stornoway are scheduled to coincide with low tide.

Outdoor Activities and Sports
Hire a cycle from **MacDougall Cycles** (✉ 29 St. Brendan Rd., Castlebay, ☎ 01871/810284).

THE NORTHERN HIGHLANDS A TO Z

Arriving and Departing

By Bus
Scottish Citylink (☎ 0990/505050) and **National Express** (☎ 0990/808080) run buses from England to Inverness, Ullapool, Thurso, Scrabster, and Wick. There are also coach connections between the ferry ports of Tarbert and Stornoway; consult the local tourist information center for details.

By Car and Ferry
The fastest route to this area is the A9 to the gateway town of Inverness. The ferry services run by **Caledonian MacBrayne,** called CalMac, link the Outer Hebrides (☞ Getting Around by Car and Ferry, *below*): ferries run from Ullapool to Stornoway (☎ 01854/612358), from Oban to Castlebay and Lochboisdale (☎ 01631/566688), and from Uig on the Isle of Skye to Tarbert and Lochmaddy (☎ 01470/542219). Causeways link North Uist, Benbecula, and South Uist.

By Plane
The main airports for the Northern Highlands are **Inverness** and **Wick** (both on the mainland). There is direct air service from Edinburgh and Glasgow to Inverness and from Edinburgh to Wick. Contact **British Airways** (☎ 0345/222111). **easyJet** (☎ 0990/292929) flies daily from London Luton to Inverness. **KLM U.K.** (☎ 0345/666777) operates a service from London Stanstead to Inverness. **Gill Air** (☎ 0191/214–6666) operates the Aberdeen–Wick service (weekdays). There are island flight connections to Stornoway (Lewis), and Barra and Benbecula in the Outer Hebrides; contact British Airways for details.

By Train
Main railway stations in the area include Oban (for Barra and the Uists) and Kyle of Lochalsh (for Skye) on the west coast or Inverness (for points north to Thurso and Wick). There is direct service from London to Inverness and connecting service from Edinburgh and Glasgow. For information contact the **National Train Enquiry Line** (☎ 0345/484950).

Getting Around

It is in the Highlands and Islands that the **Freedom of Scotland Travelpass** really becomes useful, saving you money on ferries, trains, and some buses (☞ The Gold Guide).

By Bus

Highland Country Buses (mainland and Skye, ☎ 01463/233371) provides bus service in the Highlands area. On the Outer Hebrides a number of small operators run regular routes to most towns and villages. The **post-bus** service—which also delivers mail—becomes increasingly important in remote areas; it supplements the regular bus service, which runs only a few times per week because of the small population in the region. A full timetable of services for the Northern Highlands (and the rest of Scotland) is available from the **Royal Mail** (⊠ 7 Strothers La., Inverness, IV1 1AA, ☎ 01463/256273).

By Car and Ferry

Note that in this sparsely populated area, distances between gas stations can be considerable. Although getting around is easy, even on single-lane roads, the choice of routes is restricted by the rugged terrain. Because of the infrequent bus services and sparse railway stations, a car is definitely the best way to explore this region.

The **Island Hopscotch** planned route ticket and the **Island Rover** pass, both offered by CalMac, give considerable reductions on interisland ferry fares; for details, contact **Caledonian MacBrayne Ltd.** (⊠ The Ferry Terminal, Gourock, PA19 1QP, ☎ 01475/650100).

An important caveat for visitors driving in this area: there are still some single-lane roads in this part of Scotland. These twisting, winding thoroughfares demand a degree of driving dexterity. Local rules of the road require that when two cars meet, whichever driver reaches a passing place first must stop in it or opposite it and allow the oncoming car to continue. Small cars tend to yield to large commercial vehicles. Never park in passing places, and remember that these sections of the road can also allow traffic behind you to pass; don't hold up a vehicle trying to pass you—tempers can flare over such discourtesies.

By Plane

British Regional Airways/Loganair (☎ 0345/22211) operates flights between the islands of Barra, Benbecula, and Stornoway in the Outer Hebrides (daily in high season; weekdays off-season).

By Train

Stations on the northern lines (Inverness to Thurso/Wick and Inverness to Kyle of Lochalsh) include Beauly, Muir of Ord, and Dingwall; on the Thurso/Wick line, Alness, Invergordon, Fearn, Tain, Ardgay, Culrain, Invershin, Lairg, Rogart, Golspie, Brora, Helmsdale, Kildonan, Kinbrace, Forsinard, Altnabreac, Scotscalder, and Georgemas Junction; and on the Kyle line, Garve, Lochluichart, Achanalt, Achnasheen, Achnashellach, Strathcarron, Attadale, Strome Ferry, Duncraig, Plockton, and Duirinish.

Contacts and Resources

Car Rentals

Europcar Ltd. (⊠ The Highlander Service Station, Millburn Rd., Inverness, ☎ 01463/235337). **Hertz** (⊠ Dalcross Airport, Inverness, ☎ 01667/462652).

Emergencies

For **police, fire, or ambulance,** dial ☎ 999 from any telephone. No coins are needed for emergency calls from public telephone booths.

Guided Tours

ORIENTATION

From Inverness, the following companies offer coach tours during the summer season: **Macdonald's Tours** (✉ 65 Fairfield Rd., ☎ 01463/240673). **Spa Coach Tours** (✉ Strathpeffer, ☎ 01997/421311).

SPECIAL-INTEREST

From Inverness, **Highland Insight Tours and Travel** (☎ 01463/831403) offers personalized touring holidays and full-day or half-day tours that cater to any interest. **James Johnson** (☎ FAX 01463/790179) will drive you anywhere, but he has a particularly good knowledge of the Highlands and islands, including the Outer Hebrides.

A number of small firms run boat cruises along the spectacular west-coast seaboard. On Skye there is also a broad selection of mountain guides. Contact the local tourist information center for details about local operators (☞ Visitor Information, *below*). **Dunvegan Sea Cruises**, at Dunvegan Castle (☎ 01470/521206) runs a boat trip to the nearby seal colony (£3.80) and also a spectacular trip up Loch Dunvegan to see seals and many different kinds of birds (£8). Wildlife cruises are operated from John o'Groats harbor by **John o'Groats Ferries** (☎ 01955/611353, ☉ daily from mid-June to August). The trip takes passengers into the Pentland Firth, to Duncansby Stacks and the island of Stroma, and it offers spectacular cliff scenery and bird life.

Cycle Caithness (✉ Thorval, 7 Campbell St., Thurso, KW14 7HA, ☎ 01847/896124 or 01847/894223) organizes bicycling and accommodation packages in ideal flat biking territory. **Raasay Outdoor Centre** (✉ Raasay House, Isle of Raasay reached by ferry from Sconser, Isle of Skye, ☎ 01478/660266) organizes a variety of residential or day courses in kayaking, sailing, windsurfing, climbing, abseiling (rappelling), archery, walking, and navigation skills.

Late-Night Pharmacies

These are not found in rural areas. Pharmacies in the main towns—Thurso, Wick, Stornoway—keep normal shop hours. In an emergency the police will provide assistance in locating a pharmacist. General practitioners may also dispense medicines.

Visitor Information

Dornoch (✉ The Square, Dornoch, IV25 3SD, ☎ 01862/810400). **Gairloch** (✉ Achtercairn, Gairloch, IV22 2DN, ☎ 01445/712130). **North Kessock** (✉ North Kessock, IV1 1XB, ☎ 01463/731505). **Portree,** Isle of Skye (✉ Bayfield Hous Bayfield Rd., Portree, Isle of Skye, IV51 9EL, ☎ 01478/612137). **Stornoway,** Isle of Lewis and Harris (✉ 26 Cromwell St., ☎ 01851/703088). **Wick** (✉ Whitechapel Rd., off High St., Wick, KW1 4EA, ☎ 01955/602596).

Seasonal tourist information centers can be found at Bettyhill, Broadford (Skye), Castlebay (Barra, Outer Hebrides), Durness, Helmsdale, John o'Groats, Kyle of Lochalsh, Lairg, Lochboisdale (South Uist, Outer Hebrides), Lochcarron, Lochinver, Lochmaddy (North Uist, Outer Hebrides), Shiel Bridge, Strathpeffer, Thurso, Uig, and Ullapool.

12 The Northern Isles

Orkney, Shetland

The wind and frequent mists, the exposure, and the proximity to the sea make the northern islands as much a challenge as an adventure. Orkney— a cluster of almost 70 islands, 20 inhabited—has the greatest concentration of prehistoric sites in Scotland. Shetland's islands, with their epic cliffs and dramatic "geos," or fissure-like sea inlets, and barren moors in the interior, do not feel "British" at all.

BOTH ORKNEY AND SHETLAND possess a Scandinavian heritage that gives their collective 200 islets an ambience different from any other region of Scotland. For mainland Scots, visiting this archipelago is a little like traveling abroad without having to worry about a different language or currency. Bound by the sea, both are essentially bleak and austere, with awe-inspiring seascapes and genuinely warm, friendly people. Neither Orkney nor Shetland has yet been overrun by tourism.

By Gilbert Summers

The differences between Orkney and Shetland can be summed up with the description that an Orcadian is a farmer with a boat, and a Shetlander is a fisherman with a croft (small farm). Orkney is the greener archipelago, and is rich with artifacts—stone circles, burial chambers, ancient settlements, and fortifications that emphasize many centuries of continuous settlement. Shetland, of ocean views and sparse landscapes, is endowed with a more remote atmosphere than its neighbor Orkney. However, don't let Shetland's desolate countryside fool you— it has a wealth of historic interest and is far from being a backwater island. Oil money from the mineral resources around its shores and the fact that it has been a crossroads in the northern seas for centuries have helped make it a cosmopolitan place.

Pleasures and Pastimes

Boating

There are good anchorages among Orkney's many islands. Contact the tourist information centers for details. There are also sailboats available on Shetland. Details may be obtained from the Lerwick Boating Club, which can be contacted through the tourist information center.

Dining

Seafood is first class and so is Orkney's malt whisky. At its best, dining in the islands is as good as anywhere else, but vegetable gardeners do face some extra challenges from the northerly latitude. Look out for Orkney *bere bannocks* (bere is a kind of primitive barley, bannock a kind of oatcake), Orkney-brewed ales, and local cheeses.

CATEGORY	COST*
££££	over £25
£££	£15–£25
££	£10–£15
£	under £10

per person for a three-course meal, including VAT and excluding drinks and service

Diving

Orkney, especially the former wartime anchorage of Scapa Flow, claims to have the best dive sites in Britain. Part of the attraction is the remains of the German navy, scuttled here in 1919. Many boat-rental companies offer diving charters (contact the tourist information centers). Shetland also has exceptional underwater visibility, perfect for viewing the treasure wrecks and abundant marine life.

Festivals

Shetland has quite a strong cultural identity, thanks to its Scandinavian heritage. There are, for instance, books of local dialect verse, a whole folklore contained in knitting patterns, and a strong tradition of fiddle playing. In the middle of the long winter, at the end of January, the Shetlanders celebrate their Viking culture with the Up-Helly-Aa festival, which involves much merrymaking, dressing up, and the burning of a replica of a Viking long ship. The Shetland Folk Festival, held in April, and October's Shetland Accordion and Fiddle Festival both attract large numbers of visitors. Orkney's St. Magnus Festival, a musical celebration, is based in Kirkwall and usually held the third week in June. Orkney also has an annual folk festival at the end of May.

Fishing

Sea angling is such a popular sport in Orkney that the local tourist board advises fishermen to book early. There are at least seven companies offering sea-angling boat rentals, with fishing rods available in most cases. Loch angling in Orkney is also popular; Loch of Harray and Loch of Stenness are the best-known spots. Contact the Orkney Tourist Board for information. Shetland, also renowned for sea angling, holds several competitions throughout the year. Contact the Shetland Association of Sea Anglers via the tourist information center.

Lodging

The northern isles' exoticism does not translate as "primitive": at its best, accommodations are about as good as anywhere else in Scotland.

CATEGORY	COST*
££££	over £110
£££	£80–£110
££	£45–£80
£	under £45

*All prices are for a standard double room, including service, breakfast, and VAT.

Orkney Discount Ticket

Visitors to Orkney should take advantage of a joint entry ticket to all of Historic Scotland's Orkney sights. The ticket, available at all of the sites themselves, costs only £9 and is valid until all of the sites have been visited. There is a generic telephone and fax number (☞ individual sites, *below*), which is operated daily 9–5, for all information relating to Orkney's Historic Scotland sites, so be sure to be specific when calling for information.

Shopping

Neither Orkney nor Shetland is visited expressly for shopping. However, both have attracted high-quality crafts workers, and in the United Kingdom and beyond, Shetland is almost synonymous with distinctive knitwear.

Exploring the Northern Isles

Both island groupings need at least a couple of days if you are to do more than just scratch the surface of their characters. The extra effort required to get there means that Shetland certainly deserves four or five days: the Northern Isles in any case generate their own "laid-back" approach to life, and once there you will not want to hurry around.

Numbers in the text correspond to numbers in the margin and on the Shetland Islands and the Orkney Islands maps.

Great Itineraries

Getting around is quite straightforward—the roads are good on both Shetland and Orkney. A fast and frequent interisland passenger and car ferry service makes island-hopping perfectly practical. Only at peak season are reservations advisable.

IF YOU HAVE 1 DAY

Launch yourself from Inverness (☞ Chapter 10) on a day trip to Orkney—though it will be a long one—by bus and ferry, to see some of Orkney's top historic sites. Shetland is not practicable for such a short length of time.

IF YOU HAVE 4 DAYS

You could get a good flavor of Orkney and take in the main sights—St. Magnus Cathedral and Earl Patrick's Palace and the Bishop's Palace on 🏙 **Kirkwall** ⑳—then go out to **Skara Brae** ⑯, **Maes Howe** ⑮, and the **Ring of Brogar** ⑭. (You could probably get on to one of the other islands as well.) See a bit of Shetland in this length of time, provided you get a good night's sleep on the direct Orkney–Shetland ferry, leaving you a full day as soon as you arrive to take in the south of the island: **Shetland Croft House Museum** ④, **Jarlshof** ⑤, Sumburgh Head, **St. Ninian's Isle** ⑥, and so on. Staying overnight in 🏙 **Lerwick** ①, you could make a trip up to **Esha Ness** to get the flavor of the north of Mainland, leaving Lerwick itself and **Scalloway** ⑦ for the fourth day. In theory, in this length of time it is possible to get out to the very end of Scotland at Muckle Flugga, but Shetland is such an extraordinary place that it merits more time.

IF YOU HAVE 8 DAYS

This is enough time in the Northern Isles for you to see all the main sights on Orkney and then catch a midweek ferry to Shetland, with enough time to get to the far north of Shetland as well.

When to Tour the Northern Isles

Go in the early summer when the bird colonies are at their most spectacular and the long northern daylight hours give you plenty of sightseeing time.

AROUND SHETLAND

The Shetland coastline is an incredible 900 mi owing to all the indentations, and there isn't a point on the island farther than 3 mi from the sea. Settlements away from Lerwick, the primary town, are small and scattered—ask the friendly locals for directions.

Lerwick

❶ *14 hrs by ferry from Aberdeen.*

You would be remiss if you failed to explore some of Lerwick's nearby diversions before venturing beyond it. **Fort Charlotte** is a 17th-century Cromwellian stronghold, built to protect the Sound of Bressay. ☎ *0131/668–8800.* 🎟 *Free.* ☉ *Apr.–Sept., daily 9:30–6; Oct.–Mar., Mon.–Sat. 9:30–4, Sun. 2–4.*

The **Shetland Museum** in Lerwick gives an interesting account of the development of the town, with displays on archaeology, art and textiles, shipping, and folk life. ⊠ *Lower Hillhead,* ☎ *01595/695057.* 🎟 *Free.* ☉ *Mon., Wed., Fri. 10–7, Tues., Thurs., Sat. 10–5.*

❷ **Clickhimin Broch** (*broch* are circular stone monuments), on the site of what was originally an Iron-Age fortification, can be your introduction to the mysterious Pictish monuments, whose meaning is still largely obscure. South of the broch are vivid views of the cliffs at the south end of the island of Bressay, which shelters Lerwick harbor. ⊠ *1 mi south of Lerwick,* ☎ *0131/668–8800.* 🎟 *Free.* ☉ *Apr.–Sept., daily 9:30–6; Oct.–Mar., Mon.–Sat. 9:30–4, Sun. 2–4.*

Dining and Lodging

£££ ✕🏨 **Shetland Hotel.** Modern and well-appointed (a result of the oil boom in the area and the needs of high-flying oil executives), the Shetland is directly opposite the ferry terminal in Lerwick. The hotel is done

The Shetland Islands

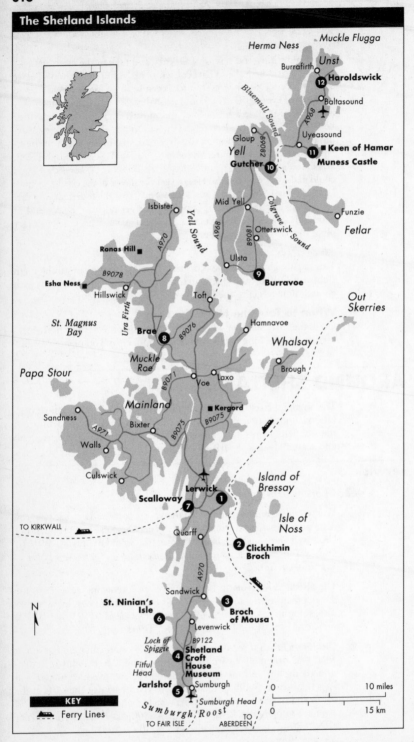

Muckle Flugga

Herma Ness

Unst

Burrafirth

12 **Haroldswick**

Baltasound

A968

Bluemull Sound

Uyeasound

Gloup

B9082

11 ■ Keen of Hamar

Yell

Gutcher

10

Muness Castle

Mid Yell

Funzie

Isbister

Otterswick

Fetlar

A970

B9081

Yell Sound

Ronas Hill ■

Ulsta

Colgrave Sound

9

B9078

Burravoe

Esha Ness ■

Hillswick

Toft

Out Skerries

St. Magnus Bay

Hamnavoe

Brae

8

B9076

Whalsay

Ura Firth

Muckle Roe

Brough

B9071

Voe

Laxo

Papa Stour

Mainland

■ **Kergord**

Sandness

Bixter

B9075

B9075

A971

Walls

Culswick

Island of Bressay

Lerwick

1

Scalloway

7

Isle of Noss

TO KIRKWALL

Quarff

2 **Clickhimin Broch**

A970

Sandwick

3

St. Ninian's Isle

6

Broch of Mousa

Levenwick

B9122

Loch of Spiggie

Shetland Croft House Museum

4

Fitful Head

Jarlshof

5

Sumburgh

Sumburgh Roost

Sumburgh Head

TO FAIR ISLE

TO ABERDEEN

KEY
⛴ Ferry Lines

N

0   10 miles

0   15 km

up in an attractive blend of peach, burgundy, and blue color schemes. The food is rich and filling, with sometimes wildly clashing flavors. One entrée consists of a folded filet of beef with Stilton cheese inside, coated in oatmeal and served with a rich red-currant sauce—enough of a meal to sink the Shetland ferry! ⊠ *Holmsgarth Rd., Lerwick, ZE1 0PW,* ☎ *01595/695515,* FAX *01595/695828. 64 rooms with bath. 2 restaurants, 2 bars. AE, DC, MC, V.*

£   🏠 **Old Manse.** The oldest inhabited building in Lerwick is now a friendly guest house on a quiet side street in town center. The house dates from 1685 and was built for Lerwick's first minister. Furnishings are traditional, in keeping with the pleasantly aged feel of the house. Dinners (for resident guests only) are in "good home-cooking" style, mostly fish, beef, and venison. ⊠ *9 Commercial St., Lerwick, ZE1 0AN,* ☎ *01595/696301. 4 rooms, 2 with shower. Restaurant. No credit cards.*

Outdoor Activities and Sports

Bicycles can be rented from **Eric Brown Cycles** (⊠ Grantfield Garage, North Rd., Lerwick, ☎ 01595/692709).

Shopping

There are many places for knitwear and woolen goods in Lerwick. **The Spider's Web** (⊠ 41 Commercial St., ☎ 01595/693299, ☉ June–Aug.) sells hand-spun and hand-knit goods in neutral earth tones, as well as pottery made in Shetland. **Anderson & Co.** (⊠ The Shetland Warehouse, 60–62 Commercial St., ☎ 01595/693714) sells handmade knitwear and has a small stock of machine-made items and tourist souvenirs. **Millers** (⊠ 116 Commercial St., Lerwick, ☎ 01595/692517) stocks machine-made knitwear in Shetland and Argyle patterns, Aran sweaters, and capes, rugs, and scarves made elsewhere in Scotland.

J. G. Rae Limited (⊠ 92 Commercial St., ☎ 01595/693686) stocks Shetland Silvercraft and gold and silver jewelry with Norse and Celtic motifs. **Hjaltasteyn** (⊠ 161 Commercial St., Lerwick, ☎ 01595/696224) handcrafts gems and jewelry in gold, silver, and enamels. **Shetland Jewelry** (⊠ Sound Side, Weisdale, ☎ 01595/830275) makes jewelry, cutlery, and other small goods, which are also stocked at J. G. Rae (☞ *above*).

Sandwick

14 mi south of Lerwick via A970.

★ ❸   The community of Sandwick is the departure point for boat trips to see the **Broch of Mousa,** the most fully extant of all the broch towers remaining in Scotland. ⊠ *Mousa,* ☎ *0131/668–8800.* 🎫 *Broch free, boat trip £5.* ☉ *Apr.–Sept., daily 9:30–6; Oct.–Mar., Mon.–Sat. 9:30–4, Sun. 2–4. Boat for hire operated by Mr. Jamieson (☎* FAX *01950/431367); times subject to his schedule.*

Shopping

Lawrence J. Smith Ltd. (⊠ Hoswick, ☎ 01950/431215) sells Shetland knitwear—both handmade and machine-made—at all prices and for all ages, in a wide range of colors.

Voe

7 mi south of Sandwick.

★ ❹   The scattered village of Voe is the home of the **Shetland Croft House Museum.** This traditionally constructed 19th-century thatched house contains a broad range of artifacts that depict the former way of life of the rural Shetlander, which the museum attendant will be delighted to discuss with you. ✉ *Voe, Dunrossness, unclassified road east of A970,* ☎ *01595/695057.* 🎟 *£1.50.* ☉ *May–Sept., daily 10–1 and 2–5.*

Sumburgh

4 mi south of Voe.

★ ❺ The big attraction at Sumburgh is **Jarlshof,** a centuries-old site that includes the extensive remains of Norse buildings, as well as prehistoric wheelhouses and earth houses representing thousands of years of continuous settlement. The site also includes a 17th-century laird's (landowner's) house built on the ruins of a medieval farmstead. ✉ *Sumburgh Head,* ☎ *0131/668–8800.* 🎟 *£2.30.* ☉ *Apr.–Sept., daily 9:30–6.*

St. Ninian's Isle

❻ *8 mi north of Sumburgh via A970 and B9122 (turn left at Skelberry).*

It was on St. Ninian's Isle—actually a tombolo, a spit of sand that moors an island to the mainland—that archaeologists in the 1950s uncovered the St. Ninian treasure, a collection of 28 silver objects from the 8th century. This Celtic silver is now in the Royal Museum of Scotland in Edinburgh (☞ Chapter 3), though good replicas are on view in the Shetland Museum in Lerwick (☞ *above*).

Scalloway

❼ *21 mi north of St. Ninian's Isle, 6 mi west of Lerwick.*

On the western coast of Mainland Island is Scalloway. Look for the information board just off the main road (A970), which overlooks the settlement and its castle. **Scalloway Castle** was built in 1600 by earl Patrick, who coerced the locals to build it for him. He was executed in 1615 for his cruelty and misdeeds, and the castle was never used again. ✉ *Scalloway,* ☎ *0131/668–8800.* 🎟 *Free.* ☉ *Apr.–Sept., daily 9:30–6; Oct.–Mar., Mon.–Sat. 9:30–4, Sun. 2–4.*

Shopping

The **Shetland Woollen Company** (✉ Castle St., ☎ 01595/880243) is one of many purveyors with a selection of Shetland knitwear.

OFF THE BEATEN PATH	Take the B9075 east off the A970, at the head of a narrow sea inlet. This leads into the unexpectedly green valley of Kergord, noted for its woodland. This would be unremarkable farther south, but here it is a novelty.

Brae

❽ *24 mi north of Scalloway.*

Brae is the home of the Busta House Hotel (☞ Lodging, *below*), probably the best hotel on the island. Beyond Brae the main road meanders past **Mavis Grind,** a strip of land so narrow you can throw a stone—if you are strong—from the Atlantic, in one inlet, to the North Sea, in another.

Dining and Lodging

£–£££   ✕🛏 **Busta House.** Busta House dates in part from the 16th century and ★   is surrounded by terraced grounds. Bedrooms are well furnished in traditional style—floral chintzes and antique furniture—and the 16th-century Long Room is a delightful place to sample the hotel's selection of malt whiskies while sitting beside a peat fire. On the Taste of Scotland menu, Shetland salmon and lamb are usually available. ✉ *Brae, Shetland, ZE2 9QN,* ☎ *01806/522506,* 📠 *01806/522588. 20 rooms*

*with bath or shower. Restaurant, bar. AE, DC, MC, V. Closed 2 wks
Christmas–New Year's.*

OFF THE
BEATEN PATH

ESHA NESS AND RONAS HILL – For outstanding views of the rugged, forbidding cliffs around Esha Ness, drive north, then turn left onto the
B9078. On the way, look for the sandstone stacks in the bay that resem-
ble a Viking galley under sail. After viewing the cliffs at Esha Ness, return to join the A970 at Hillswick and follow an ancillary road from the
head of Ura Firth. This road provides vistas of rounded, bare Ronas Hill,
the highest hill in Shetland. Though only 1,468 ft high, it is noted for its
arctic-alpine flora growing at low levels.

Yell

*11 mi northeast of Brae, 31 mi north of Lerwick via A970, A968, or
B9076, and ferry from Toft.*

After crossing to Ulsta, on the island of Yell, take the B9081 east to
⑨ Burravoe. There's not a lot to say about the blanket bog that cloaks
two-thirds of Yell, but the **Old Haa** (hall) of Burravoe, the oldest building on the island, is architecturally interesting—it was formerly a merchant's house—and has a museum upstairs. One of the displays tells
the story of the wrecking of the German sail ship, the *Bohus*, in 1924.
A copy of the ship's figurehead is displayed outside the Old Haa itself;
the original is at the shipwreck site overlooking Otterswick, along the
coast on the B9081. The Old Haa serves light meals with home-baked
buns, cakes, and other goodies; has a crafts shop; and acts as a kind
of unofficial information point. The staff is friendly and gives advice
to sightseers. ☎ 01957/722339 or 01957/702127. � *Free.* ☉ *Late Apr.–
Sept., Tues.–Thurs. and Sat. 10–4, Sun. 2–5.*

⑩ Travel to the main A968 at Mid Yell to reach **Gutcher,** the ferry pier.
If time permits, turn left on the B9082 for a pleasant drive to **Gloup,**
a cluster of houses at the end of the road. Behind a croft, in a field overlooking a long *voe* (sea inlet) is the **Gloup Fisherman's Memorial,**
which recalls an 1881 tragedy involving all the crews of 10 six-oared
local fishing boats.

Unst

49 mi north of Lerwick via ferry from Gutcher.

The ferry crosses the Bluemull Sound to Unst, the northernmost inhabited
island in Scotland. Because of its strategic location—it protrudes well
into the northern seas—Unst is inhabited by the military.

⑪ Muness Castle, Scotland's northernmost castle, was built just before
the end of the 16th century. If lucky, you'll be pleasantly surprised to
find some photogenic Shetland ponies in the field nearby. ⌗ *follow
the A968 then turn right on the B9084,* ☎ 0131/668–8800. ⌗ *Free;
ask for the key keeper.* ☉ *Apr.–Sept., daily 9:30–6; Oct.–Mar., Mon.–
Sat. 9:30–4, Sun. 2–4.*

Just to the north of Muness Castle is the **Keen of Hamar** national na-
⑫ ture reserve. In the far north of Unst is **Haroldswick,** with its post office and heritage center. If you take the B9086 at Haroldswick you will
go around the head of **Burrafirth** (a sea inlet) and eventually reach a
parking lot. From there a path goes north across moorland and up a
gentle hill. Bleak and open, this is bird-watchers' territory and is replete with diving skuas—single-minded sky pirates that attack anything
that strays near their nest sites. Gannets, puffins, and other seabirds
nest in spectacular profusion by the cliffs on the left as you look out
to sea. You should keep to the path; this is a national nature reserve.

At the top of the hills, amid the windy grasslands, you can see **Muckle Flugga** to the north, a series of tilting offshore rocks; the largest of these sea-battered protrusions has a lighthouse. This is the northernmost point in Scotland; the sea rolls out on three sides; no land lies beyond.

Lodging

£ ⊞ **Bremner's Guest House.** Comfortable and relaxed, this modern house boasts stunning sunset views that rival those anywhere in the United Kingdom. The rooms are clean and functional, much like the rest of this family-run bed-and-breakfast inn. ⊠ *Barns, Newgord, Westing, Uyeasound, Unst, ZE2 9DW,* ☎ *01957/755249. 2 rooms without bath. AE, MC, V.*

AROUND ORKNEY

Most of Orkney's many prehistoric sites are open to view, offering an insight into the life of bygone eras. At Maes Howe, for example, visitors will discover that graffiti is not solely an expression of today's youths: the Vikings left their marks here in the 12th century.

Stromness

⓭ *1 hr, 45 mins north of Thurso via ferry from Scrabster.*

You will find two points of interest in Stromness as soon as you arrive. The **Pier Arts Centre** is a former Stromness merchant's house (circa 1800) and has adjoining buildings that now serve as a gallery with a permanent collection of 20th-century paintings and sculptures. ⊠ *Victoria St.,* ☎ *01856/850209.* ▣ *Free.* ☉ *May–Aug., Tues.–Sat. 10:30–5; Sept–Apr., Tues.–Sat. 10:30–12:30 and 1:30–5.*

The **Stromness Museum** has a varied collection of natural-history material on view, including preserved birds and Orkney shells. The museum also displays exhibits on fishing, shipping, whaling, and the Hudson Bay Company, as well as ship models and a feature on the German fleet that was scuttled on Scapa Flow. ⊠ *Alfred St.,* ☎ *01856/850025.* ▣ *£2.* ☉ *May–Sept., daily 10–5; Oct.–Apr., Mon.–Sat. 10:30–12:30 and 1:30–5.*

★ ⓮ The **Ring of Brogar** is a magnificent circle of 36 stones (originally 60) surrounded by a deep ditch. When the fog descends over the stones—a frequent occurrence—their looming shapes seem to come alive. Though their original use is uncertain, it is not hard to imagine strange rituals taking place here in the misty past. The stones stand between Loch of Harray and Loch of Stenness, 5 mi northeast of Stromness. ☎ *0131/668–8800.* ▣ *Free.* ☉ *At all times.*

★ ⓯ The huge burial mound of **Maes Howe** (circa 2500 BC) measures 115 ft in diameter and contains an enormous burial chamber. It was raided by Vikings in the 12th century, and Norse crusaders sheltered here, leaving a rich collection of runic inscriptions. Maes Howe is 1 mi farther on the A965 from the Ring of Brogar. ☎ *0131/668–8800.* ▣ *£2.30; joint Historic Scotland's Orkney entry ticket, £9.* ☉ *Apr.–Sept., daily 9:30–6; Oct.–Mar., Mon.–Wed. and Sat. 9:30–4, Thurs. 9:30–1, Sun. 2–4.*

★ ⓰ At the Neolithic village of **Skara Brae** you will find houses, joined by covered passages, with stone beds, fireplaces, and cupboards that have survived since the village was first occupied around 3000 BC. The site was preserved in sand until it was uncovered in 1850, and it can be found 8 mi north of Stromness off the A967/B9056. ☎ *0131/668–8800.* ▣ *£4 (£3.20 in winter); joint Historic Scotland's Orkney entry ticket,*

The Orkney Islands

KEY

Ferry Lines

N

0 ____ 10 miles
0 ____ 15 km

ATLANTIC OCEAN

Seal Skerry
North Ronaldsay
Hollandstoun

Knap of Howar
Holland
Papa Westray

Pierowall
The North Sound

North Ronaldsay Firth

Northwall
Burness
Sanday
Kettletoft

Westray
Rapness
Calfsound
Braeswick

Westray Firth
Sanday Sound

Rousay
Brough Head
Wasbister
Eday
Whitehall

Earl's Palace
Brinyan
Backaland
Aith
Stronsay

Birsay **18**
Gurness Broch **19**
Dounby

Marwick Head Nature Reserve
17
Marwick Bay
16
Skara Brae
Stronsay Firth

Unstan Chambered Tomb
Balfour
Shapinsay

Mainland
Finstown **21**

Ring of Brogar
15
14
Maes Howe
20
Kirkwall
TO SCALLOWAY

Stromness
13
A965
Skaill

A964
Orphir Church
22
Orphir
St. Mary's

Moness
Scapa Flow
Italian Chapel
23
Lambholm
Copinsay

Old Man of Hoy
Rackwick
Scapa Flow Visitor Centre
24
Lyness
St. Margaret's Hope

Hoy
South Ronaldsay

Burwick

Pentland Firth
Old Head

Pentland Skerries

Scrabster
Gills
John o' Groats
A836
Thurso

£9. ⊙ *Apr.–Sept., daily 9:30–6; Oct.–Mar., Mon.–Sat. 9:30–4, Sun. 2–4.*

🄬 The **Marwick Head Nature Reserve,** with its spectacular seabird cliffs, is tended by the Royal Society for the Protection of Birds. The **Kitchener Memorial,** which recalls the 1916 sinking of the cruiser HMS *Hampshire* with Lord Kitchener aboard, can also be seen in the reserve, on a cliff-top site. The reserve lies to the north of Skara Brae, up the B9056; access to the reserve is along a path north from Marwick Bay. ☎ *01856/791298.* ⚏ *Free.* ⊙ *At all times.*

Nightlife and the Arts
The Pier Arts Centre (✉ Victoria St., ☎ 01856/850209) focuses on artistic life in Stromness, with an eclectic display of paintings and sculptures and changing exhibitions, often by local artists.

Outdoor Activities and Sports
Bicycles can be rented from the **Baby Linen Shop** (✉ 54 Dundas St., Stromness, ☎ 01856/850255).

Birsay

12 mi north of Stromness, 25 mi northwest of Kirkwall.

🄭 At Birsay is **Earl's Palace,** the impressive remains of a 16th-century palace built by the earls of Orkney. ✉ *Birsay,* ☎ *0131/668–8800.* ⚏ *Free.* ⊙ *At all times.*

The **Brough of Birsay,** and the remains of a Romanesque church and a Norse settlement, stand close to Birsay on an island accessible only at low tide. To ensure you won't be swept away, check the tide tables before setting out. ✉ *Birsay,* ☎ *0131/668–8800.* ⚏ *Free.* ⊙ *Daily, subject to tides.*

🄮 The **Gurness Broch** is an Iron Age tower standing more than 10 ft high, surrounded by stone huts. It is off the A966, about 8 mi from Birsay along Orkney's northern coast. ✉ *Aikerness,* ☎ *0131/668–8800.* ⚏ *£2.30; joint Historic Scotland's Orkney entry ticket, £9.* ⊙ *Apr.–Sept., daily 9:30–6.*

Kirkwall

🄯 *16 mi east of Stromness.*

In bustling Kirkwall, the main town on Orkney, there are plenty of interesting things to see in the narrow, winding streets, extending from the harbor, which retain a strong medieval feel. **Earl Patrick's Palace,** built in 1607, is perhaps the best surviving example of Renaissance architecture in Scotland. ✉ *Kirkwall,* ☎ *0131/668–8800.* ⚏ *£1.50 (includes Bishop's Palace); joint Historic Scotland's Orkney entry ticket, £9.* ⊙ *Apr.–Sept., daily 9:30–6.*

The **Bishop's Palace** nearby dates from the 13th century, though its round tower was added in the 16th century. ✉ *Kirkwall,* ☎ *0131/668–8800.* ⚏ *£1.50 (includes Earl Patrick's Palace); joint Historic Scotland's Orkney entry ticket, £9.* ⊙ *Apr.–Sept., daily 9:30–6.*

★ Founded by Jarl Rognvald in 1137 and dedicated to his uncle St. Magnus, **St. Magnus Cathedral** in Kirkwall was built between 1137 and 1200; however, additional work was carried out during the following 300 years. The cathedral is still in use and contains some of the best examples of Norman architecture in Scotland. The ornamentation on some of the tombstones is particularly striking. ⊙ *Mon.–Sat. 9–1 and 2–5, Sun. for services and 2–6.*

The **Orkney Wireless Museum** in Kirkwall tells the story of wartime communications at Scapa Flow. Thousands of service men and women were stationed here and used the equipment displayed in the museum to protect the Home Fleet. The museum also contains many handsome 1930s wireless radios, and examples of the handicrafts produced by Italian prisoners-of-war. ⊠ *Kiln Corner, Junction Rd.,* ☎ *01856/ 874272.* ⊡ *£2.* ☉ *Apr.–Sept.; check with tourist information center for opening hrs.*

㉑ The **Unstan Chambered Tomb** is a 5,000-year-old cairn containing a chambered tomb. Pottery that has been found within the tomb is now known as Unstan ware. The tomb is midway between Kirkwall and Stromness, roughly 3½ mi from each. ☎ *0131/668–8800.* ⊡ *Free.* ☉ *Apr.–Sept., daily 9:30–6; Oct.–Mar., Mon.–Sat. 9:30–4, Sun. 2–4.*

㉒ The remains of the 12th-century **Orphir Church,** Scotland's only circular medieval church (12th century), lie near the A964, 8 mi southwest of Kirkwall. ☎ *0131/668–8800.* ⊡ *Free.* ☉ *At all times.*

Dining and Lodging

££ ✕⊞ **Foveran Hotel.** Surrounded by 34 acres of grounds just outside Kirkwall, and overlooking Scapa Flow, this warm hotel has an attractive light-wood, Scandinavian-style dining room and an open fire in its sitting room. The menu features Taste of Scotland, and the homemade soups, pâtés, and seafood have helped secure the restaurant's reputation as a very dependable place to eat. ⊠ *St. Ola, Kirkwall, KW15 1SF,* ☎ *01856/872389,* ℻ *01856/876430. 8 rooms with bath or shower. Restaurant, 2 lounges. MC, V. Closed Jan.*

£ ⊞ **Polrudden Guest House.** Quietly situated yet close to the town center and public parks, this modern guest house offers a high standard of lodging for the price. Multicolored matching curtains and quilt covers complement the cream-colored rooms and pine furnishings. ⊠ *Pickaquoy Rd., KW15 1UH,* ☎ *01856/874761,* ℻ *01856/870950. 7 rooms with shower. No credit cards.*

Nightlife and the Arts

Orkney's cultural highlight is the **St. Magnus Festival** (☎ 01856/ 872669 for details), a festival of music based in Kirkwall and usually held the third week in June. Orkney also has an annual folk festival at the end of May.

Outdoor Activities and Sports

Bicycles can be rented from **Orkney Two Wheels** (⊠ Tankerness La., Kirkwall, ☎ ℻ 01856/873097).

Shopping

Kirkwall is the main shopping hub. Do not miss **Ola Gorrie at the Longship** (⊠ 7–9 Broad St., ☎ 01856/873251), which crafts gold and silver jewelry with Celtic and Norse themes, including a delightful representation of a dragon, originally drawn on the wall of the burial chamber at Maes Howe. **Ortak Jewelry** (⊠ 10 Albert St., ☎ 01856/ 873536) stocks a potpourri of gifts: Celtic-theme jewelry, crystal, barometers, and many other craft items, many made locally. At **Judith Glue** (⊠ 25 Broad St., ☎ 01856/874225) you can purchase designer knitwear with traditional patterns, as well as Orkney-made crafts. Several outlets in Kirkwall stock items made by **Joker Jewelry** (⊠ East School, Holm, ☎ 01856/781336): eye-catching and whimsical clocks, brooches, and other ceramic giftware using animal motifs (especially puffins).

South Ronaldsay

18 mi south of Kirkwall.

★ ㉓ You can reach South Ronaldsay via the A961 causeway heading south from Kirkwall. The island's first distinctive point is the **Italian Chapel,** below the small village of St. Mary's. It was here, by the shore at Lambholm, in 1943 that Italian prisoners of war, using a Nissen hut, created a beautiful chapel from scrap metal and concrete. ⊠ *Lambholm.* 🎫 *Free.* 🕓 *At all times.*

Dining and Lodging

££–£££   ✕🛏 **Creel Restaurant.** This acclaimed seafront restaurant (reserva-
★ tions essential) with a cottage-style interior serves local seafood (including lobster), prepared personally by the owner/chef. The Creel also has some modest accommodations: three spacious rooms with sea views are offered in an inexpensive B&B style. ⊠ *Front Rd., St. Margaret's Hope,* ☎ *01856/831311. 3 rooms, 1 with bath, 2 with shower. Restaurant. MC, V. Closed Jan.*

Hoy

14 mi southwest of Kirkwall, 6 mi south of Stromness via ferry.

㉔ The **Scapa Flow Visitor Centre,** on Hoy, has a growing collection of material portraying the strategic role of the sheltered anchorage of Scapa Flow (said to be Britain's best diving site) in two world wars. ⊠ *Lyness, off the B9047,* ☎ *01856/791300.* 🎫 *£1.50.* 🕓 *May–Sept., weekdays 9–4, Sat. 9–3:30, Sun. 9–6; Oct.–Apr., weekdays 9–4.*

Tended by the Royal Society for the Protection of Birds, the **North Hoy Nature Reserve,** home to vast numbers of land birds and seabirds, comprises high ground and moor. Huge cliffs nearby include the Old Man of Hoy, a 450-ft sea stack. ☎ *01856/791298.* 🎫 *Free.* 🕓 *At all times.*

OFF THE   **KNAP OF HOWAR** – This is one of the oldest inhabited sites in Europe. Its
BEATEN PATH   two 5,000-year-old dwellings—which have yielded some unusual artifacts, such as whalebone mallets, a spatula, and stone grinders—can be found on the west side of Papa Westray, off the island of Westray. ⊠ *West of Holland House,* ☎ *0131/668–8800.* 🎫 *Free.* 🕓 *At all times.*

THE NORTHERN ISLES A TO Z

Arriving and Departing

By Bus

Aberdeen and Thurso have reliable bus links to and from all over Scotland: **Scottish Citylink** (☎ 0990/505050) and **National Express**(☎ 0990/808080). **John o'Groats Ferries** (☎ 01955/611353) operates the **Orkney Bus,** a direct express coach from Inverness to Kirkwall (via ferry) that runs daily from May to early September. The same company offers a day tour from Inverness to Orkney daily from June to August.

By Car and Ferry

To get to Lerwick, Shetland, take the ferry from the port in Aberdeen. To reach Stromness, Orkney, take the passenger and car ferry from the port in Scrabster. Contact **P & O Ferries** (⊠ Orkney and Shetland Services, Box 5, Jamieson's Quay, Aberdeen, AB11 5NP, ☎ 01224/572615) for reservations. Alternatively, take the ferry from John o'Groats to Burwick, Orkney, operated by **John o'Groats Ferries,** with up to eight sailings daily from May to September (☎ 01955/611353).

By Plane
British Airways (☎ 0345/222111) provides regular service to Lerwick (Shetland) and Kirkwall (Orkney) from Edinburgh, Glasgow, Aberdeen, and Inverness.

By Train
There are no trains on Orkney or Shetland, although Aberdeen (which has a ferry to Shetland) is well served by train, and Thurso is the terminus of the far-north line. For information, contact the **National Train Enquiry Line** (☎ 0345/484950). From Thurso a bus connects to Scrabster for Orkney.

Getting Around

By Bus
The main bus services on Orkney are operated by **James D. Peace & Co.** (☎ 01856/872866), **Causeway Coaches** (☎ 01856/831444), and **Shalder Coaches** (☎ 01856/850809); on Shetland by **Shalder Coaches** (☎ 01595/880217) and **J. Leask** (☎ 01595/693162).

By Car and Ferry
Because of the oil wealth, the roads on Shetland are in very good shape. Both Orkney and Shetland are part of a network of islands with interconnecting ferries that are heavily subsidized. It's a good idea to book ferry tickets in advance. In Shetland, for ferry information, contact the tourist information center (☞ Visitor Information, *below*) or ☎ 01957/722259 or 01957/722268 if you are visiting during peak season. Shetland visitors who want to get to Orkney can do so by way of ferry from Lerwick on Shetland to Stromness, in Orkney (☞ P & O Ferries, *above*).

In Orkney, for details of ferry services operated interisland, call **Orkney Ferries** (☎ 01856/872044). Orkney also has causeways connecting some of the islands, but using these roads will, in some cases, take you on fairly roundabout routes.

By Plane
Note that because of the isolation of Orkney and Shetland there is a network of interisland flights. Tourist information centers (☞ Visitor Information, *below*) will provide details, or call **British Airways Express/Loganair** (☎ 0345/222111, or in Orkney, ☎ 01856/872494) for interisland flights.

By Train
There are no trains on Shetland or Orkney.

Contacts and Resources

Car Rentals
Although Shetland has a number of car-rental firms, you have the option of taking your car from Aberdeen by sea. The rule of thumb is that for any visit less than five days it is cheaper to rent a car in Shetland. Most of the rental companies are based in Lerwick; they include **Star Rent-a-Car** (✉ 22 Commercial Rd., Lerwick, ☎ 01595/692075) and **Bolts Car and Minibus Hire** (✉ 26 North Rd., Lerwick, ☎ 01595/693636). On Orkney try **J & W Tait** (✉ Sparrowhawk Rd., Hatston Industrial Estate, Kirkwall, ☎ 01856/872490) or **James D. Peace & Co.** (✉ Junction Rd., Kirkwall, ☎ 01856/872866).

Discount Pass
A joint entry ticket to all of **Historic Scotland's Orkney** sites is available from the sites themselves. The ticket lasts until you've seen all the sites and costs £9.

Diving

Selkie Charters (✉ Voe, ☎ 01806/588297), operated by Colin and Linda Ruthven, provide boat rentals and information.

Doctors and Dentists

Most general practitioners will see visitor patients by appointment or immediately in case of emergency. Your hotel or local tourist information center can advise you accordingly. You can also consult the Yellow Pages of the telephone directory, under "Doctor" or "Dentist."

Emergencies

For **police, fire, or ambulance,** dial ☎ 999 from any telephone. No coins are needed for emergency calls from public telephone booths.

Gilbert Bain Hospital (✉ South Rd., Lerwick, Shetland, ☎ 01595/695678). **Balfour Hospital** (✉ New Staffa Rd., Kirkwall, Orkney, ☎ 01856/885400).

Guided Tours

ORIENTATION

In addition to the bus companies mentioned above, well-run personally guided day tours are offered in Orkney by **Go-Orkney** (☎ 01856/871871). Another company that schedules general orientation tours is **Shalder Coaches** (☎ 01856/850809). The tour companies that service Shetland are **J. Leask** (☎ 01595/693162) and **Shalder Coaches** (☎ 01595/880217).

SPECIAL-INTEREST

All the companies that offer orientation tours run special-interest tours to specific places of interest on the islands, as well. Most can also tailor tours to your interests. Guided walks are available on Orkney: contact Michael Hartley, a ranger naturalist who runs **Wildabout** (☎ 01856/851011) for details of early morning, late-evening, and all-day minibus tours that combine sightseeing and the flora and fauna of the natural environment in a happy mix. In Shetland, several companies tour the spectacular Noss Bird Sanctuary—a national nature reserve—in the summer, weather permitting. The tourist information center can provide details and take reservations.

Late-Night Pharmacies

There are no late-night pharmacies on the islands. In case of emergency, police can provide assistance in locating pharmacists. Doctors in rural areas also dispense medication.

Pony Trekking

There is only one riding center on Shetland: **Broothom Ponies** (✉ Skelberry, Dunrossness, ☎ 01950/460464). There are no riding centers on Orkney.

Visitor Information

Kirkwall, Orkney (✉ 6 Broad St., ☎ 01856/872856). **Stromness, Orkney** (✉ Ferry Terminal Building, ☎ 01856/850716). **Lerwick, Shetland** (✉ Market Cross, ☎ 01595/693434).

13 Portrait of Scotland

Scotland at a Glance: A Chronology

SCOTLAND AT A GLANCE: A CHRONOLOGY

ca. 3000 BC   Neolithic migration from Mediterranean: "chambered cairn" people in north, "beaker people" in southeast.

ca. 300 BC   Iron Age: infusion of Celtic peoples from the south and from Ireland; "Gallic forts," "brochs" built.

AD 79–89   Julius Agricola (AD 40–93), Roman governor of Britain, invades Scotland; Scots tribes defeated at Mons Graupius (Grampians): "They make a desert and call it peace." Roman forts built at Inchtuthil and Ardoch.

142   Emperor Antoninus Pius orders Antonine Wall built between the Firths of Forth and Clyde.

185   Antonine Wall abandoned.

367   Massive invasion of Britain by Picts, Scots, Saxons, and Franks.

392   Ninian's mission to Picts: first Christian chapel at Whitehorn.

400–1000   Era of the Four Peoples: redheaded Picts in the north, Gaelic-speaking Scots and Britons in the west and south, Germanic Angles in the east. Origins of Arthur legend (Arthur's Seat, Ben Arthur). Picts, with bloodline through mothers, eventually dominate.

563   Columba (ca. 521–97) establishes monastery at Iona.

780–1065   Scandinavian invasions; Hebrides remain Norse until 1263, Orkney and Shetland until 1472.

1005–34   Malcolm II (ca. 953–1034) unifies Scotland and (temporarily) repels the English.

1040   Malcolm's heir, Duncan (ca. 1080–1153), is slain by his rival, Macbeth (d. 1057), whose wife has a claim to the throne.

House of Canmore

1057   Malcolm III (ca. 1031–93), known as "Canmore" ("Big Head"), murders Macbeth and assumes the throne.

1093   Death of Malcolm's queen, St. Margaret (1046–93), founder of modern Edinburgh.

1124–53   David I (ca. 1082–1153), "soir sanct" (sore saint), builds the abbeys of Jedburgh (1118), Kelso (1128), Melrose (1136), and Dryburgh (1150) and brings Norman culture to Scotland.

1290   The first of many attempts to unite Scotland peacefully with England fails when the Scots queen Margaret, "the Maid of Norway," dies on the way to her wedding to Edward (1284–1327), son of Edward I (1239–1307) of England. The Scots naively ask Edward I (subsequently known as "the hammer of the Scots") to arbitrate between the remaining 13 claimants to the throne. Edward's choice, John Balliol (1250–1325), is known as "toom tabard" (empty coat).

1295   Under continued threat from England, Scotland signs its first treaty of the "auld alliance" with France. Wine trade flourishes.

1297   Revolutionary William Wallace (1270–1305), immortalized by Burns, leads the Scots against the English.

1305   Wallace captured by the English and executed.

1306–29 Reign of Robert the Bruce (1274–1329), King Robert I. Defeats Edward II (1284–1327) at Bannockburn, 1314; Treaty of Northampton, 1328, recognizes Scottish sovereignty.

1368 Edinburgh Castle rebuilt.

House of Stewart

1371 Robert II (1316–90), son of Robert the Bruce's (1274–1329) daughter Marjorie and Walter the Steward, is crowned. Struggle (dramatized in Scott's novels) between the crown and the barony ensues for the next century, punctuated by sporadic warfare with England.

1411 Founding of University of St. Andrews.

1451 University of Glasgow founded.

1488–1515 Reign of James IV (1473–1513). The Renaissance reaches Scotland. The "Golden Age" of Scots poetry includes Robert Henryson (ca. 1425–1508), William Dunbar (ca. 1460–1530), Gavin Douglas (1474–1522), and the king himself.

1495 University of Aberdeen founded.

1507 Andrew Myllar and Walter Chapman set up first Scots printing press in Edinburgh.

1513 At war against the English, James is slain at Flodden.

1542 Henry VIII (1491–1547) defeats James V (1512–42) at Solway Moss; the dying James, hearing of the birth of his daughter, Mary, declares: "It came with a lass [Marjorie Bruce] and it will pass with a lass."

1542–67 Reign of Mary, Queen of Scots (1542–87). Romantic, Catholic, and with an excellent claim to the English throne, Mary proved to be no match for her barons, John Knox (1513–72), or her cousin, Elizabeth (1533–1603) of England.

1560 Mary returns to Scotland from her childhood in France, at the same time that Catholicism is abolished in favor of Knox's Calvinism.

1565 Mary marries Lord Darnley (1545–67), a Catholic.

1567 Darnley is murdered at Kirk o' Field; Mary marries one of the conspirators, the earl of Bothwell (ca. 1535–78). Driven from Scotland, she appeals to Elizabeth, who imprisons her. Mary's son, James (1566–1625), is crowned James VI of Scotland.

1582 University of Edinburgh is founded.

1587 Elizabeth orders the execution of Mary.

1603 Elizabeth dies without issue; James VI is crowned James I of England. Parliaments remain separate for another century.

1638 National Covenant challenges Charles I's personal rule.

1639–41 Crisis. The Scots and then the English Parliaments revolt against Charles I (1600–49).

1643 Solemn League and Covenant establishes Presbyterianism as the Church of Scotland ("the Kirk"). Civil War in England.

1649 Charles I beheaded. Oliver Cromwell (1599–1658) made Protector.

1650–52 Cromwell roots out Scots royalists.

1658 First Edinburgh–London coach: the journey took two weeks.

1660 Restoration of Charles II (1630–85). Episcopalianism reestablished in Scotland; Covenanters persecuted.

1688–89 Glorious Revolution; James VII and II (1633–1701), a Catholic, deposed in favor of his daughter Mary and her husband, William of Orange. Supporters of James ("Jacobites") defeated at Killiecrankie. Presbyterianism reestablished.

1692 Highlanders who refuse oath to William and Mary massacred at Glencoe.

1698–1700 Attempted Scottish colony at Darien fails.

1707 Union of English and Scots Parliaments under Queen Anne (1665–1714); deprived of French wine trade, Scots turn to whisky.

House of Hanover

1714 Queen Anne dies; George I (1660–1727) of Hanover, descended from a daughter of James VI and I, crowned.

1715 First Jacobite Rebellion. Earl of Mar defeated.

1730–90 Scottish Enlightenment. The Edinburgh Medical School is the best in Europe; David Hume (1711–76) and Adam Smith (1723–90) redefine philosophy and economics. In the arts, Allan Ramsay the elder (1686–1758) and Robert Burns (1759–96) refine Scottish poetry; Allan Ramsay the younger (1713–84) and Henry Raeburn (1756–1823) rank among the finest painters of the era. Edinburgh's New Town, begun in the 1770s by the brothers Adam (Robert, 1728–92; brother James, 1730–94; father William 1689–1748), provides a fitting setting.

1745–46 Last Jacobite Rebellion. Bonnie Prince Charlie (1720–88), grandson of James VII and II, is defeated at Culloden; wearing of the kilt is forbidden until 1782. James Watt (1736–1819) of Glasgow is granted a patent for his steam engine.

1771 Birth of Walter Scott (1771–1832), Romantic novelist.

1778 First cotton mill, at Rothesay.

1788 Death of Bonnie Prince Charlie.

1790 Forth and Clyde Canal opened.

1800–50 Highland Clearances: overpopulation, increased rents, and conversion of farms to sheep pasture leads to mass migration, sometimes forced, to North America and elsewhere. Meanwhile, the lowlands industrialize; Catholic Irish immigrate to factories of southwest.

1828 Execution of Burke and Hare, who sold their murder victims to an Edinburgh anatomist, a lucrative trade.

1832 Parliamentary Reform Act expands the franchise, redistributes seats.

1837 Victoria (1819–1901) accedes to the British throne.

1842 Edinburgh–Glasgow railroad opened.

1846 Edinburgh–London railroad opened.

1848 Queen Victoria buys estate at Balmoral as her Scottish residence. Andrew Carnegie emigrates from Dunfermline to Pittsburgh.

1884–85 Gladstone's Reform Act establishes manhood suffrage. Office of Secretary for Scotland authorized.

1886 Scottish Home Rule Association founded.

1901 Death of Queen Victoria.

House of Windsor

1928 Equal Franchise Act gives the vote to women. Scottish Office established as governmental department in Edinburgh. Scottish National Party founded.

1931 Depression hits industrialized Scotland severely.

1945 Two Scottish Nationalists elected to Parliament.

1959 Finnart Oil Terminal, Chapelcross Nuclear Power Station, and Dounreay Fast Breeder Reactor opened.

1964 Forth Road Bridge opened.

1970 British Petroleum strikes oil in the North Sea; revives economy of northeast.

1973 Britain becomes a member of the European Economic Community ("Common Market").

1974 Eleven Scottish Nationalist members of Parliament elected. Old counties reorganized and renamed new regions.

1979 Referendum on "devolution" of a separate Scotland: 33% for, 31% against; 36% don't vote.

1981 Europe's largest oil terminal opens at Sullom Voe, Shetland.

1988 Revival of Scots nationalism under banner of "Scotland in Europe," anticipating 1992 economic union.

1992 Increasing attention focused on Scotland's dissatisfaction with rule from London, England. Poll shows 50% of Scots want independence.

1995 In the face of a Tory Government increasingly looking like a "lame duck" and divided on the issue of Europe, Scotland continues to argue its own way forward. The Labour Party promises a Scottish Parliament but wants to keep Scotland within the United Kingdom; the Scottish National Party still wants independence and sees Labour's Scottish Parliament as a stepping-stone to full autonomy.

1997 The Labour Party wins the General Election in May. A referendum held in Scotland votes in favor of the establishment of a Scottish Parliament (with restricted powers) by the year 2000.

—Gilbert Summers

INDEX

Looking for a different kind of vacation?

Fodor's makes it easy with a full line of international guidebooks to suit a variety of interests—from adventure to romance to language help.

At bookstores everywhere.
www.fodors.com

Fodor's Special Series

Fodor's Best Bed & Breakfasts
America
California
The Mid-Atlantic
New England
The Pacific Northwest
The South
The Southwest
The Upper Great Lakes

Compass American Guides
Alaska
Arizona
Boston
Chicago
Coastal California
Colorado
Florida
Hawai'i
Hollywood
Idaho
Las Vegas
Maine
Manhattan
Minnesota
Montana
New Mexico
New Orleans
Oregon
Pacific Northwest
San Francisco
Santa Fe
South Carolina
South Dakota
Southwest
Texas
Underwater Wonders of the National Parks
Utah
Virginia
Washington
Wine Country
Wisconsin
Wyoming

Citypacks
Amsterdam
Atlanta
Berlin
Boston
Chicago
Florence
Hong Kong
London
Los Angeles
Miami
Montréal
New York City
Paris

Prague
Rome
San Francisco
Sydney
Tokyo
Toronto
Venice
Washington, D.C.

Exploring Guides
Australia
Boston & New England
Britain
California
Canada
Caribbean
China
Costa Rica
Cuba
Egypt
Florence & Tuscany
Florida
France
Germany
Greek Islands
Hawai'i
India
Ireland
Israel
Italy
Japan
London
Mexico
Moscow & St. Petersburg
New York City
Paris
Portugal
Prague
Provence
Rome
San Francisco
Scotland
Singapore & Malaysia
South Africa
Spain
Thailand
Turkey
Venice
Vietnam

Flashmaps
Boston
New York
San Francisco
Washington, D.C.

Fodor's Cityguides
Boston
New York
San Francisco

Fodor's Gay Guides
Amsterdam
Los Angeles & Southern California
New York City
Pacific Northwest
San Francisco and the Bay Area
South Florida
USA

Karen Brown Guides
Austria
California
England B&Bs
England, Wales & Scotland
France B&Bs
France Inns
Germany
Ireland
Italy B&Bs
Italy Inns
Portugal
Spain
Switzerland

Pocket Guides
Acapulco
Aruba
Atlanta
Barbados
Beijing
Berlin
Budapest
Dublin
Honolulu
Jamaica
London
Mexico City
New York City
Paris
Prague
Puerto Rico
Rome
San Francisco
Savannah & Charleston
Shanghai
Sydney
Washington, D.C.

Languages for Travelers (Cassette & Phrasebook)
French
German
Italian
Spanish

Mobil Travel Guides
America's Best Hotels & Restaurants
Arizona

California and the West
Florida
Great Lakes
Major Cities
Mid-Atlantic
Northeast
Northwest and Great Plains
Southeast
Southern California
Southwest and South Central

Rivages Guides
Bed and Breakfasts of Character and Charm in France
Hotels and Country Inns of Character and Charm in France
Hotels and Country Inns of Character and Charm in Italy
Hotels and Country Inns of Character and Charm in Paris
Hotels and Country Inns of Character and Charm in Portugal
Hotels and Country Inns of Character and Charm in Spain
Wines & Vineyards of Character and Charm in France

Short Escapes
Britain
France
Near New York City
New England

Fodor's Sports
Golf Digest's Places to Play (USA)
Golf Digest's Places to Play in the Southeast
Golf Digest's Places to Play in the Southwest
Skiing USA
USA Today The Complete Four Sport Stadium Guide

Fodor's upCLOSE Guides
California
Europe
France
Great Britain
Ireland
Italy
London
Los Angeles
Mexico
New York City
Paris
San Francisco

WHEREVER YOU TRAVEL, *H*ELP IS NEVER FAR AWAY.

From planning your trip to

providing travel assistance along

the way, American Express®

Travel Service Offices are

always there to help

you do more.

do more AMERICAN EXPRESS

Travel

www.americanexpress.com/travel

American Express Travel Service Offices are
located throughout Scotland.